Michael Quirke

New Zealand

BUG New Zealand

Third edition – October 2008

Produced by **BUG Travel Publishing Pty Ltd** for **Explore Australia Publishing Pty Ltd**

2 Coastal Rise, Kilcunda, VIC 3995, Australia
www.bug.co.uk

85 High Street, Prahran, VIC 3181, Australia
www.hardiegrant.com.au/explore_aus/

Printed in China by C & C Offset Printing Co. Ltd

ISBN 978 1 74117 264 5

Cover photos

Front cover photo: Sea kayaking at Abel Tasman National Park
Front cover credit: Kaiteriteri Kayaks *(**website** www.seakayak.co.nz)*

Back cover photos: Hiking in Abel Tasman National Park © iStockphoto/Cat London; Bungee jumping © iStockphoto/mikeuk; Lake Matheson near Fox Glacier © iStockphoto/George Clerk; Whale off coast of Kaikoura © iStockphoto/Paul Benefield; Young spring lamb © iStockphoto/Kai Fisher

Map credits

Maps are based on LINZ (Land Information New Zealand) data supplied by QuickMap/Custom Software Ltd *(**website** www.quickmap.co.nz)*.

Disclaimer

This book is current at the time of writing and information may change after the publication date. Every effort has been made to make this book as complete and accurate as possible. However, there may be mistakes, both typographical and in content.

The reviews in this book are the opinion of the BUG researcher at the time of reviewing. This information is to be used as a general guide and readers should be aware that prices, opening hours, facilities and standards may change over time.

There are many factors that may cause prices to change and establishments reviewed and listed in this book to close down or alter the services that they offer. Many hostels may also change their prices throughout the year to take advantage of variations in seasonal demand.

This book is not intended to be used as a sole source of information, but rather to complement existing sources of information such as word of mouth, travel brochures, timetables, travel magazines and other guidebooks. You are urged to read all the available material and talk to hostel staff and other travellers to learn as much as you can about your travel options.

Like anything in life, travel entails certain risks. BUG Travel Publishing Pty Ltd, Explore Australia Publishing Pty Ltd and the authors shall have neither liability nor responsibility to any person or entity with respect to any loss or damage caused, or alleged to have been caused, directly or indirectly, by the information contained within this book.

BUG provides honest and independent travel advice. BUG Travel Publishing Pty Ltd does not receive any payment in exchange for listing any establishment and BUG's researchers never accept free accommodation in exchange for favourable reviews.

Contents

TRAVEL ESSENTIALS 12

GETTING AROUND 27

AUCKLAND REGION 50

Auckland 50
Hibiscus Coast 68
Kowhai Coast 69
Helensville 70
Hauraki Gulf 71
Waiheke Island 71
Great Barrier Island 72

NORTHLAND 76

Waipu 76
Whangarei 78
Poor Knights Islands 81
Bay of Islands 81
Paihia 82
Waitangi 88
Russell 88
Kerikeri 90
Whangaroa Harbour & Kaeo 92
The Far North 92
Kaitaia 93
Ahipara 95
Pukenui, Houhora Heads & Henderson Bay 96
Cape Reinga 97
Hokianga Region 98
Kohukohu 98
Rawene 98
Opononi & Omapere 98
Kauri Coast 100
Dargaville 100
Kaihu 101

WAIKATO 102

Hamilton 102
Raglan 105
Waitomo District 106
Te Kuiti 107
Otorohanga 107
Waitomo Caves 107
Thames Valley 111
Matamata 111
Te Aroha 112
Coromandel Peninsula 113
Thames 113
Coromandel Town 116
Whitianga 119
Hahei 121
Hot Water Beach 122
Tairua 123
Opoutere 124
Whangamata 124
Lake Taupo 125
Orakei Korako 125
Taupo 126
Turangi 132

BAY OF PLENTY 136

Tauranga & Mount Maunganui 136
Whakatane 141
White Island 143
Opotiki 144
Rotorua 145

GISBORNE & EAST CAPE 155

Gisborne 155
East Cape 157
Te Urewera National Park 161

HAWKES BAY 162

Wairoa 162
Napier 163
Hastings 169
Havelock North 172
Clive 172
Cape Kidnappers 173

TARANAKI 174

New Plymouth 174
Egmont National Park 177
Stratford 178
Hawera 179

MANAWATU-WANGANUI 180

Ruapehu District 180
Tongariro National Park 180
National Park Village 183
Ohakune 186
Wanganui & Whanganui National Park 187
Wanganui 187
Whanganui National Park 190
Manawatu & Rangitikei 191
Palmerston North 191
Taihape 194

WELLINGTON REGION 196

Wellington 196
Kapiti Coast 206
Paekakariki 206
Paraparaumu 207
The Wairarapa 207
Masterton 207
Martinborough 208

MARLBOROUGH 210

Picton 210
Havelock 214
Marlborough Sounds 215
Blenheim 219
Renwick 222

NELSON-TASMAN REGION 223

Nelson 223
Motueka 230
Abel Tasman National Park 232
Golden Bay 235
Takaka 235
Collingwood & Farewell Spit 238
Kahurangi National Park 239
St Arnaud & Nelson Lakes National Park 240
Murchison 241

WEST COAST 243

Westport 243
Granity & Hector 246
Karamea 246
Charleston 247
Punakaiki 248
Greymouth 249
Hokitika 253
Ross 256
Okarito 256
Franz Josef 257
Fox Glacier 261
Haast 262

CANTERBURY 264

Kaikoura 264
Hanmer Springs 270
Christchurch 272
Akaroa & the Banks Peninsula 287
Methven & Mount Hutt 290
Arthurs Pass 293
Geraldine 294
Timaru 295
Lake Tekapo 297
Twizel 298
Aoraki/Mount Cook National Park 300

OTAGO 303

Oamaru 303
Dunedin 307
Otago Peninsula 314
Queenstown 315
Arrowtown 327
Glenorchy 328
Mount Aspiring National Park 329
Wanaka 331

SOUTHLAND 337

The Catlins 337
Gore 340
Invercargill 341
Bluff 343
Stewart Island/Rakiura 344
Riverton 346
Tuatapere & the Hump Ridge Track 347
Manapouri 348
Te Anau 349
Fiordland National Park 352

INDEX 355

Map Contents

NORTH ISLAND

Auckland Region 50
Auckland 55
Parnell 62
Ponsonby 64
Great Barrier Island 74
Northland 77
Paihia 84
Waikato 103
Coromandel Peninsula 113
Thames 114
Coromandel Town 117
Whitianga 119
Hahei 122
Lake Taupo 127
Taupo 129
Turangi 133
Bay of Plenty 136
Tauranga 139
Rotorua 148
Gisborne & East Cape 155
Gisborne 156
Hawkes Bay 162
Napier 165
Hastings 170
Taranaki 174
New Plymouth 175
Manawatu-Wanganui 180
National Park 184
Palmerston North 193
Wellington Region 196
Wellington 200

SOUTH ISLAND

Marlborough 210
Picton 212
Marlborough Sounds 216
Blenheim 220
Nelson-Tasman Region 223
Nelson 226
Motueka 231
Takaka 237
West Coast 244
Westport 245
Greymouth 251
Hokitika 255
Franz Josef 259
Canterbury 265
Kaikoura 267
Hanmer Springs 271
Christchurch 275
Akaroa 289
Methven 291
Timaru 296
Otago 303
Oamaru 305
Dunedin 309
Queenstown 319
Wanaka 333
Southland 337
Invercargill 342
Oban (Halfmoon Bay) 345
Te Anau 350

New Zealand

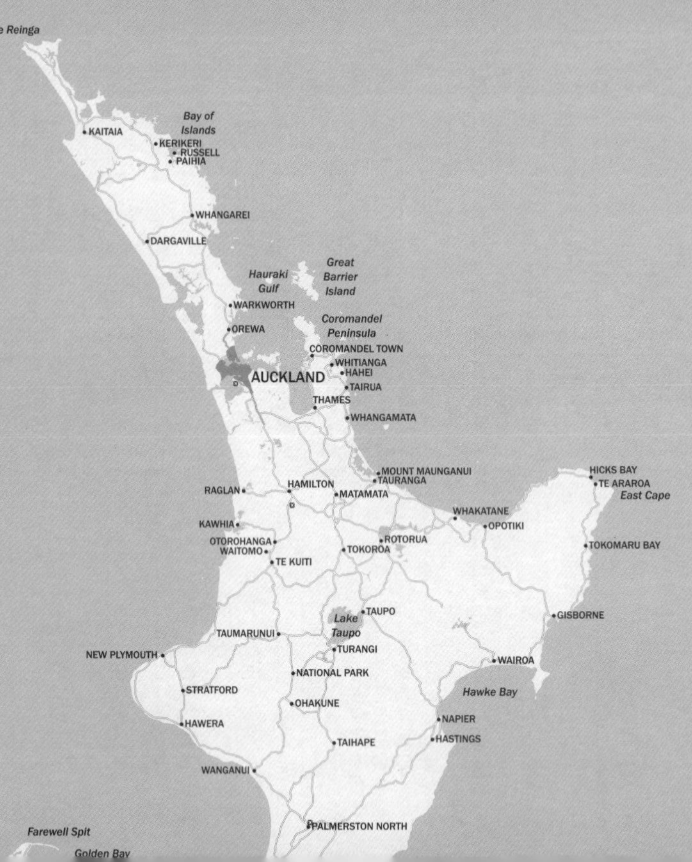

Cape Reinga
KAITAIA
Bay of Islands
KERIKERI
RUSSELL
PAIHIA
WHANGAREI
DARGAVILLE
Hauraki Gulf
Great Barrier Island
WARKWORTH
OREWA
Coromandel Peninsula
COROMANDEL TOWN
WHITIANGA
HAHEI
AUCKLAND
TAIRUA
THAMES
WHANGAMATA
MOUNT MAUNGANUI
TAURANGA
HICKS BAY
TE ARAROA
East Cape
RAGLAN
HAMILTON
MATAMATA
WHAKATANE
OPOTIKI
KAWHIA
OTOROHANGA
WAITOMO
ROTORUA
TOKOROA
TOKOMARU BAY
TE KUITI
TAUPO
Lake Taupo
GISBORNE
TAUMARUNUI
NEW PLYMOUTH
TURANGI
WAIROA
NATIONAL PARK
STRATFORD
Hawke Bay
OHAKUNE
HAWERA
NAPIER
HASTINGS
TAIHAPE
WANGANUI
PALMERSTON NORTH
Farewell Spit
Golden Bay

Tasman Bay
MOTUEKA
KARAMEA
NELSON
HAVELOCK
PICTON
PAEKAKARIKI
MASTERTON
MARTINBOROUGH
WELLINGTON
RENWICK
BLENHEIM
Cook Strait
WESTPORT
MURCHISON
ST ARNAUD
REEFTON
KAIKOURA
GREYMOUTH
HANMER SPRINGS
HOKITIKA
ARTHURS PASS
WAIPARA
OKARITO
FRANZ JOSEF
FOX GLACIER
CHRISTCHURCH
METHVEN
MOUNT COOK
AKAROA
ASHBURTON
HAAST
LAKE TEKAPO
GERALDINE
Banks
Peninsula
TWIZEL
TIMARU
MILFORD SOUND
WANAKA
GLENORCHY
ARROWTOWN
QUEENSTOWN
OAMARU
TE ANAU
MANAPOURI
DUNEDIN
PORTOBELLO
Otago
Peninsula
TUATAPERE
GORE
BALCLUTHA
RIVERTON
INVERCARGILL
OWAKA
BLUFF
Foveaux Strait
Stewart
Island
OBAN (HALF MOON BAY)

About the authors

Thomas Maresca

Thomas Maresca is from New York City, where he worked for several years as a freelance writer for television, magazines and newspapers. He left the US to travel in February 2007, and has spent time in 10 countries since. He's currently living and writing in Ho Chi Minh City but thinks fondly of mince pies, pohutukawa trees, beaches and clean air, and daydreams about going back to New Zealand soon.

Thomas researched and wrote about the North Island.

Tiffany Miller

Tiffany is a freelance travel writer living on the Big Island of Hawaii. She began travelling on surf trips in the South Pacific, and soon found herself backpacking around the world. Although her writing career began while living in Europe, the Pacific always calls her home, and updating BUG New Zealand was a very rewarding challenge.

Tiffany researched and wrote about the South Island.

Tim Uden

Tim is BUG's managing editor. He first started backpacking in 1989 when he travelled around Europe with a rail pass and he has made numerous around the world trips since then. He got hooked on travel writing while on a working holiday in the UK where he edited a travel magazine. After returning home to Australia he worked for a few years before setting off on his own to start BUG. Tim lives in the seaside village of Kilcunda, Australia with his wife and two cats, and travels as much as he can.

Tim researched the Marlborough, Taranaki and Wellington chapters.

Welcome

Welcome to BUG

BUG is the Backpackers' Ultimate Guide and we believe this is the best guidebook available for anyone backpacking around New Zealand. We set out to publish a guidebook dedicated solely for backpackers (independent budget travellers). You won't find any information about fancy hotels in this book and because of this we can better concentrate on giving you honest and detailed information about hostels and budget travel options across New Zealand. Compare us with other guides, you'll find that we have more detailed reviews of more hostels for any given destination.

This is the third edition of BUG New Zealand. Over time BUG will grow to fill a major niche in the guidebook market, but we don't plan on emulating other guidebook publishers and bringing out hundreds of different titles. Instead we will stick to a small number of guidebooks and fill them with accurate and honest information.

How to use this book

We've travelled extensively and know what should be in a guidebook and what you can find out for yourself. We've kept this in mind when putting this book together to ensure that it's packed with loads of useful information and not weighed down with stuff you don't need.

The book won't bore you with trivial details such as history or politics, which often turn out to be just a soapbox for the author to air his or her views. Instead of making you lug around an extra 100 or more pages we jump straight into the useful stuff.

The Essentials chapter has information on passports and visas, discount cards, money and keeping in touch. Boring, but important things that you need to know before you arrive.

The next chapter is Getting Around – we don't tell you how to get to New Zealand because that's what travel agents are for. The Getting Around chapter has the low-down on transport options in New Zealand including details on coach and train passes, hitchhiking, flying and driving. Read this before you go to buy your ticket so you know whether you're getting a good deal when the travel agent tries to sell you a travel pass.

After these introductory chapters it's straight into the destination chapters. There's a chapter for each region, which is organised geographically. The chapters start with Auckland, a major gateway, and are then ordered from north to south.

When you arrive in a new destination you generally want to find a place to stay, take your backpack off and start exploring. We have put details on local transport and accommodation at the start of each destination guide, so you can choose where you want to stay and find your way there.

Once you've checked into a hostel you'll find that the staff behind the front desk are experts on the local area and will be able to help you with any little questions such as where to do your laundry, check your email or grab a bite to eat. For this reason we cut out the crap such as verbose restaurant reviews and shopping information to make room for much more comprehensive accommodation reviews, although we will still point you in the right direction if you're hungry.

We have organised the information on accommodation and attractions so that every listing is followed by the address, a list of which bus routes stop nearby, telephone number, website address, prices and opening hours (reception hours for accommodation listings).

A lot of hostels give discounts to holders of BBH, VIP or HI/YHA hostel cards. When we list accommodation prices the discounted price is shown after the full price as follows: Dorm bed $25 ($23 HI/YHA, VIP). Just because a hostel offers a discount to someone holding a card from a particular hostel organisation is no indication that that hostel is affiliated with it. Where a price range is specified, for example: (Dorm bed $22-28), the low price is often the cheapest bed off-season and the high price the most expensive in the peak season. In a lot of hostels the cheapest beds are in the largest dormitories and the more expensive ones in the small dorms.

In BUG, we define a dormitory bed (or dorm bed) as any bed in a room that you share with other people who you are not travelling with. In New Zealand most dorms have four to six beds. We quote the price per person for a dorm bed and the price per room for single, double and twin rooms.

We classify a double room as a private room with one double, queen or king-size bed in it. A twin room is a private room with two single beds.

Some small hostels don't keep regular reception hours, in this case we don't list any hours. If the reception is unattended there is usually a phone number to call to speak with the manager who usually isn't far away. If you're arriving late it's a good idea to call in advance to arrange a bed for the night, in some cases you may be able to check in after reception hours if this is arranged in advance.

Each hostel review includes symbols indicating that hostel's facilities. These symbols are:

- Off street parking
- Secure off-street parking
- Wheelchair access
- Lockers for each dormitory bed
- TV lounge
- Kitchen
- Laundry
- Bar
- Swimming pool
- Tennis court
- Free use of bicycles
- Women only hostel (no male guests allowed)
- No alcohol allowed
- All indoor areas smoke-free
- Not all dormitories can be locked

BUG's hostel ratings

We wanted to provide the most comprehensive resource that could quickly describe a hostel while also providing more in depth information on hostels than any other guidebook. To achieve this we set about creating our own star rating system that highlighted the maintenance and cleanliness, facilities, atmosphere and character and security of each hostel while also providing an overall rating.

BUG's hostel reviewers fill out a two page form that collects information about various features, which are then rated to calculate that hostel's star rating. In addition to determining an objective star rating, the BUG hostel reviewer also writes a more subjective review of each hostel.

The individual ratings for particular characteristics are a handy way for travellers to choose a hostel based on what is important to them. For instance if a place with a great atmosphere is more important to you than cleanliness and maintenance, then you can just look at the atmosphere & character star rating rather than the other ratings.

When we set about creating our hostel rating system, we used what we believe are the best hostels as a benchmark for being awarded five stars. For instance we looked at the hostel we thought offered the most facilities to calculate our scoring system for this category. We did the same for security, cleanliness and atmosphere. It is very rare to find a hostel that excels in each area and because of this we have yet to award a full five stars to any hostel but any place with an overall score of four stars or higher can be considered outstanding.

The 'cleanliness and maintenance' rating shows how clean and well maintained the hostel is. A brand new purpose built place should score five stars and recently renovated hostels shouldn't be too far behind. The 'facilities' rating indicates the extent, but not necessarily the quality, of the facilities and amenities. The 'atmosphere and character' rating combines the charm of the building with the fun factor of staying at the hostel. The 'security' rating indicates the degree of security precautions that the hostel has taken.

The overall rating is calculated by averaging the other four ratings, but this is weighted to give priority to the more important aspects of the hostel.

There are other rating systems out there. The BBH hostel network has its BPP score and Qualmark, an independent rating agency that works with Tourism New Zealand, also produces a star rating system for hostels. The main differences between these and BUG's rating are that we developed our rating system from the ground up as a hostel rating (rather than an adaptation of a hotel or motel rating), we rate every hostel and the BUG score is broken into categories so you can see how the overall score is awarded. Unlike the Qualmark score, hostels don't choose to be rated and we certainly don't charge them for a rating or give advance warning that we are coming so they can make their hostel look nice for us.

We use the same criteria to rate hostels regardless of where they are in the world. No other hostel rating system has the same international consistency and you can be confident that a 3½ star hostel in Barcelona will offer a similar standard of accommodation as a hostel in Wellington that has the same BUG rating.

Help keep us up-to-date

Although everything in this guidebook is current at the time of publication, it is impossible to keep everything current for the entire life of this guide.

If you find something wrong or something that we have missed please let us know so we can keep everyone up-to-date; you can email us at tim@bug.co.uk or fax us at +61 3 5678 7033 (or (03) 5678 7033 from within Australia). If you think one our hostel reviews is way off track, you can write your own review on our website *(www.bug.co.uk)*.

We update our website with the correct details as soon as we know them. Check our website *(www.bugpacific.com or www.bug.co.uk)* for up-to-date facts.

Visit us on the Web

BUG started out in 1997 with a small website about budget travel in Europe and we have grown to become an extensive network of websites that can be accessed from our homepage *(www.bug.co.uk)*. This guide is online *(www.bugpacific.com)* and features interactive hostel reviews where you can write your own reviews of hostels all over New Zealand (and throughout the world). In fact BUG was the first website to let travellers post their own hostel reviews. There are also forums where you can share travel tips with other travellers.

Travel Essentials

Information Centres

The New Zealand Tourism Board (*website www.newzealand.com*) operates a network of visitor information centres throughout New Zealand in conjunction with regional tourism associations.

The largest regional information centres are listed below:

North Island

Auckland

Tourism Auckland, 137 Quay Street, Princes Wharf, Auckland
☎ *(09) 307 0612 or 0800 282 552*
Website *www.aucklandnz.com*
Open *Mon-Wed 8am-8am, Thu-Sun 8am-10pm*

Hawkes Bay

Hawkes Bay Tourism, 100 Marine Parade, Napier
☎ *(06) 834 1911*
Website *www.hawkesbaynz.com*
Open *Mon-Fri 8.30am-5pm, Sat-Sun 9am-5pm*

Lake Taupo

Destination Lake Taupo, Tongariro Street, Taupo
☎ *(07) 376 0027*
Website *www.laketauponz.com & www. backpacklaketaupo.com*
Open *8.30am-5pm daily*

Manawatu-Wanganui

Destination Manawatu, 52 The Square, Palmerston North
☎ *(06) 354 6593*
Website *www.manawatunz.co.nz*
Open *Mon-Fri 9am-5pm, Sat-Sun 10am-3pm*

Rotorua

Tourism Rotorua, 1167 Fenton Street, Rotorua
☎ *(07) 348 5179*
Website *www.rotoruanz.com*
Open *summer 8am-6pm daily; winter 8am-5.30pm daily*

Taranaki

Taranaki Tourism, Puke Ariki, 65 St Aubyn Street, New Plymouth
☎ *(06) 759 6060*
Website *www.taranakinz.org*
Open *Mon-Tue 9am-6pm, Wed 9am-9pm, Thu-Fri 9am-6pm, Sat-Sun 9am-5pm*

Waikato

Tourism Waikato, Transport Centre, Corner Anglesea & Bryce Streets, Hamilton
☎ *(07) 839 3580*
Website *www.waikatonz.co.nz*
Open *Mon-Thu 8.30am-5pm, Fri 8.30am-6pm, Sat-Sun 10am-4pm*

Wellington

Positively Wellington Tourism, Corner Victoria & Wakefield Streets, Wellington
☎ *(04) 802 4860*
Website *www.wellingtonnz.com*
Open *Mon 8.30am-5.30pm, Tue 8.30am-5pm, Wed-Fri 8.30am-5.30pm, Sat-Sun 8.30am-4.30pm*

South Island

Christchurch & Canterbury

Christchurch & Canterbury Marketing, Old Chief Post Office, Cathedral Square West, Christchurch
☎ *(03) 379 9629*
Website *www.christchurchnz.net*
Open *summer Mon-Fri 8.30am-6pm, Sat-Sun 8.30am-5pm; winter Mon-Fri 8.30am-5pm, Sat-Sun 8.30am-4.30pm*

Dunedin

Dunedin Visitors' Information Centre, 48 The Octagon, Dunedin
☎ *(03) 474 3300*
Website *www.cityofdunedin.com*
Open *summer Mon-Fri 8.30am-6pm, Sat-Sun 8.45am-6pm; winter Mon-Fri 8.30am-5pm, Sat-Sun 8.45am-5pm*

Marlborough

Destination Marlborough, The Foreshore, Picton
☎ *(03) 520 3113*
Website www.destinationmarlborough .com

Open *Jan-Apr 8.30am-5pm daily; May-Sep Mon-Fri 9am-5pm, Sat-Sun 9am-4.30pm*

Nelson-Tasman Region
Latitude Nelson, Corner Halifax & Trafalgar Streets, Nelson
☎ *(03) 548 2304*
Website *www.nelsonnz.com*
Open *Mon-Tue 8.30am-5pm, Wed 9am-5pm, Thu-Fri 8.30am-5pm, Sat-Sun 9am-4pm*

Queenstown
Queenstown Information Centre, Corner Camp Street and the Mall, Queenstown
☎ *(03) 442 4100*
Website *www.queenstown-vacation.com*
Open *7am-6pm daily*

Southland
Tourism Southland, 108 Gala Street, Invercargill
☎ *(03) 214 6243*
Website *www.southland.org.nz*
Open *summer 8am-7pm daily; winter 8am-5pm daily*

Department of Conservation

The Department of Conservation *(DOC;* ***website*** *www.doc.govt.nz)* operates a network of information centres throughout New Zealand with information on national parks and hiking trails.

If you are planning an overnight walk, you will need to book hut accommodation through a DOC office or information centre.

Entry Requirements

Everyone visiting New Zealand needs a valid passport and some travellers also require a visa.

Passports

It is essential that your passport does not expire within six months of entering New Zealand or you may not be allowed into the country – even if you're only planning on staying a few days.

You should allow plenty of time to apply for a new passport, although some passport agencies will rush your application for an additional cost.

Most travellers apply for a passport at the passport agency in their home country, but people living outside their country of citizenship should apply through their nearest embassy or consulate.

Australia

You can get passport application forms and apply for a passport at one of 1700 Australia Post passport agencies.

You will need to make an appointment for an interview at a post office and bring along your completed application form and original documents confirming your citizenship and identity. Australian passports cost $200 for a 32-page passport or $300 for a 64-page passport. They are usually issued within 10 days.

Contact the Australian Passport Information Service *(☎ 13 12 32;* ***website*** *www.passports.gov.au)* for further information.

Canada

To obtain a passport you will need the following: two identical passport photos; at least one document, such as a drivers' licence, to prove your identity; proof of Canadian citizenship; any previous Canadian passport, certificate of identity or refugee travel document issued to you in the last five years; a completed application form and the application fee. A Canadian passport costs CDN$87-92 and is usually issued within two weeks if you apply in person and up to a month if you apply by mail or through an agent.

You can either apply at your local passport office or by sending your application forms to the main passport office in Gatineau, Québec.

Passport Canada, 22 de Varennes Building, 22 rue de Varennes, Gatineau Québec J8T 8R1, Canada
☎ *1 800 567 6868 or (819) 997 8338*
Website *www.ppt.gc.ca*
Open *Mon-Fri 8.30am-4.30pm*

Ireland

Passport application forms are available from all Garda stations and from Post Offices that provide the Passport Express service. Completed application forms should be sent to the passport office in Cork (if you live in the counties of Clare, Cork, Kerry, Limerick, Tipperary or Waterford) or Dublin (if you live elsewhere in Ireland, including Northern Ireland). Passports should be issued within 10 working days.

A passport application should include two passport photos (which have been signed and certified) as well as proof of citizenship and the application fee. An Irish passport is valid for 10 years and costs €75 for a 32-page passport and €100 for a 48-page passport.

Dublin

Passport Office Dublin, Setanta Centre, Molesworth Street, Dublin 2
St Stephens Green
(01) 671 1633
***Website** http://foreignaffairs.gov.ie/home/index.aspx?id=253*
***Open** Mon-Fri 9.30am-4.30pm*

Cork

Passport Office Cork, 1a South Mall, Cork
(021) 494 4700
***Open** Mon-Fri 9.30am-4.30pm*

South Africa

Passport application forms are available at all Department of Home Affairs offices in South Africa and South African consulates and embassies abroad. South African passports are valid for 10 years and cost R 165. Allow six weeks for the application to be processed.
Department of Home Affairs, Civitas Building, 242 Struben Street, Pretoria
(012) 314 8911
***Website** www.home-affairs.gov.za/services_citizens.asp?topic=travel*

United Kingdom

British citizens can apply for a passport at offices of the UK Identity & Passport Service *(0870 521 0410; **website** www.ips.gov.uk/passport/)* in Belfast, Durham, Glasgow, Liverpool, London, Newport and Peterborough or at one of 76 interview offices. British passports cost £72 for a 32-page passport and £85 for a 48-page passport. Expedited passport renewal applications lodged in person at a Passport Office cost £97 for a one-week service or £114 for same day service. British passports are valid for 10 years.

Passport renewals take around three weeks but if this is your first passport you will need to allow around six weeks as you may need to attend an interview.
London Passport Office, Globe House, 89 Eccleston Square, London SW1V 1PN
Victoria Victoria
0870 521 0410
***Website** www.ips.gov.uk/passport/*
***Open** Mon-Fri 7.45am-7pm, Sat 9.15am-3.15pm*

British citizens living outside the UK should apply through the Foreign & Commonwealth Office *(FCO; **website** www.fco.gov.uk).*

United States of America

US citizens can apply for a passport at over 9,000 public places that accept passport applications, which include courthouses, and many post offices. Applications take around four weeks to be processed but applications lodged at one of 13 regional passport agencies (Aurora CO, Boston MA, Chicago IL, Honolulu HI, Houston TX, Los Angeles CA, Miami FL, New Orleans LA, New York NY, Norwalk CT, Philadelphia PA, San Francisco CA, Seattle WA and Washington DC) are processed within two weeks. Passports cost US$100 ($75 application fee plus a $25 execution fee).

For more information, contact the US Passport office *((202) 647 0518; **website** http://travel.state.gov/).*

Tourist Visas

You do not require a visa to visit New Zealand if you hold one of the following passports: Andorra, Argentina, Australia, Austria, Bahrain, Belgium, Brazil, Brunei, Bulgaria, Canada, Chile, Cyprus, Czech Republic,

Denmark, Estonia, Finland, France, Germany, Greece, Hong Kong, Hungary, Iceland, Ireland, Israel, Italy, Japan, Kuwait, Latvia, Liechtenstein, Lithuania, Luxembourg, Malaysia, Malta, Mexico, Monaco, Netherlands, Norway, Oman, Poland, Portugal, Qatar, Romania, San Marino, Saudi Arabia, Singapore, Slovak Republic, Slovenia, South Africa, South Korea, Spain, Sweden, Switzerland, United Arab Emirates, United States of America, Uruguay and Vatican City.

You will need to apply for a visitor's visa if you are not from one of the above countries. To apply for a visa you will need to supply a completed Application for Visiting New Zealand (form NZIS 1017, available from New Zealand embassies and consulates), a passport photo and evidence of access to at least $1000 for each month you intend to stay in New Zealand. You may also be asked to show an onward ticket. Visitor visas cost $100-130 depending on your nationality and where the visa is issued.

See the Working in New Zealand section later in this chapter for information on work visas.

New Zealand Embassies, Consulates & High Commissions

Australia
New Zealand Consulate General, Commonwealth Avenue, Canberra
% (02) 6270 4211
Website www.nzembassy.com
Open Mon-Fri 8.45am-5pm

There are also New Zealand consulates-general in Sydney and Melbourne plus an immigration office in Sydney.

New Zealand Immigration Service, Level 10, 55 Hunter Street, Sydney
☎ *(02) 9223 0144*
Website *www.immigration.govt.nz*
Open *Mon-Fri 10am-4pm*

Canada
New Zealand High Commission, 99 Bank Street, Suite 727, Ottawa
☎ *(613) 238 5991*
Website *www.nzhcottawa.org*

Germany
New Zealand Embassy, Friedrichstraße 60, 10117 Berlin
☎ *(030) 20621-0*
Open *Mon-Fri 9am-noon*

United Kingdom
New Zealand High Commission, New Zealand House, 80 Haymarket, London SW1
☎ *(020) 7930 8422*
Website *www.nzembassy.com*
Open *Mon-Fri 2pm-4pm*

There are also New Zealand consulates-general in Belfast and Edinburgh plus an immigration office in London.

New Zealand Immigration Service, New Zealand House, 80 Haymarket, London SW1
☎ *09069 100100 (£1 per minute) or +44 1344 71 61 99 (from outside the UK)*
Website *www.immigration.govt.nz*
Open *Mon-Fri 10am-4pm*

South Africa
New Zealand High Commission, Block C, 2nd Floor, Hatfield Gardens, 1110 Arcadia Street, Hatfield, Pretoria
☎ *(021) 342 8656*

United States of America
New Zealand Embassy, 37 Observatory Circle NW, Washington DC
☎ *(202) 328 4800*
Website *www.nzembassy.com*
Open *Mon-Fri 8.30am-12.30pm*

There are also consulates general in Los Angeles and New York and honorary consuls in Atlanta, Boston, Chicago, Honolulu, Houston, Sacramento, Salt Lake City, San Diego, San Francisco and Seattle.

New Zealand Consulate-General (Los Angeles), Suite 1150, 12400 Wiltshire Boulevard, Los Angeles
☎ *(310) 207 1605*
Website *www.nzembassy.com*
Open *Mon-Fri 9am-5.30pm*

New Zealand Consulate-General (New York), Suite 2510, 222 East 41st Street, New York
☎ *(212) 832 4038*
Website *www.nzembassy.com*

Customs & Quarantine

New Zealand's customs regulations are much like those of other countries but it has some of the toughest quarantine policies in the world.

Customs

Visitors aged over 17 are allowed to bring 1125ml of spirits or 4.5 litres of wine or beer and 200 cigarettes, 50 cigars or 250 grams of tobacco into New Zealand without paying import duties. You are also allowed to import personal items such as cameras and electronic goods without paying duties, as long as you take these items out of the country.

Like many other countries, you are not allowed to bring weapons or prohibited drugs into New Zealand.

Visit the New Zealand Customs Service website *(www.customs.govt.nz)* for more information.

Quarantine

New Zealand is free of many pests and diseases that plague other countries, therefore the Ministry of Agriculture and Forestry Quarantine Service (☎ *(09) 256 8547; website www.maf.govt.nz/quarantine/)* is extremely vigilant about keeping these out of the country.

You will have to declare any food and animal or plant products that you have with you and most unpackaged food will not be allowed into the country. Quarantine officers will also check for dirty boots or shoes as well as camping equipment that may contain dirt that could introduce pests and diseases into New Zealand. You will also be questioned if you have visited a farm or engaged in any outdoor activity or if you have visited certain African or South American countries within the past week.

Working

Because of the common language and availability of working holiday permits, New Zealand is a popular spot for travellers to find work.

Working Holiday Visas

Citizens of Argentina, Belgium, Canada, Chile, Czech, Denmark, Estonia, Finland, France, Germany, Hong Kong, Ireland, Italy, Japan, Korea, Malaysia, Malta, Mexico, Netherlands, Norway, Singapore, Sweden, Taiwan, Thailand, United Kingdom, United States of America and Uruguay are allowed to work in New Zealand on a temporary basis through the Working Holiday Scheme.

The Working Holiday Scheme allows citizens of the above countries aged between 18 and 30 to undertake temporary work to help fund their travel in New Zealand.

In most cases you are not permitted to work for the same employer for longer than three months.

Most applicants are eligible for a 12-month Working Holiday Visa, but British passport holders can get a 23-month visa and applicants from Malaysia and Singapore are only eligible for a six-month visa.

Applications from Singapore are also restricted to either undergraduate students or graduates of a Singapore university or polytechnic.

Working holidaymakers who can show that they have worked for at least three months in the horticulture or viticulture industries (picking grapes or other fruit) are eligible to apply for an additional three month stay in New Zealand.

To be eligible for a working holiday permit under this scheme, applicants must be:

- resident in the country of their passport;
- aged between 18 and 30

- not be accompanied by any children on their visit to New Zealand
- able to provide sufficient funds to cover their visit to New Zealand, in most cases this means at least $4,200.

For many nationalities there is a quota limiting the number of working holiday permits issued each year. If the quota for your nationality is full you may have to wait until the scheme recommences the following year. You can increase your chances by applying for your working holiday visa as close as possible to the scheme commencement date.

Quotas and scheme commencement dates for working holiday visas are shown in the table below:

Passport	Quota	Scheme commences
Argentina	1000	8 Dec
Belgium	2000	1 Nov
Canada	2000	1 Jan
Chile	1000	30 Sep
Czech Republic	1000	1 Mar
Denmark	2000	1 Feb
Estonia	100	2 Apr
Finland	2000	1 Aug
France	5000	1 Mar
Germany	unlimited	-
Hong Kong	200	1 Apr
Ireland	2800	1 Jul
Italy	1000	1 Apr
Japan	unlimited	-
Malaysia	1150	1 Jan
Malta	50	1 Jul
Mexico	200	31 Mar
Netherlands	unlimited	-
Norway	unlimited	-
Singapore	200	1 Nov
South Korea	1500	1 Apr
Sweden	unlimited	-
Taiwan	600	1 Jun
Thailand	100	1 Jul
United Kingdom	unlimited	-
United States	TBA	TBA
Uruguay	200	TBA

Tax

If you're working in New Zealand, you will have to pay tax to the New Zealand government. Your employer will deduct your income tax and Accident Compensation Corporation (ACC) earners' levy from your wages. The following table shows income tax rates in New Zealand:

Income	Tax rate (ex ACC)	Tax rate (incl ACC)
$0 to $38,000	19.5%	20.9%
$38,001 to $60,000	33%	34.4%
$60,001 and over	39%	40.4%

The tax year runs from April to March and you may need to file a tax return after 31 March and when you return home.

Before you start work you will need to apply for an IRD number from the Internal Revenue Department (☎ *0800 227 774; **website** www.ird.govt.nz).*

Finding Work

The easiest way to find work is to register at temporary employment agencies. Temporary assignments fit within the scope of your working holiday permit and employment agencies also line you up with reasonably well paying positions.

You could try one of the following agencies, which have a job search function on their website and offices throughout New Zealand:

Addeco
With over 6000 offices worldwide, Adecco has all sorts of office work available. Addeco also run the PicknPlay programme *(**website** www.adeccopicknplay.com)* that will organise fruit picking work for you before you arrive in New Zealand.
Level 8, Qantas House, 191 Queen Street, Auckland
☎ *(09) 309 7572*
***Website** www.adecco.co.nz*

Clayton Ford
This specialist in accounting, banking and financial related jobs has branches in Auckland and Wellington.
Level 13, 120 Albert Street, Auckland
☎ *(09) 379 9924*
***Website** www.claytonford.co.nz*

Clinical One

This recruitment agency specialises in jobs for health professionals and can help with work visas.
Level 13, 120 Albert Street, Auckland
☎ *(09) 368 1054*
Website *www.clinicalone.co.nz*

De Winter

This is an Auckland-based recruitment agency specialising in contract work in the IT field.
Level 8, Unite House, 300 Queen Street, Auckland
☎ *(09) 366 1944*
Website *www.dewinter.co.nz*

Health Recruitment International

Health Recruitment International specialises in finding work in medical related professions.
Level 9, BNZ Trust Towers, 50 Manners Street, Wellington
☎ *(09) 496 9262*
Website *www.healthrecruitment.com*

HHES Hospitality Recruitment

HHES specialises in jobs in the hospitality industry.
50 College Hill, Ponsonby, Auckland
☎ *(09) 379 7532*
Website *www.hhes.co.nz*

There are a few good general-purpose employment websites that are a good starting point. These are ideal for both reseaching the job market and lining up interviews before you leave home.

New Zealand's largest employment website is Seek *(**website** www.seek.co.nz)*; but New Zealand's main auction site, Trade Me *(**website** www.trademe.co.nz/Trade-me-jobs/index.htm)* also has job listings; and free listings site Gumtree *(**website** www.gumtree.co.nz)* has job listings in Auckland, Christchurch and Wellington. You can find seasonal work like fruit picking at Seasonal Work NZ *(**website** www. seasonalwork.co.nz)*.

To get a good idea about the availability of work, long-term accommodation and costs of living, check Gumtree *(**website** www.gumtree.co.nz)* and the classified ads in the main New Zealand newspapers. The *Dominion-Post (Wellington; **website** www.dompost.co.nz)*, the *New Zealand Herald (Auckland; **website** www.nzherald.co.nz)*, the *Press (Christchurch; **website** www.thepress.co.nz)* are particularly good places to look for work.

Fruit picking is a popular backpackers job in New Zealand. It is hard work, but it's a good way to keep fit and get a tan. Grape picking work is often available in the wine growing regions of Hawke's Bay and Marlborough, particularly in Hastings and Blenheim. Other fruit picking work is found around Kerikeri in the Bay of Islands and Motueka, near Nelson.

You can find fruit picking work through Addeco PicknPlay *(**website** www.adeccopicknplay.com)* and Seasonal Work NZ *(**website** www. seasonalwork.co.nz)*, although hostels in fruit-picking destinations will usually find work for you and a quick phone call before arriving can give you a quick rundown on the work situation.

Even if you didn't plan on picking fruit, it may be a good idea as three months fruit picking work qualifies you for a three-month extension on your visa.

Health Cover

Everyone in New Zealand, including visitors, is covered by the Accident Compensation Commission *(ACC;* ☎ *(04) 918 7700; **website** www.acc.org.nz)* for medical expenses that are a result of an accident.

The ACC only covers injuries that occur in New Zealand and treatment provided in New Zealand; it will not cover additional treatment that you may need when you get home. It does not cover illness and should not be seen as an alternative to travel insurance.

Money

New Zealand is a fairly cheap country to travel around, particularly when taking into account the quality of hostel accommodation. However prices can come as a shock if you've arrived here after a couple of months on the road in Asia.

Work out your daily budget by tripling your accommodation cost. Multiply this by the number of days you're planning on travelling, and add the cost of your airfare and bus/travel passes and you should get a pretty good idea of the costs of travelling around New Zealand.

You should be able to save some money by cooking all your own meals and drinking less alcohol, but there are lots of easy ways to blow through a wad of cash such as a few big nights out on the town or adventure activities such as bungee jumping and sky diving.

Travellers' Cheques

Travellers' cheques used to be the best way to carry travel money, but they're not as common now that ATMs and credit cards are so widespread.

It is worthwhile taking some of your money as travellers' cheques since it is a great backup if you lose your wallet with all your credit cards or if you arrive to discover that your cash card won't work in the ATM.

The beauty of travellers' cheques is that they can be replaced if they're lost or stolen. It helps if you keep a record of your travellers' cheque numbers in a safe place, preferably a copy with you (but not with your cheques) and another copy at home (or somewhere where someone can fax them to you if you need to make a claim for lost cheques).

Many travellers buy travellers cheques in British pounds, euros or US dollars, which is fine if you're travelling through lots of different countries. However travellers' cheques in New Zealand dollars have the advantage of being able to be used as an alternative to cash as long as you can find someone willing to accept them.

If you bring travellers' cheques with you, make sure that you sign them when you buy them, but do not countersign them until you are ready to cash them. You may also need to have identification such as your passport with you when you cash your cheques.

The most widely accepted brands of travellers' cheques are American Express, Thomas Cook and Visa. Don't travel with anything else as many people will not recognise or accept them.

ATMs, Credit Cards & EFTPOS

Plastic is the preferred way to access your cash while you're on the road and most cards are widely accepted throughout New Zealand.

There are several types of cards, each with their advantages. Most travellers have at least one credit card, and also a card to draw cash from an ATM (either from an account at home or from a New Zealand bank account).

Credit Cards

Credit cards are great for getting out of trouble and are often tied to a frequent flyer programme. One of the main advantages of credit cards is the favourable currency exchange rate as well the freedom to spend more money than you have. Of course this spending can get out of hand and you'll end up paying for it later on.

The most useful cards in New Zealand are MasterCard and Visa, followed by American Express and Diners Club. In tourist areas you may find some places that accept JCB and – occasionally – UnionPay cards, but Discover card is not accepted in New Zealand.

Most credit cards can be replaced quickly if they are lost or stolen. Call one of the following numbers if you need a new card:

American Express
☎ *0800 656 660*
Website *www.americanexpress.com*

Diners Club
☎ *0800 657 373*
Website *www.dinersclub.com*

MasterCard
☎ *0800 449 140*
Website *www.mastercard.com*

Visa
☎ *0508 660 300*
Website *www.visa.com*

ATM & EFTPOS Cards

ATM cards are a popular way to access your cash, particularly if your card is part of an international network allowing you to use New Zealand Automatic Teller Machines (ATMs). If the bank that issued your card is part of the Plus, Cirrus or Visa networks you should find plenty of ATMs in Australia where you can withdraw money.

Despite the favourable exchange rate and the ease of drawing your money from a cash dispenser, there are sometimes problems using your cash card abroad. Before leaving home you should check with your bank whether it is possible to use your card in New Zealand. In some cases you may need to change your PIN or even have a new card issued.

Cards issued by New Zealand banks are a lot more useful, working in virtually all ATMs and also at EFTPOS terminals in most shops, hotels, service stations and pubs.

Electronic Funds Transfer at Point of Sale (EFTPOS) terminals at cash registers at most New Zealand shops allow you to use a New Zealand issued ATM card to pay for goods and withdraw cash from your account. The combination of ATMs and EFTPOS terminals everywhere makes getting a Kiwi bank account essential if you're planning on staying in the country for more than a few months.

New Zealand Bank Accounts

If you're planning on spending a lot of time in New Zealand, your own bank account will make things a lot easier, particularly if you're planning on finding work.

The biggest banks in New Zealand are ANZ *(**website** www.anz.co.nz)*, ASB *(**website** www.asb.co.nz)*, Bank of New Zealand *(**website** www.bnz.co.nz)*, National Bank *(**website** www.nationalbank.co.nz)* and Westpac *(**website** www.westpac.co.nz)*. Since you'll be on the road, it makes sense to open an account with one of the bigger banks as they have a larger number of branches.

Tipping & Bribery

Bribery in exchange for good service isn't as widely practised in New Zealand as in other countries although tipping is starting to catch on, particularly in fancy restaurants in trendy inner-city neighbourhoods. However even in more expensive restaurants it is quite normal to pay the exact change for your meal. You never tip in a pub or bar, which also means that pub meals are tip-free.

Despite the increasing number of people tipping, the average New Zealander does not tip. Many New Zealanders equate tipping with bribery and would prefer that you save your money and not make it a custom here.

When paying taxi fares it is commonplace to round up the fare, such as paying $10 for a $9.60 fare; but it is not uncommon for a taxi driver to round a $10.20 fare down to an even $10.

Discount Cards

If you're travelling on a budget you're crazy to pay full price if there is a cheaper option. Armed with a wallet full of discount cards you should be able to drastically cut the cost of travel.

Discount cards come in two varieties – hostel cards and student/youth cards. Both types of cards are worth taking, particularly if you're travelling for a while. Student cards are generally best for getting cut-price admission to museums and other attractions and often allow for cut-price transport; with hostel cards, the emphasis is on cheaper accommodation although these also give you excellent discounts on bus and train fares.

Student & Youth Cards

It's worth bringing along several student cards if you're a student; if you're not a student but are aged under 26 you can get a youth discount card that gives you similar discounts.

Most sightseeing attractions including museums, wildlife parks and zoos allow substantial discounts for students. Many attractions throughout New Zealand refer to the discounted price as the concession rate. Some hostels will also extend the BBH, HI/YHA or VIP discount to you if you have a student card. In many cases just flashing the card issued by your university will get you these discounts; however some attractions require an internationally recognised card such as the ISIC or ISE card. This is a good reason why you should have at least two student cards.

Both ISIC and ISE publish a list of available discounts, however virtually all establishments that offer discounts will grant the discount for either card even if it that establishment is not listed in the card's discount guide.

The concession rate on the public transport networks in most New Zealand cities is not available with these cards and in most cases it is restricted to students enrolled in local schools.

ISE

The International Student Exchange (ISE) card is a good option with loads of discounts. Although this card is not as established as the ISIC, many establishments that give discounts to the ISIC will also provide the same discounts to ISE cardholders. The ISE card costs US$25 and you can order it online. See the ISE website *(www.isecards.com)* for more information.

ISIC, IYTC & ITIC

The International Student Travel Confederation *(ISTC; **website** www.isiccard.com)* produces three discount cards that give discounts to students; teachers and travellers aged under 26. Some of these cards include basic travel insurance although this is dependent on where the card is issued. ISIC, IYTC and ITIC cards each cost US$22 or £9.

The International Student Identity Card (ISIC) is the most widely accepted of the student cards. Many travellers buy fake ISIC cards while they're travelling through Asia which means non-students can sometimes pick one up; because of this the cards aren't quite as good for big discounts as they used to be and you may sometimes be asked for a secondary identification such as your student ID from your university at home. This is a good reason why you should have a couple of student ID cards.

The International Youth Travel Card (IYTC) is an alternative for travellers aged under 26 who do not qualify for an ISIC. There is a wide range of discounts, but it isn't as good as a student card.

The International Teacher Identity Card (ITIC) is a good alternative if you are a full-time teacher. Like the IYTC this isn't quite as good as a student card but it's worthwhile if you don't qualify for anything else.

Hostel Cards

Cards issued by the different hostelling organisations offer excellent discounts, particularly for transport and accommodation. Many travellers take along two cards, a YHA or Hostelling International card and one issued by an independent hostelling organisation such as Budget Backpacker Hostels (BBH) or VIP Backpackers Resorts. There is more information about hostel cards in the hostel section at the end of this chapter.

In our accommodation listings we list the price without a hostel card followed by the price charged if you have a card. Just because a hostel offers a discount to someone with a card from a particular hostel network does not mean that that hostel is part of the network.

Keeping in Touch

It is increasingly easy to keep in touch with the world. Mobile phones, voicemail and VOIP services such as Skype make it easy for people to call you and most hostels offer internet access, which is supplemented by internet cafés and wireless hotspots.

Telephone

The phone is still the easiest way to keep in touch and having your own number means that people can call you (which will save you a fortune in phone calls). Your own local phone number is also essential if you're looking for work.

Mobile phones

Virtually every backpacker travels with a mobile phone. If your mobile phone works with the GSM system (most European phones do) and is unlocked (not locked into your home network) then you can simply buy a $35 Vodafone New Zealand SIM card and stick it in your phone. If you don't already have a compatible phone, then you will need to buy a prepaid starter pack including a phone and SIM card for around $100-150.

There are two mobile phone network operators in New Zealand: Telecom New Zealand *(**website** www.telecom.co.nz)* and Vodafone *(**website** www.vodafone.co.nz)*. Of these two companies, only Vodafone use the GSM standard so you'll need to buy a Vodafone SIM to put in it your own phone or buy a new phone if you want to go with Telecom.

It is expensive to use a mobile phone in New Zealand with Telecom and Vodafone charging 89c per minute although cheaper calls are available if you're calling another number on the same carrier.

Virtually all backpackers use the Vodafone network; however travellers spending six months or longer may find that it is worth the additional up-front cost to get a new mobile with Telecom as this gives you cheaper calls to Telecom landlines.

ALTERNATIVES TO ROAMING

Roaming (leaving your home SIM card in your phone when you travel abroad) is the most expensive way to make calls. Not only are you charged exorbitant rates for your calls but you are also charged international rates when receiving calls. Usually roaming is something you use in isolated cases, such as a one-day stopover when it doesn't make sense to buy a local SIM card.

Roaming does give you the advantage of having a single number (usually in your home country) that people can contact you on regardless of what country you are travelling in. There are many cases when you need to offer a single point of contact so you can receive important calls, this is especially the case if you do freelance work and you don't want your clients to know that you are travelling down under.

One of the easiest and cheapest options is to use a SkypeIn number (or another VoIP service) that is diverted to your mobile in New Zealand. You still have to pay for the incoming call but it is a lot cheaper than roaming and you don't need to update everyone with your new number every time you visit a new country. To save on call costs give your New Zealand mobile number to people who call you frequently so they can call you directly.

Another option is to use an international SIM. This is a SIM from a small country (they usually come from Estonia, Liechtenstein, Iceland or the Isle of Man). It is free to receive calls in most countries, although New Zealand usually isn't on the list of countries with free incoming calls, and making a call is also reasonably priced. However the quality is dire and many travellers give up on the service (or lack thereof) after they realise that it is almost impossible for people to contact them.

The best option is to simply buy a local SIM in every country where you spend a week or longer and combine this with a SkypeIn number so you don't miss those really important calls.

Calling cards

Despite the popularity of mobile phones, calling cards are still the cheapest way to call home. Virtually every service station, newsagent and dairy (corner store) sells calling cards.

Rates are generally cheapest if you call a local access number rather than the toll-free number on the back of the card but this means that you may have to pay for a local call on a payphone in addition to the calling card rate.

Skype & other VoIP services

VoIP (Voice over Internet Protocol) is one of the cheapest ways to make a phone call but the quality isn't so great if you have a bad internet connection.

Generally VoIP lets you call other customers of the same VoIP service for free, which gives the biggest VoIP services the advantage of more people you can talk to for nothing.

Skype ***(website** www.skype.com)* is the biggest of the internet-based phone services and Skype software (and webcams for video calling) is installed in most internet cafes and in many hostels, which makes choosing Skype a no-brainer even though many of Skype's competitors are cheaper.

Although many travellers just sign up for the free Skype account so they can talk to other Skype users for free, it is worth the money to go for a fully fledged account with a SkypeIn number (a proper number that anyone with a phone can call) and even opt for the €3.95 monthly subscription that gives you free calls to landlines either at home or in New Zealand.

Of course you still have to pay to use the computers at the internet cafe so it's a better deal if you're staying at a hostel with free internet access or if you have your own notebook computer and a free Wi-Fi connection.

Internet

It's easy to get online virtually everywhere you travel in New Zealand, but it is cheaper in the more popular tourist destinations.

Internet cafés

It is easy to find internet cafés in popular tourist destinations like Auckland, Queenstown or Taupo. You can get online cheaply – as little as $3 an hour in bigger cities like Auckland – but in small towns and less touristy areas you may have to use slow and expensive coin-operated terminals.

Many internet cafés, including big chains like Global Gossip ***(website** www.globalgossip.com)*, are now fitted with webcams and headsets to make Skype calls and many also let you download photos from your digital camera.

We list internet cafés in the practical information section at the beginning of each destination guide.

Using your own computer

An increasing number of travellers are choosing to travel with their own notebook computer.

Wi-Fi hotspot access

New Zealand isn't as well set up with wireless hotspots as you would expect and when you do find them they tend to be expensive. However free hotspots are slowly starting to catch on.

Many backpackers use the Global Gossip Connect hotspots that are in many backpackers' hostels around New Zealand (and in Australia). They're not cheap but they are an affordable option if you can't find a free hotspot and you can use any remaining credit at other Global Gossip Connect hotspots.

Zenbu ***(website** www.zenbu.net.nz)* is another nationwide network of affordable Wi-Fi hotspots. Zenbu charge 10c per Mb. Unless you're downloading lots of bandwidth-hogging video, this works out much cheaper than Wi-Fi services that charge by the hour.

If you're really desperate to get online and can't find anywhere to connect you can use the expensive Telecom hotspots at Starbucks and many libraries.

Fortunately free hotspots are starting to catch on, although they are still a bit thin on the ground compared with other countries. Esquires Coffee Houses ***(website** www.esquires.co.nz)* is one of the only national chains to offer free Wi-Fi access.

We list free Wi-Fi hotspots in the practical information section at the beginning of each destination guide.

Hostels

Hostels are a great cheap accommodation option, however they have much more to offer than a cheap bed. A good backpackers' hostel is also a place to party, meet new friends from around the world and get information on other cool places.

Hostels provide dormitory accommodation, along with shared shower and kitchen facilities. Generally there are four to six people sharing a room and there is somewhere like a TV room or bar where you can meet other travellers. Often the people running the hostel are backpackers themselves, and are a mine of information about places to see, things to do and transport and accommodation options elsewhere in New Zealand.

New Zealand has some of the world's best hostels and they often include facilities that you would seldom find in hostels in Europe or North America such as spas, free use of bikes and courtesy buses. The New Zealand backpacking industry is very competitive and this keeps the standard of accommodation relatively high.

The best hostels are usually either small intimate hostels in historic buildings that are full of character or newer purpose-built places with first-class facilities. Small hostels in popular destinations such as the Marlborough Sounds or the Catlins tend to be excellent as the competition between hostels in these places drives up the standard of accommodation and they attract a more discerning backpacker who is less likely to trash the place. However hostels in bigger cities and less visited regional centres aren't as predictable.

A good hostel should provide a way for travellers to meet each other with common areas and a design that is conducive to meeting other people. This is one of the main features that distinguish hostels from hotels and motels, which are designed to offer their guests privacy. For this reason, many hostels with self-contained facilities (usually those that are former motels or apartment complexes) don't have as much atmosphere as your average backpackers hostel.

Hostels that are located above pubs are among the worst. In many of these places the bar downstairs is the main business and a lot less attention is paid to the accommodation.

Don't let the bed bugs bite

Bed bugs are a serious problem encountered by travellers throughout the world. They can be found on buses, on trains, in cinemas, in hostels and even in five-star hotels.

Although they are blood-sucking parasites, bed bugs do not transmit any disease and for most people the bites are no more irritating than a flea, mosquito or sand fly bite. However some people do have serious reactions to bed bug bites.

There is quite a stigma surrounding bed bugs and travellers that have been bitten often feel dirty and are ashamed to tell people about them, or they assume that it is the hostel's fault and tell other travellers to avoid the hostel. However bed bugs can prefer cleaner environments and an isolated case of bed bugs is no indication of a bad hostel.

It is impossible for hostels to completely eliminate bed bugs but they can take steps to prevent bed bugs from becoming a serious problem. These include not having carpet, wallpaper and wooden furniture where bed bugs can hide and prohibiting guests from using their own sleeping bags. However one of the best things that hostel owners can do is to admit the problem exists and react quickly whenever they discover a case of bed bugs. Hostel managers who claim to never have bed bugs are deluded and inevitably will be slow to act when bed bugs are found in their hostel.

There are a lot of misconceptions about bed bugs. A lot of people think that they are so tiny that they are virtually invisible; however they are brown flat oval insects that are around 5mm across and quite easy to spot on your bed.

It is quite easy to quickly inspect your room for bed bugs by checking for small dots of blood on the bed slats and around the seams of mattresses, but blood spots could merely indicate a previous infestation that has been cleaned up. Infested rooms may also have an unpleasant almond-like smell.

If you think you have bed bugs you should:

- Tell hostel staff so they can treat your room
- Wash all your clothes and anything else that can be washed on the highest heat setting and dry in a clothes dryer for 20 minutes
- Have a hot shower
- Empty your backpack, clean it with boiling water and (if possible) dry in a clothes dryer for 20 minutes
- Visually check anything that can't be washed for signs of bed bugs

Hostels catering to working holiday-makers are usually not that great either, existing solely to provide accommodation to backpackers picking fruit and they do little for travellers that happen to be passing through town and only staying a night or two. However the management of workers' hostels do have a lot of employment contacts and sometimes also provide transport to and from work. These hostels work for the employers as much as the backpackers and they have more rules than your standard hostel. Often there are restrictions on alcohol consumption in workers' hostels as local farms rely on them to provide a reliable, hard-working and sober workforce.

Although the hostel reviews in the BUG New Zealand guidebook are more comprehensive than any other guidebook, the reviews on BUG's website *(www.bug.co.uk)* are even more detailed and allow you to write your own hostel reviews and read reviews submitted by other travellers. A lot of the hostels reviewed on our website also allow online booking.

Top 10 small hostels

New Zealand is known for its excellent small hostels, some of which have as few as six beds. These are among the most memorable hostels you'll find anywhere. They are often just as clean as the big hostels but with a warm atmosphere that you can only get in a small place.

The following are our favourite small hostels (with less than 60 beds):

- Bay Adventurer (Paihia, Northland)
- Beaconstone (Charleston, West Coast)
- Billy Brown's (Port Chalmers, Otago)
- The Bug (Nelson, Nelson-Tasman)
- Hopewell (Marlborough Sounds, Marlborough)
- Juggler's Rest (Picton, Marlborough)
- Moana Lodge (Plimmerton, Wellington)
- Mt Cook YHA (Mount Cook, Canterbury)
- Old Slaughterhouse (Hector, West Coast)
- Tree House Backpackers Lodge (Kohukohu, Northland)

Hostel Chains

There are three main groups of hostels in New Zealand. Each of which offers its own discount/membership card that gives discounts on accommodation and transport.

Budget Backpacker Hostels (BBH)

Budget Backpacker.Hostels *(BBH; website www.backpack.co.nz)* is by far the most dominant hostel network in New Zealand with over 350 hostels.

BBH hostels tend to be smaller than those in the VIP or HI/YHA networks and in general they cater to more independently minded travellers. While VIP and HI/YHA promote travel packages and backpackers' buses, the BBH network (but not necessarily individual BBH hostels) makes a point of reminding you to 'take care not to be processed as Backpackage' in their popular blue hostel guide.

The Backpacker Perception Percentage (BPP) ratings are one of the strengths of the BBH network. Twice each year backpackers fill out a survey of hostels that they have stayed in and the results of these surveys are published in the blue BBH guide with each hostel being rated on a scale of 10 to 100 (it is not a true percentage rating since it is impossible to achieve a score less than 10). As a hostel network, introducing such a scheme was a very bold and courageous move that I'm sure annoyed a few hostels, but over time it enabled the overall standard of BBH hostels to improve as hostels competed for higher ratings and low performing hostels dropped out of the network to avoid having their BPP ratings published.

The BBH Club Card costs $45 and includes a $20 phone card. The card provides accommodation discounts of at least $3 per hostel and also offers good transport discounts. It's well worth buying the BBH Club Card if you plan on spending a month or longer in New Zealand, however the network is limited to New Zealand (with the exception of one hostel in Tonga) and it is not such great value if you're only planning on spending a week or two in New Zealand.

VIP

VIP Backpackers Resorts *(website www.vipbackpackers.com)* is a group of independently run hostels that vary enormously as far as facilities are concerned. A lot of the larger independent hostels that cater to the backpacker bus crowd are part of the VIP network.

They originally started out as an Australian hostel group but it is now a very international operation with close to 1000 hostels worldwide including around 70 hostels in New Zealand. Because of its international acceptance the VIP card is one of the most useful hostel cards and a lot of backpackers buy one although the BBH card is a better deal if you're just visiting New Zealand.

Most VIP hostels give a $1 discount per night and the card also has good transport discounts. A VIP card costs A$37 for one year and is available from VIP hostels.

Hostelling International (HI)/ Youth Hostels Association (YHA)

The Youth Hostel Association *(YHA; website www.stayyha.com)* is the New Zealand branch of Hostelling International (HI) and its hostels have a fairly consistent standard. In New Zealand the YHA's main market are independent travellers as opposed to school groups that fill a lot of European hostels and consequently youth hostels in New Zealand have a much better atmosphere than the institutional hostels that you find in Europe. The competition between hostels in New Zealand has also forced the YHA to clean up its act and you won't find any YHA hostels in New Zealand with chores, a curfew or a lockout. Although HI/YHA hostels in New Zealand are better than Hostelling International hostels elsewhere, they still have a reputation as a dull and relatively boring place to stay and very few YHA hostels fit the description of 'party hostel'.

Most travellers take along a YHA or Hostelling International card. This hostel card gives you good accommodation discounts with savings of $3 per night. The card is good at any of the thousands of hostels around the world, including over 140 in Australia and 62 in New Zealand, that are part of the Hostelling International organisation. The HI/YHA card also has good discounts on transport including discounts on car rental, bus and train travel. HI/YHA cards are available through many student travel agencies as well as at HI/YHA offices and hostels and costs NZ$40/US$28/£15.95 (England & Wales)/£8 (Scotland)/€20.

Getting Around

Air Travel

New Zealand is well connected by a dense network of air routes making it easy to travel around the country by air.

The major airlines are Air New Zealand *(☎ 0800 737 000; **website** www.airnz.co.nz)*, Qantas *(☎ 0800 808 767; **website** www.qantas.co.nz)*, Pacific Blue *(☎ 0800 670 000; **website** www.pacificblue.co.nz)* although there are minor airlines such as Soundsair *(☎ 0800 505 005; **website** www.soundsair.co.nz)*, Great Barrier Airlines *(☎ 0800 900 600; **website** www.greatbarrierairlines.co.nz)* and Stewart Island Flights *(☎ (03) 218 9129; **website** www.stewartislandflights.co.nz)*. The smaller airlines serve a limited geographic region, but can be useful for getting to places not served by the big carriers.

There are cheaper ways to get around New Zealand; but both Air New Zealand and Pacific Blue often have specials so it is worth checking whether there are any good deals going.

As New Zealand is a small country, most backpackers limit domestic flights, using them as an alternative to the ferry connection between the North and South Islands, with some airfares priced competitively with the ferry. Soundair flies from Wellington to Kaikoura and Picton and Air New Zealand flies from Wellington to Blenheim and Nelson.

Other flights popular among backpackers include flights to Great Barrier and Stewart Islands. Many travellers book the sail/fly option to visit Great Barrier Island, which involves a ferry trip one way and a flight back. Also stand by fares on flights operated by Stewart Island Flights make this an affordable alternative to the ferry journey.

When you leave the country you are required to pay a $25 departure tax at the Bank of New Zealand or Travelex branch in the airport terminal building.

Bus Travel

New Zealand is well served by a multitude of bus routes that makes buses a good way to get around the country. Virtually everywhere in New Zealand is accessible by coach although some smaller places may have more infrequent connections. The scheduled coach services include large coaches operated by national companies like Intercity as well as smaller minibuses, known as shuttle buses, that offer a cheaper and more flexible service. New Zealand also has a good choice of backpackers' buses such as Kiwi Experience, Magic Bus and Stray travel as well as a lot of smaller backpacker buses.

Scheduled Buses

The main coach operator is InterCity, which has scheduled bus services to most major cities and towns in New Zealand. Naked Bus is a smaller bus company with a nationwide network and much cheaper prices. There are also many smaller bus companies that offer frequent bus services within a limited regional area. The biggest of these is Atomic Shuttles, which has an extensive network in the South Island. The smaller companies usually offer a cheaper service and often are more flexible about dropping off or picking up from your hostel; however InterCity services are included in several travel passes making them a popular option with many backpackers.

InterCity Coachlines

InterCity Coachlines *(☎ (09) 623 1503; **website** www.intercity.co.nz)* is New Zealand's major national coach operator. Intercity coaches go to most destinations in both the North and South Islands. Although many travellers buy individual tickets, you can save up to 40% by buying one of the passes that are available. The range of passes offered by InterCity is quite confusing with specific passes valid only on certain routes.

Discounts are available with BBH, VIP and YHA hostel cards.

Travel Passes

InterCity passes include:

Pathfinder Pass

Travel in either direction from Christchurch to Auckland, via Mount Cook National Park, Queenstown, Milford Sound, Fox and Franz Josef Glaciers, Greymouth, Nelson, Picton, Wellington, Taupo, Rotorua, Waitomo Caves, Hamilton and Auckland.
***Price** $565*

New Zealand Trailblazer Pass

Travel in either direction taking in a circular loop of the South Island stopping at Picton, Kaikoura, Christchurch, Dunedin, Queenstown, Fox Glacier, Franz Josef, Greymouth and Nelson, in the North Island the pass allows travel between Wellington and Auckland stopping at Taupo, Rotorua, Waitomo Caves and Hamilton. It also includes a loop from Auckland to the Bay of Islands and the Waipoua Forest.
***Price** $585*

Total New Zealand Experience Pass

This pass covers the same destinations in the South Island as the Pathfinder Pass but it covers more destinations in the North Island. Destinations in the North Island include: Auckland, Thames and the Coromandel Peninsula, Tauranga, Hamilton, Waitomo Caves, Rotorua, Taupo, Napier, Palmerston North and Wellington.
***Price** $729*

The above passes do not include the ferry between the North and South Islands.

InterCity Coachlines also have a range of travel passes for travel in just the North or South Island. These passes include:

Bay of Islands Pass (North Island)

The Bay of Islands Pass lets you travel between Auckland and the Bay of Islands with stops in Whangarei, Paihia and Kerikeri.
***Price** $105*

Pacific Coast Highway (North Island)

This pass follows the Pacific coast from Auckland to Wellington. Stops include: the Coromandel Peninsula, Tauranga, Rotorua, Gisborne and Napier.
***Price** $209*

North Island Value Pass (North Island)

This pass allows travel in either direction between Auckland and Wellington with stopovers in Taupo, Rotorua and either Tauranga or Hamilton and Waitomo Caves.
***Price** $156*

Top Half Pass (North Island)

The Top Half Pass lets you travel between Rotorua and the Bay of Islands with stops en route in Auckland, Hamilton and Whangarei.
***Price** $145*

Milford Bound Adventurer (South Island)

The Milford Bound Adventurer allows you to travel in either direction between Christchurch and Queenstown (via Mount Cook including Milford Sound). It also includes Methven, Fairlie, Tekapo, Twizel, Omarama, Cromwell and Te Anau.
***Price** $235*

Southern Discovery (South Island)

The Southern Discovery pass allows you to travel in either direction between Greymouth and Christchurch (via Queenstown, Milford Sound and Mount Cook). This pass also includes Methven, Fairlie, Tekapo, Omarama, Twizel, Cromwell, Wanaka, Fox Glacier, Franz Josef and Hokitika.
***Price** $355*

West Coast Passport (South Island)

The West Coast Passport runs in either direction from Greymouth, Picton or Nelson to Queenstown with stops along the West Coast of New Zealand's South Island.
***Price** $125 from Greymouth, $149 from Nelson; $169 from Picton.*

FLEXI-PASSES

Intercity's Flexi-Passes (***website*** *www.flexipass.co.nz)* are an ideal option for independent travellers that don't want to be tied down to a pre-determined itinerary.

With the Flexi-Pass you buy travel time that can be used on Intercity and Newmans coaches as well as the Interislander ferry, the Kings Dolphin Cruise to Cape Brett and the Hole in the Rock cruise in the Bay of Islands. Flexi-Passes give you between 15 and 60 hours of travel and you can top up your pass in increments of five or 10 hours if you want to travel further.

Travel Time (hours)	Price
15 hours	$164
20 hours	$214
25 hours	$263
30 hours	$312
35 hours	$362
40 hours	$410
45 hours	$454
50 hours	$498
55 hours	$541
60 hours	$585
5 hour top-up (for existing pass holders)	$55
10 hour top-up (for existing pass holder	$110

The Intercity Flexi-Pass is valid for 12 months.

Naked Bus

Naked Bus (☎ *0900 62533 (0900 NAKED);* ***website*** *www.nakedbus.com)* is a new bus operator that has a nationwide network with bus services to most destinations in New Zealand. What makes Naked Bus a good deal is that – like Megabus in the UK and USA – they operate with a yield-management pricing system just like budget airlines such as easyJet and Ryanair. So basically you can ride the bus around New Zealand with prices starting at $1 per trip (plus a 70c booking fee) as long as you book far enough in advance. Although booking everything so far in advance can kill the spontaneous carefree spirit of independent travel, the cost savings make it a real bargain.

Some of the buses are old minibuses operated by affiliated companies, but newer full-size coaches operate on many routes.

It is always best to book Naked Bus online, as their phone number is an expensive 0900 number.

Atomic Shuttles

Atomic Shuttles (☎ *(03) 319 5641;* ***website*** *www.atomictravel.co.nz)* is the largest of New Zealand's smaller bus operators and has an extensive route network on the South Island that rivals InterCity and Naked Bus's services.

Other bus operators

There are a lot of small bus companies that operate scheduled services to regional New Zealand. Many of these companies operate door-to-door shuttle bus services that are often cheaper than the services offered by InterCity. Shuttle bus services are particularly widespread in the South Island.

Scheduled shuttle bus services on the North Island include:

Bay Xpress

Bay Xpress operate a daily coach service linking Wellington with Napier.
☎ *0800 4 BAYXPRESS (0800 422 997)*
Website *www.bayxpress.co.nz*

Dalroy Express

This coach line runs express services between Auckland and the Taranaki region with daily buses in each direction between Auckland and Hawera via New Plymouth, and connecting services from Hamilton to Rotorua and Taupo and from Auckland to Paihia in the Bay of Islands.
☎ *(06) 755 0009*
Website *www.dalroytours.co.nz/express.htm*

Go Kiwi Shuttles

Go Kiwi operate door-to-door minibuses on the Coromandel Peninsula with connections to Auckland, Tauranga and Rotorua. They offer a 15% discount if you have a BBH, VIP or

HI/YHA card.
☎ *0800 446 549*
Website *www.go-kiwi.co.nz*

Scheduled shuttle bus services on the South Island include:

Akaroa Shuttle
The Akaroa Shuttle operates transport between Christchurch and Akaroa on the Banks Peninsula.
☎ *0800 500 929*
Website *www.akaroashuttle.co.nz*

Astro Coachlines
Astro Coachlines operate a daily coach service from Christchurch to Akaroa and Hanmer Springs.
☎ *0800 800 575*
Website *www.akaroabus.co.nz*

Backpacker Express
Backpacker Express run bus services between Queenstown and Glenorchy, although their main business is transporting people hiking the Greenstone, Caples and Rees/Dart Tracks but both minibus and boat.
☎ *03) 442 993*
Website *www.glenorchyinfocentre.co.nz*

Citibus Newton
This Dunedin-based company runs a coach service that connects with the Taieri Gorge Railway at Middlemarch, making it possible to take the scenic train ride between Dunedin and Middlemarch and continue by coach to Queenstown.
☎ *(03) 477 5577*
Website *www.transportplace.co.nz*

The Cook Connection
The Cook Connection runs coach services between Lake Tekapo, Twizel and Aoraki/Mount Cook. They offer discounts if you have a backpackers' or student card.
☎ *025 583 211*
Website *www.cookconnect.co.nz*

Methven Travel
Methven Travel operates several daily shuttle services linking Methven with Christchurch and Christchurch Airport. They offer discounts if you have a backpackers card.
☎ *(03) 302 8106*
Website *www.methventravel.co.nz*

Mount Aspiring Express
Mount Aspiring Express run two daily services between Wanaka and Mount Aspiring National Park.
☎ *(03) 443 8422*
Website *www.adventure.net.nz*

Southern Link K Bus
Southern Link K Bus is one of the larger small bus operators with an extensive route network in the South Island. They have bus services linking Christchurch with Dunedin, Queenstown, Picton, Nelson, Golden Bay and the West Coast.
☎ *(03) 358 8355*
Website *www.kbus.co.nz*

Topline Tours
Topline Tours runs a daily coach service linking Queenstown and Te Anau.
☎ *(03) 442 8178*
Website *www.toplinetours.co.nz*

TrackNet
This company specialises mostly in transport to the main hiking tracks including the Kepler, Milford, Routeburn and Greenstone Tracks. They also operate several daily coach services linking Queenstown with Te Anau and Milford Sound.
☎ *(03) 249 7777*
Website *www.tracknet.net*

Wanaka Connexions
Wanaka Connexions run daily services linking Dunedin with Queenstown and Wanaka.
☎ *(03) 43 9122*
Website *www.wanakaconnexions.co.nz*

Backpackers' Buses

Another option for backpackers is the multitude of specialised bus services operated specifically for backpackers. Some of these are very useful services stopping off at hostels and also making detours to attractions that the conventional buses miss. However some of the so-called backpacker buses are tours, which is a different concept to independent travel.

Kiwi Experience, Magic Travellers Network and Stray Travel are the three biggest backpacker bus companies, which operate extensive route networks throughout the country and represent a good travel option. Generally the backpacker buses cater to younger backpackers and they have a reputation as party buses.

They all claim to cater to independent travellers and although you can get on and off the coach at any point en route, you are more limited than if you were travelling on a regular scheduled bus. The main constraint is that you are forced to follow the bus company's set route and you have to stay overnight at the town the bus company has chosen as its overnight stop. These compulsory overnight stops limit your freedom and the set routes make it difficult to make excursions off the set itinerary. Another drawback is that the hostels these buses stop at tend to be the bigger places, as they have to be big enough to accommodate a full bus, and backpackers travelling on these buses miss out on many of New Zealand's great little hostels. Although you are not forced to stay at any hostel, it can be difficult to go your own way when all your mates on the bus are staying at the bus company's recommended accommodation.

There's no doubt that travelling on a backpackers' bus is a lot of fun and you meet some great people, however after a while you stop making an effort to meet other people since you already know most of the other travellers on the bus.

If you're thinking about buying a pass for one of the smaller backpacker bus companies, first check whether it really caters for independent travellers, allowing you to get on and off as you please – if it doesn't offer this sort of flexibility then it is probably just a tour.

Kiwi Experience

Kiwi Experience (*☎ (09) 366 9830;* ***website*** *www.kiwiexperience.co.nz)* is the longest established of the backpacker bus companies and boasts flash new coaches with a full-on party atmosphere.

The various passes allow travel along pre-defined routes, although the names of each route provide little idea of the destinations covered. It's confusing to work out but there's bound to be something for everyone among the different passes available.

National Passes

START ANYWHERE

You can start the following national passes anywhere en route.

Full Monty

This pass covers pretty much the whole country and takes you to Cape Reinga at the tip of the North Island, Paihia in the Bay of Islands, Auckland, the Coromandel Peninsula, East Cape, Gisborne and Hawkes Bay, Rotorua, Waitomo, Taupo and Wellington on the North Island. On the South Island it goes to Picton, Nelson and Westport and then down the west coast and in to Wanaka, Queenstown, Te Anau, Milford Sound, Invercargill and through the Catlins to Dunedin and then up to Christchurch and Kaikoura.

Overnight stops *Auckland, Christchurch, Curio Bay (Catlins), Dunedin, East Cape, Franz Josef, Kaikoura, Lake Mahinapua, Mercury Bay, Napier, Nelson, Queenstown, Paihia, River Valley, Rotorua, Taupo, Te Anau, Te Kaha, Waitomo, Wanaka, Wellington and Westport*

Price *$1969 ($1899 HI/YHA, ISIC, Nomads, VIP)*

Minimum trip *31 days*

Maximum trip *six months*

Funky Chicken

This pass covers the North Island between Auckland and Wellington plus the South Island north of Queenstown. It takes you to Auckland, the Coromandel Peninsula, Rotorua, Waitomo, Taupo and Wellington on the North Island plus Picton, Nelson, the West Coast, Wanaka, Queenstown, Christchurch and Kaikoura on the South Island.

Overnight stops *Auckland, Christchurch, Franz Josef, Kaikoura, Lake*

Mahinapua, Mercury Bay, Nelson, Queenstown, River Valley, Rotorua, Taupo, Waitomo, Wanaka, Wellington and Westport
***Price** $1039 ($999 HI/YHA, ISIC, Nomads, VIP)*
***Minimum trip** 21 days*
***Maximum trip** six months*

Rangi

The Kiwi Experience Rangi pass covers most of New Zealand, although in the North Island it doesn't include Taranaki, Hawkes Bay and East Cape or anywhere north of Paihia and on the South Island it doesn't include Dunedin or anywhere south of Queenstown.
***Overnight stops** Auckland, Christchurch, Franz Josef, Kaikoura, Lake Mahinapua, Mercury Bay, Nelson, Queenstown, Paihia, River Valley, Rotorua, Taupo, Waitomo, Wanaka, Wellington and Westport*
***Price** $1129 ($1079 HI/YHA, ISIC, Nomads, VIP)*
***Minimum trip** 22 days*
***Maximum trip** six months*

Whole Kit & Kaboodle

The Whole Kit & Kaboodle pass covers most of the country except the East Cape, Hawkes Bay and Taranaki. It takes you from Auckland up to Cape Reinga, to Paihia in the Bay of Islands, to the Coromandel Peninsula, Rotorua, Waitomo, Taupo and Wellington in the North Island. On the South Island it goes to Picton, Nelson and Westport and then down the west coast and in to Wanaka, Queenstown, Te Anau, Milford Sound, Invercargill and through the Catlins to Dunedin and then up to Christchurch and Kaikoura.
***Overnight stops** Auckland, Christchurch, Curio Bay (Catlins), Dunedin, Franz Josef, Kaikoura, Lake Mahinapua, Mercury Bay, Nelson, Queenstown, Paihia, River Valley, Rotorua, Taupo, Te Anau, Waitomo, Wanaka, Wellington and Westport*
***Price** $1599 ($1549 HI/YHA, ISIC, Nomads, VIP)*
***Minimum trip** 27 days*
***Maximum trip** six months*

START AUCKLAND

The following passes start in Auckland and finish in Christchurch:

The Kitchen Sink

The Kitchen Sink takes you from Auckland to Cape Reinga and back, then over to Whitianga on the Coromandel Peninsula, down to Rotorua, Waitomo, Taupo, Tongariro National Park and Wellington, across to Picton on the South Island, then onto Nelson, Abel Tasman National Park, Westport, down the west coast to Wanaka, Queenstown, Te Anau and Milford Sound, then down to Invercargill and through the Catlins to Dunedin, then back to Queenstown and up to Christchurch.
***Starts** Auckland; **finishes** Christchurch.*
***Overnight stops** Auckland, Christchurch, Curio Bay (Catlins), Dunedin, Franz Josef, Lake Mahinapua, Mercury Bay, Nelson, Queenstown, Paihia, River Valley, Rotorua, Taupo, Te Anau, Waitomo, Wanaka, Wellington and Westport*
***Price** $1379 ($1349 HI/YHA, ISIC, Nomads, VIP)*
***Minimum trip** 23 days*
***Maximum trip** six months*

Joint Mullets

The Joint Mullets Pass lets you travel between Auckland and Christchurch. In the North Island it includes Mercury Bay on the Coromandel Peninsula, Rotorua, Waitomo and Taupo, plus the East Cape, Napier and Wellington. On the South Island it includes Nelson, then travel down the West Coast to Wanaka, Queenstown and up to Christchurch.
***Starts** Auckland; **finishes** Christchurch.*
***Overnight stops** Auckland, Christchurch, East Cape, Franz Josef, Lake Mahinapua, Mercury Bay, Napier, Nelson, Queenstown, River Valley, Rotorua, Taupo, Te Kaha, Waitomo, Wanaka, Wellington and Westport*
***Price** $1159 ($1139 HI/YHA, ISIC, Nomads, VIP)*
***Minimum trip** 20 days*
***Maximum trip** six months*

Sheep Dog

This pass takes you from Auckland to the Coromandel Peninsula, down

to Rotorua, Waitomo, Taupo, Tongariro National Park and Wellington, across to Picton, then onto Nelson, Abel Tasman National Park, Westport, down the west coast to Wanaka, Queenstown, then up to Christchurch via Twizel.
Start *Auckland;* ***finish*** *Christchurch.*
Overnight stops *Auckland, Christchurch, Franz Josef, Lake Mahinapua, Mercury Bay, Nelson, Queenstown, River Valley, Rotorua, Taupo, Waitomo, Wanaka, Wellington and Westport*
Price *$799 ($775 HI/YHA, ISIC, Nomads, VIP)*
Minimum trip *16 days*
Maximum trip *six months*

Zephyr

The Zephyr Pass takes you from Auckland to Christchurch. On the North Island it includes Paihia in the Bay of Islands, Mercury Bay in the Coromandel Peninsula plus Rotorua, Waitomo Caves, Taupo and Wellington. On the South Island it includes Nelson, then travel down the West Coast to Wanaka, Queenstown and up to Christchurch.
Start *Auckland;* ***finish*** *Christchurch.*
Overnight stops *Auckland, Christchurch, Franz Josef, Lake Mahinapua, Mercury Bay, Nelson, Queenstown, Paihia, River Valley, Rotorua, Taupo, Waitomo, Wanaka, Wellington and Westport*
Price *$889 ($869 HI/YHA, ISIC, Nomads, VIP)*
Minimum trip *17 days*
Maximum trip *six months*

START CHRISTCHURCH

The following passes start in Christchurch and finish in Auckland:

Dog Leg

The Dog Leg goes from Christchurch to Queenstown, then up to Wanaka and Franz Josef before heading back to Christchurch over Arthurs Pass, then up to Picton via Kaikoura and over to Wellington on the North Island. You then travel from Wellington to Auckland stopping en route at Taupo, Rotorua and Waitomo.
Start *Christchurch;* ***finish*** *Auckland.*
Overnight stops *Auckland, Christchurch, Franz Josef, Kaikoura, Lake Mahinapua, Queenstown, Rotorua, Taupo, Waitomo, Wanaka, Wellington and Westport*
Price *$819 ($799 HI/YHA, ISIC, Nomads, VIP)*
Minimum trip *14 days*
Maximum trip *six months*

Gumboot

The Gumboot Pass takes you from Christchurch to Auckland. In the South Island it takes you down to Queenstown and Wanaka, then up the West Coast to Westport, back to Christchurch and up to Picton via Kaikoura. Stops on the North Island include Wellington, Taupo, Rotorua, Waitomo Caves, Auckland and Paihia.
Start *Christchurch;* ***finish*** *Auckland*
Overnight stops *Auckland, Christchurch, Franz Josef, Kaikoura, Lake Mahinapua, Queenstown, Paihia, Rotorua, Taupo, Waitomo, Wanaka, Wellington and Westport*
Price *$909 ($889 HI/YHA, ISIC, Nomads, VIP)*
Minimum trip *15 days*
Maximum trip *six months*

Kea

The Kea pass allows you to circle around the South Island taking in Christchurch, Twizel, Queenstown, Wanaka, the west coast, Nelson, Picton and Kaikoura before heading over to Wellington on the North Island and up to Auckland via Taupo, Rotorua and Waitomo.
Start *Christchurch;* ***finish*** *Auckland.*
Overnight stops *Auckland, Christchurch, Franz Josef, Kaikoura, Lake Mahinapua, Nelson, Queenstown, Rotorua, Taupo, Waitomo, Wanaka, Wellington and Westport*
Price *$799 ($775 HI/YHA, ISIC, Nomads, VIP)*
Minimum trip *16 days*
Maximum trip *six months*

Top Dog

The Top Dog Pass takes you from Christchurch to Auckland. In the South Island it includes Kaikoura, Christchurch, Queenstown, Wanaka,

the West Coast and Nelson. Stops on the North Island include Wellington, Taupo, Rotorua, Waitomo Caves, Auckland and Paihia.
Start *Christchurch;* ***finish*** *Auckland*
Overnight stops *Auckland, Christchurch, Franz Josef, Kaikoura, Lake Mahinapua, Nelson, Queenstown, Paihia, Rotorua, Taupo, Waitomo, Wanaka, Wellington and Westport*
Price *$889 ($869 HI/YHA, ISIC, Nomads, VIP)*
Minimum trip *181 days*
Maximum trip *six months*

North Island Passes

The following Kiwi Experience passes are restricted to travel on the North Island:

Awesome

Awesome is a quick one-day excursion from Auckland to Paihia in the Bay of Islands.
Start/finish *Auckland*
Price *$95*
Minimum trip *1-2 days*
Maximum trip *six months*

Awesome & Top Bit

This three-day excursion from Auckland takes you all the way to Cape Reinga at the tip of the North Island with a stop in the Bay of Islands.
Start/finish *Auckland*
Overnight stop *Paihia*
Price *$189*
Minimum trip *3 days*
Maximum trip *six months*

East As

This circuit takes you to the rarely visited East Cape region. It includes East Cape, New Zealand's most eastern point, as well as Gisborne and Napier.
Overnight stops *East Cape, Napier, Taupo, Te Kaha*
Price *$375*
Minimum trip *4 days*
Maximum trip *six months*

Geyserland

This trip goes from Auckland to Whitianga on the Coromandel Peninsula, then down to Rotorua, across to Waitomo and back up to Auckland.
Start/finish *Auckland*
Overnight stops *Auckland, Mercury Bay, Rotorua*
Price *$265*
Minimum trip *4-6 days*
Maximum trip *six months*

Geyserland & Lake

This trip goes from Auckland to Whitianga on the Coromandel Peninsula, then down to Rotorua, across to Waitomo, Taupo and back up to Auckland.
Start/finish *Auckland*
Overnight stops *Auckland, Mercury Bay, Rotorua, Taupo, Waitomo*
Price *$299*
Minimum trip *4-6 days*
Maximum trip *six months*

Northern Roundup

The Northern Roundup includes the North Island between Auckland and Wellington including the Coromandel Peninsula, Rotorua, Waitomo, Taupo and Taihape.
Overnight stops *Auckland, Mercury Bay, River Valley, Rotorua, Waitomo, Wellington*
Price *$499 ($479 HI/YHA, ISIC, Nomads, VIP)*
Minimum trip *9 days*
Maximum trip *12 months*

South Island Passes

The following Kiwi Experience passes are restricted to travel on the South Island:

Back Paddock

The Back Paddock travel pass takes you across Arthurs Pass to the West Coast then down to Wanaka and Queenstown via Franz Josef and then back to Christchurch via Twizel.
Start/finish *Christchurch.*
Overnight stops *Christchurch, Franz Josef, Lake Mahinapua, Queenstown, Wanaka and Westport*
Price *$499*
Minimum trip *7 days*
Maximum trip *six months*

Bottoms Up

The Bottoms Up pass takes you to virtually every place in the South Island.

Overnight stops Christchurch, Curio Bay (Catlins), Dunedin, Franz Josef, Kaikoura, Lake Mahinapua, Nelson, Queenstown, Paihia, River Valley, Te Anau, Wanaka and Westport
Price *$939 ($919 HI/YHA, ISIC, Nomads, VIP)*
Minimum trip *14 days*
Maximum trip *six months*

Milford Explorer

This pass operates as a day excursion from Queenstown to Milford Sound and you have the option of a three-hour boat cruise on the Sound.
Start/finish *Queenstown*
Price *$169*
Minimum trip *1 day*
Maximum trip *six months*

Southern Roundup

The Southern Roundup is the southern portion of the Funky Chicken pass. It takes you to Picton, Nelson, the West Coast, Wanaka, Queenstown, Christchurch and Kaikoura on the South Island.
Overnight stops *Christchurch, Franz Josef, Kaikoura, Lake Mahinapua, Nelson, Queenstown, Wanaka and Westport*
Price *$549 ($529 HI/YHA, ISIC, Nomads, VIP)*
Minimum trip *11 days*
Maximum trip *six months*

Southlander – Bottom Bus

Kiwi Experience's Southlander pass is also known as the Bottom Bus. It links Queenstown, Invercargill and Dunedin and includes the Catlins region between Invercargill and Dunedin.
Overnight stops *Curio Bay (Catlins), Dunedin, Queenstown, Te Anau*
Price *$399*
Minimum trip *4 days*
Maximum trip *six months*

Magic Transport Network

The Magic Travellers Network (☎ *(09) 358 5600;* ***website*** *www.magicbus.co.nz)* is a good alternative to Kiwi Experience and Stray. Like the Kiwi bus, Magic runs along a fixed route giving travellers the option to get on and off whenever they wish. Travellers have up to 12 months to complete their journey.

The various passes are restricted to a particular route and there are compulsory overnight stops. The Magic Network covers most parts of the country, but some regions including the Catlins*, East Cape and Taranaki are not covered (* Magic sell travel on the Catlins Coaster as an add-on pass). Some of the passes on the Magic Network include travel on the *TranzAlpine* train between Greymouth and Christchurch.

National Passes

Magic Travellers Network passes covering both North and South Islands include:

Auckland to Queenstown

The Auckland to Queenstown pass takes you between Auckland and Queenstown. In the North Island you travel between Auckland and Wellington with stops at Waitomo, Rotorua, Taupo, Turangi and Palmerston North. In the South Island you go from Picton to Nelson and then down the West Coast to Queenstown.
Start *Auckland;* ***finish*** *Queenstown.*
Overnight stops *Auckland, Franz Josef, Greymouth, Makarora, Nelson, Rotorua, Taupo, Wellington*
Price *$412*
Minimum trip *8 days*

Kiwi Explorer

The Kiwi Explorer pass starts in Christchurch and includes travel by train to Greymouth, then bus travel down the West Coast to Wanaka and Queenstown, across to Dunedin and back up to Christchurch. Then it's back on the train to Kaikoura and Picton and across to the North Island where you can visit Wellington, Napier, Taupo, Rotorua and Thames before finishing in Auckland.
Start *Christchurch;* ***finish*** *Auckland*
Overnight stops *Christchurch, Dunedin, Franz Josef, Greymouth, Mount Maunganui, Napier, Queenstown, Tekapo, Wellington*
Price *$603*
Minimum trip *11 days*

Kiwi Traverse

Starting in Auckland and finishing in Christchurch, this pass combines coach and rail travel. In the North Island it includes transport between Auckland and Wellington with stops in Thames, Mount Maunganui, Rotorua, Taupo and Hawkes Bay. In the South Island it includes train travel on the *TranzCoastal* train between Picton and Christchurch and the *Tranz Alpine* from Christchurch to Greymouth. In Greymouth you pick up the coach, which takes you down the West Coast to Queenstown, across to Dunedin and back up to Christchurch.

Start *Auckland;* ***finish*** *Christchurch.*
Overnight stops *Auckland, Christchurch, Dunedin, Franz Josef, Greymouth, Makarora, Queenstown, Rotorua, Turangi, Wellington*
Price *$616*
Minimum trip *11 days*

Magic Adventure

Essentially this pass is the same as the Wayward Wanderer except that it doesn't include any destinations north of Auckland. It covers the North Island south of Auckland including Rotorua, Taupo, Hawkes Bay and Wellington and the east and west coasts of the South Island as far south as Dunedin and Queenstown.

Overnight stops *Auckland, Christchurch, Dunedin, Franz Josef, Greymouth, Kaikoura, Makarora, Mount Maunganui, Nelson, Queenstown, Rotorua, Taupo, Turangi, Wellington*
Price *$519*
Minimum trip *16 days*

Navigator

Starting in Christchurch, this pass covers both the east and west coasts of the South Island going as far south as Dunedin and Queenstown. In the North Island, this pass includes transport between Wellington and Auckland with stops in Napier, Taupo, Rotorua, Mount Maunganui and Thames.

Start *Christchurch;* ***finish*** *Auckland.*
Overnight stops *Christchurch, Dunedin, Franz Josef, Greymouth, Kaikoura, Makarora, Mount Maunganui, Nelson, Queenstown, Taupo, Wellington*
Price *$425*
Minimum trip *14 days*

Navigator Plus

Starting in Christchurch, this pass covers both the east and west coasts of the South Island going as far south as Dunedin, Milford Sound and Queenstown. In the North Island, this pass includes transport between Wellington and Auckland with stops in Napier, Taupo, Rotorua, Mount Maunganui and Thames. It also includes transport to Paihia in the Bay of Islands and Cape Reinga at the far north of the North Island.

Start *Christchurch;* ***finish*** *Auckland.*
Overnight stops *Christchurch, Dunedin, Franz Josef, Greymouth, Kaikoura, Makarora, Mount Maunganui, Nelson, Queenstown, Wellington, Whitianga*
Price *$927*
Minimum trip *20 days*

New Zealand Encounter

This pass starts in Auckland and includes the Coromandel Peninsula, Waitomo Caves, Rotorua, Taupo and Wellington on the North Island. On the South Island it travels to Nelson and down the West Coast to Wanaka and Queenstown, then on to Dunedin and up to Christchurch.

Start *Auckland;* ***finish*** *Christchurch*
Overnight stops *Dunedin, Franz Josef, Greymouth, Nelson, Queenstown, Rotorua, Taupo, Tekapo, Wellington, Whitianga*
Price *$468*
Minimum trip *14 days*

New Zealand North & South

This pass starts in Auckland and includes travel to Wellington with stops at Waitomo, Rotorua and Taupo. In the South Island it covers the west coast as far south as Queenstown and then continues up to Christchurch via Dunedin.

Start *Auckland;* ***finish*** *Christchurch.*
Overnight stops *Auckland, Dunedin, Franz Josef, Greymouth, Makarora, Nelson, Queenstown, Rotorua, Turangi, Wellington*

Price *$532*
Minimum trip *11 days*

Spirit of New Zealand
This pass covers most of the country including Northland and the Bay of Islands, Rotorua and Hawkes Bay in the North Island and both the east and west coast of the South Island including Queenstown and Milford Sound.
Overnight stops *Paihia, Auckland, Christchurch, Dunedin, Franz Josef, Greymouth, Kaikoura, Makarora, Mount Maunganui, Nelson, Queenstown, Rotorua, Taupo, Turangi, Wellington, Whitianga*
Price *$1035*
Minimum trip *23 days*

TranzAlpine and the North
This pass starts in Christchurch taking the scenic *TranzAlpine* train across Arthurs Pass to Greymouth on the West Coast. In Greymouth you pick up the coach, which takes you down to Queenstown, across to Dunedin, and then north to Christchurch and Picton. In the North Island, this pass includes transport between Wellington and Auckland with stops in Napier, Taupo, Rotorua, Mount Maunganui and Thames.
Start *Christchurch;* ***finish*** *Auckland.*
Overnight stops *Christchurch, Dunedin, Franz Josef, Greymouth, Kaikoura, Makarora, Mount Maunganui, Queenstown, Taupo, Wellington*
Price *$543*
Minimum trip *12 days*

Wayward Wanderer
This pass covers most of the country stopping at more or less the same places as the Spirit of New Zealand; except it doesn't include Abel Tasman National Park, Te Anau and Milford Sound in the South Island. It also doesn't go north of Thames on the Coromandel Peninsula.
Overnight stops *Auckland, Christchurch, Dunedin, Franz Josef, Greymouth, Kaikoura, Makarora, Mount Maunganui, Nelson, Queenstown, Paihia, Rotorua, Taupo, Turangi, Wellington*
Price *$804*
Minimum trip *20 days*

North Island Passes
Magic passes covering the North Island only include:

Auckland to Wellington
This Auckland to Wellington pass covers transport between Auckland and Wellington with stops in Waitomo, Rotorua, Taupo, Turangi and Palmerston North.
Start *Auckland;* ***finish*** *Wellington.*
Overnight stops *Auckland, Rotorua, Taupo, Turangi, Wellington*
Price *$219*
Minimum trip *3 days*

Northern Discovery
The Northern Discovery pass allows you to take a round-trip between Auckland and Wellington with stops in Thames, Mount Maunganui, Rotorua, Taupo, Hawkes Bay, Wellington, Turangi and Waitomo.
Overnight stops *Auckland, Mount Maunganui, Rotorua, Taupo, Turangi, Wellington*
Price *$358*
Minimum trip *6 days*

Pacific Coaster
The Pacific Coaster pass lets you travel north from Wellington to Auckland. It includes stops in Napier, Taupo, Rotorua, Mount Maunganui, Thames and Auckland.
Start *Wellington;* ***finish*** *Auckland*
Overnight stops *Auckland, Mount Maunganui, Napier, Wellington*
Price *$189*
Minimum trip *3 days*

Top of the North
This pass covers the central North Island with return transport between Auckland and Taupo. Stops include Thames, Mount Maunganui, Rotorua, Taupo and Waitomo.
Start/finish *Auckland*
Overnight stops *Auckland, Mount Maunganui, Rotorua, Taupo*
Price *$205*
Minimum trip *4 days*

South Island Passes
The following Magic passes only include the South Island:

Southern Discovery

This pass covers a circular route taking in both the east and west coasts of the South Island, going as far south as Christchurch and Dunedin.
Overnight stops *Christchurch, Dunedin, Franz Josef, Greymouth, Kaikoura, Makarora, Nelson, Queenstown*
Price *$448*
Minimum trip *9 days*

Top of the South

This pass includes bus travel from Christchurch to Kaikoura, Picton, Nelson, Westport and Greymouth and train travel between Greymouth and Christchurch.
Start/finish *Christchurch, Nelson or Picton*
Overnight stops *Christchurch, Kaikoura, Greymouth, Nelson*
Price *$284*
Minimum trip *4 days*

TranzAlpine Experience

The TransAlpine Experience starts and finishes in Christchurch and includes the scenic *TranzAlpine* train journey from Christchurch to Greymouth on the West Coast. From Greymouth, you travel by coach down the West Coast to Queenstown, then across to Dunedin, and back north to Christchurch.
Start/finish *Christchurch.*
Overnight stops *Christchurch, Dunedin, Franz Josef, Greymouth, Makarora, Queenstown*
Price *$442*
Minimum trip *7 days*

Wild West Coast

The Wild West Coast pass includes travel on the West Coast of the South Island between Nelson and Queenstown.
Start *Nelson;* ***finish*** *Queenstown.*
Overnight stops *Franz Josef, Greymouth, Nelson*
Price *$255*
Minimum trip *4 days*

Magic Coach & Jet Passes

There are also several Magic passes that encompass both islands and include a domestic flight. These passes are ideal if your time in New Zealand is limited but you want to see as much as possible. Magic coach and jet passes include:

Kaka Pass

This pass includes coach travel from Auckland, via Waitomo, to Rotorua; a flight between Rotorua and Christchurch and travel on the *TranzAlpine* train from Christchurch to Greymouth. In Greymouth you take the coach down the West Coast to Queenstown, across to Dunedin and back up to Christchurch.
Start *Auckland;* ***finish*** *Christchurch.*
Overnight stops *Christchurch, Dunedin, Franz Josef, Greymouth, Queenstown, Rotorua, Tekapo*
Price *$740*
Minimum trip *9 days*

Kea Pass

The Kea pass includes a flight between Auckland and Christchurch as well as travel on the scenic *TranzAlpine* train between Christchurch and Greymouth on the West Coast. In Greymouth you join the coach, which takes you south to Queenstown, across to Dunedin and back up to Christchurch.
Start *Auckland;* ***finish*** *Christchurch.*
Overnight stops *Auckland, Christchurch, Dunedin, Franz Josef, Greymouth, Queenstown, Tekapo*
Price *$667*
Minimum trip *8 days*

Kokako Pass

This pass includes coach travel from Auckland, via Waitomo, to Rotorua, Taupo and Wellington, ferry travel to the South Island and train travel to Kaikoura, Christchurch and across to Greymouth, then bus travel down the West Coast to Wanaka and Queenstown, then across to Dunedin, Tekapo and Christchurch and a flight back to Auckland.
Start/finish *Auckland*
Overnight stops *Auckland, Christchurch, Dunedin, Franz Josef, Greymouth, Queenstown, Rotorua, Taupo, Tekapo, Wellington*
Price *$950*
Minimum trip *12 days*

Tui Pass

This pass includes a flight between Auckland and Christchurch and coach travel around the South Island. Destinations covered include both the east and west coasts of the South Island, taking you as far south as Dunedin and Queenstown.
Start *Auckland;* ***finish*** *Christchurch.*
Overnight stops *Auckland, Christchurch, Dunedin, Franz Josef, Greymouth, Kaikoura, Nelson, Queenstown*
Price *$673*
Minimum trip *10 days*

Weka Pass

This pass includes a flight between Auckland and Wellington, the ferry from Wellington to Picton and coach travel on the South Island. Coach travel on the South Island goes from Picton to Nelson and Westport, then down the West Coast to Wanaka and Queenstown, across to Dunedin and up to Christchurch.
Start *Auckland;* ***finish*** *Christchurch.*
Overnight stops *Auckland, Christchurch, Dunedin, Franz Josef, Greymouth, Nelson, Queenstown, Tekapo, Wellington*
Price *$684*
Minimum trip *9 days*

Optional Connections

Magic Transport Network also offers a choice of add-on passes that include travel to the Coromandel Peninsula, the Catlins, Northland and transfers to Abel Tasman National Park and Milford Sound.

Stray Bus

Stray Travel (☎ *(03) 309 8772;* ***website*** *www.straytravel.com)* is the newest of the three big backpacker coach companies and they have the newest fleet. They have an excellent coverage of the South Island including the Catlins and Milford Sound on their standard passes (other backpacker coach operators sell these as an additional add-on pass). However they miss out on Mount Cook and their coverage of the North Island is more limited, for instance they do not go to Hawkes Bay or the Taranaki region; but they include Raglan, which the other coach companies miss out on.

Stray have an emphasis on active outdoor activities such as walking and spotting wildlife, so they may not be the best option if this isn't your thing.

Like Kiwi Experience, Stray's passes have cute names that don't give you any clue where they go. The ferry between Wellington and Picton is not included in Stray passes.

National Passes

Passes covering both North and South Islands include:

Arthur

The Arthur pass includes the bottom half of the South Island including Christchurch, Greymouth, Franz Josef, Queenstown and the Catlins; it also includes Kaikoura and Picton plus Wellington and Auckland in the North Island. You can upgrade to the *TranzAlpine* train over Arthurs Pass for an additional $85.
Start *Christchurch;* ***finish*** *Auckland*
Overnight stops *Auckland, Christchurch, Curio Bay, Kaikoura, Makarora, Queenstown, Tuatapere and Wellington*
Price *$950*
Minimum trip *15 days*

Short Arthur

The Short Arthur pass is basically the same as the Arthur Pass but with travel only as far south as Queenstown. It includes Christchurch, Greymouth, Franz Josef, Queenstown, Kaikoura and Picton on the South Island plus Wellington and Auckland in the North Island. You can upgrade to the *TranzAlpine* train over Arthurs Pass for an additional $85.
Start *Christchurch;* ***finish*** *Auckland*
Overnight stops *Auckland, Christchurch, Curio Bay, Kaikoura, Makarora, Queenstown, Tuatapere and Wellington*
Price *$675*
Minimum trip *10 days*

Bret

Bret covers all the South Island, plus Wellington and the central North Island. The pass includes Christchurch,

Kaikoura, Picton, Nelson, Abel Tasman National Park, the west coast between Westport and Haast, Wanaka, Queenstown, Te Anau, Milford Sound, Invercargill, through the Catlins to Dunedin, then up the east coast and across to the North Island. On the North Island, it covers travel from Wellington to Taupo, Raglan, Waitomo, the Coromandel Peninsula, Rotorua and Auckland.
Start *Christchurch;* ***finish*** *Auckland*
Overnight stops *Auckland, Barrytown, Christchurch, cultural stop (north of Rotorua), Dunedin, Franz Josef, Haast, Hahei, Invercargill, Kaikoura, Marahau (Abel Tasman National Park), Picton, Queenstown, Raglan, Taupo, Te Anau, Wellington*
Price *$1125*
Minimum trip *25 days*

Short Bret

This pass covers covers the South Island north of Queenstown and the central North Island. Destinations include Christchurch, Kaikoura, Picton, Nelson, Abel Tasman National park, the west coast between Westport and Haast, Wanaka and Queenstown in the South Island. On the North Island it covers travel from Wellington to Auckland stopping at Taupo, Rotorua, Raglan and the Waitomo Caves.
Start *Christchurch;* ***finish*** *Auckland*
Overnight stops *Barrytown, Franz Josef, Hahei, Makarora, Maketu, Marahau, Picton, Queenstown, Raglan, Taupo and Wellington*
Price *$850*
Minimum trip *20 days*

Dave

Dave includes all the South Island, plus the drive between Wellington and Auckland on the North Island.
Start *Christchurch or Picton;* ***finish*** *Auckland*
Overnight stops *Auckland, Barrytown, Christchurch, Dunedin, Franz Josef, Haast, Invercargill, Kaikoura, Marahau (Abel Tasman National Park), Picton, Queenstown, Te Anau, Wellington*
Price *$905*
Minimum trip *20 days ex Christchurch, 18 days ex Picton*

Short Dave

The Short Dave pass is similar to the Dave pass except it doesn't include the bottom of the South Island. It goes to destinations on the South Island north of Queenstown and on the North Island includes the direct route between Wellington and Auckland.
Start *Christchurch or Picton;* ***finish*** *Auckland*
Overnight stops *Auckland, Barrytown, Christchurch, Dunedin, Franz Josef, Haast, Kaikoura, Marahau (Abel Tasman National Park), Picton, Queenstown, Wellington*
Price *$630*
Minimum trip *15 days ex Christchurch, 13 days ex Picton*

Max

Max is a very extensive pass that goes to all Stray destinations south of Auckland.
Start/finish *anywhere*
Overnight stops *Auckland, Barrytown, Christchurch, cultural stop (north of Rotorua), Dunedin, Franz Josef, Haast, Hahei, Invercargill, Kaikoura, Marahau (Abel Tasman National Park), Ohakune, Queenstown, Raglan, Taupo, Te Anau, Wellington*
Price *$1200*
Minimum trip *24 days*

Short Max

Short Max is similar to the Max pass, but it doesn't go any further south than Queenstown. In other words it goes to all Stray destinations between Auckland and Queenstown.
Start/finish *anywhere*
Overnight stops *Auckland, Barrytown, Christchurch, Dunedin, Franz Josef, Haast, Hahei, Kaikoura, Marahau (Abel Tasman National Park), Ohakune, Queenstown, Raglan, Taupo, Wellington*
Price *$925*
Minimum trip *19 days*

Maximus

The Maximus pass is Stray's most extensive year-round pass. It includes travel throughout the North and South Islands from Cape Reinga at the tip of the North Island to Invercargill at the bottom of the South Island.

Start *anywhere;* ***finish*** *where you started*
Overnight stops *Auckland, Barrytown, Christchurch, Curio Bay, Franz Josef, Hahei, Kaikoura, Makarora, Maketu, Marahau, Paihia, Queenstown, Raglan, Taupo, Tongariro National Park, Tuatapere and Wellington*
Price *$1375*
Minimum trip *28 days*

Moe

Moe covers the North Island between Auckland and Wellington with stops at Raglan, Waitomo, Hahei, Rotorua, Taupo, Tongariro National Park. On the South Island, it covers transport from Picton to Nelson, Abel Tasman National Park, the west coast between Westport and Haast, plus Wanaka, Queenstown, Te Anau, Milford Sound, Invercargill, through the Catlins to Dunedin and up to Christchurch.
Start *Auckland; finish Christchurch*
Overnight stops *Auckland, Barrytown, Christchurch, Maketu, Dunedin, Franz Josef, Haast, Hahei, Invercargill, Marahau (Abel Tasman National Park), Ohakune, Queenstown, Raglan, Taupo, Te Anau, Wellington*
Price *$1050*
Minimum trip *21 days*

Short Moe

Moe covers the North Island between Auckland and Wellington with stops at Raglan, Waitomo, Hahei, Rotorua, Taupo, Tongariro National Park. On the South Island, it covers transport from Picton to Nelson, Abel Tasman National Park, the west coast between Westport and Haast, plus Wanaka, Queenstown, Te Anau, Milford Sound, Invercargill, through the Catlins to Dunedin and up to Christchurch.
Start *Auckland,* ***finish*** *Christchurch*
Overnight stops *Auckland, Barrytown, Christchurch, Maketu, Dunedin, Franz Josef, Haast, Hahei, Marahau (Abel Tasman National Park), Ohakune, Queenstown, Raglan, Taupo, Wellington*
Price *$775*
Minimum trip *16 days*

Stray Everywhere

The Stray Everywhere pass is Stray's most extensive pass but it only operates during summer. It goes everywhere that the Maximus pass goes with thye addition of the East Cape.
Start *anywhere;* ***finish*** *where you started*
Overnight stops *Auckland, Barrytown, Christchurch, Curio Bay, Franz Josef, Hahei, Gisborne, Kaikoura, Makarora, Maketu, Maraehako Bay, Marahau, Paihia, Queenstown, Raglan, Taupo, Tongariro National Park, Tuatapere and Wellington*
Price *$ 1614*
Minimum trip *31 days*

North Island Pa sses

Passes covering the North Island only include:

Go East

This add-on pass can be added to any other pass that goes through Rotorua. Go East and goes to the East Cape and Gisborne. It only operates during summer.
Start/finish *Rotorua*
Overnight stops *Hicks Bay, Rotorua, Tatapouri*
Price *$295*
Minimum trip *3 days*

Jackson

Jackson is an excursion from Auckland to Paihia in the Bay of Islands.
Start/finish *Auckland*
Price *$105 ($90 HI/YHA, Nomads, VIP)*
Minimum trip *1 day*

Jill

This pass covers most major destinations between Auckland and Wellington including stops at Raglan, Waitomo, Coromandel Peninsula, Rotorua, Taupo, Ohakune and Wellington.
Start/finish *Auckland*
Overnight stops *Hahei, Maketu, Ohakune, Raglan, Taupo*
Price *$465 ($435 HI/YHA, Nomads, VIP)*
Minimum trip *7 days*

Patch

This excursion to the Northland region visits Whangarei, Paihia in the Bay of Islands, Kiatia and includes a drive on the 90 Mile Beach to Cape Reinga at the tip of the North Island.

Start/finish *Auckland*
Overnight stop *Paihia*
Price *$195 ($180 HI/YHA, Nomads, VIP)*
Minimum trip *3 days*

Peter
This pass visits Raglan, Waitomo, the Coromandel Peninsula, Rotorua, Taupo and Ohakune (near Tongariro National Park). From Ohakune you have the option of taking an express coach to Wellington or back to Auckland.
Start *Auckland;* ***finish*** *Auckland or Wellington*
Overnight stops *Hahei, Maketu, Ohakune, Raglan, Taupo*
Price *$360 ($345 HI/YHA, ISIC, VIP)*
Minimum trip *6 days*

Tom
This pass covers the central North Island including Auckland, the Coromandel Peninsula, Rotorua, Taupo, Raglan and Waitomo.
Start *anywhere;* ***finish*** *where you started*
Overnight stops *Auckland, Hahei, Maketu, Raglan, Taupo*
Price *$285 ($270 HI/YHA, Nomads, VIP)*
Minimum trip *5 days*

South Island Passes
Passes covering the South Island only include:

Burt
The Burt pass focuses on the bottom part of the South Island and includes Queenstown, Milford Sound, Invercargill and the Catlins.
Start *anywhere;* ***finish*** *where you started*
Price *$315*
Minimum trip *3 days*

Q
The Q pass covers travel on the southern half of the South Island. It includes an express coach across Arthurs Pass to Barrytown on the West Coast and then travels down the coast to Wanaka and Queenstown, to Te Anau (with an excursion to Milford Sound), down to Invercargill, through the Catlins and back up to Christchurch. You can upgrade to the *TranzAlpine* train over Arthurs Pass for an additional $85.
Start/finish *Christchurch*
Overnight stops *Barrytown, Christchurch, Franz Josef, Haast, Invercargill, Queenstown and Te Anau*
Price *$740*
Minimum trip *12 days*

Short Q
The Short Q pass is the same as the Q pass, but without any travel south of Queenstown. It includes an express coach across Arthurs Pass to Barrytown on the West Coast and then travels down the coast to Wanaka and Queenstown and then heads back up to Christchurch. You can upgrade to the *TranzAlpine* train over Arthurs Pass for an additional $85.
Start/finish *Christchurch*
Overnight stops *Barrytown, Christchurch, Franz Josef, Haast and Queenstown*
Price *$465 ($450 HI/YHA, Nomads, VIP)*
Minimum trip *12 days*

Ron
Ron includes both the east and west coasts and covers the whole South Island including Nelson and Abel Tasman National Park, the west coast between Westport and Haast, Wanaka, Queenstown, Milford Sound, the Catlins and Christchurch.
Start *anywhere;* ***finish*** *where you started*
Overnight stops Barrytown, Christchurch, Franz Josef, Haast, Invercargill, Kaikoura, Marahau (Abel Tasman National Park), Queenstown, Picton and Te Anau
Price *$835*
Minimum trip *17 days*

Short Ron
The Short Ron pass goes everywhere that Ron goes except the north east coast between Christchurch and Picton. In other words it covers all the South Island except Kaikoura.
Start *Picton;* ***finish*** *Christchurch*
Overnight stops *Barrytown, Christchurch, Franz Josef, Haast, Invercargill, Marahau (Abel Tasman National Park), Queenstown, Picton and Te Anau*

Price *$780*
Minimum trip *15 days*

Sally

Sally starts in Queenstown and includes Milford Sound, Te Anau, Invercargill and then travels through the Catlins to Dunedin and back to Queenstown and up to Christchurch.
Start *Queenstown;* ***finish*** *Christchurch.*
Overnight stops *Dunedin, Invercargill, Te Anau*
Price *$375 ($360 HI/YHA, Nomads, VIP)*
Minimum trip *5 days*

Willy

This pass includes the east coast of the South Island between Christchurch and Picton, then heads to Nelson and the Abel Tasman National Park and down the west coast to Wanaka and Queenstown with an express coach between Queenstown and Christchurch.
Start *anywhere;* ***finish*** *where you started*
Overnight stops *Barrytown, Christchurch, Franz Josef, Haast, Kaikoura, Marahau (Abel Tasman National Park), Queenstown and Picton*
Price *$535 ($500 HI/YHA, Nomads, VIP)*
Minimum trip *12 days*

Short Willy

This pass starts in Picton and heads to Nelson and the Abel Tasman National Park and down the west coast to Wanaka and Queenstown with an express coach between Queenstown and Christchurch. It is basically the Willy pass without Kaikoura.
Start *anywhere;* ***finish*** *where you started*
Overnight stops *Barrytown, Christchurch, Franz Josef, Haast, Marahau (Abel Tasman National Park), Queenstown and Picton*
Prices *$495 ($480 HI/YHA, Nomads, VIP)*
Minimum trip *10 days*

New Zealand Travelpass

The New Zealand Travelpass (☎ *0800 33 99 66;* ***website*** *www.travelpass.co.nz)* is an excellent transport option for the independent traveller. This pass includes unlimited coach travel on InterCity and Newmans coaches as well as inter-island ferry travel and the option of rail and air transport as well depending on which pass you purchase. The New Zealand Travelpass provides the holder with a specified number of travel days within a six-month period.

This is a much easier to understand travel option than many of the other bus passes available, many of which limit which routes which you may travel on.

2-in-One Travelpass

This is the basic Travelpass allowing unlimited coach travel on InterCity and Newmans coaches for a specific number of travel days within a 12 month period. This pass also allows for either one Cook Strait ferry crossing on the InterIslander or a Kings "Hole in the Rock" Cape Brett Cruise in the Bay of Islands.

Travel Days	Price
5 days	$399
6 days	$439
7 days	$479
8 days	$521
9 days	$570
10 days	$619
11 days	$667
12 days	$715
13 days	$760
14 days	$850
15 days	$871
Additional travel day	$54

3-in-One Travelpass

The 3-in-One Travelpass allows unlimited coach travel on InterCity and Newmans coaches for a specific number of travel days within a 12 month period. This pass also allows for either one Cook Strait ferry crossing on the InterIslander or a Kings "Hole in the Rock" Cape Brett Cruise in the Bay of Islands and one rail journey.

Travel Days	Price
5 days	$504
6 days	$560
7 days	$617
8 days	$676
9 days	$716
10 days	$757
11 days	$798

12 days	$838
13 days	$867
14 days	$898
15 days	$931
Additional travel day	$54

It is essential to make seat reservations when travelling with the New Zealand Travelpass. You can call 0800 33 99 66 (toll-free within New Zealand) to make reservations on any mode of transport covered by the Travelpass. Reservations for coach travel have to be made at least three hours before travel and rail and ferry bookings need to be made at least 24 hours in advance. Reservations for air travel should be made as far in advance as possible to ensure a seat.

Train Travel

The Tranz Scenic (☎ *0800 872 467 (0800 TRAINS);* ***website*** *www.tranzscenic.co.nz)* rail network connects Christchurch to Picton and Greymouth and Auckland with Wellington. In the North Island, Tranz Scenic trains are limited to the *Overlander* connecting Auckland and Wellington and the *Capital Connection* that runs between Wellington and Palmerston North. Rail services in the South Island include the *TranzCoastal* that runs between Picton and Christchurch and the scenic *TranzAlpine* that runs over Arthurs Pass between Christchurch and Greymouth.

Many people don't consider the train because it runs infrequently and doesn't go to the big tourist destinations like Queenstown or the Bay of Islands, but it is still worth considering for the odd journey, as it is far more comfortable than the coach. The *TranzAlpine* service between Christchurch and Greymouth is considered one of the world's most scenic rail journeys and many people make this journey for the spectacular train trip.

In addition to trains operated by Tranz Scenic, there are some small tourist-oriented rail services, the most useful of which is the *Taieri Gorge Railway* (☎ *(03) 477 4449;* ***website*** *www.taieri.co.nz)* that runs from Dunedin to Middlemarch along the spectacular Taieri River Gorge with coach connections to Queenstown.

The New Zealand Travelpass includes train travel and the Scenic Rail Pass is worth considering if you plan on travelling on all the Tranz Scenic train lines.

Scenic Rail Pass

The Scenic Rail Pass gives you seven days unlimited travel on Tranz Scenic trains.

Pass	Price
South Island	$265
South Island with ferry	$299
All services	$309
All services with ferry	$359

Driving

Although New Zealand has good bus connections, driving is still the best way to see the country at your own pace. It gives you more freedom than any other mode of transport and allows you to get to some fantastic little hostels in out-of-the-way places.

In New Zealand, traffic drives on the left. The maximum speed limit is 100 km/h, although the speed limit drops to 50 km/h in built-up areas.

One-way bridges are common in rural areas. As you approach a one-way bridge there will be a sign stating who has priority. In some instances there are passing bays on long bridges.

The other major thing to remember is that you have to give way to the right – in other words, when you are at an intersection you have to let any car to the right of you go first.

Most major road atlases have a couple of pages explaining the road rules and rental car companies will often give you a flyer with diagrams explaining road rules.

Unleaded fuel is reasonably priced by European standards, but expensive in comparison with the United States.

Renting a Car

Renting a car or motor home is cheap and easy in New Zealand and it is very common among backpackers. New Zealand has all the major rental companies plus a lot of smaller car rental agencies that often have much better rates. You may need to stick with the major companies if you want a one-way rental, particularly if the car is being dropped off on a different island.

Generally inter-island rentals entail dropping the car off in Picton or Wellington ferry terminals or Blenheim, Nelson or Wellington airports and picking up another car when you get to the other side of Cook Strait. This saves having to pay to take the car on the ferry.

The price of a rental car can drop substantially if you rent for a month or more. This is particularly the case with some of the smaller car rental companies.

Because most travellers fly into Auckland and drive south, there are some very good relocation deals if you're renting a car and driving north although the cheap deals are usually only available if you complete your trip within a couple of days. It is well worth enquiring with the rental companies if you want to drive north from Christchurch to Picton or Wellington to Auckland – if you complete the trip within 24 hours you may even get the rental for free.

The standard insurance cover that comes with most car rental companies requires that you pay an excess of $2000-3000 before the insurance company pays out. Rental car companies will sell you insurance to cover this excess, but at around $20 a day this is overpriced and in many cases doubles the cost of your car rental. A much better idea is to take out travel insurance that covers this excess or arrange rental car excess insurance through your auto club before leaving home. This works out a lot cheaper than paying the excess cover that rental car companies charge.

Rental car companies in New Zealand include:

A2B Rentals
11 Stanley Street, Parnell, Auckland
☎ *0800 616 111*
Website *www.a2brentals.co.nz*

Ace Rental Cars
39 The Strand, Parnell, Auckland
☎ *(09) 303 3112 or 0800 422 771*
Website *www.acerentals.co.nz*
Open *8am-5pm daily*

Avis
17-19 Nelson Street, Auckland
☎ *(09) 379 2650 or 0800 655 111*
Website *www.avis.co.nz*
Open *Mon-Fri 7.30am-6pm, Sat-Sun 8am-5pm*

Bargain Rental Cars
99 Beach Road, Auckland
☎ *(09) 444 4573 or 0800 566 700*
Website *www.bargainrentals.co.nz*

Budget
163 Beach Road, Auckland
☎ *(09) 976 2270 or 0800 652 227*
Website *www.budget.co.nz*
Open *Mon-Fri 7am-6pm, Sat-Sun 8am-5pm*

Ezy Car Rentals
2-16 The Strand, Parnell, Auckland
☎ *(09) 374 4360 or 0800 399 736*
Website *www.ezy.co.nz*

Hertz
154 Victoria Street West, Auckland
☎ *(09) 367 6350*
Website *www.hertz.co.nz*
Open *7.30am-5.30pm daily*

National
73 Shortland Street, Auckland
☎ *0800 800 115*
Website *www.nationalcar.co.nz*
Open *8am-6pm daily*

Omega Rental Cars
75 Beach Road, Auckland
☎ *(09) 377 5573 or 0800 52 52 10*
Website *www.omegarentals.com*

Pegasus Rental Cars
83 Haven Road, Nelson
☎ *(03) 548 2852 or 0800 803 580*
Website *www.rentalcars.co.nz*

Thrifty
150 Khyber Pass Road, Auckland
☎ *(09) 309 0111*
Website *www.thrifty.co.nz*

Renting a Campervan

Motor homes or campervans are a popular alternative to a rental car since they also solve the problem of where to stay. However they are more expensive than regular car rental and you'll have to pay to stay in a motor camp (caravan/trailer park) so you can have a shower. Another drawback with travelling in a campervan is that because you're not staying in hostels you generally miss out on being part of the backpacker scene.

Campervan rental companies in New Zealand include:

Apollo
2/20 Verissimo Drive, Westney Industry Park, Mangere, Auckland
☎ *0800 113 131*
Website *www.apollocamper.co.nz*
Open *8am-4.30pm daily*

Backpacker Campervans
36 Richard Pearse Drive, Mangere, Auckland
☎ *(09) 275 0200 or 0800 422 267*
Website *www.backpackercampervans.com*
Open *7am-6pm daily*

Britz
36 Richard Pearse Drive, Mangere, Auckland
☎ *(09) 275 9090*
Website *www.britz.co.nz*
Open *7am-6pm daily*

Escape Rentals
7 Gore Street, Auckland
☎ *0800 216 171*
Website *www.escaperentals.co.nz*

Kea Campers
36 Hillside Road, Glenfield, Auckland
☎ *(09) 441 7833 or 0800 520 052*
Website *www.keacampers.com*
Open *Mon-Fri 8am-5pm, Sat-Sun 8am-1pm*

Maui
36 Richard Pearse Drive, Mangere, Auckland
☎ *(09) 275 3013 or 0800 651 080*
Website *www.maui.co.nz*
Open *7am-6pm daily*

Spaceships
31 Beach Road, Auckland
☎ *(09) 309 8777 or 0800 772 237*
Website *www.spaceships.tv*

Buying a Car

Because there is a lot to see, many travellers buy a car, drive around New Zealand for a few months and then resell the car to another group of travellers. This is a good option for a group of people with time on their hands, although both car and motor home rental are both popular options.

If you want to buy a car, check classified ad magazines in newsagents and petrol stations and notice boards in hostels. Most hostels have a few cheap cars for sale. In big cities like Auckland where there is an established backpacker scene, you may be able to buy a car from a second-hand car dealer that specialises in backpackers; the main advantages is that they can assist with all the paperwork and even arrange to buy the car back when you have finished travelling. You can also look online for a car. Gumtree *(**website** www.gumtree.co.nz)* and Trade Me *(**website** www.trademe.co.nz)* are two good places to start looking to get an idea of what you can expect to pay.

You will need to ensure that there is no money owing on the vehicle, otherwise you may find yourself in a situation where the car is repossessed to repay the previous owners debts. For $3 you can check the vehicle with the Personal Property Securities Register *(☎ 0900 90977; **website** www.ppsr.govt.nz)*. You will need to provide details of the car's registration, VIN and chassis number.

If you are buying a car it will need to have a WOF (Warrant of Fitness) certificate, which shows that minimum safety standards have been met. If the car doesn't have a WOF you will need to get the car inspected at one of 3,500 WOF agents throughout New Zealand. If you are buying a car with a WOF, you will need to have this renewed when it expires (every six months).

You will then need to fill in a MR13A form to transfer the car's ownership. This will cost $9.20 and can be done at any New Zealand Post Office. Depending on the length of registration remaining on the car, you may also need to pay for more registration and third-party insurance. Registration will cost $235.59 for six months or $323.42 for one year. This paperwork is organised by the Land Transport Safe ty Authority, check the buying & selling pages of the Motorists section of their website *(www.ltsa.govt.nz)* for more information on all the bureaucracy that you may need to deal with.

Third-party liability insurance protects you if you are involved in an accident that causes damage to someone else's property. Budget Backpackers Hostels (BBH) sells a third-party liability insurance policy that is specially tailored to the requirements of backpackers. This policy is available from the following BBH hostels:

North Island

- Bamber House (Auckland)
- Brown Kiwi (Auckland)
- City Garden Lodge (Auckland)
- Verandahs (Auckland)
- Peppertree Lodge (Paihia, Northland)
- Hone Heke Backpackers (Kerikeri, Northland)
- Sunkist Lodge (Thames, Waikato)
- Bell Lodge (Tauranga, Bay of Plenty)
- Mount Backpackers (Mount Maunganui, Bay of Plenty)
- Funky Green Voyager (Rotorua, Bay of Plenty)

South Island

- The Grapevine (Blenheim, Marlborough)
- Beach Hostel (Nelson, Nelson-Tasman)
- Charlie B's (Christchurch, Canterbury)
- Chester Street Backpackers (Christchurch, Canterbury)
- Foley Towers (Christchurch, Canterbury)

If you're buying a car and planning on doing a lot of driving you may consider joining the Automobile Association *(AA; ☎ 0800 500 444;* ***website*** *www.aa.co.nz)*. Membership in the AA has a lot of benefits including breakdown assistance, discounts and travel information. If you are already a member of an affiliated motoring organisation, excluding the AA or RAC in the UK, you are entitled to reciprocal services for up to six months; alternatively you can take out a six-month visitor's membership for $99. If you are renting a car some sort of breakdown assistance scheme may already cover you, so it is really only worth the money if you've bought a cheap old car that is likely to break down.

Hitchhiking

Hitchhiking is a great way to travel that allows you to really get to know the locals. Many people prefer hitching to other forms of transport because you can get dropped off anywhere, allowing you to discover places you may never have dreamt of visiting.

Unfortunately hitchhiking gets a lot of bad press, particularly since the widely publicised hitchhiker murders many years ago. It seems that there are a lot of people who think that you'll get murdered if you hitch. This attitude has two negative effects – people are too frightened to pick you up and a lot of other travellers are scared to hitchhike meaning less hitchers on the road, which ultimately leads to hitchhiking becoming a dying art.

Where to hitch

It is important to choose a good spot to hitchhike. A good spot makes it easier to get a ride and more importantly it is safer for both you and the driver.

If you are leaving a big city it is a good idea to take a bus or train to the outskirts of town to get to a road leading to a motorway and then choose a spot with plenty of room for the driver to safely stop. If possible try and stand in a spot where the traffic isn't too fast. It is much safer and also most drivers want to size you up before they decide whether to give you a lift.

If you've got a lift on a motorway, try and get dropped off at a service area rather than in town. If you're dropped off in town you have to wait hours in local traffic before getting a lift back on to the motorway. If you hitch at a service area you have facilities like a restaurant, shop and toilets; you can chat to truck drivers and ask about getting a lift and you can get a good safe spot to stand where all the traffic is long distance.

Don't hitchhike on motorways, stick to the entrance ramps and service areas. Not only is hitching on motorways dangerous, it is difficult for cars to safely stop and it is usually illegal.

Signs

A lot of hitchers debate whether to use signs or not. Some argue that drivers won't stop if they don't know where you want to go, while other hitchers say that it is safer to avoid using a sign. If you don't use a sign you can ask the driver where they are going before accepting a lift – the driver won't be able to lie about his destination to get you into the car.

A good compromise is to use a sign indicating the name of the road you want to travel on. This is especially useful if you are on a busy road before a major intersection, without a sign you may get a lift going in the wrong direction.

Tips for getting a ride

You'll find a lot of rides come from regular stoppers – people who've hitchhiked themselves and are repaying the favour and frequent solo travellers, like couriers and truck drivers who want some company. Although you'll find that different people have different reasons for picking you up, there are a number of things you can do to improve your chances of getting a lift.

- Look neat and respectable. Not only should you look non-threatening to any passing driver, but you also help to improve other people's impression of hitchhiking.
- Face the oncoming traffic and smile. It is important that people can see you, so avoid wearing sunglasses.
- Try and look smart and clean.
- When a car stops ask the driver where they are going to. At this point it is easy to decline the lift if you don't like the look of the driver or if they aren't going your way.
- Never smoke in someone else's car.
- Travel light. The lighter your load, the quicker you travel.
- Take an international drivers licence. Many people stop because they want someone to share the driving.

Safety

Although hitchhiking is more hazardous than bus or train travel, it's still safer than other forms of transport such as cycling.

The most dangerous thing about hitchhiking is the possibility of being involved in a car accident or being hit by a car if you stand too close to the side of the road.

There is also a very small danger posed by accepting a lift with a driver that you do not know. The driver could either be a dangerous character or simply a bad driver.

Despite the perceived danger, there are plenty of ways to minimise your risk.

If you're a single female you'll travel quickly, however you'll also attract your fair share of obnoxious drivers. It is a good idea to travel with someone else, preferably a guy. This way you will be perceived as a couple which means that you shouldn't have any sleazy old men trying to come on to you, and if they do at least there is someone to help you out.

Many hitchhikers travel with a mobile phone and only hitch where there is coverage. Being able to call for help makes hitching a safer transport option. For this to work you need to keep your phone charged and in your pocket and you need to know the emergency number (112 is the international emergency number from GSM mobile phones, although the New Zealand emergency number 111 also works).

Don't let the driver put your backpack in the car boot. Try and keep all your stuff with you, even when you stop for food and fuel.

Don't feel compelled to accept a lift just because someone has stopped for you. If it doesn't feel right, don't get in. Another ride will come along.

Ferry Travel

The ferry is the most popular way to get between the North and South Islands and it is also a good way to get to Stewart Island and the islands in the Hauraki Gulf.

Cook Strait (Inter-island Ferries)

There are two ferry companies connecting the North and South Island. Interislander is the main company that most travellers sail with, but the smaller Blue Bridge line is an alternative.

The Interislander *(☎ 0800 802 802; **website** www.interislander.co.nz)* has three big ships that connect Wellington and Picton several times a day. This ferry is the most popular option mostly because it is the one everyone knows about and also because you can use some travel passes on it. The Interislander also operates the nicest boats and with up to nine return sailings a day they are the most convenient.

The Interislander ferry sails from the Interislander ferry terminal Aotea Quay, Wellington, which is 3km from the city centre, but a free shuttle bus departs the train station 35 minutes before each sailing. There is also a shuttle bus that costs $2 and departs from the YHA hostel at 8.10am to meet the 9.30am ferry departure.

Interislander fares are $62-72 for passengers, $200-235 for cars and small campervans and $130-150 for motorcycles; however there are often special deals when you book online.

The smaller Blue Bridge line *(☎ 0800 844 844; **website** www.bluebridge.co.nz)* is an alternative that works out cheaper if you're taking a car across. Blue Bridge's fares are also easier to work out, as there is a simple flat fare that everyone pays regardless of when they book their ticket. Blue Bridge ferries depart from the wharf beside the train station. Blue Bridge fares are a flat $35 for passengers, $130 for a car or small campervan and $85 for a motorcycle.

Stewart Island Ferries

Stewart Island Experience *(☎ (03) 212 7660 or 0800 000 511; **website** www.stewartislandexperience.co.nz)* operates two 20-metre catamarans between Stewart Island and Bluff at the bottom of the South Island. This is the cheapest and most popular way to visit Stewart Island. There are two scheduled trips each day except Christmas day with extra services during peak periods such as long weekends. Stewart Island Experience ferry fares are $55 each way. Transport between Invercargill and the ferry terminal at Bluff costs an additional $18 each way.

Hauraki Gulf Ferries

Fullers *(☎ (09) 367 9111; **website** www.fullers.co.nz)* and Sealink *(☎ (09) 300 5900 or 0800 732 546; **website** www.sealink.co.nz)* operate ferry services from Auckland to the Hauraki Gulf islands including popular trips to Waiheke.

Waiheke Island is the most popular destination with both Fullers and Sealink making the half-hour journey from central Auckland. Return fares between Auckland and Waiheke cost $28.50.

Fullers also operate commuter ferries to the North Shore with the Devonport service most popular with backpackers. The Devonport ferry runs every half hour and costs $5.20 each way or $9 return.

Fullers ferries depart from behind the ferry building at the end of Queen Street in central Auckland.

Sealink Ferries sail to Great Barrier Island. The four-hour journey costs $68 one-way or $110 return. Sealink's Great Barrier Island ferries depart from Wynyard Wharf on Jellicoe Street in Freemans Bay, about a half hour walk from the Fullers ferry terminal.

Fullers also run ferries to Great Barrier Island and charge around the same as Sealink at $70 one way or $130 return, but Fullers only operate this route during peak times on long weekends and during summer.

Auckland Region

The Auckland region is a sprawling area of suburbs, beaches, harbours, and islands. It includes Auckland City, the North Shore, the cities of Manukau and Waitakere, the district of Rodney, and the islands of the Harauki Gulf.

The city of Auckland is New Zealand's metropolis, a buzzing urban centre set between two beautiful harbours. It offers both big-city thrills and a lovely, tranquil waterfront setting. Adventure activities, water-based fun, dining, art, nightlife, a strong Polynesian influence and much more give travellers a wealth of choices in Auckland. There's much more to it than the bars and clubs of the downtown area.

Although, there is definitely a charmless suburban sprawl circling Auckland, within half an hour on most sides of the city there are beaches, vineyards, islands and native bush.

The islands of the Hauraki Gulf make a great escape from the urban jungle. It's a short ride to artsy, counter-cultural Waiheke Island, a laid-back world of beaches, cafés, and forest. Further into the gulf, Great Barrier Island is an unspoiled, remote island paradise that is still easily accessible by plane or ferry.

Heading north into the Kowhai Coast, there are charming small towns, still-uncrowded beaches, wine and food trails, and some great snorkelling and diving opportunities.

Most travellers arrive in Auckland by air, but very few see any of the region surrounding the city – they don't realise what they are missing.

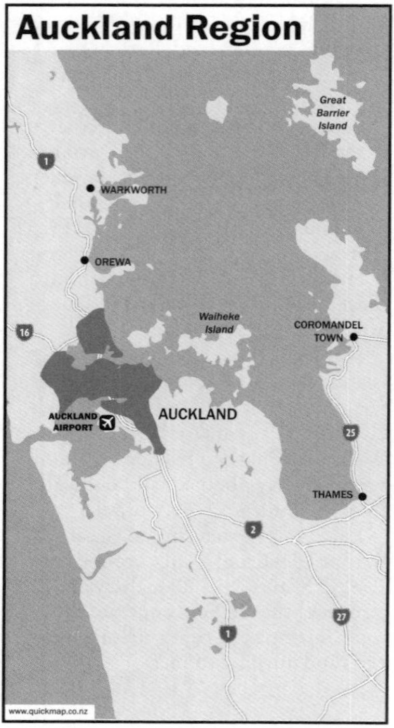

Auckland Region

Great Barrier Island
1
WARKWORTH
OREWA
16
Waiheke Island
COROMANDEL TOWN
AUCKLAND AIRPORT
AUCKLAND
25
THAMES
2
27
1
www.quickmap.co.nz

Auckland

Auckland is by far New Zealand's biggest city, with 1.3 million residents out of a country that has a population of only 4.2 million. As such, it has an outsized cultural and economic influence on New Zealand and can inspire love or hate in Kiwis, but never indifference. To much of the rest of the country Auckland folk are derided as "JAFAs" – Just Another F-ing Aucklander. But Aucklanders are probably too busy enjoying their cosmopolitan, brash, and yes, sometimes a little bit crass city to care.

Auckland is situated between the Manukau and Waitemata Harbours and is built up on a landscape of extinct volcanic cones. The suburbs of Auckland sprawl for miles and miles, with many people commuting to work from secluded bays and island communities. The centre city is not particularly charming, a kind of anonymous big-city environment of tall buildings and crowded business-hour streets. Yet there's also great nightlife to be found, excellent restaurants, and a lively cultural and artistic scene in town.

The city also has an interesting multicultural mix with a blend of Asian, European and Polynesian culture and it has the largest Polynesian population of any city in the world.

Many of Auckland's more interesting neighbourhoods are to be found in its inner suburban ring. Parnell is a short walk from the city centre and has a quaint old shopping area along with stylish restaurants and cafés. Walk a little further away from the centre and you come to Newmarket, a bustling neighbourhood which is a great place for no-nonsense shopping.

On the opposite side of the city is Ponsonby – the coolest neighbourhood in Auckland, with loads of cafés and bars lining the streets; nearby Karangahape Road (known widely as K Road), on the north end of Queen Street, is the hip centre of nightlife and alternative culture.

A big part of the city's appeal is its great harbourside location. Auckland is called the "City of Sails", with one in ten Aucklanders said to own a boat, and it's easy to believe if you get out on the water on a sunny weekend afternoon. Sailing excursions can be booked, or you can just get out and take a ferry to Auckland's many nearby islands.

Almost everyone visiting New Zealand comes and goes through Auckland at some point. Many backpackers just stay in the downtown area and hit the bars and clubs of the Fort Street/Queen Street area - decent enough fun, but there's so much more to see and do in Auckland. It's the kind of place that rewards a bit of exploration.

Practical Information

INFORMATION CENTRES

Auckland i-SITE Visitor Centre – SKYCITY Atrium
Sky City, Corner Federal & Victoria Streets, Auckland
☎ *(09) 363 7182 or 0800 AUCKLAND*
Website *www.aucklandnz.com*
Open *8am-8pm daily*

Auckland i-SITE Visitor Centre – Princes Wharf
137 Quay Street, Princes Wharf, Auckland
☎ *(09) 307 0612 or 0800 AUCKLAND*
Website *www.aucklandnz.com*
Open *Jan-Mar Mon-Fri 8.30am-6pm, Sat-Sun 9am-5pm; Apr-Sep 9am-5pm daily; Oct-Dec 8.30am-6pm, Sat-Sun 9am-5pm*

Devonport i-SITE Visitor Centre
3 Victoria Road, Devonport
☎ *(09) 446 0677*
Website *www.tourismnorthshore.org.nz*
Open *8.30am-5pm daily*

EMBASSIES & CONSULATES

Australia
Level 7, Price Waterhouse-Coopers Tower, 188 Quay Street, Auckland
☎ *(09) 921 8800*
Website *www.australia.org.nz*
Open *Mon-Fri 9am-4.30pm*

Ireland
7 Citigroup Centre, 23 Customs Street East, Auckland
☎ *(09) 977 2252*
Website *www.ireland.co.nz*

United Kingdom
17th floor, 151 Queen Street, Auckland
☎ *(09) 303 2973*
Website *www.britishhighcommission.gov.uk*
Open *Mon-Fri 9am-5pm*

United States
3rd Floor, Citibank Centre, 23 Customs Street East, Auckland
☎ *(09) 303 2724*
Website *http://newzealand.usembassy.gov/auckland/*
Open *Mon-Fri 8am-noon & 2pm-4pm*

INTERNET ACCESS

Most hostels have internet access, but you can also get online at these internet cafés:

Discount Dialing
7 Fort Street, Auckland
☎ *(09) 355 7300*
Open *8am-11.30pm daily*

Global Gossip
Base Auckland Central Backpackers, Level 3, 229 Queen Street, Auckland
☎ *(09) 358 4877*
Website *www.globalgossip.com*

Esquires Coffee *(**website** www.esquires.co.nz)* has free Wi-Fi access at many of their central Auckland stores including: the Citibank Building, 23 Customs Street East; Foodtown, 76 Quay Street;

188 Quay Street; 155 Queen Street; 57B Hobson Street; 33 Lorne Street; 291 Queen Street and Pier 1 in the Ferry Terminal. **Magnation** *(100 Queen Street, Auckland; **website** www.magnation.com)* also have free Wi-Fi.

Coming & Going

Auckland is New Zealand's main international gateway and has excellent transport connections to the rest of the country.

AIR

Auckland International Airport *(☎ (09) 256 8899; **website** www.auckland-airport.co.nz)* is on Manakau Harbour 21km south of the city centre. The airport is New Zealand's largest.

If you are leaving on an international flight you are required to pay a $25 departure tax at the Bank of New Zealand branch in the terminal building.

There is a free shuttle bus service between the international terminal and the two domestic terminals, which operates from 6am until 10.30pm; alternatively it is about a 10 minute walk between the two terminals.

There are plenty of bus services running between the airport and downtown Auckland. The main one is the AirBus *(☎ 0508 AIRBUS; **website** www.airbus.co.nz)*, which runs a set route every 20 minutes (every 30 minutes after 6pm) between the airport and the city centre with various stops at hostels and hotels in central Auckland with a free connecting bus to Parnell for $15 ($13 BBH, HI/YHA, VIP).

Some travellers arrive in New Zealand on the cheap Freedom Air flights from Australia. Freedom Air flies into Hamilton Airport, which is near Hamilton in the Waikato region about 150km south of Auckland. There are frequent buses connecting Hamilton Airport with Hamilton, which connect with bus services to downtown Auckland.

BUS

InterCity *(☎ (09) 623 1503; **website** www.intercity.co.nz)* coaches stop at the Sky City Coach Terminal at 102 Hobson Street and Naked Bus *(☎ 0900 62533 (0900 NAKED); **website** www.nakedbus.com)* stop at 172 Quay Street, about 50m from the Britomart Transport Centre. Both InterCity and Naked Bus go to most destinations throughout the North Island.

TRAIN

Auckland's Britomart Transport Centre is at the downtown end of Queen Street. This is Auckland's main station for suburban trains and the daily *Overland* service to Wellington.

HITCHHIKING

The motorway system around Auckland makes it easy for drivers to get out of town, although you may miss out on a lot of traffic that is already on the motorway if you are waiting at a motorway entrance ramp. There are a number of convenient motorway entrances in the downtown area that make it relatively easy to hitch out of Auckland.

If you're heading south, you'll want to get on the Southern Motorway. Coming from downtown Auckland, the handiest on-ramps to the motorway are at the top of Hobson Street and on Stanley Street near the Domain. Pick a safe spot to stand before the motorway entrance, preferably a spot where a car can safely stop for you. An easier option is to take a coach to the spot near Bombay where the motorway ends. Any Hamilton-bound bus should be able to drop you off here.

If you're heading north, you have two main options. You can get on the motorway at the Fanshawe Street entrance, near Victoria Park or take a bus to the Massey University campus at Albany on the North Shore. Alternatively the North-Western Motorway also takes you north – you can get on at the entrance at the top of Hobson Street or at the entrance on Newton Road.

If you're hitching from central Auckland, you'll need to use a sign indicating your destination, as the motorway junctions in the central area are quite complex and lead to more than one motorway.

Local Transport

Auckland's public transport system is made up of buses, trains and ferries. Auckland's transport system is rather disorganised, but it is currently being re-branded as MAXX Regional Transport *(☎ (09) 366 6400 or 0800 103 080; **website** www.maxx.co.nz)*, which is intended to introduce some consistency between bus, ferry and train routes.

BUS

The bus is the most convenient way for most travellers to get around the city.

There are around six different bus companies operating in the Auckland area, but Stagecoach Auckland *(☎ 0800 STAGECOACH; **website** www.stagecoach.co.nz)* is the main bus operator.

Bus fares start at 50c for a short hop in the city centre and go up to $9.70.

There are only a few routes that are useful to the average backpacker. These include the bus routes running up and down Queen Street and the Link bus. The Link bus operates a circular route taking in all the main inner-city neighbourhoods including Parnell, Newmarket, Karangahape Road and Ponsonby. You can catch The Link on Queen Street in the city centre. Each ride is $1.60. Link buses run every 10 minutes during weekdays and every 20 minutes on week nights and weekends.

Although the Link bus is a good value way to get out to Parnell, Newmarket or Ponsonby, if you just want to go up and down Queen Street it is cheaper to hop on a regular (not a Link) bus, as this will cost you just 50c.

Another popular bus service is the free City Circle bus that runs around the city centre every 10 minutes linking Viaduct Harbour, Sky City and Auckland University.

FERRY

There are frequent ferry services departing from the wharf behind the Ferry Building on Quay Street in downtown Auckland. Fullers Ferries *(☎ (09) 367 9111; **website** www.fullers.co.nz)* run affordable commuter services to Devonport and Waiheke Island. The ferry journey to Devonport is a popular day trip and costs $5.20 each way or $9 return.

TRAIN

Veolia Transport *(**website** www.veoliatransport.co.nz)* run a fairly extensive suburban rail network that is centred on the new Britomart station at the bottom of Queen Street. The most useful train route is the short hop between Britomart and Newmarket stations. Fares range from $1.40 to $9.10 for a single journey.

TRAVEL PASSES

There are several travel passes available that are good value for travellers who rely a lot on public transport. These passes include:

Auckland Discovery Day Pass

This bus service is valid for unlimited travel on the five major bus companies, plus trains and Fuller's inner-harbour ferries between 5am on the day of purchase and 4.59am the following morning. It covers a large area that encompasses the suburban area and outlying towns, but doesn't include travel to Waiheke Island. This pass costs $13.

Aucklandpass

This pass is good for one day unlimited travel on Go West, Link, North Star and Stagecoach buses and ferry services to the North Shore. This pass costs $11.

3-Day Rover

This is essentially the same as the Aucklandpass, but it is valid for three consecutive days. It costs $25.

Accommodation

CITY CENTRE

Hostels in the city centre are handy to shops, transport and the main sights.

Albert Park Backpackers

The entrance to Albert Park Backpackers is grungy and uninviting but the interior of the building is more appealing. A bright common room off of the reception area has a pool table. There are kitchen and laundry facilities, and a small courtyard in the middle of the building for smoking and sunning. The rooftop has a good view and is a definite plus in

nicer weather. It's a basic hostel and the rooms are a bit worn, but the staff are friendly, and its proximity to hilly Albert Park as well as the Central Business District is another plus.
27-31 Victoria Street East
Link, City Circuit, 210-213, 215, 219, 223, 224, 233, 241, 243, 246, 248, 249
(09) 309 0336 or 0800 220 224
Website *www.albertpark.co.nz*
Dorm bed *$18-$21;* ***single room*** *$52;* ***double/twin room*** *$62*
Credit cards *Amex, Diners, JCB, MC, Visa*
Reception open *5am-1am*

Maintenance & cleanliness	★★★½
Facilities	★★½
Atmosphere & character	★★★½
Security	★★★½
Overall rating	★★★½

Base Auckland Central Backpackers

ACB, one of the best-known hostels in Auckland, became part of the expanding Base empire a couple of years back. It's a 500+ bed self-contained travel universe with all the amenities, including a travel desk, a big bank of internet PCs, an employment office, and more. Rooms are clean and feature quality bedding, lockers for every bed, refrigerators and air-conditioning. The sixth floor Balcony Bar is only open in the summer, but is a congenial place to congregate over free sausage sizzles. The ground level Globe Bar is one of Auckland's busier and buzzier night spots. ACB shares the advantages of belonging to a big and well-funded organisation like Base – clean, well-run facilities with many perks. On the flip side there can be a kind of impersonal backpacker-factory feeling.
229 Queen Street, Auckland
Link, City Circuit, 015, 017, 024, 025, 027, 034, 042, 043, 045, 210-213, 215, 219, 223, 224, 233, 241, 243, 246, 248, 249
(09) 358 4877 or 0800 227 369 (0800 BASE NZ)
Website *www.stayatbase.com*
Dorm bed *$26-$28;* ***single room*** *$70;* ***double/twin room*** *$90;* ***family room*** *$130*
Credit cards *MC, Visa (2 night minimum stay required for credit card payment)*
Reception open *24 hours*

Maintenance & cleanliness	★★★★
Facilities	★★★
Atmosphere & character	★★★
Security	★★★½
Overall rating	★★★½

Base Auckland

Base Auckland has a bit more character than the ACB, its fellow Base hostel in Auckland. Set in a turn-of-the century building, there are some standout features including a spa pool and sauna, treats after a long day of lugging a pack around. A few original details are intact and make for nice touches, like exposed brick in the café and a fireplace in the library. Smaller common spaces give Base Auckland a slightly warmer feeling than some other Base properties, although there are still loads and loads of backpackers coming and going, and the usual party vibe. Its location on Fort Street guarantees lots of rowdy late night action at your doorstep; the in-house bar, First Base, gets pretty frisky too.
16-20 Fort Street, Auckland
Link, City Circuit *Britomart*
Downtown Ferry Terminal
(09) 300 9999
Website *www.stayatbase.com*
Dorm bed *$26-$30;* ***double room*** *$90;* ***twin room*** *$70*
Credit cards *MC, Visa*
Reception open *24 hours*

Maintenance & cleanliness	★★★★½
Facilities	★★★★
Atmosphere & character	★★★
Security	★★★★½
Overall rating	★★★★

BK Hostel

BK Hostel is a bright and tidy place located above the Subway sandwich shop right on happening Karangahape Road. Almost all the share rooms are twin single beds with real mattresses; one room has three beds. A small lounge features a great TV and a pool

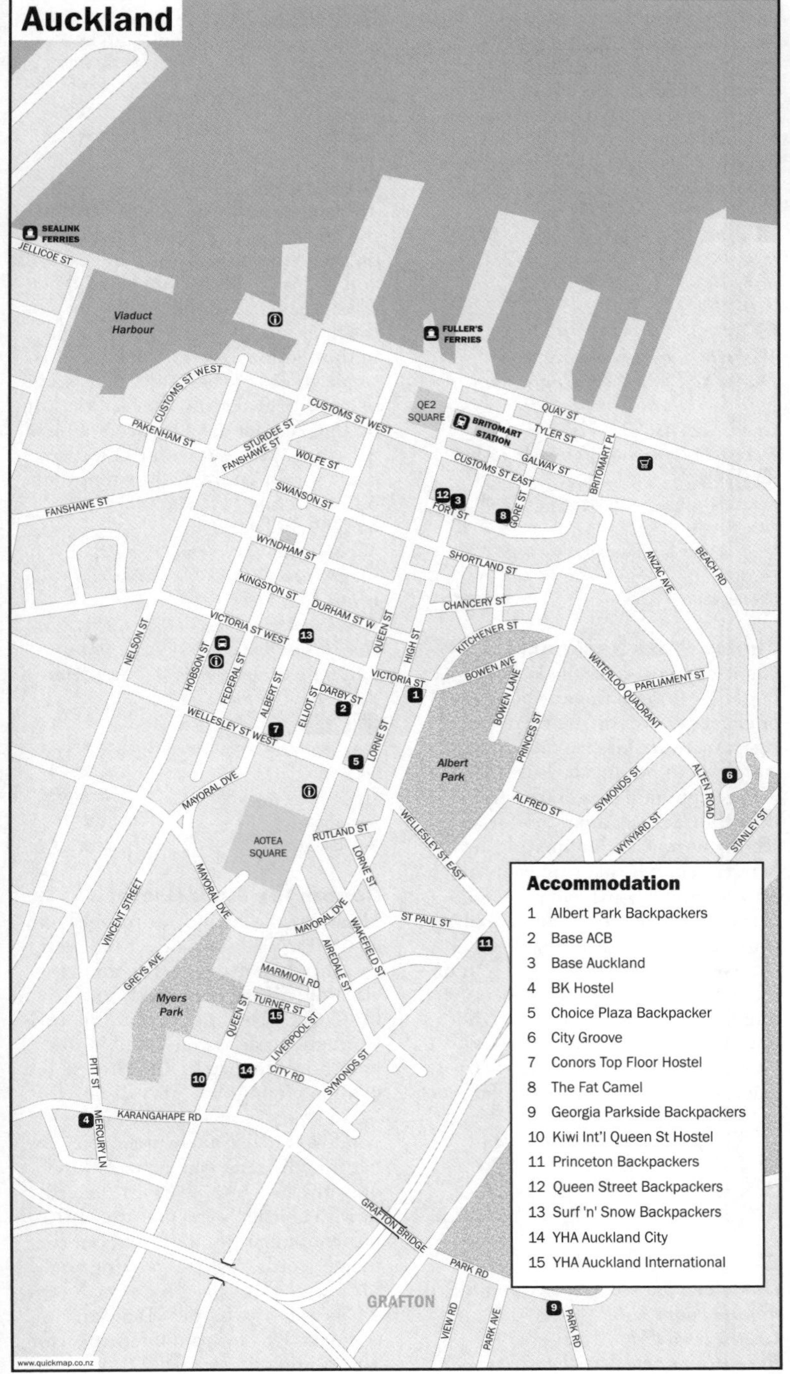

Accommodation

1 Albert Park Backpackers
2 Base ACB
3 Base Auckland
4 BK Hostel
5 Choice Plaza Backpacker
6 City Groove
7 Conors Top Floor Hostel
8 The Fat Camel
9 Georgia Parkside Backpackers
10 Kiwi Int'l Queen St Hostel
11 Princeton Backpackers
12 Queen Street Backpackers
13 Surf 'n' Snow Backpackers
14 YHA Auckland City
15 YHA Auckland International

table, and there are good kitchen facilities. Walls are white and every door is painted a different pastel colour. Overall the place has a slightly feminine vibe; the very friendly owner is in fact a woman – BK is her husband's initials. It's a quiet oasis in the midst of some of Auckland's cooler nightlife.

3 Mercury Lane, Auckland
Link, 004, 005, 012, 015, 017, 018, 024, 025, 027, 028, 035, 042, 043, 045, 190-194, 196-199, 205, 206, 207, 210-213, 215- 217, 223- 225, 229
(09) 307 0052 or 307 0056
***Website** www.bkhostel.co.nz*
***Dorm bed** $25-$29; **single room** $40-$45; **double room** $58*
***Credit cards** MC, Visa*
***Reception open** 8.30am-10.30pm*
TV K L

Maintenance & cleanliness	★★★½
Facilities	★★½
Atmosphere & character	★★½
Security	★★★
Overall rating	★★★

Choice Plaza Backpacker

Choice Plaza is centrally located but offers little in the way of charm or character. Rooms are clean and basic, there are kitchen facilities and laundry, but not much else. A TV lounge/common area on the ground floor didn't have ample comfortable seating or much of an inviting air. Some attempt is made to liven things up with brightly painted scenes of Australia & New Zealand on hallway walls. There is plug-in broadband access for laptops. Rooms are four or six beds, and showers and toilets are individual. Rates are low, though it's not much cheaper than hostels with a lot more atmosphere. Choice Plaza is a place to sleep, but it doesn't offer much more.

10 Wellesley Street East, Auckland
Link, City Circuit, 015, 017, 024, 025, 027, 034, 042, 043, 045, 822, 839, 858, 875, 879, N05, N13, N83, N97
(09) 302 0888
***Dorm bed** $20-$25; **single room** $70; **double room** $80*
***Credit cards** MC, Visa*
***Reception open** 9am-9pm*
TV K L

Maintenance & cleanliness	★★★
Facilities	★½
Atmosphere & character	★½
Security	★★
Overall rating	★★

City Groove

This small, funky house is located in the middle of a hilly park practically on the University of Auckland campus, and is close to both Parnell and downtown Auckland. Books and pillows on the floor (no TV) set a mellow tone in the common room. The kitchen is small, rooms are basic and there's a bit of a bedraggled air to the facilities. But on the plus side are a big, cool, bi-level backyard fitted out with tiki torches and a very friendly, slightly hippy vibe.

6 Constitution Hill, Auckland
(09) 303 4768
***Website** www.citygroove.co.nz*
***Dorm bed** $19-$24; **double/twin room** $58-$65*
***Credit cards** Amex, Diners, MC, Visa*
***Reception open** Mon-Sat 8.30am-12.30pm & 4pm-8.30pm, Sun 9am-12.30pm & 4pm-8.30pm*
TV K L

Maintenance & cleanliness	★★
Facilities	★½
Atmosphere & character	★★★½
Security	★½
Overall rating	★★

Conors Top Floor Hostel

Head down a laneway, turn right into a building's side entrance, take a left, then head up five flights on an old elevator with manual doors, and you'll hit Conors. Facilities here are about as worn and basic as you'll find in town, with prices to match. The kitchen and common lounge are fairly dishevelled. Rooms vary in quality; the ones with windows are definitely preferable. The bathrooms aren't bad, actually kind of sunny. A rooftop balcony (fenced in with chicken wire, presumably to prevent bungee jumping without the bungee cord) is where smoking and socialising takes place – especially over $2 Saturday barbecues. There are a couple of PCs for paid internet surfing. The location is central.

5th floor, 15-31 Wellesley Street West, Auckland
🚌 *Link, City Circuit, 288, 297, 298, 605, 606, 893-897*
☎ *(09) 374 4237*
Website *www.hostelnz.co.nz*
Dorm bed *$18;* ***single room*** *$30;* ***double/twin room*** *$52*
Reception open *8.30am-10pm*
acb

Maintenance & cleanliness	★½
Facilities	★½
Atmosphere & character	★½
Security	★★
Overall rating	★½

The Fat Camel

The Fat Camel is a busy and popular hostel right in the middle of the action on Fort Street. Dorms are separated into apartment-style units with their own lounge areas, separate kitchens, and bathroom facilities. Frankly, they aren't particularly clean or comfortable – the bedding is thin and bunks are creaky, and some rooms tend to be stuffy and airless. That said, security features are good, including key card access to rooms, and there is a free (small) evening meal each night at the downstairs bar. The social atmosphere in the hostel itself tends to be limited because of the apartment layout, but the bar is a very popular social hub, so travellers do tend to meet and hang out here.

38 Fort Street, Auckland
🚌 *Link, City Circuit* 🚆 *Britomart*
☎ *(09) 307 0181 or 0800 220 198*
Website *www.fatcamel.co.nz*
Dorm bed *$19-$28;* ***double room*** *$55;* ***twin room*** *$69*
Credit cards *JCB, MC, Visa*
Reception open *24 hours*
TV K L

Maintenance & cleanliness	★½
Facilities	★★
Atmosphere & character	★★★
Security	★★★★
Overall rating	★★½

Kiwi International Queen Street Hotel & Hostel

Tucked behind a building on Queen Street, Kiwi International is a hotel/hostel hybrid with a big drive-up entrance. Parking is available to hostel guests for $5 per day. The lobby has a travel desk and the Kiwi Kai bar/café, and there's a lounge with a pool table and air hockey table. It's an older property, more readily apparent in the backpackers' part, which could stand some renovation. Rooms are basic, and most have en suite facilities. Prices are low and the location on the uptown end of Queen Street, right by K Road is good. There's not much social atmosphere, though – it feels more like a hotel than a hostel.

411 Queen Street, Auckland
🚌 *Link, 012, 017, 018, 024, 025, 027, 028, 035, 042, 043, 045*
☎ *(09) 379 6487 or 0800 100 411*
Website *www.kiwihotel.co.nz/queenst.html*
Dorm bed *$20;* ***single room*** *$39;* ***double room*** *$79-$92;* ***twin room*** *$49*
Credit cards *MC, Visa*
Reception open *24 hours*
TV K L

Maintenance & cleanliness	★★½
Facilities	★★
Atmosphere & character	★½
Security	★★½
Overall rating	★★

Princeton Backpackers

The "backpackers" tag is a bit of a misnomer here; shared twin rooms are available, but the overwhelming majority of accommodations are single or double rooms in small, shared apartment layouts. The Princeton caters to longer-term residents, primarily university students – it's practically on the AUT (Auckland University of Technology) campus, and the University of Auckland is close by as well. As such, it has far more of a student-residence feel than a hostel. There's a great TV lounge in the basement that looks like something out of a Kubrick film. Otherwise, there's not much in the way of communal space, apart from a pair of restaurants. Each shared apartment has a kitchenette, toilet & shower. Walls are kind of thin and furnishings are basic and on the flimsy side.

30 Symonds Street, Auckland
🚌 *Link, City Circuit, 205, 210-213, 215- 217, 223-225, 229, 231, 233, 236, 238, 241, 243, 246-249, 274,*

275, 277
☎ *(09) 950 8300 or 0508 237 883 (0508 BEST DEAL)*
Website *www.princeton.net.nz*
Dorm bed *$28;* ***single room*** *$35;* ***double/twin room*** *$60-$79*
Credit cards *MC, VISA*
Reception open *8am-8pm*

Maintenance & cleanliness	★★★
Facilities	★★
Atmosphere & character	★
Security	★★
Overall rating	★★½

Queen Street Backpackers

This hostel is a few doors down the street from Base Auckland, and can't compete in terms of facilities, but it does have a personality all its own. It's a scruffy, informal place, a bit rough around the edges, but with a very friendly staff and an interesting mix of all-ages guests. Rooms are old and large, and feature windows that open; most have a sink and mirror as well. The common area has a pair of pool tables and a TV lounge with nightly movies. Kitchen facilities are decent, and showers and toilets are all individual cabins. Right off reception is the Longboard Bar, with about five stools and an old surfboard for a sign. Nightlife on Fort Street and in the bar and club-filled laneway right next door is positively frantic on the weekends.
4 Fort Street, Auckland
Link, City Circuit *Britomart*
☎ *(09) 373 3471*
Website *www.qsb.co.nz*
Dorm bed *$21-$27;* ***single room*** *$50-$52;* ***double room*** *$65-$67;* ***twin room*** *$63-$65*
Credit cards *MC, Visa*
Reception open *Mon-Fri 7am-2am, Sat-Sun 24 hours*

Maintenance & cleanliness	★★★
Facilities	★★
Atmosphere & character	★★★
Security	★★½
Overall rating	★★½

Surf 'n' Snow Backpackers

A sleek entrance with sliding glass doors welcomes visitors to Surf 'n' Snow Backpackers. It's a popular and well-located place, right in the shadow of the Sky Tower, and close enough to feel the breeze and hear the shrieks from the bungee ride. The actual hostel itself is a mixed bag, however. Things feel pinched for space inside, with a very modest common lounge, and a small basement kitchen/dining area. Ten-bed dorms are cramped as well, though some of the four-bed rooms with big windows are pleasing. Also on the positive side are good security features, including lockers for every bed, and friendly and helpful staff.
102 Albert Street, Auckland
Link, City Circuit, 085, 087, 089, 097, 102, 107, 113, 115, 134-138, 140, 154, 156, 163,173, 179, 188X, 189X, 190-194, 196, 198, 199, 207
☎ *(09) 363 8889*
Website *www.surfandsnow.co.nz*
Dorm bed *$23-$27;* ***single room*** *$55-$90;* ***double/twin room*** *$68-$90,* ***triple room*** *$120*
Credit cards *Amex, MC, Visa*
Reception open *24 hours*

Maintenance & cleanliness	★★★
Facilities	★½
Atmosphere & character	★★½
Security	★★★★
Overall rating	★★½

YHA Auckland City

Up a steep hill near the uptown end of Queen Street, this hostel isn't quite as nice as the other YHA hostel nearby, but it is still relatively clean and comfortable, if lacking a bit in atmosphere. There's cafeteria-like seating on the ground floor, where "Tommy's Bistro" serves snacks and meals in the mornings. The third floor has a TV lounge, internet room, and a nice sundeck with views and a herb garden.
Corner City Road & Liverpool Street, Auckland
Link, 012, 017, 018, 024, 025, 027, 028, 035, 042, 043, 045
☎ *(09) 309 2802*
Website *www.yha.co.nz*
Dorm bed *$23-$27 ($20-$24 HI/YHA);* ***single room*** *$67 ($64 HI/YHA);* ***double/twin room*** *$80 ($74 HI/YHA)*

***Credit cards** Amex, MC, Visa*
***Reception open** 7am-11pm*

Maintenance & cleanliness	★★★
Facilities	★★
Atmosphere & character	★★
Security	★★★
Overall rating	★★★

YHA Auckland International

This is the better-maintained of the two YHA hostels in town. The Auckland International YHA can't quite escape the institutional character of the building itself, but a bright, open dining area/lounge and excellent kitchen facilities (including a sandwich press) make up for it. There's also a cosy TV room, air hockey table, and on-site travel and employment assistance. Rooms are clean and tidy and kept in good shape. Limited parking is available if reserved in advance.

5 Turner Street, Auckland
Link, 012, 017, 018, 024, 025, 027, 028, 035, 042, 043, 045
(09) 302 8200
***Website** www.yha.co.nz*
***Dorm bed** $23-$29 ($20-$26 HI/YHA); **double/twin room** $84-$102 ($78-$96 HI/YHA); **apartment** $118 ($112 HI/YHA)*
***Credit cards** Amex, JCB, MC, Visa*
***Reception open** 7am-11pm*

Maintenance & cleanliness	★★★★½
Facilities	★★
Atmosphere & character	★★½
Security	★★★½
Overall rating	★★★½

GRAFTON & NEWMARKET

Newmarket is a popular shopping area south of Parnell that has good supermarkets and better shopping than the city centre. The residential area of Grafton is within easy walking distance of Newmarket and is also convenient to the Domain and Auckland Museum.

Georgia Parkside Backpackers

There's a nice old Victorian house somewhere in here, but it's hidden underneath a general aura of neglect. Dorm rooms themselves aren't bad – they're fairly spacious and have high ceilings – but common areas could use refurbishing. The kitchen and dining area are definitely on the grubby side, and there's something kind of discouraging about the near-empty courtyard in the middle of the house. It's too bad, because some nice old details are apparent, including a stained-glass window. On the plus side, for those looking to be away from the city centre, Georgia Parkside is well situated, on a corner between two parks: Outhwaite Park and the great Auckland Domain.

189 Park Road, Grafton
Link, 283 Boston Road
(09) 309 8999 or 0508 436 744 (0508 GEORGIA)
***Website** www.georgia.co.nz/*
***Dorm bed** $20; **single room** $44; **double room** $50; **twin room** $54; **triple room** $74; **quad room** $84*
***Credit cards** MC, Visa*
***Reception open** 8am-9pm*

Maintenance & cleanliness	★★
Facilities	★★
Atmosphere & character	★★★
Security	★
Overall rating	★★

MANGERE & THE AIRPORT

Mangere is a boring suburb a long way from the city centre, but it's only a five-minute drive to the airport and many travellers choose to stay here for their first or last night in the country.

Kiwi International Airport Hostel

Kiwi International is 5km from the airport and is more of a full-fledged hotel than hostel. Dorms are set apart from the main building on the grassy hotel grounds; all rooms are en suite and have kitchenettes. There is a TV lounge with a pool table and air hockey table, and a full restaurant and bar in the main hotel building. Facilities are generally clean and the grounds are well maintained, but there's not much in the way of atmosphere here. Free 24 hour airport transfer is offered; it's obviously a convenient choice for those late arrivals or early departures.

150 MacKenzie Road, Mangere

327, 328, 334
(09) 256 0046 or 0800 801 919
***Website** www.kiwihotel.co.nz*
***Dorm bed** $29; **double/twin room** $69-$109*
***Credit cards** Amex, Diners, JCB, MC, Visa*
***Reception open** 24 hours*

Maintenance & cleanliness	★★★½
Facilities	★★★½
Atmosphere & character	★★½
Security	★★½
Overall rating	★★★½

Skyway Lodge

Skyway Lodge is a motel/hostel just five minutes from the airport. It has a small yard with a barbecue, a swimming pool, a decent kitchen, and a TV room with videos and some furniture from the 70s time capsule. Airport pick-up and drop-off is offered for $5 a head, and they'll accommodate early and late arrivals. Staff are helpful and the lodge is reasonably clean, if dated. It is what it is – not a place you're likely to spend more than a night on your way to or from the airport but not a bad option if convenience is a key factor.

30 Kirkbride Road, Mangere
327, 328, 334
(09) 275 4443
***Website** www.skywaylodge.co.nz*
***Dorm bed** $31 ($28 BBH); **double/twin room** $59-$99 ($56-$99 BBH)*
***Credit cards** MC, Visa*
***Reception open** 8am-8pm*

Maintenance & cleanliness	★★
Facilities	★★★
Atmosphere & character	★½
Security	★
Overall rating	★★

MOUNT EDEN

Mount Eden is a pleasant suburb with a nice community feel to its high street. It is about a 10-minute bus ride from the city centre.

Bamber House

Bamber House offers a range of accommodation in a pair of houses set on large grounds in Mount Eden. The main house is a strikingly handsome colonial home with exposed beam work, fine furnishings, and well-preserved period details. Features include a book-filled common room and a great kitchen. It's simply overflowing with character. The second house doesn't have the charm of the first – as it's more recently-built – but it is also meticulously clean and comfortable. Lots of outdoor space, including a barbecue area and a trampoline, add to the appeal. There's a swimming pool as well, but it had been covered over and was being used as a sundeck when we visited; its future is uncertain. Bamber House is one of the superior hostels in Auckland, a very appealing alternative to staying downtown.

22 View Road, Mount Eden
255-258
(09) 623 4267
***Website** www.hostelbackpacker.com*
***Dorm bed** $25-$28 ($22-$25 BBH); **single room** $38 ($35 BBH); **double/twin room** $60-$66 (BBH $54-$60)*
***Credit cards** MC, Visa*
***Reception open** 8.30am-noon & 1pm-8.30pm*

Maintenance & cleanliness	★★★★½
Facilities	★★★
Atmosphere & character	★★★★½
Security	★★
Overall rating	★★★★

Oaklands Lodge

Oaklands Lodge is very well situated, right around the corner from the Mount Eden shops. It's a big old house with a backyard that has a barbecue and trampoline. There's a cute TV room as well. One nice feature is that most beds are individual single beds, not bunks, and feature real spring mattresses. The staff is friendly and helpful and Oaklands has a good reputation among backpackers.

5A Oaklands Road, Mount Eden
274, 275, 277
(09) 638 6545
***Website** www.oaklands.co.nz*
***Dorm bed** $23-$25 ($20-$22 BBH); **single room** $43 ($40 BBH); **double/twin room** $60-$66 ($54-$60 BBH)*
***Credit cards** MC, Visa*

Reception open *8.30am-1pm & 4pm-8.30pm*

Maintenance & cleanliness	★★★
Facilities	★★
Atmosphere & character	★★★
Security	★½
Overall rating	★★½

Pentlands

Pentlands is a big blue house on a quiet cul-de-sac in Mount Eden. It's kept in pretty good shape, with a nice TV/common lounge showing off a bit of charm; nice old fixtures are intact, including a fireplace. There's also a good-sized kitchen and dining area, as well as an outdoor deck for sunning and eating. A tennis court is on the grounds, but was being used for parking when we visited. A fair number of the guests at Pentlands are longer-term, doing temporary work in Auckland, which gives it a bit more of an insular feel than some other hostels. Still, it's a comfortable place away from the noise and bustle of the city centre.

22 Pentland Avenue, Mount Eden

250, 255, 256, 258, 265, 267

(09) 638 7031

Website *www.pentlands.co.nz/index.html*

Dorm bed *$23 ($20 BBH);* ***single room*** *$43 ($40 BBH);* ***double/twin room*** *$56 ($50 BBH)*

Credit cards *MC, Visa*

Reception open *Mon-Fri 6pm-8.30pm, Sat 8.30am-1.30pm*

Maintenance & cleanliness	★★★
Facilities	★★½
Atmosphere & character	★★½
Security	★½
Overall rating	★★½

Yaping House

Yaping House was built in 1875 (it claims to be the oldest house in Mount Eden), and has been operating as some sort of hostel since 1948. It's no stretch to say that it shows its years. The house and furnishings are worn and the place generally feels neglected. There's just a stale and unkempt air about the hostel. The property does offer some great views, however, as it is set high up on a hill near Mount Eden. There's also free Internet and Wi-Fi, a serious rarity in Auckland (though PC facilities are limited). Its location is not too far away from Mount Eden town; still, Yaping House would need a significant makeover to grade higher.

79 Owens Road, Epsom

274, 275, 277

(09) 623 4486

Website *www.yapinghouse.co.nz*

Dorm bed *$21-$23 ($18-$20 BBH);* ***single room*** *$39-$41 ($36-$38 BBH);* ***double room*** *$56-$62 ($50-$56 BBH);* ***twin room*** *$54-$56 ($48-$50 BBH)*

Credit cards *MC, Visa*

Maintenance & cleanliness	★
Facilities	★½
Atmosphere & character	★★½
Security	★½
Overall rating	★½

PARNELL

This quiet area east of the city centre has a lovely main street with cafés and cute shops. Hostels in this part of town have a lot of character and the city centre is just a short walk or bus ride away.

Auckland International Backpackers

Auckland International Backpackers (formerly Alan's Place) is located in a residential neighbourhood. There's something of a musty air to the place, with dated furnishings and floor coverings. A good-sized downstairs common area helps matters, however, with a big kitchen, TV lounge and common room with books and magazines. There's a decent backyard as well. It's a quiet if slightly non-descript hostel, a bit away from the action.

2 Churton Street, Parnell

Link, 635, 645, 655, 965, 966

(09) 358 4584

Website *www.alansinternational.co.nz*

Dorm bed *$20-$22 ($17-$19 BBH);* ***single room*** *$38 ($35 BBH);* ***double room*** *$52-$76 ($46-$70);* ***twin room*** *$56 ($50 BBH)*

Credit cards *MC, Visa*

Reception open *7.30am-9pm*

Maintenance & cleanliness	★★
Facilities	★½
Atmosphere & character	★½
Security	★½
Overall rating	★★

City Garden Lodge

This great old mansion crowned with finials was originally built for the Queen of Tonga as her embassy 120 years ago. Today, it's a lodge full of character and charm. A lovely lounge features high ceilings, an enormous fireplace, big comfy seats and heaps of books, board games and puzzles. Dorms are roomy, and there are lots of intact period details around the house, which rambles with little hallways and sitting areas. Out front, there's a big brick patio with barbecue and picnic tables, and a front lawn that doubles as a yoga centre. City Garden Lodge is close to the shops and cafes of Parnell Road, but feels a world away from the city centre. The owner says he gets quite a few "refugees" from the city, looking for a slice of tranquillity.

25 St Georges Bay Road, Parnell
Link, 635, 645, 655, 965, 966
(09) 302 0880
Website *www.citygardenlodge.co.nz*
Dorm bed *$24-$25 ($20-$22 BBH);* ***single room*** *$50 ($47 BBH);* ***double room*** *$64 ($58 BBH);* ***twin room*** *$54-$64 ($48-$58 BBH)*
Credit cards *MC, Visa*
Reception open *8am-1pm & 4pm-8pm*
K L

Maintenance & cleanliness	★★★★
Facilities	★★
Atmosphere & character	★★★★★
Security	★½
Overall rating	★★★½

Lantana Lodge

This old white house isn't much to look at from the outside, but things improve considerably indoors. Thick, springy mattresses feature prominently in the tidy rooms. A small, warm common room has a book-covered mantelpiece and gas fireplace. The adjacent kitchen and dining area are small also, but then there are only

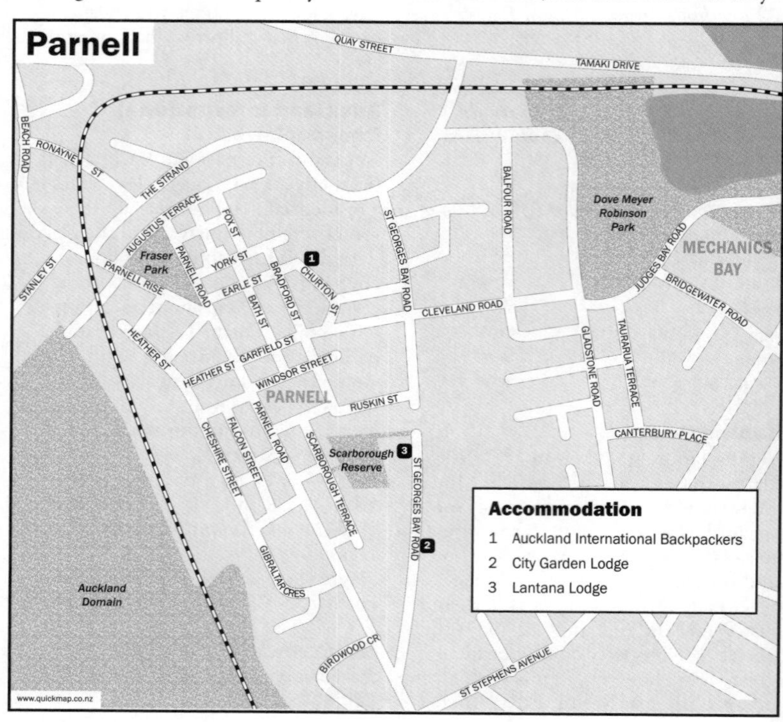

20 beds in the hostel. The Lantana Lodge also features free internet and Wi-Fi, a real rarity in Auckland and certainly a big plus for some travellers. It's located a few-minutes away from the shops and restaurants of Parnell Road.

60 St Georges Bay Road, Parnell
Link, 635, 645, 655, 965, 966
(09) 373 4546
***Website** www.lantanalodge.co.nz*
***Dorm bed** $22 ($20 BBH); **double room** $60 ($58 BBH)*
***Credit cards** MC, Visa*
***Reception open** 8am-12.30pm & 3.30pm-8pm*

Maintenance & cleanliness	★★★
Facilities	★★½
Atmosphere & character	★★★½
Security	★
Overall rating	★★★

PONSONBY

Ponsonby is an interesting neighbourhood with some good pubs and cafés. It has a less polished and more youthful feel than Parnell and is about a 20-minute walk into the city centre.

The Brown Kiwi

The Brown Kiwi is a smaller hostel (sleeping only 32) near the café action on Ponsonby Road but with a quiet ambience. Facilities are basic, but there is a great little backyard with lots of hardy foliage, hardwood tables and benches, and the sound of a small bubbling pool. It's idyllic. The kitchen is also fantastic, small but well-equipped and well laid-out. Bunks are notably sturdy. The staff are cool and friendly and the overall vibe is very appealing.

7 Prosford Street, Ponsonby
Link, 012, 017, 962, 963, 965, 966
(09) 378 0191
***Website** www.brownkiwi.co.nz*
***Dorm bed** $22-$27 (BBH $19-$24); **double/twin room** $58-$64 ($54-$58); **triple room** $72-$78 ($69-$75 BBH)*
***Credit cards** MC, Visa*
***Reception open** 8am-noon & 2.30pm-7pm*

Maintenance & cleanliness	★★★
Facilities	★★
Atmosphere & character	★★★★
Security	★★½
Overall rating	★★★

New Zealand Backpackers

You might think you've gone too far as you wander among massive car dealerships on the way to New Zealand Backpackers. But there it is; one of only a few houses on a small side street in this unlikely location right above Karanghape Road. Still, you aren't staying here for atmosphere, because there is none. It's a former rooming house now doing business as a backpackers, but it hasn't lost the doss house feel – dark and unkempt and a little bit disheartening. It is cheap, though – very cheap. And it's close to the junction of Ponsonby and K Roads.

8 Nixon Street, Newton
Link, 012, 018, 024-027, 034, 035, 102, 107, 192-199, 966
(09) 376 3871
***Dorm bed** $17; **single room** $30; **double/twin room** $50*
***Credit cards** MC, Visa*

Maintenance & cleanliness	★
Facilities	★
Atmosphere & character	-
Security	★
Overall rating	★

Ponsonby Backpackers

Ponsonby Backpackers is a 30-bed hostel in a converted old villa located right off of Ponsonby Road. Facilities include a very cosy TV lounge with a fireplace, and a small but fully-equipped kitchen. One of the dorms is set in the villa's distinctive Victorian-style tower, giving it a nice atmosphere. There's also a good backyard set in a native garden with an outdoor deck and picnic tables. A herb garden grows fresh parsley, rosemary, garlic, chives and more. The backyard has some bungalow accommodation as well. Overall, Ponsonby Backpackers is a basic but pleasant place with a relaxed and homely vibe.

2 Franklin Street, Ponsonby

Link, 012, 017, 962, 963, 965, 966
(09) 360 1311 or 0800 476 676
Website *www.ponsonby-backpackers.co.nz*
Dorm bed *$25 ($22 BBH);* ***single room*** *$39-$43 ($36-$40 BBH);* ***double room*** *$56-$63 ($50-$56 BBH);* ***twin room*** *$66 ($60 BBH)*
Credit cards *Amex, JCB, MC, Visa*
Reception open *8am-noon & 2pm-7pm*

Maintenance & cleanliness	★★★
Facilities	★★½
Atmosphere & character	★★★
Security	★★½
Overall rating	★★★½

Uenuku Lodge

Uenuku Lodge is a cute place right on Ponsonby Road with a big patio in the back and another on the side of the house. The interior of the lodge is clean and decorated with a bit of metro style. The fully-equipped kitchen is small but particularly nice. Rooms feature real spring mattresses and there are some lockers available. But our favourite part is definitely all the outdoor seating among the hardy-looking tropical foliage and goldfish pond. Also, the upstairs room has a good view of the city centre. And in case you were wondering: Uenuku means "rainbow" in Māori.

217 Ponsonby Road, Ponsonby
Link, 012, 017, 962, 963, 965, 966
(09) 3788 990
Website *www.uenukulodge.co.nz*
Dorm bed *$20-$27 ($18-$24 BBH);* ***single room*** *$40-$47 ($38-$44 BBH);* ***double room*** *$60-$82 ($56-$82 BBH)*
Credit cards *MC, Visa*
Reception open *8am-12pm, 2pm-7pm*

Maintenance & cleanliness	★★★½
Facilities	★½
Atmosphere & character	★★★½
Security	★★★½
Overall rating	★★★

Verandahs Backpacker Lodge

Verandahs is a lovely old 1900 kauri villa backing onto Western Park near the corner of Ponsonby and Karanga-

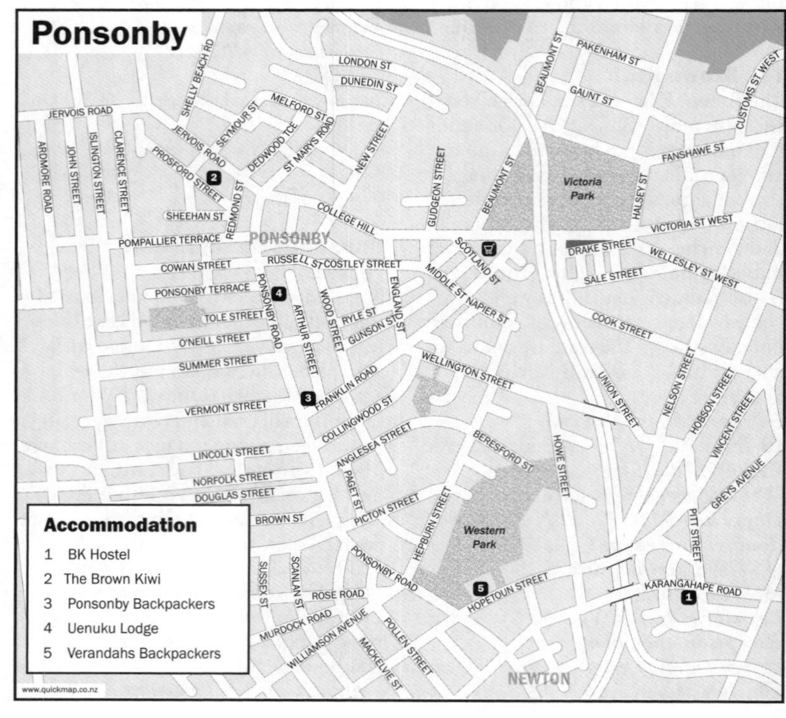

hape Roads. The house is well kept up and features many intact details like coloured-glass windows and stately fireplaces. The common lounge is homely and slightly cluttered with books and games; freshly-painted rooms feature new spring mattresses. And, as the name might suggest, there is a breezy, wraparound veranda with splendid views of the city centre; it makes a great place to while away an afternoon with a book. When we visited, the owner was in the midst of renovating a second villa next door, adding more rooms and new facilities to an already wonderful location.
6 Hopetoun Street, Ponsonby
Link 012, 018, 024-027, 034, 035, 102, 107, 192-194, 196, 198, 199, 966
(09) 360 4180
***Website** www.verandahs.co.nz*
***Dorm bed** $25-$29 ($22-$26 BBH); **single room** $48 ($45); **double/twin room** $66 ($60)*
***Credit cards** MC, Visa*
***Reception open** 8am-12pm, 2pm-7pm*

Maintenance & cleanliness	★★★★
Facilities	★★½
Atmosphere & character	★★★★★
Security	★★
Overall rating	★★★½

Eating & Drinking

Auckland has New Zealand's most diverse and sophisticated dining scene, reflecting a blend of its many influences, particularly Polynesian and Asian. It also has an abundance of cheap eating options for backpackers.

Central Auckland is an almost endless blur of kebab joints and fast food outlets. More diverse and hip cafés and restaurants abound in the surrounding neighbourhoods of Ponsonby and Parnell.

One good rule of thumb when looking for a place to eat is to follow the locals. A few doors down from Base Auckland City Backpackers, for example, is the **Green Crocodile Café** *(10 Darby Street, Auckland)*. Lines run out the door at lunchtime for their tasty and inexpensive sandwiches and salads.

The Fresh Fish & Chip Co. *(127 Ponsonby Road, Ponsonby)* serves what some consider to be Auckland's best fish & chips to an always-packed shop. There are also very good fish and chip shops in Devonport and Mount Eden.

The **Asian Food Court** on Queen Street in the centre of the city has nine different counters selling everything from Indian to Korean, with big-enough-for-two portions and cheap prices, in the $7-$10 range per dish.

For greasy late-night munchies, try the brightly-lit **White Lady** food van on Shortland Street, near the corner of Queen Street.

The main supermarkets near the centre are the **Foodtown** *(76 Quay Street, Auckland)* near Britomart Transport Centre, a **New World** *(2 College Hill, Freemans Bay)* near Victoria Park between Ponsonby and the city centre. There is also a **Foodtown** in the 277 Newmarket complex *(corner Broadway & Morrow Street, Newmarket)*.

There is no shortage of drinking options in the city centre, including several English and Irish pubs. Bars, cafés and clubs also surround Viaduct Harbour. Some of the bigger hostels have very lively bars as well, including **Base ACB** *(229 Queen Street, Auckland)*, and the **Fat Camel** *(38 Fort Street, Auckland)*. For a hipper drinking and club going experience, try Karangahape Road (also known as K Road), and Ponsonby Road.

Activities

Auckland Harbour Bridge Bungy

AJ Hackett has set up a bungee platform on the Auckland Harbour Bridge, 40m (131ft) above the harbour. Jumpers are fitted with a full body harness and then walk 10 minutes up the base of the bridge before leaping from the jump pod.
Westhaven Reserve, Curran Street, Herne Bay
(09) 361 2000 or 0800 GO BUNGY
***Website** www.bungy.co.nz*
***Cost** $100 with free t-shirt*
***Open** summer 8.30am-7pm daily; winter 9am-5pm daily*

Auckland Harbour Bridge Climb

The Auckland Bridge Climb is a 1½ hour activity that takes you up the

arched walkway to the highest point on the Auckland Harbour Bridge, while learning a lot about the bridge, going to places that are off-limits to the public and taking in lovely views of the harbour.
Curran Street, Westhaven Reserve, Herne Bay
☎ *(09) 361 2000 or 0800 GO CLIMB*
Website *www.aucklandbridgeclimb.co.nz*
Cost *$80-100*
Open *9am-5.30pm daily*

Sailing
Auckland is known as the City of Sails and it boasts the world's highest proportion of boat owners. There are several companies that offer a day out sailing on the harbour including Sail NZ, which gives you the opportunity to sail on an America's Cup yacht.
Quay Street, Auckland
☎ *(09) 359 5987 or 0800 SAIL NZ*
Website *www.sailnewzealand.co.nz*
Two hours sailing *$140*

SkyJump
Think you've done everything crazy? For those who have already tried bungee jumping and skydiving, this is a whole new way of jumping off tall things. This adventure activity involves jumping from the top of the Sky Tower fitted with a harness that is attached to a fan descender, as used for movie stunts. The 192m (630ft) jump takes 20 seconds as you drop at a rate of 75km/h.
Sky Tower, Corner Victoria & Federal Streets, Auckland
☎ *0800 SKYJUMP (0800 759586)*
Website *www.skyjump.co.nz*
Cost *$195 ($175 students); combined admission SkyJump & SkyWalk $240*

SkyWalk
There is a 1.2m-wide external walkway at the top of the Sky Tower and the SkyWalk experience lets you walk the entire 360 degrees around the tower with no handrails, just a safety harness. It is a great experience with fantastic views from this unique position 192m above the ground.
Sky Tower, Corner Victoria & Federal Streets, Auckland
☎ *(09) 368 1835 or 0800 759 586*
Website *www.skywalk.co.nz*
Cost *$115 ($95 students); combined admission SkyJump & SkyWalk $240*

Ultra Light Glider Flights
Aqua Air operates tandem flights on an ultra light glider. The glider is launched by boat or 4WD and it flies over the harbour at around 1000ft
☎ *025 288 0193*
Website *www.gethigh.co.nz*
Cost *$200-220*

Sights
Auckland Art Gallery
The Auckland Art Gallery features an excellent programme of New Zealand and international exhibits that supplement the country's most extensive art collection.
Corner Kitchener & Wellesley Streets, Auckland
🚌 *Link*
☎ *(09) 379 1349*
Website *www.aucklandartgallery.govt.nz*
Admission *free; charge for temporary exhibits*
Open *10am-5pm daily*

Auckland War Memorial Museum
This excellent museum is a good introduction to Auckland's history and its Māori Culture. Exhibits include a Māori meeting house and war canoe.
Auckland Domain, Auckland
🚌 *Link, 63-, 64-, 65-*
☎ *(09) 306 7067*
Website *www.akmuseum.org.nz*
Admission *$5*
Open *10am-5pm daily*

Auckland Zoo
Although it's not a huge attraction for international visitors, Auckland's zoo is quite good considering the city's relatively small population. The zoo has all the major African animals, but the main attraction is native animals such as the kiwi and tuatara.
Motions Road, Western Springs
🚌 *043-045*
☎ *(09) 360 3819*
Website *www.aucklandzoo.co.nz*
Admission *$18 ($14 students)*
Open *Jan-May 9.30am-5.30pm daily;*

Jun-Aug 9.30am-5pm daily; Sep-Dec 9.30am-5.30pm daily

Devonport

This seaside suburb is a popular excursion. Victoria Road, near the ferry terminus, has some good pubs and fish and chip shops while the Hauraki Gulf Maritime Park at North Head is a great place to explore with its maze of underground tunnels. There is also a Navy Museum full of nautical exhibits.

Devonport

Kelly Tarlton's Underwater World

Kelly Tarlton's is an excellent attraction despite all the glossy brochures that make it sound like a tourist trap worth avoiding. You can view an assortment of marine life from a clear underwater tube and there is now also a very good Antarctic Encounter attraction with King and Gentoo penguins.

23 Tamaki Drive, Orakei
740-769
(09) 528 0603
Website *www.kellytarltons.co.nz*
Admission *$29.50 ($22 students); reduced prices for online booking*
Open *9am-6pm daily (last entry 5pm)*

Lionzone

The Lion Brewery is New Zealand's largest brewery – it's where Steinlager and Lion Red are produced. Brewery tours include a virtual tour of the brewing process. At the end of the tour you have the opportunity to pour a pint of Steinlager and Lion Red in the Brewfloor Bar.

380 Khyber Pass Road, Newmarket
Link
(09) 358 8366, bookings recommended
Website *www.lionzone.co.nz*
Admission *$18 ($15 students)*
Tours *Tue 12.15pm, 3pm, Wed-Sat 9.30am, 12.15pm, 3pm*

Mount Eden & One Tree Hill

These two extinct volcanoes provide great views of Auckland, but are easiest reached by car.

274, 275 to Mount Eden; 30, 31 to One Tree Hill

Museum of Transport & Technology (MOTAT)

This is a fascinating place if you're in to old cars, planes, trains and steam engines. Exhibits include a Beam Engine and a recreated shopping street from the 1920s.

Great North Road, Western Springs
045
(09) 846 7020
Website *www.motat.org.nz*
Admission *$14*
Open *10am-5pm daily (last entry 4.30pm)*

National Maritime Museum

This excellent museum features exhibits on New Zealand's maritime endeavours from Māori canoes right up to the recent America's Cup yacht race. Exhibits include a replica of the America's Cup trophy.

Corner Lower Hobson & Quay Streets, Viaduct Harbour, Auckland
(09) 373 0800
Website *www.nzmaritime.org*
Admission *$16 ($9 students)*
Open *Jan-Apr 9am-6pm daily; May-Sep 9am-5pm daily; Oct-Dec 9am-6pm daily*

Rainbow's End

New Zealand's largest amusement park with a corkscrew roller coaster, log flume and pirate ship rides. Fearfall is the newest major ride, which has you plummet 18 storeys to the ground at 80km/h.

Corner Great South & Wiri Station Roads, Manakau City
(09) 262 2030 or 0800 438 672
Website *www.rainbowsend.co.nz*
Admission *$40 unlimited ride pass*
Open *10am-5pm daily*

Sky Tower

At 328m, Sky Tower is New Zealand's tallest building. The tower offers a great vantage point with excellent views of the city centre and surrounding area. The observation deck features glass floors where you can stand with the city at your feet. If you're game, you can try SkyJump and SkyWalk – two adventure activities that operate from the tower.

Corner Victoria & Federal Streets, Auckland

City Circuit, Link
(09) 912 6400
***Website** www.skytower.co.nz*
***Admission** $25 ($15 BBH, HI/YHA, VIP, students); Sky Deck extra $3*
***Open** Mon-Thu 8.30am-10.30pm, Fri-Sat 8.30am-11.30pm, Sun 8.30am-10.30pm*

Victoria Park Market

Although it isn't a huge attraction, this pleasant market is a good cheap place to poke around. You'll probably pass this market if you're walking between Ponsonby and the city centre.

210 Victoria Street West, Auckland
Link
(09) 309 6911
***Website** www.victoria-park-market.co.nz*
***Admission** free*
***Open** 9am-6pm daily*

Hibiscus Coast

This coastal area on the Hauraki Gulf is only about half an hour north of central Auckland, and its beaches and attractions make it a popular weekend and holiday getaway for Aucklanders. It's also a good weekend escape for backpackers working in Auckland, or for those who want to visit Auckland but don't want to stay in the city. The main centre on the Hibiscus Coast is Orewa, a resort town with a good selection of dining and shopping options, and a nice 3km-long beach. Windsurfing is a popular activity in the area. An indoor winter-sports recreation centre called Snow Planet in the town of Silverdale has also become an attraction.

Practical Information

Orewa i-SITE Visitor Information Centre

214a Hibiscus Coast Highway, Orewa
895, 895X
(09) 426 0076
***Website** www.rodneynz.com*
***Open** 9am-5pm daily*

Coming & Going & Local Transport

Stagecoach bus route 895 and 895X run hourly between central Auckland and Orewa. The journey takes just over an hour and costs $9.70. This bus also stops along the Hibiscus Coast and is a good way to travel between Orewa and Hatfields Beach. The short five-minute hop between Orewa and Hatfields Beach costs $1.60.

Accommodation

Marco Polo Backpackers Inn

This is a very charming place set on a hill around a very lush garden on a hill fitted out with tiki torches. Cute clean rooms line either side of the garden. Shared facilities are on a higher tier, and an outdoor deck has a nice view. The kitchen is large and well equipped, and the common room is absolutely serene: it boasts a wood-burning fireplace, a piano, bookshelves, and a general air of tranquillity. There's no TV or internet access, but this is the kind of place you go to unplug for a little while.

2D Hammond Avenue, Hatfields Beach
894, 895
(09) 426 8455
***Website** www.marcopolo.co.nz*
***Dorm bed** $26-$28 ($23-$25 BBH); **single room** $48 ($45 BBH); **double/twin room** $66 ($60 BBH); **camping** $19 ($16 BBH) per person*
***Reception open** 9am-9pm*

Maintenance & cleanliness	★★★★
Facilities	★★½
Atmosphere & character	★★★★
Security	★
Overall rating	★★★

Pillows Travellers Lodge

Pillows Travellers Lodge is a transformed motel set around a garden courtyard. The years show on the outside of the lodge, painted in a pale yellow and blue, but inside the rooms are surprisingly spic and span and nicely maintained. There's a plain common room with TV and a small fully-equipped kitchen. Laundry facilities and internet access (on one computer) are available. Depending on how you look at it, Pillows is either the last backpackers on the Hibiscus Coast Highway before returning to Auckland or the first escaping from it,

so it can make for a convenient stopping point.
412 Hibiscus Coast Highway, Orewa
894, 895, 899
(09) 426 6338
***Website** www.pillows.co.nz*
***Dorm bed** $20-$22; **double/twin room** $49-$65*
***Credit cards** MC, Visa*
***Reception open** 24 hours*

Maintenance & cleanliness	★★★
Facilities	★★
Atmosphere & character	★★
Security	★
Overall rating	★★½

Kowhai Coast

Less than an hour north of Auckland, the Kowhai Coast – named for the native kowhai tree – is home to some lots of coastline and good beaches, and excellent snorkeling and diving at Goat Island. The area is increasingly being referred to as the Matakana Coast, and the wine country centered around the town of Matakana is becoming heavily promoted as a boutique destination, with wineries, specialty shops, restaurants, a farmers' market and other upscale attractions.

Warkworth

This charming village of 3300 is the hub of the Kowhai Coast, and a popular getaway for Aucklanders, but still isn't a major stop on the international tourist trail. It's got some historical architecture and attractions, numerous cafes and galleries, and a nice riverbank walkway along the Mahurangi River. Warkworth is a good base for exploring the Kowhai Coast and the developing wine industry around nearby Matakana.

Practical Information

Warkworth i-SITE Visitor Centre

1 Baxter Street, Warkworth
(09) 425 9081
***Website** www.warkworthnz.com*
***Open** Mon-Fri8.30am-5.15pm, Sat-Sun 9am-3pm*

Accommodation

Sheepworld Caravan Park

As the name might suggest, this site caters primarily to camper vans. However, there is some backpacker-style accommodation available, so it's worth a mention. Backpackers can set up in one of the parked caravans (which have a kitschy early 60s feel) or in the four-bed "Hobbit House", a little cabin with a rounded roof and porthole windows that is actually pretty charming. There's a small, extremely rustic, indoor common area with a TV, and a big outdoor barbecue area with picnic tables and a nice view of a waterfall. There's also an indoor spa pool. Sheepworld Caravan Park is right next door to the Sheepworld attraction, so you can't get any closer to the sheep-shearing action than this.
State Highway 1, Warkworth
(09) 425 9962
***Website** www.sheepworldcaravanpark.co.nz*
***Dorm bed** $25; **single caravan** $35; **shared caravan** $25 per person; **cabin** $25 per person; **camp motel room** $120*
***Credit cards** MC, Visa*
***Reception open** 24 hours*

Maintenance & cleanliness	★½
Facilities	★½
Atmosphere & character	★★
Security	★
Overall rating	★½

Sights & Activities

Sheep World

This tourist attraction features sheep shearing demonstrations and hands-on farm themed activities however you can get a more genuine farm experience by simply staying in a farm hostel.
324 State Highway 1, Warkworth
(09) 425 7444
***Website** www.sheepworldnz.com*
***Admission** $9; $18.50 including show*
***Open** 9am-5pm daily*

Warkworth & District Museum

This small museum has exhibits of local history. It features a number of restored buildings including the old Warkworth prision.
Tudor Collins Drive, Warkworth

☎ *(09) 425 7093*
Website *www.wwmuseum.orcon.net.nz*
Admission *$6*
Open *summer 9am-4pm daily; winter 9am-3.30pm daily*

Maintenance & cleanliness	★★
Facilities	★★½
Atmosphere & character	★★★
Security	★
Overall rating	★★

Leigh & Goat Island Marine Reserve

Leigh is a small commercial fishing town with nice views over the harbour and out to Little Barrier Island. Diving and fishing activities can be arranged here, but the main attraction for travellers is the magnificent Goat Island Marine Reserve a few kilometres away. This is New Zealand's first marine reserve, established in 1975 and protecting 547 hectares of sea and shoreline. Consequently, it is teeming with aquatic life and makes one of the best diving and snorkeling sites in New Zealand; it's certainly the best this close to Auckland. There are a number of different marine habitats home to a variety of marine life. And if you don't feel like getting wet, a glass bottom boat ride is available.

Accommodation

Goat Island Camping & Backpackers

Down a very winding road on the way to the Goat Island Marine Reserve, you'll find this interesting place. Goat Island is not a backpackers' in any traditional sense; it's primarily a campsite, with a few dorm-style beds in a bunkhouse, as well as caravans and stand-alone cabins. That said, there is character and charm to the place. A big communal bonfire and tables out front are well-used and inviting. A games room/lounge inside a hangar offers a pool table, books, and a big kitchen. Views over Goat Island are awesome, and the site is just 500m away from the beach. Snorkel gear and wetsuits are available for hire, and free-range eggs are offered up by the on-site chickens.
Goat Island Road, Leigh
☎ *(09) 422 6185*
Website *www.goatislandcamping.co.nz*
Dorm bed *$22-$25;* ***camping*** *$12-$16*
Reception open *9am-9pm*

Helensville

This small town is close to the southern extremity of Kaipara Harbour. It was settled by a Scottish timber miller who built a house that he named "Helen's Villa" after his wife; shortly thereafter the settlement became known as Helensville. The town is a centre for the surrounding dairy farming and timber industries and some travellers visit the hot springs at Parakai, 3km from Helensville.

Coming & Going

Auckland's suburban rail network has recently been extended to Helensville. The one-way fare from Auckland's Britomart Transport Centre to Helensville is $9.10.

Accommodation

Malolo House

This beautifully-restored 1904 kauri villa is much more of a luxury B&B than ordinary hostel, but there is one six-bed dorm for backpackers, who get to share the lovely surroundings and facilities. The kitchen is immaculate, with breakfast and free tea and coffee provided daily. A nice veranda has good views over the valley below, and the free spa pool makes for a rare treat on the backpacker circuit. The dorm room itself is not the most spacious we've ever seen, with a pair of three-tiered bunks in close quarters. They're well-designed bunks, at least, with lockers built into them. Malolo House is definitely not a party spot, but a place to add a bit of class and refinement to your travels.
110 Commercial Road, Helensville
☎ *(09) 420 7262*
Website *www.helensville.co.nz/malolo.htm*
Dorm bed *$30 ($27 BBH);* ***double room*** *$65-120 ($60-110 BBH);* ***twin***

room *$70 ($66 BBH)*
Credit cards *MC, Visa*
Reception open *early-10pm*

Maintenance & cleanliness	★★★★★
Facilities	★★
Atmosphere & character	★★★★½
Security	★★
Overall rating	★★★★

Hauraki Gulf

The sparkling Hauraki Gulf, which lies between the Auckland region and the Coromandel Peninsula, is speckled with more than 50 islands and islets, many of which can be visited by sea or air. Its waters, which are sheltered from the Pacific Ocean by the Great Barrier Island, are great for fishing and there are many good swimming beaches along the coast.

The two biggest islands in the gulf are Waiheke Island and Great Barrier Island. Waiheke is a popular weekend retreat for Aucklanders, while Great Barrier is a rugged, unspoiled place that offers the opportunity to visit a part of the country most New Zealanders never get the chance to experience.

Waiheke Island

Waiheke Island is the second-largest of the Hauraki Gulf islands. It is the most populated, and the most easily accessible – it's a mere 35 minutes by ferry from downtown Auckland. Waiheke has a permanent population of around 8000, which swells to over 30,000 over holiday periods, particularly during the Waiheke Island Jazz Festival on Easter weekend.

There's an artsy, bohemian vibe still alive in Waiheke – you might see stickers calling it the "People's Republic of Waiheke" or spot a "Free Waiheke" t-shirt – and there's a vibrant café culture and arts scene. At the same time it's also become an upscale, fashionable place with expensive homes and vineyards.

Still, Waiheke retains plenty of natural, relaxed charm. There are more than 40km of beaches and numerous walking tracks, and a much more laid-back vibe than its big-city neighbour to the west, Auckland.

Practical Information

Waiheke i-SITE Visitor Centre
2 Korora Road, Oneroa, Waiheke Island
☎ *(09) 3721 234 or 0800 282 552*
Website *www.aucklandnz.com*
Open *9am-5pm daily*

Coming & Going

Waiheki is only a 35-minute ferry ride from central Auckland making it the most accessible of the Hauraki Gulf islands.

Most travellers take the Fullers Ferry *(☎ (09) 367 9119; **website** www.fullers.co.nz)* that runs hourly from the Auckland ferry terminal on Quay Street. The ferry costs $15.60 one-way or $28.50 return.

Sealink *(☎ (09) 534 5663; **website** www.sealink.co.nz)* also operates ferries between Auckland and Waiheke, but they depart from suburban Half Moon Bay rather than the downtown ferry terminal. Sealink's return fare is $28.50.

Local Transport

There are frequent local bus services on the island, although a rental car offers a lot more flexibility. Local bus fares range from $1.40 to $4. An all-day pass costs $8.

There are five bus routes on the island, all of which originate at the Matiatia Wharf ferry terminal. Most buses run every half hour.

Waiheke Auto Rentals *(☎ (09) 372 8998)* and Waiheke Rental Cars *(☎ (09) 372 8635; **website** www.waihekerentalcars.co.nz)* are both located at Matiatia Wharf on Waiheke Island and give you the flexibility to explore the whole island at your own pace.

Accommodation

Hekerua Lodge

Tucked down a long road and hidden in the bush, Hekerua Lodge is a fantastic little lodge with an uncommonly relaxing atmosphere and heaps of charm. A prayer flag-festooned deck overlooks a little stone swimming

pool with a waterfall and a spa pool. Accommodation is set in a pair of wooden houses; the TV-less common room is very cosy, and made-up beds are comfortable (and come with mosquito netting). It's a 10-15 minute walk into town via a path through the bush. Hekerua Lodge is close to Auckland but feels like a universe away; no wonder so many guests seem like they don't want to leave.
11 Hekerua Road, Oneroa
1, 1a, 2, 3, 4
(09) 372 8990
***Website** www.hekerualodge.co.nz*
***Dorm bed** $26-$35 ($23-$30 BBH); single room $48 ($40 BBH); **double/twin room** $75-$110 ($70-$100 BBH)*
***Credit cards** Amex, JCB, MC, Visa*
***Reception open** 8am-1pm, 4pm-8pm*

Maintenance & cleanliness	★★★½
Facilities	★★★
Atmosphere & character	★★★★★
Security	★½
Overall rating	★★★½

Waiheke Island Hostel

Waiheke Island Hostel is located high up on a hill overlooking Onetangi Beach. The exterior is bright and cheerful, painted with colourful scenes of trees, flowers and dolphins. Inside is on the spare side, however, with a common area/TV lounge feeling empty and the kitchen area kind of drab. Accommodation is basic as well, but the grassy front yard with picnic tables serves up oh-so-sweet views over the beach and the bay far below. Onetangi Beach is Waiheke's biggest, a 2.5km stretch of white sand, and is a popular spot for surfing and sea kayaking – or of course, doing nothing.
419 Seaview Road, Onetangi
1, 1a, 3, 4
(09) 372 8971
***Website** www.waihekehostel.co.nz*
***Dorm bed** $24; **single room** $36; **double/twin room** $54-$64*

Maintenance & cleanliness	★★½
Facilities	★½
Atmosphere & character	★★★½
Security	★½
Overall rating	★★½

Activities

Sea Kayaking

Ross Adventures operates sea-kayaking trips that depart from Matiatia Wharf. They offer popular two hour and half day trips and full day and two to three day trips are also available.
Matiatia Wharf, Matiatia
1, 1a, 2, 3, 4
(09) 372 5550
***Website** www.kayakwaiheke.co.nz*
***Half day trip** $70; **full day trip** $135; **two day trip** $270*

Great Barrier Island

Great Barrier Island is just 90 km from Auckland, but it feels like much, much further away. The island, known as Aotea in Māori, is the largest and most remote in the Harauki Gulf, and acts as a breakwater from the Pacific Ocean. It's a lush and rugged place, sparsely populated, with a frontier feel and a leisurely island pace. Great Barrier was the setting for the BBC reality series *Castaway* in 2007, which should give you some idea of how wild parts of the island are; yet it's only 4½hrs by ferry from downtown Auckland, or a half-hour flight.

Great Barrier Island is a great place for bush walks and bird-watching. There's a lack of predatory species on the island, particularly possums, allowing flora to flourish and many otherwise endangered bird species, like the kaka, to thrive. In guidebook-speak, there's a truly unspoiled beauty here.

Plan and pack accordingly if you're going to visit. For one thing, bring cash – there are no ATMs on Great Barrier Island, and you can't necessarily count on using credit or debit cards. All electricity is self-generated on the island as well, so a torch is a good idea, as generators generally shut down at night and there aren't exactly any streetlights around. Mobile phone coverage is limited as well.

This is definitely one of the more interesting and unique destinations in New Zealand, with a real worlds-away feel.

Coming & Going

Most travellers visit Great Barrier Island by ferry from Auckland, but there are also frequent reasonably priced flights that are ideal if you want to save time.

Sealink (☎ *(09) 373 4036;* ***website*** *www.sealink.co.nz)* ferries sail from Wynyard Wharf in Auckland to Tryphena on Great Barrier Island. The four-hour trip costs $110 return.

The island's main airport is at Claris, which is about a half hour drive north of Tryphena. Great Barrier Airlines (☎ *(09) 275 9120;* ***website*** *www.greatbarrierairlines.co.nz)* and Mountain Air (☎ *(09) 256 7026 or 0800 222 123;* ***website*** *www.mountainair.co.nz)* have frequent flights to Auckland International and Auckland North Shore airports and less frequent flights to Whangarei and Whitianga. The one-way fare is $76-96 for the 30-minute flight from Auckland.

If you're not sure whether you'd rather take the ferry or fly, it is also possible to buy a ticket for $150 that includes ferry transport to the island and a flight back to Auckland.

Local Transport

Great Barrier is a big island and most travellers find they need to rent a car to really explore the island; however there is also a local bus service that is a handy alternative if your time on the island isn't limited.

Great Barrier Travel (☎ *0800 426 832;* ***website*** *www.greatbarriertravel.co.nz/bus.html)* run "People & Post" buses that go between Tryphena and Port Fitzroy. Great Barrier Island Shuttle Services have up to five daily services between Tryphena and Claris and schedules are timed to meet ferry and plane arrivals. You can buy an unlimited day pass for $50, a weekend pass for $75 or a five-day pass for $99.

A car rental is the most flexible option and there are several companies on the island to choose from including Aotea Cars (☎ *(09) 4290 055)*, GBI Rent-A-Car (☎ *(09) 429 0062)* and Medlands Rentals (☎ *(09) 4290 861)*. Allow plenty of time to drive around the island, as it is bigger than most people realise and the 35km/h speed limit and narrow winding roads means that it can take a long time to get anywhere.

Accommodation

Crossroads Backpackers Lodge

There aren't many crossroads on Great Barrier Island, but the Crossroads Backpacker Lodge sits right on one, at the point where roads for Port Fitzroy and Whangaparapara Harbour diverge. Basic dorm rooms are set in small "blocks" in a backyard area; the great kitchen and dining room/common area are found inside the main house. There's a kind of home stay feel to the Crossroads, with long-term and repeat visitors who come back to share in the hospitality of colourful hosts Katie and Bruce. It's the most conveniently located hostel on the island to the airport, which is just 2km away. Internet facilities are also available.

1 Blind Bay Road (2km north of Claris)
☎ *(09) 4290 889*
Website *www.xroadslodge.com*
Dorm bed *$25;* ***single room*** *$40;* ***double/twin room*** *$60*

Maintenance & cleanliness	★★★½
Facilities	★½
Atmosphere & character	★★★
Security	★
Overall rating	★★½

Medlands Beach Backpackers

This basic but cute backpackers' is 4km from the airport and 500m to the beach – an enticing view of which is available from the hilltop grounds of the Medlands. Dorm beds are set in small bungalows behind the main house, which is currently inhabited by a friendly Aussie family running the place. Accommodation is simple; a bit of art livens up the bungalows, but a nice deck and scenic views are the real eye-grabbers here. Private houses and a double-bed "love shack" also dot the sprawling property, and a vegetable garden grows in front. Facilities include a small common room and kitchen. Body boards, flippers and snorkels are available to borrow.

9 Mason Road, Medlands Beach
☎ *(09) 429 0320*
Website *www.medlandsbeach.com*
Dorm bed *$25 (plus $5 one-time linen charge);* ***double room*** *$70;* ***house*** *(sleeps four) $240 ($25 per extra person)*

Maintenance & cleanliness	★★½
Facilities	★½
Atmosphere & character	★★½
Security	½
Overall rating	★★

Orama

Orama is a private Christian community on Karaka Bay, in a remote and gorgeous part of Great Barrier Island. A huge range of accommodation is available here, from tent sites to large self-contained cottages. Facilities include an outdoor swimming pool, gym with basketball hoops and badminton net and an outdoor trampoline. The backpacker dorms are as no-frills as they come, with tightly crowded beds. There's an undeniable church recreation-centre feel to some areas, such as the small common room with Christian reading material on the library shelves. Still, it doesn't appear that heavy-duty proselytizing is on the agenda. Orama does host large conferences, group outings, and spiritual retreats, though. There is a private jetty, and the Orama brochure mentions guests regularly pulling giant snapper out of the bay. As if on cue, we saw a happy fisherman holding up a whopper when we visited. Dinghies, kayaks and other gear can be rented, subject to availability.

Orama, Great Barrier Island
(09) 429 0063
Website *www.orama.org.nz*
Dorm bed *$20-$25;* ***double/twin cabin*** *$50-$70;* ***self-contained cottage*** *$50-$220;* ***camping*** *$10-$15*

Maintenance & cleanliness	★★★
Facilities	★★★
Atmosphere & character	★★
Security	★
Overall rating	★★½

Pohutukawa Lodge

Pohutukawa Lodge offers a recently renovated six-bed dorm right down the road from Pah Beach. This is about as in "town" as you'll get on Great Barrier Island, with a grocery store and bakery next door, and the Currach Irish Pub

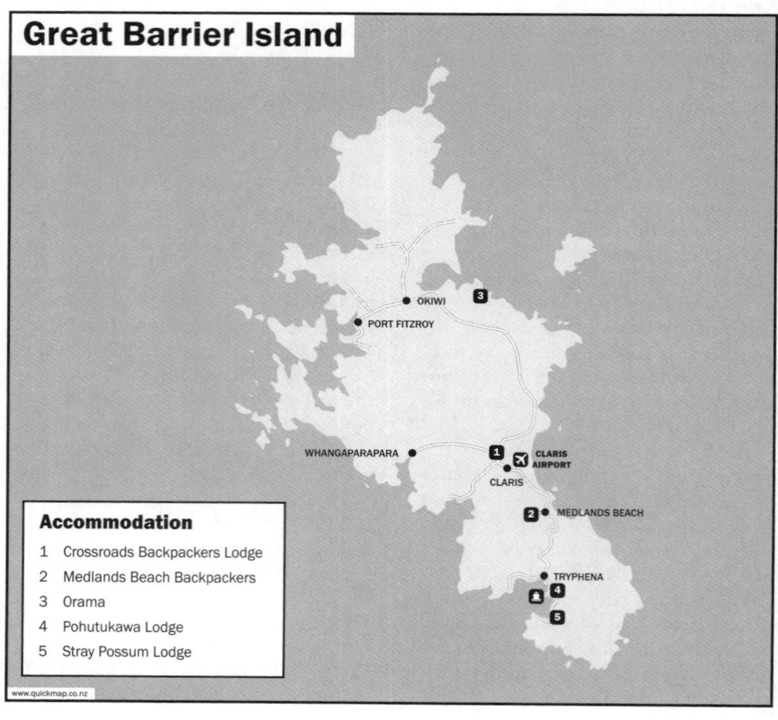

right on the premises. The Currach is the only proper pub on Great Barrier and makes a great place to get a taste of the local life. There's live entertainment some nights, a projection TV for the big rugby matches, and a small art gallery with works by locals. Accommodation and facilities are fairly basic (as is most everything on the island.) There's a decent shared kitchen and a lush backyard with nice views of hills and fields. New owners are relative newcomers to the island but seem to have settled in quite nicely.

Blackwell Drive, Pah Beach, Tryphena
☎ *(09) 429 0211*
Website *www.currachirishpub.com*
Dorm bed *$25;* ***double room*** *$120-$165;* ***family room*** *$130-$165*
Credit cards *MC, Visa*

Maintenance & cleanliness	★★★½
Facilities	★★
Atmosphere & character	★★★★
Security	★
Overall rating	★★★

Stray Possum Lodge

The Stray Possum is conveniently close to the ferry wharf, but still offers an in-the-bush experience. Dorms are set in a rustic cabin lodge on a hill surrounded by nature; the smell of a wood-burning water heater adds to the outdoors feel. Rooms are spacious and clean, and there's a good-sized shared kitchen. A bar and restaurant is open during the summer months, and can make for a lively hangout, with excellent pizzas and an even better view. The endangered parrot-like kaka bird is frequently seen – and constantly heard – round the lodge. There are some good hiking trails right out the door from the dorm cabin. Staff are friendly and helpful. The Lodge's name plays on the fact that there are no possums (or ferrets or stoats) ravaging the forests of Great Barrier Island.

64 Cape Barrier Road, Tryphena
☎ *09 429 0109 or 0800 767 786 (0800 POSSUM)*
Website *www.straypossum.co.nz*
Dorm bed *$23 (one-time linen charge $5);* ***double/family room*** *$70;* ***chalet*** *$135*
Credit cards *MC, Visa*

Maintenance & cleanliness	★★★½
Facilities	★½
Atmosphere & character	★★★★
Security	★
Overall rating	★★★

Eating and Drinking

Great Barrier Island doesn't have a wealth of cheap eating options for backpackers. Many of the restaurants on Great Barrier Island are connected to the nicer resorts.

The **Currach Pub** *(Blackwell Drive, Pah Beach, Tryphena)* has typical pub grub, and this is probably the best place for local drinking action as well.

A few doors down is **Cruisy Café**, serving up coffee and baked items, including pies. There's also a small market next door.

Claris Texas Café *(129 Hector Sanderson Road, Claris)* has decent Tex-Mex food plus public internet access.

Higher up the ladder, the restaurant at **Great Barrier Lodge** *(Whangaparapara Harbour, Whangaparapara)* is one of the better on the island, as is **Tipi and Bob's** *(38 Puriri Bay, Tryphena)*. **The Stray Possum Lodge** *(64 Cape Barrier Road, Tryphena)* serves good food as well, particularly its pizzas.

Seafood is fresh across the island, and you'll find most restaurants offering the same specials on the same day depending on a catch.

Be warned, though, eating out here is generally much more expensive than on the mainland. You may want to heed the advice of one hostel manager: "I tell people to bring their own food".

Northland

This region starts north of Auckland and stretches to the northern tip of the North Island and boasts New Zealand's warmest weather and a wealth of natural attractions including kauri forests, long sandy beaches and isolated coves and islands. The area was one of the first parts of the country to be settled by Europeans and includes the site where the Treaty of Waitangi was signed.

The Bay of Islands is the most popular destination in Northland. Other popular attractions include scuba diving at the Poor Knights Islands, off the coast from Whangarei, and driving along the 90 Mile Beach to Cape Reinga at the northern most tip of the North Island.

Must do in Northland

- Sail, cruise or kayak in the Bay of Islands
- Learn about New Zealand's history at the Waitangi Treaty Grounds

Waipu

Tiny Waipu's claim to fame, as it were, is its long and proud Scottish tradition. It was settled in the 1850s by a group of Highlanders who migrated via Nova Scotia, and the town has maintained a strong Scottish identity ever since. There are regular events such as Scottish Country Dancing in the town, and every January since 1871 the Caledonian Society holds Highland Games. The games feature piping and drumming competitions, as well as heavyweight events like the hammer throw and sheaf toss.

Waipu Museum tells the story of the town and its settlers for the truly interested; there's also a good deal of genealogical information collected here for anyone with a family connection to Waipu.

Other activities around Waipu include surfing and swimming at Waipu Cove, and the glow-worm rich Waipu Caves.

Waipu is 40km south of Whangarei.

Practical Information

Waipu Information Centre

There's a small information centre at the Waipu Museum, although the information is rather limited.
36 The Centre, Waipu
☎ *(09) 432 0746*
Website *www.waipumuseum.com*
Open *9.30am-4.30pm daily*

INTERNET ACCESS

Waipu Off-Licence

Waipu's off-licence also doubles as an internet café so you can check your email when you pop in for a six-pack.
15-17 The Centre, Waipu
☎ *(09) 432 0225*
Open *Mon-Thu 9am-6.30pm, Fri-Sat 9am-7.30pm*

Internet access is also available in the visitor information centre at the **Waipu Museum** *(36 The Centre, Waipu).*

Accommodation

Waipu Wanderers Backpackers

Waipu Wanderers is a very small house on a quiet residential street, with just seven beds in three rooms. There's a living-room common area and small kitchen, and it feels more like staying in someone's house than in a hostel. A front yard surrounded by a charmingly unkempt garden has a table for outdoor eating and socialising. The owners, who live in a separate house right next door, are friendly and have lots of local information about Waipu; one of them teaches Scottish Country Dance and on Mondays there's a dance held in the town hall, to which guests at Waipu Wanderers are often invited.
25 St Mary's Road, Waipu
☎ *(09) 432 0532*
Website *www.waipu.co.nz*
Dorm bed *$30 ($25 BBH);* ***single room*** *$45 ($40 BBH);* ***double/twin room*** *$60 ($50 BBH)*

🚗 TV K L

Maintenance & cleanliness	★★★★
Facilities	★½
Atmosphere & character	★★½
Security	★
Overall rating	★★½

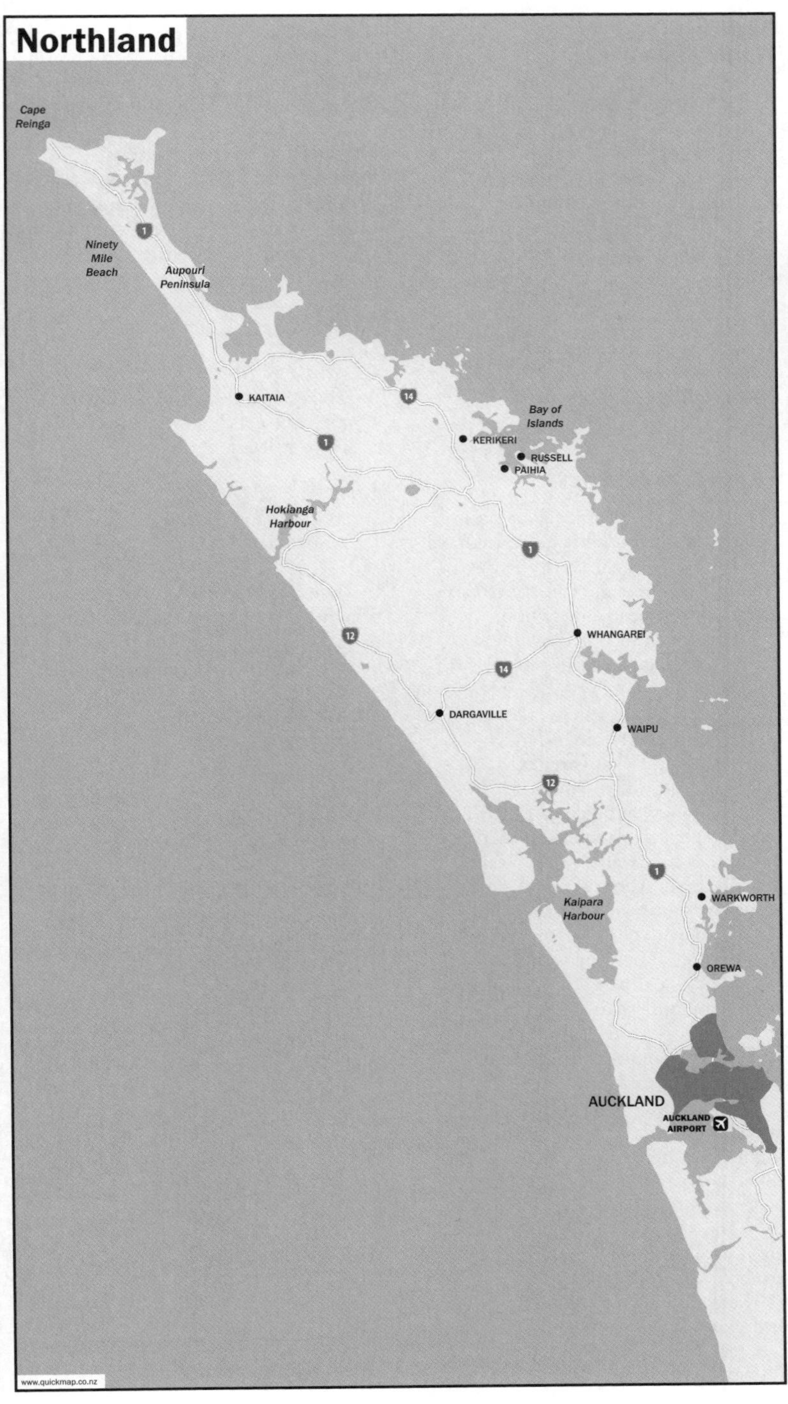
Northland
Cape Reinga
Ninety Mile Beach
Aupouri Peninsula
KAITAIA
Bay of Islands
KERIKERI
RUSSELL
PAIHIA
Hokianga Harbour
WHANGAREI
DARGAVILLE
WAIPU
Kaipara Harbour
WARKWORTH
OREWA
AUCKLAND
AUCKLAND AIRPORT
www.quickmap.co.nz

Sights

Waipu Museum

This interesting museum makes a big deal about the town's Scottish heritage with displays explaining about the migration of Scottish Highlanders who moved from Nova Scotia to New Zealand where they established Waipu. There is a genealogy centre on site where you can dive into your family's history.
36 The Centre, Waipu
☎ *(09) 432 0746*
Website *www.waipumuseum.com*
Admission *$8*
Open *9.30am-4.30pm daily*

Whangarei

Whangarei, the provincial capital of Northland, is often bypassed by travellers on their way north to the Bay of Islands, but there are some interesting attractions around this region.

The major thing that draws most people to Whangarei is its proximity to Poor Knights Islands, considered by many to be New Zealand's premier diving spot.

The easily accessible and much-photographed Whangarei Falls are just 5km from the town centre. They're not the highest or biggest in the world, but they are picturesque and there are a couple of nice walks you can take around them. About seven minutes from the town centre are the Abbey Caves, home to glow worms and 30 million year-old limestone formations.

On the coastline in the Whangarei region are more than a hundred beaches and bays with good weather year-round and plenty of opportunities for swimming, fishing, and kayaking.

Whangarei's town centre is generic and charmless (and eerily desolate at night); but there's a cute quayside area called the Town Basin, with colonial-style restaurants, arts and crafts shops, cafés and a museum with one of the largest collections of clocks in the southern hemisphere, Claphams Clocks.

There are a few very good hostels in and around town, and many Whangarei folk feel their hometown is underrated. A plan to construct a $9.5 million Hundertwasser art centre devoted to the Austrian artist's work has locals hoping that Whangarei will become more of a destination in its own right.

Practical Information

Whangarei i-SITE Visitor Centre

This information centre, located south of the city centre, features a combination tourist information centre and Department of Conservation information centre and there is also a café on site.
Tawera Park, 92 Otaika Road, Whangarei
☎ *(09) 438 1079*
Website *www.whangareinz.org.nz*
Open *Mon-Fri 8.30am-5pm, Sat-Sun 9.30am-4.30pm*

Coming & Going

InterCity *(☎ (09) 623 1503;* ***website*** *www.intercity.co.nz)* and Naked Bus *(☎ 0900 62533 (0900 NAKED);* ***website*** *www.nakedbus.com)* operate scheduled buses to Auckland. Coaches depart from the Northland Coach & Travel Centre at 3C Bank Street.

Accommodation

Bunkdown Lodge

This nice 1903 kauri villa has a pair of lounges, two kitchens, a dining room with a log fire, pianos, guitars, a fish tank, and loads of character. It's very homely and lived-in, and probably the best place in town to get the scoop on local info and history. The lovely owners have put together several books with photos and articles on all things Whangarei; they're incredibly, painstakingly detailed, and a treasure trove of information. The Bunkdown Lodge sleeps only 22 and the accommodation is fairly basic. There's a little courtyard in the back that has an aviary filled with finches and canaries; dogs and cats are also roaming around. In all, it's a very charming and welcoming place.
23 Otaika Road, Whangarei
☎ *(09) 438 8886*
Website *www.bunkdownlodge.co.nz*
Dorm bed *$22-$24 ($20-$22 BBH);* ***double room*** *$55 ($50 BBH);* ***twin room*** *$50 ($48 BBH)*
Credit cards *MC, Visa*

Maintenance & cleanliness	★★★
Facilities	★★
Atmosphere & character	★★★★
Security	★½
Overall rating	★★★

Little Earth Lodge

Little Earth Lodge is a lovely hostel in a rural setting. It's right next to the limestone Abbey Caves, 6km from Whangarei town centre. The house was purpose-built with furnishings and décor shipped in from Bali. Animals wander the grounds – chickens provide free-range eggs and a pair of miniature horses, Tom and Jerry, nibble on the grass (the owner calls them his "lawnmowers"). A separate thatched-wall house holds a small kitchen and common room with games, books, and DVDs. Torches and helmets are supplied for exploring the caves and checking out the glow-worms. The owners are really friendly and enthusiastic about the area; overall, this is an excellent, unique, eco-aware hostel with tonnes of atmosphere and charm.

85 Abbey Caves Road, Whangarei
☎ *(09) 430 6562*
***Website** www.littleearthlodge.co.nz*
***Dorm bed** $25 ($22 BBH); **single room** $49 ($45 BBH); **double room** $58 ($50 BBH)*
***Seasonal opening** Jan-Jun & Sep-Dec Sep-Jun; **reception open** 8.30am-8.30pm daily*

Maintenance & cleanliness	★★★★½
Facilities	★★½
Atmosphere & character	★★★★½
Security	★★
Overall rating	★★★½

The Mural (Whangarei Backpackers)

The Mural is easy enough to spot, with its bright orange façade and location right on Whangarei's main street. Inside, you'll quickly discover where its name comes from – walls are covered in an eclectic mix of paintings, all done by backpackers. The quality ranges, as do the themes – there's sci-fi, fantasy, beach scenes, and more on display. The building itself is deceptively large – it seems like a one-storey affair at street level, but it goes down, down, down a few floors to a big, very cool bar called Ibanez and backs onto a great outdoor courtyard with a wood-burning pizza oven. There's a true backpacker spirit to the place, with communal activities like the wall-painting, shared dinners, group outings, and more. No surprise to learn that one of the managers actually grew up in a hostel – she's got a lot of good ideas about how to run a place. The Mural is a very interesting addition to a town that's been somewhat overlooked on the backpacker trail.

90 Bank Street, Whangarei
☎ *(09) 459 7070*
***Website** www.whangareibackpackers.co.nz*
***Dorm bed** $20-$25; **single room** $45-$50; **double room** $55-$60*
***Credit cards** MC, Visa*
***Reception open** 7.30am-noon & 4.30pm-late evening daily*

Maintenance & cleanliness	★★★
Facilities	★★½
Atmosphere & character	★★★★½
Security	★★
Overall rating	★★★

Whangarei Falls Backpackers

Whangarei Falls Backpackers is part of a holiday park and motor camp right next to the waterfall and walking trails, about 5km from the city centre. There's a good range of facilities on the property, including a swimming pool, spa pool, trampoline, and a big covered barbecue area with picnic tables. Bunk rooms are clean and basic. There's a decent kitchen and a simple TV lounge with books, puzzles, and games and coin-operated internet PCs. Sharing space with the motor camp doesn't give it much of a typical hostel feel, but it's a pleasant enough place.

12-16 Ngunguru Road, Whangarei
☎ *(09) 437 0609 or 0800 227 222*
***Website** www.whangareifalls.co.nz*
***Dorm bed** $22 ($19 BBH); **single room** $32-$50 ($29-$47 BBH); **double/twin room** $46-$54 ($40-$48 BBH)*
***Credit cards** MC, Visa*
***Reception open** 8am-8.30pm daily*

Northland

Maintenance & cleanliness	★★★
Facilities	★★★
Atmosphere & character	★★
Security	★
Overall rating	★★½

Whangarei Manaki Tanga YHA

This YHA-owned hostel is a simple, clean place on a hill overlooking the city centre and the town basin. It's not overflowing with charm, but is cosy and friendly with good bedding (nice new linen when we visited) and a TV room with a log fire. Other facilities include a decent kitchen, internet access and an outdoor deck with barbecue. It's about a 15-minute walk into town. The YHA also provides maps and torches for a glow-worm walk backpackers can take from the hostel; it's around 30 minutes each way.

52 Punga Grove, Whangarei
☎ *(09) 438 8954*
Website *www.stayyha.com*
Dorm bed *$22-$25 ($19-$22 YHA/HI);* ***double room*** *$56-$66 ($50-$60 YHA/HI)*
Credit cards *MC, Visa*
Reception open *8am-1pm & 5pm-8pm daily*

Maintenance & cleanliness	★★★½
Facilities	★★
Atmosphere & character	★★½
Security	★★
Overall rating	★★★

Eating & Drinking

Whangarei's city centre has a collection of pubs, pizza and Asian restaurants, along with a few nicer cafés and restaurants. Night time in Whangarei can have a bit of an edgy feel to it, but there are a number of bars around. The **Ibanez Bar** inside Mural Backpackers *(90 Bank Street, Whangarei)*, is a popular spot with locals and backpackers alike. Or if you're feeling adventurous check out **Danger! Danger!** *(37 Vine Street, Whangarei)*, a big local party barn of a place with a cool sign and lots of nightly specials. There are also several places to eat on Quality Street, where the main shopping centre is located.

The Town Basin, by the marina, is where the more conspicuously charming and upmarket places are located, including nice waterfront cafés and restaurants.

Whangarei's supermarkets include a **Countdown** *(Okara Drive, Whangarei)*, a **New World** *(167 Bank Street, Whangarei)* and a **Pak'n Save** *(Walton Street, Whangarei)*.

Sights

Abbey Caves

These caves near Whangarei are home to glow worms and 30 million year old limestone formations.

Abbey Caves Road, Parahaki

Clapham's Clocks

Clapham's Clocks is an unusual museum that has been around for 100 years and now boasts a collection of over a thousand timepieces.

Dent Street, Town Basin, Whangarei
☎ *(09) 438 3993*
Website *www.claphamsclocks.co.nz*
Admission *$8*
Open *9am-5pm daily*

Whangarei Falls

Located 6km north of the city centre, the 26.3m Whangarei Falls are one of New Zealand's most photogenic waterfalls.

Ngungurua Road, Tikipunga

Whangarei Art Museum

The Whangarei Art Museum is the major art gallery in the Northland region. It hosts a variety of temporary exhibits.

Calfler Park Rose Gardens, Water Street, Whangarei
☎ *(09) 430 4240*
Website *www.whangareiartmuseum.co.nz*
Admission *by donation*
Open *Mon-Fri 10am-4pm, Sat-Sun noon-4pm*

Whangarei Museum & Kiwi House

This museum complex comprises both indoor and outdoor exhibits and is set on 25ha of parkland, 5km west of the city centre. It features a nocturnal kiwi

house with live kiwi, a colonial homestead dating from 1886 and exhibits on the region's Polynesian and European history.
4 State Highway 14, Maunu
☎ *(09) 438 9630*
Website *www.whangareimuseum.co.nz*
Admission *$10*
Open *10am-4pm daily*

Poor Knights Islands

The Pacific Ocean around the Poor Knights Islands is home to New Zealand's most diverse range of marine life, which includes a colourful mix of subtropical and tropical fish. Common species include rays, Moray eels and Kingfish (some as big as 40kg).

This marine reserve was famously named by Jacques Cousteau as one of the top 10 dive sites in the world, thanks to its rare subtropical fish species, sponge gardens and gorgonian fields, underwater caves and arches, and incredible visibility.

Whangarei and Tutukaka, 30 minutes drive from Whangarei, are the main places to organise trips out to the islands.

Companies that organise dive trips include:

Knightdiver

30 Whangarei Heads Road, Whangarei
☎ *(09) 436 2584 or 0800 766 756*
Website *www.poorknights.co.nz*
Full day trip with two dives *$190;* ***snorkelling trip*** *$90*

Dive Tutukaka

Marina Road, Tutukaka
☎ *(09) 434 3867 or 0800 288 882*
Website *www.diving.co.nz*
Full day trip with two dives *$225;* ***snorkelling trip*** *$130*

Poor Knights Divers

Unit 11, Oceans Resort, Tutukaka Marina, Tutukaka
☎ *(09) 434 4678*
Website *www.pkdive.co.nz*
Full day trip with two dives *$215;* ***snorkelling trip*** *$115*

Bay of Islands

The Bay of Islands is the major tourist region in the Northland, and one of the most popular destinations in all of New Zealand. Its appeal is instantly obvious to any visitor with mile after mile of beach and rock coastline surrounding a bay dotted with 144 islands – a dazzling, sparkling world of blue and green.

There are a number of towns in the Bay of Islands, each with a very distinct character. Paihia is the main tourist centre, a place of late-night fun, excellent hostels, and heaps of activities. Russell is its refined and historic neighbour, which is just a short ferry ride away. Kerikeri is a large town with fruit-picking work and a café culture. Waitangi is New Zealand's most important historic site; it's where the Treaty of Waitangi was signed, which effectively handed New Zealand over to British rule.

The Bay of Islands is a popular getaway for New Zealanders, who come here for big-game fishing and to sail among the various coves and islands. But countless activities in the Bay of Islands are geared towards backpackers, from affordable cruises and fishing trips to sea kayaking and excursions where you can swim with dolphins. The Bay of Islands is one of the easiest and yet most rewarding places to travel in New Zealand.

Coming & Going & Local Transport

Paihia is the main centre in the Bay of Islands and consequently handles most coach services that arrive and depart from the Maritime Building on Marsden Road.

Much of the transport around the region radiates from Paihia with frequent buses and ferries to other towns in the Bay of Islands. In addition to the backpacker buses, InterCity *(☎ (09) 623 1503;* ***website*** *www.intercity.co.nz)* operates coaches to other areas in Northland and also to Auckland. InterCity coaches depart from the Maritime Building on Paihia's waterfront.

There are also several places in Paihia where you rent a car to explore the region.

Ferries operate between Paihia and Russell; the 15 minute trip costs $5 each way and departs every half hour. If you have your own car you can take it on the car ferry, which runs between Opua (6km from Paihia) and Okiato near Russell. The car ferry runs every 10 minutes and costs $8 each way or $15 return for a car and driver, plus $1 each way for each additional passenger. With a couple of passengers, this can be cheaper than the direct passenger ferry between Russell and Paihia.

The region's airport is in Kerikeri *(**website** www.kerikeri-airport.co.nz)* and has up to five daily flights from Auckland.

Paihia

Paihia is a pretty town that is the tourist capital of the Bay of Islands, with a highly-developed infrastructure catering to backpackers. Paihia's hostels have a consistently high quality with several truly outstanding choices, and the nightlife here is the most high-spirited in the Bay of Islands.

There's a seemingly infinite number of water-based activities available from Paihia. Cruises are big here, and the choices range from high-speed crafts to small yachts. Many cruises sail out to Motukokako Island, famous for the "Hole in the Rock", which most of the bigger and faster boats sail through. Boats that make it out this far also sail past the picturesque Cape Brett lighthouse.

Sea kayaking is another popular option in Paihia, with guided tours available; more casually, many hostels offer free use of kayaks. For a more hands-on experience than cruising, there are several sailing tours available; and there are the ever-popular swimming with dolphins trips.

For land-based activities, some good walks are available in the area, including through the Opua Forest and in the bush around Waitangi.

And when you've had your fill of exploring land and sea and learning about New Zealand history, the backpackers' area around Kings and Marsden Roads becomes a nightly playground of drinking and dancing until the wee hours.

Practical Information

Awesome Adventure Centre

This tour booking office provides information geared towards backpackers. They also offer internet access.

Maritime Building, Marsden Road, Paihia
☎ *(09) 402 6985*
Website *www.awesomeadventures.co.nz*
Open *Jan-Mar 7am-8pm daily; Apr-Oct 8am-4.30pm daily; Sep-Dec 7am-8pm daily*

Bay of Islands i-SITE Visitor Centre

The Wharf, Marsden Road, Paihia
☎ *(09) 402 7345*
Open *8am-5pm daily*

INTERNET ACCESS

Boots Off

13 Selwyn Road, Paihia
☎ *(09) 402 8262*
Website *www.bootsoff.net.nz*
Open *Mon-Fri 9am-7pm, Sat-Sun 10am-7pm*

6 Kings Road, Paihia
☎ *(09) 402 8262*
Website *www.bootsoff.net.nz*
Open *Mon-Fri 9am-late, Sat-Sun 10am-late*

Accommodation

Paihia is one of the main centres of New Zealand's backpacker party scene and most action happens on Kings Road, which is also where many of Paihia's hostels are located. If you want to party then a Kings Road hostel should be your first choice, otherwise you should stay at a hostel away from Kings Road.

Base Backpackers Paihia

This recent addition to the Base family (it was formerly the Pipi Patch Lodge) keeps up the Base tradition of being a social, party-oriented hostel. Dorm rooms themselves are clean and all come with en suite bathrooms. There's

a relatively small common room with a TV and a sunny, little outdoor deck. The attached Pipi Patch bar has a castaway, beach-bum vibe, decorated as it is with driftwood, barrels, fishing nets and the like. Most evenings, it's one of the more thumping party spots in town. Other facilities include a swimming pool, spa pool, free use of bicycles and access to the nearby tennis court.
18 Kings Road, Paihia
☎ *(09) 402 7111 or (0800) 227 369 (0800 BASE NZ)*
Website *www.stayatbase.com*
Dorm bed *$26;* ***double room*** *$67-$85*
Credit cards *MC, Visa*
Reception open *7am-7pm daily*

Maintenance & cleanliness	★★★★
Facilities	★★★★
Atmosphere & character	★★★★
Security	★½
Overall rating	★★★★

Bay Adventurer

Bay Adventurer is a great, well-run hostel with a cool atmosphere and an incredible range of facilities. Dorm rooms are comfortable and nicely maintained. Beds have real mattresses and individual reading lights (a nice touch), and all come with a locker. The kitchen is clean and fully-equipped and there's a sweet flat-screen TV in the adjoining lounge. Wireless internet is also available (10c per Mb; Zenbu). Outdoors, a swimming pool and a spa pool await in the courtyard. Guests have free use of bicycles and kayaks, and if all that doesn't give you enough to do, free access to the tennis court next door is thrown in as well. The owners and staff are very friendly and helpful; it's obvious a great deal of thought and care has gone into the Bay Adventurer, making it one of the top hostels we've seen.
26-28 Kings Road, Paihia
☎ *(09) 402 5163 or (0800) 112 127*
Website *www.bayadventurer.co.nz*
Dorm bed *$20-$25 ($19-$24 VIP/Nomads);* ***double/twin room*** *$50-$85;* ***studio*** *$75-$125;* ***apartment*** *$99-$225*
Credit cards MC, Visa
Reception open 8am-8pm daily

Maintenance & cleanliness	★★★★½
Facilities	★★★★★
Atmosphere & character	★★★★
Security	★★★
Overall rating	★★★★½

Captain Bob's Beachhouse

Captain Bob's is a well-known and popular Paihia hostel with a great view of the bay from its upstairs balcony and sitting area. It's located a few minutes' walk from both the town centre and the Woolworths supermarket. The atmosphere here is on the quieter side, and there's perhaps less of a warm and friendly vibe from the management as well. Rooms are clean and tidy and the kitchen is fully equipped. The upstairs dining and sitting area are very charming and comfortable, and the view can't be beat.
44 Davis Crescent, Paihia
☎ *(09) 402 8668*
Website *www.capnbobs.co.nz*
Dorm bed *$25 ($22 BBH);* ***single room*** *$47 ($44 BBH);* ***double/twin room*** *$58-$78 ($54-$74 BBH)*
Credit cards *MC, Visa; $1 credit card surcharge*
Reception open *8am-8pm daily*

Maintenance & cleanliness	★★★½
Facilities	★★½
Atmosphere & character	★★★
Security	★½
Overall rating	★★★

Centabay Lodge

Centabay Lodge is located right in the town centre and features a nice big outdoor garden area with a spa pool. It's a little bit scruffier than the other hostels in Paihia, although not in poor shape. Rooms are plain and the kitchen is big and fully-equipped, though it could be better maintained. Guests have free use of bicycles and kayaks; there's an outdoor barbecue as well. A fair number of long-term and repeat visitors stay here, which gives it a familiar, perhaps slightly clique-y social vibe.
27 Selwyn Road, Paihia
☎ *(09) 402 7466*
Website *www.centabay.co.nz*
Dorm bed *$22-$24 ($20-$22 BBH);* ***double room*** *$55-$80 ($50-$80 BBH);*

twin room *$55-$70 ($50-$66 BBH)*
Credit cards *MC, Visa*
Reception open *7.30am-8pm daily*

Maintenance & cleanliness	★★
Facilities	★★★
Atmosphere & character	★★★
Security	★
Overall rating	★★½

Mayfair Lodge

Mayfair Lodge is Paihia's smallest hostel, with just 25 beds. It's set in an old motel right next door to the Woolworths supermarket on the north side of town, away from the Kings Road hostels. Dorms and common areas are brightly painted with colourful images of sailboats and fishes. Everything is very clean and looked after, if a bit basic. A covered patio offers all-weather outdoor living and there's a pool table inside as well as a TV lounge and the usual assortment of games and puzzles. Guests also have use of free bikes, kayaks, and fishing gear. It's not as new and feature-rich as some of the other hostels in town, but the Mayfair offers a quieter alternative.

7 Puketona Road, Paihia
☎ *(09) 402 7471*
Website *www.mayfairlodge.co.nz*
Dorm bed *$23-$25 ($20-$22 BBH);* ***single room*** *$52 ($45 BBH);* ***double room*** *$62 ($54 BBH);* ***twin room*** *$60 ($52 BBH);* ***camping*** *$14 ($12 BBH) per person*
Credit cards *MC, Visa*
Reception open *7.30am-8pm daily*

Maintenance & cleanliness	★★★½
Facilities	★★½
Atmosphere & character	★★★
Security	★
Overall rating	★★★

Mousetrap Backpackers

Mousetrap Backpackers has heaps of character and maybe the homeliest vibe of all the Paihia hostels. The house is full of all sorts of nautical bric-a-brac – shells and whalebones, old tools, coloured glass bottles, buoys, driftwood, etc. The house is tucked among a hilly

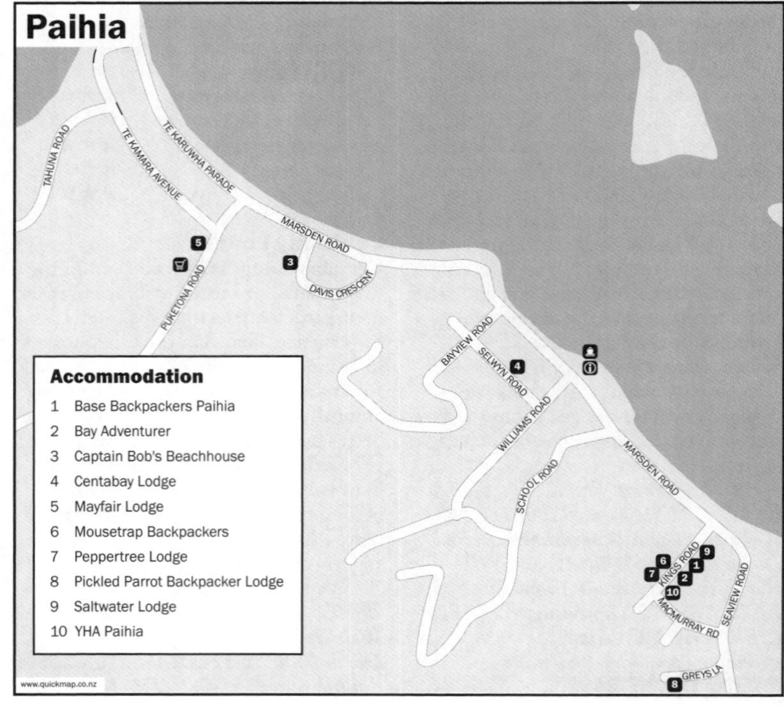

garden, lush with figs, passion fruit, guavas, bananas, grapes, and more, along with vine-shaded sitting areas. The very friendly owners like to call it "the quiet hostel in the street" (there's a quiet policy from 11pm onwards). There's also a great balcony with a nice view. Rooms and facilities are nice, although one nine-bed dorm is a bit crowded. Guests have free use of bikes and the tennis court across the road, and there's even a pétanque piste in front of the house. In all, the Mousetrap has a good atmosphere.

11 Kings Road, Paihia
(09) 402 8182 or (0800) 402 8182
***Website** www.mousetrap.co.nz*
***Dorm bed** $22-$24 ($19-$21 BBH); **double/twin room** $60 ($52 BBH)*
***Credit cards** MC, Visa; 50c-$1 credit card surcharge*
***Reception open** 7.30am-7.30pm daily*

Maintenance & cleanliness	★★★
Facilities	★★★
Atmosphere & character	★★★★★
Security	★★½
Overall rating	★★★½

Peppertree Lodge

The Peppertree Lodge doesn't look like much from the outside, but there's a nice hostel with some very good facilities hidden on the inside. Particularly impressive is the big split-level common room, all sunny with light wood and a great TV screen. The kitchen is also high quality. The dorm rooms are kept tidy and feature very sturdy bunk frames that don't rattle or shake. Extras include free use of bikes and kayaks, a barbecue outside, and free access to the tennis court across the road.

15 Kings Road, Paihia
(09) 402 6122
***Website** www.peppertree.co.nz*
***Dorm bed** $23-$26 ($20-$23 BBH); **double room** $65-$75 ($59-$69 BBH)*
***Credit cards** MC, Visa*
***Reception open** 7.30am-8pm daily*

Maintenance & cleanliness	★★★★
Facilities	★★★½
Atmosphere & character	★★★
Security	★
Overall rating	★★★½

Pickled Parrot Backpacker Lodge

Just around the corner from all the Kings Road hostels, the Pickled Parrot manages to have a quiet and secluded feel. Facilities include a kitchen and TV lounge and a nice outdoor garden with lots of trees and flowers and a barbecue. There's a parrot hanging around, but it wasn't talking when we visited. Guests have free use of fishing gear and free access to the tennis court on Kings Road. Free breakfast is included as well. It's definitely a more laid-back option than many of the other hostels in town, but still very close to the action.

Greys Lane, Paihia
(09) 402 6222 or 0508 727 768 (0508 PARROT)
***Website** www.pickledparrot.co.nz*
***Dorm bed** $23-$25 ($20 BBH); **double/twin/single room** $60 ($54 BBH); **camping** $16 ($14 BBH) per person*
***Credit cards** MC, Visa*
***Reception open** 8am-8pm daily*

Maintenance & cleanliness	★★★★
Facilities	★★★
Atmosphere & character	★★★
Security	★
Overall rating	★★★½

Saltwater Lodge

Saltwater Lodge is an impressive, purpose-built hostel with top-notch facilities. It is easily the most distinctive looking place on the Kings Road strip, with its red and blue corrugated metal exterior and porthole windows. Inside, everything is maintained to a very high standard. Dorm rooms are clean and modern and all come with en suite bathrooms. A big common room has plenty of good couches and a great TV. The brilliant kitchen has restaurant-style stainless steel refrigerators and fixtures. There's something of a view to the harbour on the upstairs verandas, but it's been partially blocked by the newer buildings springing up. Guests have free use of bikes, a free gym and free use of the nearby tennis courts. Throw in a friendly and helpful management, and you have a top-class hostel all around.

14 Kings Road, Paihia

☎ *(09) 402 7075 or 0800 002 266*
Website *www.saltwaterlodge.co.nz*
Dorm bed *$26-$30 ($23-$27 BBH);* ***double/twin room*** *$75-$120 ($65-$90 BBH)*
Credit cards *Amex, MC, Visa*
Reception open *7.30am-7.30pm daily*

Maintenance & cleanliness	★★★★½
Facilities	★★★★½
Atmosphere & character	★★★★
Security	★★½
Overall rating	★★★★½

YHA Paihia

The local YHA is a good quality hostel right at the end of busy Kings Road. It doesn't have the facilities or atmosphere of some of its neighbours, but it's a solid option, particularly if you're looking for less of a party atmosphere. Things are kept clean and well maintained. Dorms feature beds with real mattress and there's a nice, fully-equipped kitchen. A TV lounge and Internet access are there for guests, as well as free access to the tennis court next door. There is a pleasant outdoor sitting area with a barbecue.

Corner Kings & MacMurray Roads, Paihia
☎ *(09) 402 7487*
Website *www.yha.co.nz*
Dorm bed *$25-$28 ($22-$25 YHA);* ***double/twin room*** *$65-$90*
Credit cards *MC, Visa*
Reception open *8am-8pm daily*

Maintenance & cleanliness	★★★★
Facilities	★★★
Atmosphere & character	★★½
Security	★½
Overall rating	★★★

Eating & Drinking

As the backpacker capital of the Northland, Paihia has plenty of drinking and dining options for the budget traveller.

The thumping nightlife in Paihia is centred on Kings and Marsden Roads. A couple of the more popular places for backpackers are connected with hostels including the **Saltwater Bar** *(14 Kings Road, Paihia)*, part of the Saltwater Lodge; and the **Pipi Patch Bar** *(18 Kings Road, Paihia)*, part of Base Paihia. Just follow the crowds and the noise.

Cheap eating options are more abundant on Williams Road and opposite the Maritime Building in the town centre. Eating options in town include pizzerias, cafés, fish and chips and other takeaways.

Woolworths *(9 Blackbridge Road, Paihia)* is the big supermarket in Paihia. It's on the other side of town from Kings Road.

Activities

The Bay of Islands has plenty of water-based activities.

BOAT CRUISES

The Bay of Islands is a popular spot for a cruise and there is a large variety to choose from, ranging from high-speed craft to small yachts. Many cruises sail out to Motukokako Island, which is famous for the 'Hole in the Rock' that most of the bigger and faster boats sail through. Boats that make it out this far also sail past the picturesque Cape Brett lighthouse. Many of the bigger, slower boats cater to the blue rinse set but the high-speed boats like the *Excitor* and *Mack Attack* have more of a backpacker focus.

Excitor

No, it's not the latest product from Durex. It's an 18-metre speedboat that jets out to the Hole in the Rock in just 1½ hours.

Maritime Building, Paihia
☎ *(09) 402 7020*
Website *www.excitor.co.nz*
Cost *$77*
Departure times *Jan-Apr 8am, 10.30am, 12.30pm, 2.30pm, 4.30pm daily; May-Sep 10.30am, 2.30pm daily; Oct-Dec 8am, 10.30am, 12.30pm, 2.30pm, 4.30pm daily*

Mack Attack

No, it's not the latest McDonalds promotional menu. It's another boat that claims to be the fastest to the rock (also 1½ hours).

Maritime Building, Paihia
☎ *(09) 402 8180 or 0800 622 528*
Website *www.mackattack.co.nz*
Cost *$75*
Departure times *10.30am, 12.30pm, 2.30pm, 4.30pm daily*

The Rock

This big boat offers overnight cruises that feature island treks, snorkelling, kayaking and a phosphorescence swim. It gets mixed reports from travellers, but generally if you are looking for a good time you will have a good time on this boat. It's a good value trip and the price includes a night's accommodation on board plus a barbecue dinner and breakfast.

Corner Marsden & Williams Roads, Paihia
☎ *0800 762 527*
Website *www.rocktheboat.co.nz*
24-hour overnight cruise *$178 including dinner and breakfast*

SEA KAYAKING

There are several companies in the Bay of Islands that offer sea kayaking that range from a half day to two-day overnight trips.

Coastal Kayakers

This company operates guided sea kayak trips that take you past the Waitangi treaty grounds, through mangrove forests to the Haruru Falls. The two-day trip goes further afield and allows you to experience islands in the bay.

Te Karuwha Parade, Ti Bay, Waitangi
☎ *(09) 402 8105*
Website *www.coastalkayakers.co.nz*
Half day trip *$55;* ***full day trip*** *$75;* ***two day trip*** *$130*

Island Kayaks

Island Kayaks runs half day trips that take you past mangroves to secluded bays where you can snorkel or relax on the beach.

Marsden Road, Paihia
☎ *(09) 402 6078*
Website *www.baybeachhire.co.nz*
Half day trip *$60;* ***full day trip*** *$150*

SAILING

If you're looking for a slower paced, but more hands-on experience than a simple boat cruise, then sailing a yacht on the Bay of Islands may be for you. There are several companies that operate yacht trips that range from one to three-day cruises. Most of the one-day cruises depart Paihia or Russell around 10am, returning around 4pm. Some of the sailing companies only operate during summer.

Bay of Islands Sailing/Gungha II

A trip on this 60ft maxi-yacht is loads of fun and many people regard it as the best of the one-day cruises. You have the opportunity to help crew the yacht or you can let others do the work. There is an island stop over and you have the chance to see dolphins. This trip operates Oct-May.

☎ *(09) 407 7930 or 0800 478 900*
Website *www.bayofislandssailing.co.nz*
Full day sailing *$85 including lunch.*
Departs Paihia *9.30am,* ***departs Russell*** *10am*

Carino Sailing

Carino operate full day sailing trips on a spacious 12m (40ft) catamaran. This boat makes plenty of island stops where you can swim or snorkel and there are often opportunities to swim with dolphins.

☎ *(09) 402 8040*
Website *www.sailinganddolphin.co.nz*
Full day sailing *$90*
Departs Paihia *9.30am,* ***departs Russell*** *9.40am*

Ecocruz

This fantastic three-day sailing trip aboard a 22m (72ft) ocean-going yacht allows you plenty of time to really experience the Bay of Islands. The trip includes sea kayaking, snorkelling and fishing and you get to explore islands. There's also the opportunity to see marine wildlife, including dolphins. The trip is fully inclusive and includes all meals and accommodation on board.

☎ *0800 4 ECOCRUZ (0800 432 6278)*
Website *www.ecocruz.co.nz*
Three day cruise *$495-575, includes all meals and accommodation*
Departs Paihia *Tues 8am, Fri 8am*

She's a Lady

This yacht makes full day trips on the bay with lunch on an island and opportunities for snorkelling, swimming, fishing and knee boarding.

Northland

☎ *0800 724 584*
***Website** www.bay-of-islands.com/sailing/*
***Full day sailing** $90 includes lunch*
***Departs Paihia** 10am; **departs Russell** 10.15am*

Straycat

Straycat is a fast stable catamaran that does full day trips on the bay. You have an opportunity to see dolphins and penguins and participate in activities that include fishing, swimming and snorkelling.
☎ *(09) 402 6130 or 0800 101 007*
***Website** www.bayofislandsdaysailing.co.nz*
***Full day sailing** $79 including lunch*
***Departs Russell** 9.30am; **departs Paihia** 10am*

SWIMMING WITH DOLPHINS
Awesome Adventures

Awesome Adventures run small (35 seat) catamarans out on the Bay of Islands, which have the warmest waters in New Zealand where you can swim with dolphins. Bottlenose and Common dolphins can both be seen from the boat and you have a 90% chance of seeing them. The best time to see dolphins is Apr-Jun, Orca are frequently spotted Apr-Oct, Brydes whales May-Jun and migrating whales including Blue, Humpback and Pilot whales are often spotted May-Apr and Aug-Sep.
Maritime Building, Marsden Road, Paihia
☎ *(09) 402 6985*
***Website** www.awesomenz.com/dolphin.php*
***Cost** $115*
***Departs Paihia** 8am & 12.30pm daily*

SKYDIVING
NZ Skydive

The Bay of Islands Skydive Centre offers tandem skydives in the country's warmest drop zone where you are treated to views of both the east and west coasts. Jumps are from 6000, 9000 or 12,000ft.
☎ *(09) 402 6744 or 0800 427 593*
***Website** www.nzskydive.co.nz/bay_of_islands/*
***Tandem jump from 6,000ft** $200; **tandem jump from 9,000ft** $245; **tandem jump from 12,000ft** $295*

Waitangi

Waitangi, immediately to the north of Paihia, is New Zealand's most important historic site. The Treaty of Waitangi was signed here in 1840, which effectively handed New Zealand over to British rule. The Treaty House and adjoining visitor centre is the highlight of a visit to the Bay of Islands and offers a crash course in New Zealand history. Waitangi is also home to a Māori meetinghouse and a huge waka (war canoe).

Sights
Waitangi Treaty Grounds

The Waitangi Treaty Grounds were the scene of the signing of Waitangi. They feature an elaborate traditional carved Māori meeting house, the Treaty House and a canoe house that features *Ngātokimatawhaorua* – one of the largest ceremonial war canoes in the world with a hull carved from two huge kauri trees.
1 Tau Henare Drive, Waitangi
☎ *(09) 402 7437*
***Website** www.waitangi.net.nz*
***Admission** $12, one hour guided tour $10*
***Open** summer 9am-6pm daily; winter 9am-5pm daily*

Russell

Russell, just a short ferry ride across the bay from Paihia has a very different feel from its party-town neighbour. Russell was the first capital of New Zealand, and has a great deal of historical buildings and sites that are worth a visit. Pompallier is a Catholic mission that was used as a printer, tannery, and storehouse; it's New Zealand's oldest remaining Roman Catholic building and is now a museum. Christ Church is the oldest church in New Zealand, and still has musket-ball holes from the Māori Wars. There are good beaches and walks around here as well.

The town likes to call itself "Romantic Russell", and it has a kind of antique charm that generally appeals to an older crowd. It's a long way from Russell's rough and ready past, when it was once known as the "Hellhole of the Pacific", a lawless town teeming with criminals and prostitutes. Nowadays, Russell makes a good alternative to Paihia if you want to avoid the noise and drunken revelry but still partake in all the activities the region has to offer.

Accommodation

The End of the Road Backpackers

The End of the Road Backpackers is a little cottage with no regular on-site staff. Visitors let themselves in and, if a bed is available, simply stay there. The owner stops in to collect money and perform maintenance. There are two single beds in one room and a double bed in the other. Everything is very basic. A small living room has a TV, there's a little kitchen, a small dining room table, a few books and that's about it. One thing the End of the Road does have going for it is a great view over the Matauwhi Bay. It's an unusual, self-catering situation, which could hold a certain appeal for some.

13 Brind Road, Russell
☎ *(09) 403 8827*
***Dorm bed** $30; **double/twin room** $60*

Maintenance & cleanliness	★★
Facilities	★
Atmosphere & character	★½
Security	-
Overall rating	★½

Pukeko Cottage Backpackers

This small cottage sleeps up to seven in three rooms: the Blue Room, the Gold Room, and the "Sunshine Supervan", a groovy 1950s caravan set up in the backyard. The cottage itself is cluttered but in a cosy way, filled with books and all sorts of interesting knick-knacks. Barry, the owner, is a fount of local knowledge and history. Actually, many pieces of the cottage have an interesting history of their own; the fireplace, for instance, was salvaged from the original Bank of New Zealand. The Pukeko is a swamp hen common to New Zealand, in case you were wondering.

14 Brind Road, Russell
☎ *09 403 8498*
***Website** www.pukekocottagebackpackers.co.nz*
***Dorm bed** $25; **double room** $50*

Maintenance & cleanliness	★★½
Facilities	★½
Atmosphere & character	★★★★
Security	★
Overall rating	★★½

Sheltered Waters Backpackers

Sheltered Waters is the biggest backpackers in Russell, with all of 16 beds. It's set in a nice house with a front patio and a big backyard with lots of lush flora. There's a spa pool, trampoline and a barbecue in the back courtyard, as well as an aviary and a cat prowling around. The living room has a homely, lived-in feel, with portraits and family photos, and there are very good kitchen facilities. The dorm room itself seemed a bit on the crowded side with 10 beds, but the overall atmosphere is warm and inviting.

18 Florance Avenue, Russell
☎ *(09) 403 8818*
***Website** www.russellbackpackers.co.nz*
***Dorm bed** $25; **double room** $65-$75; **twin room** $60*

Maintenance & cleanliness	★★★½
Facilities	★★½
Atmosphere & character	★★★½
Security	★
Overall rating	★★★

Activities

Many of the activities available in Paihia can also be done through Russell, this includes many of the cruises, which pick up passengers here. See the preceding Paihia section for more information.

Sights

Pompallier

New Zealand's oldest building associated with the Catholic Church has been used as a printer's workshop as well as a tannery and storehouse. It is unique in the fact that it is the oldest surviving example of a rammed earth building. There is a museum on site

featuring demonstrations of printing, binding, leatherwork and tanning.
The Strand, Russell
☎ *(09) 403 7861*
***Admission** $7.50*
***Open** Jan-Apr 10am-5pm daily; May-Nov 10am-4pm daily; Dec 10am-5pm daily*

Russell Museum

This interesting museum recounts the history of the early years of Māori-European contact and also has some fascinating displays about the whaling industry. One of the museum's main attractions is the 1:5 scale model of Captain Cook's ship the *Endeavour.*
2 York Street, Russell
☎ *(09) 403 7701*
***Website** www.russellmuseum.org.nz*
***Admission** $5*
***Open** Jan 10am-5pm daily; Feb-Dec 10am-4pm daily*

Kerikeri

Located slightly inland at the northern end of the bay, fast-growing Kerikeri's main draw for backpackers is its abundance of casual work picking fruit in the nearby orchards. Most hostels will arrange work and transport pretty much all year.

There is more than fruit-picking to Kerikeri, however. It's the site of the first permanent mission station in the country, and is home to several historic buildings, including New Zealand's oldest house, the 1821 Kemp House. Another local icon is the 1832 stone store.

For the more upscale traveller, Kerikeri also has a thriving arts and food scene. There are a surprising number of art and craft studios, workshops and galleries for such a small town. Cafés, restaurants, gourmet food shops, wineries and a farmer's market are part of a developing and serious food culture here. Return visitors to Kerikeri after a number of years have commented on how dramatically the town has changed.

Coming & Going

InterCity *(☎ (09) 623 1503; **website** www.intercity.co.nz)* coaches stop outside Subway *(9 Cobham Street, Kerikeri).*

Accommodation

Aranga Backpackers

Aranga Backpackers is part of the sprawling Top 10 Holiday Park campgrounds, which include tent sites, cabins, and lots of campervans. The grounds are pretty nice, with the river running alongside, but the backpacker lodges have a rough and ready feel to them. There's a large common room with a huge TV, but the couches and furniture are in disrepair. The kitchen isn't in the greatest shape, either. Dorms themselves are basic and functional. That said, a major reason backpackers stay here is for work; Aranga finds them jobs and offers free transport to and from work. The staff seem friendly and helpful in looking after backpackers. Guests have free use of kayaks and there is also a volleyball net and a massive, truly impressive covered barbecue area.
Kerikeri Road, Kerikeri
☎ *(09) 407 9326 or (0800) 272 642*
***Website** www.aranga.co.nz*
***Dorm bed** $23 ($110 per week); **double/twin room** $46 ($240 per week)*
***Credit cards** MC, Visa*
***Reception open** 7.30am-8pm daily*
TV K L

Maintenance & cleanliness	★½
Facilities	★★★½
Atmosphere & character	★★½
Security	★
Overall rating	★★½

Hideaway Lodge

Hideaway Lodge is a caravan park and hostel that's good at finding temporary work for travellers. Dorms are decent-sized and come with a refrigerator, but overall the facilities and common areas are in poor shape. There's a swimming pool, a TV lounge and a barbecue area, but all the furnishings are old and falling apart. A small shop sells canned and packaged food in the reception. Daily rides into town are free; transport to jobs is offered for $3 round trip.
Wiroa Road, Kerikeri
☎ *(09) 407 9773*
***Website** www.hideawaylodge.co.nz*
***Dorm bed** $20 pernight, $155 per*

week; ***double/twin room*** *$55 per night, $205-$210 per week;* ***camping*** *$12 per night, $70 per week per person*
Credit cards *MC, Visa*
Reception open *Mon-Fri 8am-10pm, Sat-Sun 9am-10pm*

Maintenance & cleanliness	★½
Facilities	★★
Atmosphere & character	★½
Security	★
Overall rating	★½

Hone Heke Lodge

Hone Heke Lodge is set in an old motel around a gravel courtyard; the place was totally refurbished a few years ago and is still in quite good shape. Rooms are large and all come with a refrigerator. There are indoor and outdoor kitchen facilities and a big, covered outdoor barbecue/dining/hanging out area with a pool table. The TV lounge has a nice big flat screen on the wall; internet and Wi-Fi access is available in a separate lounge. Other facilities include table tennis and a trampoline. Free pick-up is offered from the bus station and a security guard patrols in the evening. It's generally a hostel for backpackers working in the area, but Hone Heke is cleaner and has a bit more atmosphere than many similar places.

65 Hone Heke Road, Kerikeri
☎ *(09) 407 8170*
Website *www.honeheke.co.nz*
Dorm bed *$23-$35 ($20-$32 BBH);* ***single room*** *$35-$55 ($32-$52 BBH);* ***double room*** *$50-$70 ($44-$64 BBH)*
Credit cards *MC, Visa*
Reception open *8am-8pm daily*

Maintenance & cleanliness	★★★★
Facilities	★★★½
Atmosphere & character	★★★½
Security	★½
Overall rating	★★★

Kerikeri Farm Hostel

This is a small, 10-bed hostel on a working organic citrus farm. It is set in a lovely old farmhouse with wooden floors and ceilings and has loads of character. There's a very nice kitchen and dining/sitting area, along with a fireplace lounge and grapevine-covered patio with a barbecue. There's a whole lot more atmosphere than in the working hostels in town. It's about a ten-minute drive from the town centre. No TV or Internet is available, making Kerikeri Farm Hostel just a quiet place to relax and reflect among the orchards.

State Highway 10, Kerikeri
☎ *(09) 407 6989*
Dorm bed *$23 ($20 BBH);* ***single room*** *$38 ($35 BBH);* ***double/twin room*** *$56 ($50 BBH)*

Maintenance & cleanliness	★★★★½
Facilities	★★½
Atmosphere & character	★★★★
Security	½
Overall rating	★★★½

Eating & Drinking

Kerikeri has a serious café culture, with much of the action centred on and around Kerikeri Road, the main street that runs through town. There almost seem too many cafés to count. A few are: **Café Jerusalem** *(Cobblestone Mall, Kerikeri)*, which has Middle Eastern food to eat in or take away. **Café Zest** *(73 Kerikeri Road, Kerikeri)* is an organic/vegetarian café; the **Fishbone Café** *(88 Kerikeri Road, Kerikeri)* is another popular spot.

There's not a lot of nightlife in Kerikeri; the **Citrus Bar** *(corner Cobham and Kerikeri Roads, Kerikeri)* is the main venue in the area.

There's a farmers' market featuring the great local produce every Sunday morning on Hobson Avenue.

Kerikeri's supermarkets include a **New World** *(99 Kerikeri Road, Kerikeri)* and a **Woolworths** *(corner Fairway Drive & Kerikeri Road, Kerikeri)*.

Sights

Kemp House & Stone Store

New Zealand's oldest European building (Kemp House) and the country's oldest stone building (the Stone Store) are located at the Kerikeri River Basin, a 20-minute walk from the town centre. It is a fascinating site if you're interested in New Zealand history.

246 Kerikeri Road, Kerikeri Basin
☎ *(09) 407 9236*

Website *www.historic.org.nz*
Admission *$5*
Open *Jan-Apr 10am-5pm daily; May-Oct 10am-4pm daily; Nov-Dec 10am-5pm daily*

Rewa's Village

This reconstructed Maori fishing village depicts how Maori lived in the Kerikeri area before the arrival of missionaries.
1 Landing Road, Kerikeri
☎ *(09) 407 6454*
Admission *$2.50*
Open *summer 9am-5pm daily; winter 10am-4pm daily*

Whangaroa Harbour & Kaeo

Whangaroa is a town set on the shore of the very deep Whangaroa Harbour, on a slightly secluded location off State Highway 1. Big-game fishing is the main activity here; Whangaroa calls itself the Marlin Capital of New Zealand and fishing expeditions and charters can be arranged here. Social life seems revolves around the Whangaroa Big Gamefish Club, which hosts many fishing tournaments and has a restaurant and bar in its atmospheric old clubhouse.

There are some nice secluded beaches around Whangaroa and some great views to be had from surrounding hillsides, particularly St Pauls Peak, which requires some basic rock climbing up the last several metres. Nearby Matauri Bay is an excellent diving spot and is the watery resting place of the original Greenpeace flagship, the *Rainbow Warrior*. The wreck can be dived.

The tiny service town of Kaeo is at the southern end of Whangaroa Harbour, on State Highway 1. It has a single hostel but almost nothing else. It's about 32km north of Kerikeri and a 8km from Whangaroa.

Accommodation

KAEO

Kaeo Backpackers

Kaeo Backpackers is a new hostel right on State Highway 10, about 32km north of Kerikeri and 8km from Whangaroa, in the tiny one-street village of Kaeo. It's above a laundromat and internet shop that also has a pool table. The hostel sleeps 13. One room, called the "woofers' room" is set in a small cabin outside the main house. The rest of the accommodation is in a simple home with a living room, TV and kitchen. Facilities are basic and reasonably clean. There's not really any reason to stay in Kaeo, but if Kerikeri and Whangaroa are full, or you just get tired of driving, there it is.
Leigh Street, Kaeo
☎ *(09) 405 0821*
Dorm bed *$22;* ***double/twin room*** *$44*
TV K L

Maintenance & cleanliness	★★½
Facilities	★½
Atmosphere & character	★½
Security	★½
Overall rating	★★

WHANGAROA

Sunseeker Lodge

Sunseeker Lodge offers simple backpacker accommodation on a property high up on a hill with spectacular views of Whangaroa Harbour. Dorm rooms are set in a small house and are brightly painted in aqua and orange, but the bedding is very basic and thin. There's a small common lounge with a fireplace and cheap internet access on a single PC. Other facilities include a guest kitchen and outdoor spa pool. There are pricier options, including motel units and a holiday house on the grounds, but the view is free and shared by everyone.
Old Hospital Road, Whangaroa
☎ *(09) 405 0496*
Website *www.sunseekerlodge.co.nz*
Dorm bed *$22 ($18 BBH);* ***double room*** *$65-$75*
Reception open *8am-8pm*
🚗 TV K L

Maintenance & cleanliness	★★★
Facilities	★★½
Atmosphere & character	★★★
Security	★
Overall rating	★★½

The Far North

Around the glum provincial capital of Kaitaia, the North Island narrows into the Aupouri Peninsula, a 10km-wide strip of land that projects out into the Tasman Sea and the Pacific Ocean. Moving northward travellers encounter an increasingly isolated and sparsely-populated subtropical landscape.

The main reason visitors press onward from the Northland is to reach Cape Reinga, a spiritually important Maori location, and a dramatic point from which to watch the ocean and sea churn together. Running along virtually the entire west side of the peninsula, from lovely beach town Ahipara to Scott Point is Ninety Mile Beach (which is really only 88km long).

The beach is actually a highway, but rental car companies generally won't let their vehicles drive on it and many people get their cars stuck in the sand. Tours are a better idea; a number that drive up the beach to Cape Reinga can be arranged from Kaitaia (tours are also available from the Bay of Islands, but they make for a much longer day). On the east side of the peninsula, the state highway winds through tiny towns, bays, and forest.

This is a remote and un-touristy part of New Zealand where the journey is as much a part of the experience as any actual destination. The Far North can be a very refreshing alternative to the beaten tourist trail.

Kaitaia

Kaitaia, the largest town in the Far North region, has a bad reputation among travellers and it's hard to say much to dispel that impression. It is simply a dreary and depressed-looking town, not the kind of place that pops into your head when you're sitting in class or at work daydreaming about your holiday in New Zealand.

That said, it does make a good spot to arrange travel up to Cape Reinga. You'll definitely pay less and spend less time on the bus if you start your journey here rather than in Paihia. The town itself has both a strong Māori and Dalmatian presence, the latter reflecting the days of Kaitaia's gum-digging boom. If you're interested to learn more about the local history, Kaitaia is home to the Far North Regional Museum.

If you're making the drive yourself up north, Kaitaia make sure to fuel up, hit the ATM, and get supplies here.

Practical Information

Far North i-SITE Visitor Centre

Jaycee Park, South Road, Kaitaia
☎ *(09) 408 0879*

Coming & Going

InterCity *(☎ (09) 623 1503; **website** www.intercity.co.nz)* coaches stop at the visitor information centre in Jaycee Park.

Accommodation

Hike & Bike Hostel

This dispiriting place on Kaitaia's main street feels more like a low-rent lodging house than a hostel. It looks absolutely worn out from the outside, but is somewhat cleaner inside. Facilities include a common room with a pool table, a small TV room, and kitchen facilities that are not half bad. Still, overall, there's just a stale feeling to the Hike & Bike Hostel, like the curtains haven't been opened in years. This is the kind of place that lives up (or down) to Kaitaia's dreary reputation.

160 Commerce Street, Kaitaia
☎ *(09) 408 1840*
***Dorm bed** $20; **single room** $24; **double/twin room** $40*

Maintenance & cleanliness	★½
Facilities	★
Atmosphere & character	½
Security	★
Overall rating	★

Main Street Lodge

The yellow, purple, and black house out front is not the most attractive thing in the world, but backpackers stay in a newer wing behind it, set around a courtyard. Main Street Lodge has the most "backpacker" feel of any place in Kaitaia and owners Claire and Allen are knowledgeable about the region. Rooms are simple and clean, and were being renovated when we visited, and there's a big outdoor barbecue and wood-fired pizza oven. Other facilities include a large

kitchen and a TV room. There's also a Māori whare on-site that is sometimes used as a cultural centre and a bone-carving workshop. Internet access is available.
235 Commerce Street, Kaitaia
☎ *(09) 408 1275*
***Website** www.mainstreetlodge.co.nz*
***Dorm bed** $25-$27 ($20-$23 BBH); **single room** $50-$60 ($45-$55 BBH); **double/twin room** $56-$64 ($50-$58 BBH)*
***Credit cards** MC, Visa*
***Reception open** 7am-9.30pm daily*

Maintenance & cleanliness	★★★½
Facilities	★★
Atmosphere & character	★★
Security	★½
Overall rating	★★½

Pirates Backpackers (Kaitaia Hotel)

Pirates Backpackers is part of an old hotel that's been partially renovated. From the outside, it's eye-catching; the entrance is sleek and black and the attached bar/restaurant, Nero, is probably the most glamorous place in a decidedly un-posh town. The inside is a mixed bag, however. Some rooms seem like they're straight out of a time capsule from 1964, with fuzzy chairs, garish bedspreads and wallpaper and ancient television sets. Carpeting throughout the backpacker wings is pretty psychedelic, too. Kitchen facilities are adequate, as is a TV lounge (although it also has the furry shag chairs). Wireless internet is also available (10c per Mb; Zenbu). A small outdoor courtyard is comfortable and new. All rooms have en suite bathrooms.
25 Commerce Street, Kaitaia
☎ *(09) 408 0360*
***Dorm bed** $23-$25 ($20-$22 BBH); **single room** $54 ($48 BBH); **double room** $80; **twin room** $65 ($58 BBH)*
***Credit cards** MC, Visa*
***Reception open** 7am-10pm/midnight*

Maintenance & cleanliness	★★★
Facilities	★★
Atmosphere & character	★★
Security	★½
Overall rating	★★½

Sights

Far North Regional Museum

This small museum features displays relating to local history. These include the de Surville anchor, which was left in New Zealand in 1769, earlier than any other item of European origin. The other main attraction at this museum is a replica of the ancient Kaitaia carving.
6 South Road, Kaitaia
☎ *(09) 408 1403*
***Website** www.farnorthmuseum.co.nz*
***Admission** $4*
***Open** 10am-4pm daily*

Cape Reinga Tours

Most travellers visit Kaitaia to organise a tour to Cape Reinga. The best way to experience the cape is to drive along Ninety Mile Beach, however rental car companies prohibit this and people frequently get their cars stuck in the sand. If you don't have a 4WD and experience driving in sandy conditions, it's best to leave the driving to a tour company. Some of these trips also have departures from the Bay of Islands, however leaving from Kaitaia means that you can sleep in an extra couple of hours.

Cape Reinga Adventures

Cape Reinga Adventures runs short kayaking trips plus longer tours that are a good option for outdoorsy people. Activities include fishing, kayaking and sand boarding.
☎ *(09) 409 8445*
***Website** www.capereingaadventures.co.nz*
***3 hour kayak to Cape Reinga** $95; **half day harbour kayak trip** $85; **full day harbour kayak trip** $125*

Dune-Rider

The Dune-Rider runs trips to Cape Reinga in custom-built 4WD coaches, which include a drive on Ninety Mile Beach and boogie boarding on the sand dunes. These trips depart from Paihia, but picking the tour up at the Big River Café in Awanui, near Kaitaia, is a better option if you don't want to wake up too early.
Big River Café, Awanui
☎ *(09) 402 8681 or 0800 494 868*

Website *www.dunerider.co.nz*
One-day tour *$65-110 from Awanui, $110 from Paihia/Kerikeri*
Pick up *7.15am from Paihia, 7.50am from Kerikeri, 10am from Awanui (near Kaitaia)*

Harrisons Cape Runner

Harrisons Cape Runner operates daily trips between Kaitaia and Cape Reinga that include a drive along Ninety Mile Beach and tobogganing on sand dunes.

123 North Road, Kaitaia
☎ *(09) 408 1033*
Website *www.ahipara.co.nz/caperunner*
One-day tour *$45*

Sand Safaris

Sand Safaris run trips between Kaitaia and Cape Reinga that feature a drive along the Ninety Mile Beach and through the Te Paki quicksand stream.

221 Commerce Street, Kaitaia
☎ *(09) 408 1778 or 0800 869 090*
Website *www.sandsafaris.co.nz*
One-day trip *$65*
Departs *Kaitaia 9am*

Ahipara

Ahipara is 14km from Kaitaia, but this small village at the southern end of Ninety Mile Beach feels like it's on another planet. This is a ruggedly blissful beach town with awesome surf at Shipwreck Bay and gorgeous sunset views. Surfcasting, dune surfing, and quad biking are big activities here; you can also ride horses or sand yachts on the beach. It's not as easily accessible as Kaitaia, but Ahipara makes a great alternative if you plan to base yourself in the area while arranging travel up farther north.

Accommodation

Endless Summer Lodge

Right across the road from the southern end of Ninety Mile Beach, Endless Summer Lodge is great little place set in a gorgeously-maintained 1880 kauri villa. Rooms are sunny and clean and have excellent beds. There's a small, cute lounge (without a TV) and a big front yard with a veranda looking out over the beach and Shipwreck Bay. A number of rooms also have sea views. The backyard features a covered barbecue area and a long, grapevine-shaded table. Full kitchen facilities, including a dishwasher, are absolutely top-notch. If you have your own transport, this makes a fantastic alternative to staying in Kaitaia.

245 Foreshore Road, Ahipara
☎ *(09) 409 4181*
Website *www.endlesssummer.co.nz*
Dorm bed *$26 ($23 BBH);* ***double room*** *$62-$68 ($56-$62 BBH);* ***twin room*** *$62 ($56 BBH)*

Maintenance & cleanliness	★★★★★
Facilities	★★
Atmosphere & character	★★★★★
Security	★
Overall rating	★★★★

YHA Ahipara Backpackers & Motor Camp

This YHA associate offers a range of accommodation options, from campers, tents, and cabins to dorm beds. It's set among a pine forest and has a real campground feel and the standard of accommodation is basic and rustic. Facilities include a kitchen/dining area and a big common room with an enormous projection TV. Internet access and Wi-Fi is available and there's a barbecue area outdoors. Snacks and various sundries are sold at reception. The Ahipara Backpackers & Motor Camp is a five minute walk to Ninety Mile Beach and about 15 km from Kaitaia.

168 Takahe Street, Ahipara
☎ *(09) 409 4864*
Website *www.ahiparamotorcamp.co.nz*
Dorm bed *$26 ($23 YHA);* ***double room*** *$60 ($54 YHA);* ***twin room*** *$56 ($50 YHA); cabin $55-$75 ($49-$69 YHA);* ***camping*** *$14*
Credit cards *MC, Visa*
Reception open *8am-9pm daily*

Maintenance & cleanliness	★★★
Facilities	★★
Atmosphere & character	★★
Security	★
Overall rating	★★½

Northland

Pukenui, Houhora Heads & Henderson Bay

This area about halfway up the Aupouri Peninsula is a popular spot for travellers to stay while making their way up to Cape Reinga. Pukenui is the most northern town of any size; make sure you fill up with fuel here if you're driving and this is a good spot to buy any supplies you might need.

There are a few cafés, shops and a bar in Pukenui, and there are some very nice hostel choices nearby. There is excellent wharf fishing in Houhoura Harbour and there are nice beaches on Henderson Bay with excellent surfing.

Accommodation

HOUHORA HEADS

Houhora Backpackers' Heaven

"Heaven" is a definite exaggeration here. Backpacker dorms are up on top of a hill overlooking the large Wagener Holiday Parks campsite and facilities are basic at very best. Rooms are spartan and the limited kitchen/common room is in rough shape. Showers are coin-operated. Meals are available at a café on site as is (pricey) internet access. There is a saving grace to this heaven, however, and that is its waterfront location. The views are absolutely gorgeous and access to the beach couldn't be much closer.

Wagener Holiday Park, Houhora Heads Road, Houhora Heads
☎ *(09) 409 8564*
Website *www.northlandholiday.co.nz*
Dorm bed *$18-$20*
Credit cards *MC, Visa*
Reception open *7.30am-9pm daily*

Maintenance & cleanliness	★½
Facilities	★½
Atmosphere & character	★★
Security	½
Overall rating	★½

PUKENUI

Farmstay Backpackers

Farmstay Backpackers is a working dairy farm (which also grows watermelons in season), but accommodation is not nearly as rustic as you might imagine. The small house for backpackers is relatively new and modern, with a nice, well-equipped kitchen and a TV room with log fire. There is one six-bed dorm room, a double room and a twin. Camping is also available if you have a tent. You can check email on a single computer inside the main house. Views out over the farm are great for catching sunsets and there are lots of stars to see at night. There is just a very nice, cosy feeling here as the fog comes rolling up the hills in the early morning.

Lamb Road, Pukenui
☎ *(09) 409 7863*
Dorm bed *$21 ($18 BBH);* ***double/twin room*** *$56 ($50 BBH)*

Maintenance & cleanliness	★★★★
Facilities	★★
Atmosphere & character	★★★½
Security	★
Overall rating	★★★

Pukenui Lodge Hostel

The backpacker part of this motel complex is set in an historic 1891 house. There is a pair of very basic four-bed dorms and a few doubles inside, along with a simple kitchen and TV room. Internet access is available (but expensive, like most places in this area). On a front lawn, picnic tables overlook the Houhora Harbour, which is right down the hill. A general store, bar and café are across the road. Backpackers are able to use the motel facilities, including the swimming pool and trampoline (though a sign says it's for children only). Kayaks and sand boards are available for hire.

Corner State Highway 1 & Wharf Road, Pukenui
☎ *(09) 409-8837*
Website *www.pukenuilodge.co.nz*
Dorm bed *$22.50 ($20 BBH);* ***double room*** *$60 ($54 BBH)*
Credit cards *MC, Visa*
Reception open *8.30am-8.30pm daily*

Maintenance & cleanliness	★★½
Facilities	★★½
Atmosphere & character	★★
Security	★
Overall rating	★★½

HENDERSON BAY
North Wind Lodge

North Wind Lodge is a nice house a few kilometres off the main road, on a 4ha property that stretches down to the Henderson Bay waterfront. Rooms are clean and comfortable and a few parts of the house were being renovated when we visited. There's a pleasant backyard patio along with the usual kitchen/TV facilities, including internet access. Owners John and Cathleen (and their twins) are very friendly and a great source of information about hikes and tours in the area. Free boogie boards and sand boards are available for guests. A small shop sells essential food items. At certain times of the year, Henderson Bay is a top surf spot.

Otaipango Road, Henderson Bay
☎ *(09) 409 8515*
Website *www.northwind.co.nz*
Dorm bed *$25-$27 ($20-$25 BBH);* ***single room*** *$45-$55 ($40-$50 BBH);* ***double room*** *$64 ($54 BBH)*

Maintenance & cleanliness	★★★½
Facilities	★★
Atmosphere & character	★★★½
Security	★
Overall rating	★★★

Cape Reinga

Cape Reinga is as far north is New Zealand as you can go (although it is not the northernmost point; North Cape is, but that is a scientific reserve closed to the public). It has a true end-of-the-road feel, as the land tapers away and yields to unbroken sea. Here, by its iconic lighthouse, you can actually see the Pacific Ocean and the Tasman Sea meet, their waters visibly churning together and merging in a tidal race.

You can instantly feel the power that Māori ascribe to this place. They traditionally believe it is the place where spirits of the dead leave this world for the underworld (Reinga means "underworld", and Māori call the Cape Te Rerenga Wairua, the "leaping-place of the spirits"). The final departure point is said to be from an 800 year-old pohutukawa tree that juts out from the cliffs beneath the lighthouse. A sense of decorum and respect is expected of visitors here.

The closest facilities to Cape Reinga are at Waitiki Landing, 21km of unsealed road away, a tiny outpost with a small market, some accommodation and a service station with an unreliable supply of fuel. Making the drive yourself can be a dramatic way to approach the Cape, but caution is advised on the winding gravel roads; it's easier to slide off the road or flip a car than you might think.

In addition to the rewarding sense of accomplishment of reaching Cape Reinga, there are some good hiking trails around that offer spectacular coastal views. This is one of New Zealand's special places.

Accommodation
Waitiki Landing

This is the last place to stay, eat and fill up the tank before heading the final, unpaved 21km north to Cape Reinga, and there is a real end-of-the-road feeling to Waitiki Landing. The basic dorms and common areas in the main structure are about as tired and droopy as they come. Rooms in the log cabin are significantly nicer, however, and there are camping facilities as well. A restaurant serves food until 8pm, a bar stays open later, and there's an off-licence and grocery store on the premises. Hot showers are $1 a pop. The Waitiki Landing can arrange different Cape Reigna/Ninety Mile Beach tours, hikes, quad bike rentals, and more.

Word of caution: Waitiki Landing does not reliably have petrol; it's wiser to fill up back in Pukenui.

Far North Road, Waitiki Landing (21km south of Cape Reinga)
☎ *(09) 409 7508*
Dorm bed *$20;* ***cabin*** *$55-$85*
Credit cards *MC, Visa*

Maintenance & cleanliness	★½
Facilities	★
Atmosphere & character	★
Security	★
Overall rating	★½

Northland

Hokianga Region

This region on the Northland's west coast is seldom visited, but makes a good alternative route south if you've already gone up the east coast through the Bay of Islands. It's one of the less developed areas of the North Island and boasts some great scenery including Hokianga Harbour and the sand hills near Opononi.

Hokianga is also home to some of the oldest European settlements in New Zealand, including Horeke and the ferry town of Rawene. The area is a very relaxing alternative to the more touristy action of the Bay of Islands.

Kohukohu

This small town is at the northern terminus of the Hokianga Harbour vehicle ferry and home to a great little hostel a couple of kilometres past the ferry wharf. Kohukohu has a long history, and was once the heart of New Zealand's timber industry. Some historic buildings remain, but many were lost to fire over the years.

There's a good café, a general store, a couple of art galleries, and not a whole lot else to do in this sleepy town. A van serves surprisingly good Cuban coffee at the vehicle queue for the ferry.

Coming & Going

Because there's no bridge across the Hokianga Harbour you will have to take the Hokianga car ferry *(**website** www.fndc.govt.nz/Maritime/iHokiangaFerry.asp)*, which sails between Kohukohu and Rawene about once an hour between 7.45am and 8pm (the last sailing from Rawene is at 7.30pm). The crossing takes around 15 minutes and the one-way fare costs $14 per car, $2 for foot passenger and $3.50 for a motorcycle.

Accommodation

Tree House Backpackers Lodge

The Tree House Lodge is set in lush, flowery wilderness 2km from the car ferry. The wood house is owner-built, and the land surrounding it was cultivated – rescued, really – by the owners as well, as a restoration/conservation project that's been going on for 27 years. These guys were eco-conscious before it was cool, and they're very low-key about it. The lodge itself is a great, relaxing place to stay, with a lovely kitchen and a comfy reading nook filled with beanbag chairs and cushions. You can practically reach out the dorm window and grab limes off a tree. Walks in the area are magnificent, all the more so considering the unseen work that's gone in to making the area so vital and abundant. This is a very special place.

168 West Coast Road, Kohukohu
☎ *(09) 405 5855*
Website *www.treehouse.co.nz*
Dorm bed *$23-$30 ($20-$27 BBH);* ***single room*** *$50 ($45 BBH);* ***double/twin room*** *$66 ($56 BBH),* ***camping*** *$17 ($14 BBH) per person*
Credit cards *MC, Visa*
Reception open *8.30am-8.30pm daily*
[Car] [K] [L]

Maintenance & cleanliness	★★★★★
Facilities	★★
Atmosphere & character	★★★★★
Security	★
Overall rating	★★★★

Rawene

The Southern terminus of the Hokianga vehicle ferry is a pleasant spot to have a coffee while waiting for the ferry.

Coming & Going

The Hokianga car ferry *(**website** www.fndc.govt.nz/Maritime/iHokiangaFerry.asp)* sails between Rawene and Kohukohu about once an hour between 7.30am and 7.30pm. The crossing takes 15 minutes and the one-way fare costs $14 per car, $2 for foot passenger and $3.50 for a motorcycle.

Opononi & Omapere

Opononi and Omapere are neighbouring villages at the entrance of Hokianga Harbour. There are some good accommodation options and beautiful ocean and harbour views, otherwise activities and facilities are fairly limited.

The massive sand dunes at the North Heads are very cool natural phenomena that you can ride down on a sand board. Ferry rides to the dunes can be arranged in Opononi and the Hokianga Information Centre and Museum is in Ompaere.

Practical Information

Hokianga i-SITE Visitor Centre

State Highway 12, Omapere
☎ *(09) 405 8869*
Website *www.hokiangatourism.org.nz*

Accommodation

Globetrekkers Lodge

Globetrekkers is a very friendly, relaxed place overlooking the beautiful blue waters of Hokianga Harbour and the sand dunes on the opposite shore. Dorm rooms are simple but comfortable. The common room has a great atmosphere and is set up with a big telescope, chess set and good songs on the stereo, but no TV (the owners, Mike and Sue, have guests vote every year whether to get a TV, and the verdict is always against it). The kitchen is extremely sunny and airy, with big windows on two walls. An outdoor deck has a barbecue, and tables shaded by grape vines – as well as a simply gorgeous view. Guests have access to the swimming pool at the hotel next door.
281 State Highway 12, Omapere
☎ *(09) 405 8183*
Dorm bed *$23-$25 ($20-$22 BBH);* ***single room*** *$48 ($45 BBH);* ***double/twin room*** *$56 ($50 BBH);* ***family room*** *$75-$85*
Credit cards *MC, Visa*
Reception open *8.30am-7.30pm daily*

Maintenance & cleanliness	★★★★
Facilities	★★★½
Atmosphere & character	★★★★
Security	★★½
Overall rating	★★★★½

House of Harmony

Located across the road from beautiful Hokianga Harbour, House of Harmony is a cheery white house with blue trim. It has a really casual, beach-y air. The four rooms (two dorms, a double and a twin) are sturdy and clean and each has been given a name: "Tropical Fish", "Seagull", "Dolphin", and "Rainbow", with décor to match. The sun deck is a nice place to chill out over great views of the harbour. The jetty is right down the road, where you can catch a boat across the water for some sand dune sledding. A grocery store and bar/restaurant are down the road as well. Camping is available on the property.
State Highway 12, Opononi
☎ *(09) 405 8778*
Website *www.houseofharmony.co.nz*
Dorm bed *$23 ($20 BBH);* ***double room*** *$50 ($44 BBH)*
Credit cards *MC, Visa*

Maintenance & cleanliness	★★½
Facilities	★★
Atmosphere & character	★★★½
Security	★
Overall rating	★★½

Okopako Lodge

High up a gravelly mountain road, Okopako Lodge rewards the drive with spectacular panoramic views. Accommodation is nothing fancy, but there's a definite rustic charm throughout. Facilities include laundry, a kitchen and common room. There's no TV, but that's exactly the point of a place like this; the wraparound sundeck offers plenty to look at day or night. Okopako Lodge has 27 beds total, among share rooms, doubles, and three caravans; camping is also available. Farmhouse breakfasts and dinners are offered (but must be ordered in advance), and fresh produce from an organic garden is for sale.
140 Mountain Road, Opononi
☎ *(09) 405 8815*
Website *http://homepages.paradise.net.nz/okopako/index.html*
Dorm bed *$24 ($21 BBH);* ***single room*** *$40 ($36 BBH);* ***double/twin room*** *$58 ($52 BBH)*
Credit cards *MC, Visa*
Reception open *8am-8pm daily*

Maintenance & cleanliness	★★★
Facilities	★★
Atmosphere & character	★★★
Security	★
Overall rating	★★½

Kauri Coast

The west coast between the Hokianga and Kaipara Harbours was once densely forested with its majestic namesake kauri trees. It was the centre of New Zealand's booming 19th century timber and gum industry and was heavily logged for shipbuilding and for house building in Australia and the west coast of the United States. Kauri trees were instrumental in rebuilding San Francisco after the devastating 1906 earthquake.

Impressive kauri forests do still remain, however, including ancient Waipoua Forest, which is home to the awesome Tāne Mahuta, the largest tree in New Zealand. Today, the Kauri Coast is mainly a farming region, specialising in kumara (sweet potato), but the kauri forests, the 100km drivable Ripiro Beach, and overall unspoiled feel make it an interesting, off-the-beaten track place to visit. There's a Kauri Museum in the town of Matakohe.

Dargaville

Dargaville's not a place for adrenalin junkies, as one resident put it, but this rural service town does make a good base for exploring the surrounding region. It's the gateway to Waipoua Forest, home of Tāne Mahuta (the Lord of the Forest), the largest tree in New Zealand. It's also close to Baylys Beach, on the 100km-long drivable Ripiro Beach, and the dune lakes of Kai Iwi.

And of course, Dargaville has the distinction of being the kumara capital of New Zealand.

Practical Information

Kauri Coast Information Centre

Normanby Street, Dargaville
(09) 439 8360 or 0800 528 744
***Website** www.kauricoast.co.nz*
***Open** Mon-Fri 8.30am-5pm, Sat-Sun 10am-4pm*

Coming & Going

InterCity (*(09) 623 1503; **website** www.intercity.co.nz*) coaches stop at the AD Focus Carpark at the corner of Kapia and Totara Streets.

Accommodation

Dargaville Holiday Park

This large site close to the centre of town has areas for tents and campervans as well as accommodation in motel units and small cabins. Backpackers are generally put in the cabins, which are little more than wooden boxes with a big window and simple beds inside. They're clean, anyway. Motel units are significantly nicer. Facilities include a big outdoor barbecue area and a spa pool ($6 per ½ hour). The kitchen is not bad, but showers are coin-operated and the TV room is in an outdoor lean-to with crumbling furniture. With the mixed use of the park, it doesn't have a real "hostel" feel.

10 Onslow Street, Dargaville
(09) 439 8296
***Dorm bed** $25; **motel unit** $85*
***Credit cards** MC, Visa*
***Reception open** 8am-10pm daily*

Maintenance & cleanliness	★★
Facilities	★★½
Atmosphere & character	★★½
Security	★
Overall rating	★★½

Greenhouse Backpackers

Greenhouse Backpackers is in a former schoolhouse and walking in is very likely to trigger some memories (whether good or bad). It's a unique environment, at the very least. The TV lounge/common area is in one former classroom, with a colourfully-decorated chalkboard on the wall and primary-school bright colours all around. Dorms beds are in another big classroom. There are no bunks; single beds are arranged around the room, partitioned off into small groups. Internet access is available, and there's a small outdoor area out the back with a barbecue.

13 Portland Street, Dargaville
(09) 439 6342
***Dorm bed** $21 ($18 BBH); **double/twin room** $50 ($44 BBH)*

Maintenance & cleanliness	★★★½
Facilities	★★
Atmosphere & character	★★
Security	★
Overall rating	★★½

Kaihu

This rural locality lies 30km north of Dargaville and is a good accommodation alternative if you have a car.

Accommodation

Kaihu Farm

Kaihu Farm is a quiet, isolated place on 5.6ha of farm and bush. There's no TV or radio here (although internet is available), just cattle, sheep, pigs, chickens, and Buster the farm dog. Facilities are basic, but there are nice touches, like slab kauri tables and benches on the outdoor patio. Free bush walks and a glow worm walk right on the Kaihu Farm property are offered, and offsite guided treks are available. The gruff-but-friendly, bearded owner prepares hearty farm breakfasts and roast dinners on request.

State Highway 12, Kaihu
☎ *09 439 4004*
Website *www.kaihufarm.co.nz*
Dorm bed *$23-$25 ($20-$22 BBH);* ***single room*** *$48 ($45 BBH); double/* ***twin room*** *$56 ($50 BBH)*

Maintenance & cleanliness	★★★
Facilities	★★½
Atmosphere & character	★★★
Security	★½
Overall rating	★★★½

Waikato

This farming region south of Auckland features lots of green, rolling landscape and the powerful Waikato River. At 425km, the Waikato (Māori for "flowing water") is the longest river in New Zealand. It flows from Mount Ruapehu into the Tasman Sea, and in addition to hydrating the region's broad plains, the Waikato generates clean hydroelectric power.

The biggest attractions for travellers to Waikato are the world-class surf and laid-back culture in the beach town of Raglan and the limestone glow-worm caves farther south in Waitomo. You can do lots of adventure activities in Waitomo, from abseiling (rappelling) to cave tubing. Hamilton is the area's largest city, and is a university town with good nightlife.

Waikato is the region that Peter Jackson chose to create the town of Hobbiton for his *Lord of the Rings* trilogy (near the town of Matamata), and there is indeed that kind of bucolic charm to be found here.

Hamilton

Hamilton is New Zealand's largest inland city and its fourth largest urban area overall, with a population of around 131,000. It's traditionally been an agricultural centre, but Hamilton is also a university town, with more than 40,000 tertiary students enrolled at the University of Waikato, Waikato Institute of Technology and Te Wānanga o Aotearoa. Hamilton is young and fast-growing and has a surprisingly vibrant nightlife and restaurant scene.

Hamilton is known for its impressive botanic gardens. Hamilton also has a good zoo and the Waikato Museum, as well as several art galleries. The town hosts several events throughout the year, including a V8 supercar race and a hot-air balloon festival, both in April.

Also, *Rocky Horror Picture Show* fans take note: a bronze statue of the character Riff Raff *(**website** www.riffraffstatue.org)* can be found at the south end of Victoria Street, in commemoration of Hamilton resident Richard O'Brien, who dreamed up the cult hit.

The Waikato River flows through the town and makes for a pleasant riverfront setting.

Must do in Waikato

- Surf at Raglan
- Go on a 'wet' trip at the Waitomo Caves
- Dig yourself into a hole in the sand at Hot Water Beach on the Coromandel Peninsula
- Go tandem skydiving in Taupo

Practical Information

Hamilton i-SITE Visitor Centre

Transport Centre, Corner Anglesea & Bryce Streets, Hamilton
☎ *(07) 958 5960*
***Website** www.visithamilton.co.nz*
***Open** Mon-Thu 8.30am-5pm, Fri 8.30am-6pm, Sat-Sun 10am-4pm*

INTERNET ACCESS

There are two branches of **Esquires** *(**website** www.esquires.co.nz; 9 Ward Street, Hamilton & 501 Victoria Street, Hamilton)* with free Wi-Fi access.

Coming & Going

Hamilton is a major transport hub and many people who visit the city come here to make connections.

AIR

Hamilton International Airport *(☎ (07) 848 9027; website www.hamiltonairport.co.nz)*, 12km south of Hamilton, is becoming a popular alternative to Auckland Airport particularly with cut-price flights from Australia. Chesters Airport Shuttles *(☎ (07) 843 4538; **website** www.chestershuttles.co.nz)* and Supershuttle *(☎ 0800 748 885 (0800 SHUTTLE)*; website www.supershuttle.co.nz) run between the airport and central Hamilton.

Minibus Express *(☎ (07) 8563191 or 0800 64 64 28 (0800 MINIBUS); **website** www.minibus.co.nz)* runs shuttle buses to Auckland Airport.

BUS

InterCity *(☎ (09) 623 1503; **website** www.intercity.co.nz)* Coachlines and Naked Bus *(☎ 0900 62533; **website** www.nakedbus.com)* have services from Hamilton to most destinations in the North Island and Metrowide *(☎ 0800 2163876 (0800 21METRO); **website** www.metrowide.co.nz)* have buses to Tauranga and Waitomo. Environment Waikato *(**website** www.ew.govt.nz/regionalservices/passengertransport/)* runs regional bus services to towns in the Waikato region including Raglan, Taupo and the Coromandel Peninsula.

Buses stop at the Hamilton Travel Centre at the corner of Anglesea and Bryce Streets.

TRAIN

Tranz Scenic's *(☎ 0800 872 467 (0800 TRAINS); **website** www.tranzscenic.co.nz) Overlander* service between Auckland and Wellington stops in Hamilton.

Local Transport

Hamilton has a good local bus network operated by Environment Waikato *(**website** www.ew.govt.nz/regionalservices/passengertransport/)* that is comprised of 24 city routes including the CBD shuttle, a free bus route that runs a loop through the city centre every 10 minutes. A single cash fare costs $2.60 for other bus routes in Hamilton city,

Accommodation

Eagle's Nest Backpackers

Located above a sports store on Hamilton's main street, Eagle's Nest is a simple, clean hostel close to everything in town. Rooms are on either side of a single corridor and feature skylights. There's a kitchen and a TV area with lots of couches. A small balcony overlooks the action on the street below. Internet access is available. Check out the world map marked up by many of the guests who have stayed at Eagle's Nest.

937 Victoria Street, Hamilton
🚌 CBD shuttle, 1, 2, 4, 5, 6, 9, 10, 11, 12, 13, 16, 17, 18, 50
☎ (07) 838 2704
***Dorm bed** $25; **double/twin room** $60*

Waikato

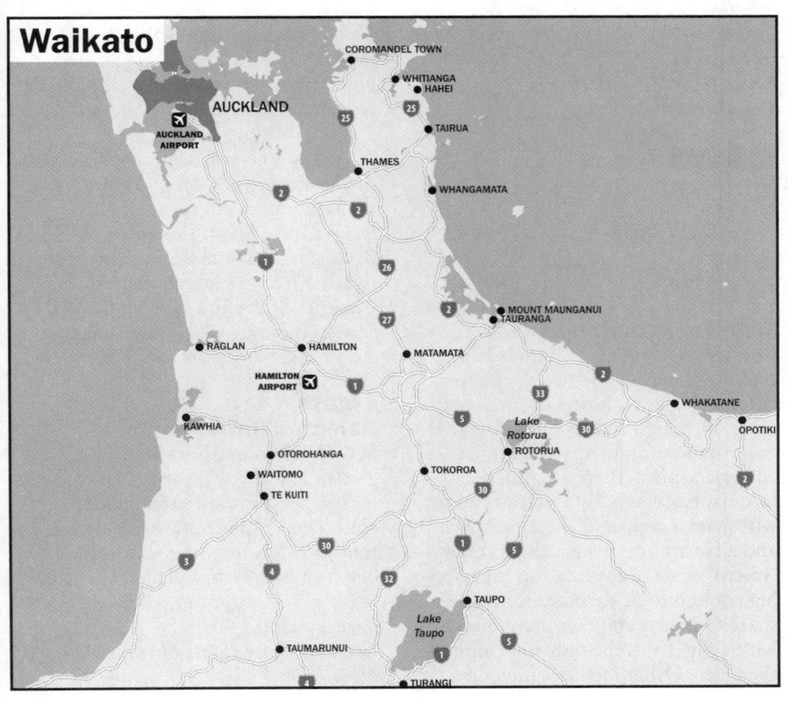

***Credit cards** MC, Visa*
***Reception open** 8am-10pm daily*
TV K L

Maintenance & cleanliness	★★★
Facilities	★★
Atmosphere & character	★★
Security	★★
Overall rating	★★½

J's Backpackers

Out in East Hamilton, close to the university and Hamilton Gardens, J's Backpackers is set in a modest house with a big backyard area. Rooms are basic and clean. There isn't a ton of indoor space, with a couple of small common areas, but the back patio features a nice outdoor fireplace and there's a front yard as well. The staff are friendly and there's a good backpacker vibe here. Some shops and pubs are close by on Grey Street and the centre of Hamilton is about a half-hour walk. There is a free pick-up and drop off service to the bus station.

8 Grey Street, Hamilton
2, 10, 17
(07) 856 8934
***Website** www.jsbackpackers.co.nz*
***Dorm bed** $25 ($22 BBH); **double/twin room** $60 ($54 BBH); **triple room** $75 ($66 BBH)*
***Credit cards** MC, Visa*
***Reception open** 8am-8pm daily*
TV K L

Maintenance & cleanliness	★★★
Facilities	★½
Atmosphere & character	★★½
Security	★★
Overall rating	★★½

MicroTel Hamilton

Located in a stretch of motels and motor lodges outside the city centre, MicroTel is not a hostel in the strict sense, although it does offered shared accommodation in apartment-style configurations. There are different layouts, but generally a pair of rooms will share a common entrance space and a bathroom. Everything is on a "micro" scale indeed; rooms are barely big enough to fit their beds. There's a shared kitchen and common lounge with a big TV – the only big thing in the place. Other facilities include a sauna and spa pool. There's not a real hostel feel at all, but Hamilton has limited facilities and backpackers will sometimes end up here.

40 Ulster Street, Hamilton
(07) 957 1848
***Website** www.microtel.co.nz*
***Dorm bed** $25; **single room** $35; **double room** $59; **twin room** $40*
***Credit cards** MC, Visa*
***Reception open** 7.30am-8.30pm daily*
TV K L

Maintenance & cleanliness	★★½
Facilities	★★½
Atmosphere & character	½
Security	★
Overall rating	★★

Eating & Drinking

Hamilton has a good variety of restaurants, from fast food and pub fare to Indian, Japanese, Chinese and Thai. Victoria Street is the main street for food and nightlife, with the overwhelming range of places located on or right off of this busy stretch. Centre Place shopping centre on Victoria Street has a food court. Bars and clubs tend to cluster around Victoria and Hood Streets. It can get lively here thanks to Hamilton's large student population. There is also a smattering of bars and cafés on Grey Street in East Hamilton.

There are several centrally located supermarkets including a Countdown at the corner of Anglesea and Liverpool Streets and a Foodtown at the corner of Bryce and Tristram Streets. There are two Pak'n Save supermarkets; one on Clarence Street and another on Mill Street. There are also several specialty Asian and gourmet markets in the city.

Sights

Hamilton Gardens

Hamilton's impressive 58ha botanic garden features a "Story of Gardens" theme, with five different garden collections exploring garden design traditions, history, the relationships between people and plants, and more. It is a pleasant spot to relax, walk or have a picnic.

Cobham Drive (State Highway One), Hamilton

☎ *(07) 856 3200*
Website *www.hamiltongardens.co.nz*
Admission *free*
Open *7.30am-½hr before sunset daily*

Hamilton Zoo

Situated on 21ha of parkland, Hamilton Zoo is impressive for a small town zoo and is home to a variety of wildlife from Africa, Asia and Latin America. The zoo also boasts a huge walk-through aviary, which is home to many rare and endangered New Zealand birds.
Brymer Road, Hamilton
☎ *(07) 838 6720*
Website *www.hamiltonzoo.co.nz*
Admission *$12*
Open *9am-5pm daily (last entry 3.30pm)*

Waikato Museum of Art & History

Hamilton's main museum has a large collection of exhibits with a focus on local history and Maori culture.
1 Grantham Street, Hamilton
☎ *(07) 838 6606*
Website *www.waikatomuseum.org.nz*
Admission *free; charge for temporary exhibits*
Open *10am-4.30pm daily*

Raglan

Raglan, aka Ragtown, is an awesome, laid-back beach town with some of the best surf in New Zealand. It has a seductive power for many – chances are the people working at your hostel were originally just passing through, but have ended up staying for months to ride the waves and bask in Raglan's unique ambience.

Raglan is home to black sand beaches and world-famous left-hand surf breaks. The breaks are found at three main points: Whale Bay, the Indicators, and Manu Bay. Manu Bay, 8km from Raglan, is probably the most famous; it hosts international surfing competitions and was featured in the 1966 cult classic surf film the *Endless Summer*. The left-hand break here is one of the longest in the world.

Raglan is about a 45-minute drive west from Hamilton and features several nice cafés and shops on its main street, as well as a few surfing schools. Be warned, you may get bitten by the Raglan bug and not want to leave.

Practical Information

Raglan Visitor Information Centre

4 Wallis Street, Raglan
☎ *(07) 825 0556*
Website *www.raglan.org.nz*
Open *Mon-Fri 9am-3pm, Sat-Sun 10am-4pm*

Coming & Going

Raglan is far enough off the main highway to be left off the schedules of the main coach operators such as InterCity and Naked Bus, and Stray is the only backpacker bus that comes here. However, Environment Waikato *(**website** www.ew.govt.nz/regionalservices/passengertransport/)* run regular bus services from Hamilton that cost $5.50 from Hamilton's Transport Centre. This bus has several stops in Raglan including the library and visitor information centre.

Accommodation

Karioi Backpackers Lodge

The very fun Karioi Lodge sprawls over the grounds of an old youth camp, the remnants of which are used to entertain backpackers today. For instance, there's a flying fox, a low ropes course and a "sports barn" with table tennis and air hockey (as well as lots of space to party). The Raglan Surfing School operates from here as well, and they have package deals with lessons and accommodation. There's a really good vibe here; it seems that the ethos is to surf by day and party by night. Other facilities include a pool table, internet access and a sauna. Be sure to check out "Inspiration Point", a platform with incredible views over Whale Bay.
5B Whaanga Road, Whale Bay, Raglan
☎ *(07) 825 7873*
Website *www.karioilodge.co.nz*
Dorm bed *$27 ($24 BBH);* ***single room*** *$69 ($60 BBH);* ***double/twin room*** *$69 ($60 BBH)*
Credit cards *MC, Visa*
Reception open *Jan-Mar 8am-8pm daily; Apr-Nov 9am-5pm daily; Dec 8am-8pm daily*

Maintenance & cleanliness	★★½
Facilities	★★★½
Atmosphere & character	★★★★★
Security	★
Overall rating	★★★

Raglan Backpackers & Waterfront Lodge

Raglan Backpackers is a friendly place right in the middle of town. Clean rooms (some with electric blankets) are arranged around a small courtyard with plenty of hammocks. Like everywhere in Raglan, surfing is the central activity and boards, wetsuits and lessons are all available. There are many free extras too, like the use of bikes, kayaks, fishing gear, golf clubs and an infrared sauna. A lounge with log fire is a nice place to relax and it offers lovely sea views. A kitchen, small TV room, and internet access on a couple of PCs round out the offerings. The vibe here is very relaxed and laid back.

9 Nero Street, Raglan
23
(07) 825 0515
***Website** www.raglanbackpackers.co.nz*
***Dorm bed** $22-$23 ($19-$20 BBH); **double/twin room** $52-$59 ($46-$53 BBH)*
***Reception open** 9am-9pm daily*

Maintenance & cleanliness	★★★½
Facilities	★★★½
Atmosphere & character	★★★★
Security	★★
Overall rating	★★★½

Solscape

Solscape is easily one of the most interesting and unusual hostels we've seen, with a serious eco-focus. Dorm accommodation and shared facilities are housed in old train carriages and cabooses on a hill overlooking famous Manu Bay. There is also a tepee site that is entirely "off the grid" – lights are solar-powered, there are compost toilets, earth ovens, etc. Even the tepees themselves were built with low environmental impact materials. Renovations were underway on other areas of the site to make it as low-impact and self-sustaining as possible when we visited. It is a true example of green-consciousness being put into action. Plus, the views are spectacular, surfing lessons are available and it's a great location to just chill out.

611 Wainui Road, Raglan
(07) 825 8268
***Website** www.solscape.co.nz*
***Dorm bed** $20-$24; **double/twin room** $58; tepee $34 per person*
***Credit cards** MC, Visa*

Maintenance & cleanliness	★★★
Facilities	★★
Atmosphere & character	★★★★½
Security	★½
Overall rating	★★★

Eating & Drinking

Bow Street is where you'll find practically all of Raglan's small selection of restaurants and bars. For such a small town there's a nice variety. There are some cool cafés – particularly **Tongue & Groove** *(19 Bow Street, Raglan)* and **Aqua Velvet** *(17 Bow Street, Raglan)* – as well as an Asian restaurant, a pizzeria and a fish & chip shop. **Vinnie's** *(7 Wainui Road, Raglan)* is an Italian pizza restaurant/café run by a real New Yorker. There's also an off-licence on Wainui Road. **Four Square** *(16-18 Bow Street, Raglan)* is the only supermarket in town.

Surfing

Most travellers come to Raglan for its world-class surfing. Experienced surfers head to Manu Bay, but beginner surfers are advised to start at Ocean Beach. Please note that access is now restricted to Whale Bay as Māori regard this as a sensitive spiritual area.

Raglan Surfing School *((07) 825 7873; **website** www.raglansurfingschool.co.nz)* is popular with many backpackers. It is run by Karioi Backpacker Lodge and they also rent surfboards and wetsuits.

Waitomo District

The main attraction in this region are the Waitomo Caves, although some travellers also visit Otorohanga and Te Kuiti.

Te Kuiti

If you've ever wanted to try the Running of the Bulls in Pamplona but were afraid of getting trampled or gored, Te Kuiti may be the place for you. Every year on the weekend after Easter, this small town, a 15-minute drive south of Waitomo, hosts the New Zealand Shearing Championships, which includes the very silly "Running of the Sheep". Over 2,000 of the soft, woolly critters are let loose on Te Kuiti's main street – a much safer alternative to Pamplona.

Other than being the sheep shearing capital of New Zealand, there's not a lot going on in Te Kuiti, but it makes a decent base for exploring the Waitomo Caves.

Practical Information

Te Kuiti i-SITE Visitor Centre

Rora Street, Te Kuiti
☎ *(07) 878 8077*
***Website** www.destinationwaitomo.co.nz*

Coming & Going

InterCity Coachlines *(☎ (09) 623 1503; **website** www.intercity.co.nz)* stop outside Tiffany's Tearooms *(241 Rora Street, Te Kuiti)*.

Accommodation

Casara Mesa

Casara Mesa is a small hostel up on a hill 3km from Te Kuiti's town centre. It's on a farm and offers fairly basic accommodation with excellent views of the town and the valley below. There's a small, fully-equipped kitchen and a TV lounge with old furniture but a surprisingly extensive collection of VHS videos – some obscure stuff here. It's a very quiet and relaxing place, and the wraparound veranda makes an especially nice place to chill out. Free pick-up and drop-off to town is available and transport to Waitomo caves is offered for a small charge.
Mangarino Road, Te Kuiti
☎ *(07) 878 6697*
***Dorm bed** $25 ($20 BBH); **single room** $35 ($30 BBH); **double room** $55-$60 ($45-$50 BBH); **twin room** $55 ($45 BBH)*

Maintenance & cleanliness	★★★
Facilities	★★
Atmosphere & character	★★★½
Security	½
Overall rating	★★½

Otorohanga

Otorohanga is known as New Zealand's kiwi capital and some travellers use it as a base for visiting the Waitomo Caves. Otorohanga's main attraction is the kiwi house and adjoining native bird park, which is a must if you've got your heart set on seeing a real live kiwi.

Practical Information

Otorohanga i-SITE Visitor Centre

21 Maniapoto Street, Otorohanga
☎ *(07) 873 8951*
***Website** www.otorohanga.co.nz*
***Open** Mon-Fri 9am-5.30pm, Sat-Sun 10am-4pm*

Coming & Going

InterCity Coachlines *(☎ (09) 623 1503; **website** www.intercity.co.nz)* stop on Wahanui Crescent near the visitor information centre.

Sights

Otorohanga Kiwi House & Native Bird Park

Oto's main attraction is the kiwi house where you have the opportunity to see New Zealand's national bird along with other native birds and native wildlife including tuataras and wetas.
Alex Telfer Drive, Otorohanga
☎ *(07) 873 7391*
***Website** www.kiwihouse.org.nz*
***Admission** $15*
***Open** Jan-May 9am-4.30pm daily; Jun-Aug 9am-4pm daily; Sep-Dec 9am-4.30pm*

Waitomo Caves

The Waitomo Caves are the most popular attraction in the Waikato region and a major stop on the tourist trail in New Zealand. The extensive cave system features limestone formations and the magical, bioluminescent glow-worms, which hang like little fairy lights from cave walls and ceilings.

Many tourists take a fairly sedate tour and boat trip through the caves, but there are loads of adventure activities centred around the caves as well. Caving, abseiling and black water rafting are all popular among backpackers; some of the adventure packages can get pretty extreme and can last several hours.

Waitomo is the village close to the caves. It has a couple of hostels, one bar and a few eating and shopping options.

Practical Information

Waitomo i-SITE Visitor Centre

21 Caves Road, Waitomo
☎ *(07) 878 7640*
Website *www.waitomo-museum.co.nz*
Open *8am-5pm daily*

Coming & Going

Waitomo has good bus connections. InterCity Coachlines *(☎ (09) 623 1503; **website** www.intercity.co.nz)* go to Auckland, Hamilton and New Plymouth. Naked Bus *(☎ 0900 62533; **website** www.nakedbus.com)* has direct services to Auckland, Rotorua, Taupo, Tauranga and Whangarei and Metro Wide *(☎ 0800 216 3876; **website** www.metrowide.co.nz)* have three daily services from Hamilton.

Buses depart from the information centre at 21 Waitomo Caves Road.

Accommodation

Juno Backpackers

Juno Hall is a lodge close to Waitomo Caves with a charming, rustic feel and a good range of facilities. It's a purpose-built log hostel decorated with lots of old farm equipment. An open, airy common room has shabby but comfortable furnishings and there's a big fully-equipped kitchen. The hostel is set on farmland and has plenty of outdoor activities available, like a swimming pool, trampoline and volleyball court. Tennis courts are up on a hill, and you can play while horses, which are available for treks, graze around you.

600 Waitomo Caves Road, Waitomo
☎ *(07) 878 7649*
Website *www.junowaitomo.co.nz*
Dorm bed *$25 ($22 BBH);* ***double room*** *$60-$70 ($50-$60 BBH);* ***camping*** *$15 ($13 BBH) per person*
Credit cards *MC, Visa*
Reception open *8am-8pm daily*

Maintenance & cleanliness	★★½
Facilities	★★★★
Atmosphere & character	★★★
Security	-
Overall rating	★★★

Kiwipaka YHA

The Kiwipaka YHA is a very sharp, purpose-built hostel in walking distance to the glow-worm caves and the Waitomo information centre. It's modern and nicely maintained. Rooms are clean and feature real mattresses and individual bedside lights. There's a small TV/game room downstairs with a pool table and a kitchen and dining area upstairs. A pizzeria and café, the Morepork Café, is on site and has indoor and outdoor seating. There's also a reading/internet room and Wi-Fi access is available. Backpacker buses stop here, so it's often filled up with ready-to-party groups of travellers. Luckily, Kiwipaka is also in walking distance to the only bar in Waitomo.

School Road, Waitomo
☎ *(07) 878 3395*
Website *www.kiwipaka-yha.co.nz*
Dorm bed *$27;* ***single room*** *$60;* ***double/twin room*** *$62*
Credit cards *MC, Visa*
Reception open *summer 8am-9pm daily; winter 8am-8pm daily*

Maintenance & cleanliness	★★★★
Facilities	★★½
Atmosphere & character	★★★½
Security	★★½
Overall rating	★★★½

Rap, Raft 'n' Rock (Waitomo Backpackers)

Rap, Raft 'n' Rock is a very small hostel right off the main road to Waitomo Caves. There are only three rooms – two four-share dorms, and a double room – sleeping a total of 10 people. Rooms are plain and the bedding is a bit tired. The owners run a rafting and caving business on-site, offering special combination packages of adrenalin-pumping activities. There's also a

high-ropes course on the property and a small climbing wall. Hostel facilities are very basic with a small, limited kitchen and TV room with outdated furnishings. Rap, Raft 'n' Rock is 8km from Waitomo Caves.
95 Waitomo Caves Road, Waitomo
☎ *(07) 873 9149*
Website *www.caveraft.com*
Dorm bed *$23 ($20 BBH);* ***double/ twin room*** *$51 ($45 BBH)*
Credit cards *MC, Visa*
Reception open *8am-7pm*

Maintenance & cleanliness	★★★½
Facilities	★★½
Atmosphere & character	★★½
Security	★★½
Overall rating	★★

Sights

Aranui Cave

Aranui Cave is a quieter alternative to the Glowworm Cave and is favoured by people who want to experience the cave's amazing subterranean rock formations.
Caves Road, Waitomo
☎ *(07) 878 8227 or 0800 456 922*
Website *www.waitomocaves.co.nz*
Admission *$35;* ***Aranui Cave & Glowworm Cave combined admission*** *$50*
Tours depart *10am, 11am, 1pm, 2pm, 3pm daily*

Waitomo Glowworm Cave

This is the main cave, which was first opened to tourists in 1889. It is the most touristy and least adventurous option and for many years was the only way to visit the caves. Admission is by a 45-minute tour that culminates in a boat ride through the glow-worm grotto.
Caves Road, Waitomo
☎ *(07) 878 8227 or 0800 456 922*
Website *www.waitomocaves.co.nz*
Admission *$35;* ***Aranui Cave & Glowworm Cave combined admission*** *$50*
Open *Jan-Easter Mon 9am-5.30pm daily; Easter Tue-Oct 9am-5pm; Nov-Dec 9am-5.30pm; tours depart every half hour*

Waitomo Museum

This small, but interesting, museum specialises in caves and karst landscape.
21 Caves Road, Waitomo
☎ *(07) 878 7640*
Website *www.waitomo-museum.co.nz*
Admission *$5*
Open *8am-5pm daily*

Activities

TOUR OPERATORS

There are four companies that operate various caving activities. All four companies offer underground rafting and adventure caving.

Cave World

This company offers cave rafting plus two different abseiling adventures.
Waitomo Caves Road, Waitomo
☎ *(07) 878 6577 or 0800 CAVEFUN (0800 228 386)*
Website *www.caveworld.co.nz*

The Legendary Black Water Rafting Co

This is the original cave rafting company that coined the phrase "black water rafting". The three cave activities they offer are the dry Spellbound trip and, for the more adventurous, the wet Black Abyss and Black Labyrinth adventures.
Waitomo Caves Road, Waitomo
☎ *(07) 878 6219 or 0800 228 464*
Website *www.blackwaterrafting.co.nz*

Waitomo Adventures

Waitomo Adventures offer a large range of caving activities including Haggas Honking Holes, Lost World and Tumu Tumu Toobing.
Waitomo Caves Road, Waitomo
☎ *(07) 878 7788 or 0800 924866*
Website *www.waitomo.co.nz*

Waitomo Wilderness Tours

This smaller operator runs Rap, Raft 'n' Rock, which combines abseiling, cave rafting and rock climbing in one tour.
95 Waitomo Caves Road, Waitomo Caves
☎ *(07) 873 9149*
Website *www.caveraft.com*

'DRY' TRIPS

'Dry' tours refer to activities where you don't get very wet. These activities can include abseiling and rafting in a regular raft (not an inner tube).

The Canyon
This daytime abseiling adventure is a challenging abseil into a 46m (150ft) deep canyon.
Cave World
☎ *(07) 878 6577 or 0800 CAVEFUN (0800 228 386)*
Website *www.caveworld.co.nz*
Price *$120*
Duration *2 hours*

Lost World Abseil
The Lost World Abseil involves a 100m abseil down a massive shaft followed by a journey through the Lost World Cave, reaching the surface via a 30m ladder.
Waitomo Adventures
☎ *(07) 878 7788 or 0800 924866*
Website *www.waitomo.co.nz*
Price *$245*
Duration *4 hours*

Night Abseil
This nighttime abseiling adventure is a challenging abseil into a 46m (150ft) deep canyon. The nighttime abseil gives you the opportunity to witness spectacular glow-worm displays.
Cave World
☎ *(07) 878 6577 or 0800 CAVEFUN (0800 228 386)*
Website *www.caveworld.co.nz*
Price *$160*
Duration *2 hours*

Spellbound
This trip involves rafting on a regular raft (not in an inner tube) through the breathtaking Mangawhitikau cave system. It is one of the cheapest ways to see the glow-worms, but it's not as much fun as the other trips.
Spellbound
☎ *(07) 878 7640 or 0800 773 55*
Website *www.waitomospellbound.co.nz*
Price *$55*
Duration *3-3½ hours (1 hour underground)*

St Benedict's Caverns
St Benedict's Caverns are described as 'the prettiest piece of known cave in New Zealand'. Waitomo Adventures' trip is a must for people who come to Waitomo to see spectacular caves. It involves two abseils and a bit of caving.
Waitomo Adventures
☎ *(07) 878 7788 or 0800 924866*
Website *www.waitomo.co.nz*
Price *$145*
Duration *3 hours (1½ hours in cave)*

'WET' TRIPS
Many 'wet' trips involve rafting in an inner tube, also known as Black Water Rafting, although some 'wet' trips involve swimming or abseiling down waterfalls. Some of the more tame 'wet' trips are just a leisurely float through the cave, but there are some that also involve other more adventurous activities such as abseiling or rock climbing.

Black Abyss
This is the most challenging of the Legendary Black Water Rafting Co's cave trips. It starts with an abseil into the Ruakuri Cave where you can go cave tubing among the glow-worms and finishes off with a swim followed by squeezing and climbing out of the cave.
The Legendary Black Water Rafting Co.
☎ *(07) 878 6219 or 0800 228 464*
Website *www.blackwaterrafting.co.nz*
Price *$185*
Duration *5 hours (2-3 hours underground)*

Black Labyrinth
Black Labyrinth is based on the original Black Water Rafting trip. After climbing into the Ruakuri Cave you float down the underground river in an inner tube. The trip includes a drop down a waterfall as you float past thousands of glow-worms.
The Legendary Black Water Rafting Co.
☎ *(07) 878 6219 or 0800 228 464*
Website *www.blackwaterrafting.co.nz*
Price *$95*
Duration *3 hours (1 hour underground)*

Black Magic
This trip is a leisurely float through Te Anaroa (the Long Cave) in an inner-tube. This cave boasts unbeatable glow-worm displays.
Cave World
☎ *(07) 878 6577 or 0800 CAVEFUN (0800 228 386)*
Website *www.caveworld.co.nz*

Price *$99*
Duration *2½-3 hours*

Haggas Honking Holes

Unlike other wet trips, Haggas Honking Holes doesn't involve cave rafting, but it is definitely an adventure. This fast paced trip involves three abseils in waterfalls while exploring the caves.
Waitomo Adventures
☎ *(07) 878 7788 or 0800 924866*
Website *www.waitomo.co.nz*
Price *$195*
Duration *4 hours (2 hours underground)*

Lost World Epic

This seven-hour adventure starts with a 100m abseil into the Lost World Cave, which is followed by walking, swimming and climbing through vast caverns where you can see fossils, waterfalls and lots of glow-worms.
Waitomo Adventures
☎ *(07) 878 7788 or 0800 924866*
Website *www.waitomo.co.nz*
Price *$395*
Duration *7 hours*

Rap, Raft 'n' Rock

This cave adventure combines a 27m abseil into the cave entrance with cave rafting and a 20m rock climb back. It is one of the best value cave trips.
Waitomo Wilderness Tours
☎ *(07) 873 9149*
Website *www.caveraft.com*
Price *$125*
Duration *4½ hours*

Tumu Tumu Toobing

This trip combines cave rafting in inner tubes with swimming and climbing through the dry sections of the Tumutumu Cave. It is the most active of the easy wet trips.
Waitomo Adventures
☎ *(07) 878 7788 or 0800 924866*
Website *www.waitomo.co.nz*
Price *$125*
Duration *4hrs*

NON-CAVE ACTIVITIES

Most people come to Waitomo for cave-based activities, but there are also plenty of options for people who would rather stay above ground. These include horse riding, jet boating and 4WD biking.

Big Red 4WD Bikes

Big Red runs 4WD quad bikes trips through farmland near the Waitomo Caves. The Legendary Black Water Rafting Co bundles this with their cave trips for an under/over experience.

Big Red can be booked through Waitomo Museum *(☎ (07) 878 7690;* ***website*** *www.waitomo-museum.co.nz)* or the Legendary Black Water Rafting Co. *(☎ (07) 878 6219 or 0800 228 464;* ***website*** *www.blackwaterrafting.co.nz)*
Price *$105*
Duration *2 hours*

Horse Riding

These horse-riding trips go through Waikato farmland. Most people take the one or two hour rides.
Waitomo Caves Horse Treks.
☎ *(07) 878 5065.*
Price *$50 30 minutes, $80 1½ hours*

Thames Valley

This area is south of Thames and northeast of Hamilton. It's primarily a dairy farming region. Its main attractions are Te Aroha, a charming town with hot mineral spas; Paeroa, home to New Zealand's famous L&P (Lemon & Paeroa) soft drink, originally made with the town's therapeutic spring water; and Matamata, a rural town that has re-branded itself as Hobbiton, thanks to its scenic role in Peter Jackson's *LOTR* trilogy.

Matamata

Matamata is a small town serving the surrounding farming region. There's not much here to interest most travellers, but many people come here to see the original Hobbiton village set from the *Lord of the Rings* film trilogy.

Practical Information

Matamata i-SITE Visitor Centre
45 Broadway, Matamata
☎ *(07) 888 7260*
Website *www.matamatanz.co.nz*

Coming & Going

InterCity Coachlines *(☎ (09) 623 1503; **website** www.intercity.co.nz)* has direct services to Auckland, Hamilton and Tauranga and Naked Bus *(☎ 0900 62533; **website** www.nakedbus.com)* has direct buses from Matamata to Auckland, Hamilton, Tauranga and Waitomo.

Buses stop outside the visitor information centre (45 Broadway, Matamata).

Sights

Hobbiton Movie Set

The Hobbiton village from the *Lord of the Rings* film trilogy was filmed on farmland near Matamata. After shooting the film the set was returned to its natural state, but the hobbit holes are still there. Rings Scenic Tours operate pricey tours to the set where you can see the hobbit holes and discover trivia about the movie.

Tours depart from The Shire's Rest *(501 Buckland Road, Matamata)* and also from the visitor information centre *(45 Broadway, Matamata).*

☎ (07) 888 6838

***Website** www.hobbitontours.com*

***Price** $58*

Te Aroha

Te Aroha is 53km northeast of Hamilton and 50km south of Thames, set at the base of lovely Te Aroha mountain. The Waihou River runs through Te Aroha, eventually emptying into the Firth of Thames.

Te Aroha took off as an Edwardian spa town in the 19th century, its natural hot mineral springs widely sought after for bathing and drinking. "Taking the waters" at one of Te Aroha's hot pools is still a relaxing and therapeutic activity, especially after doing one of the many walking or biking trails in the surrounding hills

The Mokena Geyser, in the historic Te Aroha Hot Springs Domain, is the world's only hot soda geyser. Te Aroha is also home to the oldest pipe organ in the southern hemisphere, dating back to 1769. It can be found at St Mark's Anglican Church.

Practical Information

Te Aroha i-SITE Visitor Information Centre

102 Whitaker Street, Te Aroha

☎ (07) 884 8052

***Website** www.tearohanz.co.nz*

Coming & Going

InterCity Coachlines *(☎ (09) 623 1503; **website** www.intercity.co.nz)* stop next to Econo Honda on Kenrick Street.

Accommodation

Te Aroha Holiday Park

This holiday park has tent and campervan sites, caravans, cabins and private cottages. It doesn't have a proper hostel feel, but it does have some good facilities and seems to be well looked after. One block holds a very basic kitchen, bathrooms and laundry facilities. Another has a TV/common room and some gym equipment. There's also an outdoor swimming pool, a spa pool and a very nice natural hot mineral pool. There is free Wi-Fi access on the grounds, which have nice views of Mount Te Aroha.

217 Stanley Road, Te Aroha

☎ (07) 884 9567

***Website** www.tearoha-info.co.nz/HolidayPark*

***Dorm bed** $15; **single room** $25-$30; **double/twin room** $35-$40*

***Credit cards** MC, Visa*

TV K L

Maintenance & cleanliness	★★½
Facilities	★★★
Atmosphere & character	★★
Security	★
Overall rating	★★½

YHA Te Aroha

The YHA Te Aroha is a very charming small house on a hill near the town centre. There are only two dorm rooms and a double/family room, along with a small kitchen and cosy common room that has books, games and a guitar. A very nice outdoor yard has hammocks and good views over the town and surrounding area. The kitchen is well stocked with herbs and spices. There's also lots of good local information provided here. Mountain

bike and walking trails are easily accessible.
Miro Street, Te Aroha
☎ *(07) 884 8739*
Website *www.yha.co.nz*
Dorm bed *$21 ($18 HI/YHA);*
double/twin room *$50 ($44 HI/YHA)*
Reception open *5pm-8pm daily*

Maintenance & cleanliness	★★★
Facilities	★★
Atmosphere & character	★★★½
Security	-
Overall rating	★★½

Coromandel Peninsula

The Coromandel Peninsula is a popular weekend getaway for many Aucklanders. This peninsula at the eastern end of the Hauraki Gulf is home to dense forest that is perfect for hiking; horse riding and mountain biking while the coastal areas have beautiful secluded beaches including the unique Hot Water Beach.

Thames

Thames is the gateway to the Coromandel Peninsula and is the most accessible and best-equipped town in the area, if not the most charming. Many historical buildings still remain from the gold rush days of the 1860s and -70s on the Grahamstown end of town. Thanks to gold and the kauri logging industry, at one point little Thames was one of the biggest cities in New Zealand.

These days, Thames has the peninsula's busiest main street – Pollen Street – which is well-stocked with pubs, bars, restaurants and shops. There's also the large Goldfields shopping centre, the one only of its type on the peninsula. If you're heading up the peninsula, Thames is the best place to refuel the car, stock up on supplies and use the ATM; facilities aren't as good further north.

Thames isn't only a gateway town, however. It does have some attractions of its own, primarily the biking, hiking and canyoning in nearby Kauaeranga Valley. The Goldmine Experience takes visitors on a tour of an old mine and through an operational 19th century Stamper Battery. There's also the Historical Museum and the School of Mine Museum in town, and a cool Butterfly and Orchid Garden – the only of its type in New Zealand – located on the grounds of Dickson Holiday Park.

Practical Information

Thames i-SITE Visitor Centre
209 Pollen Street, Thames
☎ *(07) 868 7284*
Website *www.thamesinfo.co.nz*
Open *Mon-Fri 8.30am-5pm, Sat-Sun 9am-4pm*

Coming & Going

InterCity Coachlines *(☎ (09) 623 1503; **website** www.intercity.co.nz)* and Naked Bus *(☎ 0900 62533; **website** www.nakedbus.com)* stop at the visitor information centre (206 Pollen Street, Thames).

Coromandel Peninsula

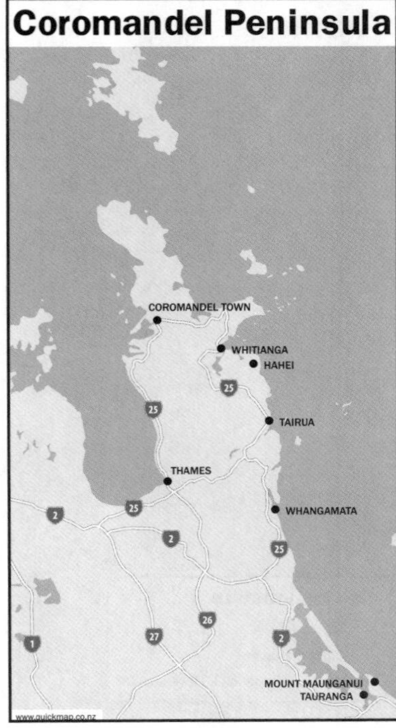

Waikato

Go Kiwi Shuttles *(☎ 0800 446 549;* ***website*** *www.go-kiwi.co.nz)* operate minibuses to Auckland and Auckland Airport. The fare to Auckland is $21-36 and the trip to the airport costs $38-50.

Sunkist Backpackers run the Sunkist Pinnacles Shuttle *(☎ (07) 868 8808)* between Thames and the Kauaeranga Valley. This is ideal if you want to hike around the Pinnacles in the Coromandel Forest Park. The return shuttle costs $30.

Accommodation

Dickson Holiday Park

Dickson Holiday Park is a large camp with accommodation ranging from tent and camper van sites to cabins and motel units. It's set along a stream and has a number of bush walks you can take through the surrounding forest. There's a games room with table tennis and table soccer, a swimming pool and free bikes to use. A butterfly and orchid garden is also on-site, and you can pick up small snacks and goods at a shop in the reception office. Backpackers generally stay in the small cabins and caravans; there's one large dorm bunk but we're told it's hardly ever used. In all, there's lots of space and some good facilities, although it lacks a real hostel atmosphere and has lots of families and groups coming through.

Victoria Street, Taruru, Thames
☎ (07) 868 7308
Website *www.dicksonpark.co.nz*
Dorm bed *$20;* ***double/twin room*** *$50-$65*
Credit cards *MC, Visa*
Reception open *8.30am-10am & 4pm-6pm daily*

Maintenance & cleanliness	★★½
Facilities	★★½
Atmosphere & character	★½
Security	★
Overall rating	★★½

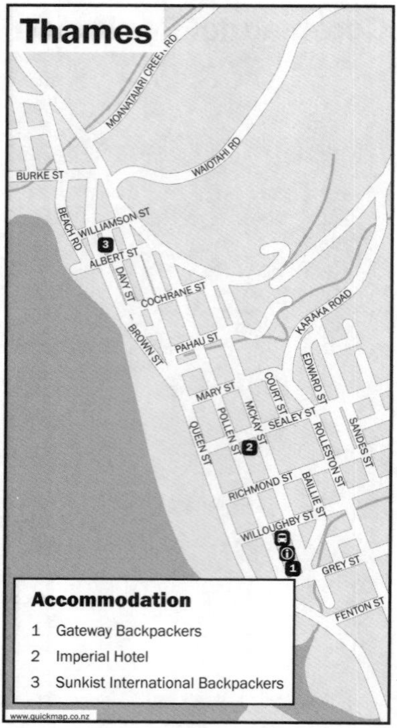

Gateway Backpackers

Gateway Backpackers is made up of a pair of houses directly behind the Thames information centre. It's not much to look at – rooms are basic and bedding seemed old. Kitchen facilities were adequate, but the TV room looked frozen in time from the 1970s. There's a little courtyard around a feijoa tree with a barbecue with picnic tables and a badminton net in the yard. Internet access is available on a coin-operated terminal. Guests have free use of bikes and free laundry, both nice touches, and you can't beat the location if you're getting off the bus and don't want to walk anywhere.

209 Mackay Street, Thames
☎ (07) 868 6339
Website *www.gatewaybackpackers.co.nz*
Dorm bed *$23 ($20 BBH);* ***single room*** *$40;* ***double room*** *$56-$66 ($50-$60 BBH);* ***twin room*** *$56 ($50 BBH)*

Maintenance & cleanliness	★★
Facilities	★★
Atmosphere & character	★½
Security	★½
Overall rating	★★

Imperial Hotel

The Imperial Hotel is above a bar in the centre of town; it's not a real hostel,

Thames

Accommodation
1 Gateway Backpackers
2 Imperial Hotel
3 Sunkist International Backpackers

www.quickmap.co.nz

but it does have some share rooms. The place is dark with long hallways and has kind of a spooky, old hotel feel. Most of the furnishings and facilities are dated and tired. There is a small smokers' courtyard with a barbecue and an outdoor jukebox (a genius idea if you ask us), and there are several internet PCs (Wi-Fi is also available). The downstairs Udder Bar attracts a local crowd and has lots of events like quiz nights and live bands.
476 Pollen Street, Thames
☎ *(07) 868 6200*
***Dorm bed** $20-$25; **single room** $30; **double room** $50*
TV K L

Maintenance & cleanliness	★★
Facilities	★★
Atmosphere & character	★★½
Security	★★½
Overall rating	★★

Sunkist International Backpackers

Sunkist International is one of the oldest houses in Thames, a kauri hotel that dates back to the gold rush days. It's been nicely renovated and maintained and easily has the most charm of any of Thames' hostels. There's a very cosy TV lounge with a piano, a solid kitchen, lots of nice old fixtures, and nice wooden-slab sinks in the bathrooms. Rooms are clean and comfortable. The best feature is a great courtyard with a deck, hammocks, a barbecue and lots of lovely trees and plants. Owners are very good about arranging tours and travel in the region, and rent 4WD vehicles as well.
506 Brown Street, Thames
☎ *(07) 868 8808*
***Website** www.sunkistbackpackers.com*
***Dorm bed** $21-$27 ($18-$24 BBH, HI/YHA); **double/twin room** $60 ($54 BBH, HI/YHA)*
***Credit cards** MC, Visa*
***Reception open** 7.30am-9pm daily*
TV K L

Maintenance & cleanliness	★★★★
Facilities	★★
Atmosphere & character	★★★★
Security	★★
Overall rating	★★★½

Eating & Drinking

Almost all of Thames' drinking and dining options are on the main commercial strip of Pollen Street. There are a few pubs and taverns, some takeaways, a fish and chip shop and several cafés. **Char-coal Cafe & Bar** *(206 Pollen Street, Thames)* right next to the information centre is a decent place to hang out while waiting for your bus. If you happen to be in Thames on a Saturday morning, there's a market on the Grahamstown end of Pollen Street with local produce, as well as arts and crafts and other souvenirs.

The Goldfields Shopping Centre is on Mary Street, a couple of blocks over from Pollen Street. It's the biggest of its kind on the Coromandel and has a McDonalds, a Pak'n Save supermarket and a Warehouse as well as a food court. It is a good place to stock up on food and supplies if you're heading up the peninsula.

Sights

Butterfly & Orchid Garden

This butterfly enclosure at Dickson Holiday Park is the only butterfly house in New Zealand. It is home to around 400 butterflies as well as birds and up to 200 orchids.
Dickson Holiday Park, Victoria Street, Tararu, Thames
☎ *(07) 868 8080*
***Website** www.butterfly.co.nz*
***Admission** $9 ($8 students)*
***Open** summer 10am-4pm daily; winter 10am-3pm daily*

Goldmine Experience

This re-created gold mine sits on the original site of the 1868 Golden Crown claim and features working mining equipment dating from the 1870s. A visit includes a tour of three original tunnels.
Tararu Road, Thames
☎ *(07) 868 8514*
***Website** www.goldmine-experience.co.nz*
***Admission** $10*
***Open** 10am-4pm daily*

Thames Historical Museum

The Thames Historical Museum is a small museum that has displays about

the town's colourful history including exhibits about the gold rush, the timber industry and the life of early settlers.
Corner Cochrane & Pollen Streets, Grahamstown, Thames
☎ *(07) 868 8509*
***Admission** $4*
***Open** 1pm-4pm daily*

Coromandel Town

An hour north of Thames on State Highway 25, little Coromandel Town has a laid-back atmosphere and a good deal of charm and local flavour. It was a major centre during the height of the gold rush, but those days are long gone. Today, Coromandel Town has a notably artsy character, some good cafés, excellent local fish and shellfish and the dramatic coastal scenery of the northern peninsula.

There isn't a great deal to do in Coromandel Town. The most popular activity is probably the Driving Creek Railway, a narrow-gauge railway that passes through a wildlife sanctuary and pottery complex; and the Coromandel Gold Stamper Battery, an authentic old machine that miners used to crush rocks into sand. It's powered by New Zealand's largest working water wheel.

Shuttle buses from Coromandel Town can bring you farther north to the rugged, beautiful Coromandel Coastal Walkway, which links Fletcher Bay to Stony Bay. It's a 3-4 hour walk over remote farmland, coastline and bush, and it takes in views of the Hauraki Gulf, Great Barrier Island and the Pacific Ocean.

Practical Information

Coromandel i-SITE Visitor Centre

355 Kapanga Road, Coromandel
☎ *(07) 866 8598*
***Website** www.coromandeltown.co.nz*
***Open** Mon-Sat 9am-5pm, Sun 10am-2pm*

Coming & Going

InterCity Coachlines *(☎ (09) 623 1503; **website** www.intercity.co.nz)* stop at the visitor information centre *(355 Kapanga Road, Coromandel).*

Go Kiwi Shuttles *(☎ 0800 446 549; **website** www.go-kiwi.co.nz)* operate minibuses between Coromandel and Whitianga.

Accommodation

Anchor Lodge

Anchor Lodge is an excellent hostel with accommodation ranging from dorm rooms to high-end self-contained units. Everything is relatively new and kept in top shape. Facilities include a good kitchen, TV lounge, and internet access (including Wi-Fi). Backpackers can also rub shoulders with the rest of the guests, some of whom are towing massive boats, around the great swimming pool or in the tropical-themed "Ooga Booga Hut". There's also a spa pool and a nice outdoor deck with a barbecue. The Anchor Lodge is right across the road from Coromandel Harbour and out back is some nice native bush.
448 Wharf Road, Coromandel
☎ *(07) 866 7992*
***Website** www.anchorlodgecoromandel.co.nz*
***Dorm bed** $22 ($18 BBH); **double room** $55-$60 ($50-$55 BBH)*
***Credit cards** MC, Visa*
***Reception open** 8am-9pm daily*

Maintenance & cleanliness	★★★★½
Facilities	★★★
Atmosphere & character	★★★½
Security	★½
Overall rating	★★★½

Coromandel Town Backpackers

Coromandel Town Backpackers is small hostel with only six rooms, but not much character or atmosphere. One structure houses the rooms, and there's a separate, high-ceilinged shed with common areas. A very small TV lounge is located near the reception and a big open kitchen and sitting area are in the main space. It's all very clean, but there really is no ambience, and its location right on a main road gives it a sort of motel-like feeling. Guests have free use of bicycles.
732 Rings Road, Coromandel
☎ *(07) 866 8327*
Dorm bed** $20 ($18 BBH); **double/

twin room *$46 ($40 BBH)*
Reception open *7am-11pm daily*

Maintenance & cleanliness	★★★★
Facilities	★★½
Atmosphere & character	★★½
Security	★★½
Overall rating	★★★½

Lion's Den

Lion's Den is a very cool, funky, cluttered-in-a-good-way hostel with a whimsical safari motif. All the bedspreads have lion prints on them and there's safari art and prints and knickknacks spread around the house. Inside, a nice kitchen is well laid out and there's a big solid dining table. Dorm rooms are pleasant and comfortable with lots of character. A common room has a TV and heaps of magazines lying around. There's plenty of cool outdoor space too; with lots of plants, flowers, fruit trees, fairy lights and Tibetan prayer flags strung up. It's definitely a hostel with an uncommon amount of personality.

126 Te Tiki Street, Coromandel
☎ *(07) 866 8157*
Dorm bed *$24 ($22 BBH);* ***double room*** *$55 ($50 BBH)*

Maintenance & cleanliness	★★★½
Facilities	★★½
Atmosphere & character	★★★★★
Security	★
Overall rating	★★★

Tidewater Tourist Park (YHA)

Tidewater Tourist Park is a small hostel attached to a motel about 400 metres from the town centre. Backpacker accommodation is limited to a pair of single-gender six-bed dorms; there's camping and a couple of double and twin rooms, but most of the facility is comprised of self-contained motel and studio units. Backpacker facilities are very basic – clean, but without too much charm. There's a TV lounge with old furniture, a kitchen and a sauna available for a $5 fee. Bikes and kayaks can also be rented.

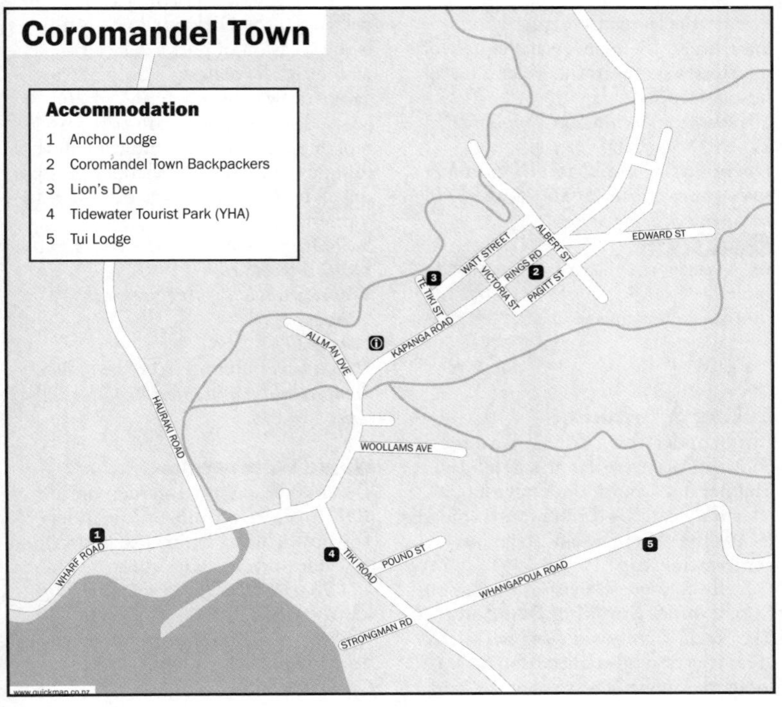

270 Tiki Road, Coromandel
☎ *(07) 866 8888*
Website *www.tidewater.co.nz*
Dorm bed *$28 ($21 HI/YHA);* ***single room*** *$35;* ***double room*** *$58 ($52 HI/YHA);* ***twin room*** *$60*
Credit cards *MC, Visa*

Maintenance & cleanliness	★★½
Facilities	★★
Atmosphere & character	★★
Security	★
Overall rating	★★

Tui Lodge

Set among big grounds with extensive gardens, Tui Lodge is a very nice hostel a little under 1km from the town centre. There are a couple of separate buildings, two kitchens, a big gazebo out in the front yard and different fruit trees including apple, feijoa, grapefruit and orange. Guests have free use of nice mountain bikes, and there's also a trampoline and small sauna on site. A wide range of accommodation is available, ranging from tent sites to self-contained motel units; the backpacker dorms are clean and feature good mattresses. There are even a couple of mattresses set up in the gazebo for al fresco sleeping.

60 Whangapoua Road, Coromandel
☎ *(07) 866 8237*
Dorm bed *$25 ($22 BBH);* ***double/twin room*** *$55-$75 ($50-$70 BBH);* ***camping*** *$12 per person*

Maintenance & cleanliness	★★★½
Facilities	★★½
Atmosphere & character	★★★½
Security	★
Overall rating	★★★

Eating & Drinking

Coromandel Town doesn't have the choice of places to eat and drink that Thames does, but it does have a few charming cafés and restaurants, mostly located on Wharf Road, the main commercial strip.

Definitely worth a visit is the famous **Coromandel Smoking Company** *(70 Tiki Road, Coromandel)*, which sells a great selection of smoked fish and seafood; the smoked mussels are the stuff of local legend. They're a little bit more than the ordinary backpacker budget might allow, but if you can splurge, go for it – you won't regret it.

There's a **Four Square** supermarket *(18 Kapanga Road, Coromandel)*, near Wharf Road.

Sights

Coromandel Gold Stamper Battery

If you missed the one in Thames, Coromandel's Gold Stamper Battery is a good spot to learn about the region's gold mining heritage. The museum features working 100-year mining machinery including New Zealand's biggest working water wheel.

410 Buffalo Road, Coromandel
☎ *025 2464 898*
Website *www.webtrails.co.nz/coromandel/coromandeltown/stamperbattery/*
Admission *$5*
Open *summer 10am-5pm daily; winter Sat-Sun 10am-5pm*

Driving Creek Railway

Located just 3km north of Coromandel Town, the Driving Creek Railway is the creation of potter Barry Brickell, who built the country's only narrow gauge railway over a period of 26 years. The one-hour train trip passes replanted kauri forest and it includes a unique double-decker viaduct plus two spirals and a great view from the ridge-top terminus.

380 Driving Creek Road, Coromandel
☎ *(07) 866 8703*
Website *www.drivingcreekrailway.co.nz*
Fare *$20*
Departures *summer 10.15am, noon, 2pm, 4pm daily; winter 10.15am, 2pm daily*

Waiau Waterworks

The unique sculpture garden on the 309 Road, 9km from Coromandel Town, features a whimsical collection of water-powered sculptures.

471 The 309 Road, Coromandel
☎ *(07) 866 7191*
Website *www.waiauwaterworks.co.nz*
Admission *$12*
Open *10am-5pm daily*

Whitianga

Whitianga is the main town on Mercury Bay, on the east coast of the Coromandel Peninsula. This former timber port is a popular holiday town for Kiwis, and gets quite busy during the summer months. The development along its harbour front is becoming conspicuous. Whitianga has a nice selection of restaurants and bars, and good local seafood.

There are a number of good beaches around town. Whitianga's main one, Buffalo Beach (named for the 1840 wreck of the *HMS Buffalo*) has excellent swimming and fishing, and is home to frolicking dolphins. All sorts of recreational activities are available in the area: kayaking, diving, windsurfing, horse trekking. Whitianga's deep harbour makes it a popular big game fishing spot; charters and fishing trips are available.

Cathedral Cove and Hot Water Beach are the main attractions around Whitianga. Hahei is closer, but there are several boat trips to Cathedral Cove that depart from Whitianga.

Practical Information

Whitianga i-SITE Visitor Centre

66 Albert Street, Whitianga
☎ *(07) 866 5555*
Open *Mon-Fri 9am-5pm, Sat-Sun 9am-4pm*

Coming & Going

InterCity Coachlines *(☎ (09) 623 1503; **website** www.intercity.co.nz)* and Naked Bus *(☎ 0900 62533; **website** www.nakedbus.com)* stop outside the information centre *(66 Albert Street, Whitianga)* in the town centre. Naked Bus also have a stop outside Buffalo Beach Backpackers *(46 Buffalo Beach Road, Whitianga)*. InterCity and Naked Bus go to Auckland and Go Kiwi Shuttles *(☎ 0800 446 549; **website** www.go-kiwi.co.nz)* have services to Auckland and Tauranga/Mount Maunganui.

Accommodation

IN TOWN

Baywatch Backpackers

Baywatch Backpackers is part of a motel that has some units converted to dorms. Rooms have en suite bathrooms, and there's a small common room/kitchen/dining area. The location is good, right across the road from Mercury Bay, but there's not much in the way of facilities or atmosphere here. A small barbecue area occupies a little patch of grass, but otherwise there's a concrete car-park ambience to the place. The Anchorage Motel on the same property has doubles and self-contained units with kitchenettes and TVs. Internet access and Wi-Fi are available.

22 The Esplanade, Whitianga
☎ *(07) 866 5481*
Website *www.whitianga.co.nz/baywatch/*
Dorm bed *$25;* ***double room*** *$65-$75*
Credit cards *Amex, JCB, MC, Visa*
Reception open *Mon-Sat 8am-8pm, Sun 9am-8pm*

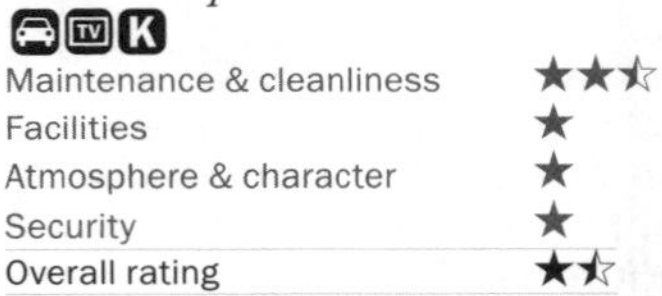

Maintenance & cleanliness	★★½
Facilities	★
Atmosphere & character	★
Security	★
Overall rating	★½

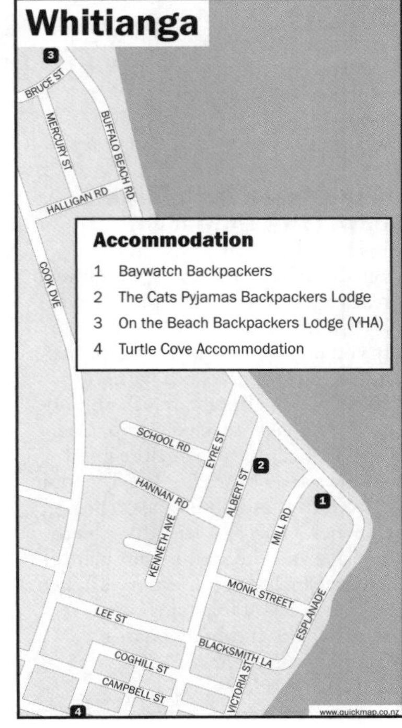

The Cats Pyjamas Backpackers Lodge

The Cats Pyjamas is on the site of a former hostel called Buffalo Peaks. There used to be another Cats Pyjamas in Whitianga, the original, but it closed. The owners of Buffalo Peaks then bought the name. Confused? That's the point – the old Cats Pyjamas had a better reputation and good guidebook write-ups. Anyway, tricky naming aside, the present hostel is not too bad. Dorms are kind of crowded, but there's a big, comfy common room and a brick courtyard area with a barbecue and spa pool. They're clearly trying to give it a bit of a social atmosphere, with $5 barbecue meals and a wall for backpackers to decorate. There's internet and Wi-Fi access and guests have free use of body boards.

12 Albert Street, Whitianga
☎ *(07) 866 2933*
Website *www.cats-pyjamas.co.nz*
Dorm bed *$23 ($21 BBH);* ***double room*** *$55-$65 ($52-$62 BBH)*
Credit cards *MC, Visa*
Reception open *7.15am-8pm daily*

Maintenance & cleanliness	★★½
Facilities	★★½
Atmosphere & character	★★½
Security	★½
Overall rating	★★½

On the Beach Backpackers Lodge (YHA Whitianga)

This hostel is right across the road from Buffalo Beach and sports some great views from the big picture windows in its upstairs dorms – the staff say you can sometimes see dolphins and orcas from here, but we couldn't verify this. In either case, it's an unusually nice view to wake up to, even if the 12-bed dorms with the good windows are a bit tight. The TV room is also fairly small but boasts the same view. There's a friendly vibe to the place and the staff is very helpful. Facilities include an ordinary kitchen, internet access, table tennis and free use of kayaks and body boards.

46 Buffalo Beach Road, Whitianga
☎ *(07) 866 5380*
Website *www.coromandelbackpackers.com*
Dorm bed *$24-26 ($21-23 BBH, HI/YHA);* ***single room*** *$49-55 ($46-52 BBH, HI/YHA);* ***double room*** *$66-96 ($60-90 BBH, HI/YHA);* ***twin room*** *$66 ($60 BBH, HI/YHA)*
Credit cards *MC, Visa*
Reception open *7am-8pm daily*

Maintenance & cleanliness	★★★
Facilities	★★½
Atmosphere & character	★★★★
Security	★½
Overall rating	★★★

Turtle Cove Accommodation

Turtle Cove is a very nice and fairly new hostel on a residential street a couple of minutes' walk to the town centre. It's clean and features hotel mattresses in the spacious dorms. Downstairs, there's a big kitchen and a nice TV lounge; out back is a covered patio with tables, a barbecue, and darts, as well as a small bar that promises the cheapest drinks in town. There's a spa pool as well. Turtle Cove gets the Kiwi Experience coming through every night, so it's generally got a built-in crowd of ready-to-party backpackers – a plus or a minus, depending on what you're looking for.

14 Bryce Street, Whitianga
☎ *(07) 867 1517*
Website *www.turtlecove.co.nz*
Dorm bed *$25;* ***double room*** *$65-$68*
Credit cards *MC, Visa*
Reception open *7.15am-7.30pm daily*

Maintenance & cleanliness	★★★★
Facilities	★★★
Atmosphere & character	★★★
Security	★
Overall rating	★★★½

OUT OF TOWN

Black Jack Lodge

This small, charming hostel is a recently-built house on the site of an old bakery dating from the gold rush days. There are vegetable gardens and fruit trees on the property, and a small river runs past; guests can take kayaks right onto it and paddle out to sea. A small bridge connects the hostel to the few shops in town, including a nice

café and art gallery. Accommodation is clean and very comfortable, with lots of nice touches. Facilities are fairly limited – there's no TV or internet – but this is the kind of place you go to switch off. A veranda out front has wonderful views over the beach.
201 State Highway 25, Kuaotunu (near Whitianga)
☎ *(07) 866 2988*
Website *www.black-jack.co.nz*
Dorm bed *$30 ($25 BBH);* ***double room*** *$75-$95 ($65-$85 BBH)*

Maintenance & cleanliness	★★★★½
Facilities	★★
Atmosphere & character	★★★★½
Security	★
Overall rating	★★★½

Eating & Drinking

Whitianga has a reasonable selection of cafés, restaurants and bars, although most cater to an older, more upscale crowd. You can find the majority of places to eat and drink on Albert Street. **Snapper Jacks** *(26 Albert Street, Whitianga)* is a bar/restaurant with fast food such as fish and chips; there's a small **Four Square** market *(Albert Street, Whitianga)* here as well. The nearby Esplanade has several larger bars and restaurants.

Several small cafés are spread around the Whitianga area; a few are in Hahei, and some are right across the wharf in Flaxmill Bay.

Sights & Activities

Boat trips to Cathedral Cove

Although Hahei is closer to the Cathedral Cove Marine Reserve, there are several boat trips that depart from Whitianga. **Cave Cruzer** *(☎ (07) 866 2574;* ***website*** *www.cavecruzer.co.nz)* operates cruises departing Whitianga Wharf; cruises cost $50-100.

High Zone

This high ropes course has a selection of activities such as trapeze and high wire exercises 12m above the ground.
49 Kaimarama Road, Whitianga
☎ *(07) 866 2113*
Website *www.highzone.co.nz*
Price *$15-60 depending on activity*

Mercury Bay Museum

This small museum has displays on local history, including exhibits on shipwrecks and Māori history.
11 The Esplanade, Whitianga
☎ *(07) 866 0730*
Website *www.mercurybaymuseum.co.nz*
Admission *$5*
Open *10am-4pm daily*

Hahei

Hahei is a tiny town with a smattering of cafés, a bar, an ice cream parlour and a general store. It has a fantastic swimming beach. On the southern end of the beach one end is the Te Pare Historic Reserve, which are the remnants of two ancient pā (Māori village) sites.

At the north end of the beach, there's a walking track to Cathedral Cove, about an hour away by foot. Cathedral Cove is a big attraction in this area, so named because its massive arch gives the cove a dramatic, solemn, church-like air. Its Māori name is Te Whanganui-A-Hei. The cove is also a marine reserve, the first on the Coromandel, and makes a good diving and snorkelling spot.

The main attraction for tourists, however, is Hot Water Beach, 10km south of Hahei.

Accommodation

Cathedral Cove Backpackers

Cathedral Cove is part of the Hahei Holiday Resort; the hostel has been in operation since 1960. The large grounds have tent and campervan sites as well as stand-alone villas and studios, and lead directly down to the beach. Guests can walk to 500m of beachfront without having to cross the road. Dorm accommodation varies – some rooms are in an older house and are clean but a little worn; newer annexes are in better shape. There's a big TV in a common room with old furniture. The Stray Bus stops here frequently, so there are often large groups of backpackers travelling together staying here.
41 Harsant Avenue, Hahei
☎ *(07) 866 3889*
Website *www.cathedralcove.co.nz*
Dorm bed *$22-$25;* ***double room***

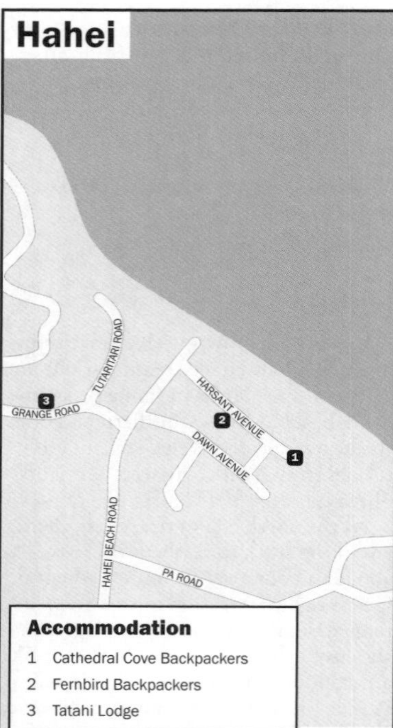

$54-59
Credit cards *Amex, JCB, MC, Visa*

Maintenance & cleanliness	★★★½
Facilities	★★½
Atmosphere & character	★★★½
Security	★
Overall rating	★★

Fernbird Backpackers
Fernbird Backpackers is a tiny hostel down the road from Hahei Beach. There are only two rooms: one twin/share room and a double room. The host family lives on the premises as well, so there's something of a home stay feeling. Facilities include a shared kitchen and TV lounge. There are big lush gardens in front, with plants and flowers helpfully identified; the backyard has a big silk tree growing in it and there is a very cute patio with a barbecue. Guests have free use of bicycles and body boards.
24 Harsant Avenue, Hahei
☎ *(07) 866 3080*
Website *www.cathedralcove.com/fernbird*
Dorm bed *$23 ($20 BBH);* ***double/twin room*** *$46 ($40 BBH)*

Maintenance & cleanliness	★★★½
Facilities	★★
Atmosphere & character	★★
Security	★
Overall rating	★★

Tatahi Lodge
Tatahi Lodge is a lovely all-pine house designed in an airy Lockwood-style. The property runs the gamut of accommodation from dorm beds to luxury motel units. Six-bed dorm rooms are fairly small but feel open with high, sloping ceilings and large windows. They come with sturdy pine bunks. There's a cosy common room and a nice kitchen as well. Tatahi Lodge is set on nice grounds and is very close to a little cluster of cafés, an ice-cream parlour, a bar and a general store. Internet and Wi-Fi access are available, and there's a barbecue on the back deck.
Grange Road, Hahei
☎ *(07) 866 3992*
Website *www.dreamland.co.nz/tatahilodge/*
Dorm bed *$22 (BBH $20);* ***double/twin room*** *$65-$75 ($55-$65 BB)*
Credit cards *Amex, MC, Visa*
Reception open *8.30am-6.30pm daily*

Maintenance & cleanliness	★★★★½
Facilities	★★½
Atmosphere & character	★★★★
Security	★
Overall rating	★★★

Hot Water Beach
This unique beach, 10km south of Hahei, allows you to dig your own hot spring-fed thermal pool in the sand two hours on either side of low tide. The water temperature can get up to around 65°C. In the summer, the beach gets quite crowded with people digging away, an amusing sight in itself. Shovels can easily be hired at the beach.

Conditions aren't always favourable and the hot water doesn't appear around 30% of the time, particularly in winter.

Tairua

This small seaside town on the east coast of the peninsula has a nice harbour and good surfing. Its most striking feature is the extinct volcanic cone of Mount Paku at the head of Tairua Harbour, the top of which gives great views of Tairua and the surrounding areas. It's a short walk to the top, and according to Māori legend, if you climb Mount Paku, you will return to Tairua within seven years.

Tairua has a pretty decent selection of restaurants, cafés, and shops and there's a supermarket as well. It's a popular holiday resort for Kiwis, but there are things for the international traveller to do. Some use the town as a base for visiting Hot Water Beach, which is a 20-minute drive away. Diving is nearby at the Alderman Islands, and there's good fishing around Tairua; both activities can be booked in town. Tairua is also a good spot to learn how to windsurf. Some nice hiking trails are also available in nearby Broken Hills Recreation Area.

Practical Information

Tairua Information Centre

Main Road, Tairua
☎ *(07) 864 7575*
***Open** 8.30am-3.30pm daily*

Coming & Going

InterCity Coachlines (☎ *(09) 623 1503; **website** www.intercity.co.nz)* and Naked Bus (☎ *0900 62533; **website** www.nakedbus.com)* buses go to Auckland and Go Kiwi Shuttles (☎ *0800 446 549; **website** www.go-kiwi.co.nz)* have a services to Auckland and Tauranga/Mount Maunganui. Eastbound coaches stop at the Tairua Information Centre and westbound coaches stop at the Landing Bar & Café.

Accommodation

Beach Villa Backpackers

Beach Villa Backpackers is a hostel with lots of charm and some magnificent views over the beach out to Mount Paku. One dorm in particular has a jaw-dropping, postcard scene perfectly framed by a massive picture window. There's a great deck out back for chilling and enjoying the sights, and lots of flowers and fruit trees growing on the property. The interior has a homely, lived-in feeling, with lots of art and knick-knacks around. The beach is just steps away and guests have free use of bikes, body boards, windsurfers and kayaks. The owner runs a windsurfing school from here as well (and mentions that girls learn much more quickly than guys). Māori legend has it that if you scale Mount Paku, you will return within seven years. After staying at this excellent hostel, you might want to come back sooner.

200 Main Road, Tairua
☎ *(07) 864 8345*
***Dorm bed** $26 ($23 BBH); **single room** $45 ($40 BBH); **double/twin room** $55-$59 ($50-$55 BBH)*
***Credit cards** MC, Visa*

Maintenance & cleanliness	★★★½
Facilities	★★½
Atmosphere & character	★★★★★
Security	★½
Overall rating	★★★½

The Pinnacles Backpackers

If one pinnacle is just not enough for you, you know where to come. This nice hostel is easy to spot, with a big painted Obelix sign out front. Inside, it has two lounges and two kitchens, and offers basic accommodation in a very homely environment. The upstairs lounge sports a pool table (with a chalkboard on the wall for keeping score) and a nice big TV. It also leads to an outdoor deck with a barbecue. There are lots of books and DVDs lying around and internet access is available.

305 Main Road, Tairua
☎ *(07) 864 8448*
***Website** www.pinnaclesbakpak.co.nz*
***Dorm bed** $23 ($20 BBH); **double room** $54-$60 ($50-$56 BBH); **twin room** $54 ($50 BBH)*
***Credit cards** MC, Visa*

Maintenance & cleanliness	★★★½
Facilities	★★
Atmosphere & character	★★½
Security	★
Overall rating	★★½

Tairua Beach House

Tairua Beach House is a basic wooden lodge with plain white walls and simple dorm accommodation. There's a plain kitchen and a common room with a pool table, table tennis, a TV and mismatched furniture. Otherwise, there is nothing much in the way of décor or atmosphere here and something feels empty and institutional about the place. Outside, there are fairly extensive grounds with a spa pool and – something we haven't seen elsewhere – a small cement skateboard park (it's apparently a holdover from a church/community group that used to own the place). Guests also get free use of kayaks.

342A Main Road, Tairua
(07) 864 8313
***Website** http://tairuabeachhouse.50g.com/*
***Dorm bed** $19-$22; **double room** $60-$80*
***Credit cards** Amex, Diners, JCB, MC, Visa*

Maintenance & cleanliness	★★½
Facilities	★★½
Atmosphere & character	★½
Security	★½
Overall rating	★★½

Hiking

There are several good hiking trails, including the Collins Creek Drive and Gem of Boom Creek walks, in the Broken Hills Recreation Area. You will need a car to get to these tracks.

Collins Creek Drive (3hrs) is a unique walk that passes through a 500-metre tunnel complete with glow-worms. It's dark in the tunnel so you will need to bring along a torch.

The Gem of Boom Creek Loop Walk (30mins) is a shorter walk that goes through the bush to an old mining settlement.

Opoutere

Located between Tairua and Whangamata, this quiet town has an estuary and a 5km white sand surf beach that is protected from development by a forested reserve.

The Opoutere Wildlife Refuge Reserve is a popular spot with bird-watchers. It's a nesting site for the rare New Zealand dotterel, a small wading bird. There are also bushwalks and fishing in the area, but mainly Opoutere is a nice place to come and relax.

Coming & Going

InterCity Coachlines *((09) 623 1503; **website** www.intercity.co.nz)* have buses to Auckland and Go Kiwi Shuttles *(0800 446 549; **website** www.go-kiwi.co.nz)* go to Auckland and Tauranga/Mount Maunganui. Buses stop outside Opoutere YHA *(389 Opoutere Road, Opoutere).*

Accommodation

Opoutere YHA

The Opoutere YHA is a nice little hostel hidden away next to an estuary among native bush and gardens. There are four- and five-share rooms in a house that has a cosy common room with log fire and books. There's also a big kitchen and dining room. A big 12-bed dorm is in a separate structure, an old school house. Other accommodation includes tent sites and a few double rooms in private cabins. The grounds are quite nice, with a little gazebo and a barbecue, as well as table tennis in a small shed. Guests have free use of kayaks.

389 Opoutere Road, Opoutere
(07) 865 9072
***Website** www.yha.co.nz*
***Dorm bed** $23-$26 ($20-$23 YHA); **double/twin room** $76-$86 ($70-$80 YHA); **camping** $15 per person*
***Credit cards** MC, Visa*
***Open** Dec-Apr; **reception open** 8.30am-10am & 5pm-8pm daily*

Maintenance & cleanliness	★★★
Facilities	★★½
Atmosphere & character	★★★
Security	★½
Overall rating	★★★

Whangamata

Whangamata is a gold-rush town of 3,555 people on the southeast coast of the Coromandel Peninsula, and is known as one of New Zealand's best surf spots. The town and its 4km of white sand beach are overrun by surfers during the summer holidays (Dec-Jan), but is quiet otherwise throughout the year.

Whangamata borders the Coromandel Forest Park and Tairua Forest and there are bush walks, mountain biking trails and old gold mining sites to visit. There are some islands easily accessible from Whangamata as well. Hauturu (or Clark) Island can be waded out to during low tide, or reached by kayak. And about 1km away is Whenuakura, or Donut Island, so called because of a large collapsed blow hole that has formed a beach inside the island.

Practical Information

Whangamata i-SITE Visitor Centre

616 Port Road, Whangamata
☎ *(07) 865 8340*
Website *www.whangamatainfo.co.nz*
Open *9am-5pm daily*

Coming & Going

InterCity Coachlines *(☎ (09) 623 1503;* ***website*** *www.intercity.co.nz)* goes to Auckland and Whitianga and Go Kiwi Shuttles *(☎ 0800 446 549;* ***website*** *www.go-kiwi.co.nz)* have services to Auckland and Tauranga/Mount Maunganui. Buses stop outside the library *(620 Port Road, Whangamata)*.

Accommodation

Southpacific Accommodation (Garden Tourist Lodge)

Southpacific Accommodation is an excellent, purpose-built tourist lodge connected to an adjoining motel. The hostel is a cool, big, curved-roof structure in a distinctive green colour. The common room is wide open, like an aeroplane hangar and there's a nice fully-equipped kitchen and dining area sharing the airy space. Upstairs dorm rooms are clean and in very good shape and their ceilings share the curve of the roof, giving them a bit of character. Out front is a large barbecue area and there's also a covered spa pool. Body boards are free to use, and the owner gives surf lessons and hires boards.

245 Port Road, Whangamata
☎ *(07) 865 9580*
Website *www.thesouthpacific.co.nz*
Dorm bed *$28 ($24 BBH);* ***single room*** *$49 ($39 BBH);* ***double/twin room*** *$63 ($57 BBH)*
Credit cards *MC, Visa*

[Car] [TV] [K] [L]

Maintenance & cleanliness	★★★★½
Facilities	★★½
Atmosphere & character	★★★
Security	★½
Overall rating	★★★½

Whangamata Backpackers Hostel

The Whangamata Backpackers Hostel is a dreary little place with an air of neglect that is located down a residential street. All the furnishings are second-hand and kind of mushy. Rooms are worn and tired, and the TV lounge is dark and depressing; it looks like hasn't been updated since the 1950s. There's a small kitchen as well; a little upstairs deck gives a slight respite from the gloom, but not much.

227 Beverley Terrace, Whangamata
☎ *(07) 865 8323*
Dorm bed *$20-$23 ($17-$20 BBH);* ***single room*** *$25 ($22 BBH);* ***double room*** *$50 ($44 BBH);* ***twin room*** *$56 ($50 BBH)*

[Car] [TV] [K] [L] [Key]

Maintenance & cleanliness	★
Facilities	★
Atmosphere & character	½
Security	★
Overall rating	★

Lake Taupo

The area around Lake Taupo has some of the world's best trout fishing and many backpackers stay a few days here to take advantage of excellent value adventure activities such as bungee jumping and sky diving.

Orakei Korako

Located around mid-way between Taupo and Rotorua, Orakei Korako (also known as the Hidden Valley) is one of the world's largest geothermal

Waikato

areas, famed for both its geysers and its silica terraces including the jade-green Emerald Terrace.

Although two-thirds of the active thermal area – some 200 hot springs and 70 geysers – were flooded when a lake was formed for a hydro power plant in 1961, Orakei Korako remains the largest geyser field in New Zealand with 35 active geysers.

The most famous geyser is the Diamond Geyser, an unpredictable geyser whose eruptions of up to 9m sometimes last for several hours and other times only for a few minutes.

Orakei Korako is also home to the Ruatapu Cave – one of only two caves in the world to exist in a geothermal field.

Coming & Going

The park is around a half-hour drive north of Taupo and is inaccessible unless you have a car.

Sights

Orakei Korako Cave & Thermal Park

Access to the park is by a ferry trip across Lake Ohakuri. This impressive thermal park features a dazzling array of thermal features that include hot springs, geysers and silica terraces and there is also a rare geothermal cave with a warm mineral pool.

494 Orakei Korako Road, Reporoa (25min north of Taupo)
☎ *(07) 378 3131*
Website *www.orakeikorako.co.nz*
Admission *$28*
Open *summer 8am-4.30pm daily; winter 8am-4pm daily*

Taupo

This town of more than 22,000 sits on the northeastern corner of Lake Taupo, New Zealand's largest lake. The attractions of the lake itself and the huge range of adventure activities on offer make this one of the most popular backpacker stops in all of New Zealand.

Lake Taupo was formed by a volcanic eruption in 186 AD, which blew a 660m^2 hole in the earth, and there's still plenty of volcanic and geothermal activity going on in the area. The active geothermal field called Karapiti, or Craters of the Moon, is a lunar landscape of steam vents, craters, and mud pools close to Taupo on State Highway 1. Orakei Korako, about 25 minutes from Taupo on the way to Rotorua and across the Waikato River, is considered one of the best geothermal areas in New Zealand.

Trout fishing is a major attraction on Lake Taupo, and there's a wide range of fly-fishing guides and trips available, many of which can be booked from hostels. You'll need to buy a fishing license from the visitor centre or one of the angling or sports shops in town. You have a choice of spinning or fly-fishing on Lake Taupo, but only fly-fishing is allowed on the nearby rivers. Many restaurants will cook up your catch for you if you contact them in advance.

Nearby is the ever-popular Huka Falls, which is one of New Zealand's most powerful (and definitely the most-visited) waterfalls. Although most buses and motorists stop off here to and from Taupo, the most rewarding way to visit is by hiking the Huka Falls Track that begins at the Spa Thermal Centre on Spa Road in Taupo.

But it's the adrenalin-pumping adventure activities that draw backpackers in droves to Taupo. Bungee jumping, skydiving, kayaking, jetboating and Rock 'n' Ropes courses are all on offer. Taupo is considered to be the cheapest place to skydive in New Zealand, and attracts many backpackers for that fact alone. As such, there's a very good backpacker infrastructure set up, with a wide range of restaurants, nightlife, transport and accommodation options.

Practical Information

Taupo i-SITE Visitor Centre

Tongariro Street, Taupo
☎ *(07) 376 0027*
Website *www.laketauponz.com & www.backpacklaketaupo.com*
Open *8.30am-5pm daily*

INTERNET ACCESS

Cybershed

117 Tongariro Street, Taupo
☎ *(07) 377 4168*
Open 9am-8pm daily

Internet Outpost
11 Tuwharetoa Street, Taupo
☎ *(07) 376 9920*
Website *www.internet-outpost.com*
Open *9am-11pm daily*

Log On
71 Tongariro Street, Taupo
☎ *(07) 376 5901*
Open *9am-9pm daily*

Coming & Going
Taupo has good coach connections to destinations throughout the North Island. InterCity Coachlines *(☎ (09) 623 1503; **website** www.intercity.co.nz)* stop at 16 Gascoigne Street and Naked Bus *(☎ 0900 62533; **website** www.nakedbus.com)* stops outside the i-Site visitor information centre on Tongariro Street.

Alpine Hotbus *(☎ 0508 468 287; **website** www.alpinehotbus.co.nz)* operates a daily shuttle bus for hikers tackling the Tongariro Crossing. It departs Taupo at 6.15am with an additional 5.30am service during summer (Nov-Apr). The return fare is $45.

Hitchhiking in and out of Taupo is easy with State Highways 1 and 5 passing through town.

Local Transport
Environment Waikato *(☎ (07) 378 2172; **website** www.ew.govt.nz/regionalservices/passengertransport/taupo.htm)* run an urban bus service in Taupo. There is only one route and it only runs a few times a day. A single trip costs $1.50.

Accommodation
Action Down Under YHA
There's a very congenial vibe at this large YHA hostel. Action Down Under is comprised of two buildings; one is set around a small courtyard with a ping-pong table and features a huge kitchen and nice outdoor deck. The other is a smaller house with a volleyball net and spa pool in the yard, as well as space for tents. There are a few small lounge areas. Rooms are relatively clean and some feature en suite bathrooms and hair dryers. Internet and Wi-Fi are available as well. Action Down Under is not the newest place in town but there's a good social atmosphere and the staff are very attentive.
56 Kaimanawa Street, Taupo
☎ *(07) 378 3311*
Website *www.yha.co.nz*
Dorm bed *$26-$28 ($23-$24 YHA/HI); **single room** $38 ($35 YHA/HI); **double room** $76-$96 ($70-$90 YHA/HI)*
Credit cards *MC, Visa*
Reception open *7.30am-8.30pm daily*
[car] [TV] K L

Maintenance & cleanliness	★★★
Facilities	★★★
Atmosphere & character	★★★★
Security	★★
Overall rating	★★★

Base Backpackers Taupo
This is the newest member of the Base empire and it fits in quite nicely. Everything is clean and new and done up in the Base red-and-black colour scheme, with many of the nicer touches that Base brings to its hostels – lockers for every bed, good mattresses

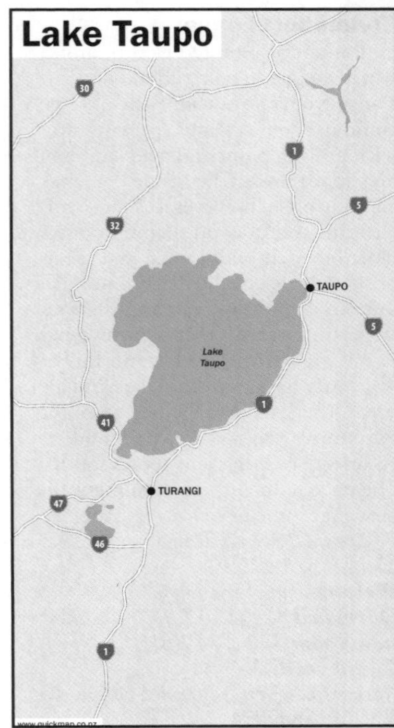

Waikato

and bedding, individual reading lights and key-card security. There is a girls-only Sanctuary wing as well, which features fluffy towels and girly bath products. The kitchen is big and well-equipped. The literature brags about the attached sun deck, however, which is nothing special. Like many Base hostels, this is a definite place to party, with a huge and lively bar/nightclub, Element, attached. It's within walking distance to pretty much all of Taupo's other nightlife options.
7 Tuwharetoa Street, Taupo
☎ *(07) 377 4464 or 0800 227 369 (0800 BASE NZ)*
Website *www.stayatbase.com*
Dorm bed *$26-$29;* ***double/twin room*** *$65-$76;* ***family room*** *$100*
Credit cards *MC, Visa*
Reception open *24 hours*

Maintenance & cleanliness	★★★★★
Facilities	★★★★½
Atmosphere & character	★★★★½
Security	★★★★
Overall rating	★★★★

Berkenhoff Lodge

You might be tempted to turn around when you get a look at Berkenhoff Lodge from the outside. The old house could use some serious sprucing up, with peeling paint and a general hang-dog appearance. The inside comes as a big surprise, however. It's clean and cheerful and in good shape. Rooms are older but well-maintained and most of them have en suite bathrooms. The kitchen is big and clean and there's a large dining room that features a pair of talking parrots, Tickle and Lolly. A TV room has comfy couches and a log fire. Other facilities include an outdoor swimming pool and spa pool and an on-site bar that also serves food. There's just an authentic, homely vibe here that some newer places lack.
75 Scannell Street, Taupo
☎ *(07) 378 4909*
Website *www.berkenhofflodge.co.nz*
Dorm bed *$24 ($20 BBH);* ***double/twin room*** *$62 ($54 BBH)*
Credit cards *MC, Visa*
Reception open *8.30am-8.30pm daily*

Maintenance & cleanliness	★★★
Facilities	★★★½
Atmosphere & character	★★★½
Security	★★
Overall rating	★★★

Burke's Lodge

This is a basic hostel that used to be a motel. It has a spa pool, a small kitchen and a TV lounge with a pool table with rooms around a courtyard. It's located close to the Pak 'n' Save supermarket and the Warehouse. Nothing too special about the place, but it's got a decent, quiet atmosphere and clean rooms. We were told that there are plans for a complete overhaul, with an eye towards making it a more upmarket hostel; time will tell if it actually materialises.
69 Spa Road, Taupo
☎ *(07) 378 9292*
Website *www.burkesbp.co.nz*
Dorm bed *$23-$24 ($20-$21 BBH);* ***single room*** *$52 ($47 BBH);* ***double room*** *62-$66 ($52- $56 BBH);* ***twin room*** *$56 ($46 BBH)*
Credit cards *MC, Visa*
Reception open *8am-8pm daily*

Maintenance & cleanliness	★★½
Facilities	★★
Atmosphere & character	★★½
Security	★
Overall rating	★★½

Go Global Backpackers

Go Global is located right above an enormous Irish pub, Finn MacCuhal's, on Taupo's main nightlife street. Years ago it was a hotel, and traces like old radiators in the rooms and tile bath-rooms are still evident. It's a pretty basic place and could be better-maintained. One nice touch is an absolutely enormous outdoor deck that looks over the town park and a little slice of the river.
Corner Tongariro & Tuwharetoa Streets, Taupo
☎ *(07) 377 0044*
Website *www.go-global.co.nz*
Dorm bed *$22-$25;* ***single room*** *$53;* ***double/twin room*** *$58*
Credit cards *MC, Visa*
Reception open *8am-10pm daily*

Maintenance & cleanliness	★★
Facilities	★★★½
Atmosphere & character	★★
Security	★★★½
Overall rating	★★

Rainbow Lodge

This is a great little hostel with a very friendly staff and atmosphere. Rooms are clean and in good shape and there's a cosy common room with a piano and log fire. Some en suite rooms are in a separate cottage on the property. The TV room features a sizable flat screen and the kitchen is fully equipped. Other facilities include a barbecue and a sauna. Internet is limited to one PC in the office, however. The Rainbow has been around for a while and deservedly enjoys a good reputation among travellers.

99 Titaraupenga Street, Taupo

☎ *(07) 378 5754*

Website *www.rainbowlodge.co.nz*

Dorm bed *$22-$25 ($19-$22 BBH);* ***single room*** *$45-$55 ($42-$52 BBH);* ***double/twin room*** *$56-$62 ($50-$56 BBH);* ***triple room*** *($66 BBH)*

Credit cards *MC, Visa*

Reception open *8am-10pm daily*

TV K L

Maintenance & cleanliness	★★★
Facilities	★★★
Atmosphere & character	★★★★
Security	★★
Overall rating	★★★

Silver Fern Lodge

The Silver Fern is a very clean, well-maintained and totally antiseptic place. It's going after the flashpackers aesthetic, with lots of steel and black, but it really misses the mark when it comes to atmosphere. This doesn't feel like a hostel at all; it's more like a business hotel. There is a TV room and a kitchen with a dining area, but neither is an inviting place to hang out. The quality of the mattresses and beds are quite good, and the kitchen has nice touches like a fish smoker and a dish steriliser; but the entire place shouldn't be as sterile as the dishware.

Corner Kaimanawa & Tamamutu

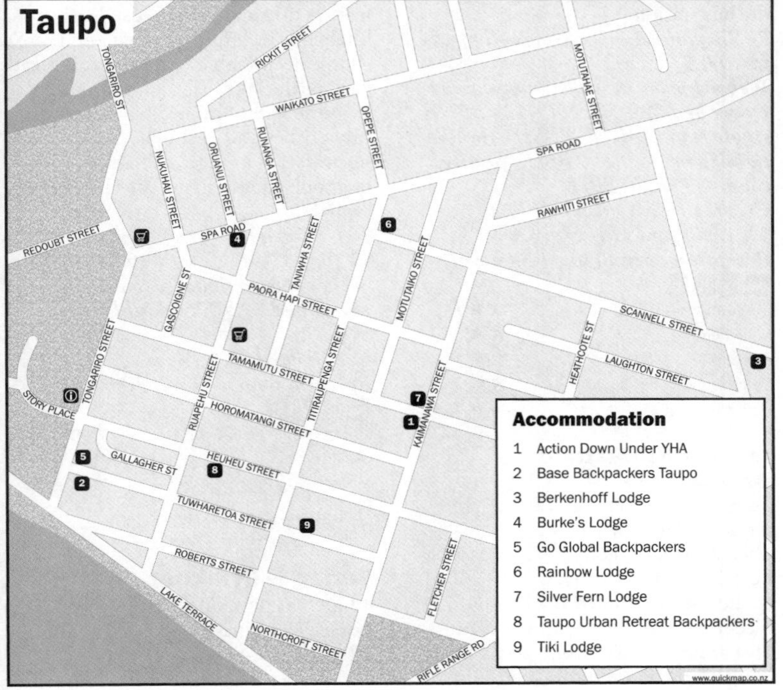

Streets, Taupo
☎ *(07) 377 4929*
Website *www.silverfernlodge.co.nz*
Dorm bed *$25;* ***double room*** *$99-$110*
Credit cards *Amex, MC, Visa*
Reception open *7.30am-9.30pm daily*

Maintenance & cleanliness	★★★★★
Facilities	★★
Atmosphere & character	½
Security	★★½
Overall rating	★★★

Sunset Lodge

Sunset Lodge is a small hostel close to the lakefront 3½km from the town centre. There's a quieter vibe here than the places in town. The common room has a log fire and a veranda with views of the lake, which is nice. The house and some of the facilities are on the old side, however. There's a small kitchen (with a couple of dorm rooms practically inside it) and a chill outdoor sitting area with a barbecue. Internet access is available on a single PC. The Sunset Lodge picks up and drops off at the bus station.

27 Tremaine Avenue, Gradwell
☎ *(07) 378 5962*
Website *www.sunsetlodgetaupo.co.nz*
Dorm bed *$22-$24 ($19-$22 BBH);* ***single room*** *$40 ($35 BBH);* ***double/twin room*** *$55 ($50 BBH);* ***family room*** *$75 ($70 BBH)*
Credit cards *Amex, MC, Visa; 5% credit card surcharge*
Reception open *8.30am-8pm daily*

Maintenance & cleanliness	★★½
Facilities	★★
Atmosphere & character	★★½
Security	★½
Overall rating	★★½

Taupo Urban Retreat Backpackers

Taupo Urban Retreat is a clean and modern place with a social atmosphere. It's not exactly clear where the hostel ends and the lively bar – billed as the cheapest in town – begins. The reception, the large common/dining area and the grassy front yard all overlap with the bar. Four-bed en suite rooms are comfy and some feature a pretty good view of the lake. There is one 18-bed dorm in a separate, high-ceilinged extension; it feels spacious and airy, but still, that is a lot of beds for one room. Security features are good, including lockers for all the beds. Free use of a nearby gym is included, maybe to sweat out those cheap drinks.

65 Heuheu Street, Taupo
☎ *(07) 378 6124 or 0800 872 261*
Website *www.tur.co.nz*
Dorm bed *$22-$26;* ***double/twin room*** *$60-$65*
Credit cards *MC, Visa*
Reception open *24 hours*

Maintenance & cleanliness	★★★½
Facilities	★★★
Atmosphere & character	★★★★
Security	★★★½
Overall rating	★★★½

Tiki Lodge

Tiki Lodge is a relatively up-market hostel on the quieter end of Taupo's main street. All dorms sleep seven and feature tidy, made-up beds. The big kitchen is in fully-equipped and there's a large deck with a barbecue and great view of the lake. The common room is comfortable and neat, with colourful couches and cushions. There's a separate TV lounge, and an outdoor spa pool. Internet and Wi-Fi access are available.

104 Tuwharetoa Street, Taupo
☎ *(07) 377 4545 or 0800 845 456*
Website *www.tikilodge.co.nz*
Dorm bed *$22-$26;* ***double room*** *$70-$75*
Credit cards *MC, Visa*
Reception open *8am-8.30pm daily*

Maintenance & cleanliness	★★★★½
Facilities	★★★
Atmosphere & character	★★★½
Security	★★½
Overall rating	★★★½

Eating & Drinking

Taupo has developed a varied and extensive dining scene, ranging from sophisticated restaurants to more backpacker budget-friendly cafés and takeaways. There are burger and pizza joints, and fish and chip shops all within the city centre. There's also a backpacker-centric nightlife with a good selection of bars and clubs to drink and dance.

Most of the action takes place on and around Tongariro and Tuwharetoa Streets. **Finn MacCuhal's** *(Tuwharetoa Street, Taupo)* is an enormous Irish pub near the corner of Tongariro Street; right across the street is **Element** *(7 Tuwharetoa Street, Taupo)*, the Base Taupo bar and nightclub that gets jumping most nights. **Holy Cow** *(11 Tongariro Street, Taupo)* is a legendary Taupo backpacker spot and **Taupo Urban Retreat** *(65 Heuheu Street, Taupo)* claims to have the cheapest bar in town.

There are some restaurants and fast food places around Lake Terrace and Tongariro Street, right across from the waterfront, which are nice places to grab a bite.

Or you can hit the **Pak'n Save** *(Ruapehu Street, Taupo)* or the **Woolworth's** *(corner Spa Road & Tongariro Street, Taupo)* supermarket and have a picnic in the Taupo Domain right on the lakefront.

Sights

Craters of the Moon

This unique lunar landscape is the result of the 1954 explosion during construction of the Wairakei geothermal power station. There is a loop track (1 hour) that takes you through this active thermal area that features craters, mud pools and steam vents.
Karapiti Road, 7km north of Taupo
***Admission** free*

Volcanic Activity Centre

This small science museum has exhibits on geothermal and volcanic activity. The centre boasts an earthquake simulator, a live model geyser and an interactive tornado machine.
Karetoto Road, Wairakei Park
☎ *(07) 374 8375*
***Website** www.volcanoes.co.nz*
***Admission** $9.50*
***Open** Mon-Fri 9am-5pm, Sat-Sun 10am-4pm*

Activities

Apart from Huka Falls and the lovely view across the lake, there's not a lot to see in Taupo. However there are loads of things to do with an emphasis on great value adventure activities.

BUNGEE JUMPING

Taupo Bungy is a popular jump from a 47m platform above the Waikato River, north of town near the Huka Falls.
202 Spa Road, Taupo
☎ *(07) 377 1135 or 0800 888 408*
***Website** www.taupobungy.co.nz*
***Solo jump** $109; **tandem jump** $218 for two people*

HIGH ROPES COURSE

The Rock 'n' Ropes high ropes course features a number of activities that are designed to both build confidence and scare the shit out of anyone with a fear of heights. The three main activities are the high beam, the giant trapeze and the thrilling giant swing. It is a good value half day and a highly recommended activity that many people say is scarier than bungee jumping or skydiving.
Crazy Catz Adventure Park, State Highway 5, 10 minutes north of Taupo
☎ *(07) 374 8111 or 0800 244 508*
***Website** www.rocknropes.co.nz*
***Half day** $65*

JET BOATING

Two jet boating operators are based in Taupo, both offer exciting trips on the Waikato River.

Huka Jet

Huka Jet is the most popular of Taupo's two jet boat companies. They are based at Wairakei Park and go right up to the base of the Huka Falls.
Huka Jet, Wairaki Park
☎ *(07) 374 8572 or 0800 485 2538*
***Website** www.hukajet.co.nz*
***30-minute ride** $95*

Rapids Jet

Rapids Jet is the other jet boat operator in Taupo. They operate further upstream where they surf the Ngaawapurua Rapids – New Zealand's

biggest commercially jet boated rapids.
☎ *(07) 378 5828 or 0800 RAPIDS.*
Website *www.rapidsjet.com*
35-minute ride *$85*

KAYAKING

There are a couple of kayaking companies based in Taupo that run kayaking trips both on Lake Taupo and on the Waikato River.

The Māori carving on the cliff face overlooking Lake Taupo is one of the highlights of the region and the best way to see it is on a half-day kayaking trip run by **Kayaking Kiwi** (☎ *(07) 378 0909 or 0800 529 255;* ***website*** *www.kayakingkiwi.com)*. A half-day trip costs $95.

Kiwi River Safaris (☎ *(07) 377 6597 or 0800 723 8577;* ***website*** *www.krs.co.nz)*, is another kayaking company that offers kayaking trips from Taupo. Rather than kayaking on the lake, Kiwi River Safaris runs trips on the Waikato River that let you see bungee jumpers from underneath the platform and also give you the opportunity to try a cliff jump or just soak in hot pools. A two-hour trip costs $40.

SKYDIVING

Skydiving is Taupo's most popular activity. It is the cheapest place in New Zealand to jump out of a plane and the scenery is spectacular with views over Lake Taupo and the snow capped mountain peaks of Tongariro National Park.

Competition between the three skydive companies keeps the prices low and you usually get the choice of several jump heights. Generally the ripcord gets pulled at 1524m (5000ft); so a 1829m (6000ft) jump gives you five seconds freefall, a 2743m (9000ft) jump gives you 30 seconds of freefall, a 3658m (12000ft) jump gives you 45 seconds and a 4572m (15000ft) jump gives you one minute. However the 15000ft jump is not always possible, particularly in cold weather and most people choose to jump at 12000ft. Skydiving operators in New Zealand advertise their jump altitudes in feet, rather than metres.

The quality of video footage is one of the main differences between the different operators. Lots of travellers recommend Skydive Taupo because it features a one-on-one video of your jump as opposed to a group video of everyone on the plane. Also the video is of the entire parachute jump and not just the freefall.

Skydiving companies only operate when the weather conditions are right, so be prepared to spend an extra day or two in Taupo waiting for the right conditions. Most tandem skydive companies impose a maximum weight of 100kg.

Great Lake Skydive Centre

☎ *(07) 378 4662 or 0800 FREEFLY (0800 373 335)*
Website *www.freefly.co.nz*
12000ft tandem jump *$219, $409 including freefall DVD;* ***15000ft tandem jump*** *$314, $489 including freefall DVD*

Taupo Tandem Skydiving

☎ *0800 275934*
Website *www.taupotandemskydiving.com*
12000ft tandem skydive *$219, $398 including freefall DVD;* ***15000ft tandem skydive*** *$314, $489 including freefall DVD*

Skydive Taupo

☎ *0800 JUMP NOW (0800 586 766)*
Website *www.skydivetaupo.co.nz*
12000ft tandem skydive *$220;* ***15,000ft tandem skydive*** *$315; freefall DVD extra $149*

Turangi

Turangi, 50km southwest of Taupo, bills itself as the "Trout Fishing Capital of the World"; if that thought turns you on, this is the place to go. If you're really, really into trout there's even the Tongariro National Trout Centre nearby, a hatchery with a viewing chamber and picnic areas.

But if fishing on the Tongariro River is not your thing, Turangi doesn't offer much else to attract backpackers. There are a couple of very good hostels, and it's a quieter alternative to the touristy scene in Taupo; many of the activities in Taupo can be booked from here.

Turangi also makes a base for tackling the Tongariro Crossing or any of the other walks in Tongariro National Park. It's less than an hour to the Whakapapa ski area on Mt Ruapehu. The Tokaanu Thermal Pools are five minutes away. Turangi is the midpoint between Auckland and Wellington.

Practical Information

Turangi i-SITE Visitor Centre

1 Ngwaka Place, Turangi
☎ *(07) 386 8999*
Website *www.laketauponz.com*
Open *8.30am-5pm daily*

Department of Conservation

Turanga Place, Turangi
☎ *(07) 386 8607*
Open *Mon-Fri 8am-5pm*

Coming & Going

InterCity Coachlines *(☎ (09) 623 1503; **website** www.intercity.co.nz)* and Naked Bus *(☎ 0900 62533; **website** www.nakedbus.com)* stop in Turangi en route between Auckland and Wellington. They stop at the Turangi i-SITE Visitor Centre *(1 Ngwaka Place, Turangi).*

Alpine Hotbus *(☎ 0508 468 287; **website** www.alpinehotbus.co.nz)* operates a daily shuttle bus for hikers tackling the Tongariro Crossing. It departs Turangi at 7am with an additional 6.15am service during summer (Nov-Apr). The return fare is $35.

Accommodation

A Plus Lodge

Formerly called Samurai Lodge, this hostel is on a residential street, around a ten-minute walk from the town centre. A Plus is a clean but charmless cinderblock affair. Facilities are basic; there's a good-sized kitchen and a not-very-homely TV/dining room. A large back yard is available for camping but otherwise is not an inviting place to hang out. Rooms are clean and very plain. Internet access is available on one PC in the office.
41 Iwiheke Place, Turangi
☎ *(07) 386 8979*
Dorm bed *$21-$22 ($18-$19);* ***single room*** *$32 ($29 BBH);* ***double room*** *$49-$52 ($43-$46 BBH);* ***twin room*** *$48 ($42 BBH)*
Reception open *7am-10pm daily*
🚗 TV K L

Maintenance & cleanliness	★★★
Facilities	★★½
Atmosphere & character	★
Security	★★½
Overall rating	★★

Backpackers Habitat (YHA Turangi)

Backpackers Habitat is part of a sprawling holiday park complex, with accommodation options including tents, campervans, dorms, motel rooms and cabins. It feels like a self-contained village with around 185 beds spread around the property. Facilities include a sauna (for an additional fee) and spa pool, a small TV lounge, playground equipment and a minimarket by the reception. There's also a large bar with three pool tables, an air hockey table and a big projection TV.

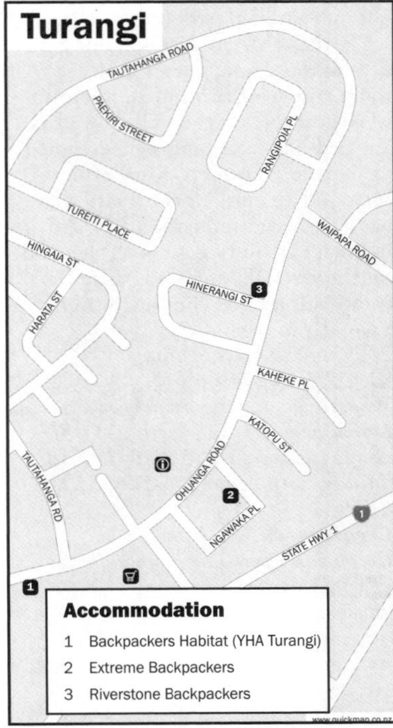

Waikato

It's so spread out and varied that there's not much backpacker atmosphere here. Facilities and accommodation could also be in better shape. The entire camp is often hired out by large groups for meetings, retreats, and other outings.

25 Ohuanga Road, Turangi
☎ *(07) 386 7492*
***Website** www.yha.co.nz*
***Dorm bed** $22-$26 ($21-$25 HI/YHA); **single room** $29; **double/twin room** $52-$80*
***Credit cards** MC, Visa*
***Reception open** 7am-10pm daily*

Maintenance & cleanliness	★★
Facilities	★★★½
Atmosphere & character	★
Security	★
Overall rating	★★

Extreme Backpackers

This excellent purpose-built hostel is hard to miss if you're near the Turangi town centre. It's a big aluminium-and-wood structure that's supposed to resemble an oversized camping hut in a national park (not sure if we see it, though). Inside, everything is kept in top shape. There's a nice TV room with a log fire and an interesting Maori carving on the wall, as well as a few bed-like seats purposely designed as an exile for snorers. Most rooms surround an outdoor courtyard that has a barbecue and hammocks. An internet café/restaurant is on site, and, for the vertically-inclined, there is a competition-rated climbing wall that is a wonder to behold.

26 Ngawaka Place, Turangi
☎ *(07) 386 8949*
***Website** www.extremebackpackers.co.nz*
***Dorm bed** $23-$25 ($20-$22 BBH); **single room** $46-$56 ($40-$50 BBH); **double/twin room** $56-$66 ($50-$60 BBH)*
***Credit cards** MC, Visa*
***Reception open** 7am-8pm daily*

Maintenance & cleanliness	★★★★★
Facilities	★★½
Atmosphere & character	★★★★
Security	★★
Overall rating	★★★★

Riverstone Backpackers

Riverstone is a relatively new "boutique" backpackers' hostel close to the town centre. Everything is well designed and carefully thought out inside this renovated house, which can hold up to 20 guests. A very comfy TV lounge has a wood fire. The kitchen is excellent, with nice appliances and sharp knives. Rooms feature real mattresses and quality bedding. Outside, there's a peaceful garden and sundeck decorated with lanterns and Tibetan prayer flags (an outdoor fireplace and wood-burning pizza oven were being added when we visited). There are also good facilities for all the sports activities Turangi has on offer – a drying room for all that wet skiing and fishing gear, an outdoor fish-cleaning area, even a fish smoker. The owner is an excellent source of local information, as well.

222 Tautahanga Road, Turangi
☎ *(07) 386 7004*
***Website** www.riverstonebackpackers.com*
***Dorm bed** $27 ($22 BBH); **double room** $66-$78 ($56-$68); **twin room** $66 ($56 BBH); **family room** $90-$120 ($75-$100 BBH)*
***Credit cards** MC, Visa*
***Reception open** 8am-11pm & 4pm-7pm daily*

Maintenance & cleanliness	★★★★★
Facilities	★★★
Atmosphere & character	★★★★
Security	★½
Overall rating	★★★★

Eating & Drinking

Turangi doesn't have the variety of restaurants or the nightlife that Taupo does, but there are a number of places for backpackers to grab a bite. There's a **Burger King** *(corner State Highway 1 & Pihanga Street, Turangi)* right on the State Highway at the Turangi turnoff. **Grand Central Fry** *(Ohuanga Road, Turangi)* in the town centre is the locally famous place for fish and chips. Close by is **Four Fish** *(corner Ohuanga & Pihanga Roads, Turangi)*, a bistro/pizza joint that's pricier. **Thyme for Food** *(35 Ohaunga Road, Turangi)* is a café in the town centre.

If you're preparing your own food, there's a **New World** supermarket *(Ohuanga Road, Turangi).*

Of course, you can always catch and smoke or fry up your own trout here in New Zealand's trout fishing capital.

Activities

Most travellers use Turangi as a base for hiking in the Tongariro National Park (see Manuwatu-Wanganui chapter). White water rafting is the other main activity.

White Water Rafting

Rapid Sensations *(☎ 0800 35 34 35; **website** www.rapids.co.nz)*, **River Rats** *(☎ 0800 333 900; **website** www.riverrats.co.nz)* and **Tongariro River Rafting** *(☎ (07) 386 6409; **website** www.trr.co.nz)* operate rafting trips on the Tongariro River.

The Tongariro river has over 50 grade 3+ rapids that make a fun day of rafting although there are wilder rivers elsewhere in New Zealand. Trips cost $99-115.

Bay of Plenty

The bay stretching from the Coromandel Peninsula to East Cape includes many great beaches plus Rotorua and the twin cities of Tauranga and Mount Maunganui. It's one of the top holiday regions for Kiwis, and maintains a strong Māori culture.

The Bay of Plenty was named by Captain Cook when he noted its abundant fruit-growing properties (he also named Poverty Bay, for opposite reasons). The Bay still maintains a vibrant agricultural industry, growing kiwifruit in its temperate climate. Many backpackers doing seasonal fruit picking work come up this way during the winter months.

The area inland from the Bay is a geothermal playground with boiling mud pools and hissing geysers. Rotorua is one of the biggest tourist attractions in New Zealand and the primary base for checking out the geothermal action, and is also a centre for performance of traditional Māori heritage.

Tauranga is a fast-growing and sophisticated coastal city; its neighbour Mount Manganui is a top surf spot, particularly among Kiwis.

Must do in Bay of Plenty

- Visit the geothermal sites in Rotorua
- Go white water rafting or sledging (hydrospeed) on the Kaituna River
- Visit White Island, 50km offshore from Whakatane

The Bay of Plenty holds an abundance of attractions for travellers; no trip to the North Island would be complete without stopping here.

Tauranga & Mount Maunganui

With a population of 109,000, the port city of Tauranga is the largest in the Bay of Plenty, and one of New Zealand's fastest growing areas. The Strand area along the waterfront has become home to cafés, restaurants, bars and a buzzing nightlife over the last several years. Tauranga is also a major centre for the surrounding kiwifruit growing region; most of the work is available during the winter harvest months.

Mount Maunganui, on a peninsula just north of its twin city of Tauranga, is a more popular holiday destination with Kiwis than with international travellers. Its main feature is the large dormant volcano that dominates the landscape. The 16km white sandy surf beach is considered one of the top surf spots in New Zealand. There's a good selection of shops and eateries along the Mount's main street, and the town is home to the massive Bayfair shopping centre. Other attractions include hot salt water pools and hikes up to the top of the volcano cone, a rewarding experience.

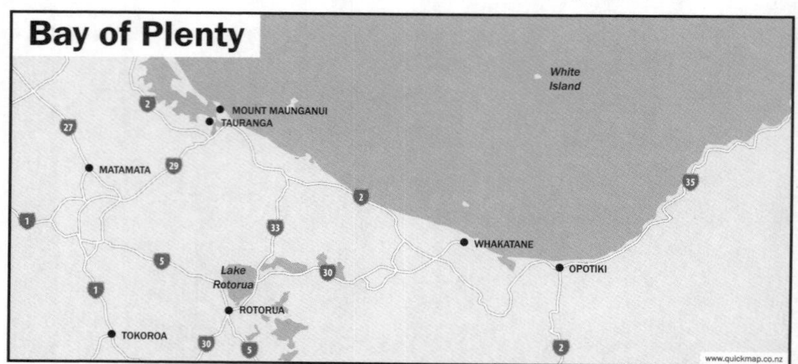

Both Tauranga and Mount Maunganui have their unique attractions and both cities offer good accommodation options. Mount Maunganui has the beach and a resort-town feel, but Tauranga offers a more vibrant urban setting. Your choice, but it's hard to go too far wrong either way.

Practical Information

INFORMATION CENTRES

Tauranga i-SITE Visitor Centre

95 Willow Street, Tauranga
☎ *(07) 578 8103*
Website *www.bayofplentynz.com*
Open *Mon-Fri 7am-5.30pm, Sat-Sun 8am-4pm*

Mount Maunganui i-SITE Visitor Centre

Salisbury Avenue, Mount Maunganui
☎ *(07) 575 5099*
Website *www.bayofplentynz.com*
Open *Mon-Fri 9am-5pm*

Department of Conservation

253 Chadwick Road, West Greerton
☎ *(07) 578 7677*
Website *www.doc.govt.nz*
Open *8am-4.30pm daily*

INTERNET ACCESS

Cybersurf

Piccadilly Arcade, Grey Street, Tauranga
☎ *(07) 578 0140*
Website *www.cybersurf.co.nz*
Open *Mon-Fri 9am-6pm, Sat 10am-4pm, Su 11am-4pm*

Esquires Coffee in the Goddards Centre *(**website** www.esquires.co.nz; 21 Devonport Street, Tauranga)* has free Wi-Fi access.

Coming & Going

InterCity Coachlines *(☎ (09) 623 1503; **website** www.intercity.co.nz)* and Naked Bus *(☎ 0900 62533; **website** www.nakedbus.com)* have buses to Auckland, Opotiki and Rotorua and Naked Bus also has direct services to Waitomo. Go Kiwi *(☎ (07) 866 0336; **website** www.go-kiwi.co.nz)* also have a shuttle service from Tauranga and Mount Maunganui to Auckland, Hamilton and the the Coromandel Peninsula.

In Tauranga, InterCity stops outside the i-SITE Visitor Centre *(95 willow street, Tauranga)* and Naked Bus stops at the Wharf Street bus terminal. In Mount Maunganui, both InterCity and Naked Bus stop outside the i-SITE Visitor Centre *(Salisbury Avenue, Mount Maunganui)*.

Bayline Coaches *(☎ 0800 422 9287 (0800 BAYBUS); **website** www.baylinebus.co.nz)* run regional bus services within the Bay of Plenty with services to Opotiki, Rotorua and Whakatane.

Local Transport

Bayline Coaches *(☎ 0800 422 9287 (0800 BAYBUS); **website** www.baylinebus.co.nz)* run the Bay Hopper bus service in the Tauranga and Mount Maunganui area. A one-way trip costs between $1.50 and $3 or you can buy a Day Saver ticket for $6, which lets you travel on any Tauranga and Mount Maunganui buses. The most popular bus routes for most backpackers are routes 1, 2 and 6, which run between Tauranga and Mount Maunganui; route 3, which runs from Just the Ducks Nuts hostel into central Tauranga and routes 3 and 10, which run between Bell Lodge and central Tauranga.

Accommodation

TAURANGA

Bell Lodge

Outside of the city centre (but closer to the beaches), Bell Lodge is a motel/hostel (a mostel?) built around a small courtyard with a barbecue. Like most hostels in this area, it's much busier during the winter season thanks to the kiwifruit picking work available, and they'll help you arrange jobs. The place itself is clean and basic and many of the dorm rooms have en suite bathrooms. There's a TV room, a lounge with a pool table and a fully-equipped kitchen. They provide free pickup from the city centre, about 4km away, and offer weekend trips to the Mount Maunganui beaches, but this location is far more convenient if you have your own transport.

39 Bell Street, Judea
🚌 *3, 10*

(07) 578 6344
Website *www.bell-lodge.co.nz*
Dorm bed *$25-$27 ($22-$24 BBH);* ***double room*** *$65 ($59 BBH);* ***twin room*** *$60 ($54 BBH);*
Credit cards *MC, Visa*
Reception open *8am-8.30pm daily*

Maintenance & cleanliness	★★★
Facilities	★★
Atmosphere & character	★★★½
Security	★½
Overall rating	★★★½

Harbourside City Backpackers

This hotel right on The Strand is one of the oldest buildings in Tauranga (dating from 1913) and has a fair bit of character. There are 80 beds on two floors; rooms are generally clean and well-maintained, but some parts of the building are a bit worn. The main attraction here is the fabulous rooftop deck, with tremendous views over the harbour. It makes a great place to hang out. The attached common room and big kitchen are sunny and very inviting as well. Internet PCs are near reception, there are also free bikes, and the management is good at finding temporary work for travellers.

105 The Strand, Tauranga
all Bay Hopper routes
(07) 579 4066
Website *www.backpacktauranga.co.nz*
Dorm bed *$23-$26 ($20-$23 BBH);* ***double room*** *$64-$70 ($58-$64 BBH);* ***twin room*** *$64-$68 ($56-$60 BBH)*
Credit cards *MC, Visa; 2% credit card surcharge*
Reception open *8am-9pm daily*

Maintenance & cleanliness	★★★
Facilities	★★★½
Atmosphere & character	★★★★½
Security	★★★½
Overall rating	★★★

Just the Duck's Nuts

On a hill a few minutes' drive (or a 20-minute walk) from the city centre, Just the Duck's Nuts is made up of a pair of suburban houses. There's a log fire and cosy TV room with books and games, a second downstairs common lounge and two kitchens. The yard has a table shaded by a tree and good views of Mount Maunganui (about a 20-minute bike ride away). There's internet and Wi-Fi access available. It's not a bad spot, although it's not the tidiest and cleanest place we've ever seen either. The owners will help you find local work.

6 Vale Street, Otumoetai
3, 4, 5
(07) 576 1366
Website *www.justtheducksnuts.co.nz*
Dorm bed *$21-$23 ($18-$21 BBH);* ***double room*** *$50-$56 ($44-$50);* ***twin room*** *$50 ($44 BBH)*
Reception open *8.30am-9pm daily*

Maintenance & cleanliness	★★
Facilities	★★
Atmosphere & character	★★★½
Security	★½
Overall rating	★★

Loft 109

Loft 109 is a small, cool hostel on a commercial street a couple of minutes from The Strand, with shopping and a cinema right nearby. It's up a flight of stairs from the street and has a small balcony overlooking the action below, as well as a little kitchen and TV/common room. A couple of deck areas feature a barbecue. The décor has some style, with exposed brick and nautical flourishes. There's also a log fire, and an all girls' dorm on another floor. Like most hostels in Tauranga, seasonal work can also be arranged here.

109 Devonport Road, Tauranga
all Bay Hopper routes
(07) 579 5638
Website *www.loft109.co.nz*
Dorm bed *$23 ($20 BBH);* ***double/twin room*** *$54-$60 ($48-$54 BBH)*
Credit cards *MC, Visa*
Reception open *8am-8.30pm daily*

Maintenance & cleanliness	★★★
Facilities	★½
Atmosphere & character	★★★½
Security	★★
Overall rating	★★★½

Tauranga Central Backpackers

Tauranga Central Backpackers is right in the city centre, close to the visitor information centre, and the hostel has an urban feel to it. There are many coin-operated internet PCs near the entrance. The basic common room has mismatched furniture, a pool table, table tennis and a decent-sized TV. Rooms are basic and run around an inner ring in the building; hence, no windows. Some have small skylights, but if you're really into natural light this might be a problem for you. It's actually something of a trade-off, because the rest of the facilities are open and sunny. The owner is quite friendly.

62-64 Willow Street, Tauranga
all Bay Hopper routes
(07) 571 6222
***Website** www.tgabackpack.co.nz*
***Dorm bed** $24; **single room** $45; **double room** $56*
***Reception open** 9am-10pm daily*
TV K L

Maintenance & cleanliness	★★★½
Facilities	★★
Atmosphere & character	★★
Security	★★
Overall rating	★★★½

YHA Tauranga

This YHA-owned hostel is very clean and has a bit of a quirky personality, something you don't always find in YHA hostels. There's a good-sized kitchen and dining area, as well as a small TV lounge, but the real standout here is the backyard. It's large, with nice gardens, a picnic table, and a small pond. There are whimsical wooden sculptures throughout, including a giant kiwifruit and a boat on the pond. The hostel is a few minutes from the centre of town and has off-street parking available.

171 Elizabeth Street, Tauranga
(07) 578 5064
***Website** www.yha.co.nz*
***Dorm bed** $26-$27 ($23-$24 HI/YHA); **single room** $49 ($46 HI/YHA); **double room** $62 ($56 HI/YHA)*
***Credit cards** MC, Visa*
***Reception open** 8am-2pm & 4pm-9pm*
TV K L

Maintenance & cleanliness	★★★★
Facilities	★★
Atmosphere & character	★★★
Security	★★★½
Overall rating	★★★★½

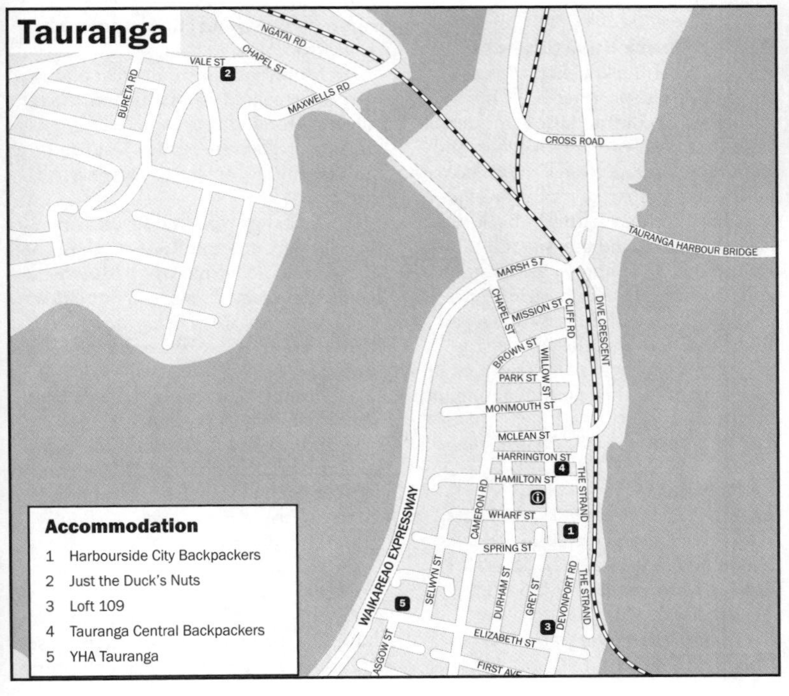

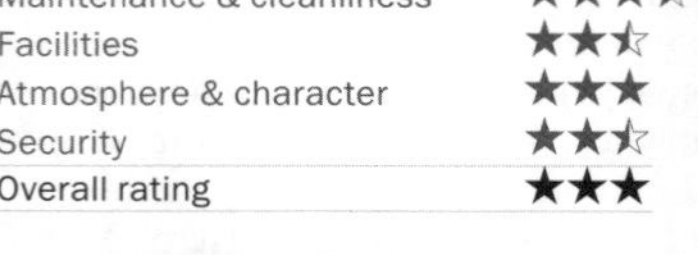

Maintenance & cleanliness	★★★½
Facilities	★★½
Atmosphere & character	★★★
Security	★★½
Overall rating	★★★

MOUNT MAUNGANUI

Mount Backpackers

Mount Backpackers is a small, basic hostel, well located right in the heart of Mount Maunganui's commercial stretch just a couple of minutes from the beach. There are only a few rooms: a pair of six-bed dorms, a four-bed dorm, and one nine-bed dorm, which is kind of crowded but has a very high ceiling and a skylight, so it feels airier. There's a small central courtyard with picnic tables and a TV room with an Xbox. An internet café downstairs has plenty of coin-operated internet PCs.

87 Maunganui Road, Mount Maunganui
Bay Hopper 1, 2
(07) 575 0860
Website *www.mountbackpackers.co.nz*
Dorm bed *$24-$26 ($21-$23 BBH);* ***double room*** *$70 ($60 BBH)*
Credit cards *MC, Visa*
Reception open *8am-8pm daily*
TV K L

Maintenance & cleanliness	★★½
Facilities	★½
Atmosphere & character	★★
Security	★★
Overall rating	★★

Pacific Coast Backpackers

Pacific Coast Backpackers is a big, silver-and-blue purpose-built hostel with good accommodation and facilities. There's an excellent kitchen and big dining area, a cosy TV lounge with books and a separate room for reading and internet surfing. A back patio has a barbecue and a few small tables. Rooms are clean and well-maintained and wall murals with nature scenes give the place a bit of atmosphere. Bikes and body boards are free for guests to use. There's also free pick up and drop off at the Mount Maunganui information centre.

432 Maunganui Road, Mount Maunganui
Bay Hopper 1, 2
(07) 574 9601 or 0800 666 622
Website *www.pacificcoastlodge.co.nz*
Dorm bed *$24-$28 ($21-$25 BBH);* ***double/twin room*** *$70 ($64 BBH)*
Credit cards *MC, Visa*
Reception open *8am-9pm daily*
TV K L

Eating & Drinking

The majority of Tauranga's restaurants and bars can be found along The Strand, although many of the surrounding streets have little cafés and restaurants as well. **Orange Zephyr** *(15 Wharf Street, Tauranga)* is a cool little restaurant/bar/music venue. A few doors down is the **Crown & Badger** *(corner The Strand & Wharf Street, Tauranga)*, a traditional British pub.

The **Grumpy Mole** *(41 The Strand, Tauranga)* is a popular late-night backpacker spot, part of a Wild West, saloon-themed chain. The **Coyote Bar** *(107 The Strand, Tauranga)* is another late-night party place, this time with a South-western US, Santa Fe-style theme.

The **Sunrise Café** *(10 Wharf Street, Tauranga)* does great breakfasts. One of the most highly-recommended spots for a cheap bite is the **Fresh Fish Market** *(Dive Crescent, Tauranga)*, serving up fresh-as fish and chips right on the waterfront.

In Mount Maunganui, most places are concentrated on Maunganui Road; there's a good selection including Chinese restaurants, cafés, fast food and takeaways, as well as more stylish options.

In Tauranga, you find several supermarket on Cameron Road south of the city centre including: **Countdown** *(618 Cameron Road, Tauranga)*, **Foodtown** *(683 Cameron Road, Tauranga)* and **Pak'n Save** *(476 Cameron Road, Tauranga)*.

In Mount Maunganui there's a **New World** supermarket *(corner Tweed and Maunganui Roads, Mount Maunganui)* and also branches of **Countdown** and **Woolworths** in the Bayfair shopping centre *(Girvan Road, Mount Maunganui)*.

Activities

Tauranga and Mount Maunganui don't have any major sights, but there are several things to do. Apart from climbing the Mount, the most popular activity is swimming with the dolphins.

Climbing Mount Maunganui

This 232m extinct volcano dominates the centre of Mount Maunganui. At the end of the Mall take the walking track to the summit for a great view. It's a 45-minute walk to the top and 25 minutes back down.

Learn to Surf

Mount Maunganui is a popular surfing destination. **Hibiscus Surf School** *(☎ (07) 575 3792; **website** www.surfschool.co.nz)* and **New Zealand Surf School** *(☎ (07) 574 1666; **website** www.nzsurfschools.co.nz)* hold surf lessons several times a day during summer (Nov-mid Apr). A two-hour lesson costs $80.

Skydiving

You can jump from between 8000 and 12000ft above Mount Maunganui with **Tauranga Tandem Skydiving** *(☎ (07) 576 7990; **website** www.tandemskydive.co.nz)*. Tandem jumps start at $220 for an 8000ft jump and go up to $310 for a 12000ft jump; a freefall video is an additional $150.

Swimming with Dolphins

Several companies offer boat trips where you can swim with dolphins. Sometimes you can also see fur seals, blue penguins, whales and turtles on these trips.

Dolphin Seafaris *(☎ (07) 575 4620 or 0800 326 8747; **website** www.nzdolphin.com)* trips depart from Mount Maunganui, take three to four hours and cost $120.

Tauranga Dolphin Company *(☎ (07) 578 3197 or 0800 836 574; **website** www.swimwithdolphins.co.nz)* trips depart from both Tauranga and Mount Maunganui, usually last for at least five hours and cost $120.

Whakatane

Whakatane is a buzzing little town of 18,000 on the eastern side of the Bay of Plenty. It's a sunny place with a busy stretch of shops, bars and restaurants in the town centre. But its main draw for travellers is its proximity to White Island, New Zealand's only live marine volcano, 50km away. Tours depart from Whakatane by helicopter or launch and sometimes include dolphin or whale encounters.

Other popular activities include swimming with dolphins and jet boating on the Matahina Dam and the Rangitaiki River. Whakatane is also one of the best all-around fishing destinations in New Zealand and is considered NZ's yellowfin capital.

Practical Information

Whakatane Visitor Information Centre

Corner Kakahoroa Drive & Quay Street, Whakatane
☎ (07) 308 6058 or 0800 942 528
***Website** www.whakatane.com*
***Open** Mon-Fri 8.30am-5pm, Sat 9am-4pm, Sun 10am-4pm*

Coming & Going

InterCity Coachlines *(☎ (09) 623 1503; **website** www.intercity.co.nz)* have buses to Rotorua, Opotiki and Gisborne and Naked Bus *(☎ 0900 62533; **website** www.nakedbus.com)* have buses to Auckland, Gisborne, Opotiki, Rotorua and Tauranga. Bayline Coaches *(☎ 0800 422 9287 (0800 BAYBUS); **website** www.baylinebus.co.nz)* run regional bus services within the Bay of Plenty with services from Whakatane to Ohope Beach, Opotiki and Tauranga.

InterCity and Naked Bus stop outside the visitor information centre *(corner Kakahoroa Drive & Quay Street, Whakatane)*; Naked Bus also stops on Boon Street.

Accommodation

Karibu Backpackers

Karibu Backpackers is a small, friendly hostel in a house a fifteen-minute walk from the centre of town. It's got a common room with a TV, books and board games, and a chess set. There's a decent kitchen. Outside is a nice backyard with a thatched hut, a barbecue, picnic table and a separate cottage with

a dorm room. It's all seen a bit of wear and tear but is reasonably tidy. Internet access is available, and there are free bikes and a free pick-up and drop-off at the bus stop in town.
13 Landing Road, Whakatane
Bay Hopper
(07) 307 8276
***Website** www.karibubackpackers.co.nz*
***Dorm bed** $23 ($20 BBH); **double room** $58 ($52 BBH)*
***Reception open** 7am-8pm daily*

Maintenance & cleanliness	★★★½
Facilities	★★
Atmosphere & character	★★★½
Security	★★★½
Overall rating	★★★½

Lloyds Lodge

Who is Lloyd? We forgot to ask. It's not the name of the owner, but whoever he is, this hostel is a very clean, charming place about a 10-minute walk to the town centre. The interior is very homely, with lots of floral print wallpaper and plants. There are only four rooms, for up to 20 people; each is quite cosy and named with a different Māori word. There are lots of Māori accents around, including art and a chart that teaches the alphabet. A nice backyard has a barbecue and garden with lots of fresh herbs. There's also a good kitchen, a TV room, books and board games, and internet access available.
10 Domain Road, Whakatane
Bay Hopper
(07) 307 8005
***Website** www.lloydslodge.com*
***Dorm bed** $25 ($22 BBH); **double/twin room** $62 ($56 BBH)*

Maintenance & cleanliness	★★★★½
Facilities	★½
Atmosphere & character	★★★½
Security	★
Overall rating	★★★

Whakatane Hotel

The Whakatane is an old hotel right on The Strand, across the road from the information centre and bus stop. The hotel itself feels pretty worn out and lacks charm, but there are party opportunities right underneath your feet. An Irish pub, the Craic, is directly downstairs, and a couple of doors down is a massive party bar called The Boiler Room. The Kiwi Experience bus stops here, so there's a built-in crowd of backpackers ready to roll, but there's really not much of a hostel feeling to the place itself. A small kitchen and sparsely furnished TV room are there for guests to use, as well as a balcony with views of the waterfront, but most of the action is outside the hostel.
79 The Strand, Whakatane
Bay Hopper, Beach Runner
(07) 307 1670
***Dorm bed** $20; **single room** $30; **double/twin room** $50*
***Credit cards** Amex, Diners, MC, Visa*

Maintenance & cleanliness	★★
Facilities	★½
Atmosphere & character	★★★½
Security	★½
Overall rating	★★

The Windsor

This fairly new Whakatane hostel doesn't exactly jibe with its regal-sounding name. It's a very clean place but there isn't much in the way of atmosphere. It's set around a concrete courtyard; inside the rooms are very tidy, if on the small side. The bathrooms are meticulous. There's a breeze-block games/TV room with a pool table and a signature wall for backpackers that looked pretty bare when we visited. Outdoor seating and a barbecue are available in the courtyard, but it has a kind of car-park ambience. Still, it is very clean.
10 Merritt Street, Whakatane
(07) 308 8040
***Dorm bed** $25 ($22 BBH); **single room** $35; **double room** $50*
***Credit cards** Amex, JCB, MC, Visa*

Maintenance & cleanliness	★★★★
Facilities	★½
Atmosphere & character	★
Security	★
Overall rating	★★½

Eating & Drinking

In Whakatane, pretty much all the nightlife and dining centres around

The Strand. A few of the biggest and most popular night spots are right across the road from the information centre underneath the Whakatane Hotel *(79 The Strand, Whakatane)*; these include **The Craic** pub and **The Boiler Room** bar.

Try **NZ's Finest Fish and Chips** right at the wharf on The Strand. Cafés, takeaways, bars, and an ice cream parlour can be found further along down The Strand.

Some fast food outlets are clustered around Domain Road and Commerce Street. Whakatane has a **Countdown** *(corner King & Stewart Streets, Whakatane)* and a large **New World** supermarket *(51 Kakahoroa Drive, Whakatane)*.

Sights & Activities

Swimming with Dolphins

Thousands of dolpins visit the water off Whakatane during the warmer months (Nov-Apr) and several Whakatane-based companies operate dolphin and whale watching trips that allow you to swim with the dolphins.

Dolphins Down Under *(☎ (07) 308 2001 or 0800 354 7737; **website** www.dolphinswim.co.nz)* runs 3-4 hour trips where you can swim with dolphins for $150 ($110 if you just want to watch).

Whale Island Tours *(☎ (07) 308 5896; **website** www.whaleislandtours.com)* also run dolphin swim tours that cost $140 (or $110 if you just want to watch).

Whakatane District Museum

This small museum has exhibits about local history and environment including displays on Māori culture and early European settlement.

11 Boon Street, Whakatane
☎ (07) 306 0505
***Website** www.whakatanemuseum.org.nz*
***Admission** by donation*
***Open** Mon-Fri 10am-4.30pm, Sat-Sun 11am-3pm*

White Island

Located 50km offshore from Whakatane, New Zealand's only active marine volcano offers a barren lunar landscape and amazing geothermal activity. Visiting White Island is an expensive day trip and you have the option of visiting either by boat or air. With the exception of the helicopter, flights are purely scenic and you don't get the chance to walk around on the island. Visiting by boat also offers the opportunity to see (and perhaps swim with) dolphins.

Tours

Most tours depart from Whakatane although some may also pickup from Tauranga or Rotorua.

AIR

Air Discovery

Air Discovery has scenic flights over White Island departing from either Rotorua or Whakatane Airports. They use fixed-wing planes that are a better value option to the more pricy helicopter tours.

Discovery Base, 224 Aerodrome Road, Whakatane Airport
☎ (07) 308 7760
***Website** www.airdiscovery.co.nz*
***55-minute White Island scenic flight** $199; **two-hour White Island/Mt Tarawera flight** $399; **half-day White Island/Mt Tarawera/Lake Taupo/Mt Ruapehu flight** $599*

Vulcan Helicopters

Vulcan offers a pricey, but spectacular trip out to the island that includes a landing as well as a flight over the island.

Whakatane Airport
☎ (07) 308 4188 or 0800 804 354
***Website** www.vulcanheli.co.nz*
***2½ hour trip** (with 45 minute flight) $435*

SEA

PeeJay Charters

PeeJay takes you out to White Island on a luxury launch where you have the unique opportunity to walk on the island. This trip takes five to six hours.

15 The Strand East, Whakatane
☎ (07) 308 9588 or 0800 242 299
***Website** www.whiteisland.co.nz*
***Price** $175*

White Island Dive

This dive company runs diving and snorkelling trips to the island but the focus is on the marine life around the island, rather than the island itself.
186 The Strand, Whakatane
☎ *(07) 308 9588 or 0800 348 394*
Website *www.divewhite.co.nz*
Snorkelling *$180;* ***dive with full gear*** *$340*

Opotiki

Opotiki is the gateway to the East Cape, and has more in common with that region's remote, country feel than with the thriving Bay of Plenty to the west. Most travellers stop off here on the way to or from the Cape; if you're heading into the Cape, this is definitely a place to stock up on cash, fuel and supplies.

There's not a great deal to detain you in Opotiki for long, but it does offer some attractions. The region's strong Māori presence is obvious on the town's main street, which is bedecked with the work of master carvers. The beaches nearby are also fantastic, and there are some good accommodation options around.

Practical Information

Opotiki i-SITE Visitor Centre

Corner Elliot & St John Streets, Opotiki
☎ *(07) 315 8484*
Website *www.opotikinz.com*
Open *Mon-Fri 8am-5pm*

Coming & Going

InterCity Coachlines *(☎ (09) 623 1503;* ***website*** *www.intercity.co.nz)* have buses to Gisborne and Whakatane and Naked Bus *(☎ 0900 62533;* ***website*** *www.nakedbus.com)* have buses to Gisborne, Tauranga, Rotorua and Auckland. The Bay Hopper *(☎ 0800 422 9287 (0800 BAYBUS);* ***website*** *www.baylinebus.co.nz)* bus goes to Tauranga via Whakatane.

InterCity and Naked Bus stop outside the hot bread shop *(43 St Johns Street, Opotiki)* and Naked Bus has an additional stop outside the Opotiki i-SITE Visitor Centre *(corner Elliot & St John Streets, Opotiki).*

Accommodation

Central Oasis Backpackers

Central Oasis Backpackers is a small kauri villa right in the centre of town. It's a cute, high-ceilinged older house that has had some renovation and is generally well maintained. There are only a few rooms – a seven-bed dorm, a three-bed share, and a double. Guests share a small kitchen and a common room with a little TV. There's an internet room as well; cupboard-sized, really, with a single PC. A backyard has a barbecue, a nice big table, and there's room for tents as well. Bikes are free to use. The very friendly German owners are a good source of information about the town and the region. There's just a very charming vibe to the place. Free popcorn, too.
30 King Street, Opotiki
☎ *(07) 315 5165*
Website *www.centraloasisbackpackers.co.nz*
Dorm bed *$18-$20 ($16-$18 BBH);* ***double room*** *$44 ($40 BBH);* ***twin room*** *$40 ($36 BBH)*

Maintenance & cleanliness	★★★½
Facilities	★★
Atmosphere & character	★★★½
Security	★
Overall rating	★★★

Hunters Backpackers

Hunters Backpackers is located inside the Royal Hotel, on Opotiki's main street. The Hunters Bar and Lounge downstairs is quite nice and modern; however, the hotel itself is old and unevenly restored. Some rooms and common areas have been renovated, but most of it when we visited had a dated and musty feel, with furnishings from a bygone era. There really isn't much of a hostel feel here; the rooms are generally small and there's not much in the way of common space: a small sitting room with mismatched furniture, a small kitchen and dining table and a balcony out front. It's definitely looking to become more of a hotel than hostel.
Corner Church & King Streets, Opotiki
☎ *(07) 315 5760*
Website *www.huntersbackpackers.co.nz*

***Dorm bed** $20-$25; **single room** $30; **double room** $50*
***Credit cards** MC, Visa*

Maintenance & cleanliness	★★
Facilities	★★
Atmosphere & character	★½
Security	★½
Overall rating	★★

Opotiki Backpackers Beach House

The Beach House is the kind of place you arrive at and just say "ahhh..." Forget TV or internet – there isn't any – just check out the views over the beach metres away. Go surfing, fishing or swimming, or lie around and do nothing. This is a cute little place 4km outside Opotiki, decorated with beach house décor – driftwood and shells and the like. It's clean and has just 12 beds. There's a kitchen, a lounge with books, a couple of sun decks, a barbecue and table football. The owners are very friendly, and the atmosphere is absolutely relaxed.
7 Appleton Road, Waiotahi Beach
(07) 315 5117
***Dorm bed** $23 ($20 BBH); **double/twin room** $56 ($50 BBH)*

Maintenance & cleanliness	★★★½
Facilities	★★½
Atmosphere & character	★★★★
Security	★
Overall rating	★★★

Rotorua

Rotorua is one of the few cities in the world that you may actually smell before you see; depending on the wind you may catch a whiff of its signature, sulphurous rotten-egg smell well before you actually reach it. But whenever you do encounter the smell for the first time, it makes a strong impression. You'll get used to it quickly enough, though, and soon be on your way to taking in all the things that make Rotorua one of New Zealand's most unique, and most visited, cities.

Geothermal activity is what makes Rotorua such a special place. There are bubbling mud pools in the city's parks and steam rising from suburban front yards. Geothermal attractions within day trip distance of Rotorua include Wai-O-Tapu, Hell's Gate and the Waimangu Volcanic Valley; the most accessible, however, is the Te Whakarewarewa Thermal Village just 3km from the city centre. Te Whakarewarewa includes a Māori cultural centre as well as Pohutu geyser, New Zealand's largest and most well-known.

Kuirau Park at the western edge of the city centre is a free city park which holds bubbling mud pools and steaming lakes and is easier on the budget than the entrance fee to Te Whakarewarewa.

The area's thermal activity also means that there are several hot spas. Polynesian Spa near the Government Gardens in the city centre is a popular and reasonable option for soaking in thermally-heated luxury in an idyllic outdoor setting. It's been frequently chosen as a world top 10 spa by readers of *Conde Nast Traveller*. Many hostels in town also offer free thermally-heated spa pools.

Māori cultural performances are another main Rotorua attraction, and part of the reason Rotorua also goes by the nickname "Rotovegas". Māori concerts and hangi meals are mainstays of the Rotorua tourist trade, and while they may be a bit overdone (the shows, not the food) for some tastes, they can also be good fun and might be a casual traveller's best introduction to Māori tradition.

Rotorua boasts a beautiful location on Lake Rotorua, and is considered by many to the best mountain-biking region in the country.

Because Rotorua is so popular with budget travellers, a whole industry has popped up catering to the needs of the backpacker with plenty of fast-paced activities. There's bungee jumping, skydiving, white water rafting, jet boating, and luge rides, which were invented in Rotorua. Another Rotorua original is zorbing, where you roll down a hill inside an inflatable plastic ball.

Rotorua has a highly developed food and drink scene, and a plethora of hostels to choose from, of widely varying quality. It's on seemingly every traveller to New Zealand's itinerary and it can feel overly touristy, but people visit it for a reason – it's a one-of-a-kind place.

Practical Information

Rotorua i-SITE Visitor Centre

1167 Fenton Street, Rotorua
☎ *(07) 348 5179*
Website *www.rotoruanz.com*
Open *summer 8am-6pm daily; winter 8am-5.30pm daily*

Department of Conservation

1144 Pukaki Street, Rotorua
☎ *(07) 349 7400*
Website *www.doc.govt.nz*

Coming & Going

InterCity Coachlines *(☎ (09) 623 1503; **website** www.intercity.co.nz)* and Naked Bus *(☎ 0900 62533; **website** www.nakedbus.com)* connect Rotorua with most major North Island destinations. Bayline Coaches' *(☎ 0800 422 9287 (0800 BAYBUS); **website** www.baylinebus.co.nz)* Twin City Express runs between Rotorua and Tauranga twice each weekday. Buses stop at the Rotorua i-SITE Visitor Centre *(1167 Fenton Street, Rotorua)*.

Local Transport

Rotorua's local Cityride bus service *(☎ 0800 4BAYBUS (0800 422 928); **website** www.baybus.co.nz)* consists of 10 routes running every half hour (Mon-Fri) covering city and suburbs. All buses stop on Amohau, Fenton and Puketua Streets in the city centre. The more useful routes include bus 1 to Ngongotaha and bus 10 to the airport. A single cash fare is $2 and a Day Saver pass costs $6.

Accommodation

Base Hot Rock Rotorua

This is an older property that Base took over, and so it doesn't have the same level of cleanliness and maintenance of some of the purpose-built Base hostels. But it does have good facilities, including a nice geothermal-heated outdoor swimming pool and a pair of indoor spa pools. Like most Base hostels, there's a party-oriented vibe – the attached and newly rebuilt Lava Bar is definitely one of the busiest backpacker boozing spots in town. Rooms are generally clean, and all come with a balcony or outdoor sitting area. Base Hot Rock is right across the road from Kuirau Park, so you've got easy access to some free geothermal action as well.
1286 Arawa Street, Rotorua
🚌 *all Cityride routes*
☎ *(07) 347 9469 or 0800 227 369 (0800 BASE NZ)*
Website *www.stayatbase.com*
Dorm bed *$26-$28;* ***double/twin room*** *$70*
Credit cards *MC, Visa*
Reception open *7am-8pm*
🚗 TV K L 🏊

Maintenance & cleanliness	★★★
Facilities	★★★
Atmosphere & character	★★★½
Security	★★½
Overall rating	★★★

Base Rotorua

This Base hostel is in the city centre and is clean and well-looked after, sharing a building with a climbing wall and cinema. The kitchen is small but very nicely appointed, and a common room looks directly out onto the climbing wall. The familiar Base red colour scheme is apparent, as are its Sanctuary girls-only dorm rooms featuring fluffy towels and bath products. Beds are fully made-up, and some of the dorm rooms have big windows over the city below. It's a nice enough place, if a bit on the sterile side. One quirk is that there are ramps between floors instead of stairs; apparently the building used to be a shopping centre.
1140 Hinemoa Street, Rotorua
🚌 *all Cityride routes*
☎ *(07) 350 2040 or 0800 227 369*
Website *www.stayatbase.com*
Dorm bed *$26-$28; double room $70*
Credit cards *Amex, JCB, MC, Visa*
Reception open *7.30am-7.30pm daily*
TV K L 🚭

Maintenance & cleanliness	★★★★
Facilities	★★
Atmosphere & character	★★½
Security	★★★
Overall rating	★★★

Blarneys Rock

Blarneys Rock is a small, 40-bed hostel in the city centre next door to a large Irish pub. There are several internet PCs and a small reception area on the ground floor; the accommodation and facilities – a cosy TV lounge, a small kitchen and dining area – are upstairs. Rooms are named for Irish towns, and there's a leprechaun-and-shamrocks theme to the painted walls. Blarneys Rock doesn't compete in terms of facilities with most of the Rotorua hostels, though it does have a friendly, personal touch to it that some might enjoy.

1210 Tutanekai Street, Rotorua
all Cityride routes
(07) 343 7904
***Website** www.blarneysrock.com*
***Dorm bed** $21-$24 ($18-$21); **double room** $52 ($46 BBH)*
***Credit cards** MC, Visa*
***Reception open** 8.30am-8.30pm daily*

Maintenance & cleanliness	★★★
Facilities	★½
Atmosphere & character	★★½
Security	★★
Overall rating	★★½

Cactus Jacks

Cactus Jacks is easy enough to spot – just look for the cacti growing out front and the giant gun-toting bandito on the wall. The theme carries on inside – most rooms are set around a courtyard that's done up to look like a Wild West town, in a sort of Disney-meets-Deadwood vibe. Rooms are given different names and façades – the all-guys dorm is done up like the town jail; the all-girls room is called "Madame Fifi's", and so on. Looking for the toilet? It's in the "Shit House". It's a fun and different concept. The dorm is a bit old and tired, however, and it seems like a lot of buckaroos have passed through over the years. Facilities include a big TV lounge and a good-sized kitchen as well as the requisite spa pool.

1210 Haupapa Street, Rotorua
all Cityride routes
(07) 348 3121 or (0800) 122 228
***Website** www.cactusjackbackpackers.co.nz*
***Dorm bed** $22 ($20 BBH); **single room** $37 ($35 BBH); **double room** $55 ($50 BBH); **twin room** $50 ($45 BBH)*
***Credit cards** MC, Visa*
***Reception open** 8am-8pm daily*

Maintenance & cleanliness	★★
Facilities	★★½
Atmosphere & character	★★★★
Security	★★
Overall rating	★★½

Crash Palace Backpackers

Crash Palace is an old building that could stand some renovation, but it has a friendly, quirky vibe. The courtyard is a nice place to hang out, with old furniture and picnic tables set among the barbecue and spa pool (a pet rabbit lives here too). Basic dorm rooms range from four beds to ten. Internet and Wi-Fi are available and there's also a TV lounge with second-hand furniture. A small bar behind reception serves up cheap drinks to thirsty travellers. Secure off-street parking is a nice plus, especially in the centre of town.

1271 Hinemaru Street, Rotorua
all Cityride routes
(07) 348 8842
***Website** www.qsb.co.nz*
***Dorm bed** $20-$22 ($19-$21 BBH, HI/YHA, ISIC, VIP); **single room** $45 ($44 BBH, HI/YHA, ISIC, VIP); **double room** $55-$75 ($53-$73 BBH, HI/YHA, ISIC, VIP)*
***Credit cards** MC, Visa*
***Reception open** 7.30am-8pm daily*

Maintenance & cleanliness	★★½
Facilities	★★½
Atmosphere & character	★★½
Security	★★
Overall rating	★★½

Funky Green Voyager

Funky Green Voyager is a cool, friendly hostel on a quiet street. It's been around for a while but is very clean and well maintained. Facilities include a great kitchen and a sunny common room with lots of books (and no TV). The walls are covered with photos, art and framed articles. Outside is a nice big yard with a barbecue, picnic tables and a separate smokers' gazebo. A second building across the road houses a few

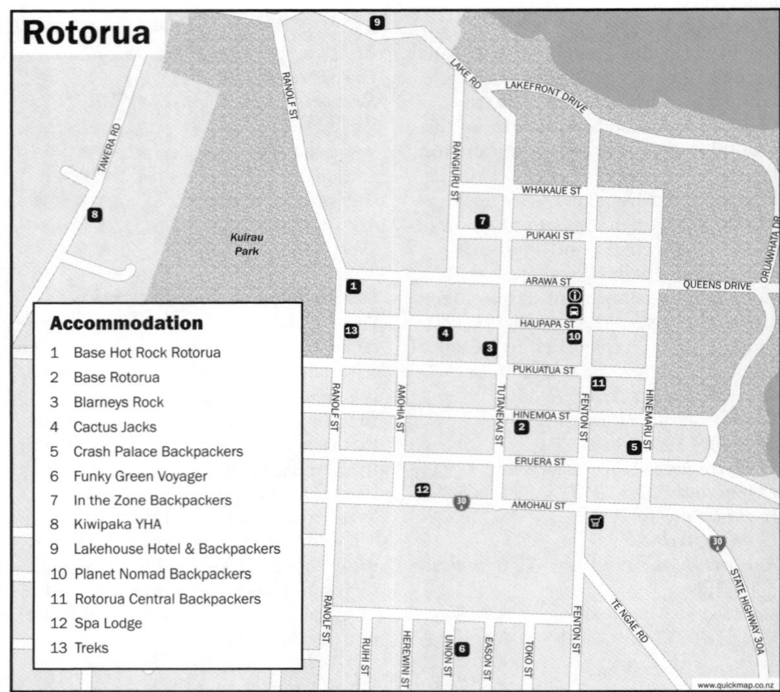

internet PCs and more dorm rooms, as well as another kitchen and common room – it's not as atmospheric as the original house but is quiet and has its own charm. The 'green' in the name refers to the colour of the house, but this is also an environmentally-friendly hostel, with loads of recycling and composting bins. Rooms are clean and comfortable, and there's just an overall great vibe here. The owners are fun to talk to and great sources of local information.

4 Union Street, Rotorua
(07) 346 1754
Website *www.funkygreenvoyager.com*
Dorm bed *$22-$23 ($19-$20 BBH);* ***double room*** *$51-$59 ($45-$53);* ***twin room*** *$49-$51 ($43-$47 BBH)*
Credit cards *MC, Visa*
Reception open *8am-11pm daily*
TV K L

Maintenance & cleanliness	★★★★★
Facilities	★★
Atmosphere & character	★★★★★
Security	★★
Overall rating	★★★★

In the Zone Backpackers

In the Zone is a very clean, recently renovated hostel right around the corner from Tutanekai Street, Rotorua's main dining area. The dorm rooms (all four-bed) are comfortable and roomy, with nice innerspring mattresses. There's a small common room with a TV and leather couches and bean bags, and a smaller kitchen/dining area. A little outdoor patio has a barbecue. There is also a pair of individual mineral pools. Bathrooms are particularly sleek and well-appointed, with the nice touch of automatic lights – on when you walk in. The main thing missing is a sense of atmosphere; small common areas would seem to limit social interaction, and there's not a particularly friendly vibe to the place.

1181 Pukaki Street, Rotorua
all Cityride routes
(07) 348 3338
Website *www.inthezonebackpackers.co.nz*
Dorm bed *$25*
Credit cards *MC, Visa*
Reception open *8am-6pm daily*

Maintenance & cleanliness	★★★★½
Facilities	★★½
Atmosphere & character	★★
Security	★★
Overall rating	★★★

Kiwipaka YHA

This YHA-associate hostel is set on large grounds on the other side of Kuirai Park from the centre of town. Accommodation ranges from tent and campervan sites to lodge dorms and private chalets. Rooms were reasonably clean but had clearly seen some wear and tear, as have most of the facilities. There's a big thermal pool on site, as well as a café and bar. Kitchen facilities were large but not fully equipped; there are barbecues available, but they cost 50c to use. Many large school groups and backpacker buses come through, and it has something of a holiday camp feel to it.

60 Tarewa Road, Rotorua
5
(07) 347 0931
Website *www.kiwipaka-yha.co.nz*
Dorm bed *$25;* ***single room*** *$42;* ***double/twin room*** *$58-$70;* ***camping*** *$9 per person*
Credit cards *MC, Visa*
Reception open *7.30am-9.30pm daily*

Maintenance & cleanliness	★★★½
Facilities	★★★
Atmosphere & character	★★★½
Security	★½
Overall rating	★★★½

Lakehouse Hotel & Backpackers

This big old hotel is set right on Lake Rotorua and clearly has history, but it makes for a very strange hostel. The house is massive and sprawling with a kind of spooky and deserted feeling. The bar downstairs has a local, rough-and-ready vibe to it. Dorm accommodation is in three- or four-share rooms with single beds and bedspreads straight out of the 1960s. There are limited kitchen facilities and a few internet PCs for use. On the plus side, a big veranda out back has terrific views of the lake; otherwise, it's tough to shake the odd vibe of the place.

37-45 Lake Road, Rotorua
6
(07) 348 5585
Dorm bed *$22-$25;* ***single room*** *$36;* ***double room*** *$58;* ***twin room*** *$56*
Credit cards *Amex, MC, Visa*

Maintenance & cleanliness	★½
Facilities	★★
Atmosphere & character	★
Security	★½
Overall rating	★½

Little Village Backpackers

This is a dark, strange and dispiriting place right near the entrance to the Whakarewarewa thermal village. There's more of a doss house feel here than an ordinary hostel, and the entire place feels neglected. It's set around a small courtyard full of plants and little cacti. There's a small balcony out front, internet access on a single PC and free bikes for guests to use. But the only possible reason to stay here would have to be the price, or if everywhere else in town was full.

15 Tryon Street, Rotorua
2
(07) 348 3305
Dorm bed *$15-$18;* ***single room*** *$20;* ***double room*** *$50-$55*
Reception open *9am-9pm daily*

Maintenance & cleanliness	-
Facilities	★½
Atmosphere & character	-
Security	★
Overall rating	½

Lyons Lakestay

Lyons Lakestay, is a small eight-bed house located across the road from Lake Okareka, about 12km from Rotorua city centre. It's a peaceful and very well-maintained place, with much more of a home stay or bed and breakfast feel than a hostel. Rooms are cosy and nicely appointed. The small kitchen and sitting room are pleasant, and there's a lovely garden out front with organic produce; the owners are very eco-conscious and into promoting sustainable tourism. This makes an interesting alternative to staying right in Rotorua; for one thing, the (in)famous sulphur smell doesn't make it out here. There

are lots of walking and biking trails around and lake activities on Okareka and other nearby lakes. Lyons Lakestay provides free pick-up from town.
8 Okareka Loop Road, Lake Okareka
(07) 362 8790 or 0800 258 996
Website *www.lakestayrotorua.co.nz*
Dorm bed *$26-$30;* ***single room*** *$50-$60;* ***double/twin room*** *$75-$85*
K L

Maintenance & cleanliness	★★★★
Facilities	★½
Atmosphere & character	★★★★
Security	★★
Overall rating	★★★

Planet Nomad Backpackers

Right down the street from the information centre, Planet Nomad is a no-frills, urban-feel hostel. It's short on facilities compared with many of its Rotorua neighbours; with a simple kitchen, a TV lounge with mismatched furnishings, and a small smokers' courtyard with barbecue. A few coin-operated internet PCs round out the offerings. It doesn't look like it's been renovated in a while, but colourfully-painted walls and doors give a bit of cheer to the place.
1193 Fenton Street, Rotorua
all Cityride routes
(07) 346 2831
Website *www.planetnomad.co.nz*
Dorm bed *$22-$23;* ***single room*** *$45;* ***double/twin room*** *$50*
Credit cards *MC, Visa*
Reception open *8am-8pm daily*
TV K L

Maintenance & cleanliness	★★½
Facilities	★½
Atmosphere & character	★★
Security	★★★
Overall rating	★★

Rotorua Central Backpackers

This row of flats from 1936 makes for a comfortable, well-located Rotorua hostel. The exterior is a dull, grey colour but it is warmer indoors with pastel walls and some nice old period fixtures and detailing still remaining. Dorms all feature single beds with real mattresses – no bunks – and double rooms have massive, king-sized slabs for beds. The facilities are a bit rambling, as they're spread over six former flats. There's a reading lounge with internet access and a very nice sunny sitting room. A separate TV lounge is comfortable as well. The concrete courtyard has a barbecue and, like many Rotorua hostels, there's a geothermal spa pool. Off-street parking is available.
1076 Pukuatua Street, Rotorua
all Cityride routes
(07) 349 3285
Dorm bed *$22-$25 ($18-$21 BBH);* ***double/twin room*** *$52 ($44 BBH)*
Credit cards *MC, Visa*
Reception open *8am-7pm daily*
TV K L

Maintenance & cleanliness	★★★
Facilities	★★½
Atmosphere & character	★★★
Security	★½
Overall rating	★★★

Spa Lodge

Occupying a pair of houses on Amohau Street, Spa Lodge is one of the smaller hostels in Rotorua, with 42 beds. The houses are old and badly in need of an exterior paint job. Things are in somewhat tidier shape on the inside, but the hostel is still generally quite worn. There is a geothermal-heated pool in the paved courtyard and there are two kitchens, a small TV room and a lounge with a few coin-operated internet PCs. A backpacker-scrawled wall near the entrance makes for some fairly interesting reading. Seagulls like to congregate on the roof of the shopping centre across the road and make a racket at dusk.
1221 Amohau Street, Rotorua
all Cityride routes
(07) 348 3486
Website *www.spalodge.co.nz*
Dorm bed *$20-$21 ($17-$18 BBH);* ***single room*** *$33 ($30 BBH);* ***double room*** *$46-$50 ($40-$44 BBH);* ***twin room*** *$42-$48 ($36-$42 BBH)*
Credit cards *MC, Visa*
Reception open *7.30am-10pm daily*
TV K L

Maintenance & cleanliness	★★
Facilities	★★
Atmosphere & character	★★
Security	★★
Overall rating	★★

Treks

Treks is a purpose-built hostel that offers a very high standard of accommodation. The exterior is a reddish-brown corrugated metal, and the interior common spaces are airy, open and very clean. A big spacious lounge features nice leather couches and beanbags. There's a large kitchen and cafeteria-like dining area, as well as an outdoor deck with a barbecue. Rooms feature clean, made-up single beds – no bunks. Treks is right across the street from Kuirai Park, full of free-to-visit geothermal pools. Heaps of off-street parking is available in a separate lot. Treks is not dripping with atmosphere, but it's about as crisp and clean of a hostel as you'll find in Rotorua.

1278 Haupapa Street, Rotorua
all Cityride routes
(07) 349 4088 or (0508) 487 357
***Website** www.treks.co.nz*
***Dorm bed** $27 ($26 BBH, HI/YHA, VIP); **double room** $64-$74 ($62-$72 BBH, HI/YHA, VIP); **twin room** $74 ($72 BBH, HI/YHA, VIP)*
***Credit cards** MC, Visa*
***Reception open** 7.30am-7.30pm daily*

Maintenance & cleanliness	★★★★★
Facilities	★★★½
Atmosphere & character	★★★
Security	★★★★½
Overall rating	★★★★

Eating & Drinking

Rotorua's dining and nightlife scene has something for everyone, befitting Rotorua's status as one of New Zealand's major tourist destinations. Choices range from fine dining and cafés to takeaways and fast food. There's Thai, Indian, Middle Eastern, several Japanese places, Italian, Chinese and more. Restaurants and bars are spread all over the centre of town, but the main stretch of places to eat is along Tutenakai Street.

Popular cafés among the backpacker set are **Zippy Central** *(1153 Pukuatua Street, Rotorua)* and **Fat Dog Café** *(1161 Arawa Street, Rotorua)*. Both are cool, laid-back and not too expensive. Fast food chains can be found around town; a few are clustered on Fenton Street.

There's a good choice of supermarkets in Rotorua including **Countdown** *(246 Fenton Street, Rotorua)*, **New World** *(247 Old Taupo Road, Rotorua)*, **Pak'n Save** *(corner Fenton & Amohau Streets, Rotorua)* and a massive **Woolworths** supermarket *(Rotorua Central Mall, Victoria Street, Rotorua)*. An Asian specialty supermarket, purportedly the largest in the Bay of Plenty, can be found on Hinemoa Street.

As for nightlife, there are a few good places around. The **Pig and Whistle** *(corner Haupapa & Tutanekai Streets, Rotorua)* is a popular and well-known British pub with food, their own microbrew beer, and live bands. **The Shed** *(1166 Amohau Street, Rotorua)* is another popular watering hole with pool tables and sport on TV screens. Probably the liveliest backpacker nightspot is the recently-renovated **Lava Bar** *(1286 Arawa Street, Rotorua)*, part of the Base Hot Rock hostel.

Sights

Agrodome

This popular agricultural theme park features live sheep shows where you can watch sheep shearing demonstrations, sheep auctions and sheep dog trials. There's also the opportunity to milk a cow on stage. The whole show is pretty touristy and doesn't appeal much to backpackers, but the Agrodome is also home to several more backpacker-focused activities that include bungy jumping, jet boating, swoop ride and zorbing (details of these are in the following Activities section).

Western Road, Ngongotaha
1
(07) 357 1050
***Website** www.agrodome.co.nz*
***Admission** $24-46*
***Shows** 9.30am, 11am, 2.30pm daily*

The Blue Baths

Established in the 1930s, the Blue Baths is New Zealand's first unisex swimming pool and is still one of the most elegant. It houses a museum with displays detailing the pool's history.

Government Gardens, Rotorua
(07) 350 2119

Website *www.bluebaths.co.nz*
Museum admission *$11 (includes admission to Rotorua Museum)*
Museum open *10am-5pm daily*
Pool admission *$9*
Pool open *Mon-Thu 10am-7pm, Fri-Sun 10am-8pm*

Buried Village of Te Wairoa

In June 1886, Mount Tarawera erupted and destroyed Te Wairoa and two smaller villages under a flood of hot ash and mud. New Zealand's equivalent of Pompeii features excavated village dwellings and a museum detailing the events surrounding Tarawera's eruption.
Tarawera Road, Te Wairoa
☎ *(07) 362 8287*
Website *www.buriedvillage.co.nz*
Admission *$26*
Open *Jan-Mar 8.30am-5.30pm daily; Apr-Oct 9am-4.30pm daily; Nov-Dec 8.30am-5.30pm daily*

Hells Gate

This huge 10ha site is home to a large array of geothermal features including boiling mud pools, New Zealand's only accessible mud volcano and the Kakahi Falls – the largest hot waterfall in the Southern Hemisphere. The complex also includes mud baths and a sulphur spa.
State Highway 30, 15km west of Rotorua
☎ *(07) 345 3151*
Website *www.hellsgate.co.nz*
Admission *$25; $35 including sulphur spa*
Open *9am-8.30pm daily*

Paradise Valley Springs

This animal park has lots of trout as well as New Zealand wildlife and a lion enclosure.
Paradise Valley Road, Rotorua
☎ *(07) 348 9667*
Website *www.paradisev.co.nz*
Admission *$25*
Open *8am-6pm daily (last entry 5pm)*

Rainbow Springs

This animal park features sheep shearing and sheep dog shows plus trout feeding and native New Zealand wildlife including kiwis and tuatara.
Fairy Springs Road, Rotorua
🚌 *1*
☎ *(07) 350 0440*
Website *www.rainbownz.co.nz*
Admission *$24.50*
Open *8am-9.30pm daily*

Rotorua Museum

This excellent museum describes the culture, environment and history of Rotorua. It gives you a better understanding of the city making it an excellent place to start before tackling other attractions.
Government Gardens, Rotorua
☎ *(07) 349 4350*
Website *www.rotoruamuseum.co.nz*
Admission *$11*
Open *Jan-Mar 9.30am-6pm daily; Apr-Sep 9.30am-5pm daily; Oct-Dec 9.30am-6pm daily*

Wai-O-Tapu Thermal Wonderland

This geothermal reserve, 30km south of Rotorua, is home to an impressive array of thermal wonders including volcanic craters and bubbling mud pools but the highlights are the huge Champagne Pool and Lady Knox Geyser, which erupts daily at 10.15am.
State Highway 5, 30km south of Rotorua
☎ *(07) 366 6333*
Website *www.geyserland.co.nz*
Admission *$27.50*
Open *8.30am-5pm daily (last entry 3.45pm)*

Waimangu Volcanic Valley

Waimangu was created on 10 June 1886 by the eruption of Mt Tarawera, making it a relative baby compared with other thermal areas. It features Echo Crater, the world's larges hot water spring, and Inferno Crater, the world's largest geyser-like feature. The park has several walkways and you can also take a boat cruise on Lake Rotomahana.
Waimangu Road, 20km south of Rotorua
☎ *(07) 366 6137*
Website *www.waimangu.co.nz*
Admission *$30 walking tour; $37.50 boat cruise; $67.50 boat cruise and walking tour*
Open *Jan 8.30am-6pm daily (last entry*

4.45pm); Feb-Dec 8.30am-5pm daily (last entry 3.45pm)

Whakarewarewa Thermal Village

Whakarewarewa combines a geothermal reserve with an authentic Māori village. Thermal features include boiling mud pools, silica terraces, a steaming hot lake and the Pohutu and Prince of Wales geysers. At the village you can see demonstrations of Māori craftspeople at work and twice daily cultural performances.

Sala Street, Whakarewarewa, Rotorua
🚌 *2*
☎ *(07) 349 3463*
Website *www.whakarewarewa.com*
Admission *$25*
Open *8.30am-5pm daily; guided tours 9.30am, 10.30am, 11.45am, 12.30pm, 1.30pm, 3.30pm; cultural performances 11.15am, 2pm; hangi meals noon, 2.30pm*

Activities

AgroJet

This exciting jet boat ride at the Agrodome claims to be New Zealand's fastest, reaching 100km/h in 4.5 seconds.

Agrodome, Western Road, Ngongotaha
🚌 *1*
☎ *(07) 357 2929*
Website *www.agrojet.co.nz*
Price *$45*
Open *9am-5pm daily*

Bungee Jumping

Rotorua Bungy operates bungee jumps from a purpose-built 43m-high tower at the Agrodome complex.

Agrodome, Western Road, Ngongotaha
🚌 *1*
☎ *(07) 357 4747*
Website *www.rotoruabungy.co.nz*
Price *$90*

Four Wheel Driving

Off Road NZ offer a range of activities that include a 4WD Bush Safari where you drive small 4WDs through a muddy course and a Monster 4WD Thrill Ride where you come along for the ride in an expertly driven specially modified vehicle.

Amoore Road, Rotorua
☎ *(07) 332 5748*
Website *www.offroadnz.co.nz*
4WD Bush Safari $85; Monster 4WD Thrill Ride $40

Freefall Xtreme

This is the only skydive simulator in the southern hemisphere. It involves leaping into a 150km/h column of wind that is generated by a DC3 aircraft engine. There's a safety net to prevent you from falling into the engine plus a 12m wide air cushion.

Agrodome, Western Road, Ngongotaha
🚌 *1*
☎ *(07) 357 5856*
Website *www.freefallxtreme.com*
Price *$49-79*

Shweeb

Shweeb is a suspended monorail that you pedal like a bicycle. The Shweeb track near the Agrodome consists of two 200m-long overhead rails with suspended pedal-powered pods. The aerodynamic design of the pods mean that you can reach speeds of 45 km/h and it is possible to race, as there are two parallel rails.

Paradise Valley Road (500m off State Highway 5), Ngongotaha
🚌 *1*
☎ *(07) 357 5856*
Website *www.shweeb.com*
Shweeb ride *$45*
Open *9am-5pm*

Skyline Skyrides (Gondola & Luge)

This complex, south of the town centre, features gondola and luge rides. The gondola is aimed mostly at older tourists, but the luge is a cheap and fun activity for many backpackers. There is 5km of luge track including a 1km advanced track for thrill seekers.

Fairy Springs Road, Rotorua
🚌 *1*
☎ *(07) 347 0027*
Website *www.skylineskyrides.co.nz*
Gondola Ride *$24;* ***luge ride*** *$9;* ***five luge rides*** *$30;* ***gondola ride & five luge rides*** *$45*

Swoop Ride

This ride at the Agrodome involves up to three people being hoisted in

sleeping bag-like harnesses 40m above the ground and then falling at 130kmh as you swoop above the ground.
Agrodome, Western Road, Ngongotaha
🚌 *1*
☎ *(07) 357 4747*
Website *www.rotoruabungy.co.nz*
Price *$45*

White Water Rafting

Several companies offer white water rafting trips around Rotorua with the Kaituna, Rangitaiki and Wairoa Rivers being the most popular. The Rangitaki boasts grade 4 rapids and is perhaps the most scenic option, but the Wairoa and especially the Kaituna River offers grade 5 rapids with more excitement. The Kaituna River features the legendary Tutea Falls with its massive seven-metre drop, which is claimed to be the world's highest commercially rafted waterfall.

Rafting trips cost $89 on the Kaituna River, $110 on the Rangitaiki River and $99 on the Wairoa River.

The main rafting companies operating in Rotorua are **Kaitiaki Adventures** *(☎ (07) 357 2236;* ***website*** *www.kaitiaki.co.nz)*, **Raftabout** *(☎ (07) 343 9500 or 0800 RAFTABOUT (0800 723 822);* ***website*** *www.raftabout.co.nz)*, **River Rats** *(☎ (07) 345 6543 or 0800 333 900;* ***website*** *www.riverrats.co.nz)*, **Wet 'n' Wild Rafting** *(☎ (07) 348 3191 or 0800 462 7238;* ***website*** *www.wetnwildrafting.co.nz)* and **Whitewater Excitement** *(☎ (07) 345 7182 or* ***website*** *www.raftnz.co.nz)*.

White Water Sledging (Hydrospeed)

White water sledging, or hydrospeed, involves riding a custom-designed river sledge through rapids. Hydrospeed puts you in control, as opposed to rafting where the guide does the steering.

Kaitiaki Adventures *(☎ (07) 357 2236 or 0800 338 736;* ***website*** *www.kaitiaki.co.nz)* and **Sledgeabout** *(☎ (07) 343 9500;* ***website*** *www.raftabout.co.nz)* run white water sledging (hydrospeed) trips on the Kaituna River. A 3½ hour trip on Kaituna River costs $99. Kaitiaki Adventures also run eight hour trips on the Rangitaiki River that cost $149.

Zorbing

This unique activity was invented in Rotorua and involves rolling down a hill inside a big inflatable ball. There's the option of a wet zorb, where a bucket of water is tossed into the zorb before rolling down the hill.
Agrodome, Western Road, Ngongotaha
🚌 *1*
☎ *(07) 357 5100 or 0800 227 474*
Website *www.zorb.com*
Price *$59*

Gisborne & East Cape

New Zealand's remote East Cape is one of the first places in the world to see the sun rise. It is one of the country's least visited places and it offers a spectacular rugged coastline and is a great place for travellers who want to get off the beaten track.

Must do in Gisborne & East Cape

- Watch the sunrise at East Cape
- Hike the Lake Waikaremoana Track

Gisborne

Gisborne is the main centre of the Eastland region, and boasts of being the first place in the world to see the sun each day, thanks to its proximity to the International Date Line. With around 33,000 residents, it's a rural town wrapped in increasingly cosmopolitan and affluent packaging. Gisborne calls itself the Chardonnay capital of New Zealand, and there are numerous boutique vineyards in the region, as well as a restaurant culture in the heart of the palm-tree lined city.

Gisborne has one of the sunniest climates in New Zealand and there are some good beaches nearby. Kaiti Beach was the site of Captain Cook's first landing in New Zealand, an event memorialised by statues of both Cook and his cabin boy Nick Young, who was the first crew member to spot land.

As in most of the East Cape, there is a strong Māori presence around Gisborne.

If you're on your way to travel around the East Cape, this is a good place to stock up on cash, fuel and supplies, and maybe a good meal in a fine restaurant; Gisborne is the most developed city you'll see for a while.

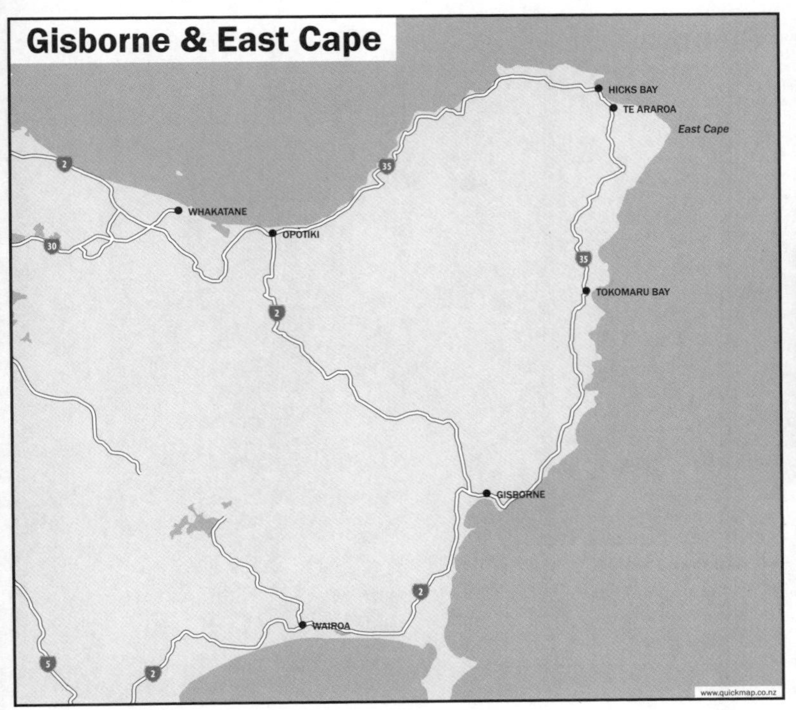

Gisborne & East Cape

Practical Information

Gisborne i-SITE Visitor Centre

209 Grey Street, Gisborne
☎ *(06) 868 6139*
Website *www.gisbornenz.com*
Open *Mon-Fri 8.30am-5.30pm, Sat-Sun 10am-5pm*

Department of Conservation

63 Carnarvon Street, Gisborne
☎ *(06) 869 0460*
Open *Mon-Fri 8am-4.30pm*

Coming & Going

InterCity Coachlines *(☎ (09) 623 1503; **website** www.intercity.co.nz)* go to Hawkes Bay, Opotiki and Whakatane, and Naked Bus *(☎ 0900 62533; **website** www.nakedbus.com)* goes to Auckland via Opotiki and Rotorua. Buses stop at the Gisborne i-SITE Visitor Centre *(209 Grey Street, Gisborne)*.

Accommodation

Flying Nun Backpackers

Flying Nun Backpackers has a unique setting – it's an old convent transformed into a hostel. If that doesn't give you nightmares, then there's plenty of character in the old building (as well as some benign black-and-white ghosts, allegedly). It's pretty well kept and has lots of great original details, though it's a bit rough around the edges in places. Facilities include a big kitchen and a common room inside, and a back patio with a barbecue. There are also a few caravans outside – two are TV rooms (one for smokers) and the other is a games room with a pool table and table tennis. There is free internet access (including Wi-Fi), which is very rare in New Zealand, and there are lockers for every bed. An historical footnote: the legendary Dame Kiri Te Kanawa received her first singing lessons from the nuns here.
147 Roebuck Road, Gisborne
☎ *(06) 868 0461*
Website *www.flynun.co.nz*
Dorm bed *\$21-\$23 (\$18-\$20 BBH);* ***single room*** *\$33 (\$30 BBH);* ***double/twin room*** *\$52 (\$46 BBH)*
Reception open *8am-8pm daily*
TV K L

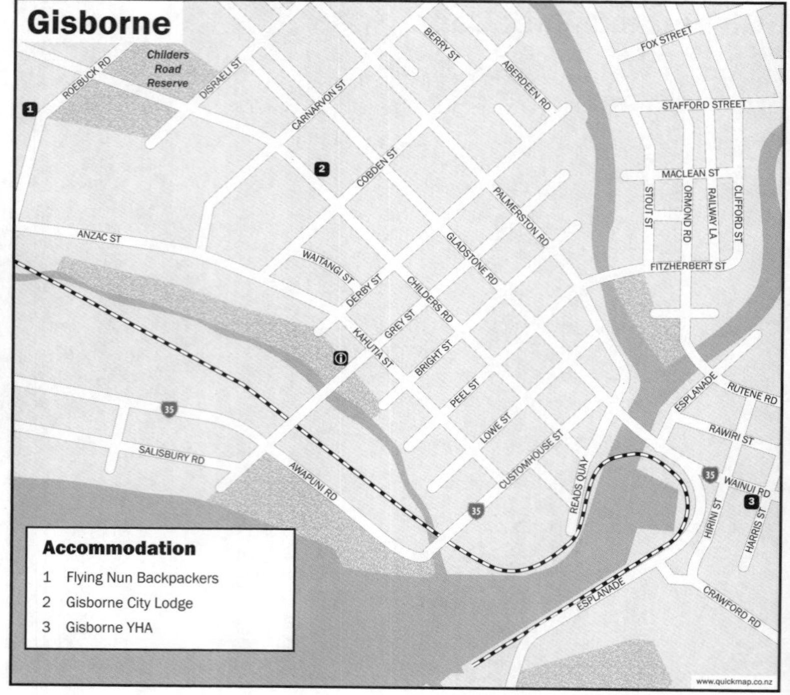

Maintenance & cleanliness	★★★
Facilities	★★½
Atmosphere & character	★★★★½
Security	★★★
Overall rating	★★★

Gisborne City Lodge

Gisborne City Lodge is an old doss house that has recently started doing business as a hostel, but it hasn't done much to change its dreary atmosphere. There are still a number of long-term residents here, and furnishings are old and mismatched, if kept reasonably clean. There's a small kitchen and a TV lounge, as well as a backyard with some ratty furniture and a cabin (the nicest place on the premises). Only stay here if you're desperate.

335 Childers Road, Gisborne
☎ *0800 999 004*
***Dorm bed** $20; **double/twin room** $50*

Maintenance & cleanliness	★½
Facilities	★
Atmosphere & character	½
Security	★½
Overall rating	★

Gisborne YHA

The Gisborne YHA is a big peach-coloured house and separate cottage close to Kaiti Hill, about a 10-minute walk to the information centre. It's set on large grounds with lots of outdoor space for hanging out. There's a standard kitchen and a TV lounge. Things are pretty clean and well-maintained, though some of the furnishings are older. Bikes and wetsuits are available for hire.

32 Harris Street, Gisborne
☎ *(06) 867 3269*
***Website** www.stayyha.co.nz*
***Dorm bed** $24-$26 ($21-$23 YHA); **double/twin room** $56 ($50 YHA)*
***Reception open** 7am-10pm daily*

Maintenance & cleanliness	★★½
Facilities	★★
Atmosphere & character	★★★
Security	★½
Overall rating	★★½

Eating & Drinking

Gladstone Road is the main commercial strip of "Gizzy", and it has numerous fast food, Asian, and takeaway joints, as well as cafés and restaurants. **Captain Morgan's** *(285 Grey Street, Gisborne)* near Waikanae Beach is well-known for its burgers and ice cream. **Smash Palace Wine Bar** *(24 Banks Street, Gisborne)* is a wacky memorabilia-filled bar serving beer, wine and pizza, with a DC3 aeroplane on the roof and live music.

Upscale dining and drinking has sprung up all over Gisborne, with some particularly nice places along the waterfront by the wharf. If you're in the mood to splurge after a trip through the East Cape, this is the place to do it.

The **Pak'n Save** supermarket *(Childers Road, Gisborne)* is a good place to stock up on supplies before heading up through the East Cape.

Sights

Tairawhiti Museum

This excellent museum complex features exhibits on local history with a fine collection of Māori artefacts. The maritime exhibits include displays of shipwrecks including the bridge house of the *Star of Canada*, which ran aground on Kaiti Beach in 1912. It also has an exhibit of historic surfboards.

10 Stout Street, Gisborne
☎ *(06) 867 3832*
***Website** www.tairawhitimuseum.org.nz*
***Admission** $5*
***Open** Mon-Sat 10am-4pm, Sun 1.30pm-4pm*

East Cape

The East Cape is one of the most strikingly beautiful, rugged, and untouristed areas of the North Island. A drive along the Pacific Coast Highway (State Highway 35) reveals one awesome vista after another along a landscape of crooked pohutukawa trees, craggy cliffs, coastal toitoi plants, beaches, forests, mountains and endless sea.

As captivating as the landscape is, it is the people who make the East Cape even more special. The Māori presence here is stronger than anywhere else in

New Zealand; and not in the Rotorua-performance way, but as an everyday living culture. Marae and wharenui (meeting houses) dot the countryside and opportunities abound for cultural interaction in real Māori communities. The connection between the people and the land here is palpable, and offers a powerful lesson of conservation and respect for nature.

A trip to catch the sunrise at the East Cape lighthouse, the easternmost point of New Zealand is a memorable experience. Gisborne is the main city of the East Cape, a provincial but increasingly cosmopolitan capital at the northern end of Poverty Bay.

Some of the hostels along the East Cape coast can boast the most beautiful settings anywhere on the North Island as well as some of the friendliest and most interesting owners.

This is a laid-back region of fishing and horseback riding, where you will quickly realise things move on "Cape Time". So slow down when you're here, and savour the rewards of this special, off-the-beaten-track corner of New Zealand.

Local Transport

There isn't much local transport around the East Cape and it is best enjoyed at your own pace in a rental car. If you don't have a car; your best option is Kiwi Experience's East As bus, which does a good job of getting you around the cape. East As travels along State Highway 35 from Taupo to Rotorua and around the East Cape.

Accommodation

TOLAGA BAY

This small village is just 45km north of Gisborne, halfway between Gisborne and Tokomaru Bay. It has New Zealand's longest wharf, which is necessary because of its unusually shallow bay.

Tolaga Bay Inn

The Tolaga Inn (formerly Pacificka Backpackers) is a 1932 Tudor-style hotel with a bar and café on premises. It's a large, rambling old house with a TV lounge and balcony upstairs and a decent guest kitchen below (with great smells coming from the attached café/bakery kitchen). There's definite atmosphere here, but the house and furnishings show their age, with worn floor coverings and a generally tired air to the facilities. The bar is one of the more happening spots in this otherwise quiet town.

Corner Solander Street & Cook Street (SH 35), Tolaga Bay
☎ *(06) 862 6856*
Dorm bed *$20;* ***single room*** *$30-$40;* ***double/twin room*** *$50-$60*
Credit cards *MC, Visa*

Maintenance & cleanliness	★★
Facilities	★★
Atmosphere & character	★★★★½
Security	★½
Overall rating	★★★½

TOKOMARU BAY

This small seaside town is most travellers' first (or last) stop on the road around the cape. It is a laid back place with a couple of shops.

Brians Place

Set high up on a hill overlooking Tokomaru Bay, Brian's Place likes to say that it's the first hostel in the world to see the sun rise. We're not geographically astute enough to verify this claim, but a look at the map says it's plausible. In any case, the view is absolutely stellar up here, and the hostel itself is friendly and full of a rough charm. Accommodation includes a downstairs dorm in the main house, as well as a couple of great little two – and three-bed sleeping lofts with sweet views. There are small standalone doubles on the property, as well as space for tents. A nice open kitchen is available for guests and the common/TV room is really cosy and rustic. Brian, the friendly owner, has been at it for a while and knows what he's doing. He can arrange fishing charters, horse treks and will take guests possum hunting in the evenings. It's a lovely place.

21 Potae Street, Tokomaru Bay
☎ *(06) 864 5870*
Website *www.briansplace.co.nz*
Dorm bed *$25 ($22 BBH);* ***double/twin room*** *$56 ($50 BBH);* ***camping*** *$18 ($15 BBH)*

Credit cards *MC, Visa*

TV K L

Maintenance & cleanliness	★★★
Facilities	★★½
Atmosphere & character	★★★★
Security	★
Overall rating	★★★

Footprints in the Sand

Footprints in the Sand is a small hostel right down the road from the beach. It consists of a double room in a home stay and a separate nine-bed dorm in a cottage (another four-bed structure was being built on the site when we visited). There are also camping facilities in the big backyard, which has flowers and fruit trees (lemon and feijoa) growing in it. It's a simple place, but clean, recently renovated and well-maintained. The owner is very friendly and arranges fishing charters as well a traditional Māori flax weaving lessons. Kayaks and bikes are also available for hire.

13 Potae Street, Tokomaru Bay

(06) 864 5858

Website *www.footprintsinthesand.co.nz*

Dorm bed *$20;* ***double room*** *$60;* ***camping*** *$15*

K

Maintenance & cleanliness	★★★½
Facilities	★½
Atmosphere & character	★★★
Security	★
Overall rating	★★½

RANGITUKIA/EAST CAPE

This rural location is the closest you can stay to East Cape, but Te Araroa is a shorter driving distance.

Eastender Backpacker & Horse Treks

Eastender Backpacker is set on a horse and sheep farm, and has a few basic eight-bed bunkhouses and some cabins. The East As bus stops here, and activities are set up to cater to groups of travellers – there are sheep-shearing demonstrations and bone-carving lessons and you can also go horse trekking. The big shearing shed also holds a games room with a pool table and table tennis. There's a basic kitchen and TV room, and an outdoor fireplace and barbecue. It's a rustic place but it's pretty clean and is guaranteed a regular crowd a few times a week thanks to the bus.

836 Rangitukia Road, Rangitukia

(06) 864 3820

Website *www.eastenderbackpackers.co.nz*

Dorm bed *$23 ($20 BBH);* ***camping*** *$10*

TV K

Maintenance & cleanliness	★★
Facilities	★½
Atmosphere & character	★★★½
Security	½
Overall rating	★★

TE ARAROA & HICK'S BAY

Te Araroa is the closest town with direct road access to East Cape and Hick's Bay is just up the road.

Mel's Place

Mel's Place is located on the ancestral pā (Māori village) of owners Marilyn (Mel) and Joe, a gorgeous spot that pokes out into the bay and is bounded by a hillock behind. Facilities are basic, but the views and surroundings are absolutely magnificent. Accommodation is offered in a five-bed dorm with a nice big window, a double room in a caravan and a few tent sites. They've also just built a standalone luxury suite with its own deck. Mel and Joe run a fishing charter and offer cultural tours as well; they're very interesting hosts and good at articulating Māori traditions and their relationship with the land. They practice sustainable fishing, and Mel's Place is totally green, with solar and wind power, recycling, composting etc. There's swimming and snorkelling on calm Onepoto Beach. Also check out the "loo with a view", an outdoor toilet with an eye-level window to take in the scenery. This is a special place in a beautiful spot.

Onepoto Beach Road, Hicks Bay

(06) 864 4694

Website *www.eastcapefishing.co.nz*

Dorm bed *$28 ($25 BBH);* ***double room*** *$72 ($66 BBH)*

K

Maintenance & cleanliness	★★★★
Facilities	★★
Atmosphere & character	★★★★★
Security	½
Overall rating	★★★½

Sunrise Lodge

Sunrise Lodge is the closest hostel to East Cape, about a 45-minute drive to the lighthouse. It's just a basic house, set among tall grass and toitoi plants, with direct access to the beach close by. It sleeps up to eight, with a four bed dorm and a couple of private rooms, and has a small kitchen and TV lounge. It's clean and tidy, but a little frilly and it feels a bit dated. A little deck has very nice views over the beach and ocean; in the winter months the sun rises directly over the horizon, making the view even more spectacular, and giving the Sunrise Lodge a reasonable claim for being the first hostel in the world to see the sun rise.

State Highway 35, Te Araroa
☎ *(06) 864 4854*
Dorm bed *$25;* ***single room*** *$35;* ***double/twin room*** *$70*

Maintenance & cleanliness	★★★
Facilities	★
Atmosphere & character	★★½
Security	★½
Overall rating	★★

WHANARUA BAY

This beautiful seaside setting near the Opotiki end of the coastal highway is home to what may travellers describe as the best situated of the hostels in the East Cape region.

Maraehako Bay Retreat

The Maraehako Bay Retreat bills itself as "absolute sea front accommodation", and it's no exaggeration. If you were any closer to the bay, you'd be underwater. The setting here is absolutely stunning, a secluded paradise hidden among craggy rocks and cliffs and giant pohutukawa trees. The hostel itself is a quirky, owner-built wooden house with tons of idiosyncratic charm; it slopes and slants over multiple levels with lots of decks, and is decorated with nautical flourishes like heavy rigging, fishing nets, and driftwood. The whole place almost doesn't seem real. Accommodation is basic but clean and there are good facilities like an outdoor spa pool with a view, hammocks, a barbecue and free use of kayaks and boogie boards. The Maraehako Bay Retreat simply has to rank as one of the most beautiful locations on the North Island.

State Highway 35, Te Kaha, Whanarua Bay
☎ *(07) 325 2648*
Website *www.maraehako.co.nz*
Dorm bed *$28 ($25 BBH);* ***double room*** *$66 ($60 BBH)*
Reception open *8am-10pm daily*

Maintenance & cleanliness	★★★★
Facilities	★★½
Atmosphere & character	★★★★★
Security	½
Overall rating	★★★½

TE KAHA

This small community near Opotiki has a strong Māori culture and staying at the hostel here is a great way to experience it.

Te Kaha is the first overnight stop if you're starting the East Cape trail in Opotiki.

Te Kaha Homestead Lodge

It's all about good times with a dash of Māori culture in this fun and friendly hostel, which calls itself a traditional whanau (family) home stay. Guests are greeted with a hongi nose-press and sung a welcome song (and are expected to reply with a song of their own!) When the lights go down and the East As bus comes through, the party atmosphere commences. A communal meal is offered and Paul, the host, is great at breaking the ice and getting people to participate in a night of ribald sing-alongs and story-telling. Dorms are simple and clean. Facilities include a TV lounge and kitchen, a small bar, free use of kayaks, and – best of all – a spa pool right on the ocean, with simply spectacular views.

State Highway 35, Te Kaha
☎ *07 325 2194*
Dorm bed *$30;* ***double room*** *$70*

Maintenance & cleanliness	★★★★
Facilities	★★½
Atmosphere & character	★★★★★
Security	★
Overall rating	★★★½

Te Urewera National Park

This remote national park is comprised of a large swathe of rugged wilderness and is home to two beautiful lakes – Lake Waikaremoana and the smaller Lake Waikareiti.

It is the country's fourth largest national park and the largest in the North Island.

The park has several good walking tracks that range from short walks to Lake Waikareiti to the brilliant Lake Waikaremoana Track (see below).

Practical Information

Aniwaniwa Visitor Centre

State Highway 38, Aniwaniwa
☎ *(06) 837 3900*
Open *8am-4.45pm daily*

Coming & Going

Big Bush Holiday Park *(☎ (06) 837 3777; **website** www.lakewaikaremoana.co.nz)* run a shuttle bus to the park from Rotorua and Wairoa. The one-way fare to/from Wairoa is $30.

Local Transport

Big Bush Water Taxi *(☎ (06) 837 3777; **website** www.lakewaikaremoana.co.nz)* run a drop off and pick up service to the trailheads of the Lake Waikaremoana Track.

Hiking

Lake Waikaremoana Track

Lake Waikaremoana Track (48km, 3-5 days) is one of DOC's Great Walks. It is a varied trek through the wilderness surrounding Lake Waikaremoana that allows you to see many of New Zealand's unique birds. The track offers splendid views over the lake.

There are five huts on the track. Each hut costs $25 per night, camp sites are $12, and must be booked in advanced through the Aniwaniwa Visitor Centre *(☎ (06) 837 3900)*.

The track can be hiked in either direction and the last three sections can be combined in one day.

The challenging first section of the track, from Onepoto to Panekiri Hut (8.8km, 5 hours), involves a steep 600m climb to the top of the Panekiri Bluff where you are rewarded by breathtaking views. The track then follows the ridge to Panekiri Hut.

The second day, Panekiri Hut to Waiopaoa Hut (7.6km, 3-4hrs), is mostly downhill through beech and kamahi forest.

The third section of the track passes through kanuka forest by the lakeshore and there is a short detour to the dazzling Korokoro Falls. This section runs between Waiopaoa Hut and Marauiti Hut (12.1km, 4½ hours).

The section from Marauiti Hut to Waiharuru Hut (6.2km, 2 hours) is an easy walk along the lakeshore. The area is home to kiwi and it is common to hear them at night if you're staying at either the Marauiti or Waiharuru Huts.

The stretch between Waiharuru Hut and Whanganui Hut (5.3km, 2½ hours) crosses the neck of the Puketukutuku Peninsula and then follows the lake shore.

The final stretch of the track, from Whanganui Hut to Hopuruahine Bridge (5.2km, 1½hrs), takes in lovely views of the Huiarau Inlet before crossing the Hopuruahine suspension bridge.

Hawkes Bay

This region on the North Island's east coast is the source of much of the country's fresh produce, and for many travellers the region's major attraction is the abundance of casual fruit picking work, particularly around Hastings.

The other main attraction for visitors is the region's architecture. The twin cities of Napier and Hastings were severely damaged by a 1931 earthquake and rebuilt in the latest style of the day – Art Deco – leaving the two cities, particularly Napier, with some of the world's best intact examples of the style. There are several distinctive Spanish Mission buildings as well.

Hawkes Bay is one of New Zealand's major wine producing regions, particularly reds, and food and wine tourism is a big drawcard for the area. There are more than 40 wineries, several farmers' markets, and fine dining options throughout the region. Havelock North is a prosperous country village in the heart of the wine producing region.

The climate here is sunny and dry – tourism officials like to call it "Mediterranean" – and there are good beaches and outdoor activities as well. A gannet colony at Cape Kidnappers is a big hit with bird watchers.

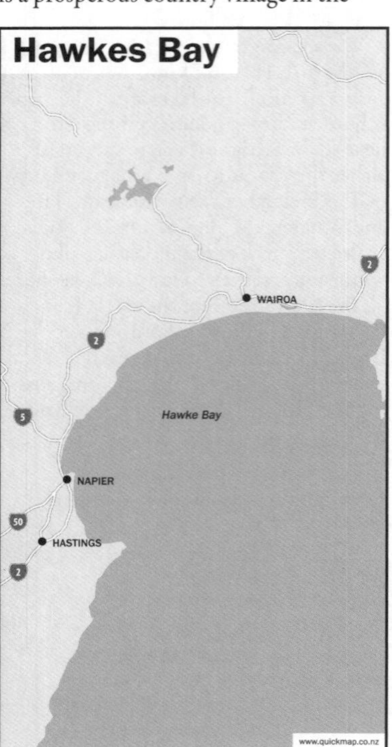

Must do in Hawkes Bay

- Walk around Art Deco Napier
- See the world's largest gannet colony at Cape Kidnappers

Wairoa

This small town in northern Hawkes Bay is the midway point on the drive between Napier and Gisborne. It's set on the banks of the Wairoa River, but there's not much in the way of ambience here, nor much to hold a backpacker's attention. Wairoa is the closest town to Te Urewera National Park and travellers use it as a gateway. Supplies, food and guides for the park are all available here.

Practical Information

Wairoa i-SITE Visitor Centre

Corner State Highway 2 & Queen Street, Wairoa

☎ *(06) 838 7440*

***Website** www.hawkesbaynz.com*

Coming & Going

InterCity Coachlines *(☎ (09) 623 1503; **website** www.intercity.co.nz)* stop in Wairoa en route between Napier and Gisborne. Coaches stop at i-SITE Visitor Centre at the corner State Highway 2 and Queen Street.

Accommodation

Bushdale Farm Backpackers

Bushdale Farm Backpackers is a quaint blue farmhouse set on a horse and sheep farm 15km from Wairoa and 4km off the main road. There are only a couple of rooms inside the

house, and a small kitchen with a wood-burning stove and antique spoon collection. A rustic back patio has a barbecue. Internet access is available in the owner's main house, which also has a swimming pool. Riding lessons and horse treks are offered to guests. This is a very quiet and charming spot.
438 Cricklewood Road, Wairoa
☎ *(06) 838 6453*
Website *www.bushdalefarm.co.nz*
Dorm bed *$30 ($25 BBH);* ***single room*** *$30 ($25 BBH);* ***double/twin room*** *$60 ($50 BBH)*

Maintenance & cleanliness	★★½
Facilities	★★
Atmosphere & character	★★★½
Security	½
Overall rating	★★½

Haere Mai Cottage
There are just six beds and a couple of tent sites at this tiny hostel on the edge of town. It's really a home stay, as facilities are shared with the family (parents and two kids) who live there. Rooms are clean, though furnishings are kind of frilly and old. A log fire, a TV, and board games are on offer in the living room. Internet and Wi-Fi access are available too, though kitchen facilities for guests are limited. If you crave privacy or don't want to mingle with a host family, this is probably not the place for you.
49 Mitchell Road, Wairoa
☎ *(06) 838 6817*
Dorm bed *$25 ($22 BBH);* ***single room*** *$25 ($22 BBH);* ***double room*** *$50 ($44 BBH)*

Maintenance & cleanliness	★★
Facilities	★★
Atmosphere & character	★★½
Security	★
Overall rating	★★

Riverside Motor Camp
Riverside is a motor camp (caravan park) with an eight-bed dorm plus some beds in caravans available to backpackers. There's not much atmosphere here, although rooms and shared facilities are uncommonly clean for a motor camp. The bathroom is spotless, with a frilly little skirt running the length of the stainless steel sink. The kitchen is clean as well, and there's a whimsical barbecue (called the "Barbie Q") set in the boot of a fake old 50's Chevy. Facilities are otherwise pretty limited, and showers are coin-operated, but there aren't many options in Wairoa, so it's worth a look if you find yourself needing a place to stay in town.
19 Marine Parade, Wairoa
☎ *(06) 838 6301*
Dorm bed *$20*
Credit cards *MC, Visa*

Maintenance & cleanliness	★★★½
Facilities	★
Atmosphere & character	★½
Security	★
Overall rating	★★

Napier

Arriving in Napier can feel like walking onto a 1930s film set where any second bootlegging gangsters in town cars are going to come peeling around the corner, tommy guns blazing. The centre of town is a shrine to Art Deco architecture, with some of the best intact examples in the world.

When a 1931 earthquake devastated Napier, the city was rebuilt in the prevailing style of the day. Today, one of the biggest attractions of this cosmopolitan town of nearly 58,000 is the town itself, drawing architecture buffs to admire its Art Deco and Spanish Mission buildings. Every February, the city holds an Art Deco weekend to celebrate its unique heritage.

Many of Napier's Art Deco buildings line Emerson Street; Marine Parade, with its shady Norfolk Island Pines, is home to some more recent tourist attractions. There's a Kiwi House at the northern end of the street, which may be your best chance to see a real live kiwi. Further south along Marine Parade is the Hawkes Bay Museum, and then there's the ever popular Marineland and the Hawkes Bay Aquarium.

Napier has a fairly refined dining and café scene for a small city. The city's cosmopolitan air is reflected in its street names, many of which are British authors: Carlyle, Thackeray, Tennyson, Dickens and Shakespeare.

Practical Information

Napier i-SITE Visitor Centre

100 Marine Parade, Napier
☎ *(06) 834 1911*
Website *www.hawkesbaynz.com*
Open *Mon-Fri 8.30am-5pm, Sat-Sun 9am-5pm*

INTERNET ACCESS

Cybers Internet Café

98 Dickens Street, Napier
☎ *(06) 835 0125*
Website *www.cybers.co.nz*
Open *Mon-Fri 8.30am-midnight, Sat-Sun 9am-midnight*

Esquires Coffee *(**website** www.esquires.co.nz; Emerson Street, Napier)* has free Wi-Fi access.

Coming & Going

InterCity Coachlines *(☎ (09) 623 1503; **website** www.intercity.co.nz)* go to Gisborne, Taupo and Wellington and Naked Bus *(☎ 0900 62533; **website** www.nakedbus.com)* has direct buses to Auckland, Waitomo, Wellington and Whangarei. BayXpress *(☎ 0800 422 997; **website** www.bayxpress.co.nz)* is a good alternative if you're going to Palmerston North or Wellington.

InterCity coaches depart from 85 Munroe Street. BayXpress and Naked Bus depart from outside the i-SITE Visitor Centre *(100 Marine Parade, Napier)*.

Local Transport

The Hawkes Bay area has a good local bus service with most bus routes running every half hour. Most fares in Napier are $2.40 although it costs $4.30 to go to Hastings and and $5.70 to Havelock North.

Accommodation

Aqua Lodge

Aqua Lodge consists of three houses on a residential street a few minutes' walk from the town centre, near the cricket stadium. One of the houses is generally used by long-term guests. Each building has its own kitchen (with dishwasher) and common areas. Cleanliness and maintenance varies throughout the property, but things are generally on the tattered and worn side. There's an outside yard with tables and a barbecue and a swimming pool (which didn't look all that inviting when we visited). Still, there's a friendly and social atmosphere to the place.

53 Nelson Crescent, Napier
🚌 *14*
☎ *(06) 835 4523*
Dorm bed *$24 ($21 BBH);* ***double room*** *$58-$72 ($52-$66 BBH);* ***twin room*** *$58 ($52 BBH);* ***camping*** *$16 ($13 BBH) per person*
Credit cards *MC, Visa*
Reception open *8am-10pm daily*

Maintenance & cleanliness	★★
Facilities	★★½
Atmosphere & character	★★★
Security	★½
Overall rating	★★½

Archies Bunker

If you can forgive the bad pun for a name (or even better, if you don't get the reference to a 1970s US television character), this is a clean and well-maintained hostel right in the centre of Napier. There are a pair of common lounges; a small one downstairs with a piano, and a much larger with a big TV and pool table, along with the usual games and books. A small outdoor deck has a barbecue and a picnic table, and there a couple of kitchens. Internet and Wi-Fi access are available as well. The building doesn't have the great Art Deco façade of some others in Napier, but it dates from that era and has some nice interior spaces.

14 Hershell Street, Napier
🚌 *12, 13, 14*
☎ *(06) 833 7990 or 0800 272 4437 (0800 ARCHIES)*
Website *www.archiesbunker.co.nz*
Dorm bed *$23 ($20 BBH);* ***single room*** *$30-$38;* ***double/twin room*** *$52-$56*
Credit cards *MC, Visa*
Reception open *7.45am-9.30pm daily*

Maintenance & cleanliness	★★★½
Facilities	★★
Atmosphere & character	★★★
Security	★★½
Overall rating	★★★

Bay Booziee Backpackers

Bay Booziee – yes, that's the spelling – is located in Bayview, 8km north of Napier city centre. There's a working-class vibe out here compared to its cosmopolitan city cousin. This is a sprawling place with sites for camper vans and tents, as well as rooms in an older house; most backpacker rooms, however, are five-bed dorms in new pre-fabricated cabins. Bay Booziee is also a massive bar known in the area for its Sunday night pig-on-a-spit roast. The bar has live music, pool tables, pokie machines and horse betting, and it attracts a local crowd. There were about 40 dorm beds when we visited, but we're told it should be up to 100 by the time you read this.

47 Petane Road, Bayview
(06) 836 6007

***Dorm bed** $21 ($18 BBH); **double room** $56 ($50 BBH)*

Maintenance & cleanliness	★★★
Facilities	★★½
Atmosphere & character	★★
Security	★
Overall rating	★★½

Criterion Art Deco Backpackers

Enter this stylish hostel and take a step back in time; it's set in Napier's largest Spanish Mission/Art Deco style building, an old hotel that opened in 1932. The lobby is nicely restored, with big red couches and lots of great period details on display, including great windows and fireplaces. There's also an excellent kitchen, a dining room and a small separate TV lounge. Rooms are good-sized, if a little bit more tired than the common areas. A downstairs bar and café, "The Cri" caters to backpackers, but gets lots of local action as well, and is a lively and popular place right in the centre of town. It is a unique place.

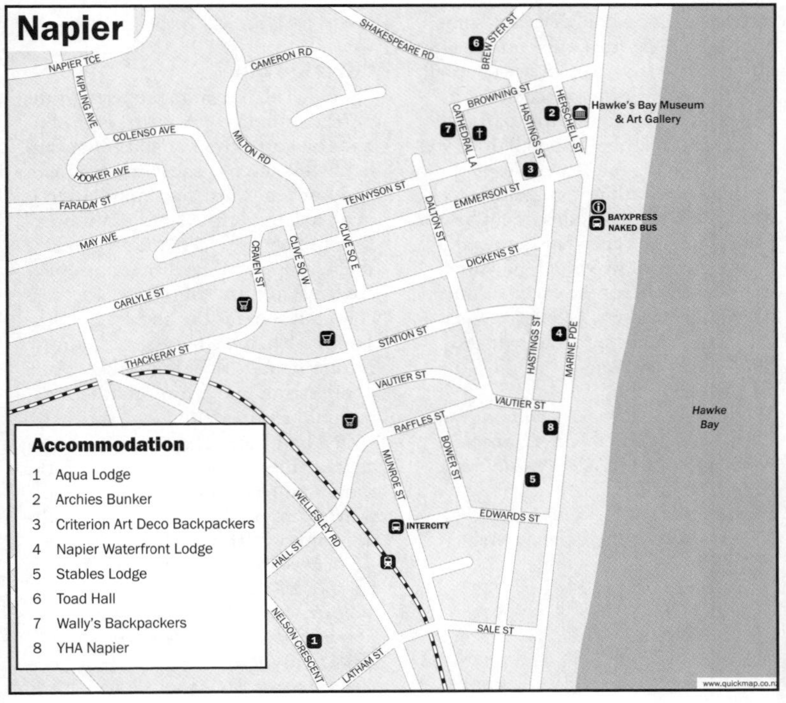

48 Emerson Street, Napier
🚌 *12, 13, 14*
☎ *(06) 835 2059*
Website *www.criterionartdeco.co.nz*
Dorm bed *$26 ($24 VIP, Magic Bus);* ***single room*** *$45 (VIP, Magic Bus);* ***double/twin room*** *$60-$80 ($55-$75 VIP, Magic Bus)*
Credit cards *MC, Visa*
Reception open *8.30am-8.30pm daily*

Maintenance & cleanliness	★★★½
Facilities	★★
Atmosphere & character	★★★★
Security	★★★
Overall rating	★★★

Napier Prison

Well, it's original. This hostel is set in New Zealand's oldest prison, which operated from 1862 to 1993. It's got quite a bit of atmosphere, to say the least, which you'll either like or be spooked out by. There's definitely a morbid sense of humour around the place – for instance, laundry is hung out to dry in the actual old hanging yard. Facilities include a big TV room, internet access, a pool table and some gym equipment (this was a prison, after all). Rooms are very basic, as you might expect, and the whole place shows its years; which, again, is either part of appeal or something that will drive you away. If you dig the idea of sleeping in an old cell with prison graffiti still carved into the walls, this might be your place. But check ahead if they're taking bookings: when we visited, the hostel was booked out for the entire summer by seasonal workers. Guests get to take the prison tour at a discounted rate.

55 Coote Road, Napier
☎ *(06) 835 9933*
Website *www.napierprison.com*
Dorm bed *$23 ($20 BBH);* ***single room*** *$43 ($40 BBH);* ***double/twin room*** *$56 ($50 BBH)*
Credit cards *MC, Visa*
Reception open *9am-5pm daily*

Maintenance & cleanliness	★★
Facilities	★★
Atmosphere & character	★★★½
Security	★★★
Overall rating	★★½

Napier Waterfront Lodge & Backpackers

As the name might suggest, this hostel is right across the road from the beach. It's an older, rambling colonial house that was an earthquake survivor. The hostel is generally well-maintained, and has a TV lounge, a nice kitchen and front veranda for watching the action on Marine Parade. There's also a backyard with a barbecue and an internet room. It's only about a five-minute walk to the city centre, but free pick up from the bus is offered.

217 Marine Parade, Napier
🚌 *12, 13, 14*
☎ *(06) 835 3429*
Website *www.napierbackpackers.co.nz*
Dorm bed *$25 ($23 BBH);* ***single room*** *$45 ($42 BBH);* ***double/twin room*** *$66 ($64 BBH)*
Credit cards *Amex, MC, Visa*
Reception open *8am-10am & 1pm-9pm*

Maintenance & cleanliness	★★★
Facilities	★★
Atmosphere & character	★★½
Security	★½
Overall rating	★★½

Portside Inn

Portside Inn is a large property in the portside suburb of Ahuriri. Part of it was converted from an old restaurant/bar, which houses the common areas and kitchen. Most accommodation is in a separate purpose-built building. Rooms here are clean and in good shape; the shared facilities, however, are neglected and worn-out. The common room is big and open, with a pool table, table tennis, and dumpy, second-hand furnishings. There's outdoor seating in the front that looks out onto the road, and courtyard area with a barbecue. There's not really any character to the place. It's close to the shops and restaurants by the Ahuriri waterfront, but isn't convenient without your own transport.

52 Bridge Street, Ahuriri
☎ *(06) 833 7292*
Website *www.portsideinn.co.nz*
Dorm bed *$20;* ***single room*** *$25;* ***double room*** *$50*
Credit cards *MC, Visa*

Reception open *7am-10am & 3pm-8pm daily*

TV K L

Maintenance & cleanliness	★★★½
Facilities	★½
Atmosphere & character	★★
Security	★½
Overall rating	★★

Stables Lodge

Stables Lodge is a friendly place with a loopy, hand-made charm and outgoing owner. Art and craft projects seem to be constantly underway, with guests and the owner working on wall murals of flags and planets, and doors to rooms painted to look like horse stables. There's a courtyard with hammocks, a barbecue and lots of relaxed-looking people hanging out; also guests have use of a nice fully-equipped kitchen and free internet access on a single PC. Like many places in town, seasonal work can be arranged, and there's generally a mix of longer-term guests and backpackers. Overall, there's lots of character and social atmosphere here.

370 Hastings Street, Napier

12, 13, 14

(06) 835 6242

Website *www.stableslodge.co.nz*

Dorm bed *$20-$24 ($17-$21 BBH);* ***double/twin room*** *$51 ($48 BBH)*

TV K L

Maintenance & cleanliness	★★★
Facilities	★★
Atmosphere & character	★★★★
Security	★½
Overall rating	★★★

Toad Hall

Even though it's got an Art Deco façade, Toad Hall is set in a building that actually predates the earthquake that levelled most of Napier. It's an old hotel, and while it has a friendly vibe, it's poorly maintained. There's a kitchen and a TV lounge with old, mismatched furniture. The best area is definitely the rooftop patio, which has decent views over the city. Dorms are small, with only two beds (and a couple with three), but these too are pretty tired. Free laundry and free internet on a single PC (and pay Wi-Fi) are pluses.

11 Shakespeare Road, Napier

(06) 835 5555

Website *www.toadhall.co.nz*

Dorm bed *$22;* ***single room*** *$35;* ***double room*** *$45-$70;* ***twin room*** *$48*

Credit cards *Amex, MC, Visa*

Reception open *9am-9pm daily*

TV K L

Maintenance & cleanliness	★½
Facilities	★★
Atmosphere & character	★★★½
Security	★★
Overall rating	★★

Wally's Backpackers

Wally's Backpackers is a pair of 1920s wooden villas (plus a cottage) on a quiet street behind Napier's Art Deco cathedral. It's right in the middle of town, a five-minute walk to either the sea or the city centre, but it's set back from the street and feels nicely secluded. Rooms and facilities are very clean; there's an excellent, full kitchen, and a nice outdoor patio shaded by vines and fruit trees. The property is bounded by a big lush hill and other native growth, which adds to the feeling of being out of the city. Off-street parking is a plus for this area as well. Overall, Wally's is an elegant and well-located hostel.

7 Cathedral Lane, Napier

12, 13, 14

(06) 833 7930

Website *www.wallysbackpackers.co.nz*

Dorm bed *$23 ($20 BBH);* ***double room*** *$66 ($60 BBH);* ***twin room*** *$56 ($50 BBH)*

Credit cards *MC, Visa*

Reception open *9am-9pm daily*

TV K L

Maintenance & cleanliness	★★★★
Facilities	★★
Atmosphere & character	★★★½
Security	★★★
Overall rating	★★★

YHA Napier

YHA Napier is right across the road from the waterfront and the Marineland complex. It's an old wooden house that is clean and well-maintained and has some charm. There's a nice kitchen and a backyard area with a barbecue. An upstairs TV lounge has a couple of cosy window seats that look out over the sea and some rooms have sea views as well. Rooms are basic and clean and extra hooks and shelves are a nice touch. Internet and Wi-Fi access are available. The downstairs dining area is a bit on the institutional side, but overall this is a homely place with a helpful staff.

277 Marine Parade, Napier
12, 13, 14
(06) 835 7039
***Website** www.yha.co.nz*
***Dorm bed** $27-$29 ($24-$26 HI/YHA); **single room** $35 ($32 HI/YHA); **double/twin room** $64 ($58 HI/YHA)*
***Credit cards** MC, Visa*
***Reception open** 8am-10am; 4pm-7.30pm daily*

Maintenance & cleanliness	★★★½
Facilities	★★
Atmosphere & character	★★★
Security	★★
Overall rating	★★★

Eating & Drinking

Napier takes its food and drink culture seriously and there's a vast selection of upscale places around town, as well as some lower-budget options. The main clusters are in the city centre, around Hastings and Emerson Streets, with a few places along Marine Parade. There are several fine restaurants and cafés quayside in the suburb of Ahuriri as well.

For drinks, **Rosie O'Grady's** *(corner Marine Parade & Tennyson Street, Napier)* is a well-known Irish pub. **The Cri** *(48 Emerson Street, Napier)* is a popular backpacker-oriented spot, with cheap meals, drink specials and theme nights. It's located below Criterion Art Deco Backpackers.

There are several supermarkets around Munroe Street; including **Countdown** *(corner Munroe & Dickens Streets, Napier)*, **Pak'n Save** *(5 Munoe Street, Napier)* and **Woolworths** *(36 Carlyle Street, Napier)*.

Sights

Art Deco Walking Tours

Napier's architecture is the city's main attraction. Just walking around town will give you a good idea of the Art Deco craze that swept through Napier in the 1930s. The Art Deco Trust conducts walking tours of the city that departs from the Art Deco Shop in Tennyson Street. Alternatively you can buy a self-guided walk booklet for $5 and do the walk yourself. The tour is 1½km long and takes up to two hours to complete.

Art Deco Shop, 163 Tennyson Street, Napier
(06) 835 0022
***Website** www.artdeconapier.com*
***Tours cost** $14-20*
***Tours depart** 10am, 2pm, 5.30pm*

Hawke's Bay Museum & Art Gallery

This museum has a wide variety of exhibits including dinosaurs, Māori culture and local history. The exhibits relating to the 1931 earthquakes are particularly interesting.

9 Herschell Street, Napier
(09) 835 7781
***Website** www.hbmag.co.nz*
***Admission** $7.50*
***Open** 10am-6pm daily*

Marineland

New Zealand's only marine zoo is home to marine animals that include little blue penguins, seals, sea lions and dolphins. It also features dolphin shows and you have the option of getting in the pool and swimming with the dolphins.

Marine Parade, Napier
(06) 834 4027
***Website** www.marineland.co.nz*
***Admission** $11-18; **swim with dolphins** $50*
***Open** summer Mon 10am-4.30pm, Tue-Wed 10am-5.30pm, Thu 10am-4.30pm, Fri-Sun 10am-5.30pm; winter 10am-4.30pm daily*

National Aquarium

New Zealand's National Aquarium features a wide variety of marine life. It includes a walk-through tunnel in one of the tanks plus enclosures with kiwis, glow-worms, tuatara and New Zealand Geckos.

Marine Parade, Napier

☎ *(06) 834 1404*
***Website** www.nationalaquarium.co.nz*
***Admission** $14.60*
***Open** Jan 9am-9pm daily; Feb-Easter 9am-7pm daily; Easter-24 Dec 9am-5pm daily; 26-31 Dec 9am-9pm daily*

Hastings

Like Napier, Hastings also has some lovely Art Deco and Spanish Mission architecture, but it doesn't share the same cosmopolitan feel as its neighbour. There's a distinctly agricultural feel to the place, a rougher, less polished vibe.

Most backpackers come to Hastings for fruit picking work (available Nov-May). People also come to Hastings to check out the wineries in the area, but probably the main attraction is Splash Planet, a big family-oriented water park.

Practical Information

Hastings i-SITE Visitor Centre

Russell Street, Hastings
☎ *(06) 873 5526*
***Website** www.hastings.co.nz*
***Open** Mon-Fri 8.30am-5pm, Sat 9am-4pm, Sun 9am-3pm*

Coming & Going

InterCity Coachlines *(☎ (09) 623 1503; **website** www.intercity.co.nz)* go to Gisborne, Taupo and Wellington and Naked Bus *(☎ 0900 62533; **website** www.nakedbus.com)* has direct buses to Auckland, Waitomo, Wellington and Whangarei. BayXpress *(☎ 0800 422 997; **website** www.bayxpress.co.nz)* is a good alternative if you're going to Palmerston North or Wellington.

Buses depart from Russell Street near the Police kiosk.

Local Transport

The Hawkes Bay area has a good local bus service with most bus routes running every half hour. Most fares in Hastings are $2.40 although it costs $2.90 to go to Havelock North and $4.30 to go to Napier.

Accommodation

Most backpackers come to Hastings for fruit picking work (available Nov-May) and almost all the hostels in town cater to temporary workers. It's worth mentioning that some hostels this past year were completely or almost completely full for the entire season. Briefly, a change to the TRSE (Transitioning to Recognised Seasonal Worker) work policy has required large employers such as Watties or Mr Apple to provide accommodation for their TRSE workers (who are frequently Pacific Islanders).

The employers are turning to hostels to house their workers and for some hostels the prospect of a fully-booked season is too good to resist. So in short, check ahead. And it's always worthwhile to arrive before the season starts if you're serious about getting work.

A1 Backpackers

A1 Backpackers is a lovely house west of the city centre that was converted to a hostel a few years ago. It's in great shape, with clean tasteful rooms, a nice kitchen and TV lounge, and interesting little details like decorative coloured glass windows. There's a big, peaceful backyard as well, with tables and a barbecue, as well as a couple of small campervans. The owners are very friendly, and in this case, the name doesn't lie – A1 Backpackers is undoubtedly the cleanest, homeliest hostel in Hastings.

122 Stortford Street, St Leonards, Hastings
16A, 20
☎ *(06) 873 4285*
***Dorm bed** $23 ($20 BBH); **double/twin room** $46 ($40 BBH)*
***Credit cards** MC, Visa*
***Reception open** 9am-9pm daily*

Maintenance & cleanliness	★★★★½
Facilities	★★
Atmosphere & character	★★★★
Security	★½
Overall rating	★★★½

AJ's Backpackers Lodge

AJ's Backpackers is a large old house that is generally clean but in uneven shape. Bedding is good quality, some rooms are recently renovated and painted, and some bathrooms have nice new fixtures. But in other places, the house and furnishings really show their age. It's an ongoing project, but the owner seems genuinely interested in improving the quality of the place. Facilities include a coin-operated internet on a single PC, a small TV room and a kitchen that is busy and a little worn. Jobs can be arranged here, and many people who stay at AJ's are working.

405 Southland Road, Hastings
16A, 20
(06) 878 2302
Dorm bed *$25*
Reception open *9am-noon, 1pm-5.30pm & 7.30pm-9pm daily*
TV K L

Maintenance & cleanliness	★★★
Facilities	★½
Atmosphere & character	★★★½
Security	★★
Overall rating	★★★½

Hastings Backpackers Hostel

The generic name belies the quirky character of this hostel. Hastings Backpackers is yet another working hostel, but it's got some personality – brightly painted dorms, a cute covered courtyard with loads of fruit trees (mandarin, grapefruit, lemon, apricot and plum). There's a decent kitchen and a common room with TV, table tennis, a dart board and games. It's definitely a place to find work, but at least there's some colour and charm to it.

505 Lyndon Road East, Hastings
21
(06) 876 5888
Website *www.medcasa.co.nz*
Dorm bed *$21-$22 ($18-$19 BBH);* ***single room*** *$27 ($24 BBH);* ***double/twin room*** *$40-$50 ($36-$44 BBH)*
Reception open *9am-noon & 2pm-8pm daily*
TV K L

Maintenance & cleanliness	★★★
Facilities	★½
Atmosphere & character	★★★★½
Security	★★
Overall rating	★★★½

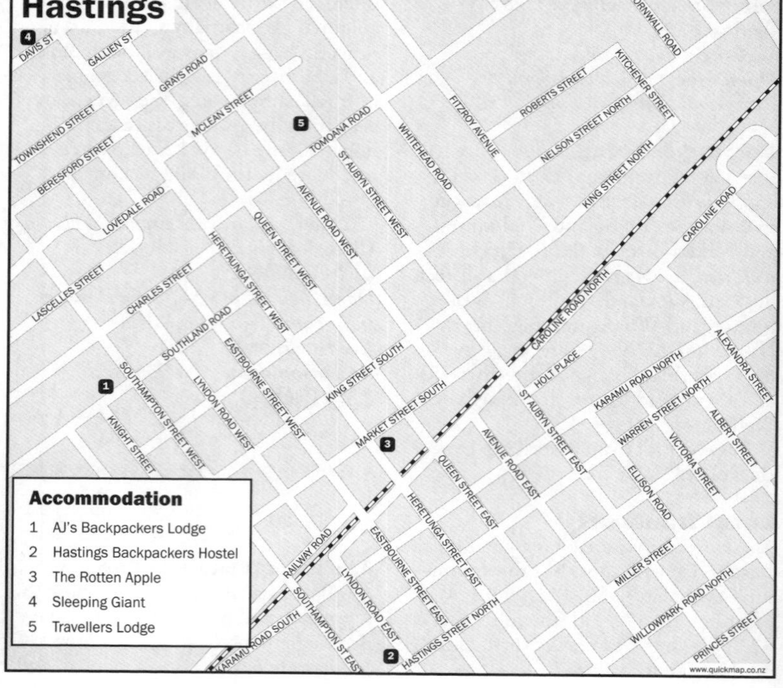

The Rotten Apple

The Rotten Apple is on the top floor of an old hotel right in the centre of town. Dorm rooms are basic and named after famous figures in New Zealand and world history – Captain Cook, Jacques Cousteau, etc. There's a big open TV room with a pool table and a separate quiet reading room. A small outdoor deck has a barbecue and there's a kitchen with nice freezers and good storage. Like every hostel in Hastings, fruit-picking work is arranged here; but there's more of a true backpacker hostel feeling to The Rotten Apple than most, and an overall friendly, fun vibe.

114 Heretaunga Street, Hastings
16A, 16B, 17, 20, 21
(06) 878 4363
***Website** www.rottenapple.co.nz*
***Dorm bed** $20-$24 ($17-$21 BBH); **double/twin room** $52 ($46 BBH)*
***Credit cards** MC, Visa*
***Reception open** 9am-9pm daily*

Maintenance & cleanliness	★★★½
Facilities	★★
Atmosphere & character	★★★
Security	★★★½
Overall rating	★★★½

Siesta Backpackers

Siesta Backpackers is part of a converted motel east of the city centre. Every room comes with a TV and an en suite bathroom, and the biggest has four beds. There's a small shared kitchen, not fully-equipped, and a courtyard area with a trampoline, swings and picnic tables. It's clean and quiet, although it doesn't have any kind of hostel atmosphere, with very limited opportunities for socialising. Still, if you're just looking for a place to catch a siesta, it makes an alternative to the busier working hostels in Hastings.

911 Heretaunga Street East, Hastings
21
(06) 870 8112
***Dorm bed** $30; **single room** $30; **double/twin room** $60*
***Credit cards** MC, Visa*
***Reception open** 8am-8pm daily*

Maintenance & cleanliness	★★★
Facilities	★★½
Atmosphere & character	★
Security	★★½
Overall rating	★★

Sleeping Giant

Sleeping Giant is an older house with old, worn furnishings and facilities that aren't very well maintained. It's a working hostel, and when we visited, it was entirely booked out for the summer with seasonal workers from the Pacific Islands. Beds for casual travellers may not be available again this coming season. Facilities include free laundry, a basic kitchen and TV room and an outdoor patio with a pool table. There's not much atmosphere at all, but the owner can arrange work.

109 Davis Street, St Leonards, Hastings
16A, 20
(06) 877 4445
***Dorm bed** $20; **twin room** $50*
***Reception open** 8am-10pm daily*

Maintenance & cleanliness	★½
Facilities	★½
Atmosphere & character	★½
Security	★½
Overall rating	★½

Travellers Lodge

Travellers Lodge is spread around several small buildings among a large yard area, including cottages, cabins, a couple of campervans, and two villas. Some facilities are newer and nicer than others – the newest dorms are particularly clean and in good shape, though older facilities are somewhat worn. All beds have real innerspring mattresses, at least. There's a small kitchen and TV lounge. The owner is friendly and good at finding work for guests; overall, it's a decent place with the atmosphere of a working hostel.

606 St Aubyn Street West, Hastings
17, 20
(06) 878 7108
***Website** www.tlodge.co.nz*
***Dorm bed** $21 ($18 BBH); **single room** $30 ($27 BBH); **double/twin room** $52 ($46 BBH)*
***Credit cards** MC, Visa*
***Open** Nov-May*

Maintenance & cleanliness	★★★
Facilities	★★½
Atmosphere & character	★★
Security	★★½
Overall rating	★★½

Eating & Drinking

Hastings doesn't have the same upscale dining scene as Napier; however there are a few top-class restaurants in town, as well as several budget options on and around Heretaunga Street, including Indian, Asian, kebabs and fish-and-chip takeaways.

Nearby Havelock North also has several fine cafés, restaurants, and places to sample the local wines, if you feel like blowing a little of your fruit-picking earnings.

Supermarkets in Hastings include **Countdown** *(corner Queen Street West & King Street North, Hastings)*; **New World** *(400 Heretaunga Street East, Hastings)* and **Pak'n Save** *(corner Heretaunga & Westend Streets, Hastings).*

Sights

Splash Planet

This 6.5ha aqua theme park is Hastings' top attraction although it is targeted mostly towards families. It features plenty of waterslides and some land-based attractions such as mini-golf and mini jeeps.

Grove Road, Hastings
☎ *(06) 876 9856*
Website *www.splashplanet.co.nz*
Admission *$25*
Open *summer 10am-6pm daily*

Havelock North

Havelock North is a small, prosperous village just five minutes southeast of Hastings. It has a decidedly more upscale feel than Hastings and is not a magnet for backpackers so much as for older visitors doing the wine and food trail in the region. The town centre features gourmet olive and cheese shops, boutiques, local art galleries, and see-and-be-seen cafés and restaurants.

Havelock North is situated at the base of impressive Te Mata Peak, said in Māori legend to be the body of a giant chief. The village is also the closest settlement to Cape Kidnappers, home to the largest mainland gannet colony in the world.

Coming & Going & Local Transport

The Hawkes Bay area has a good local bus service with most bus routes running every half hour. Route 21 runs between Hastings and Havelock North. Local travel in Havelock North costs $2.40 and it costs $2.90 to go to Hastings.

Accommodation

Peak Backpackers

The upscale charm of Havelock North does not extend to Peak Backpackers, a rundown place very out of step with its surroundings. The furnishings and facilities are extremely tired – exhausted is more like it – with thrift-store couches and crazy old car-seat chairs littering the halls and common spaces. Facilities include a messy kitchen, a small TV and internet access. Rooms are reasonably tidy, although the bedding is old. There's more the character of a doss house than a hostel here.

33 Havelock Road, Havelock North
21
☎ *(06) 877 1170*
Dorm bed *$20;* ***single room*** *$30;* ***double/twin room*** *$50*
Reception open *8am-8pm daily*

Maintenance & cleanliness	★
Facilities	★½
Atmosphere & character	½
Security	★½
Overall rating	★

Clive

Clive is a small village 10km south of Napier. There's not really anything in particular for the traveller here, but it offers a quiet, rural alternative to staying in one of the twin cities, as it is almost midway between Napier or Hastings. Clive is home to the Hawkes Bay Rowing Club.

Accommodation

Gannet Cottage

Gannet Cottage is a charming little house set on farmland with a tiny vineyard. There are only four rooms, the largest sleeping four, and all are clean and cosy. The rest of the house is just a small TV/living room, and a fully-equipped kitchen with dining area. There's a small porch out front, and a larger wraparound deck on the side and back of the house with a barbecue. It's a simple, homely place, and is a much quieter alternative to most hostels in Napier and Hastings, both of which are about 10km away.

77 School Road, Clive
☎ *(06) 870 1222*
Website *www.gannetcottage.co.nz*
Dorm bed *$23 ($20 BBH);* ***single room*** *$31 ($28 BBH);* ***double room*** *$56 ($50 BBH);* ***twin room*** *$52 ($46 BBH)*

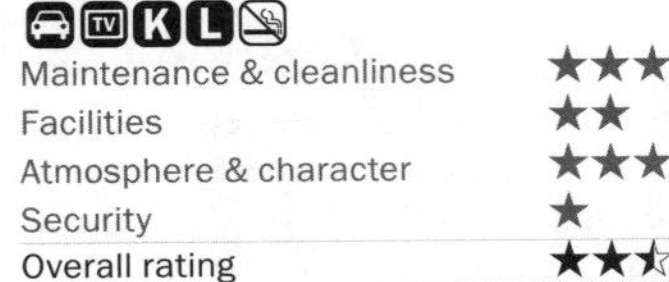

Maintenance & cleanliness	★★★
Facilities	★★
Atmosphere & character	★★★
Security	★
Overall rating	★★½

Cape Kidnappers

Located near Clive, about midway between Napier and Hastings, Cape Kidnappers is known as the world's largest and most accessible gannet colony.

It is a popular destination for bird watchers, who come here in droves during the nesting season (Sep-Mar), when 15,000 of the birds nest here.

Taranaki

Taranaki comprises the western tip of the North Island, which is dominated by the snow-capped cone of Mount Egmont (also known as Taranaki). New Plymouth is the main centre of this dairy farming region, which is also home to some great surf beaches.

New Plymouth

This is the major centre in the Taranaki region and is a very pleasant city with nice parks and open spaces and the Puke Ariki museum. New Plymouth has a great location with ski slopes and great surf beaches within a one-hour drive of the city centre.

New Plymouth is off the beaten track and none of the three main backpackers buses come here. The city doesn't attract many travellers, which is a pity as it is one of New Zealand's most underrated places.

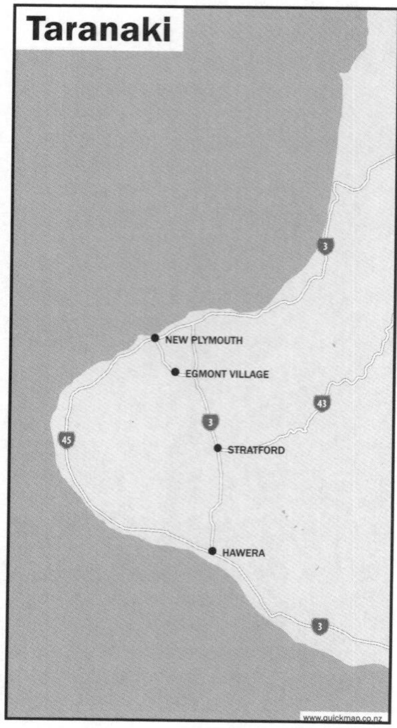

Must do in Taranaki

- Climb Mount Egmont (Taranaki)

Practical Information

New Plymouth i-SITE Visitor Centre
Puke Ariki, 65 St Aubyn Street, New Plymouth
☎ *(06) 759 6060*
Website *www.taranakinz.org*
Open *Mon-Tue 9am-6pm, Wed 9am-9pm, Thu-Fri 9am-6pm, Sat-Sun 9am-5pm*

Department of Conservation
220 Devon Street West, New Plymouth
☎ *(06) 758 0433*
Website *www.doc.govt.nz*
Open *Mon-Fri 8am-4.30pm*

INTERNET ACCESS

All New Plymouth's hostels have internet access. **Esquires Coffee** *(**website** www.esquires.co.nz; 98 Devon Street East, New Plymouth)* has free Wi-Fi access.

Coming & Going

AIR

New Plymouth Airport has several daily Air New Zealand flights to Auckland and Wellington. New Plymouth Airport Shuttles *(☎ 0800 373 001; **website** www.npairportshuttle.co.nz)* run an airport shuttle service that can pick up and drop off at your hostel.

BUS

InterCity Coachlines *(☎ (09) 623 1503; **website** www.intercity.co.nz)* have services to Auckland and Wellington. Dalroy Tours *(☎ (06) 759 0197; **website** www.dalroytours.co.nz)* run express coach services to Hawera, Hamilton, Auckland and Paihia. White Star Bus *(☎ (06) 759 0197; **website** www.whitestarbus.co.nz)* operate services between New Plymouth and Wellington with stops in Wanganui and Palmerston North. Buses depart from the New Plymouth Travel Centre on Ariki Street.

Local Transport

New Plymouth City Bus *(☎ (06) 753 9646; **website** www.okatobus.co.nz/citybus/index.htm)* operate seven bus routes in the New Plymouth area. A single fare is $3 ($20 for 10 trips) within New Plymouth or $5 ($35 for 10 trips) between New Plymouth and Oakura. The central bus terminus is on Ariki Street next to Puke Ariki.

Accommodation

Egmont Eco-Lodge YHA

Egmont Eco-Lodge YHA is a clean hostel in a natural setting in suburban New Plymouth and it backs onto a stream where you can feed the eels. It has all the amenities you would expect including a lounge near the reception with internet access and a fully-equipped kitchen. Accommodation is in tidy dormitories. The manager serves Egmont Cake every evening.

12 Clawton Street, New Plymouth

444, 555

☎ *(06) 753 5720*

***Website** www.taranaki-bakpak.co.nz*

***Dorm bed** $26-28 ($23-25 BBH, HI/YHA); **single room** $48 ($45 BBH, HI/YHA); **double/twin room** $66 ($60 BBH, HI/YHA)*

***Credit Cards** MC, Visa*

TV K

Maintenance & cleanliness	★★★
Facilities	★½
Atmosphere & character	★★★½
Security	★½
Overall rating	★★½

Seaspray House

Seaspray House is a nice small hostel about a five-minute walk west of the city centre. It is tastefully decorated with polished floorboards and has a nice big common room with lots of games, a fully-equipped kitchen. Accommodation in mostly double and twin rooms, but there is also a very spacious four-bed dorm. It only sleeps 14, but the building is big enough to accommodate many more. It is very clean and well

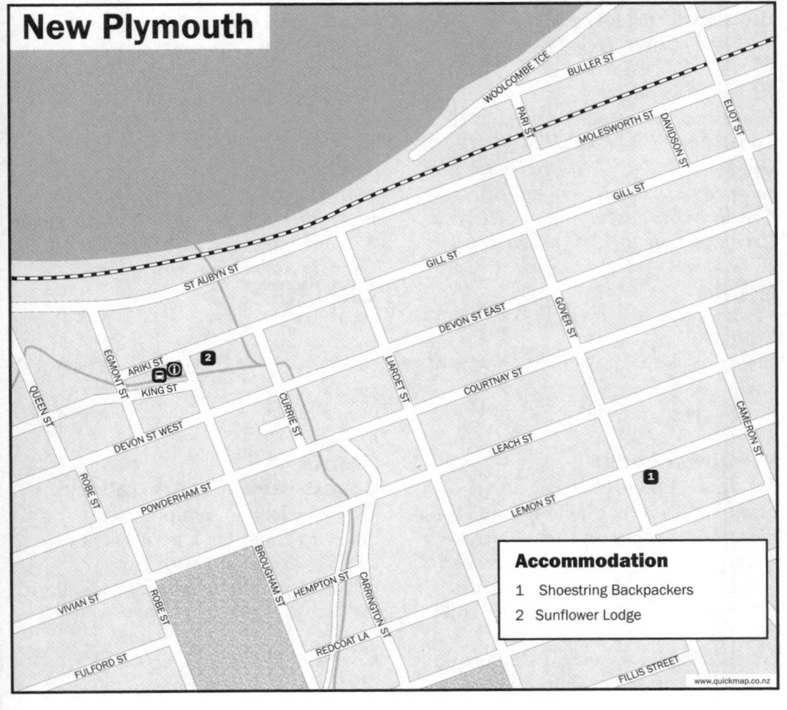

maintained and there is a great atmosphere because there is no TV, which encourages people to talk to each other.

13 Weymouth Street, New Plymouth
333
(06) 759 8934
***Website** www.seasprayhouse.co.nz*
***Dorm bed** $27-29 ($22-24 BBH); **single room** $43 ($38 BBH); **double/twin room** $66 ($56 BBH)*
***Reception open** 8am-9pm daily*

Maintenance & cleanliness	★★★★★
Facilities	★★½
Atmosphere & character	★★★★★
Security	★★½
Overall rating	★★★½

Shoestring Backpackers

Shoestring Backpackers is a big old wooden hostel south of the town centre that features a lounge with a fireplace, a sun room and balcony, a fully-equipped kitchen and a dining room with a long wooden table. There is also a sauna and a barbecue area outside. Accommodation is in tidy dormitories and comfortable double rooms and there is also a small area for camping.

48 Lemon Street, New Plymouth
444, 555, 888
(06) 758 0404
***Website** www.shoestring.co.nz*
***Dorm bed** $25-26 ($22-24 BBH); **single room** $43 ($40 BBH); **double/twin room** $62-66 ($56-60 BBH)*
***Credit cards** Amex, Diners, MC, Visa*
***Reception open** 7.30am-9.30pm; late check in with prior arrangement*

Maintenance & cleanliness	★★★★
Facilities	★★
Atmosphere & character	★★★★
Security	★★½
Overall rating	★★★

Sunflower Lodge

Sunflower Lodge is a basic hostel with dated facilities that include a quiet lounge near the reception, internet access in the corridor, plus a kitchen and a TV lounge. The best feature is the sun deck with a barbecue and views of the city and the sea. It is a very central location near Puke Ariki and the Centre City shopping centre.

25 Ariki Street, New Plymouth
14, 222, 333, 444, 555, 777, 888
(06) 759 0050
***Website** www.sunflowerlodge.co.nz*
***Dorm bed** $22-25 ($20-23 BBH); **single room** $55 ($50 BBH); **double/twin room** $63-78 ($55-70 BBH)*
***Credit cards** Amex, MC, Visa*
***Reception open** 8am-10pm daily*

Maintenance & cleanliness	★★
Facilities	★★
Atmosphere & character	★★
Security	★★★½
Overall rating	★★

Wave Haven Backpackers

Wave Haven is a laid-back place that's got a great atmosphere a bit like a big shared house. The hostel has a TV lounge with surround sound projector TV; internet access (including Wi-Fi) and a fully-equipped kitchen with an espresso machine. There is a big garden with a sauna and even a glow worm walking trail. The hostel is in a state of ongoing maintenance but it has clean and comfortable rooms. It is near the beach about 16km south of New Plymouth and it's a popular spot for surfers.

1518 Main Road, Oakura (15km from New Plymouth)
14
(06) 752 7800
***Website** www.thewavehaven.co.nz*
***Dorm bed** $20; **single room** $35 first night, then $30 per night; **double room** $50 first night, then $40 per night*
***Credit cards** Amex, MC, Visa*

Maintenance & cleanliness	★★★½
Facilities	★★½
Atmosphere & character	★★★★★
Security	★
Overall rating	★★★½

Sights

Govett-Brewster Art Gallery

This excellent contemporary art museum combines a permanent collection with a variety of temporary exhibitions. It is an impressive gallery for such a small city.

Queen Street, New Plymouth
(06) 758 5149
***Website** www.govettbrewster.com*

Admission *free*
Open *10.30am-5pm daily*

Puke Ariki

This brilliant museum is the city's top attraction. It features excellent displays on the region's geological and cultural history.
1 Ariki Street, New Plymouth
☎ *(06) 759 6060*
Website *www.pukeariki.com*
Admission *free*
Open *Mon-Tue 9am-6pm, Wed 9am-9pm, Thu-Fri 9am-6pm, Sat-Sun 9am-5pm*

Egmont National Park

New Zealand's second national park is centred on Mount Egmont (Taranaki), which towers above the surrounding farmland. The mountain is one of the country's most striking, maintaining its snow-capped crater year round. Although hiking trails in the national park are popular, treks up the mountain shouldn't be taken lightly if you are not an experienced mountaineer, as Mount Egmont (Taranaki) is New Zealand's most dangerous mountain. It has claimed the lives of more than 60 people over the years.

If you don't feel like climbing to the summit, there are plenty of shorter walks, some of which are only 30 minutes long.

Practical Information

Dawson Falls Visitor Centre

Manaia Road, Kaponga
☎ *025 430 248*
Open *summer 8am-4.30pm daily; winter Wed-Sun 8.30am-4.30pm*

North Egmont Visitor Centre

Egmont Road, Inglewood
☎ *(06) 756 0990*
Open *8am-4.30pm daily*

Accommodation

Most people visiting Egmont National Park stay in Egmont Village or drive up from Stratford or New Plymouth

The Missing Leg

The Missing Leg is a small hostel offering basic facilities that include a small kitchen and a main common area with a fireplace, a big dining table and a piano. Furnishings and bedding are old and worn and the place could be better maintained, but the hostel has lots of character. It is on the edge of Egmont Village. It's easy to find; just look for the collection of aging bicycles on the fence.
State Highway 3, Egmont Village
☎ *(06) 752 2570*
Website *www.missinglegbackpackers.co.nz*
Dorm bed *$23 ($18 BBH);* ***single room*** *$56 ($22 BBH);* ***double room*** *$50-56 ($44-50 BBH);* ***twin room*** *$50 ($44 BBH);* ***camping*** *$10 per person*

Maintenance & cleanliness	★½
Facilities	★
Atmosphere & character	★★★½
Security	-
Overall rating	★★

Hiking

Egmont National Park has over 140km of hiking trails including multi-day hikes around the mountain and the popular, and often dangerous, one-day climb.

Climbing Mount Egmont/Taranaki

One of the most popular activities in the park involves climbing Mount Egmont/Taranaki, however it is dangerous and over 60 people have died attempting it. The best time to climb is in autumn (Feb-Apr) when there is very little snow on the mountain. The ascent can be done in one day with the return climb taking around eight hours.

There are several routes to the summit with the most popular departing from the North Egmont Visitor Centre.

It is recommended that inexperienced hikers go along with a guide. **Ian MacAlpine** (☎ *(06) 765 6234; website www.macalpineguides.com)* and **Taranaki Outdoor Professionals** (☎ *0800 448433; website www.topguides.co.nz)* conduct guided climbs of the mountain.

Around the Mountain Circuit
This popular five-day walk circles the mountain and during summer there is a shorter three-day version at a higher altitude. There are huts located at one-day intervals along the track.

Dawson Falls
The 16.5m high Dawson Falls are a 20-minute walk from the Dawson Falls visitor centre.

Stratford

Stratford is the closest major town to Egmont National Park and some travellers use the town as a base for visiting the park.

Practical Information

Stratford i-SITE Visitor Centre
Prospero Place, Broadway, Stratford
☎ *(06) 765 6708 or 0800 765 6708*
Website *www.stratfordnz.co.nz*
Open *Mon-Fri 8.30am-5pm, Sat-Sun 10am-3.30pm*

Department of Conservation
Pembroke Road, Stratford
☎ *(06) 765 5144*
Website *www.doc.govt.nz*
Open *Mon-Fri 8am-4.30pm*

Coming & Going

InterCity Coachlines *(☎ (09) 623 1503; **website** www.intercity.co.nz)* have services to Auckland and Wellington. Dalroy Tours *(☎ (06) 759 0197; **website** www.dalroytours.co.nz)* run express coach services to Hawera, New Plymouth, Hamilton, Auckland and Paihia. White Star Bus *(☎ (06) 759 0197; **website** www.whitestarbus.co.nz)* have services to New Plymouth, Palmerston North, Wanganui and Wellington. Buses depart from the i-SITE Visitor Centre *(Prospero Place, Broadway, Stratford)*.

Accommodation

Stratford Top 10 Holiday Park
This motor camp/caravan park offers accommodation for backpackers in a bunkhouse with common areas that include a lounge with a pool table and TV but normally the bunkhouse is kept for groups while independent travellers stay in cabins. It is primarily a caravan park and the management don't really have a clue about backpackers so there is virtually no atmosphere.
10 Page Street, Stratford
☎ *(06) 765 6440*
Dorm bed *$20*
Credit cards *MC, Visa*
Reception open *8am-10pm*
[car] [TV] [K]

Maintenance & cleanliness	★★½
Facilities	★★
Atmosphere & character	½
Security	★½
Overall rating	★★

Taranaki Accommodation Lodge
Taranaki Accommodation Lodge is a dreadful hostel with a depressing institutional feel and many of the fittings and furnishings are old and worn. Facilities include a lounge with a pool table and table tennis, a kitchen and a TV lounge with old ratty sofas. It is a dilapidated former nurses' home dating from the 1950s with accommodation in mostly double and twin rooms with limp sagging mattresses, although there are a couple of small dorms.
7 Romeo Street, Stratford
☎ *(06) 765 5444*
Website *www.mttaranakilodge.co.nz*
Dorm bed *$20 ($18 BBH);* ***single room*** *$27 ($25 BBH);* ***double room*** *$48-54 ($44-50 BBH);* ***twin room*** *$44 ($40 BBH);* ***camping*** *$10 per person*
Reception open *8am-10pm*
[car] [TV] [K] [L]

Maintenance & cleanliness	★
Facilities	★★
Atmosphere & character	-
Security	-
Overall rating	★

Sights

Glockenspiel
Stratford's Tudor-style clock tower is home to New Zealand's only glockenspiel, which features six figures of Romeo and Juliet and performs for five minutes daily at 10am, 1pm and 3pm.
Broadway, Stratford

Taranaki Pioneer Village

This open-air museum depicts life 100 years ago and features 40 historic buildings including Mangatoki Church, Okato Cottage, Pembroke School, Stratford Courthouse and Tariki Railway Station.

3912 Main South Road, Stratford
☎ *(06) 765 5399*
Website *www.pioneervillage.co.nz*
Admission *$10*
Open *10am-4pm daily*

Hawera

This small town serves the surrounding dairy farms and is the gateway to the southern Taranaki region.

The town's name is Māori for 'the burnt place' and it has suffered the wrath of four major fires. After a particularly devastating fire in 1912, insurance companies demanded that a water tower be erected as a fire-fighting reservoir. The tower was completed in 1914 and remains the town's major landmark.

Practical Information

Hawera i-SITE Visitor Centre

55 High Street, Hawera
☎ *(06) 278 8599 or 0800 111 323*
Open *Mon-Fri 8.30am-5pm, Sat-Sun 10am-3pm*

Coming & Going

InterCity Coachlines *(☎ (09) 623 1503; **website** www.intercity.co.nz)* go to Auckland and Wellington; Dalroy Tours *(☎ (06) 759 0197; **website** www.dalroytours.co.nz)* have express coach services to New Plymouth, Hamilton, Auckland and Paihia and White Star Bus *(☎ (06) 759 0197; **website** www.whitestarbus.co.nz)* go to New Plymouth, Palmerston North, Wanganui and Wellington. Buses depart from the i-SITE Visitor Centre *(55 High Street, Hawera).*

Accommodation

Wheatly Downs Farmstay Backpackers

Wheatly Downs is a great little farm hostel in a small house with polished wooden floorboards and a cosy lounge and a small kitchen/dining area. The friendly manager knows a lot about the region and encourages you to get involved in farm activities.

484 Ararata Road, 8km north of Hawera
☎ *(06) 278 6523*
Website *www.taranaki-bakpak.co.nz/hawera.htm*
Dorm bed *$28 ($25 BBH);* ***double room*** *$65 ($60 BBH)*
Credit cards *MC, Visa*

Maintenance & cleanliness	★★★★½
Facilities	★
Atmosphere & character	★★★★
Security	★
Overall rating	★★★

Sights

Tawhiti Museum

Many people regard Tawhiti Museum as New Zealand's best small privately run museum. It uses brilliant dioramas to cover the history of South Taranaki.

401 Ohangi Road, Hawera
☎ *(06) 278 6837*
Website *www.tawhitimuseum.co.nz*
Admission *$10*
Open *Jan 10am-4pm daily; Feb-May Fri-Mon 10am-4pm; Jun-Aug Sun 10am-4pm; Sep-Dec Fri-Mon 10am-4pm*

Activities

Dam Dropping

One of the craziest things you can do in New Zealand is to sledge the world's first commercially sledged hydro dam. Dam Dropping involves sledging over an 8m waterfall and then spending around three hours sledging on the Waingongoro River. One of the attractions of white water sledging, or hydrospeed, (compared with white water rafting) is that you are in control of a buoyant and highly manoeuvrable water sledge rather than being guided on a raft.

Kaitiaki Adventures, 436 Stent Road, Okato
☎ *(06) 752 8242*
Website *www.damdrop.com*
Dam drop *$100*

Manawatu-Wanganui

Manawatu-Wanganui is a large region in the lower half of the North Island. It covers a big chunk of th e middle area between Taupo and Wellington, and therefore gets lots of travellers passing through. It isn't as big of a tourist draw as some of its neighbouring regions, but there's a slower-paced "real New Zealand" feeling to much of the area, as well as diverse natural attractions, some interesting small towns and the cities of Wanganui and Palmerston North.

Some travellers come here to kayak the brilliant Whanganui River Journey in the Whanganui National Park. The Whanganui continues down and runs through the historic river town of Wanganui. Palmerston North is a provincial capital with the country's second-biggest university, giving it an interesting mix of people and a good nightlife and café culture.

Rafting the Rangitikei River is another popular attraction. Close to Taihape is Mokai Gravity Canyon, home to the North Island's highest bungee jump and an incredibly fast flying fox. There are also dunes, mountain ranges, the beautiful Manawatu Gorge and some fine gardens.

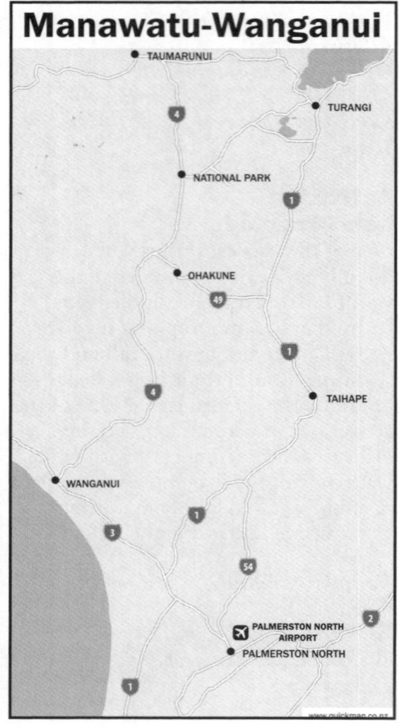

Must do in Manawatu-Wanganui

- Hike the Tongariro Alpine Crossing
- Visit Wanganui
- Canoe or kayak on the Whanganui River

Much of Manawatu-Wanganui is rural and opportunities exist to get up close and personal with the farming way of life. The town of Feilding has been voted "New Zealand's Most Beautiful Town" multiple times, and travellers can catch a traditional livestock auction there.

If you're on the North Island, you'll almost definitely be going through Manawatu-Wanganui; spending some time here can make an interesting diversion from the more beaten-down tourist trails.

Ruapehu District

This area in the central North Island contains Tongariro National Park, the tourist towns of National Park Village and Ohakune. The biggest draw card for backpackers is the Tongariro Alpine Crossing hiking trail, which is said to be New Zealand's best one-day hike.

Tongariro National Park

Tongariro National Park – New Zealand's first, and the world's fourth, national park – encompasses several of the North Island's largest active volcanoes, including Mounts Ruapehu, Ngauruhoe and Tongariro. The majestic Mount Ngauruhoe is perhaps the most easily recognisable with its distinct conical features, while neighbouring Mount Ruapehu is the largest skiing and snowboarding area in New Zealand, home to the Whakapapa and Turoa ski resorts. The park is a UNESCO World Heritage Site.

There are several excellent hiking trails in Tongariro National Park including the four-day Tongariro Northern Circuit, the six-day Round the Mountain and the Tongariro Alpine Crossing, widely considered New Zealand's best one-day walk. The Tongariro Alpine Crossing traverses a spectacular volcanic setting of craters, lava flows and thermal lakes.

Several companies operate transport to and from the trailhead from Taupo, Turangi, Ohakune and National Park Village, making the Tongariro Alpine Crossing a popular day trip. The park also has some good shorter walks from Whakapapa village as well as the climb to Mount Ngauruhoe's summit.

In April 2008, tragedy hit when a group of students and a teacher were swept away by a flash flood while canyoning in Tongariro National Park. Six students and one teacher were killed.

Practical Information

Whakapapa Visitor Centre

State Highway 48, Whakapapa Village
☎ *(07) 892 3729*
***Open** 8am-5pm daily*

Coming & Going

Although both Taupo and Turangi make good bases for Tongariro National Park, the smaller towns of National Park and Whakapapa Village are a more convenient alternative. National Park is on the rail line for trains between Auckland and Wellington and is also a stop for long-distance coach services. There are shuttle buses connecting National Park and Whakapapa Village.

Several hostels in Taupo organise transport to and from Tongariro National Park specifically aimed at day-trippers hiking the Tongariro Alpine Crossing.

Hiking

Hiking is the main attraction at Tongariro National Park. There is a wide selection of walks that range from an easy 15-minute stroll to demanding multi-day treks.

SHORT WALKS FROM WHAKAPAPA VILLAGE

There are several day walks from Whakapapa Village, with most of them departing from near the information centre.

The shortest is the **Whakapapa Nature Walk** (15 minutes) that starts 250m from the information centre taking in some of the regions unique flora.

The **Mounds Walk** (20 minutes) starts 5km south of the information centre. This interpretive walk takes you past mounds that were formed thousands of years ago by Ruapehu's volcanic activity.

The **Ridge Track** (30-40 minutes) is another short walk that departs from the information centre. This walk climbs through beech forest to the ridge where you are rewarded by panoramic views.

The varied **Silica Rapids Walk** (7km, 2½ hours) leaves from the information centre and follows a stream before arriving at Silica Rapids.

Taranaki Falls Walk (6km, 2 hours) is a longer walk that takes you to Taranaki Falls, which drop over a lava flow into a pool surrounded by boulders.

Whakapapaiti Valley Walk (4-5 hours) is a diverse walk through beech forest and along mountain ridges with fabulous views.

TONGARIRO ALPINE CROSSING

The Tongariro Alpine Crossing (17km, 6-8 hours) is the most popular hiking trail in the park and many people describe it as the world's best one day hike. It starts with a climb up to the saddle between the summits of Mount Ngauruhoe and Mount Tongariro and passes breathtaking scenery and then travels downhill to the finish line at Ketetahi car park.

There are several side trips that you can take; these include climbing to the summits of both Mount Ngauruhoe and Mount Tongariro and a short hike to Soda Springs.

You can walk this trail in either direction but most people start in the Mangatepopo Valley as this route involves less climbing. Much of the hike is over steep volcanic rock and it is recommended that you only undertake this trek if you're reasonably fit.

Most people complete the Crossing in one day, but there are two huts and campsites on the track so you may want to make it a two-day hike if you plan on tackling some of the side trips. Some people spend the first night at Mangatepopo hut so they can get an early start the following morning and beat the crowds that arrive by bus between 7.30am and 8.30am. It is possible to combine part of the Northern Circuit with the Tongariro Crossing, which enables you to start the walk from Whakapapa Village – this option involves hiking between Whakapapa and Mangatepopo Hut and adds an extra 8.5km (3-5 hours) to the hike.

Transport to the Crossing

Several companies operate shuttle buses for hikers tackling the Crossing.

There are several shuttle bus services between National Park Village and the Tongariro Alpine Crossing including a daily shuttle operated by Plateau Lodge (☎ *(07) 892 2993;* ***website*** *www.plateaulodge.co.nz)*, which costs $25 return.

Tongariro National Park Shuttle Transport (☎ *(06) 385 8561)* run a shuttle from Ohakune. The return trip costs $25.

Alpine Hotbus (☎ *0508 468 287;* ***website*** *www.alpinehotbus.co.nz)* operates a daily shuttle bus for hikers tackling the Tongariro Crossing. It departs Taupo at 6.15am with an additional 5.30am service during summer (Nov-Apr) and Turangi at 7am with an additional 6.15am service during summer (Nov-Apr). The return fare is $35 from Taupo and $45 from Turangi.

The car park at the trailheads is notorious for theft and even if you have your own car it is advisable to take one of the shuttle buses.

TONGARIRO NORTHERN CIRCUIT

The Department of Conservation (DOC) classifies the Tongariro Northern Circuit (50km, 3-4 days) as one of New Zealand's Great Walks. It takes in the more spectacular parts of the Tongariro Crossing, including the saddle between Mount Ngauruhoe and Mount Tongariro. Most people start and finish the Northern Circuit at Whakapapa Village, but some people start at Mangatepopo as this ties in nicely with many of the shuttle bus operators who drop off here for hikers doing the Tongariro Crossing.

The Northern Circuit is broken into four main sections, each ending at a hut making it possible to spend four days on the Circuit.

If you're starting at Whakapapa, the first section goes from Whakapapa Village to Mangatepopo Hut (8.5km, 3-5 hours) where it meets up with the Tongariro Crossing. You get a nice view of Mount Ngauruhoe and Mount Tongariro but this stretch can get muddy after wet weather.

The next section goes between Mangatepopo Hut and Oturere Hut (11km, 5½ hours). The stretch between Mangatepopo Hut and Emerald Lake follows the same route as the Tongariro Crossing along the saddle between the two mountains. It is possible to make side trips from here to the summit of both Mount Ngauruhoe (3 hours return) and Mount Tongariro (2 hours return). At Emerald Lake the track splits between the Tongariro Alpine Crossing and Northern Circuit, which descends into the Oturere Valley with views of the valley and the Rangipo Desert.

The section between Oturere Hut and Waihohonu Hut (8.5km, 3 hours) is a fairly easy day that passes several streams and open fields of volcanic gravel.

The home stretch from Waihohonu Hut back to Whakapapa Village (15½km, 5½ hours) follows the Waihohonu Stream before climbing the often windswept Tama Saddle. The track passes the lovely Taranaki Falls about an hour before it ends back at Whakapapa Village.

MOUNT RUAPEHU CRATER CLIMB

The Mount Ruapehu Crater Climb (5 hours) is the most challenging one-day hike on the national park. You need to take the Waterfall Express chairlift to the start of the walk. There are two main routes to the crater, but they are unmarked making it essential to bring along a good map and compass. During winter you'll need crampons, an ice axe and to be experienced in hiking and climbing in extreme conditions.

ROUND THE MOUNTAIN

The Round the Mountain hike (4-6 days) circumnavigates Mount Ruapehu and is accessible from either Turoa Ski Area (near Ohakune) or from Whakapapa Village. This hike features great mountain views, particularly of Mount Ruapehu, and is ideal for people who find the more popular walks too crowded.

Skiing & Snowboarding

The Mount Ruapehu Ski Area *(**website** www.mtruapehu.co.nz)* is New Zealand's largest and has two resorts, one on either side of the mountain.

Snowboarders and skiers alike love Turoa, which features long runs and New Zealand's longest vertical drop (720m). Most people skiing at Turoa stay at Ohakune, which is only 17km away.

On north western side of the mountain is Whakapapa. It boasts great views of Mt Taranaki and is a popular resort for beginners while still providing challenging runs for more advanced skiers. Whakapapa has its own village on the mountain but many people base themselves at National Park Village, which is only a short distance away.

There are several lift passes available that allow you to ski at both ski areas. The Rocket Pass is designed for beginners and features three days of lessons, ski or snowboard rental and lift tickets for $285. Alternatively a one-day lift pass is $83 or $113 for a lift pass with ski rental or $123 for a lift pass and snowboard rental.

National Park Village

There's not much to National Park Village, a small town on the main north-south train line. It was set up as an accommodation base for hikers and skiers visiting the national park. It has excellent transport connections and good accommodation, but there's very little character to the town; a few restaurants and a service station with a minimart make up are about all there is to this place.

But then, it's all about location here, and you're right at the doorstep to Tongariro National Park, making it an ideal base for park activities.

Coming & Going

The *Overlander* train stops at National Park Village en route between Auckland and Wellington.

InterCity Coachlines *(☎ (09) 623 1503; **website** www.intercity.co.nz)* stop at Ski Haus, and some services also stop at Howards Lodge; both on Carroll Street.

There are several shuttle bus services between National Park Village and the Tongariro Alpine Crossing including a daily shuttle operated by Plateau Lodge *(☎ (07) 892 2993; **website** www.plateaulodge.co.nz)*, which costs $25 return.

Accommodation

Adventure Lodge & Motel

Adventure Lodge and Motel is a former ski lodge with a great split-level lounge and big fireplace. Rooms are well-maintained and comfortable, with fully made-up beds. Internet and Wi-Fi access are offered, and there's a spa pool and drying room. There's also a restaurant and bar on-site, as well as a covered outdoor barbecue area. They have their own package deal to Tongariro Alpine Crossing, including accommodation, breakfast and dinner. In all, the Adventure Lodge has a nicer atmosphere than most other hostels in town.

Carroll Street, National Park
☎ (07) 892 2991
***Website** www.adventurenationalpark.co.nz*
***Dorm bed** $25-$30; **double room** $60*
***Credit cards** MC, Visa*
***Reception open** 7am-10pm daily*

Maintenance & cleanliness	★★★½
Facilities	★★½
Atmosphere & character	★★★★
Security	★½
Overall rating	★★★

The Crossing Backpackers

The Crossing Backpackers is situated 6km outside of National Park Village. This hostel is a sprawling property that includes a paintball arena and horse riding barn and stables. It feels more a part of Tongariro National Park than some of the other hostels in town, though the accommodation is definitely on the rustic side. Dormitories and common areas are in simple lodges with painted plywood walls and mismatched, secondhand furniture. There is a movie room with a big projection screen, and a huge outdoor fireplace that used to be part of a long-demolished building. Internet access is available.

Erua Road East, National Park
☎ *(07) 892 2894*
Website *www.thecrossingbackpackers.co.nz*
Dorm bed *$22-$24 ($19-$21 BBH);* ***double room*** *$61 ($55 BBH);* ***twin room*** *$51 ($45 BBH)*
Credit cards *MC, Visa*

Maintenance & cleanliness	★★
Facilities	★★★½
Atmosphere & character	★★
Security	★
Overall rating	★★

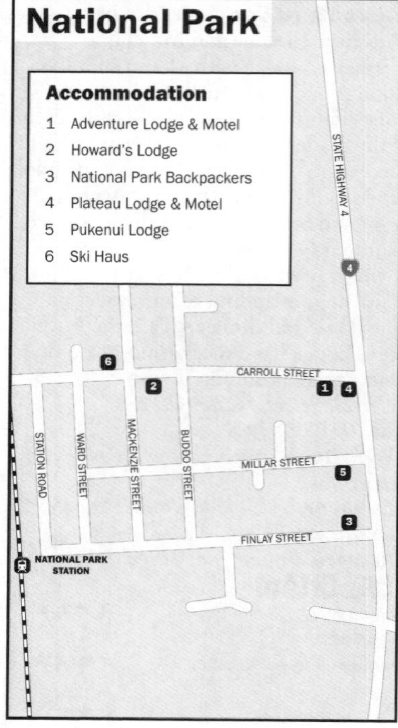

Howard's Lodge

This clean and well-maintained hostel features a couple of comfy lounges with great TVs and a pair of kitchens. Howard's runs one of the most comprehensive outdoor shops in town right on site, with ski gear, hiking boots and outdoor gear for hire. They're also the only mountain bike hire place in town. Accommodation is very clean and tidy. Other facilities include internet and Wi-Fi access, a spa pool, a drying room and an outdoor area with a barbecue.

Carroll Street, National Park
☎ *(07) 892 2827*
Website *www.howardslodge.co.nz*
Dorm bed *$22;* ***double/twin room*** *$60-$85;* ***triple room*** *$75-$105;* ***quad room*** *$90-$130*
Credit cards *Amex, MC, Visa, UnionPay*
Reception open *7am-8pm daily*

Maintenance & cleanliness	★★★★
Facilities	★★★½
Atmosphere & character	★★★
Security	★
Overall rating	★★★½

National Park Backpackers

This YHA associate is a little more worn than some of the other hostels in town. It does, however, offer probably the only rainy-day activity in National Park Village, an impressive climbing wall with five different grades. There's also a small shop with snacks and drinks on the premises, which is handy in a town where the only market (at the service station), closes at 7pm. Accommodation is otherwise basic and the layout is kind of a labyrinth but it's not a bad place overall. Facilities include a hot tub, internet access and a dining room/kitchen area with a log fire.

Finlay Street, National Park
☎ *(07) 892 2870s*
Website *www.npbp.co.nz*
Dorm bed *$22-$27 ($19-$22 YHA);* ***double/twin room*** *$59-$77 ($53-$71 YHA);* ***camping*** *$14 per person*

Credit cards *MC, Visa*
Reception open *7am-8pm daily*

Maintenance & cleanliness	★★½
Facilities	★★½
Atmosphere & character	★★
Security	★
Overall rating	★★½

Plateau Lodge & Motel

This is a small, very clean hostel that offers basic facilities. Rooms have nice, fully made-up beds and there is a spa pool as well as an outdoor barbecue. A common room has a dining area, log fire and a large flat-screen TV. The kitchen is on the small side. Internet and Wi-Fi access are available. The Plateau Lodge and Motel sleeps 56.

Carroll Street, National Park
(07) 892 2993
Website *www.plateaulodge.co.nz*
Dorm bed *$20-$22 ($17-$19);* ***double room*** *$60 ($54 BBH);* ***triple room*** *$87 ($78 BBH)*
Credit cards *MC, Visa*
Reception open *7am-8pm daily*

Maintenance & cleanliness	★★★★
Facilities	★★½
Atmosphere & character	★★½
Security	★
Overall rating	★★★

Pukenui Lodge

Pukenui Lodge is a nice, clean place with a sunny common room and big fireplace. Kitchen and dining facilities are on the small side, although meals are available. Rooms feature quality, made-up beds. There is a drying room and outdoor barbecue. One nice bonus is free internet access. The owner, Chris, is a good source of advice and information about activities around the area.

1 Millar Street, National Park
(07) 892 2882 or 0800 785 368
Website *www.tongariro.cc*
Dorm bed *$25;* ***double room*** *$55-$75*
Credit cards *Amex, Diners, MC, Visa*

Maintenance & cleanliness	★★★½
Facilities	★★
Atmosphere & character	★★★
Security	★½
Overall rating	★★★

Ski Haus

Ski Haus is an older lodge that has quite a bit of charm. The common area has a real alpine feel, with a big log fire and lots of cushions and cosy seating. The dorm rooms themselves are quite basic and the premises in general haven't been renovated in a while. There's a spa pool and drying room (like most places in town), and a new bar and restaurant on site.

Carroll Street, National Park
(07) 892 2854
Website *www.skihaus.co.nz*
Dorm bed *$20-$22 ($17-$19 BBH);* ***double room*** *$60 ($54 BBH);* ***triple room*** *$87 ($78 BBH)*
Credit cards *MC, Visa*
Reception open *7am-8pm daily*

Maintenance & cleanliness	★★½
Facilities	★★★
Atmosphere & character	★★★★
Security	★½
Overall rating	★★★

Eating & Drinking

There are only a few dining restaurants in National Park Village, and none of them are particularly cheap.

The Station *(Findlay Street, National Park)* is a very nice, slightly upscale joint right by the railway station. **Schnapps** *(corner State Highway 4 & Findlay Street, National Park)* is a very popular pub/restaurant. Many of the hostels in town also have on-site bars with food menus. The **Ski Haus** *(Carroll Street, National Park)* was in the process of totally revamping its restaurant when we visited, so this might be worth a look. The most backpacker budget-friendly spot in town, **Basekamp** *(Carroll Street, National Park)*, which does burgers and pizzas, is only open during the winter season.

There's no supermarket in town, just a mini-mart at the fuel station right at the intersection of State Highways 4 and 47. It closes at 7pm. There's a small shop at the reception of the National Park Backpackers on Findlay Street with packaged foods and sundries, which is open later. It's a good idea to stock up on groceries before coming here.

Ohakune

Ohakune is an attractive little ski town on the southern slopes of Mount Ruapehu, at the foot of the road leading to the Turoa Ski Resort. It's far, far busier in the winter, when most skiers and snowboarders tend to congregate in the lodges, bars and restaurants at the northern end of town, called the Junction. However, the main commercial strip in the southern part has some nice restaurants, bars, and shops as well, and there's more atmosphere than in National Park Village, which is 20 minutes away.

In the summer, the town can get very quiet and most hostel facilities are kind of barebones. There seems to be little incentive for hostels to court traditional backpacker crowds, as they get most of their business in the ski season

In addition to skiing, Ohakune is widely known as the carrot capital of New Zealand, and the giant carrot sculpture in town makes a kitschy photo-op.

Practical Information

INFORMATION CENTRES

Ruapehu i-SITE Visitor Information Centre

54 Clyde Street, Ohakune
☎ *(06) 385 8427*
Website *www.visitruapehu.com*
Open *Mon-Fri 9am-5pm, Sat-Sun 9am-3.30pm*

Department of Conservation

Ohakune Mountain Road, Ohakune.
☎ *(06) 385 0010*
Website *www.doc.govt.nz*
Open *Mon-Fri 9am-12.30pm & 1pm-3pm*

Coming & Going

Ohakune has good transport connections. The daily Overlander train on the Auckland-Wellington line stops here and InterCity Coachlines *(☎ (04) 385 0520;* ***website*** *www.intercity.co.nz)* stop opposite the Holiday Shop *(27 Clyde Street, Ohakune).*

Tongariro National Park Shuttle Transport *(☎ (06) 385 8561)* run a shuttle from Ohakune to the trailhead of the Tongariro Alpine Crossing. The return trip costs $25.

Accommodation

Alpine Backpackers

The Alpine Backpackers is in an arch-shaped building right in the heart of Ohakune. It is connected to the Alpine Motel and Sassi's Restaurant, and frankly feels like an afterthought to both. It is as basic as possible with a small kitchen and TV set just about the only facilities. Rooms are basic and small as well. It is, like all of Ohakune, much busier during the winter than the summer.

7 Miro Street, Ohakune
☎ *(06) 385 8758*
Dorm bed *$20-$27;* ***motel unit*** *$95*
Credit cards *Diners, MC, Visa*
Reception open *7am-late daily*

Maintenance & cleanliness	★★
Facilities	★
Atmosphere & character	★
Security	★
Overall rating	★★½

The Hobbit

The Hobbit is an attractive property, but one that is geared more towards its higher-end lodging. The backpackers' section is clean and beds are nicely made up with electric blankets but there is almost no communal space and kitchen facilities are minimal. All dorm rooms come with TVs, which just adds to the lack of any social atmosphere. There's a nice outdoor spa pool surrounded by trees, and room to hang out outside, but there is very little real backpacker feel here. It is better-suited for those looking for quiet and not particularly hoping to mingle with and meet other travellers.

Corner Goldfinch & Wye Streets, Ohakune
☎ *(06) 385 8248*
Website *www.the-hobbit.co.nz*
Dorm bed *$22-$44;* ***studio room*** *$90-$175*
Credit cards *MC, Visa*

Maintenance & cleanliness	★★★★½
Facilities	★★
Atmosphere & character	★
Security	★½
Overall rating	★★★

Matai Lodge

The Matai Lodge is a basic YHA youth hostel right in the centre of Ohakune. Facilities and accommodation are reasonably clean but on the worn side. Facilities include a common room with a log fire, a TV room with a nice flat-screen set and an outdoor area with a barbecue and volleyball net. One of the Matai's main attractions is that it operates its own shuttle service that offers flexible transport and pick-up all over the region. They also have an in-house tour company for river tours, the Tongariro Alpine Crossing and a rental vehicle service. It's more equipped for the summer activities in Ohakune than any of the other hostels in town.

1 Rata Street, Ohakune

(06) 385 9169 or (06) 385 8724

***Website** www.matailodge.co.nz*

***Dorm bed** $26 ($23 YHA/BBH); **double/twin room** $60 ($54 YHA/BBH)*

***Credit cards** MC, Visa*

***Reception open** 7am-9pm daily*

Maintenance & cleanliness	★★★½
Facilities	★★★½
Atmosphere & character	★★
Security	★½
Overall rating	★★★½

Rimu Park Lodge

Rimu Park Lodge is located on the Junction end of town, which buzzes in the winter but is quiet during the summer. It offers a very wide range of accommodation, from dorms and cabins to apartments and renovated train carriages. The backpacker facilities are located in a big, old villa with high ceilings, which is up kept fairly well and certainly has some charm. There's a big kitchen/dining area and a living room with a fireplace. Facilities include an outdoor spa pool and free internet access on a single PC.

27 Rimu Street, Ohakune

(06) 385 9023

***Website** www.rimupark.co.nz*

***Dorm bed** $20-$32; **cabin** $50-$80; **motel unit** $80-$120; **railway carriage** $80-$190*

Maintenance & cleanliness	★★★½
Facilities	★★
Atmosphere & character	★★★★½
Security	★½
Overall rating	★★★½

Station Lodge

Station Lodge is only open during the winter ski season and is generally known as the first place to fill up in Ohakune. Beds are mainly taken up by skiers travelling together in groups, so it doesn't strictly have a backpacker feel. The hostel is located in a big house on the Junction end of town, right next to the actual train station. Rooms are clean and fairly cosy, and the facilities are basic, though well looked after. A kitchen and TV lounge with pool table are available, as are an outdoor spa pool and drying room. Prices are the lowest in town for ski season. The owners also operate one of the most popular and cheapest ski shops in Ohakune next door.

60 Thames Street, Ohakune

(06) 385 8797

***Website** www.stationlodge.co.nz*

***Dorm bed** $23-$27*

***Credit cards** MC, Visa*

***Open** ski season (mid Jun-Nov)*

Maintenance & cleanliness	★★★★½
Facilities	★★
Atmosphere & character	★★★½
Security	★
Overall rating	★★★½

Wanganui & Whanganui National Park

This is one of the most underrated destinations in New Zealand. Wanganui, the region's main town, is one of New Zealand's nicest cities and the Whanganui River Journey canoe trip is one of the country's best outdoor activities.

Wanganui

Wanganui is one of New Zealand's oldest European settlements and possibly the country's most underrated destination. It is a small city of around 50,000 with a lively cultural scene that you would expect in a much larger city. It is also a pretty town with lovely architecture, including some great Art Deco buildings and a nice riverfront promenade that hosts a great Saturday morning market.

There's not a lot to do in town unless you like visiting glass blowing studios; and let's face it, that isn't high on the backpackers' list of things to do. However Wanganui is a great place to stock up on supplies and make arrangements for the Whanganui River Journey – an epic three to five-day canoe trip on the Whanganui River, which incidentally is probably New Zealand's most underrated outdoor activity.

Practical Information

Wanganui i-SITE Visitor Centre

101 Guyton Street, Wanganui
☎ *(06) 349 0508*
Website *www.wanganuinz.com*
Open *Mon-Fri 8.30am-5pm, Sat-Sun 9am-3pm*

Department of Conservation

74 Ingestre Street, Wanganui
☎ *(06) 345 2402*
Website *www.doc.govt.nz*
Open *Mon-Fri 8am-5pm*

Coming & Going

InterCity Coachlines *(☎ (04) 385 0520; **website** www.intercity.co.nz)* has buses to Auckland, New Plymouth and Wellington and White Star Bus *(☎ (06) 759 0197; **website** www.whitestarbus.co.nz)* stop in Wanganui en route between New Plymouth and Wellington. Buses stop outside the Travel Centre at 156 Ridgway Street.

Accommodation

Anndion Lodge

Anndion Lodge is a new hostel on the north bank of the river, although it is a bit far from the centre of town. It has excellent facilities that include a fully-equipped kitchen, a dining room, free internet access (including Wi-Fi) and a lounge room with a TV, pool table and fireplace. There is also a salt water swimming pool, a sauna and spa. Everything here is brand new and very clean. However there are TVs in the rooms, which keep people away from the common areas and dampens the atmosphere.

143 Anzac Parade, Wanganui
☎ *(06) 343 3593 or 0800 343056*
Website *www.anndionlodge.co.nz*
Dorm bed *$30;* ***double room*** *$80-120;* ***twin room*** *$80*
Credit cards *Amex, MC, Visa*

Maintenance & cleanliness	★★★★★
Facilities	★★★★½
Atmosphere & character	★★½
Security	★★
Overall rating	★★★★

Braemar House YHA

Wanganui's YHA hostel consists of just 10 beds at the rear of a B&B, by the riverfront not far from Tamara Lodge. It is a neat and tidy hostel with facilities that include a small lounge with a TV, internet access including Wi-Fi (pay) and a kitchen. There is also an outdoor area where you can sit and have a few drinks.

2 Plymouth Road, Wanganui
☎ *(06) 347 2529*
Website *www.braemarhouse.co.nz*
Dorm bed *$25 ($22 HI/YHA);* ***double room*** *$56 ($54 HI/YHA)*
Credit cards *MC, Visa*
Reception open *8am-9pm daily*

Maintenance & cleanliness	★★★
Facilities	★★
Atmosphere & character	★★★
Security	★
Overall rating	★★½

Tamara Backpackers

Tamara Backpackers Lodge is in a large wooden house by the riverfront not too far from the city centre and there is a newer building out the back with en suite rooms. There is the usual kitchen; a TV lounge with a piano; plus a dining room with internet access and laundry and a nice back garden with a trampoline, hammocks and a nice sitting area. It is a grand old building with tall ceilings and there is a great atmosphere, but many of

the fittings and furnishings look a bit tired and the kitchen could do with an overhaul (however it would be a great hostel with new furniture and bedding). Rory, the manager, is a fount of information about things to see and do around Wanganui.
24 Somme Parade, Wanganui
☎ *(06) 347 6300*
Website *www.tamaralodge.com*
Dorm bed *$24 ($21 BBH);* ***single room*** *$43-53 ($40-50 BBH);* ***double/twin room*** *$56-66 ($50-60 BBH)*
Credit cards *MC, Visa*
Reception open *8am-9pm daily*

Maintenance & cleanliness	★★★½
Facilities	★★★
Atmosphere & character	★★★★★
Security	★★½
Overall rating	★★★

Eating & Drinking

Victoria Avenue is Wanganui's main restaurant and café strip, particularly between Maria Place and the City Bridge.

Stellar Restaurant & Bar *(3 Victoria Avenue, Wanganui)* is a good choice with a bar, quality pub-style food, a great atmosphere and free Wi-Fi. **Vega** *(49 Taupo Quay, Wanganui)* is another bar with good food specials. Vega has a brilliant riverfront location, right across the road from Stellar. Your best bet, however, is to buy fish and chips – there are a couple of fish and chip shops on Victoria Avenue – to eat on the riverbank.

Wanganui's most centrally located supermarket is **Countdown** *(corner Taupo Quay & Wilson Street, Wanganui)*. Other supermarkets in Wanganui include **New World** *(374 Victoria Avenue, Wanganui)*, **Pak'n Save** *(167 Glasgow Street, Wanganui)* and **Woolworths** *(Upper Victoria Avenue, Wanganui)*.

Sights

Durie Hill Elevator & Memorial Tower

If you walk across the Wanganui City Bridge you'll come to the Durie Hill tunnel, which takes you 205m into the hill where it meets the Durie Hill Elevator. Built in 1919, this historic lift takes you 66m up to the top of the hill. Once at the top, you can climb the 33.5m Memorial Tower for spectacular views of the city. On a clear day you can see Mounts Ruapehu and Taranaki.
Access to tunnel from Anzac Parade, Wanganui
Open *Mon-Fri 7.30am-6pm, Sat 9am-5pm, Sun 10am-5pm*

Queens Park

Originally the site of a Māori pā, this city park is home to several of Wanganui's main sights including the Sarjeant Gallery and the Whanganui Regional Museum.

Sarjeant Gallery

The world-renowned Sarjeant Gallery occupies an imposing neo-classical building in Queens Park. It is one of New Zealand's best regional art galleries and is host to a varying exhibition programme.
Queens Park, Wanganui
☎ *(06) 349 0506*
Website *www.sarjeant.org.nz*
Admission *free*
Open *10.30am-4.30pm daily*

Whanganui Regional Museum

This imposing regional museum is home to an extensive collection of exhibits with a focus on Maori culture, local and natural history. It is noted for its collection of Lindauer portraits and Maori taonga.
Watt Street, Wanganui
☎ *(06) 345 7443*
Website *www.wanganui-museum.org.nz*
Admission *$5*
Open *10am-4.30pm daily*

Whanganui Riverboat Centre

The Whanganui Riverboat Centre consists of the restored 100 year-old steam-powered paddle steamer *Waimarie* and a small museum. *Waimarie* plied the waters of the Whanganui River between 1899 and 1949 and she capsized and sank in 1952. In 1993 *Waimarie* was salvaged and after a seven-year restoration programme she was re-launched in 2000. *Waimarie* now runs regular cruises 13km upriver

to the small settlement of Upokongoro.
1A Taupo Quay, Wanganui
☎ *(06) 347 1863 or 0800 STEAMER*
***Website** www.riverboat.co.nz*
***Cruise** $33*
***Open** Mon-Sat 9am-4pm, Sun 10am-4pm*

Whanganui National Park

The mighty Whanganui River flows from the slopes of Mount Tongariro to Wanganui and much of its rugged grandeur is contained within the Whanganui National Park.

The national park has some great hiking trails and it is also home to the Great Walk that isn't really a walk – the Whanganui River Journey.

Hiking

Atene Skyline Track

The Atene Skyline Track (6-8 hours) starts on the Whanganui River Road, 35km from Wanganui. It is an excellent day hike that takes in magnificent views of Mount Ruapehu, Mount Taranaki and the Whanganui River.

Mangapurua Track

The Mangapurua Track (3-4 hours one-way) starts at either Ruatiti or Whakahoro and follows the Manapurua Valley via the Bridge to Nowhere. The track ends up at the Mangapurua Landing on the Whanganui River. Most people walk one way and take a jet boat back. There are several jet boat operators that offer this service including **Bridge to Nowhere Tours** *(☎ (06) 348 7122; **website** www.bridgetonowhere-lodge.co.nz)* and **River Spirit Jet Tours** *(☎ (06) 342 1718; **website** www.riverspirit.co.nz).*

Matemateonga Track

The Matemateonga Track (3-4 hours one-way) is a brilliant half-day hike that follows an old Maori trail into the wilderness of Whanganui National Park. Most people walk one way and take a jet boat back. There are several jet boat operators that offer this service including **Bridge to Nowhere Tours** *(☎ (06) 348 7122; **website** www.bridgetonowhere-lodge.co.nz)* and **River Spirit Jet Tours** *(☎ (06) 342 1718; **website** www.riverspirit.co.nz).*

Whanganui River Journey

The longest navigable river in New Zealand is the site of an outstanding canoe trip through the wilderness of the Whanganui National Park. Although it is a canoe trip, DOC classifies the Whanganui River Journey (145km; 3-5 days) as one of New Zealand's Great Walks – it's the walk you do sitting down.

The River Journey offers a lot more experiences than your regular hiking trail. You get to sit down and paddle down-river for five days (although there is a shorter three-day alternative), during this time you pass 249 named rapids (mostly grades one and two), paddle under the famous Bridge to Nowhere and you have the chance to experience Māori culture at the Tieke Kāinga marae.

Because it is a canoe trip it requires a bit more organisation than your average hike. You have the option of taking a guided canoe trip or hiring the canoes and finding your own way down river. You can hire either a kayak or Canadian canoe; many people prefer the open canoes, as they are more convenient for carrying camping gear.

If you're making the journey in the peak season (Oct-Apr), you have to buy a hut and campsite pass ($45 for six nights) from a DOC office before starting your journey. Camping is free off-season (May-Sep) and you only need hut tickets ($10), or an annual hut pass, if you're staying in huts.

THE JOURNEY

The River Journey starts at Cherry Grove near Taumaruni and finishes at Pipiriki, 68km north of Wanganui, and usually takes five days. There are only three huts along the route so you'll need to bring along a tent to camp the first night. The following description of the River Journey is broken into the four sections between the huts, however the first section is rather long and most people break it into two (making it a five day journey). The *Guide to the Whanganui River*, available from DOC offices, describes the journey in more detail.

Cherry Grove to Whakahoro Hut (57km)

Most of the rapids occur in the first part of the journey between Cherry Grove and Whakahoro Hut (57km), which most people take two days to complete.

There are three camping options on this stretch of the journey, these are Ohinepane, Poukaria and Maharanui – most people camp at either Ohinepane or Poukaria.

During the second day you'll pass the Niu Poles, where warriors would worship before battle.

Whakahoro Hut to John Coull Hut (37.5km)

During second part of the journey the river becomes a little calmer as you pass prominent cliffs. There is a small cave with glow worms located across the river from the Ohauora campsite, about two thirds of the way to John Coull Hut.

John Coull Hut to Tieke Kāinga (29km)

At Mangapurua, 19km from John Coull Hut, you can make a short detour up the Mangapurua Stream to the famous Bridge to Nowhere. This concrete bridge would otherwise be fairly ordinary if it wasn't sitting in the middle of the wilderness. It was built shortly after World War I as an access route to new farming areas that were being developed at the time, however the project failed and the bridge now is just a rather surreal part of the Mangapurua Track.

Tieke Kāinga is the highlight of this section of the journey. Tieke was originally an old pā (fortified village), which has been revived as a marae (Māori meeting place). It is a unique opportunity to experience Māori culture as you get to participate in a powhiri (welcome ceremony). You will be met at the riverbank and the protocol of the powhiri will be explained to you before you enter the marae. It is customary to present a koha (gift) during the powhiri, this may be anything such as food or money.

Tieke Kainga to Pipiriki (21.5km)

The final leg of the journey has some of the biggest rapids and the wilderness gives way to farmland as you approach Pipiriki.

GEAR RENTAL & GUIDED TRIPS

There are several companies that offer kayak and canoe rental; some of these companies also operate guided trips. These companies provide transport to and from the river. They include:

Blazing Paddles Canoe Adventures
1033 State Highway 4, Taumarunui
☎ *(07) 895 5261 or 0800 BLAZING (0800 252 946)*
Website *www.blazingpaddles.co.nz*
Canoe or kayak rental *$210 three days, $240 five days*

Canoe Safaris
☎ *(06) 385 9237 or 0800 2 PADDLE*
Website *www.canoesafaris.co.nz*
Three-day guided trip *$595;* ***five-day guided trip*** *$840*

Yeti Tours
☎ *(06) 385 8197 or 0800 322 388*
Website *www.canoe.co.nz*
Canoe/kayak rental *$165 three days, $215 five days;* ***three-day guided trip*** *$575,* ***six-day guided trip*** *$850*

Manawatu & Rangitikei

This area is fertile sheep and dairy farming country. Palmerston North is the region's major town, which you will no doubt pass through if you're travelling through the North Island. Further north youll find the rugged Rangitikei River and Taihape.

Palmerston North

Palmerston North is on the banks of the Manawatu River and has a population of almost 80,000, making it the main city in the Manawatu-Wanganui region. "Palmy" is home to Massey

University, New Zealand's second largest, and has a sizable student population, giving it a youthful energy and cultural life.

The heart of Palmerston North is The Square, a 7ha park at the centre of town that includes a war memorial and clock tower. The streets leading into and surrounding The Square are concentrated with restaurants, bars, bookstores, shops, boutiques and theatres. Other attractions in town are the Rugby Museum and Te Manawa, a unique facility that combines a history museum, art gallery and interactive science centre.

Palmerston North is not a major tourist attraction, but it does offer an opportunity to meet and mingle with a big university crowd when school's in session, and can make for an interesting stopover.

Practical Information

Palmerston North i-SITE Visitor Centre

52 The Square, Palmerston North
☎ *(06) 350 1922*
***Website** www.manawatunz.co.nz*
***Open** Mon-Fri 9am-5pm, Sat-Sun 10am-3pm*

Department of Conservation

717 Tremaine Avenue, Palmerston North
☎ *(06) 350 9700*
***Website** www.doc.govt.nz*
***Open** Mon-Fri 8am-4.30pm*

INTERNET ACCESS

Palmerston North City Library

Not only does the flash new library have internet access, but there are lockers and showers too.
The Square, Palmerston North
☎ *(06) 351 4100*
***Website** http://citylibrary.pncc.govt.nz/*
***Internet access** $6 per hour; **showers** $1*

Coming & Going

Palmerston North is located at the crossroads of several air, coach and rail routes and many people pass through here to make transport connections.

AIR

Palmerston North International Airport *(☎ (06) 351 4415; **website** www.pnairport.co.nz)* has domestic flights to Auckland, Christchurch, Hamilton, Nelson and Wellington. The airport is only 5km north east of the city centre and Super Shuttle *(☎ 0800 SHUTTLE (0800 748 885); **website** www.supershuttle.co.nz)* run minibuses to meet all flights.

BUS

InterCity Coachlines *(☎ (04) 385 0520; **website** www.intercity.co.nz)* go to Auckland, Napier, New Plymouth, Tauranga, Wanganui, Wellington; Naked Bus *(☎ 0900 62533; **website** www.nakedbus.com)* has services to Auckland, Napier, Taupo, Rotorua and Wellington; BayXpress *(☎ 0800 422 997; **website** www.bayxpress.co.nz)* goes to Hawkes Bay and Wellington and White Star Bus *(☎ (06) 759 0197; **website** www.whitestarbus.co.nz)* has services to New Plymouth, Wanganui and Wellington.

Buses stop on Main Street near The Square. InterCity stops on the west side of The Square near the corner of Main and Pitt Streets and most other buses including Naked Bus stop on Main Street just east of The Square. Buses also stop at Massey University.

TRAIN

The daily *Overlander* train on the Auckland-Wellington line and the *Capital Connection* service to Wellington stop in Palmerston North. The train station is on Matthews Avenue, about 1km north of The Square.

Accommodation

Grandma's Place

The name doesn't lie – there is definitely a "grandma's" feel here, with the old vanities, quilted bedspreads and linen doilies decorating the rooms. It may make you nostalgic for those Sunday visits to Granny's. Everything feels kind of timeworn, however, and facilities are limited. There isn't much social atmosphere either, with a small kitchen and TV lounge the extent of the common spaces.
146 Grey Street, Palmerston North
☎ *(06) 358 6928*
***Website** www.grandmas-place.com*

Dorm bed *$25 ($22 BBH);* ***single room*** *$45 ($42 BBH);* ***double/twin room*** *$60 ($54 BBH)*
Credit cards *Amex, MC, Visa*

Maintenance & cleanliness	★★½
Facilities	★
Atmosphere & character	★★½
Security	★½
Overall rating	★★

Pepper Tree Hostel

They've been at it for 17 years at the Pepper Tree Lodge but the house and accommodation has been very well taken care of. Rooms are simple, colourful and bright. A lounge area has comfortable couches, a TV, books and a log fire. The kitchen is very well laid out, with utensils easy to reach and easy to see – the kind of touch that makes this a very good hostel. There's a small outdoor area with a smokers' porch and a herb garden. The owners are very keen on recycling, so separate your rubbish. Plus, for you gear heads, they run a racing team out of their garage and there are some really cool cars about.
121 Grey Street, Palmerston North
☎ *(06) 355 4054*
Dorm bed *$26 ($23 BBH, HI/YHA);* ***double/twin room*** *$60 ($54 BBH, HI/YHA)*
Reception open *8am-9.30pm daily*

Maintenance & cleanliness	★★★½
Facilities	★★
Atmosphere & character	★★★
Security	★★
Overall rating	★★★

Eating & Drinking

Palmerston North is a big university town and has numerous cheap places to eat and drink that cater to its student population; hence, they're great for backpackers as well.

Food and nightlife centres on the streets around The Square, the park right at the heart of Palmy. The streets to the west side of the square, particularly George and Cuba Streets, are where most of the bar and café action is. Some popular places include **Moxies Café** *(81 George Street, Palmerston North)* and **Mao Bar** *(64 George Street, Palmerston North).* **Bar Mode** *(1 Coleman Place, Palmerston North)* is the best indie/punk/eclectic live music venue in town, with local and international touring acts passing through. The **Fitz Bar** *(Ferguson Street, Palmerston North)*, is Palmy's quintessential student bar.

Supermarkets in Palmerston North include **Countdown** *(corner Ashley & Ferguson Streets, Palmerston North)*; **New World** *(179-197 Main Street, Palmerston North)*; **Pak'n Save** *(335 Ferguson Street, Palmerston North)* and **Woolworths** *(corner Featherston & Rangitikei Streets, Palmerston North).* Pop into Pak'n Save to stock up on picnic fixings to eat in The Square.

Sights

New Zealand Rugby Museum

The world's oldest museum devoted to rugby features an extensive collection of rugby memorabilia from around the world.
87 Cuba Street, Palmerston North
☎ *(06) 358 6947*

Website *www.rugbymuseum.co.nz*
Admission *$5*
Open *Mon-Sat 10am-noon & 1.30pm-4pm, Sun 1.30pm-4pm*

Te Manawa

This excellent regional museum combines exhibits in the fields of art, history and science. It is a well laid out museum with many interactive exhibits.

396 Main Street, Palmerston North
☎ *(06) 355 5000*
Website *www.temanawa.co.nz*
Admission *ART & LIFE galleries free; MIND galleries $8*
Open *10am-5pm daily*

Owlcatraz

This wildlife park focuses on owls, but there are also other animals. Visitors to Owlcatraz go on a guided tour that takes them into the enclosure with the owls. A full tour takes a couple of hours.

State Highway 57, Shannon (½hr south of Palmerston North)
☎ *(06) 362 7872*
Website *www.owlcatraz.co.nz*
Admission *$10-20*
Open *10am-3pm daily*

Taihape

Taihape is a small service town on State Highway 1 that bills itself as the "gumboot capital of New Zealand" – but then you already knew that. Or maybe not, but it's kind of hard to miss the enormous gumboot statue on the north side of town. Each year in October, Taihape holds a Gumboot Day festival, with events like gumboot throwing and gumboot races.

Taihape has a small main street with shopping and a few restaurants and cafés. It's about a 45-minute drive from Mount Ruapehu, making it a potential base for skiing. Twenty minutes southeast of Taihape is an extreme sports complex, Mokai Gravity Canyon, with an 80m bungee jump, the highest tandem swing in the world, and what they claim is the world's most extreme flying fox, which goes over the Rangitikei River at speeds up to 160 km/h.

Coming & Going

InterCity (☎ *(09) 623 1503;* ***website*** *www.intercity.co.nz)* and Naked Bus (☎ *0900 62533;* ***website*** *www.nakedbus.com)* stop opposite the BP Service Station on Kuku Street. Buses go to Auckland, Tauranga and Wellington.

Accommodation

River Valley Lodge

River Valley Lodge is a destination in itself. Thirty minutes outside Taihape, it's all about outdoor recreation and adventure here – white water rafting, horse trekking, golf, kayaking, fly fishing… the list of activities goes on and on. The lodge is in an absolutely gorgeous valley right on the Rangitikei River. A sauna and spa pool is available, and you can shell out for serious spa massage treatments as well. The backpacker accommodation is nothing special, and the kitchen is positively miniscule, but there is a bar/café on site, and a grand common area with a great log fire in the middle. But then, you'll most likely spend most of your time outdoors anyway.

RD2, Pukeokahu, Taihape
☎ *(06) 388 1444 or 0800 248 666*
Website *www.rivervalley.co.nz*
Dorm bed *$22-$27;* ***single room*** *$55;* ***double/twin room*** *$65*
Credit cards *MC, Visa*

Maintenance & cleanliness	★★★★
Facilities	★★★★
Atmosphere & character	★★★★½
Security	★
Overall rating	★★★★

Stockman's Lodge

This is a small, charming log house on a hill just outside Taihape. The lodge is filled with lots of solid-wood furnishings; the kitchen is especially attractive with sturdy chopping blocks and counters and a big solid breakfast bar. The dorm rooms themselves are pretty bare and rustic. An outdoor deck has great views over the town, with Mount Ruapehu in the background. A common room is quite cosy as well. Meals are available, as are laundry and internet.

9 Dixon Way, Taihape
☎ *(06) 388 1584*

***Website** www.stockmanslodge.co.nz*
***Dorm bed** $20 ($18 BBH); **double room** $50 ($46 BBH)*
***Credit cards** MC, Visa*

Maintenance & cleanliness	★★★
Facilities	★★
Atmosphere & character	★★★★
Security	½
Overall rating	★★½

Activities

Mokai Gravity Canyon

This extreme sports complex, 20 minutes southeast of Taihape, features an 80m bungee jump (New Zealand's tallest bridge bungee jump), the highest tandem swing in the world (with a 50m freefall) and what they claim is the world's most extreme flying fox, which is 1km-long and goes at speeds up to 160 km/h over the Rangitikei River.

Mokai Bridge, Taihape
☎ (06) 388 9109 or 0800 802 864
***Website** www.gravitycanyon.co.nz*
***One activity** $110, **two activities** $175, **three activities** $240, **repeat an activity on the same day** $65*
***Open** 9am-5pm daily*

Wellington Region

New Zealand's capital is a vibrant city and virtually all backpackers pass through here, both to make transport connections between the North and South Islands and to explore the city. However most travellers seldom see the region beyond the city, including the Kapiti Coast and the Wairarapa Region.

Wellington

New Zealand's bustling capital is often seen as a transit point to make connections between the North and South Islands. However there is much more to Wellington, with its pleasant harbour front area that includes the excellent Te Papa museum.

Wellington is built around a hilly landscape; houses cling to steep hills and high rises occupy the precious flat space in the downtown area. Due to

Wellington Region

PALMERSTON NORTH AIRPORT
PALMERSTON NORTH
1
56
57
57
1
OTAKI
PARAPARAUMU
MASTERTON
PAEKAKARIKI
2
53
MARTINBOROUGH
WELLINGTON AIRPORT
WELLINGTON
Cook Strait
www.quickmap.co.nz

Must do in Wellington Region

- Visit Te Papa
- Ride the cable car
- Take a day trip to Martinborough

the lack of flat space Wellington began building multi-storey office buildings early on, and the town has a real big-city feel even though there are only 380,000 residents. The hilly terrain also prevented a lot of the suburban sprawl that you find in Auckland, making it an easily walkable city.

Like Auckland, New Zealand's windy city is built around a spectacular harbour. This isn't as big a feature in Wellington but the suburban ferry services make good day trips.

Apart from Te Papa, Wellington's attractions include the Bond Store, a maritime museum; the Beehive, Wellington's parliament house and the popular cable car ride between Lambton Quay and Kelburn.

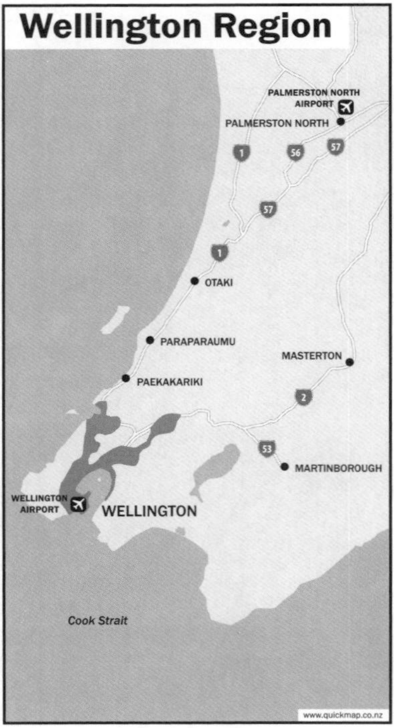

Practical Information

INFORMATION CENTRES

Wellington i-SITE Visitor Centre

Corner Victoria & Wakefield Streets, Wellington

☎ *(04) 802 4860*

Website *www.wellingtonnz.com*

Open *Mon 8.30am-5.30pm, Tue 8.30am-5pm, Wed-Fri 8.30am-5.30pm, Sat-Sun 8.30am-4.30pm*

Department of Conservation Visitor Centre

18 Manners Street, Wellington

☎ *(04) 384 7770*

Website *www.doc.govt.nz*

Open *Mon-Fri 9am-5pm, Sat 10am-3.30pm*

EMBASSIES

British Embassy

44 Hill Street, Wellington

☎ *(04) 924 2888*

Website *www.britain.org.nz*

Open *Mon-Fri 8.45am-5pm*

Canadian High Commission
61 Molesworth Street, Wellington
☎ *(04) 473 9577*
Website *www.dfait-maeci.gc.ca/newzealand/*
Open *Mon-Fri 8.30am-12.30pm & 1.30pm-4.30pm*

United States Embassy
29 Fitzherbert Terrace, Thorndon
☎ *(04) 472 2068*
Website *http://newzealand.usembassy.gov*
Open *Mon-Fri 9am-5pm*

INTERNET ACCESS

Cyberspot Internet Café
Lambton Square, 180 Lambton Quay, Wellington
☎ *(04) 473 0098*
Website *www.cyberspot.co.nz*
Open *Mon-Fri 9am-7pm, Sat 11am-3pm*

iPlay
49 Manners Street, Wellington
☎ *(04) 494 0088*
Website *www.iplaynz.com*
Open *24 hours*

Esquires Coffee *(**website** www.esquires.co.nz; 75 Featherston Street, Wellington & Courtenay Central, 100 Courtenay Place, Wellington)* has free Wi-Fi access.

Coming & Going

AIR

Wellington International Airport *(☎ (04) 385 5100; **website** www.wellington-airport.co.nz)* is a great airport to fly from – it's only 5km from the city centre, it's newly renovated and it is small enough to make checking in a breeze. It is New Zealand's busiest airport in terms of the number of flights, but most flights are domestic and the only international flights are to Australia and Fiji.

Many backpackers fly to the South Island from Wellington as an alternative to the ferry. There are a couple of options including Air Zealand flights to Blenheim or Nelson and Sounds Air flights between Wellington and Picton. Sounds Air provide a shuttle bus service at both ends, which will pick you up and drop you off at your hostel.

The Stagecoach Flyer *(**website** www.stagecoach.co.nz/flyer/)* bus departs for the airport from spots in the city centre. The fare is $5.50. Alternatively shuttle buses such as those operated by Super Shuttle *(☎ 0800 748 885 (0800 SHUTTLE); **website** www.supershuttle.co.nz)* charge around $15 but they will pick up or drop off wherever you want.

BUS

InterCity Coachlines *(☎ (04) 385 0520; **website** www.intercity.co.nz)* and Naked Bus *(☎ 0900 62533; **website** www.nakedbus.com)* have services from Wellington to most major destinations around the North Island.

InterCity coaches depart from platform nine at the train station on Bunny Street. Naked Bus has two Wellington stops: on outside the train station on Bunny Street, near Waterloo Quay and on Wakefield Street, opposite the Duxton Hotel.

Backpacker buses serve most hostels although Wellington is a hilly city and buses may not be able to drop you off right at the door of some places.

TRAIN

Wellington's train station is located on Bunny Street. There are trains to Auckland via Palmerston North, National Park and Hamilton. The Wairarapa Line has several trains a day to Masterton.

FERRY

There are several ferries that sail between Wellington and Picton on the South Island.

Blue Bridge
Blue Bridge *(☎ 0800 844 844; **website** www.bluebridge.co.nz)* provides an alternative to the more popular Interislander ferry service. They are usually the cheapest option if you are taking a car across. They sail from Waterloo Quay near the train station.

Interislander
The Interislander *(☎ 0800 802 802; **website** www.interislander.co.nz)* ferry

sails from Aotea Quay, which is just north of the Westpac Trust Stadium.

A free shuttle bus departs from the train station 35 minutes before each departure. This bus departs from the bus station at platform nine. There is also a direct bus that will transfer you to the ferry terminal from Base Backpackers and the YHA hostel for $3.

HITCHHIKING

Although the Wellington Urban Motorway is an easy way to drive out of town, it is difficult to hitch a ride at the downtown entrances, as much of the traffic is local and there are few places for cars to safely stop for you.

Your best bet is to take a train out of town and try your luck outside the city. The price of the train fare is worth the time you will save. Take a train to Paraparaumu or Otaki and wait for a lift on State Highway 1. It should be fairly easy hitching once you're out of town.

Local Transport

Metlink *(☎ 0800 801 700; **website** www.metlink.org.nz)* is Wellington's integrated public transport network, which is comprised of buses, trolley buses, trains, ferries and a cable car.

BUS

Buses and trolley buses are the best way to get around central Wellington. The bus is also the best way to get around the Miramar Peninsula and other areas not served by train routes.

Stagecoach Wellington *(☎ 0800 801 700; **website** www.stagecoach.co.nz)* operates most bus services although Newlands Coach Service, Mana Coach Services and Cityline Hutt Valley operate services to some suburban areas. One-way fares cost between $1 and $3.50.

A Stagecoach Wellington Daytripper ticket costs $5, and gives you unlimited travel on Stagecoach buses after 9am Mon-Fri and all day on weekends.

The STAR pass is a slightly more flexible travel pass giving you unlimited travel for one day on Cityline, Hutt Valley, Stagecoach Flyer and Stagecoach Wellington services (excluding After Midnight buses). The STAR pass costs $10.

CABLE CAR

Wellington's cable car *(☎ (04) 472 2199; **website** www.wellingtoncablecar.co.nz)* is one of the city's major attractions. The vintage cable car runs from the terminus on Cable Car Lane (off Lambton Quay) to the Botanic Gardens at Kelburn, via the university. The cable car runs every ten minutes (Mon-Fri 7am-10pm, Sat-Sun 8.30am-10pm). A one-way fare is $2.50, return fare $4.50.

FERRY

The *Dominion Post* ferry *(☎ (04) 499 1282; **website** www.eastbywest.co.nz)* departs Queen's Wharf for Days Bay and Matiu Somes Island. This is a popular day excursion from Wellington and worth considering if you want to escape the city. The fare to Days Bay is $8.50 each way.

TRAIN

Wellington's train station is conveniently located in the heart of the city making the train a good way to get around – particularly if you want to visit the Kapiti Coast or Hutt Valley.

Tranz Metro *(☎ (04) 801 7000; **website** www.tranzmetro.co.nz)* runs four train lines with most services running at 30-minute intervals.

Example one-way fares from the city centre are $4.50 ($3.50 off-peak) to Porirua, $6 ($4.50 off-peak) to Mana or Plimmerton and $8 ($6 off-peak) to Paekakariki. There are savings if you buy a 10-trip or monthly ticket. A Day Rover ticket costs $10 and is good for unlimited train travel after 9am on weekdays and all day on weekends.

Accommodation

CITY CENTRE

Base Backpackers

Base's Wellington hostel is a top quality backpackers' hostel near Courtney Place. It has a big reception area with bike hire and internet access including Wi-Fi (Global Gossip Connect) plus the main common area upstairs has a kitchen, dining room, a TV lounge and a courtyard. There is a basement bar, although alcohol is not allowed within the hostel. The rooms are clean and the reception area is welcoming, although the main common areas on the first floor don't have quite as much atmosphere as they could have.

21-23 Cambridge Terrace, Wellington

☎ *(04) 801 5666 or 0800 BASE NZ*

Website *www.basebackpackers.com*

Dorm bed *$26-29;* ***double room*** *$85-95*

Credit cards *Amex, Diners, MC, Visa*

Reception open *24 hours*

Maintenance & cleanliness	★★★★
Facilities	★★
Atmosphere & character	★★★
Security	★★★★★
Overall rating	★★★½

Beethoven House

This small hostel in Mount Victoria is messy and cluttered with Beethoven memorabilia scattered around the hostel. Some travellers find that the mess adds to the character but most backpackers prefer to stay somewhere a bit cleaner. Common areas include a small kitchen and some outdoor sitting areas.

89 Brougham Street, Mount Victoria

☎ *(04) 384 2226*

Dorm bed *$24 ($21 BBH);* ***double/twin room*** *$58 ($52 BBH)*

Maintenance & cleanliness	★
Facilities	★
Atmosphere & character	★★★½
Security	-
Overall rating	★½

The Cambridge Hotel

The Cambridge Hotel offers comfortable backpackers accommodation behind a pub on Cambridge Terrace. It has a big welcoming reception area and nice bathrooms. The common areas include a kitchen and a lounge with internet access and a TV.

28 Cambridge Terrace, Wellington

☎ *(04) 3858829*

Website *www.cambridgehotel.co.nz*

Dorm bed *$23-25 ($21-23 BBH);* ***single room*** *$59 ($55 BBH);* ***double/twin room*** *$75-95 ($70-90 BBH)*

Credit cards *Amex, Diners, MC, Visa*

Reception open *24 hours*

Maintenance & cleanliness	★★★★
Facilities	★½
Atmosphere & character	★★★½
Security	★★★★
Overall rating	★★★

Downtown Backpackers

Located across the road from the train station, Downtown Backpackers is the only hostel in the northern end of the city centre and its close proximity to the train station and ferry terminal makes this hostel handy if you're travelling by public transport. It is a big hostel in the old Hotel Waterloo (which hosted the Queen's entourage during the 1953 Coronation Tour, although the Queen wisely chose to stay elsewhere).The overall standard at Downtown Backpackers isn't very high; everything here feels old and worn and the atmosphere is a little gloomy. Facilities include a restaurant with internet access, a kitchen with an assortment of aging utensils, a TV lounge and a bar.

1 Bunny Street, Wellington

☎ *(04) 473 8482*

Website *www.downtownbackpackers.co.nz*

Dorm bed *$23-26 ($20-23 BBH, 22-25 VIP);* ***single room*** *$58 ($55 BBH, $57 VIP);* ***double room*** *$75-85 ($69-79 BBH, $73-83 VIP);* ***twin room*** *$56-85 ($50-79 BBH, $54-79 VIP)*

Credit cards *Amex, Diners, MC, Visa*

Reception open *24 hours*

Maintenance & cleanliness	★½
Facilities	★½
Atmosphere & character	★★½
Security	★★½
Overall rating	★★

Lodge in the City

This big drab building on Taranaki Street can sleep up to 200 people. Facilities include a large lounge with a fish tank, piano and internet access. It is clean enough but the furnishings are old and worn and there is very little atmosphere as the building is barren and charmless.

152 Taranaki Street, Te Aro, Wellington

☎ *(04) 385 8560*

Website *www.lodgeinthecity.co.nz*

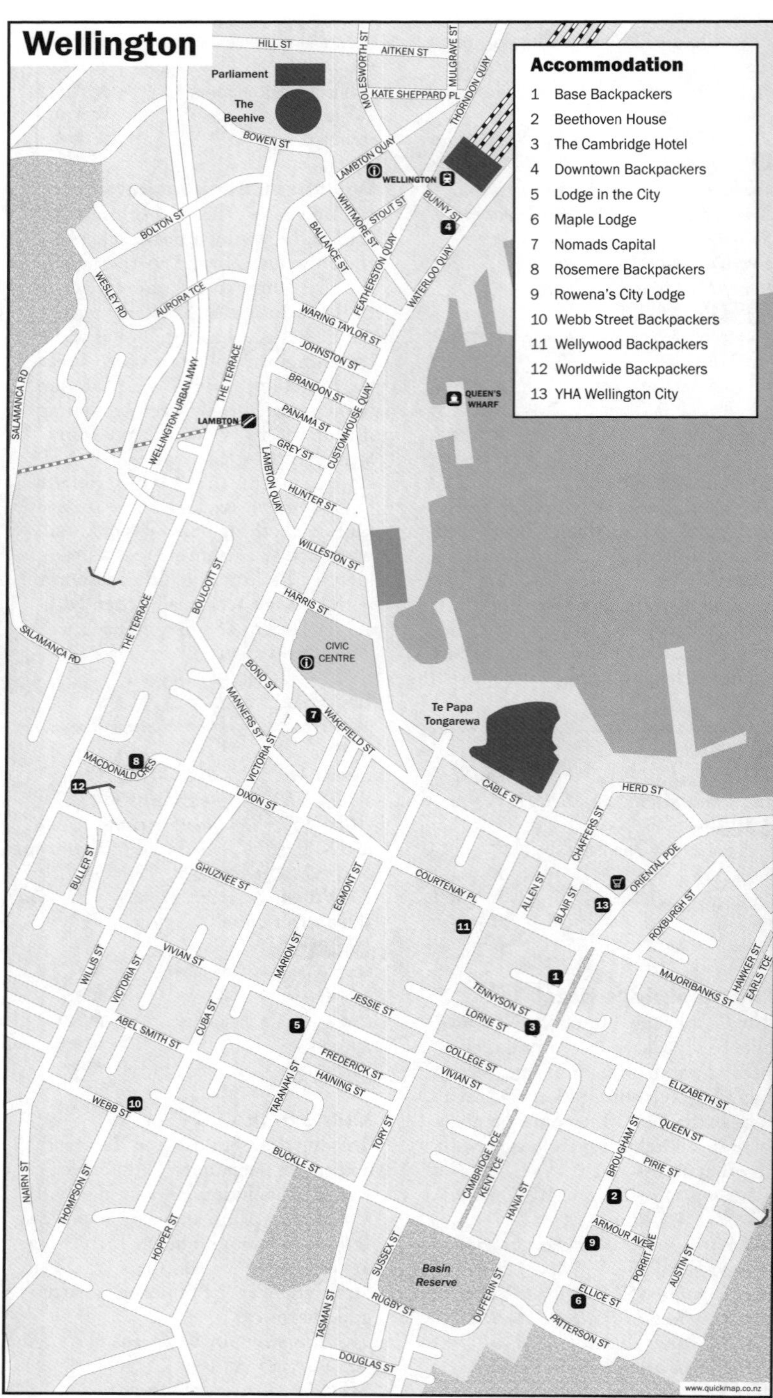
Wellington
Accommodation
1 Base Backpackers
2 Beethoven House
3 The Cambridge Hotel
4 Downtown Backpackers
5 Lodge in the City
6 Maple Lodge
7 Nomads Capital
8 Rosemere Backpackers
9 Rowena's City Lodge
10 Webb Street Backpackers
11 Wellywood Backpackers
12 Worldwide Backpackers
13 YHA Wellington City
Parliament
The Beehive
Queen's Wharf
Civic Centre
Te Papa Tongarewa
Basin Reserve
Lambton
Wellington
www.quickmap.co.nz

***Dorm bed** $23 ($22 VIP); **single room** $45; **double room** $65 ($63 VIP); **twin room** $59-69 ($57-67 VIP)*
***Credit cards** MC, Visa*
***Reception open** 8am-11pm daily*

Maintenance & cleanliness	★★
Facilities	★½
Atmosphere & character	★
Security	★★★
Overall rating	★★

Maple Lodge

Maple Lodge is a small hostel on a residential street south of the city centre that offers very basic accommodation. Common areas include a small lounge and a small, poorly equipped, kitchen. The overall standard is pretty low and the furnishings and fittings are old and worn.

52 Ellice Street, Mount Victoria
1, 3, 22, 23 (stop: Basin Reserve)
(04) 385 3771
***Dorm bed** $25 ($23 BBH); **single room** $48 ($43 BBH); **double room** $53-62 ($49-56 BBH); **twin room** $56 ($52 BBH)*
***Reception open** 9am-12.30pm & 5pm-9pm daily*

Maintenance & cleanliness	★
Facilities	½
Atmosphere & character	★★★
Security	★½
Overall rating	★½

Nomads Capital

Nomads Capital is Nomads' New Zealand flagship "flashpackers" hostel. It is a really nice place that is clean and well maintained with a high standard of accommodation. Facilities include internet access near the 24-hour reception and a Wi-Fi connection (Global Gossip Connect); a TV lounge; laundry; a small, but fully-equipped kitchen and a courtyard area. Alcohol isn't allowed in the hostel, but the hostel runs its own bar next door (but it's not really an in-house bar as you have to go outside and enter off the street) where you can get a free evening meal every night between 6pm and 7pm. This no-alcohol rule combined with the fact that there are TVs in the rooms, means that this hostel doesn't have quite the atmosphere that it could have. However if you're willing to overlook this, it is an excellent hostel with the added bonus of being Wellington's most centrally located budget accommodation.

118 Wakefield Street, Wellington
(04) 978 7810 or 0508 NOMADS
***Website** www.nomadscapital.com*
***Dorm bed** $19-31; **double/twin room** $69-99; prices include an evening meal in the Blend Bar next door*
***Credit cards** Amex, MC, Visa*
***Reception open** 24 hours*

Maintenance & cleanliness	★★★★★
Facilities	★★½
Atmosphere & character	★
Security	★★★★★
Overall rating	★★★½

Rosemere Backpackers

This hostel in a rambling old house on the edge of the city centre offers basic accommodation. Facilities include a kitchen, a lounge with a piano and a TV lounge. The rooms are clean enough but some dorms have three-tier bunks. It has improved over recent years but there are better places to stay in Wellington.

6 MacDonald Crescent, Wellington
(04) 384 3041
***Website** www.backpackerswellington.co.nz*
***Dorm bed** $27-28 ($24-25 BBH); **single room** $50-51 ($45-46 BBH); **double room** $66-67 ($60-61 BBH); **twin room** $62-63 ($56-57 BBH); prices include breakfast*
***Credit cards** MC, Visa*
***Reception open** 7.45am-10pm daily*

Maintenance & cleanliness	★½
Facilities	★½
Atmosphere & character	★★★
Security	★½
Overall rating	★★

Rowena's City Lodge

Rowena's City Lodge is one of Wellington's long-established hostels. It is an old house in the Mount Victoria neighbourhood that feels a bit tired, although the building does have some character. Facilities include a lounge with a grand piano and internet access, a kitchen (no oven), a room with a pool table and a TV lounge with city views. There is also decking outside the front of the hostel, which is probably a nice place to enjoy a few beers while looking over Wellington. It is one of the few hostels in Wellington with parking.

115 Brougham Street, Wellington
☎ *(04) 385 7872 or 0800 801 414*
Website *www.wellingtonbackpackers.co.nz*
Dorm bed *$21 ($20 VIP);* ***single room*** *$50 ($48 VIP);* ***double room*** *$60 ($58 VIP);* ***camping*** *$12 per person*
Credit cards *MC, Visa*
Reception open *7am-10pm daily*
TV K

Maintenance & cleanliness	★½
Facilities	½
Atmosphere & character	★★★
Security	★½
Overall rating	★½

Webb Street Backpackers

Webb Street Backpackers is a small hostel not far from the centre of Wellington. It is an old wooden house that feels a bit tired with old furnishings and dated décor. Facilities include a small kitchen, a TV lounge, internet access and a small barbecue area.

72 Webb Street, Wellington
☎ *(04) 803 3237*
Website *www.webbpackers.co.nz*
Dorm bed *$23;* ***single room*** *$33;* ***double room*** *$48*
Credit cards *MC, Visa*
Reception open *8am-10pm daily*
TV K L

Maintenance & cleanliness	★★
Facilities	★½
Atmosphere & character	★½
Security	★★
Overall rating	★★

Wellywood Backpackers

Wellywood Backpackers (formerlly Wildlife House) is big centrally located hostel near Courtney Place. There is a big common area on the fourth floor with free internet access, a TV lounge, reading areas, a pool table and a big kitchen. Accommodation is of a pretty high standard and it is a good place to stay.

58 Tory Street, Wellington
☎ *(04) 381 3899 or 0508 00 58 58*
Website *www.wellywoodbackpackers.co.nz*
Dorm bed *$25-27;* ***double room*** *$65-80*
Credit cards *MC, Visa*
Reception open *7.30am-10.30pm daily*
TV K L

Maintenance & cleanliness	★★★½
Facilities	★★
Atmosphere & character	★★★
Security	★★
Overall rating	★★★

Worldwide Backpackers

Worldwide Backpackers is in an old house on the fringe of the city centre. It looks unassuming from the outside but it is actually quite charming inside and it has a good atmosphere. Facilities include a kitchen and dining area with free internet access, a comfortable TV lounge and a barbecue area on the front deck.

291 The Terrace, Wellington
☎ *(04) 802 5590 or 0508 888 555*
Website *www.worldwidenz.co.nz*
Dorm bed *$27 ($24 BBH);* ***double room*** *$66 ($60 BBH);* ***twin room*** *$62 ($56 BBH); prices include breakfast*
Credit cards *MC, Visa*
Reception open *7.45am-noon & 3pm-8.45pm daily*
TV K L

Maintenance & cleanliness	★★★
Facilities	★½
Atmosphere & character	★★★★
Security	★½
Overall rating	★★½

YHA Wellington City

Wellington's YHA hostel is a big place with 320 beds over six floors with a good selection of facilities that include two fully-equipped kitchens, several lounges including a quiet reading room with massage chairs, a TV room with a projection screen and a games room with a pool table and there is also a laundry with a view of the harbour. The accommodation is of a high standard and all the four-share dorms have en suite facilities. It is on the corner of Cambridge Terrace and Wakefield Street, right across the road from the New World supermarket.

Corner Cambridge Terrace & Wakefield Street, Wellington
☎ *(04) 801 7280*
Website *www.yha.co.nz*
Dorm bed $29-32 ($26-29 HI/YHA); ***double room*** *$80-104 ($74-98 HI/YHA);* ***twin room*** *$80-100 ($74-94 HI/YHA)*
Credit cards *Amex, MC, Visa*
Reception open *summer Mon-Fri 6.45am-11pm Sat-Sun 6.45am-2am; winter 6.45am-11pm daily*

Maintenance & cleanliness	★★★★½
Facilities	★★½
Atmosphere & character	★★★
Security	★★★½
Overall rating	★★★½

NEWTOWN
Newtown Heights Lodge

Newtown Heights Lodge is a former nurse's dormitory a few minutes drive from the city centre. The buildings date from the 1970s and it's obvious some of the décor and furnishings haven't been changed since. Backpacker rooms are generally twin shares, except for a single six-bed dorm. There's a small kitchen and TV lounge and free internet access available on a single PC. A rooming-house feeling pervades, more so than in a traditional hostel. Plenty of off-street parking is a plus and Newtown has a smaller-town feel than the city centre. Newtown Heights Lodge is also closer to the airport than the city hostels, another reason some choose to stay here. But it doesn't have much appeal otherwise.

113 Coromandel Street, Newtown
11
☎ *(04) 389 8623*
Dorm bed *$20;* ***single room*** *$30;* ***double room*** *$50*
Credit cards *MC, Visa*
Reception open *Mon 11am-3pm, Tue 11am-1pm, Wed 6pm-8pm, Thu 11am-3pm, Fri 11am-3pm, Sat 1pm-3pm, Sun 1.30-3pm*

Maintenance & cleanliness	★½
Facilities	★½
Atmosphere & character	★
Security	★½
Overall rating	★½

MANA
Stillwater Lodge

Stillwater Lodge is a small, basic hostel in a house right by the sea in Mana. Dorm rooms are clean but spare. There's an upstairs common room with a TV, pool table and an assortment of books. Internet access is offered on a single PC in the downstairs office. An outdoor patio has a barbecue, and there are free kayaks for the guests' use on the inlet. The Stillwater Lodge is a few minutes walk from Mana train station (about a 25-minute ride into the city centre). It's not overflowing with charm, but it is close to the beach and makes a reasonable alternative to staying in the heart of Wellington, particularly if you have a car and don't want to deal with parking.

34 Mana Esplanade, Mana
Mana
☎ *(04) 233 6628*
Website *www.stillwaterlodge.co.nz*
Dorm bed *$23-$27 ($21-$25 BBH);* ***double room*** *$60*
Credit cards *MC, Visa*
Reception open *9am-noon & 4pm-7pm*

Maintenance & cleanliness	★★★
Facilities	★★
Atmosphere & character	★★
Security	★½
Overall rating	★★½

PLIMMERTON
Moana Lodge

Moana Lodge is a lovely house right across the road from the beach in Plimmerton, 30-minutes north of Wellington city centre. Every detail of the place is carefully thought out and well presented, and the hostel has loads of atmosphere. The kitchen is roomy and well-equipped. The dining room is charming, with candles in wine bottles, a fireplace, a guitar and keyboard. Interesting wall hangings are made from wine corks signed by guests over the years. The lounge is even better with stunning, picture-window views of the sea – on a clear day you can see the South Island from here. In the backyard, there's a garden patio with a barbecue and outdoor fire. Kayaks and bicycles are free to use, and the owner

often takes guests out on his sailboat. It doesn't get much better than this.
49 Moana Road, Plimmerton
Plimmerton
(04) 233 2010
***Website** www.moanalodge.co.nz*
***Dorm bed** $27 ($24 BBH); **single room** $48 ($45 BBH); **double room** $58-$78 ($52-$72 BBH); **twin room** $64-$78 ($58-$72 BBH)*
***Credit cards** MC, Visa*
TV K L

Maintenance & cleanliness	★★★★★
Facilities	★★★
Atmosphere & character	★★★★★
Security	★½
Overall rating	★★★★

Eating & Drinking

Wellington has a reputation as one of the country's best places for eating and drinking with an excellent choice of good restaurants and bars, including many that fit within the backpackers' budget.

There are plenty of good value eateries in the city; particularly along Cuba Street and around Courtney Place. There are also plenty of food courts in the area around Lambton Quay and Willis Street, which cater to the office workers on their lunch break.

Wellington has New Zealand's best café scene and the bar scene is pretty good as well. The neighbourhoods around Courtney Place and Cuba Street have developed a thriving bar culture. Cuba Street tends to be a bit more alternative with plenty of funky bars while the pubs on Courtenay Place are another good choice for a night out. The free listings papers, *Capital Times* and *City Voice*, are a good place to turn for up-to-date information on nightlife in Wellington.

There are three **New World** supermarkets in the city centre. The one across the road from the YHA hostel *(279 Wakefield Street, Wellington)* is the most convenient supermarket for many backpackers although the most central is the New World Willis Street Metro *(70 Willis Street, Wellington)*. There is also a New World inside the train station *(Bunny Street, Wellington)* that may be convenient if you're staying at Downtown Backpackers or if you want to get some snacks for your journey.

Sights

Archives of New Zealand

Many of New Zealand's most important documents are held in the National Archives. These include the original Treaty of Waitangi and the 1893 Women's Suffrage Petition that are on display in the Constitution Room.
10 Mulgrave Street, Thorndon
14, 81, 84, 85
(04) 499 5595
***Website** www.archives.govt.nz*
***Admission** free*
***Open** Mon-Fri 9am-5pm, Sat 9am-1pm*

Beehive & Parliament House

The eye-catching Beehive (a government building) and the adjoining Parliament House and Parliamentary Library lie at the heart of Wellington's parliamentary district, a short walk from the train station. Although parts of these buildings are usually closed to the public it is possible to take a free guided tour to discover where New Zealand's politicians work.
Bowen Street, Lambton Quay & Molesworth Street, Wellington; tours depart from the Visitor Centre on Lambton Quay.
1, 2, 4, 5, 6, 12, 13, 14, 21, 22, 23, 25, 27, 43, 44, 45, 49, 51, 52, 81, 84, 85 Lambton Quay Wellington
(04) 471 9503
***Admission** free*
***Guided tours depart** hourly Mon-Fri 10am-4pm, Sat 10am-3pm, Sun noon-3pm*

Botanic Gardens

The Botanic Gardens are a peaceful place to kick back and relax. It's just a short cable car ride from the heart of the city.
Glenmore Street, Kelburn
12 Kelburn
***Admission** free*

Colonial Cottage Museum

This museum housed in Central Wellington's oldest building features interesting exhibits about life in colonial Wellington.

68 Nairn Street, Mount Cook
7, 8
(04) 384 9122
Website *www.colonialcottagemuseum.co.nz*
Admission *$5*
Open *1 Jan-17 Feb 10am-4pm daily; 18 Feb-23 Dec Sat-Sun noon-4pm; 24-31 Dec 10am-4pm daily*

Government Buildings Historic Reserve

This impressive wooden government building is situated across the road from the Beehive. This building has a beautiful interior with cast-iron fireplaces, sweeping staircases and native timbers.
Lambton Quay, Wellington; entrance from Department of Conservation Visitor Centre
1, 2, 4, 5, 6, 12, 13, 14, 21, 22, 23, 25, 27, 43, 44, 45, 49, 51, 52, 81, 84, 85 *Lambton Quay* *Wellington*
(04) 472 7356
Admission *free*
Open *Mon-Fri 9am-4.30pm, Sat-Sun 10am-3pm*

Karori Wildlife Sanctuary

This conservation project is a unique natural area not far from Wellington that is home to rare and endangered New Zealand wildlife including kiwi, saddleback, kaka and weka, which have been released inside a 252ha pest-free valley. The sanctuary has over 35km of tracks offering scenic walks and the site also has two dams and a 19th century goldmine to explore.
Waiapu Road, Karori
12, 17, 18, 21, 22
(04) 920 9200
Website *www.sanctuary.org.nz*
Admission *$12*
Open *10am-5pm daily (last entry 4pm)*

Katherine Mansfield Birthplace

The birthplace and childhood home of New Zealand's most famous writer has been restored to show life in Wellington during late 1800s.
25 Tinakori Road, Thorndon
14
(04) 473 7268
Website *www.katherinemansfield.com*
Admission *$5.50*
Open *Tue-Sun 10am-4pm*

New Zealand Cricket Museum

This small museum has exhibits relating to New Zealand's involvement in the game of cricket.
The Old Grandstand Basin Reserve, 2 Rugby Street, Mount Cook
(04) 385 6602
Website *www.wmt.org.nz*
Admission *$5 ($2 students)*
Open *Jan-Apr 10.30am-3.30pm daily; May-Oct Sat-Sun 10.30am-3.30pm; Nov-Dec 10.30am-3.30pm daily*

National Tattoo Museum

Wellington's National Tattoo Museum features pictures of tattoo designs with the focus on the Māori moko.
42 Ablesmith Street, Wellington
(04) 384 6444
Website *www.mokomuseum.org.nz*
Admission *$5*
Open *Tue-Sun noon-5.30pm*

Museum of Wellington City & Sea

The Museum of Wellington City and Sea is an excellent introduction to New Zealand's capital. The museum is housed in an 1892 warehouse and contains six galleries over three floors. There are exhibits on the city's history including interactive exhibits and three audio-visual areas showing short films about Wellington.
Queens Wharf, Wellington
(04) 472 8904
Website *www.museumofwellington.co.nz*
Admission *free*
Open *10am-5pm daily*

Old St Paul's

This old cathedral is an excellent example of colonial Gothic architecture and was built from native timbers.
34 Mulgrave Street, Thorndon
14, 81, 84, 85
(04) 473 6722
Admission *free*
Open *Mon-Sat 10am-5pm*

Te Papa

Museum of New Zealand Te Papa Tongarewa, commonly referred to

Te Papa (Māori for Our Place), is New Zealand's leading museum and Wellington's top attraction. This popular museum has a lot of excellent and interactive exhibits, as well as interesting displays about New Zealand culture and history.
Cable Street, Wellington
14, 24
(04) 381 7000
***Website** www.tepapa.govt.nz*
***Admission** free*
***Open** Mon-Wed 10am-6pm, Thu 10am-9pm, Fri-Sun 10am-6pm*

Wellington Zoo

New Zealand's oldest zoo has a large range of African, Asian and native wildlife. Some of the zoo's more popular residents include meerkats, Sumatran tigers and the red panda.
200 Daniel Street, Newtown
10, 23, 83
(04) 381 6750
***Website** www.zoo.wcc.govt.nz*
***Admission** $15*
***Open** 9.30am-5pm daily*

Kapiti Coast

The Kapiti Coast starts around a 40-minute drive northwest of Wellington and stretches from Paekakiriki to Otaki. It's a region of smaller towns and beaches, easily accessible from Wellington by car or train.

Kapiti Island lies 5km offshore and is a nature reserve for rare and endangered bird species. A permit from the Department of Conservation is required which can be purchased online *(**website** www.doc.govt.nz)* or at the Wellington DOC office *(18 Manners Street, Wellington)*. Ferry service to the island runs from Paraparaumu. Visitors are restricted to a maximum of 50 per day,

The Kapiti Coast is a popular daytrip from Wellington, but it can be a pleasant stopover to/from the capital city as well.

Paekakariki

This sleepy seaside village is the southern gateway to the Kapiti Coast, and is very easily accessible from Wellington. The lovely beachfront, a few shops and restaurants and accommodation are all within walking distance of the train station. There's a laid-back, arts-oriented, sort of hippy vibe here and it makes a great day trip or place to chill out for a little while. There are a couple of nice parks in Paekakariki as well.

Coming & Going

Wellington's TranzMetro *((04) 801 7000; **website** www.tranzmetro.co.nz)* suburban rail system makes getting to Paekakariki a breeze. The one-way fare to Paekakariki is $8 ($6 off peak), however a day trip is better value with the $10 Day Rover travel pass, which makes it an affordable excursion from the city. Trains run approximately every half hour.

Accommodation

Paekakariki Backpackers

High up on a hill among lush, overflowing gardens, Paekakariki Backpackers offers a range of funky accommodation – shared dorm rooms, en suite double rooms, cabins, even a Mongolian yurt in the backyard. Antique furnishings and cluttered décor give the place a friendly, homely character. Backpackers stay in a small house with a kitchen and a warm little dining area and lounge. There's a tiny TV alcove and a single PC with internet access. All beds come with colourful mosquito netting – occasionally necessary but also exotically decorative. There are lots of little indoor and outdoor nooks to hang out in and the views over the sea are great. There is just a really good, unique vibe here.
11 Wellington Road, Paekakariki
Paekakariki
(04) 902 5967
***Website** www.wellingtonbeachbackpackers.co.nz*
***Dorm bed** $25-$26 ($22 BBH); **double room** $60-$68 ($54-$60 BBH)*
***Credit cards** MC, Visa*
TV K L

Maintenance & cleanliness	★★★
Facilities	★★
Atmosphere & character	★★★★★
Security	★★★
Overall rating	★★★

Paraparaumu

Paraparaumu is the largest town on the Kapiti Coast, and has lots of good shopping and eating options; once primarily a holiday resort, "Paraperam" has become home to residents who commute to Wellington. It doesn't quite have the charm of some of the other Kapiti Coast towns but it makes a good base for exploring the area.

Paraparaumu Beach lies a little to the west of the main area of development around the train station. It's a very good swimming beach and has more of a small-town atmosphere. Ferries to Kapiti Island depart from here. Another attraction, though maybe not a big one for backpackers, is the Paraparaumu Beach Golf Club, which is considered by many to be New Zealand's best golf course. *Lord of the Rings* fans take note: director Peter Jackson attended secondary school at Kapiti College in Paraparaumu.

Coming & Going

Wellington's TranzMetro *(☎ (04) 801 7000; **website** www.tranzmetro.co.nz)* suburban rail system has regular trains to Paraparaumu. The one-way fare is $9 ($6.50 off peak), but a day trip is better value with the $10 Day Rover travel pass, making it an affordable excursion from the city. Trains run approximately every half hour.

Accommodation

Barnacles Seaside Inn (YHA Paraparaumu)

Barnacles is a basic, fairly tired YHA-associate hostel set in a 1923 guest house, but it has a nice location right by the sea. There's a small downstairs kitchen, with a randomly furnished and decorated dining area and TV lounge. On the ground level is a small sitting room with a single coin-operated internet PC. Rooms are standard but not uncomfortable and most beds are made up. There's a pretty friendly vibe here and some awesome sunsets to be caught from the beach right across the road.

3 Marine Parade, Paraparaumu Beach
☎ (04) 902 5856 or 0800 555 856
***Website** www.seasideyha.co.nz*
***Dorm bed** $25 ($22 BBH, HI/YHA); **single room** $45 ($42 BBH, HI/YHA); **double room** $60-$70 ($54-$64 BBH, HI/YHA); **twin room** $54-$58 ($48-$52 BBH, HI/YHA)*
***Credit cards** MC, Visa*
***Reception open** 7.30am-8.30pm daily*

Maintenance & cleanliness	★★
Facilities	★½
Atmosphere & character	★★★½
Security	★½
Overall rating	★★

The Wairarapa

This largely rural region north of Wellington produces some good wines and is home to the Mount Bruce National Wildlife Centre. Masterton is the Wairarapa's major town.

Masterton

Home to around 20,000 people, Masterton is the largest town in the region and is worth a stop if you're driving through. It has a couple of interesting sights but is probably best known as the home of the annual Golden Shears sheep shearing competition *(**website** www.goldenshears.co.nz)* held at the end of February.

Practical Information

Masterton i-SITE Visitor Centre

5 Dixon Street, Masterton
☎ (06) 377 7577
***Website** www.wairarapanz.com*
***Open** Mon-Fri 9am-5pm, Sat-Sun 10am-4pm*

Coming & Going

The train is the best way to get to Masterton. TranzMetro *(☎ (04) 801 7000; **website** www.tranzmetro.co.nz)* trains go to Wellington and depart from the train station on Perry Street, north west of the town centre. The one-way fare is $14; a day return is only $15 although it is not valid on some early morning services.

Local buses connect Masterton with other towns in the Wairarapa region. Bus 200 goes to Featherston where you can transfer to bus 205 to Martinborough.

Accommodation

Chanel Court Backpackers

This is a motel that also has a section set aside for backpackers. Accommodation is in nice small rooms but the common areas such as the kitchen and TV lounge are very basic and there isn't much atmosphere.

14-18 Herbert Street, Masterton
☎ *(06) 378 2877*
Dorm bed *$35*
Credit cards *MC, Visa*
Reception open *8am-9.30pm daily*

Maintenance & cleanliness	★★★½
Facilities	★★½
Atmosphere & character	★★½
Security	★★½
Overall rating	★★

Empire Lodge

This centrally-located hostel on Queen Street in the town centre offers basic accommodation. It has accommodation mostly in single and double rooms but there is also a spacious dorm with single beds (no bunks). Facilities include a kitchen, a large dining room and a TV lounge and there is also a small rooftop deck with views of the Tararua Range. It is a dreary place with not much atmosphere and the fittings and furniture is old and worn.

94 Queen Street, Masterton
☎ *(06) 377 1902*
Website *www.empirelodge.co.nz*
Dorm bed *$20-35;* ***double room*** *$45-75*

Maintenance & cleanliness	★★
Facilities	★★½
Atmosphere & character	★★½
Security	★
Overall rating	★★½

Sights

Aratoi Museum

Masterton's Aratoi Museum has exhibits on local history plus artworks by local artists.

Corner Bruce & Dixon Streets, Masterton
☎ *(03) 370 0001*
Website *www.aratoi.co.nz*
Admission *$1-2 donation*
Open *10am-4.30pm daily*

Mount Bruce National Wildlife Centre

This conservation centre, 25 minutes north of Masterton, is where endangered wildlife including kiwi, kaka and tuatara are bred and looked after before being released into the wild.

State Highway 2, Mount Bruce
☎ *(06) 375 8754*
Website *www.mtbruce.org.nz*
Admission *$10*
Open *9am-4.30pm daily*

Martinborough

This small town lies at the heart of the Martinborough wine region, which is renowned for its excellent pinot noirs. It is a lovely small town with restored buildings and a charming village square and there are several upmarket cafés and wine bars. It is a popular destination with day trippers from Wellington.

Practical Information

Martinborough i-SITE Visitor Centre

18 Kitchener Street, Martinborough
☎ *(06) 306 9043*
Website *www.wairarapanz.com*
Open *10am-4pm daily*

Coming & Going

Local buses connect Martinborough with other towns in the Wairarapa region.

The most useful route is bus 205, which goes to Featherston where you can transfer to train services to Wellington.

Accommodation

Kate's Place

At first glance Kate's Place is an unassuming house on a quiet residential street just a few blocks from the centre of Martinborough. However once you're inside you'll find a friendly and cosy backpackers' hostel with hardwood floors and accommodation in bright spacious rooms. It is a small

hostel and facilities include a cosy TV lounge with a fireplace, internet access, a small but fully-equipped kitchen and a nice back deck with a barbecue.
7 Cologne Street, Martinborough
☎ *(03) 306 9935*
***Website** www.katesplace.co.nz*
***Dorm bed** $30; **double room** $80*

Maintenance & cleanliness	★★★½
Facilities	★★
Atmosphere & character	★★★★★
Security	★
Overall rating	★★★

Sights

Martinborough Wine Centre

While it's lots of fun to crawl from one winery to another sampling their produce, if time or access to transport is an issue you can come to the Martinborough Wine Centre and taste wines from a variety of Martinborough and Wairarapa wineries. A produce and craft market is held here every Sunday.
6 Kitchener Street, Martinborough
☎ *(06) 306 9040*
***Website** www.martinboroughwinecentre.co.nz*

Marlborough

Most people arrive in the Marlborough region by ferry from Wellington.

This wine-producing region is known for its excellent sauvignon blanc wine, particularly the famed Cloudy Bay and the popular Montana wines. Although some travellers stay in the region to pick up fruit picking work, most of those who decide to linger in Marlborough usually stay on to explore the breathtaking Marlborough Sounds. Many backpackers choose to hike the Queen Charlotte Track.

Must do in Marlborough

- Walk the Queen Charlotte Track
- Drink the local sauvignon blanc

Picton

As the southern terminus for the Cook Strait ferries, this pretty little town is most people's first impression of the South Island. Although most people come here to make transport connections, Picton is also the launching pad for exploring the Marlborough Sounds with many hiking trails starting nearby including the popular Queen Charlotte Track.

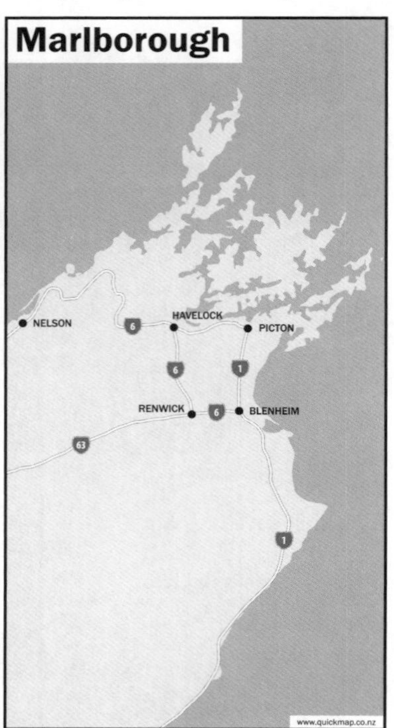

Practical Information

Picton i-Site Visitor Centre

The Foreshore, Picton
☎ *(03) 520 3113*
Website *www.destinationmarlborough.com*
Open *Jan-Apr 8.30am-5pm daily; May-Sep Mon-Fri 9am-5pm, Sat-Sun 9am-4.30pm; Oct-Nov 8.30am-5pm daily*

Coming & Going

AIR

Flights from Wellington are competitively priced, often working out at around the same price as the ferry. Sounds Air *(☎ 0800 505 005; **website** www.soundsair.co.nz)* fly from the small Koromiko airfield 9km south of town and operate their own shuttle bus to and from Picton. Air New Zealand *(☎ 0800 737 000; **website** www.airnz.co.nz)* fly from the busier Blenheim Airport, about half an hour south of Picton.

BUS

There are frequent bus connections with Atomic Shuttles, InterCity and Naked Bus plus several smaller bus operators having services to Christchurch, Nelson and elsewhere in the South Island.

Atomic Shuttles *(☎ (03) 349 0697; **website** www.atomictravel.co.nz)* have buses to Christchurch and Nelson. InterCity Coachlines *(☎ (03) 365 1113; **website** www.intercity.co.nz)* go to Christchurch, Greymouth and Nelson and Naked Bus *(☎ 0900 62533; **website** www.nakedbus.com)* go to Christchurch, Greymouth, Motueka and Nelson.

Naked Bus stop at the ferry terminal and other buses stop outside the i-Site Visitor Centre on the foreshore.

TRAIN

Picton is the northern terminus for the South Island's rail network. The train station is on Auckland Street only 200m from the ferry terminal.

FERRY

The ferry terminal handles Blue Bridge and Interislander ferries to Wellington. Most rental car agencies have their offices outside the ferry terminal and along nearby Auckland Street.

There are also water taxis that connect Picton with various spots in the Marlborough Sounds. Many backpackers use these to get to the Queen Charlotte Track and some of the more remote hostels in the Sounds.

Accommodation

Atlantis Backpackers' Hostel

This hostel near the Interislander ferry terminal is in a charmless building but its low prices (it's the cheapest hostel in town) and extensive facilities (it has a swimming pool) make it a good choice for the value conscious traveller. It feels a bit disorganised and the furniture is old and mismatched. Facilities include a fully-equipped kitchen, a TV lounge, internet access and an indoor swimming pool.

London Quay, Picton
(03) 573 7390
Website *www.atlantishostel.co.nz*
Dorm bed *$18-22 ($15-19 BBH);* ***single room*** *$48 ($45 BBH);* ***double room*** *$52 ($46 BBH);* ***twin room*** *$48 ($42 BBH); prices include breakfast*
Credit cards *MC, Visa*
Reception open *8am-10pm daily*

Maintenance & cleanliness	★★½
Facilities	★★½
Atmosphere & character	★★
Security	★★
Overall rating	★★½

Bayview Backpackers

Although nothing special compared with some of Picton's more popular hostels, this hostel overlooking Waikawea Bay, about 5km north of the town centre, is a nice place to stay with a home-style atmosphere. There are two common areas, both of which have kitchens although the main upstairs lounge is a quieter room with internet access while the downstairs lounge has a TV. Guests have free use of bicycles and kayaks.

318 Waikawa Road, Picton
(03) 573 7668
Website *www.truenz.co.nz/bayview backpackers*
Dorm bed *$23-26 ($20-23 BBH);* ***single room*** *$43 ($40 BBH);* ***double/twin room*** *$54-66 ($48-60 BBH)*
Credit cards *MC, Visa*
Reception open *8.30am-2pm & 4pm-8.30pm daily*

Maintenance & cleanliness	★★★
Facilities	★★★
Atmosphere & character	★★★
Security	★★
Overall rating	★★★

The Juggler's Rest

This gem of a hostel is a nice small place (that only sleeps 15) in an old cottage that has loads of charm. It has an excellent fully-equipped kitchen with loads of pots and pans plus a veggie patch and herb garden so it's a great place to stay if you're feeling gastronomically adventurous. There is also a lounge room with a fireplace and internet access including Wi-Fi ($4 per hour). The front garden has hammocks and a fire bath and there are plenty of balls around if you feel like a juggle. It has the best atmosphere of Picton's hostels and is located on a quiet residential street south of Nelson Square.

8 Canterbury Street, Picton
(03) 573 5570
Website *www.jugglersrest.com*
Dorm bed *$27 ($24 BBH);* ***double room*** *$58-66 ($52-60 BBH); prices include breakfast*

Maintenance & cleanliness	★★★★★
Facilities	★★★
Atmosphere & character	★★★★★
Security	-
Overall rating	★★★★

Picton Lodge

Picton Lodge is the closest hostel to the Interislander ferry terminal. It is a basic hostel with facilities that include the standard kitchen, TV lounge, internet and laundry. It has old furniture that makes it feels a bit dated but it is clean and it has everything a traveller needs.

9 Auckland Street, Picton
(03) 573 7788
***Website** www.pictonlodge.co.nz*
***Dorm bed** $22-24 ($21-23 VIP); **double room** $55 ($53 VIP)*
***Credit cards** Amex, MC, Visa*
***Reception open** 8.30am-2pm & 4pm-10pm daily*

Maintenance & cleanliness	★★½
Facilities	★½
Atmosphere & character	★★★
Security	★½
Overall rating	★★½

Sequoia Lodge

Sequoia is a good medium-size hostel on Nelson Square, a short walk or bike ride from the town centre. There are several common areas including a fully-equipped kitchen, a dining area, two lounges (one with internet access and the other with a fireplace) plus a TV room. There is also a covered outdoor barbecue area and a spa pool. Guests have free use of bikes and hot chocolate pudding and ice cream is served every night.

3a Nelson Square, Picton
(03) 573 8399
***Website** www.sequoialodge.co.nz*
***Dorm bed** $24-25 ($21-22 BBH); **double room** $60-75 ($54-69 BBH); **twin room** $75 ($69 BBH); prices include chocolate pudding and ice cream each evening*
***Credit cards** MC, Visa*
***Reception open** 8.30am-1.30pm & 3.30pm-9pm daily*

Maintenance & cleanliness	★★★
Facilities	★★★★
Atmosphere & character	★★★
Security	★
Overall rating	★★★

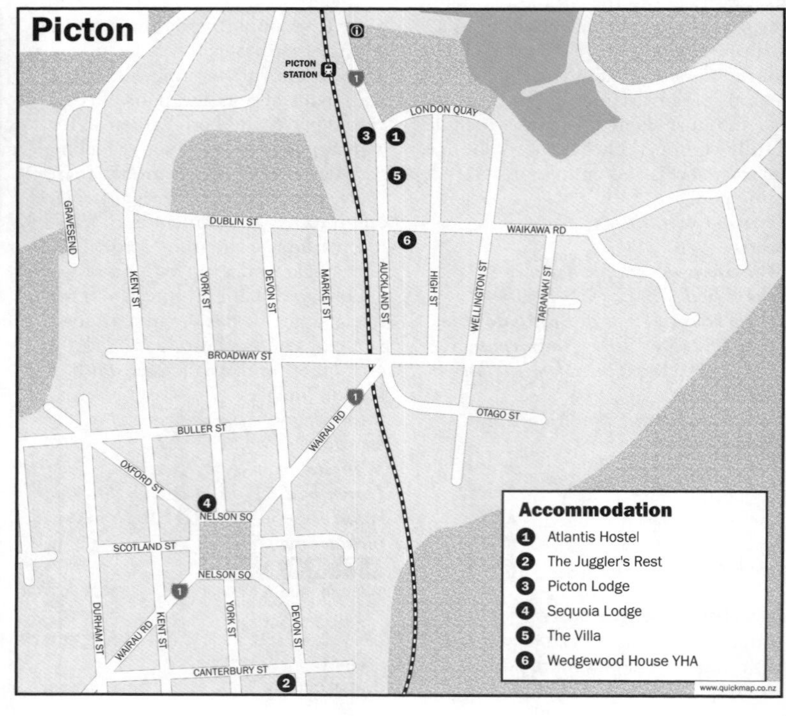

Marlborough

Tombstone Backpackers

This excellent hostel is a great budget accommodation option for travellers visiting Picton. It is comprised of an old house, where you'll find the common areas, plus a purpose-built accommodation block; this setup works well and keeps the noise away from people who want to get some sleep. There are several lounge areas including one with a piano and dining tables, another quiet reading room, a TV lounge, an enclosed outdoor space with a pool table and a long natural wooden bench where you can sit with a beer while watching the boats come in. There is also a fully-equipped kitchen, a barbecue area and spa pool overlooking the harbour. Tombstone Backpackers is on a hill near the cemetery and is very close to the Blue Bridge ferry terminal, but it is around a 10-minute walk through an industrial area to get to the town centre.

16 Gravesend Place, Picton
☎ *(03)573 7116*
Website *www.tombstonebackpackers.co.nz*
Dorm bed *$25 ($22 BBH);* ***double room*** *$66-70 ($60-64 BBH);* ***twin room*** *$66 ($60 BBH); prices include breakfast*
Credit cards *MC, Visa*

Maintenance & cleanliness	★★★★★
Facilities	★★★★½
Atmosphere & character	★★★★★
Security	★½
Overall rating	★★★★½

The Villa

The Villa is a nice hostel with a good atmosphere. It is comprised of several houses and includes a fully-equipped kitchen, a dining room with a big wooden table and a quiet lounge with a fireplace. There is also a TV lounge but this is away from the main common areas. Outside there is a garden area and a spa pool.

34 Auckland Street, Picton
☎ *(03) 573 6598*
Website *www.thevilla.co.nz*
Dorm bed *$24-30 ($21-26 BBH);* ***double room*** *$63-72 ($57-66 BBH);* ***twin room*** *$72 ($66 BBH)*
Credit cards *MC, Visa*
Reception open *8.15am-2pm & 4.30pm-9.30pm daily*

Maintenance & cleanliness	★★★
Facilities	★★★½
Atmosphere & character	★★★★
Security	★½
Overall rating	★★★

Wedgewood House YHA

This small 20-bed hostel in the centre of Picton is in a poky old house that shows its age. It feels very dated with furnishings that look like they've been there since the 1950s. Facilities are minimal and include a small lounge, a tiny kitchen and a small backyard with a barbecue. There are much better hostels in Picton and it seems that this hostel stays in business solely because of a handful of travellers who are loyal to the YHA brand.

10 Dublin Street, Picton
☎ *(03) 573 7797*
Website *www.stayyha.com*
Dorm bed *$25 ($22 HI/YHA);* ***double/twin room*** *$60 ($54 HI/YHA)*
Credit cards *JCB, MC, Visa*
Reception open *8.30am-10am, 1pm-2pm, 5pm-6.30pm & 8pm-10pm daily*

Maintenance & cleanliness	★½
Facilities	★½
Atmosphere & character	★★★
Security	★★★½
Overall rating	★★

Eating & Drinking

Although Picton is just a small town, the constant movement of travellers through town means that it has a relatively good choice of places to eat. Most restaurants and cafés are clustered on High Street and there are a few places on London Quay.

Le Café Picton *(London Quay, Picton)* was the first place to town to serve real espresso and also serves nice meals. **Gusto** *(33 High Street, Picton)* is a smaller place that also serves good coffee.

There are several bars in town including **Seamus's Irish Bar** *(25 Wellington Street, Picton)*, which is one of Picton's more popular places for a drink.

If you're preparing your own food, there is a **SuperValue** supermarket in Mariners Mall *(High Street, Picton).*

Sights

Edwin Fox Maritime Centre

The *Edwin Fox* is the world's ninth oldest ship and is the focal point of this small maritime museum near Picton's ferry terminal. This ship was built in Calcutta in 1853 and is the only surviving wooden ship to carry immigrants to New Zealand and convicts to Australia. It is also the oldest surviving troopship from the Crimean War.
Foreshore, Picton
☎ *(03) 573 6868*
Website *www.edwinfoxsociety.com*
Admission *$8*
Open *9am-5pm daily*

Havelock

This small town between Picton and Nelson is a good base for exploring the Marlborough Sounds and many people stay here to hike the Nydia Track.

Apart from hiking, Havelock is famous for two things – its mussels and Ernest Rutherford. The Noble prize winning scientist grew up in Havelock and went to school in the building that is now the YHA hostel. He is best known for splitting the atom and his other achievements include the discovery of radon and work that has led to the invention of the smoke detector and Geiger counter.

Coming & Going

Havelock lies on the main bus route linking Blenheim and Nelson and is served by Atomic Shuttles *(☎ (03) 349 0697; **website** www.atomictravel.co.nz)*, InterCity Coachlines *(☎ (03) 365 1113; **website** www.intercity.co.nz)* and Naked Bus *(☎ 0900 62533; **website** www.nakedbus.com)*. Buses stop outside the Mussel Pot restaurant *(73 Main Road, Havelock).*

Accommodation

Blue Moon

Blue Moon Backpackers is a nice hostel on Havelock's main street. It is an old wooden house but it's kept nice and clean. Facilities include a good kitchen; a lounge room with internet access, a TV and fish tank and there is a lovely deck with a barbecue and a nice view of the marina. They also have good value bike hire ($10 half day, $20 full day).
48 Main Road, Havelock
☎ *(03) 574 2212*
Website *www.bluemoonhavelock.co.nz*
Dorm bed *$23 ($20 BBH);* ***double/twin room*** *$52 ($46 BBH)*
Credit cards *Amex, Diners, MC, Visa*

Maintenance & cleanliness	★★★
Facilities	★★½
Atmosphere & character	★★★½
Security	★½
Overall rating	★★★

Rutherford Lodge YHA

The Rutherford Lodge YHA is a long established hostel – it has been a YHA hostel since 1963 – in an historic former schoolhouse. It has a lot of character with a nice big lounge containing a TV, a piano, fireplace and a big wooden dining table. There is also a fully-equipped kitchen and a laundry plus some lockers. The staff are very knowledgeable about the Nydia Track and it's a good place to stay if you're planning to hike the Nydia Track.
46 Main Road, Havelock
☎ *(03) 574 2104*
Website *www.rutherfordtravel.co.nz*
Dorm bed *$25-28 ($22-25 HI/YHA);* ***double/twin room*** *$58 ($55 HI/YHA)*
Credit cards *MC, Visa*
Reception open *8am-1pm & 4.30pm-9pm daily*

Maintenance & cleanliness	★★★
Facilities	★★
Atmosphere & character	★★★★
Security	★★
Overall rating	★★★

Eating & Drinking

Havelock proudly boasts of being the "Green-lipped Mussel Capital of the World" so it makes sense that mussels should be on the menu. That means dining at the **Mussel Pot** *(73 Main Road, Havelock)*, easily recognisable by the giant pot of mussels clinging precariously to the roof.

Because Havelock is just a small village, there is only a small **Four Square** supermarket *(Main Road, Havelock).*

Marlborough Sounds

You'll notice the Marlborough Sounds' myriad coves and inlets if you arrive in Picton by ferry (or by plane on a clear day); many of which harbour small resorts and backpackers' hostels.

The best way to explore the Marlborough Sounds is to hike the Queen Charlotte Track, although the less energetic can drive or take a local ferry or water taxi to some of the remote backpackers' resorts.

Local Transport

Various hostels in Picton can arrange boat transport to Ship Cove with a pick up from Anakiwa for hikers walking the Queen Charlotte Track. Packs can be carried between accommodation spots by boat operators; this means that you only need to walk with a daypack, making the trek a little easier.

Cougar Line *(☎ (03) 573 7925; **website** www.queencharlottetrack.co.nz)* and Endeavour Express *(☎ (03) 573 5456; **website** www.boatrides.co.nz)* are two of the main transport operators. They both combine the ferry trip from Picton to Ship Cover with pack transfer to jetties along the track and pick up from Anakiwa. Cougar Line cost $90 and Endeavour Express costs $80 for the return trip including pack transfer.

It is also possible to use the boat connections to complete a chosen section of the track, but this usually costs more than the full return trip.

Accommodation

In addition to several campsites in the region, including seven on the Queen Charlotte Track, there are a number of excellent hostels, many of which are within easy access to the Track. The following hostels are listed geographically from south to north. All of them, with the exception of Hopewell and Te Mahoerangi Eco-lodge, are within walking distance from the Queen Charlotte Track. There are no DOC huts on the Queen Charlotte Track.

QUEEN CHARLOTTE TRACK

Anakiwa Backpackers

This small backpackers' hostel has only three rooms plus common areas that comprise a TV lounge and a fully-equipped kitchen with an espresso machine. It is a very clean hostel with a warm and cosy atmosphere and a view of Queen Charlotte Sound. It is located right at the southern end of the Queen Charlotte Track so it is a popular spot for trampers walking the track.

401 Anakiwa Road, Anakiwa
☎ (03) 574 1388
***Website** www.anakiwabackpackers.co.nz*
***Dorm bed** $33 ($30 BBH); **double room** $66-90 ($60-80 BBH); **twin room** $66 ($60 BBH)*

Maintenance & cleanliness	★★★★
Facilities	★★
Atmosphere & character	★★★★
Security	★
Overall rating	★★★

Bunkhouse at the Portage Resort

The Bunkhouse at the Portage Resort is the backpackers' accommodation at the Portage Resort Hotel. It is a big resort with a wide variety of accommodation ranging from backpackers' to upmarket hotel rooms and the mix of accommodation means that it doesn't really have much of a backpackers' feel to it. The backpackers' area includes a small kitchen and lounge with internet access and accommodation in clean rooms. Other resort facilities include a swimming pool, volleyball court, a bar and two restaurants.

Kenepuru Road, Portage Bay, Kenepuru Sound
☎ (03) 573 4309
***Website** www.portage.co.nz*
***Dorm bed** $40; **double room** $80-100; **twin room** $110*
***Credit cards** Amex, Diners, JCB, MC, Visa*
***Reception open** 7am-10pm daily*

Maintenance & cleanliness	★★★★★
Facilities	★★★
Atmosphere & character	★★
Security	★
Overall rating	★★★½

Debretts

Debretts has the best atmosphere of the three hostels in Portage. It is a small clean hostel, at the top of a very steep hill, which only sleeps around six people. Accommodation is in a few double/twin or two-bed dorm rooms, which makes it a good option for couples. Facilities are limited to a small kitchen and lounge room with a TV. There is a brilliant view of Portage Bay and Kenepuru Sound from the deck.

Portage Bay, Kenepuru Sound
☎ *(03) 573 4522*
Website *www.stayportage.co.nz*
Dorm bed *$35-40;* ***double/twin room*** *$70-80; prices include bag transfer for guests hiking the Queen Charlotte Track*
Credit cards *MC, Visa*

Maintenance & cleanliness	★★★★★
Facilities	★½
Atmosphere & character	★★★
Security	-
Overall rating	★★★

Mahana Homestead Lodge

This is a really nice hostel next door to Punga Cove Resort. It is a small clean and well-maintained hostel overlooking Endeavour Inlet in Queen Charlotte Sound. It is comprised of two double/twin rooms and eight dorms beds plus a lounge and a fully-equipped kitchen and most rooms have a sea view. The hostel provides meals and the evening meal is usually served on the veranda. Guests have free use of kayaks and fishing gear.

Endeavour Inlet, Marlborough Sounds
☎ *(03) 579 8373*
Website *www.mahanahomestead.com*
Dorm bed *$33 ($28 BBH);* ***double room*** *$95 ($85 BBH)*
Credit cards *MC, Visa*
Reception open *until sunset (arrive before it gets dark)*

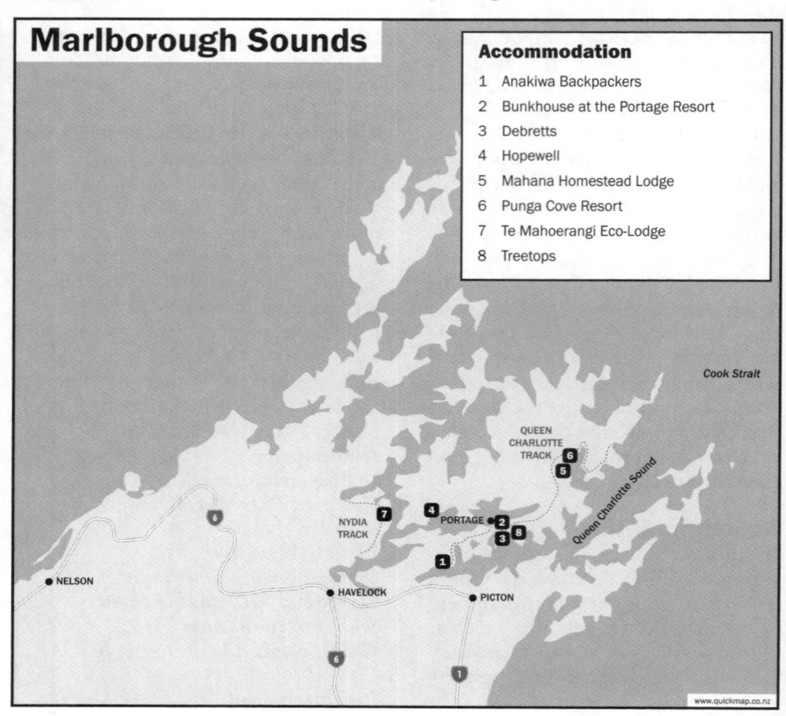

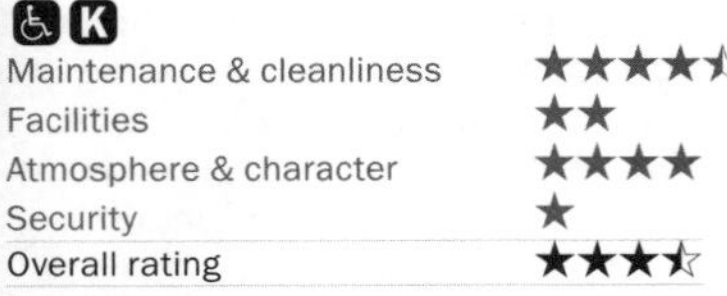

Maintenance & cleanliness	★★★★½
Facilities	★★
Atmosphere & character	★★★★
Security	★
Overall rating	★★★½

Punga Cove Resort

Punga Cove Resort – next to Mahana Lodge on Endeavour Inlet – is a big resort complex that offers a wide range of accommodation options ranging from luxury cabins to more basic backpackers' accommodation. The backpackers' accommodation is in small two-bed dorms in tidy – but charmless – prefabricated units and the backpackers' common areas are a little basic compared with the rest of the complex and include a very basic kitchen and small lounge with outdated furnishings. However the rest of the complex is very nice and includes a swimming pool, spa pool, volleyball court, bar and two restaurants. It is located right on the waterfront and most rooms have brilliant views of Queen Charlotte Sound.

Punga Cove, Queen Charlotte Sound
☎ *(03) 579 8561*
Website *www.pungacove.co.nz*
Dorm bed *$35*
Credit cards *Amex, MC, Visa*
Reception open *8am-5pm, check in at restaurant after reception has closed*

Maintenance & cleanliness	★★★½
Facilities	★★★½
Atmosphere & character	★½
Security	★½
Overall rating	★★★

Treetops

This small hostel at the top of a very steep hill has just a few rooms with accommodation in double/twin or two-bed dorm rooms, which makes it a good option for couples. Facilities are limited to a small kitchen and lounge room with a TV. There is a brilliant view of Kenepuru Sound from the deck.

Portage Bay, Kenepuru Sound
☎ *(03) 573 4522*
Dorm bed *$35-40;* ***double/twin room*** *$70-80*

Maintenance & cleanliness	★★★★½
Facilities	★
Atmosphere & character	★★★
Security	-
Overall rating	★★★

NYDIA TRACK

Te Mahoerangi Eco-Lodge

This unique volunteer-built eco-hostel is a great place to stay. It is a sprawling complex that includes a large wooden building with the main common areas along with some dormitories as well as cabins with additional accommodation. The common areas include a cosy lounge, a fully-equipped kitchen and a nice outdoor area with a seating around a big fireplace/pizza oven. There's no TV so everyone sits around every night chatting, which makes for a great atmosphere. The hostel provides cooked meals (and home brewed beer), which is great as it a long way to the nearest shop. It is accessible only by boat or by a four-hour walk (it is located midway along the Nydia Track) and it is popular with both hikers and environmentalists.

Nydia Track, Nydia Bay
☎ *(03) 579 8411*
Website *www.nydiatrack.org.nz*
Dorm bed *$28 ($25 BBH);* ***double/twin room*** *$66 ($60 BBH);* ***camping*** *$12 per person*

Maintenance & cleanliness	★★★★
Facilities	★★
Atmosphere & character	★★★★★
Security	★
Overall rating	★★★½

ELSEWHERE IN THE MARLBOROUGH SOUNDS

Hopewell

This small remote hostel is among the best in New Zealand – if not the world. It is comprised of several buildings including accommodation and a flash new common area with a brilliant fully-equipped kitchen (with top quality appliances), a dining area and a nice lounge area with a fireplace. There is also a semi-outdoor barbecue dining area, a trampoline, laundry and internet access plus a spa pool overlooking Kenepuru Sound, not to mention its own private beach. For a one-off $10 charge each, guests can have unlimited use of mountain bikes, kayaks, row-boats and fishing gear. You can collect shellfish nearby, which makes it one of those rare hostels where you regularly see backpackers dining on mussels and oysters. There are no shops nearby so you should bring supplies with you although you can buy beer, wine, fresh bread and pizzas here. It has an idyllic waterfront location at the very end of the Kenepuru Road (which includes 20km of unsealed road) and it's at least a two hour drive from Havelock. In New Zealand many of the most remote hostels are worth the trip, and this is especially the case with Hopewell.

Hopewell, Double Bay, Kenepuru Sound
☎ *(03) 573 4341*
Website *www.hopewell.co.nz*
Dorm bed *$30 ($27 BBH);* ***double room*** *$62-92 ($56-86 BBH);* ***twin room*** *$62-72 ($56-66 BBH)*
Credit cards *MC, Visa*
Open *Jan-May & Oct-Dec*

Maintenance & cleanliness	★★★★★
Facilities	★★★½
Atmosphere & character	★★★★★
Security	½
Overall rating	★★★★

Hiking

NYDIA TRACK

The Nydia Track (27km; 2 days) connects Tennyson Inlet with Kaiuma Bay, near Havelock. It follows the shoreline of Nydia Bay and crosses the Kaiuma and Nydia Saddles.

The Havelock YHA *(☎ (03) 375 2104; **website** www.havelockinfocentre.co.nz)* organises transport packages with a bus or ferry drop off at Shag Point near the start of the track and pick up at Duncan Bay. This transport package costs $60. There is a DOC hut on the track; but most backpackers prefer to stay at the Te Mahoerangi Eco-lodge, on Nydia Bay about halfway along the track.

QUEEN CHARLOTTE TRACK

The Queen Charlotte Track (71km; 3-5 days) takes in beautiful scenery on the stretch of land between Kenepuru and Queen Charlotte Sounds. Although the trail can be hiked in either direction, most people start at Ship Cove (where Captain James Cook took shelter between 1770 and 1777) and walk back toward Anakiwa near Picton.

The Queen Charlotte Track is also popular with mountain bikers, except in summer (Dec-Feb) when bikes are not permitted. It takes around 13 hours to ride the length of the track.

Ship Cove to Resolution Bay *(4.5km; 2 hours)*

The track begins at Ship Cove, a 1hr boat ride from Picton. Captain James Cook took shelter here on five separate occasions between 1770 and 1777. There is an historic reserve here that features Cook's Monument.

From Ship Cove, the track climbs through native bush to a lookout that offers breathtaking views to Mount Egmont (Taranaki) in the North Island and then descends to Resolution Bay where there are cabins and a campsite.

Resolution Bay to Endeavour Inlet *(10.5km; 3 hours)*

The track from Resolution Bay follows an old bridle path to Endeavour Inlet where there are a couple of accommodation options, but no campsite.

Endeavour Inlet to Camp Bay *(11.5km; 4 hours)*

From Endeavour Inlet, the track follows the shoreline to Camp Bay where there is a DOC campsite and backpackers' accommodation at Mahana Homestead Lodge and the Punga Cove Resort.

Camp Bay to Torea Saddle *(20.5km; 8 hours)*

This is the hardest part of the track, but you are rewarded by breathtaking views of the sounds from the ridge-top walk. Although there are a couple of campsites on this section, most people hike it all in one day and stay at one of the three backpackers' hostels in Portage, near Torea Saddle.

Torea Saddle to Mistletoe Bay *(7.5km; 4 hours)*

This section climbs out of Torea Saddle and follows the ridge along the highest points of the track offering more spectacular views. There is a DOC campsite at Mistletoe Bay.

Mistletoe Bay to Anakiwa *(12.5km; 4 hours)*

The final leg of the walk follows old bridle paths descending to a DOC campsite at Davies Bay (Umungata) before the final easy walk into Anakiwa. At Anakiwa there's a backpackers' hostel and a shelter with a toilet and payphone where you can wait for your transport back to Picton.

Blenheim

Blenheim is the largest town in the Marlborough region and it is the commercial centre for New Zealand's top wine producing district. Marlborough wines – particularly sauvignon blanc – have an excellent reputation internationally and the locally produced Cloudy Bay is considered one of the best.

The attraction for many budget travellers is the abundance of work in the vineyards, especially during the grape harvest. The managers of the local backpackers' hostels are a tremendous source of knowledge when it comes to looking for work.

Practical Information

Blenheim i-SITE Visitor Centre

Blenheim Railway Station, Sinclair Street, Blenheim
☎ *(03) 577 8080*
***Website** www.destinationmarlborough.co.nz*
***Open** Mon-Fri 9am-5pm, Sat-Sun 9am-4pm*

Coming & Going

AIR

Blenheim Airport, on State Highway 6 near Renwick, handles Air New Zealand *(☎ 0800 737 000; **website** www.airnz.co.nz)* flights to Auckland, Christchurch and Wellington and Air2there *(☎ (04) 904 5130; **website** www.air2there.com)* flights from Wellington and Paraparaumu.

Both airlines' service to and from Wellington is a good alternative to the ferry.

BUS

Blenheim lies on State Highway 1, which runs down the east coast of the South Island. State Highway 6 starts in Blenheim and goes to Invercargill via Nelson and the West Coast.

It is well served by coach and shuttle bus services linking Picton with Kaikoura and Christchurch as well as Nelson and the West Coast. These include Atomic Shuttles *(☎ (03) 349 0697; **website** www.atomictravel.co.nz)*, InterCity Coachlines *(☎ (03) 365 1113; **website** www.intercity.co.nz)* and Naked Bus *(☎ 0900 62533; **website** www.nakedbus.com)*. Buses stop at i-SITE Visitor Centre/train station on Sinclair Street.

TRAIN

The TranzCoastal train linking Christchurch and Picton stops at Blenheim. The train station is on Sinclair Street in the town centre.

Accommodation

Arrow Backpackers

This hostel in a dilapidated old house on a residential street on the northern edge of town caters to backpackers working on the vineyards around Blenheim. It is furnished with a shabby-looking odd assortment of second-hand furniture. Facilities include the usual kitchen, TV lounge, and laundry plus free internet access. The kitchen is a sorry collection of aging appliances and, like many workers' hostels, the dorm rooms are a mess.

107 Budge Street, Blenheim
☎ *(03) 577 9857*
***Dorm bed** $21-23 ($18-20 BBH); **single room** $33 ($30 BBH); **double room** $56 ($50 BBH)*

[car] [TV] K L

Maintenance & cleanliness	★
Facilities	★★
Atmosphere & character	★★★
Security	★
Overall rating	★★

BKH Limited

BKH is a small hostel that caters mostly to workers. The dorms are very basic with two bunks, and they can get cluttered and stuffy. The bathrooms are well maintained, but get very dirty,

Marlborough

and there is a kitchen that could also use some attention. The TV lounge is old and plain. The hostel offers internet access and a laundry, but not much else in the way of facilities. There is no real backpacker atmosphere here.
71 Budge Street, Blenheim
(03) 578 4599
***Dorm bed** $95-100 per week*
***Reception open** 8.30am-9.30pm daily*

Maintenance & cleanliness	★★½
Facilities	★
Atmosphere & character	★
Security	★★
Overall rating	★★

Copper Beech House

This big old wooden house on Maxwell Road offers basic accommodation for travellers picking fruit and working in the vineyards. It has the usual TV lounge, internet access and a fully-equipped kitchen. However it feels like it has been put together on the cheap with a hotchpotch of mismatched old second-hand furnishings.
73 Maxwell Road, Blenheim
(03) 579 2246
***Dorm bed** $21 ($18 BBH) per night, $120 ($110 BBH) per week; **double/twin room** $44 ($38 BBH) per night, $230 per week*
***Reception open** 8am-8pm daily*

Maintenance & cleanliness	★★
Facilities	★★
Atmosphere & character	★★★
Security	★
Overall rating	★★

The Grapevine

The Grapevine is one of Blenheim's few hostels that caters to short-term guests as well as the backpackers working in the vineyards and staying long-term (which makes up the bulk of hostel beds in Bleheim). Facilities include a good kitchen, TV lounge and internet access (including Wi-Fi) plus free laundry. There is also a lovely riverfront backyard barbecue area. The hostel rents bikes for $15 per day, but also has some free bikes if you just need to ride into town. There

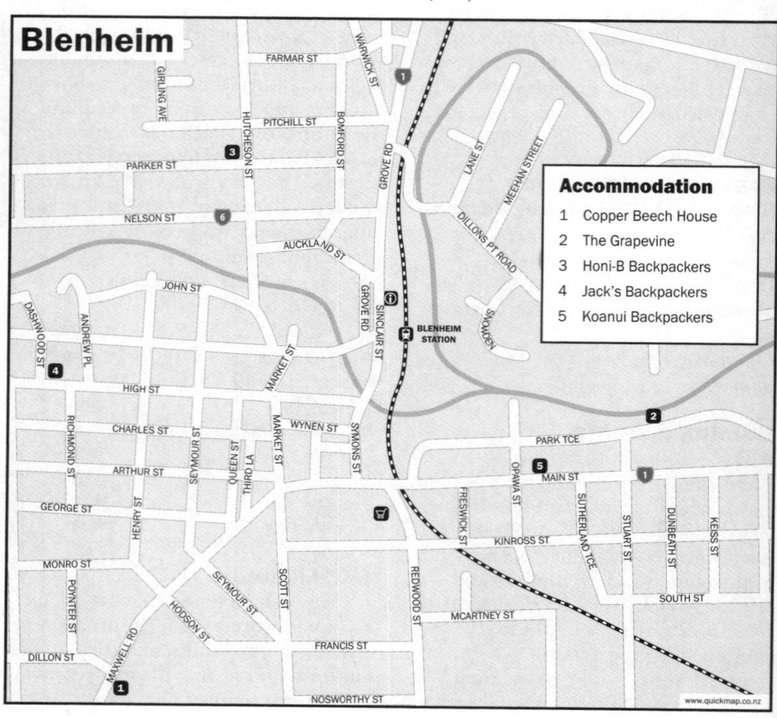

are also free canoes for guests to use. Although the dormitories don't lock, there are lockers for each bed, which makes it a bit more secure than the average New Zealand hostel.

29 Park Terrace, Blenheim
(03) 578 6062
***Website** www.thegrapevine.co.nz*
***Dorm bed** $22-24 ($19-21 BBH); **double room** $48-58 ($42-52 BBH); **twin room** $48-54 ($42-48 BBH)*
***Credit cards** MC, Visa*

Maintenance & cleanliness	★★★
Facilities	★★★
Atmosphere & character	★★★
Security	★★
Overall rating	★★★

Honi-B Backpackers

This hostel caters mostly to travellers working on the vineyards, but also has a fair share of independent travellers. It consists of four houses converted into dorm rooms, with kitchens, lounges and internet access ($4 per hour). They are nothing flash, but they are kept clean and would be a good place to call home if you are working in the area. The main building is more suited for individual travellers, with a clean communal kitchen and large TV lounge. The dorm beds and carpets are new, and there are large shelves that keep the rooms from getting too cluttered. The only problem is the lack of security as the dorm rooms don't lock. The manager is an honest and friendly guy who will help you find work.

18 Parker Street, Blenheim
(03) 577 8441
***Dorm bed** $23-29 ($20-24 BBH) per night, $120-140 per week; **double room** $58 ($48 BBH)*
***Credit cards** MC, Visa*
***Reception open** 7.30am- 9pm daily*

Maintenance & cleanliness	★★★
Facilities	★★
Atmosphere & character	★★
Security	★★½
Overall rating	★★★½

Jack's Backpackers

Jack's has a central location and a bit of character, but that's about it. It is really just part of a home with old fittings and barely any facilities. The dorms are dark and tired, with old beds and older duvets. There is a large sitting room with a nice log fire and lots of books, but it gets a bit musty. They do offer laundry facilities and cheap internet access. Security is not up to par and there is little to no atmosphere.

144 High Street, Blenheim
(03) 578 7375
***Dorm bed** $20*
***Reception open** 8am-8pm daily*

Maintenance & cleanliness	★★
Facilities	★½
Atmosphere & character	★
Security	★½
Overall rating	★½

Koanui Backpackers

Koanui is comprised of two buildings. The nicer new building is aimed mostly at short term visitors staying a day or two and the older building is used for travellers working in the vineyards. Both buildings have common areas including TV lounges and kitchens and the old building also has a lounge with a fireplace. There is also internet access including a Wi-Fi (Zenbu, 10c per MB) connection. The long-term guests mean that the dorms in the older building are much messier than the new one. The hostel rents bikes for the bargain price of $10 per day.

33 Main Street, Blenheim
(03) 578 7487
***Website** www.koanui.co.nz*
***Dorm bed** $23-26 ($20-23 BBH); **double/twin room** $54-70 ($48-64 BBH)*
***Credit cards** MC, Visa*
***Reception open** 8am-2pm & 4pm-9pm daily*

Maintenance & cleanliness	★★★
Facilities	★★★½
Atmosphere & character	★★★
Security	★½
Overall rating	★★★

Leeways Backpackers

This big house near the sports ground north of town has been converted into a hostel. It is a really shoddy job with old mismatched furniture including old ratty sofas and an assortment of limp mattresses that are well beyond their use-by date. Facilities include a fully-equipped kitchen, TV lounge and free laundry and there is also a games room with table tennis, called the Shed.

33 Landsdowne Street, Blenheim
☎ *(03) 579 2213*
***Dorm bed** $21 ($18 BBH); **double room** $50 ($44 BBH)*
***Reception open** 8am-8pm daily*

Maintenance & cleanliness	★
Facilities	★★
Atmosphere & character	★★★½
Security	★½
Overall rating	★½

Sights

Marlborough Musem

This large regional museum has exhibits of local history and culture. A new gallery with displays about Marlborough's wine industry is scheduled to open in 2009.

Brayshaw Park, 26 Arthur Baker Place, Blenheim
☎ *(03) 578 1712*
***Website** www.marlboroughmuseum.org.nz*
***Admission** $5*
***Open** 10am-4pm daily*

Omaka Aviation Heritage Centre

The excellent Omaka Aviation Heritage Centre, 5km south of Blenheim, is home to a large collection of rare aircraft.

93 Aerodrome Road, Omaka
☎ *(03) 579 1305*
***Website** www.omaka.org.nz*
***Admission** $18*
***Open** 10am-4pm daily*

Renwick

Renwick is a great location for exploring the surrounding vineyards with many wineries within an easy bike ride.

Coming & Going

AIR

Blenheim Airport is only 3km from Renwick and has Air New Zealand *(☎ 0800 737 000; **website** www.airnz.co.nz)* flights to Auckland, Christchurch and Wellington and Air2there *(☎ (04) 904 5130; **website** www.air2there.com)* flights to Wellington and Paraparaumu.

BUS

Renwick is well served by coach and shuttle bus services linking Blenheim with Nelson and the West Coast. These include Atomic Shuttles *(☎ (03) 349 0697; **website** www.atomictravel.co.nz)*, InterCity Coachlines *(☎ (03) 365 1113; **website** www.intercity.co.nz)* and Naked Bus *(☎ 0900 62533; **website** www.nakedbus.com)*. Buses stop outside the dairy/superette *(63 High Street, Renwick)*.

Accommodation

Watson's Way

This neat and tidy hostel is a great place to stay. It features a lovely outdoor sitting area under the veranda plus a nice garden with fruit trees and a petanque piste and guests have use of three tennis courts. The hostel's common area has internet access, a TV and a good kitchen (with lot of utensils but no oven). Accommodation is in mostly double and twin rooms – there is only one dormitory. The bathrooms are very clean and there is also a semi-outdoor safari bath, which is a nice luxury if you haven't had a good soak in a bath for a while. It is near the centre of Renwick and it's close to Blenheim Airport and the vineyards. The hostel rents bikes for $25 per day.

56 High Street, Renwick
☎ *(03) 572 8228*
***Website** www.watsonswaybackpackers.co.nz*
***Dorm bed** $25 ($22 BBH); **double room** $52-68 ($46-62 BBH); **twin room** $58 ($52 BBH); prices include breakfast*
***Credit cards** MC, Visa*
***Open** Jan-Aug & Oct-Dec*

Maintenance & cleanliness	★★★★½
Facilities	★★½
Atmosphere & character	★★★★
Security	★½
Overall rating	★★★½

Nelson-Tasman Region

The north western tip of New Zealand's South Island includes the Abel Tasman, Kahurangi, and Nelson Lakes National Parks. These are well known for their kayaking and hiking opportunities, and walking the Abel Tasman and Heaphy Tracks are extremely popular. The main towns in the region are Motueka and Takaka, while the pleasant city of Nelson is the main hub for accommodation, dining and nightlife. This is a varied and rugged landscape offering scenic drives, outdoor activities and working holidays on farms and vineyards.

Nelson

Nelson is a small regional city at the geographic centre of New Zealand. It is the South Island's oldest city, and one of the sunniest places in the country. It has excellent cafes, restaurants and pubs.

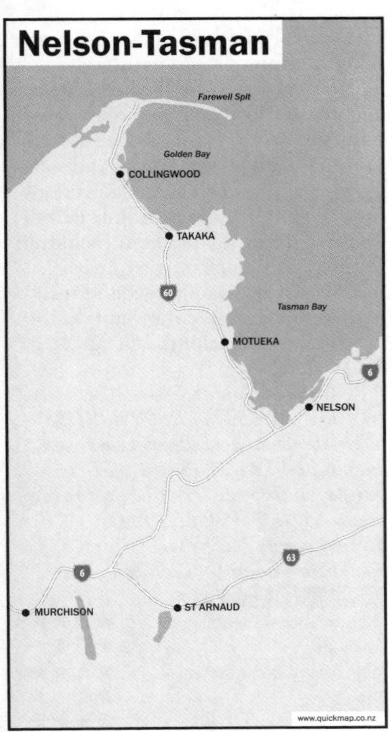

Must do in Nelson-Tasman Region

- Kayak to Tonga Island Marine Reserve in Abel Tasman National Park
- Hike the Abel Tasman Coastal Track

Christ Church Cathedral dominates Trafalgar Square and acts as a point of reference in the city centre. It is backed by beautiful gardens, and Trafalgar Street, which is loaded with shops and alfresco restaurants, runs out from here. The main attractions in the city are the Suter Art Gallery and the World of WearableArt Museum. The Nelson Provincial Museum in the centre of the city is an excellent account of the region's history, and is much too often skipped over.

There are plenty of adventure activities that you can do within a short distance of Nelson. To the south is Nelson Lakes National Park, where you can hike, ski, kayak or go jet boating. To the north are Golden Bay and the scenic Abel Tasman National Park, with waterfalls, beaches, and forests that are great for hiking and kayaking.

Practical Information

Nelson i-SITE Visitor Centre

Corner Halifax & Trafalgar Streets, Nelson
☎ *(03) 548 2304*
Website *www.nelsonnz.com*
Open *Mon-Tue 8.30am-5pm, Wed 9am-5pm, Thu-Fri 8.30am-5pm, Sat-Sun 9am-4pm*

Department of Conservation Visitor Centre

79 Trafalgar Street, Nelson
☎ *(03) 546 9339*
Website *www.doc.govt.nz*
Open *Mon-Fri 8am-4.30pm*

SHOWERS

Showers are available at the Superloo on Montgomery Square in the city centre.

INTERNET ACCESS

Aurora Internet Café
161 Trafalgar Street, Nelson
☎ *(03) 5456 6867*
Open *9am-5pm daily*

Boots Off Travel Centre
53 Bridge Street, Nelson
☎ *(03) 546 8789*

KiwiNet Café
93 Hardy Street, Nelson
☎ *(03) 548 8095*
Website *www.kiwinetcafe.com*

Coming & Going

Nelson is well connected to the rest of the country and some people opt to fly into Nelson from the North Island as an alternative to the Picton ferry.

AIR

Nelson boasts New Zealand's fourth busiest airport, which is 8km west of the centre near Tahunanui Beach. Air2there *(☎ (04) 904 5130; **website** www.air2there.com)* fly to Paraparaumu and Wellington and Air New Zealand *(☎ 0800 737 000; **website** www.airnz.co.nz)* fly to Auckland, Christchurch, Hamilton, Palmerston North and Wellington. The Super Shuttle *(☎ 0800 748 885 (0800 SHUTTLE); **website** www.supershuttle.co.nz)* connects the airport with the city centre and costs $15.

BUS

Atomic Shuttles *(☎ (03) 349 0697; **website** www.atomictravel.co.nz)*, InterCity Coachlines *(☎ (03) 365 1113; **website** www.intercity.co.nz)* and Naked Bus *(☎ 0900 62533; **website** www.nakedbus.com)* are the main coach operators with services to most South Island destinations including direct services to Blenheim, Christchurch, Motueka, Picton and the West Coast.

Abel Tasman Coachlines *(☎ (03) 548 0285; **website** www.abeltasmantravel.co.nz)* have coaches to Abel Tasman National Park and Golden Bay.

InterCity and Abel Tasman Coachlines depart from the Travel Centre at 27 Bridge Street, but Atomic Shuttles, Naked Bus and some InterCity services leave from the visitor information centre at the corner of Halifax and Trafalgar Streets.

Local Transport

Nelson Suburban Bus Lines *(SBL; ☎ (03) 548 3290; **website** www.nelsoncoaches.co.nz)* run local bus services from Nelson to the southern suburbs of Stoke and Richmond and THE BUS run four local bus routes within Nelson city. You'll need to take the bus if you want to visit the museums in Stoke or if you're staying in one of the hostels in Tahunanui.

SBL buses leave from the bus terminal at 27 Bridge Street and THE BUS services depart from Wakatu Square. Most buses run hourly.

Accommodation

Accents on the Park

This is a brilliant accommodation choice for Nelson. Accents has a central location and a high standard of accommodation. The dorms are immaculate, with comfortable made up beds. The bathrooms are spotless, with nice showers and hairdryers. There is a large, fully stocked kitchen, and an excellent small bar with cheap food and drink. It is in a century-old building with warm colours and soft lighting and a small veranda overlooking the park. Facilities include laundry, internet access ($5 per hour including Wi-Fi) and a cute courtyard with a barbecue. Everything is wonderfully maintained and reception staff are welcoming and helpful. It's a great value hostel.

335 Trafalgar Square, Nelson
☎ *(03) 548 4335 or 0800 888 335*
Website *www.accentsonthepark.com*
Dorm bed *$23-28 ($20-25 BBH);* ***single room*** *$42 ($39 BBH);* ***double room*** *$57-89 ($54-86 BBH)*
Credit cards *MC, Visa*
Reception open *6.30am-9pm daily*

Maintenance & cleanliness	★★★★★
Facilities	★★★
Atmosphere & character	★★★★
Security	★★
Overall rating	★★★★

Nelson-Tasman

Almond House Backpackers

Almond House is a small and well maintained hostel. Dorm rooms are spacious with large wooden bunks and single beds made up with duvets. The kitchen is small but very clean, and there is also a small TV lounge with books and new couches. The bathrooms are new and nicely decorated. It features a peaceful garden area with a barbecue and a large and inviting swimming pool. It has a quiet atmosphere and it is family-run and friendly. It's a few minutes' walk from town and just across from an organic market.

63 Grove Street, Nelson
☎ *(03) 545 6455*
Website *www.almondbackpackers.co.nz*
Dorm bed *$23 ($20 BBH);* ***double/twin room*** *$56 ($50 BBH)*
Credit cards *MC, Visa*
Reception open *8am-noon & 2pm-8pm*

Maintenance & cleanliness	★★★★½
Facilities	★★½
Atmosphere & character	★★★
Security	★
Overall rating	★★★½

Beach Hostel

Nelson's Beach Hostel is in a large old house that could be better maintained, but it has a homely atmosphere and is kept clean. The bathrooms are nice and clean, but the kitchen is a bit old. There is a comfy lounge with log fire, books and guitars, and a good upstairs veranda with wooden breakfast tables. Dorms are comfortable and relatively clean. This hostel caters mostly to workers. Reception staff are pleasant.

25 Muritai Street, Tahunanui
☎ *(03) 548 6817*
Website *http://nelsonbeachhostel.50megs.com/*
Dorm bed *$23 (20 BBH);* ***double/twin room*** *$55 ($50 BBH);* ***camping*** *$12 per person*
Credit cards *MC, Visa*
Reception open *9am-8.30pm daily*

Maintenance & cleanliness	★★★
Facilities	★★★
Atmosphere & character	★★
Security	★½
Overall rating	★★½

The Bug

Besides its great name, this hostel is a great choice for several reasons. It is a small, smartly decorated hostel with great atmosphere and facilities. The common areas and dorms are sleek and clean, with new, comfortable mattresses and beds made up with nice duvets and bedside lights. The fully-equipped kitchen is spacious and the bathrooms are new and spotless. Double rooms are exceptionally well appointed. They offer laundry facilities, free use of bicycles, free airport pickup and unlimited free internet (including Wi-Fi access). There is a laid-back, convivial atmosphere here, and the owner is friendly and interesting.

226 Vanguard Street, Nelson
☎ *(03) 539 4227*
Website *www.thebug.co.nz*
Dorm bed *$23-25 ($20-22 BBH);* ***double/twin room*** *$29 ($26 BBH)*
Credit cards *MC, Visa*
Reception open *7.30am-10.30pm daily*

Maintenance & cleanliness	★★★★
Facilities	★★★★
Atmosphere & character	★★★★
Security	★½
Overall rating	★★★★

Bumbles Backpackers

Bumbles Backpackers is right in the centre of town, but it is a poorly maintained hostel. The dorms (some of which are in old motel rooms) are quite dated but they have good mattresses, and the bathrooms are dirty and need serious maintenance. The kitchen is well equipped and tidy, and there is a large TV lounge with heaps of DVDs, a pool table and internet access. They also have a barbecue and laundry. There is not much atmosphere here and security could be a lot better.

8 Bridge Street, Nelson
☎ *(03) 548 2771*
Dorm bed *$20-25;* ***single room*** *$45;* ***double/twin room*** *$60 ($50 for two-night stay)*
Credit cards *MC, Visa*
Reception open *6am-11pm daily*

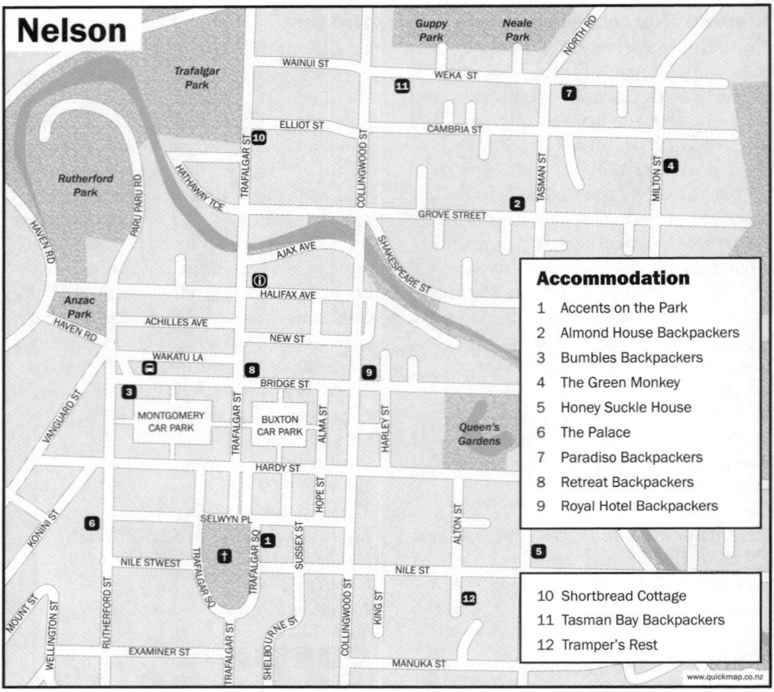

Nelson

Accommodation

1 Accents on the Park
2 Almond House Backpackers
3 Bumbles Backpackers
4 The Green Monkey
5 Honey Suckle House
6 The Palace
7 Paradiso Backpackers
8 Retreat Backpackers
9 Royal Hotel Backpackers
10 Shortbread Cottage
11 Tasman Bay Backpackers
12 Tramper's Rest

www.quickmap.co.nz

Maintenance & cleanliness	★★★½
Facilities	★★
Atmosphere & character	★★★½
Security	★★
Overall rating	★★★½

Footprints by the Sea

Footprints by the Sea is a small, modern hostel in front of the beach in Tahunanui, 5km southwest of the city centre. Facilities include a dated, but well equipped, kitchen; a laundry; internet access and a mediocre lounge with books and Sky TV. Accommodation is in small dorms and bathrooms are clean and each guest gets a towel, soap and shampoo on arrival. The hostel is under new management, who are outgoing and nice.

31 Beach Road, Tahunanui
(03) 546 5441
***Website** www.footprints.co.nz*
***Dorm bed** $20-25; **single room** $40; **double room** $70-95*
***Credit cards** MC, Visa*
***Reception open** 8am-10.30pm daily*

Maintenance & cleanliness	★★★
Facilities	★★
Atmosphere & character	★★
Security	★½
Overall rating	★★

Gingerbread House

Gingerbread House is a small hostel in an inconvenient location, 2.3km south of the city centre. It has two dorms that get pretty cluttered, and a large well-equipped kitchen. The bathrooms are lovely and clean. It has a small outdoor garden area with hammocks where you can pitch a tent. The atmosphere here is a bit dull, although some may find it peaceful. They offer laundry, internet access and free use of bicycles. The reception staff are very friendly.

42 Westbrook Terrace, Nelson
(03) 548 4854
***Dorm bed** $25 ($20 BBH); **double room** $55 ($50 BBH)*
***Reception open** 9.30am-7.30pm daily*

Maintenance & cleanliness	★★★½
Facilities	★★★½
Atmosphere & character	★★½
Security	★
Overall rating	★★

The Green Monkey

This is a cute little hostel with nice fittings and a quiet atmosphere. The dorm rooms are nicely painted and well maintained, and the bathrooms are very clean. There is a common area with TV, log fire, books and guitars, and the kitchen is small but well equipped and tidy. They also have a laundry, internet access and a barbecue. Outside there are lemon and lime trees in the garden. The location is about a five-minute walk from the centre.

129 Milton Street, Nelson
☎ *(03) 545 7421*
***Website** www.thegreenmonkey.co.nz*
***Dorm bed** $24 ($21 BBH); **double room** $58 ($52 BBH)*
***Reception open** 8.30am-8pm daily*

Maintenance & cleanliness	★★★★½
Facilities	★★★½
Atmosphere & character	★★★½
Security	★★½
Overall rating	★★★

Honey Suckle House

Honey Suckle House is a very homely hostel not far from the centre. It is a large house, but they only have 10 dorm beds. The common room is spacious with a few couches and books. The large dorms are nicely maintained with good beds. The kitchen is small but well-kept and the bathrooms are clean and tidy. They offer laundry and free pickup service. There is an outdoor garden with a barbecue and a nice view.

125 Tasman Street, Nelson
☎ *(03) 548 7576*
***Dorm bed** $24 ($21 BBH); **double room** $55 ($52 BBH); **twin room** $57 ($54 BBH)*
***Reception open** 8.30am-9pm daily*

Maintenance & cleanliness	★★★
Facilities	★★
Atmosphere & character	★★
Security	★
Overall rating	★★★½

The Palace

This is a great hostel perched on top of a hill and surrounded by thick gardens. It is in a restored old house with loads of character. There are several common rooms with chandeliers, log fires, pianos and guitars. The dorms have single beds with good mattresses. Bathrooms are newly (and rather creatively) renovated, and the showers have great water pressure. They offer internet access, an international book exchange, laundry, free tea and real coffee, and a great free breakfast. There are two other buildings with slightly lower standards, but overall it is a central, good value place to stay. The reception staff are extremely warm and friendly.

114 Rutherford Street, Nelson
☎ *(03) 548 4691*
***Website** www.thepalace.co.nz*
***Dorm bed** $23 ($20 BBH); **single room** $45 ($40 BBH); **double/twin room** $56 ($50 BBH); **triple room** $75 ($66 BBH); prices include breakfast*
***Reception open** 6am-9pm daily*

Maintenance & cleanliness	★★★½
Facilities	★★½
Atmosphere & character	★★★★
Security	★½
Overall rating	★★★

Paradiso Backpackers

The Paradiso is known as Nelson's "party hostel", but it is not typical of one. It is in a nice large restored house and everything is well maintained. It offers heaps of facilities including two TV lounges, a pool table, swimming pool, spa, sauna and a beach volleyball court. The large outdoor kitchen is fully-equipped, clean and well maintained. Dorms have comfortable beds, bedside lamps and clean en suite bathrooms. They also offer laundry, internet access and tour bookings. Every night they have free vegetable soup, plus a free breakfast every morning. The atmosphere here is cheerful and fun, but not as impersonal as most party hostels. Management and staff are very friendly and helpful.

42 Weka Street, Nelson
☎ *(03) 546 6703*

Website *www.backpackernelson.co.nz*
Dorm bed *$22-26 ($20-24 BBH);* ***double room*** *$56 ($54 BBH)*
Credit cards *Amex, Diners, MC, Visa*
Reception open *7.45am-9pm daily*

Maintenance & cleanliness	★★★½
Facilities	★★★★½
Atmosphere & character	★★★★★
Security	★★★
Overall rating	★★★★

Retreat Backpackers

This hostel is very poorly maintained. It has a great location in the centre of town, but dorm rooms are untidy, and the bathrooms need maintenance. It has a well-equipped kitchen, although it is a bit dated. There is a small TV room and a common room with a table and a few chairs. The outside patio is not very inviting, and overall it has a slightly dodgy atmosphere.

163 Trafalgar Street, Nelson
☎ *(03) 548 9001*
Dorm bed *$20-24 ($17-21 BBH);* ***single room*** *$40;* ***double room*** *$48 ($45 BBH)*
Reception open *9am-9pm daily*

Maintenance & cleanliness	★★
Facilities	★½
Atmosphere & character	★★
Security	★★
Overall rating	★★

Royal Hotel Backpackers

This hostel consists of several dormitories above an old Irish pub. It is absolute no-frills accommodation. The dorms are in a horrid state, with old beds and dirty duvets. Bathrooms are appalling, and the kitchen is barely a kitchen – it is just a hot plate and microwave plus a few plates and pans. It has no atmosphere and management are just looking to lure you in to buy food and drinks at the bar. It is basically just a place to crash if you can't find anything else.

Corner Bridge & Collingwood Streets, Nelson
☎ *(03) 546 9279*
Dorm bed *$20;* ***single room*** *$30;* ***double room*** *$50*
Credit cards *MC, Visa*
Reception open *11am-3am daily*

Maintenance & cleanliness	★
Facilities	★
Atmosphere & character	★★½
Security	★½
Overall rating	★

Shortbread Cottage

This is a quaint 13-bed hostel with a good amount of charm. It has a small but well equipped kitchen, a cosy TV lounge with a log fire, and a simple outdoor common area. The dorms have thick mattresses and duvets, and though they are small, they are cared for. Bathrooms are very nicely maintained with good showers, and there are nice polished wood floors. It has a very quiet atmosphere and the management are friendly.

33 Trafalgar Street, Nelson
☎ *(03) 546 6681*
Dorm bed *$25 ($20 BBH);* ***double room*** *$57 ($50 BBH)*
Reception open *9.30am-7.30pm daily*

Maintenance & cleanliness	★★★½
Facilities	★★½
Atmosphere & character	★★★
Security	★★
Overall rating	★★★

Tasman Bay Backpackers Hostel

This is a colourful and clean hostel with a good amount of character. It features a cosy lounge with nice artwork and log fireplace, a large kitchen, and a small outdoor garden and common area. It is laid-back but cheery. The dorms are spacious with single beds, freshly painted walls and bedside lamps. The bathrooms are very clean, and they offer internet access and a laundry. The reception staff are nice; every night they offer guests free chocolate pudding and ice cream.

10 Weka Street, Nelson
☎ *(03) 548 7950*
Website *www.tasmanbaybackpackers.co.nz*
Dorm bed *$24-25 ($21-22 BBH);* ***double room*** *$30-37.50 ($27-34.50 BBH)*
Credit cards *MC, Visa*
Reception open *8am-1pm & 3pm-9pm daily*

Maintenance & cleanliness	★★★½
Facilities	★★½
Atmosphere & character	★★★½
Security	★★½
Overall rating	★★★

Tramper's Rest

This is a home-style hostel in an old house that shows its age, but is cared for by the lovely family who own it. It is small, and has a cosy lounge area with log fire, a great international book exchange and internet access. Dorms are a bit cramped, but they have new mattresses and nice duvets. The kitchen is also small, but is kept very clean, and the bathrooms are nice and new. The atmosphere here is quiet and very convivial, and management are the friendliest and most helpful around.

31 Alton Street, Nelson

☎ *(03) 545 7477*

***Dorm bed** $25 ($22 BBH); **single room** $41 ($38 BBH); **double room** $58 ($52 BBH)*

***Credit cards** MC, Visa*

***Reception open** 9am-9pm daily*

Maintenance & cleanliness	★★★
Facilities	★★½
Atmosphere & character	★★★½
Security	★½
Overall rating	★★★

YHA Nelson Central

Nelson's YHA hostel has a great location and facilities, but it is lacking atmosphere. The dorm rooms have comfortable beds, bedside lights, and some have skylights. Bathrooms are average but very clean, and there are two huge fully-stocked kitchens. Although the kitchens are nice, the dining areas feel a bit bleak. They offer internet access (including wireless) and a full tour desk. There is also a nice outdoor barbecue and a TV lounge with two pianos. They are the only hostel with an infrared sauna, but it costs $10.

59 Rutherford Street, Nelson

☎ *(03) 545 9988*

***Website** www.yha.co.nz*

***Dorm bed** $22-25; **single room** $41; **double/twin room** $62-78*

***Credit cards** Amex, JCB, MC, Visa*

***Reception open** 8am-9pm daily*

Maintenance & cleanliness	★★★★
Facilities	★★★
Atmosphere & character	★★
Security	★★★½
Overall rating	★★★½

Eating & Drinking:

Eating cheaply in Nelson is easy. There are lots of little sandwich shops, bakeries and cafés with lunch specials, and some pubs have backpackers' specials. **Zest Café** *(56 Bridge Street, Nelson)* has yummy quiches and sandwiches, and next door is a great Turkish café. For great vegetarian and vegan fare, head to **Zippy's Vegetarian Café** *(276 Hardy Street, Nelson)*. If you want to go to a pub, the **Victorian Rose Pub** *(281 Trafalgar Street, Nelson)* has backpacker meal and drink deals.

For dinner, self-catering is the cheapest. There is a **Countdown** *(35 St Vincent Street, Nelson)*, a **FreshChoice** *(69 Collingwood Street, Nelson)*, a **Woolworths** *(corner Paru Paru Road & Halifax Street, Nelson)* and a **New World** supermarket *(corner Vanguard Road & Gloucester Street, Nelson)* to the west of the centre.

Sights

Nelson Provincial Museum

This museum features exhibits on local history in Nelson City and the Tasman District.

Corner Hardy and Trafalgar Streets, Nelson

☎ *(03) 547 9740*

***Website** www.museumnp.org.nz*

***Admission** $5*

***Open** Mon-Fri 10am-5pm, Sat-Sun 10am-4.30pm*

The Suter Art Gallery

New Zealand's third largest art museum has an impressive collection with works by John Gully, Sir Tosswill Woollaston and Gottfried Lindauer. A vibrant programme of temporary exhibitions complements its permanent collection.

208 Bridge Street, Nelson

☎ *(03) 548 4699*
Website *www.thesuter.org.nz*
Admission *$3*
Open *10.30am-4.30pm daily*

World of WearableArt (WOW)

The World of WearableArt complex near the airport combines art, fashion and a classic car museum.

95 Quarantine Road, Annesbrook
☎ *(03) 548 9299*
Website *www.worldofwearableart.com*
Admission *$18*
Open *10am-5pm daily*

Motueka

Motueka is a lively little town that stretches just a few kilometres in the midst of large expanses of farmland and scenic mountain ranges. It is a great place to stay with easy access to the Abel Tasman National Park, as there are cheap places to stay and eat and tours can easily be booked from here. Some backpackers also come here to work on farms in the area. There is a good museum in town with exhibits on the town's history and Māori culture.

Practical Information

Motueka i-SITE Visitor Centre

20 Wallace Street, Motueka
☎ *(03) 528 6543*
Website *www.motuekaisite.co.nz*
Open *8am-5pm daily*

INTERNET ACCESS

Kiwi Konnection

113 High Street, Motueka
☎ *(03) 528 5325*
Website *www.kiwiconnection.co.nz*
Open *10am-10pm daily*

Coming & Going

InterCity Coachlines *(☎ (03) 365 1113; **website** www.intercity.co.nz)* have buses to Blenheim, Christchurch, Nelson, Picton and the West Coast.

Abel Tasman Coachlines *(☎ (03) 548 0285; **website** www.nelsoncoaches.co.nz)* and Southern Link K Bus *(☎ (03) 358 8355 or 0508 458 835; **website** www.southernlinkkbus.co.nz)* have shuttle buses to destinations around Abel Tasman National Park and Golden Bay.

Buses stop at Motueka i-SITE Visitor Centre *(20 Wallace Street, Motueka).*

Accommodation

Bakers Lodge YHA

Bakers Lodge is a purpose-built hostel in a nice building. It has a large fully equipped kitchen and a nice wood and brick outdoor common area with a barbecue. Dorms are standard, with bedside lights and nice duvets. Bathrooms are clean, but need an update. They offer tour bookings, laundry, internet access and a TV lounge. It is a good choice for Motueka, but it has that characteristic institutional feel of a YHA. There is a quiet atmosphere here.

4 Poole Street, Motueka
☎ *(03) 528 0102*
Website *www.yha.co.nz*
Dorm bed *$23-26 ($20-23 HI/YHA)*
Reception open *summer 8am-10am & 2pm-9pm; winter 8am-10am & 2pm-8pm*

Maintenance & cleanliness	★★★★
Facilities	★½
Atmosphere & character	★★★½
Security	★½
Overall rating	★★★

Happy Apple Backpackers

This is a cheerful hostel just south of the town centre. It features a large, cosy TV lounge with a pool table, and a clean fully-equipped kitchen. Shared rooms are well maintained with good beds and nice furnishings. The bathrooms are newly refurbished, perfectly clean and with good showers. There is internet access, laundry and an outside common area with a barbecue and a big backyard. Management are caring and friendly, and the atmosphere is easygoing.

500 High Street, Motueka
☎ *(03) 528 8652*
Website *www.happyapplebackpackers.co.nz*
Dorm bed *$23-26 ($20-23 BBH);* ***single room*** *$35-38 ($32-35 BBH);* ***double room*** *$28 ($25 BBH);* ***twin room*** *$26-29 ($23-26 BBH)*

Nelson-Tasman

Credit cards *MC, Visa*
Reception open *7.30am-9.30pm daily*

Maintenance & cleanliness	★★★★½
Facilities	★★½
Atmosphere & character	★★★
Security	★★
Overall rating	★★★½

Hat Trick Lodge

The Hat Trick Lodge is a nice purpose-built hostel in the centre of town. It has modern furnishings and attractive décor. Dorms are nice, but small, so they can get cluttered. There is a good upstairs common lounge and a tidy kitchen, and an outside veranda with a barbecue. Bathrooms are shiny and new. Internet is available at reception and they also offer laundry facilities. The atmosphere is very low-key here and management are nice enough.

25 Wallace Street, Motueka
☎ *(03) 528 5353*
Website *www.hattricklodge.co.nz*
Dorm bed *$23-25 ($20-22 BBH)*
Credit cards *MC, Visa*
Reception open *7.45am-10.30pm daily*

Maintenance & cleanliness	★★★★½
Facilities	★★
Atmosphere & character	★★
Security	★★
Overall rating	★★★

The Laughing Kiwi

The Laughing Kiwi is made up of two houses that are bright and nicely maintained with great travel photography and good furnishings throughout. Dorms are colourful with made-up beds and the clean bathrooms have great showers. There are two fully-equipped kitchens. They offer laundry, internet access, and an outdoor spa. Location is good and there is a convivial atmosphere.

310 High Street, Motueka
☎ *(03) 528 9229*
Website *www.thelaughingkiwi.co.nz*
Dorm bed *$23-25 ($20-22 BBH);* ***double/twin room*** *$56-62 ($50-56 BBH)*
Credit cards *MC, Visa*
Reception open *7.30am-12.30pm & 2.30pm-8pm daily*

Maintenance & cleanliness	★★★★
Facilities	★★
Atmosphere & character	★★★½
Security	★
Overall rating	★★★

Motueka Backpackers

The only thing good about this hostel is its location. It is an extension of a house just off the main street in town, but it offers barely any facilities and it is in a serious state of disrepair. The

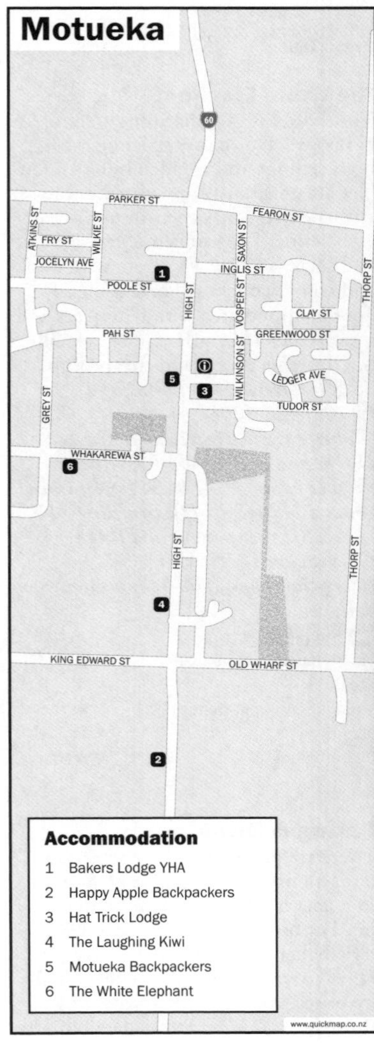

common area is a dirty room with tattered couches, and the kitchen is poorly maintained. Dorms are old and uninviting. There is no internet, no atmosphere and bad security.
200 High Street, Motueka
☎ *(03) 528 7581*
***Dorm bed** $18; **double room** $40; **camping** $10 per person*
***Reception open** 8am-9pm daily*

Maintenance & cleanliness	★
Facilities	★½
Atmosphere & character	★
Security	★
Overall rating	★

The White Elephant

This hostel is in a charmingly restored old house. Dorms are spacious with high ceilings and wooden bunks. Doubles are gorgeously appointed, some with log fires and others in new separate cabins. The kitchen is very clean and there is a tiny TV room with books and comfy couches. There is an outdoor common area with fruit trees and a barbecue. They offer laundry facilities, internet access and free pickup.
55 Whakarewa Street, Motueka
☎ *(03) 528 6208*
***Website** www.whiteelephant.co.nz*
***Dorm bed** $22-25 ($19-22 BBH); **double room** $50-70 ($44-64); **twin room** $54 ($48 BBH); **camping** $15 ($12 BBH) per person; **bed linen** $3*
***Credit cards** MC, Visa*
***Reception open** 8am-1pm & 3pm-8pm daily*

Maintenance & cleanliness	★★★½
Facilities	★★
Atmosphere & character	★★★
Security	★½
Overall rating	★★★

Eating & Drinking

There are plenty of cafés and restaurants along High Street in Motueka, so it isn't hard to find a cheap place to eat. For breakfast try the European-style bakery **Patisserie Royale** *(152 High Street, Motueka)* for cheap quality baked goods. The **Rolling Pin Bakery** *(100 High Street, Motueka)* also has great cheap sandwiches, pies and smoothies. For lunch, The **Swinging Sultan** *(172 High Street, Motueka)* offers good coffee and kebabs. It is just next to the CyberWorld Internet Café on High Street. For Italian lunch or dinner, the **Bakehouse Café and Pizzeria** *(21 Wallace Street, Motueka)* serves relatively cheap food in an atmospheric setting. At night, many backpackers head to the **Dodgy Ref Sports Bar** *(121 High Street, Motueka)* for cheap pub food and drink specials.

If you are on a strict budget, there is a **FreshChoice** supermarket *(108 High Street, Motueka)*. There are also a few good organic fruit and vegetable markets scattered through the town. This is a good way to eat cheaply while sampling some of the locally grown produce.

Sights

Motueka District Museum

This regional museum is housed in the town's old school building and it features displays on local history, genealogy and Māori culture.
140 High Street, Motueka
☎ *(03) 528 7660*
***Admission** $1-2 donation*
***Open** summer 10am-3pm daily; winter Mon-Fri 10am-3pm*

Abel Tasman National Park

New Zealand's smallest national park boasts spectacular coastline and a rugged interior with waterfalls and streams. It is extremely popular with backpackers who come to hike the Abel Tasman Coastal Track and to kayak along the park's 91km of pristine coastline, which is home to dolphins, fur seals, penguins and a variety of bird life.

Coming & Going

The park has good transport connections from Nelson, Motueka and Takaka.

Shuttle bus companies that serve the park include Abel Tasman Coachlines *(☎ (03) 548 0285; **website** www.*

nelsoncoaches.co.nz) and Southern Link K Bus *(☎ (03) 358 8355 or 0508 458 835; **website** www.southernlinkkbus.co.nz).*

Local Transport

There are several water taxi companies that offer shuttle services within the national park. These include Abel Tasman Sea Shuttle *(☎ 0800 732 748 (0800 SEA SHUTTLE); **website** www.abeltasmanseashuttles.co.nz)* and Aqua Taxi *(☎ (03) 527 8083 or 0800 278 282 (0800 AQUA TAXI); **website** www.aquataxis.co.nz).* One way fares generally range from $25 to $36.

Accommodation

There are several campgrounds in the park and DOC operates huts on the Inland and Coastal Tracks (reservations are essential in summer). DOC huts on the Abel Tasman Coastal Track cost $14 between October and April and $10 between May and September. Camping costs $7 year round.

In addition to DOC accommodation within the park, there are a couple of backpackers hostels at Marahau, near the edge of the park, and many backpackers stay at one of the hostels in nearby Motueka or Takaka.

The Barn

The Barn consists of a main house and a campground near the entrance to the Abel Tasman National Park. The main hostel has a large dormitory with a row of queen-size mattresses laid out side-by-side on a long bunk. The kitchen is relatively clean but poorly maintained, although there is a camp kitchen on the other side of the property as well. It has a cosy veranda with couches and log fire, and an internet room with a few new computers. The bathrooms in the main house are newly renovated and very clean, while the rest of the house is a bit tired. There is a barbecue and laundry, and reception staff are knowledgeable and friendly. You can't get closer to Abel Tasman, and this is a good choice if you don't mind sleeping right next to ten other people.

Harvey Road, Marahau
☎ (03) 527 8043
***Website** www.barn.co.nz*
***Dorm bed** $25; **double room** $52-62; **twin room** $62; **camping** $13 per person*
***Credit cards** MC, Visa*
***Reception open** summer 8am-9pm daily; winter 9am-6pm daily*

Maintenance & cleanliness	★★★
Facilities	★★½
Atmosphere & character	★★★
Security	★
Overall rating	★★½

Kanuka Ridge Abel Tasman Backpackers

This is a very peaceful place made up of a few cabins and campsites, perched on a hill and surrounded by mountains and pastures. There is a nice small kitchen as well as a camp kitchen with a barbecue. Bathrooms are renovated and spotless and there is a cute lounge with a log fire. Other facilities include a laundry, internet access ($4 per hour) and a small shop in the office. Guests have free use of bicycles and the helpful staff organise loads of tours.

Moss Road, Marahau
☎ (03) 527 8424
***Dorm bed** $23 ($20 BBH); **single room** $40-60 ($37-57 BBH); **double room** $56-76 ($50-70 BBH); **camping** $13 per person*
***Credit cards** MC, Visa*
***Reception open** summer 8am-7pm daily; winter 8am-6pm daily*

Maintenance & cleanliness	★★★★
Facilities	★★★½
Atmosphere & character	★★★
Security	★½
Overall rating	★★★

Kayaking

Abel Tasman National Park is New Zealand's top sea kayaking spot. It is an extremely popular activity with many backpackers and there are a large number of kayaking operators to choose from. Most companies rent kayaks and also operate guided trips. One of the highlights is the Tonga Island Marine Reserve where you can often see seals between March and October.

If you're considering a multi-day trip, rentals are by far the cheapest option; but guided trips are a good option if you're new to kayaking. A one-day guided trip followed by a multi-day rental is a good compromise that gives you the best of both worlds.

Many companies prohibit solo hire and require that at least someone in your group have some kayaking experience. Many kayak rental companies offer the fifth day free.

The following companies run guided kayaking trips and many also rent kayaks.

Abel Tasman Kayaks *(☎ (03) 527 8022 or 0800 732 529; **website** www.abeltasmankayaks.co.nz)* operate guided kayaking trips, which cost $560-890 for a three-day trip.

Kaiteriteri Kayak *(☎ (03) 527 8383 or 0800 2 52925 (0800 2 KAYAK); **website** www.seakayak.co.nz)* run highly recommended day trips that cost $110. They also have the option of water taxi assisted day trips where you are taken by water taxi to some of the best areas in the park to explore by kayak. These trips give you the best experience you can get on a single day trip. Kaiteriteri's Aqua Taxi assisted day trips cost $165-185.

Kaiteriteri also have kayak and walk combos that combine hiking and kayaking, allowing you to experience both the park from both the land and sea. One day kayak and walk trips cost $99-135 and two day trips cost $175-185.

Kiwi Kayaks *(☎ (03) 528 7705 or 0800 695 494; **website** www.kiwikayaks.co.nz)* rent kayaks and run guided kayaking trips. One day kayaking trips cost $115-185 and kayak and walk combos that cost $99-129 for a day trip. Rental costs are one day $55, two days $99, three days $140, four days $170; the fifth rental day is free.

Marahau Sea Kayaks *(☎ (03) 527 8551 or 0800 808 018; **website** www.marahauseakayaks.co.nz)* run guided one day kayaking trips and they also rent kayaks for overnight trips. One day guided kayaking trips cost $95-160 and rental costs are one day $65, two days $100, three days $140, four days $180; the fifth rental day is free.

Ocean River Sea Kayaking *(☎ (03) 527 8022 or 0800 732 529; **website** www.seakayaking.co.nz)* rent kayaks. Rental costs are one day $55, two days $99, three days $140, four days $170; the fifth rental day is free.

The **Sea Kayak Company** *(☎ (03) 528 7251 or 0508 252 925; **website** www.seakayaknz.co.nz)* runs guided single and multi-day trips and also rents kayaks. One day kayaking trips cost $99-165; kayak and walk day trip combos cost $165; two day trips cost $330; three day trips cost $410-490; five day trips cost $950. Rental costs are two days $100, three days $145, four days $180; the fifth rental day is free.

Hiking

There are some excellent hiking trails in the park. The two most popular long walks are the Abel Tasman Inland Track and the easier Abel Tasman Coastal Track. The Department of Conservation classes the Coastal Track as a Great Walk.

ABEL TASMAN COASTAL TRACK

The easy Abel Tasman Coastal Track (51km; 3-5 days) is one of New Zealand's most popular hiking trails.

For the most part it hugs the coast and allows plenty of opportunity to take a break on some lovely sandy beaches.

Like the Queen Charlotte Track, the coastal nature of the Abel Tasman Coastal Track means that you can let a water taxi carry your backpack between overnight stops allowing you to walk with only a daypack.

You will need to refer to a tide table when planning your walk as the track passes several estuaries that can only be crossed a couple of hours either side of low tide.

There are four DOC huts on the track that provide dormitory accommodation. In the peak season (Oct-Apr) you will need to book your hut accommodation by buying a summer season hut pass from a DOC office.

The track is divided into the following sections:

Marahau to Anchorage *(11.5km, 4 hours)*

The first leg of the track leaves Marahau at the southern entrance to the park, passing four beachside campsites before arriving at Anchorage Bay where there is another campsite and also a DOC hut.

Anchorage to Bark Bay
(9.5km, 3 hours)

This section of the track involves crossing the Torrent Bay estuary, which can only be crossed two hours either side of low tide. After crossing the estuary, the track climbs through pine forest and crosses the Falls River before descending back to sea level and the Bark Bay hut.

Bark Bay to Awaroa
(11.5km, 4 hours)

After crossing Bark Bay estuary, the track climbs to a saddle and through manuka bush before returning to the shore at Tonga Quarry in the Tonga Island Marine Reserve. At Onetahuti Beach you have to cross a tidal stream that is only passable three hours either side of low tide. After leaving the beach the track climbs over the Tonga Saddle before descending to Awaroa hut. The classy Awaroa Lodge is located close to Awaroa Hut and offers the opportunity for a nice meal.

Awaroa to Totaranui
(5.5km, 1½ hours)

This part of the track starts by crossing the Awaroa estuary. This can only be crossed 1½-2 hours either side of low tide, although Awaroa Lodge operates a barge ($5) during high tide. The track goes inland for a short distance before returning to the beach. Again, the track goes inland for a short distance before arriving at the DOC campsite at Totaranui.

Totaranui to Wainui Bay
(13km, 4½ hours)

Much of the last section of the track alternates between the beach and rocky headlands. You also have the option of making a one hour side trip to the lighthouse at Separation Point. After passing the Whariwharangi DOC hut, the track cuts inland for 5km before following an estuary for the final 500m to the trailhead at Wainui Bay.

ABEL TASMAN INLAND TRACK

The more demanding Abel Tasman Inland Track (4 days) is a less travelled alternative to the Coastal Track that shares the same start and finishing points, however you miss out on the spectacular coastal scenery. It passes through regenerating forest and has four DOC huts spaced along the track.

Golden Bay

Golden Bay lies between Abel Tasman and Kahurangi National Parks. It was the first place in New Zealand to be spotted by Abel Tasman in 1624 and 214 years later it was the site of the country's first gold rush.

Today it is popular with travellers as a base to explore the Kahurangi National Park, Farewell Spit, and the Wanganui Inlet Rainforest Estuary. It is also home to Tewaikoropupu Springs (aka Pupu Springs) – one of the largest freshwater springs in the world. The area is full of small towns and alternative communities, yoga retreats and rural pubs. This interesting mix makes the area worth exploring in depth – at least for a day or two. Takaka has charming little cafés and great vegetarian and organic options, and is the last stop for cheap groceries if you are heading north.

Takaka

Takaka is the main hub of Golden Bay. It is a small town with strong hippy culture and an alternative vibe, which gives it a lot more character than the average New Zealand town. There are lots of art and craft shops, but not much in the way of attractions. The main reasons travellers come here are to work on farms and to travel north to Farewell Spit.

Practical Information

Golden Bay i-SITE Visitor Centre
Willow Street, Takaka
☎ *(03) 525 9136*
Website *www.nelsonnz.com*
Open *9am-5pm daily*

Coming & Going

Abel Tasman Coachlines (☎ *(03) 548 0285; **website** www.nelsoncoaches.co.nz)*, InterCity Coachlines (☎ *(03) 365 1113; **website** www.intercity.co.nz)* and Southern Link K Bus (☎ *(03) 358 8355 or 0508 458 835; **website** www.southernlinkkbus.co.nz)* connect Takaka with Motueka and Nelson. Buses stop outside the i-SITE visitor information centre on Willow Street.

Accommodation

Annie's Nirvana Lodge

Annie's is a funky little hostel with colourful, well maintained, dorms. It has two small, but well equipped, kitchens and nice new bathrooms. There are lovely gardens in the back with a chair swing and barbecue area, and a cosy lounge with a log fire. There laundry facilities and internet access ($6 per hour) and guests have free use of bicycles. It has a chilled-out vibe, a good location, and a friendly, outgoing manager.

25 Motupipi Street, Takaka
☎ *(03) 525 8766*
***Dorm bed** $25 ($22 BBH, HI/YHA); **double room** $56 ($50 BBH, HI/YHA); no children under 3 years.*
***Credit cards** MC, Visa*
***Reception open** 8.30am-8pm daily*

Maintenance & cleanliness	★★★
Facilities	★★
Atmosphere & character	★★★½
Security	★½
Overall rating	★★½

Carlconna House

This is really just a home that has some double rooms and two dorm-priced beds available. But it is a real gem. The place is full of character and surrounded by beautiful gardens. Rooms have single, made-up and extremely comfortable beds. Décor is charming and it is all very clean. Doubles are absolutely lovely and have a big veranda overlooking the gardens. The kitchen is small but perfectly clean and well equipped. It is a quiet place, and the owner is kind and welcoming. They offer free internet access and laundry facilities.

104 Commercial Street, Takaka
☎ *0800 580 480*
***Website** www.carlconna.co.nz*
***Dorm bed** $30; **double room** $65-70; **twin room** $60*
***Reception open** 7am-8pm daily*

Maintenance & cleanliness	★★★★
Facilities	★★½
Atmosphere & character	★★★
Security	★½
Overall rating	★★★

The Gazebo

The Gazebo is a small home with just five dorm beds. It features a great lounge with plush couches, a log fire, large-screen TV with surround sound and an enormous DVD library. There is an outside deck with a spa pool and vegetable and herb gardens plus a small gym in the garage, and they also offer internet access. The dorm is a bit cluttered, but has comfortable made-up beds. Bathrooms are new and clean, and one of them has an awesome high tech shower. It has a very quiet with slightly alternative atmosphere. It is located a few minutes out of town.

7 Hiawatha Lane, Takaka
☎ *(03) 525 7055*
***Website** www.gazebo.pohara.com*
***Dorm bed** $22; **double room** $55*
***Open** Jan-Apr & Nov-Dec*

Maintenance & cleanliness	★★½
Facilities	★★★★
Atmosphere & character	★½
Security	★½
Overall rating	★★½

Golden Bay Barefoot Backpackers

This hostel is in a small home to the north of the town centre. It has a TV lounge with log fire and a well equipped kitchen, plus a spa pool and an outside deck. Dorms are clean and bright with good beds. Everything is kept clean, but it could use an update, as the carpets are old and some of the furnishings are rather tired-looking. They offer internet access ($6 per hour) and guests have free use of bicycles. There is a friendly and quiet atmosphere.

114 Commercial Street, Takaka
(03) 525 7005
***Website** www.bare-foot.co.nz*
***Dorm bed** $24-25 ($22-23 BBH); **double room** $50; **twin room** $48; **camping** $15 per person*
***Reception open** 9am-8pm daily*

Maintenance & cleanliness	★★½
Facilities	★★½
Atmosphere & character	★★★
Security	★
Overall rating	★★½

Kiwiana

Kiwiana is an intimate hostel with good facilities. Dorms are small but well maintained, and bathrooms are sparkling clean. There is a pleasant garden and a cosy lounge with TV, pool table, table tennis, internet access ($6 per hour), some guitars and a log fire. They also have laundry facilities, a nice spa pool on the deck and guests have free use of bikes. The kitchen could use a renovation, but otherwise it is a homely, clean place with friendly management. It is just a few minutes' walk to the main street.
73 Motupipi Street, Takaka
(03) 525 6261 or 0800 80 KIWIANA
***Dorm bed** $24; **single room** $40; **double/twin room** $60; **camping** $15 per person*
***Reception open** 8am-9pm daily*

Maintenance & cleanliness	★★★
Facilities	★★★
Atmosphere & character	★★★
Security	★½
Overall rating	★★★

The Nook

The Nook is a nice hostel in a cute little house a five-minute walk from the beach at Pohara. It features a small kitchen and a cosy lounge with a log fire. There is also a nice garden area with lots of little places to sit. Accommodation is in double and twin rooms and small dorms – the biggest has only three beds – and there is also a straw cottage behind the hostel.
678 Abel Tasman Drive, Clifden, Pohara
(03) 525 8501
***Website** www.thenookguesthouse.co.nz*
***Dorm bed** $25 ($22 BBH); **double room** $60 ($50 BBH); **twin room** $50 ($44 BBH)*

Maintenance & cleanliness	★★★★
Facilities	★½
Atmosphere & character	★★★★½
Security	-
Overall rating	★★★

The River Inn

The River Inn is an old pub with hostel accommodation. It is dated and could be better maintained, although it could also be described as "authentic". The kitchen is quite a mess; bathrooms are cute and clean and the dorms are clean but a bit austere, and it may be a boring place to stay for someone travelling alone. However, that gives you a reason to mingle with the locals in the downstairs bar, which has an eccentric crowd on occasion. The management are friendly and offer free use of bicycles.

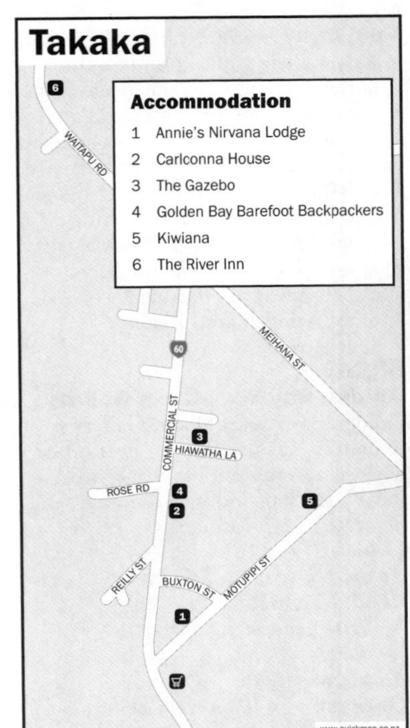

Waitapu Road, Takaka
☎ *(03) 525 9425*
Website *www.riverinn.co.nz*
Dorm bed *$25 ($22 BBH);* ***double/ twin room*** *$60 ($56 BBH)*
Credit cards *MC, Visa*
Reception open *10am- till late*

Maintenance & cleanliness	★★½
Facilities	★★½
Atmosphere & character	★★½
Security	★½
Overall rating	★★½

Eating & Drinking

Takaka is a health nut's paradise. There are organic shops and fruit and veggie markets everywhere, plus lots of healthy cafés and restaurants. Most places to eat and drink are clustered around Commercial Street.

Unfortunately, eating healthy usually comes with a high price tag. An exception is the **Wholemeal Café** *(60 Commercial Street, Takaka)* in the centre of town, where you can get quiches and lasagnes at takeaway prices. For a quick bite, head to **Bay Take Away** *(46A Commercial Street, Takaka)* where you can find all the usual snacks and lunch fare, plus some really good cheap fish and chips.

If you don't want to blow the budget at the organic market in town, there is a **FreshChoice** supermarket *(13 Willow Street, Takaka)* near the beginning of Motupipi Street. You will probably need to stock up on cheap supplies here if you are heading out to Abel Tasman or another secluded destination.

Sights

Golden Bay Museum & Gallery

Golden Bay Museum and Gallery is housed in Takaka's former post office. This small museum has displays on local history including a diorama depicting Abel Tasman's fateful visit to Golden Bay in 1642 .
Commercial Street, Takaka
☎ *(03) 525 6268*
Website *www.virtualbay.co.nz/ gbmuseum/*
Admission *free*
Open *summer 10am-4pm daily; winter Mon-Sat 10am-4pm*

Collingwood & Farewell Spit

At the far north corner of the South Island is Farewell Spit, which is the world's longest sandbar at 35km.

It extends out into the Tasman Sea and provides a coastal barrier where wetland birds come to nest. It has some nice walking tracks and is popular with cyclists despite the sometimes dangerous winding roads. A few kilometres south of the Spit is Collingwood, a tiny historic gold rush town with great views.

Accommodation

FAREWELL SPIT

The Innlet

This hostel is in an old but well-maintained house. It has a large fully-equipped kitchen and a very cosy lounge with a nice log fireplace and plenty of books. Dorms are spacious and have made-up beds with good quality mattresses. The bathrooms are small but clean. The house is surrounded by forests and herb gardens, and there are "bush baths" – heated bathtubs to relax in down by the river. It has a very quiet, retreat-like atmosphere, but at night there is plenty of socialising among guests. There are laundry facilities, internet access and lots of tours to take in the area. They hire kayaks for $35 a day.
Main Road, Pakawau
☎ *(03) 524 8040*
Website *www.goldenbayindex.co.nz/ theinnlet.html*
Dorm bed *$26 ($23 BBH);* ***double/ twin room*** *$62-80 ($56-74 BBH),*
Credit cards *MC, Visa; 2.75% credit card surcharge*
Reception open *8am-9.30pm daily*

Maintenance & cleanliness	★★★½
Facilities	★★½
Atmosphere & character	★★★½
Security	★
Overall rating	★★★

COLLINGWOOD

Somerset House

Somerset House is a homely place in Collingwood. It has large dorms

with good made-up beds and polished floorboards. The clean fully-equipped kitchen has a large wooden table and TV; the bathrooms are clean and there is a nice balcony in the front with views of a church and the mountains, and the barbecue area is a good place for socialising. It is a cheerful little place with friendly staff.
Gibbs Road, Collingwood
☎ *(03) 524 8624*
Website *www.backpackerscollingwood.co.nz*
Dorm bed *$25 ($22 BBH);* ***single room*** *$38 ($35 BBH);* ***double/twin room*** *$28 ($25 BBH)*
Credit cards *MC, Visa*
Reception open *7.30am-9pm daily*

Maintenance & cleanliness	★★★½
Facilities	★★★½
Atmosphere & character	★★★
Security	★
Overall rating	★★★

Kahurangi National Park

This large park at the South Island's northwest corner is home to the most diverse habitat of any New Zealand national park. The biggest attraction in this park is the Heaphy Track, one of the lesser walked of DOC's Great Walks.

The park's diverse environment allows over half of New Zealand's plant species to thrive here including 80% of its alpine flora.

Coming & Going

Abel Tasman Coachlines (☎ *(03) 548 0285;* ***website*** *www.nelsoncoaches.co.nz)* and Southern Link K Bus (☎ *(03) 358 8355 or 0508 458 835;* ***website*** *www.southernlinkkbus.co.nz)* run a shuttle bus to the Brown Hut trailhead of the Heaphy Track from Motueka and Takaka.

At the other end of the track, the Karamea Express (☎ *(03) 782 6757)* runs a shuttle bus that picks up at the Kohaihai River Mouth, and takes you down to Karamea and Westport.

Accommodation

The Department of Conservation maintains seven huts and seven campsites along the Heaphy Track.

You have to buy a Heaphy Track hut or camp pass from a DOC office to walk along the track. Huts on the Heaphy Track cost $20 in the peak season (Jan-Apr & Oct-Dec) and $10 off peak (May-Sep). Camping costs $10 (Jan-Apr & Oct-Dec), $7 (May-Sep).

Hiking

There are several excellent hiking tracks in the park, but the Heaphy Track is by far the most popular.

HEAPHY TRACK

The Heaphy Track (82km, 4-6 days) offers beautiful scenery and crosses a diverse landscape that includes tussock downs, forest and rugged coastal scenery.

Although it is a long hike, the track is well formed making it relatively easy going.

Most people hike from north to south, reaching the highest point on the first day and allowing for a mostly downhill hike.

Brown Hut to Perry Saddle Hut *(17km, 5 hours)*

After leaving Brown Hut, the track crosses the Brown River and then traverses a grassy plain before climbing and reaching the track's highest point (915m) half an hour before reaching Perry Saddle Hut.

Perry Saddle Hut to Gouland Downs Hut *(8km, 2 hours)*

The track crosses Perry Saddle shortly after leaving Perry Saddle Hut and then continues along windswept plains.

Gouland Downs Hut to Saxon Hut *(5km, 1½ hours)*

The track crosses tussock plains for most of this section.

Saxon Hut to Mackay Hut *(14km, 3 hours)*

This part of the track crosses the border between the Tasman District and West

Coast Region. The track gently climbs through the Mackay Downs and the ground can get boggy after rain.

Mackay Hut to Lewis Hut
(13.5km, 3½ hours)

The gradual descent to sea level begins after leaving Mackay Hut. This section sees the environment change from beech forest to incorporate nikau palms and the taller trees that are associated with the West Coast.

Lewis Hut to Heaphy Hut
(8km, 2½ hours)

The track now follows the path of the Heaphy River and passes through forests of tall rata and rimu trees before reaching the Heaphy Hut on the West Coast.

Heaphy Hut to Kohaihai River Mouth
(16.5km, 5 hours)

The final leg of the track follows the sea through nikau palm rainforest. This section offers a few opportunities to walk along the beach.

St Arnaud & Nelson Lakes National Park

The focus of the Nelson Lakes National Park are Lakes Rotoiti and Rotoroa. It is also home to the northernmost peaks of the Southern Alps, and many travellers come here for the superb hiking and walking trails around Mount Robert. St Arnaud is a small alpine village with a laid-back atmosphere and a couple of good hostels. There is a kiwi sanctuary here, so it is a good place to come if you want to spot these endangered birds. There are also kayaking tours, as well as rafting trips on the river. The scenery in the surrounding valleys, mountains and hills is excellent.

Nelson-Tasman

Practical Information
Nelson Lakes Department of Conservation Visitor Centre

View Road, St Arnaud
☎ *(03) 521 1806*
Website *www.doc.govt.nz*
Open *8am-4.30pm daily*

Coming & Going

St Arnaud lies on State Highway 63, which is the main route connecting Blenheim and the West Coast. Atomic Shuttles *(☎ (03) 322 8883; **website** www.atomictravel.co.nz)* and Southern Link K Bus *(☎ (03) 358 8355 or 0508 458 835; **website** www.southernlinkk-bus.co.nz)* stop in St Arnaud on their Greymouth to Picton route.

Local Transport

Nelson Lakes Shuttles *(☎ (03) 521 1900; **website** www.nelsonlakesshuttles.co.nz)* operates a transport service around the national park with connections to neighbouring towns.

Accommodation
Alpine Lodge

The Alpine Lodge is a nice hotel/hostel with a relaxing atmosphere. The dorms are above a café, and have long rows of bunks with good mattresses laid out side-by-side. The bathrooms and the fully-equipped kitchen are clean and there is a spacious TV lounge with new sofas and a wooden veranda. Guests can use the laundry facilities and there is a bar and restaurant in the adjoining hotel building. It is a bit institutional and basic, but if you are staying in St Arnaud, it is a good choice.

Main Road, St Arnaud
☎ *(03) 521 1869*
Website *www.alpinelodge.co.nz*
Dorm bed *$23 ($20 BBH);* ***double/twin room*** *$61 ($55 BBH)*
Credit cards *Amex, Diners, JCB, MC, Visa*
Reception open *8am-9.30pm daily*

Maintenance & cleanliness	★★★
Facilities	★★
Atmosphere & character	★★★
Security	★
Overall rating	★★★

Travers-Sabine Lodge

This hostel is a large alpine cottage with a good amount of charm. There are spacious dorms with made-up beds; a large, clean kitchen and a

couple of cosy lounges with internet, flat screen TV and log fires. It is a great place to stay if you plan to visit the mountains and lakes, but it often caters to large groups, so call ahead. Management are very friendly.
Main Road, St Arnaud
☎ *(03) 521 1887*
Website *www.nelsonlakes.co.nz*
Dorm bed *$26;* ***double room*** *$59*
Credit cards *MC, Visa*
Reception open *8.30am-8.30pm daily*

Maintenance & cleanliness	★★★★½
Facilities	★★
Atmosphere & character	★★★
Security	★★★
Overall rating	★★★½

Hiking

There is an excellent network of hiking trails in the national park.

TRAVERS-SABINE CIRCUIT

The most well known track in the park is the Travers-Sabine Circuit (8km, 5 days). This is a challenging tramp that passes through river valleys and crosses the Travers Saddle.

SHORT WALKS

There are many short walks departing from St Arnaud. These include **Black Valley Walk** *(30 minutes)*, which runs from Kerr Bay and has several exit points that lead into the village centre; the **Honeydew Walk** *(45 minutes)*, which offers great views of the lake with its backdrop of the Southern Alps and the **Loop Track** *(1½ hours)*, which stars at Kerr Bay and passes through the Rotoiti Nature Recovery Project area.

DAY WALKS

Longer day walks departing from St Arnaud include the hike up **Mount Robert** *(5 hours return)*, the **St Arnaud Range Track** *(5 hours return)*, which climbs through beech forest from Kerr Bay above the tree line (1400m) to a height of 1650m offering spectacular views. The **Lake Rotoiti Circuit** *(6-9 hours return)* combines the Lakehead and Lakeside Tracks to circumnavigate Lake Rotoiti.

Murchison

Murchison is a former gold mining town on the Buller River. It is an uninteresting town without many attractions in itself, but travellers use it as a base to go jet boating and white water rafting. It is also a good place to go fishing, horse trekking and kayaking. There is a small museum and a few old pubs in town, which have historical significance. There is just one hostel in town, and some backpackers stay here to break up the drive to Westport.

Coming & Going

InterCity Coachlines *(☎ (03) 365 1113;* ***website*** *www.intercity.co.nz)* and Southern Link K Bus *(☎ (03) 358 8355 or 0508 458 835;* ***website*** *www.southernlinkkbus.co.nz)* stop in Murchison en route between Nelson and Greymouth. InterCity stop at Beechwood's Cafe *(32 Waller Street, Murchison)* and Southern Link K Bus stops at the Midwest Cafe *(67 Fairfax Street, Murchison)*.

Accommodation

The Lazy Cow

The Lazy Cow is a small home with two dorm rooms. It has a sitting room with log fire, a TV with DVDs and a piano. The tiny, run down kitchen is often untidy and dorms are simple with good thick duvets on the beds. There is a barbecue and clean bathrooms (one with a spa bath), but otherwise there are not many facilities. There is no laundry, but they offer internet access and bike hire. It has a very quiet atmosphere.
36 Waller Street, Murchison
☎ *0800 5299 269*
Dorm bed *$23-25 ($20-22 BBH);* ***single room*** *$55 ($52 BBH);* ***double room*** *$60 ($54 BBH)*
Credit cards *MC, Visa*
Reception open *9am-5pm daily*

Maintenance & cleanliness	★★½
Facilities	★★
Atmosphere & character	★★
Security	★
Overall rating	★★

Sights & Activities

Buller Gorge Swingbridge

The Buller Gorge Swingbridge (New Zealand's longest) and a variety of other activities that include gold panning and river cruises plus more action-packed pursuits like jet boat rides, white water rafting and the high speed Comet Line ride are the highlight of this adventure and heritage park, 14km west of Murchison.

State Highway 6, Upper Buller Gorge, 14km west of Murchison
☎ *(03) 523 9809*
Website *www.bullergorge.co.nz*

Jet Boating

The Buller Experience Jet zips through the mighty Buller Gorge. Trips depart from the Buller Gorge Swingbridge.

State Highway 6, Upper Buller Gorge
☎ *(03) 523 9880*
Website *www.murchison.co.nz*
Price *$85*

Murchison Museum

The Murchison Museum has varied exhibits on local history including vintage machinery and exhibits on agriculture, gold mining and forestry. The museum's highlight is the exhibit on the earthquake that shook Murchison in 1929.

60 Fairfax Street, Murchison
☎ *(03) 523 9392*
Admission *by donation*
Open *10am-4pm daily*

White Water Rafting

Ultimate Descents operate white water rafting trips among the granite canyons of the Buller Gorge. This 4½ hour trip on the Buller River features grade 3-4 rapids.

51 Fairfax Street, Murchison
☎ *(03) 523 9899 or 0800 RIVERS (0800 748377)*
Website *www.rivers.co.nz*
4½ hour trip on Buller River *$120*

West Coast

The South Island's rugged and sparsely populated West Coast is home to some of New Zealand's most beautiful scenery. It lies between the Tasman Sea and the Southern Alps and stretches 600km from Kahurangi Point in the north to Awarua Point in the south.

It is divided into the three districts of Buller, Grey, and Westland. In the north, the famous Heaphy Track lets out at the diminutive settlement of Karamea, where travellers then continue south to Westport to explore the seal colonies at Cape Foulwind. The stunning and unique Pancake Rocks and blowholes can be found at Punakaiki in the Paparoa National Park. This is a popular stop on the way to Greymouth, the departure point for the scenic TranzAlpine train that goes to Christchurch via Arthurs Pass. Most travellers make quick stops in Greymouth and the beachside town of Hokitika before heading to the picturesque Franz Josef and Fox Glaciers, which are undeniably the highlight of the West Coast.

Must do on the West Coast

- Walk on Franz Josef or Fox Glacier
- Make your own jade carving in Hokitika

Westport

This old coal mining town is the largest town on the North West Coast. The town itself offers little for the visitor, but is often used as a jumping off point for the rugged Kahurangi National Park, the Buller Gorge or the beautiful Paparoa National Park. Westport has some rich history, which is detailed in the Coaltown Museum. It is also close to fur seal colonies at Cape Foulwind.

Practical Information

Westport i-Site Visitor Centre

1 Brougham Street, Westport
☎ *(03) 789 6658*
Website *www.westport.org.nz*
Open *Mon-Fri 9am-5pm, Sat-Sun 9am-4pm*

INTERNET ACCESS

The Web Shed

204 Palmerston Street, Westport
☎ *(03) 788 8002*
Website *www.thewebshed.co.nz*
Open *1 Jan-15 Feb Mon-Fri 8.30am-7pm, Sat 9.30am-4pm, Sun 10am-3pm; 16 Feb-15 Apr Mon-Fri 8.30am-6pm, Sat 9.30am-1pm; 16 Apr-31 Oct Mon-Fri 8.30am-5pm, Sat 9.30am-12.30pm; 1 Nov-31 Dec Mon-Fri 8.30am-6pm, Sat 9.30am-1pm*

Coming & Going

Atomic Shuttles *(☎ (03) 349 0697; **website** www.atomictravel.co.nz)* and Southern Link K Bus *(☎ (03) 358 8355 or 0508 458 835; **website** www.southernlinkkbus.co.nz)* stop outside the visitor information centre *(1 Brougham Street, Westport)*. InterCity Coachlines *(☎ (03) 365 1113; **website** www.intercity.co.nz)* stop outside the Caltex service station *(197 Palmerston Street, Westport)*.

Accommodation

Bazil's Hostel YHA

Bazil's Hostel is an old complex with plenty of dormitory accommodation. The kitchen and common areas are not very well maintained and have outdated furniture and fittings; although the dorms are nice, with new bunks, made-up beds and new carpet. Amenities include laundry, internet access (including Wi-Fi) and a barbecue. Conviviality fluctuates, as Westport is not a usual destination unless there is a festival or event in the region. Security is poor for a YHA, but staff are very warm and friendly.
54-56 Russell Street, Westport
☎ *(03) 789 6410*
Website *www.yha.co.nz*
Dorm bed *$ 25; **double/twin room** $60-80*
Credit cards *MC, Visa*
Reception open *7.30am-9.30pm daily*

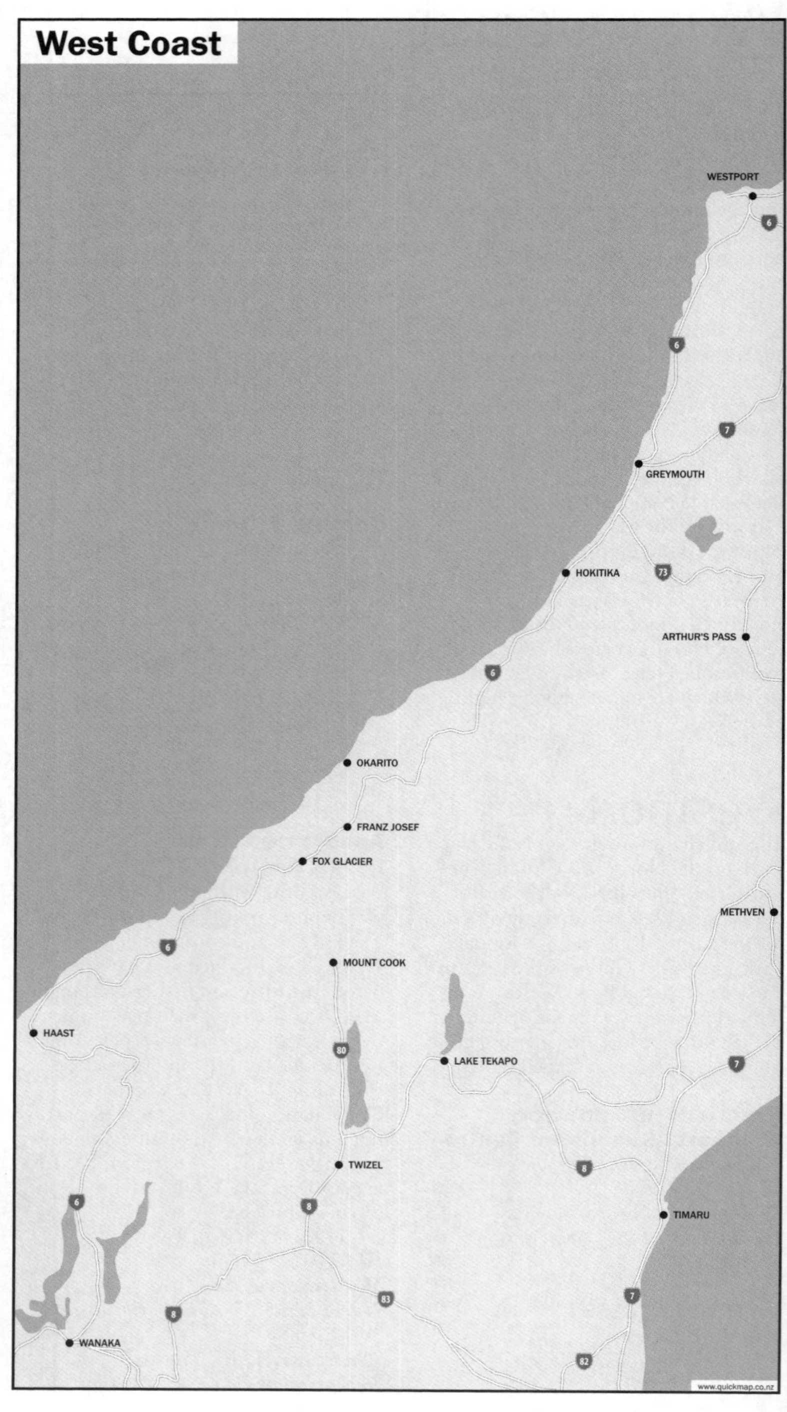
West Coast
WESTPORT
6
6
7
GREYMOUTH
HOKITIKA
73
ARTHUR'S PASS
6
OKARITO
FRANZ JOSEF
FOX GLACIER
METHVEN
6
MOUNT COOK
HAAST
80
LAKE TEKAPO
7
TWIZEL
8
6
8
TIMARU
83
8
7
WANAKA
82
www.quickmap.co.nz

Maintenance & cleanliness	★★★
Facilities	★★
Atmosphere & character	★★
Security	★
Overall rating	★★½

Berlins Café & Bar
This place is out in the middle of nowhere between Murchison and Westport, but you will see signs for it along the highway so won't miss it if you are driving. Berlins is mostly a newly restored old bar, with old photographs and memorabilia on the walls, but there are two large dorms with nice furnishings and comfortable beds, and a nice small kitchen and common area. There is a television plus laundry facilities and internet access is available. They used to run kayaking tours from here, but now there is talk of jet boating. It is near some nice walking trails, but otherwise there is not much of a reason to stay here unless you feel like breaking up the drive to Westport.
State Highway 6, Buller Gorge
☎ *(03) 789 0295*
Website *www.xtremeadventures.co.nz*
Dorm bed *$28 ($27 BBH);* ***double room*** *$60 ($59 BBH)*
Credit cards *MC, Visa*
Reception open *9.30am-7.30pm daily*

Maintenance & cleanliness	★★★½
Facilities	★
Atmosphere & character	★★★
Security	★½
Overall rating	★★½

Trip Inn
This hostel is a big old house with lots of character. It is clean but the furnishings are very outdated and the bathrooms are cramped and poorly maintained. The dorm beds are comfortable with nice thick duvets; there is a large fully-equipped kitchen and a dining/lounge room with old sofas, a log fire, piano and internet access. The hostel is surrounded by nice gardens, and there is a small area for camping in the back. There is not much of an atmosphere, but management are extremely pleasant.
72 Queen Street, Westport
☎ *(03) 789 7367*
Website *www.tripinn.co.nz*
Dorm bed *$25-28 ($22-25 BBH);* ***double room*** *$55-60 ($50-55 BBH)*
Credit cards *MC, Visa*
Reception open *8.30am-9pm daily*

Maintenance & cleanliness	★★★
Facilities	★★½
Atmosphere & character	★★★½
Security	★½
Overall rating	★★★

Eating & Drinking
Cheap restaurants and cafés line the main street in town, and you also find cheap meals in Westport's pubs.

Dirty Mary's Café *(198 Palmerston Street, Westport)* is a popular place for breakfast and lunch, and they also have great coffee. **Currtino's Yellow House Café** *(243 Palmerston Street, Westport)* has a friendly ambience and relatively cheap lunch options. For tight budgets, there is a **New World** supermarket *(244 Palmerston Street, Westport)* in the centre of Palmerston Street.

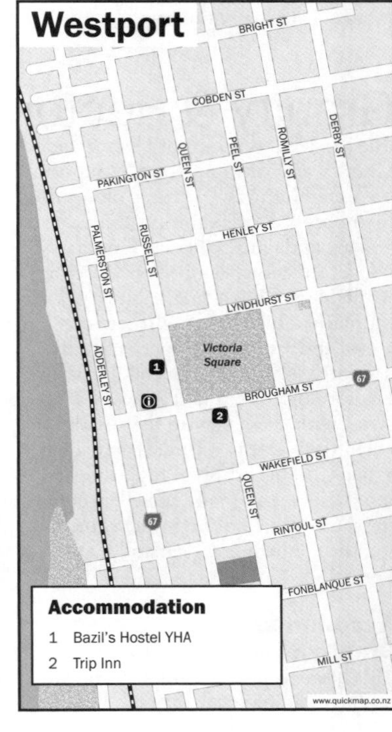

West Coast

Sights & Activities

Coaltown

This museum focuses on Westport's coal mining heritage with interesting exhibits of mining equipment in addition to displays about transport and brewing.
Upper Queen Street, Westport
☎ *(03) 789 8204*
Website *www.geocities.com/coaltownnz/*
Admission *$8*
Open *9am-4.30pm daily*

Jet Boating

Buller Adventure Tours (☎ *(03) 789 7286 or 0800 697 286;* ***website*** *www.adventuretours.co.nz/rafting/)* run jet boating trips through the Lower Buller Gorge. The trips cost $75 and last for 1¼ hours, which makes it one of New Zealand's best value jet boating trips.

White Water Rafting

Buller Adventure Tours (☎ *(03) 789 7286 or 0800 697 286;* ***website*** *www.adventuretours.co.nz/jetboating/)* operate white water rafting trips on the Buller River, 50km from Westport. This section of the river has grade 3-4 rapids. The three hour trip costs $110.

Granity & Hector

The seaside townships of Hector and Granity are 35km north of Westport on State Highway 67. These old mining towns are full of quaint little cottages and art and craft galleries. Granity houses the Northern Buller Museum, while Hector has a small country music museum, a nice beach with picnic areas, and a summertime beach café. This area is home to the endangered Hector dolphins, and it is possible to swim with these playful mammals when the water is warm. The area has a beautiful backdrop of high forested mountains, and many travellers come for the famous walking tracks, including the Charming Creek and Cape Foulwind Walkways.

Accommodation

Granity Sands Backpackers

This hostel is part of a small home just off the main highway through Granity. It has a very cosy lounge with sofas, a big fireplace and stereo with CDs. Bathrooms are small but adequately maintained, dorm rooms are nicely decorated and there is a well equipped kitchen. There are nice gardens with a small pond outside, and there's a short walkway to the beach. It is a quiet little place with very sweet owners and a cute dog.
94 Torrea Street, Granity
☎ *(03) 7828 558*
Dorm bed *$20;* ***double room*** *$40-50*
Reception open *8am-7pm daily*

Maintenance & cleanliness	★★★
Facilities	★★½
Atmosphere & character	★★½
Security	★
Overall rating	★★

The Old Slaughterhouse

This is an excellent purpose-built hostel. You have to walk up a long dirt track to get there, but it is worth it. The dorms are painted in warm colours and have made-up beds. Facilities include a brilliant fully-equipped kitchen; a nice common room with comfy sofas and lots of books; laundry; internet access; spacious bathrooms and a huge veranda that affords gorgeous views of the ocean. It has a quiet atmosphere and the owners are very welcoming and friendly.
State Highway 67, Hector
☎ *(03) 782 8333*
Dorm bed *$27-30;* ***double room*** *$68*
Reception open *8am-8pm daily*

Maintenance & cleanliness	★★★★
Facilities	★★★½
Atmosphere & character	★★★★
Security	★★½
Overall rating	★★★½

Karamea

Karamea is a meagre settlement at the north eastern corner of the South Island. An old mining town, it is just recently gaining recognition among backpackers as an unspoilt area of natural beauty perfect for a relaxing getaway. It is surrounded by lush rainforest and sandy beaches, and it is a good base for exploring the exquisite Oparara Basin and Kahurangi Gorge. There is great hiking, swimming, kayaking, fishing and surfing in the area. Its isolation means that facilities are limited for backpackers, so it is best to bring food supplies if you are on a strict budget. There is a supermarket and an excellent hostel in town and the area is full of attractions, so it is worth spending a few days to explore.

Practical Information

Karamea Information & Resource Centre

Bridge Street, Market Cross, Karamea
☎ *(03) 782 6652*
Website *www.karameainfo.co.nz*

Coming & Going

The Karamea Express *(☎ (03) 782 6757)* run a shuttle bus that picks up hikers coming off the Heaphy Track at the Kohaihai River Mouth, and takes them down to Karamea and Westport.

Accommodation

Rongo Backpackers

Rongo is a great hostel, and a welcome treat for those coming off the Heaphy Track. It is nicely maintained and creatively decorated with local and global art, mostly the product of previous guests, and there is a hallway with graffiti and postcards from around the world. The dorms are clean and spacious, the bathrooms are well maintained, and there is a good kitchen. Outside there is a large barbecue area, hammocks, a fire pit and a fire bath, and a huge cactus garden. There is also internet access (including wireless), an international library. Rongo is also home to the local FM radio station and a cinema room where bands from around the country have gigs. Guests have free use of bicycles. The place has a great vibe, and the staff are friendly and offer plenty of helpful advice on the area's activities.

130 Waverly Street, Karamea
☎ *(03) 7826 667*
Website *www.livinginpeace.com*
Dorm bed *$30 ($27 BBH);* ***double/twin room*** *$76 ($73 BBH); every 4th night free*
Credit cards *MC, Visa*
Reception open *8am-10pm daily*

Maintenance & cleanliness	★★★
Facilities	★★
Atmosphere & character	★★★★½
Security	★
Overall rating	★★★

Wanapeka Backpackers Retreat & Farmstay

This place is down a long gravel road about 20km south of Karamea. It is mainly a place to stay for WWOOFers and trampers coming or going on the Wangapeka and Heaphy Tracks. Accommodation is in a large dorm room with rustic furnishings and single beds. It is quite run down, but has a log fire and thick duvets. The bathrooms in the house are nice and clean and there is a cosy TV lounge and dining area. There are also bush baths and internet access. Guests use the clean fully-equipped kitchen in the owners' house. The owners are warm and friendly.

Atawhai Farm, Wangapeka
☎ *(03) 782 6663*
Website *www.wangapeka.com*
Dorm bed *$20;* ***double room*** *$55*
Reception open *8am-8pm daily*

Maintenance & cleanliness	★½
Facilities	★
Atmosphere & character	★★½
Security	★★
Overall rating	★½

Charleston

Charleston is a small village 30km south of Westport. The most popular activity here is caving although there are also extensive rock climbing opportunities in the area. You can stop at Mitchell's Gully Gold Mine to experience goldmining, or take a walk along the Flagstaff or Lookout walks. There is easy access to the beach and Cape Foulwind from here.

Coming & Going

Atomic Shuttles *(☎ (03) 349 0697;* ***website*** *www.atomictravel.co.nz),*

InterCity Coachlines (☎ *(03) 365 1113;* ***website*** *www.intercity.co.nz)* and Southern Link K Bus (☎ *(03) 358 8355 or 0508 458 835;* ***website*** *www.southernlinkkbus.co.nz)* stop in Charleston en route between Greymouth and Nelson. Buses stop on Main Road (State Highway 6).

Accommodation

Beaconstone

Staying at Beaconstone feels like you are at a retreat, while not being far away from civilisation. Accommodation is in a small lodge with only 11 beds and there is another cabin with a double bed tucked away in the forest. It is a self-sufficient eco-hostel that runs on solar power and it has spotless eco-friendly bathrooms. Amenities include a large cosy lounge and a charming kitchen. There are bush walking trails starting from different points around the property as well as swimming holes and the beach is close by. The owners are kind and helpful, and it has a very relaxing atmosphere.

Birds Ferry Road, Big Totara River
☎ *027 431 0491*
Website *www.beaconstone.co.nz*
Dorm bed *$28 ($25 BBH);* ***double/twin room*** *$64-66 (58-60BBH)*
Reception open *9am-9pm daily*

Maintenance & cleanliness	★★★★½
Facilities	★★
Atmosphere & character	★★★★½
Security	½
Overall rating	★★★½

Pounamu Backpackers

This hostel is in a dire state. The dorms have large rows of bunks with old stained mattresses and tattered carpet, the kitchen is a mess and bathrooms are just awful. There are laundry facilities and a nice spa pool and guests have free use of bicycles, but that doesn't make up for the dirtiness and poor maintenance. There is no internet access and the atmosphere is gloomy. Female backpackers in particular may not feel comfortable staying here.

State Highway 6, Charleston
☎ *(03) 789 8011*
Dorm bed *$22 ($20 BBH);* ***double room*** *$54 ($50 BBH)*
Credit cards *MC, Visa*
Reception open *24 hours*

Maintenance & cleanliness	★
Facilities	★½
Atmosphere & character	★
Security	★
Overall rating	★

Pyramid Farm Hostel

This hostel caters to a lot of WWOOFers, as well as some casual travellers. It is in an old home that is not very well maintained. The dorms and bathrooms are grimy and the kitchen is messy. There is a TV lounge with a large selection of movies and books, and internet access is also available. It is cheap, no-frills accommodation with a fair amount of character since it is on a farm. There are bush walking trails in the surrounding hills.

Coast Road, Charleston
☎ *(03) 789 8487*
Dorm bed *$20;* ***double room*** *$65*
Reception open *9am-7pm daily*

Maintenance & cleanliness	★★
Facilities	★½
Atmosphere & character	★
Security	★½
Overall rating	★½

Sights & Activities

Metro Cave

The 8km long Metro Cave is a beautiful subterranean world of stalactites, stalagmites and glow worms. Norwest Adventures operate several different tours of the caves, which range from an easy scenic tour to cave rafting and adventure caving where you abseil into the cave, climb up waterfalls and squeeze through tight spaces.

☎ *(03) 789 6686*
Website *www.caverafting.com*
Cave tour *$90;* ***cave rafting*** *$145;* ***adventure caving*** *$295*

Punakaiki

Punakaiki is located in the coastal forests of Paparoa National Park halfway between Greymouth and Westport on a scenic portion of State Highway 6 – one of the most scenic drives on the island. Punakaiki really only consists of scattered residences, hotels, restaurants and a few hostels set around the famed Pancake Rocks and blowholes. The Pancake Rocks are the jewel of the limestone country, unique rock formations that are a must-see for most visitors. On a day with rough seas, the blowholes are a sight to behold. There are some great walking trails in the park, most notably the Punakaiki Cavern Track and the Truman Track. Other activities include canoeing, horse trekking and caving, and there are guided tours available from the visitor's centre.

Practical Information

Punakaiki DOC Field Centre

Paparoa National Park
☎ *(03) 731 1895*
Website *www.doc.govt.nz*
Open *Jan-Mar 9am-6pm daily; Apr-Oct 9am-4.30pm daily; Nov-Dec 9am-6pm daily*

Coming & Going

Atomic Shuttles *(☎ (03) 349 0697; **website** www.atomictravel.co.nz)*, InterCity Coachlines *(☎ (03) 365 1113; **website** www.intercity.co.nz)* and Southern Link K Bus *(☎ (03) 358 8355 or 0508 458 835; **website** www.southernlinkkbus.co.nz)* stop in Charleston en route between Greymouth and Nelson. Buses stop at the Punakaiki Rocks Hotel and also outside the Wild Coast Café.

Accommodation

Punakaiki Beach Hostel

This bright yellow and green hostel has a great beachfront location. It also has a good amount of character, but unfortunately it could be better maintained. Facilities are basic, but there is a spa pool and a barbecue and a gorgeous view from the upstairs veranda. The communal kitchen is relatively clean, though the bathrooms could use some work. It has a nice atmosphere and management/staff are friendly.

Webb Street, Punakaiki
☎ *(03) 731 1852*
Website *www.punakaikibeachhostel.co.nz*
Dorm bed *$24-25 ($21-22 BBH);* ***single room*** *$40 ($37 BBH);* ***double/twin room*** *$60 ($54);* ***camping*** *$18 ($15 BBH) per person*
Credit cards *MC, Visa*
Reception open *7.30am-11pm daily*

Maintenance & cleanliness	★★★
Facilities	★★★
Atmosphere & character	★★★½
Security	★★
Overall rating	★★★

Te Nikau Retreat

Te Nikau Retreat is a good place to get away from it all. It consists of several main lodges, cottages, and small cabins strewn throughout the rainforest and connected by narrow dirt paths. They are nicely furnished and well maintained. The common areas are warm and colourful with log fires, sofas and books. The bathrooms are clean and cutely decorated. They also offer laundry facilities, internet access and freshly baked bread and muffins for sale daily. It has a nice atmosphere and the staff are friendly.

Harmount Place, Punakaiki
☎ *(03) 731 1111*
Website *www.tenikauretreat.co.nz*
Dorm bed *$20-22;* ***double room*** *$60-110*
Reception open *8.30am-8.30pm daily*

Maintenance & cleanliness	★★★★
Facilities	★★
Atmosphere & character	★★★½
Security	★
Overall rating	★★★

Greymouth

Greymouth is a large town at the mouth of the Grey River with a lively central shopping area. It can be a rather dreary town most of the time, but the centre has some nice historic buildings and there are a few worthwhile activities in the area. At the top of the list of things to do in Greymouth is a tour of Monteith's brewery. Learn a bit about the history and brewing process and enjoy the samples at the end. Greymouth is also a good base for white water rafting. The station on Mawhera Quay is the western terminus of the scenic *TranzAlpine* railway.

Practical Information

Greymouth i-SITE Visitor Centre

Corner Herbert & Mackay Streets, Greymouth
☎ (03) 768 5101
Website *www.greydistrict.co.nz*
Open *summer Mon-Fri 8.30am-7pm, Sat 9am-6pm, Sun 10am-5pm; winter 8.30am-5.30pm, Sat 9am-5pm, Sun 10am-4pm*

INTERNET ACCESS

Dp:One

108 Mawhera Quay, Greymouth
☎ (03) 768 4005
Open *9am-6pm daily*

Duke Backpackers Internet Café

27 Guinness Street, Greymouth
☎ (03) 768 9470
Website *www.duke.co.nz*
Open *8am-8pm daily*

Coming & Going

Greymouth is a busy transport hub with the *TranzAlpine* train to Christchurch and numerous coach and shuttle bus services to destinations throughout the South Island.

BUS

There are bus services from Greymouth to Nelson, Queenstown and Wanaka via the West Coast and Christchurch via Arthurs Pass.

InterCity Coachlines *(☎ (03) 365 1113; **website** www.intercity.co.nz)* stop at the train station *(164 MacKay Street, Greymouth)*. All other buses including Atomic Shuttles *(☎ (03) 349 0697; **website** www.atomictravel.co.nz)*, Naked Bus *(☎ 0900 62533; **website** www.nakedbus.com)* and Southern Link K Bus *(☎ (03) 358 8355 or 0508 458 835; **website** www.southernlinkkbus.co.nz)* stop outside the i-SITE Visitor Centre at the corner of Herbert and Mackay Streets.

TRAIN

Greymouth is the terminus for the *TranzAlpine* train from Christchurch. For many people this breathtaking train trip is the highlight and the only reason for visiting Greymouth.

Accommodation

The Duke Backpackers

This bright purple building in the centre of town has a good range of facilities. The kitchen is clean and well maintained and there is a large common area with an internet café. It is a bit run down, but manages a good atmosphere since it has a huge bar with TV, pool table, a jukebox, darts, and a free second beer. They also have plenty of free DVDs to watch. Dorms are rather basic and a bit weathered, but the bathrooms are clean. It could use some more renovations, but it is good value.

27 Guinness Street, Greymouth
☎ (03) 768 9470
Website *www.duke.co.nz*
Dorm bed *$20-24;* ***single room*** *$33-37;* ***double/twin room*** *$46-68;* ***triple room*** *$66-75*
Credit cards *MC, Visa*
Reception open *8am-8pm daily*

Maintenance & cleanliness	★★★½
Facilities	★★
Atmosphere & character	★★★★
Security	★★
Overall rating	★★★½

Global Village

This is a brilliant hostel decked out in a gorgeous global theme with tapestries and African masks adorning the warmly coloured walls. The main lounge has big sofas, a piano, a huge map, and tribal art, and there is a separate TV lounge with DVDs. The theme continues in the dorms, which are richly coloured with comfortable beds with thick duvets. The newly-renovated bathrooms are excellent, and there is a large fully-equipped kitchen which is one of the tidiest we've seen. There is also a spa pool, a sauna and a gym. It is next to a river, and guests have free use of kayaks and brand new mountain bikes. It has a great atmosphere and friendly staff.

42-54 Cowper Street, Greymouth
☎ *(03) 768 7272*
Dorm bed *$23;* ***double room*** *$56-60*
Credit cards *MC, Visa*
Reception open *9am-2pm & 5pm-9.30pm daily*

Maintenance & cleanliness	★★★★★
Facilities	★★★★½
Atmosphere & character	★★★★½
Security	★½
Overall rating	★★★★½

Kainga-ra YHA

This hostel is in a large old restored monastery with loads of character. The dorms are nice and clean, as is the kitchen and bathrooms. There is a pleasant lounge with a log fire, a huge library, and an excellent view of the town and the river mouth. The old chapel was converted into a large bedroom with good beds and individual bedside lamps. There is also an outdoor barbecue area. They offer internet access, individual lockers and laundry facilities and the staff are very kind.

15 Alexander Street, Greymouth
☎ *(03) 768 4951*
Website *www.yha.co.nz*
Dorm bed *$27 ($24 HI/YHA);*
double/twin room *$70 ($64 HI/YHA)*
Credit cards *MC, Visa*
Reception open *8am-noon, 1pm-4pm & 5pm-8pm daily*

Maintenance & cleanliness	★★★★
Facilities	★★★
Atmosphere & character	★★★½
Security	★★½
Overall rating	★★★½

Neptune's International Backpackers

This hostel in an old restored pub has a great aquatic theme throughout. The dorms have single made-up beds and guests are supplied with towels and soap. There is a bright clean kitchen and newly renovated bathrooms with bubble bath and a nice outdoor barbecue area with a spa pool. There is also internet access, a pool table, free tea and coffee and every day around 4pm

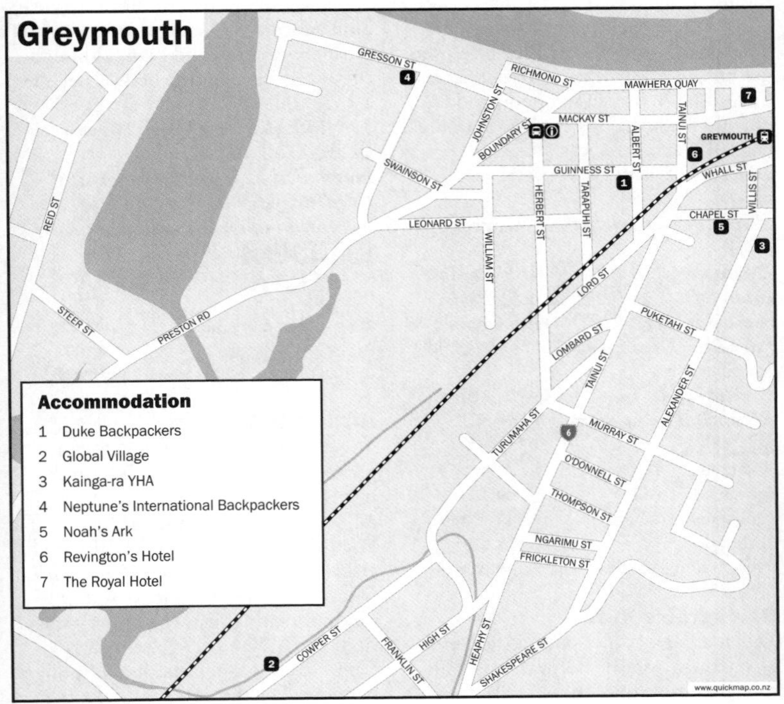

they get the unsold items from the bakery and offer them to guests.
43 Gresson Street, Greymouth
☎ *(03) 768 4425*
Website *www.neptunesbackpackers.co.nz*
Dorm bed *$20-23;* ***single room*** *$40-43;* ***double/twin room*** *$50-56;* ***triple room*** *$66-75;*
Reception open *7am-10pm daily*

Maintenance & cleanliness	★★★
Facilities	★★★
Atmosphere & character	★★★½
Security	★½
Overall rating	★★★

Noah's Ark

This hostel offers a good standard of accommodation in a huge restored farmhouse. It features animal themed dorm rooms and it has a good kitchen and dining area that gets quite lively at night. There is also a comfy TV room and two levels of wraparound verandas with wooden furniture and a backyard garden with hammocks. The bathrooms are average, but the showers are great. It is in the centre of town and has a good atmosphere. They offer free use of mountain bikes, internet access (including Wi-Fi), a spa pool, and free pick up from the bus station. Staff are helpful and attentive.
16 Chapel Street, Greymouth
☎ *(03) 768 4868*
Website *www.noahsarkbackpackers.co.nz*
Dorm bed *$23-25 ($20 BBH);* ***single room*** *$40 ($33 BBH);* ***double/twin room*** *$56 ($48 BBH);* ***triple room*** *$78 ($69 BBH);* ***camping*** *$17 ($14 BBH) per person*
Credit cards *Amex, JCB, MC, Visa*
Reception open *8am-9pm daily*

Maintenance & cleanliness	★★★½
Facilities	★★
Atmosphere & character	★★★½
Security	★½
Overall rating	★★★

Revington's Hotel

This is a huge corner pub in the centre of town with sterile dorm rooms and moderately clean bathrooms in need of maintenance. The kitchen is awful and there is not much of a common area besides the pub downstairs, which is mainly a local workers hangout. They also have internet access, laundry and a pool table, and there is a restaurant downstairs. Despite the location, it does not have a good backpackers' atmosphere. Check in at the bar.
Tainui Street, Greymouth
☎ *(03) 768 7055*
Dorm bed *$20*
Credit cards *MC, Visa*
Reception open *8am-1am daily*

Maintenance & cleanliness	★★½
Facilities	★
Atmosphere & character	½
Security	★★
Overall rating	★★

The Royal Hotel

This hostel is in an old building near the river. It has a large bar and a nice café on the ground floor, and outdated accommodation upstairs. There is a very nice kitchen, and the bathrooms are newly renovated but not very clean. Some dorms are better than others, but most are tattered and plain although they do have made-up beds. They have a pool table and laundry facilities.
128-130 Mawhera Quay, Greymouth
☎ *(03) 768 4022*
Dorm bed *$25;* ***double room*** *$90*
Credit cards *MC, Visa*
Reception open *7am-midnight daily*

Maintenance & cleanliness	★★★
Facilities	★½
Atmosphere & character	★★★
Security	★½
Overall rating	★★½

Eating & Drinking

The centre of Greymouth has some great pubs and bars. For cheap pub meals, head to the **Hog's Head** *(9 Tainui Street, Greymouth)*. The **Wild Olive Café** in the Royal Hotel *(128-130 Mawhera Quay, Greymouth)* has great cheap lunch food and nice outdoor seating near the railway station. **Café 124** *(124 Mackay Street, Greymouth)* is a popular lunch spot and hangout. For the best beer, take the tour of Monteith's Brewery and get a few to go. You may then want to head down to **Bonzai Pizzeria** *(31 Mackay Street, Greymouth)* for relatively cheap pizzas and pasta in a groovy setting.

Greymouth has several supermarkets including **FreshChoice** *(174B Mawhera Quay, Greymouth)* and **New World** *(corner High & Marlborough Streets, Greymouth)*.

Sights & Activities

4WD Quad Bike Adventure

There's a series of muddy tracks just north of town where you can drive a 4WD quad bike or ride an amphibious Argo 8WD vehicle.
State Highway 6, Coal Creek
☎ *(03) 762 7438*
Website *www.onyerbike.co.nz*
4WD quad bikes *$95-155;* ***8WD Argo tour*** *$40-80*

Kayaking & White Water Rafting

Eco-rafting operate a number of white water rafting and kayaking trips departing from Greymouth. These include a relaxing half day rafting or sit-on kayaking trip on the Arnold River (grade 2+ rapids). Full day trips feature spectacular scenery on the Upper Grey River (grade 3 & 4 rapids) or adrenaline charged heli-rafting experiences on the Hokitika, Perth, Whitcombe, Whataroa and Wanganui Rivers (grade 4 & 5 rapids). Multi-day trips are also available.
108 Mawhera Quay, Greymouth
☎ *(03) 768 4005*
Website *www.ecorafting.co.nz*
Full day trip *$130*

Monteith's Brewery

The West Coast's biggest brewery produces some of the country's best beer. It offers tours where you can see the beer being brewed and you get to taste each style of beer.
Corner Murray & Turumaha Streets, Greymouth
☎ *(03) 768 4149*
Website *www.monteiths.co.nz*
Admission *$15*
Tours depart *Mon-Fri 10am, 11.30am & 2pm, Sat-Sun 11.30am & 2pm; Bookings essential*

Shantytown

This open-air museum, 10km from Greymouth, is a recreation of a 1860s gold mining settlement. It features over 30 buildings including a sawmill, pub and general store and there is also a steam train and horse and cart rides for the kiddies.
Rutherglen Road, Paroa
☎ *(03) 762 6634*
Website *www.shantytown.co.nz*
Admission *$25*
Open *8.30am-5pm daily*

Taniwha Caves

Wild West Adventures operate cave-rafting trips in the Taniwha Caves. You get the choice of abseiling 40m into the cave or walking down a track to the entrance, and then it's into the inner tubes for a float through the caves.
Clifton Road, Greymouth
☎ *(03) 768 6649 or 0800 223 456*
Price *$105-185*

Hokitika

Hokitika is one of the nicest towns on the West Coast. It has a beach and a few old buildings from the gold rush era, but the main attraction is greenstone jade (pounamu), which is mined nearby and carved in town. The jade shops cater for the tourist coaches that pass through, although otherwise it is a fairly quiet place.

Hokitika is also home to the annual **Wild Foods Festival** *(**website** www.wildfoods.co.nz)*, which is held each March when around 20,000 people descend upon the small town to try such delicacies as earthworms, grasshoppers, huhu grubs, snails, sheep's eyes and hare's testicles.

If you're heading south, Hokitika is the last sizable town before Wanaka, so take the opportunity to buy groceries, fill the car with fuel and use the ATM machines since you may not have the chance to do this for a while.

Practical Information

Westland i-SITE Visitor Centre

Carnegie Building, 7 Tancred Street, Hokitika

☎ *(03) 755 6166*
***Open** summer Mon-Fri 8.30am-6pm, Sat-Sun 10am-4pm; winter Mon-Fri 8.30am-5pm, Sat-Sun 10am-4pm*

INTERNET ACCESS
Aim West Sports
20 Weld Street, Hokitika
☎ *(03) 755 8947*
***Open** Mon-Fri 9am-5pm, Sat 9am-1pm*

Kodak Express Internet Outpost
15 Weld Street, Hokitika
☎ *(03) 755 7768*
***Open** Mon-Fri 8am-5.30pm, Sat 8.30am-3pm, Sun 10am-2pm*

Coming & Going

There are buses from Hokitika to Christchurch, Nelson and Queenstown. InterCity Coachlines *(☎ (03) 365 1113; **website** www.intercity.co.nz)* stop at the Hokitika Travel Centre and Kiwi House *(64 Tancred Street, Hokitika)*. Other buses including Atomic Shuttles *(☎ (03) 349 0697; **website** www.atomictravel.co.nz)* and Naked Bus *(☎ 0900 62533; **website** www.nakedbus.com)* stop outside the i-SITE Visitor Centre *(7 Tancred Street, Hokitika)*.

Accommodation

Birdsong

This is a small and lovely hostel with a laid-back atmosphere. The dorms are nicely maintained with tiered wooden bunks and thick comfy duvets. The kitchen is new, fully stocked and immaculate. There is a great dining/common area with log fire, internet access and a panoramic ocean view. Throughout the hostel and in dorms there is beautiful artwork, and they have their own small gallery/shop downstairs. They have laundry facilities, a nice deck with a barbecue that's perfect for social dinners, and a garden with wonderful enclosed bush baths. It is a 10-minute walk to town, and close to the beach and the glow-worm dell. It has a warm and cosy feel, and staff are extremely amiable.
124 State Highway 6, Hokitika
☎ *(03) 755 8445*
***Website** www.birdsong.co.nz*
***Dorm bed** $27 ($24 BBH); **double/twin room** $66-78 ($60-72 BBH)*
***Reception open** 9am-1pm & 4.30pm-7.30pm daily*

Maintenance & cleanliness	★★★★
Facilities	★★★½
Atmosphere & character	★★★★
Security	★½
Overall rating	★★★½

Drifting Sands Backpackers

This hostel is in a small house in a residential area not far from the centre. It has a small untidy kitchen and a common area with old furniture. The dorms are ordinary, with single beds and duvets. There is a TV lounge and a washing machine but no dryer. There is free tea and coffee and guests have free use of bicycles. There is no internet access. This hostel is currently changing ownership, so it should see some changes in the near future.
197 Revell Street, Hokitika
☎ *(03) 755 7612*
***Website** www.driftingsands.co.nz*
***Dorm bed** $25 ($21 BBH); **double room** $58 ($50 BBH)*
***Credit cards** MC, Visa*
***Reception open** 8.30am-11pm daily*

Maintenance & cleanliness	★★★
Facilities	★★
Atmosphere & character	★★
Security	★½
Overall rating	★★½

Mountain Jade

This hostel above the Mountain Jade souvenir shop in the town centre has facilities that are limited to a small kitchen and a TV lounge with internet access ($6 per hour, including wireless). The hostel is very clean, but the décor is a bit dated and it has a dreary atmosphere. Some of the dorm rooms don't lock and there are no lockers.
It is nothing special, but for the price and location, it can't be beat. Staff are friendly, too.
41 Weld Street, Hokitika
☎ *(03) 755 8007*
***Dorm bed** $21 ($18 BBH); **double room** $55 ($52 BBH); **twin room** $38 ($35 BBH); **self-contained unit** $95*

***Credit cards** MC, Visa*
***Reception open** summer 8am-10pm daily; winter 8.30am-7pm daily*

Maintenance & cleanliness	★★★
Facilities	★★½
Atmosphere & character	★★★½
Security	★★½
Overall rating	★★★½

Railway Hotel

This pub in the town centre offers basic backpackers accommodation in motel-style self-contained units, each with a fridge, microwave and en suite bathroom. It isn't very well maintained and it doesn't have much of a proper backpackers' atmosphere.

Corner Sewell & Weld Streets, Hokitika
(03) 755 8116
***Dorm bed** $25; **double room** $60*
***Credit cards** MC, Visa*
***Reception open** 10am-late*

Maintenance & cleanliness	★★
Facilities	★★½
Atmosphere & character	★
Security	★
Overall rating	★★½

Riverview Cabins

Riverview Cabins is a small building 3½km west of town. It is a quiet place with 14 beds with accommodation in well maintained rooms with beds made up with duvets and electric blankets. There is a small TV lounge with books, and a quaint clean kitchen.

154 Kaniere Road, Hokitika
(03) 755 7440
***Website** www.hokitika.com/riverview cabins/*
***Dorm bed** $28 ($24 BBH); **single room** $43 ($40 BBH); **double/twin room** $64 ($58 BBH)*
***Reception open** 8am-7.30pm daily*

Maintenance & cleanliness	★★
Facilities	★★½
Atmosphere & character	★★★½
Security	★
Overall rating	★★

Eating & Drinking

There are quite a few good places to eat in Hokitika's town centre. **Adz Café** *(39 Tancred Street, Hokitika)* has great fish and chips and all day breakfast. For drinks and bar meals, **Stumper's Bar** *(2 Weld Street, Hokitika)* has the cheapest quality food in town and a great atmosphere, especially at night when locals and visitors alike drink and mingle in the bar.

For groceries, head to the **New World** supermarket at 116 Revell Street.

Sights & Activities

Jade Carving

There are several places in Hokitika where you can create your own jade carving. These include **Bonz n Stonz** *(16 Hamilton Street, Hokitika; (03) 755 6504; **website** www.bonz-n-stonz.co.nz)*, which has jade carving workshops for $95 ($90 BBH) and bone carving for $75 ($70 BBH) and **Just Jade Experience** *(197 Revell Street, Hokitika; (03) 755 7654; **website** www.madkiwi.co.nz/jadex.html)*, which charges from $20 to $180 depending on the complexity of the design.

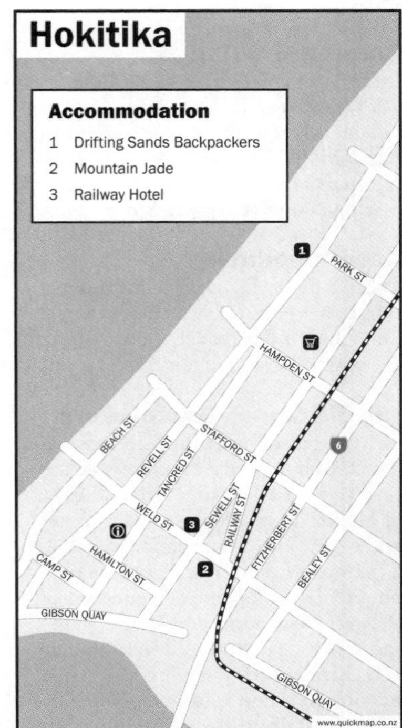

West Coast Historical Museum

The West Coast Historical Museum has exhibits on local history and culture with displays on greenstone jade (pounamu) and the region's pioneer beginnings.
Corner Hamilton & Tancred Streets, Hokitika
☎ *(03) 755 6898*
Admission *$5*
Open *Jan-Mar 9.30am-5pm daily; Apr-Dec Mon-Fri 9.30am-5pm, Sat-Sun 10am-2pm*

Ross

This historic gold mining town, 20 minutes south of Hokitika on State Highway 6, is where New Zealand's largest gold nugget was found in 1909. Today it is a sleepy township with little to do, but lots of lovely scenery. There are a few nice historic buildings, and access to the Totara and Mikonui Valleys. There are some nice beaches in this area, as well as a good heritage walk.

Coming & Going

InterCity Coachlines *(☎ (03) 365 1113;* ***website*** *www.intercity.co.nz)* stop outside Maneras Store and Naked Bus *(☎ 0900 62533;* ***website*** *www.nakedbus.com)* stops outside the visitor information centre *(4 Aylmer Street, Ross).*

Accommodation

There is no backpackers' accommodation in town, but if you have a car the Old Church Backpackers and Pukekura Accommodation are not too far away.

The Old Church Backpackers

This hostel is in a beautifully renovated old church in a peaceful riverside location about a 10-minute drive south of Hokitika. Inside, it is warm, cosy and clean. The common room has a huge stone fireplace, comfy sofas, a pool table and an extensive record collection. Bathrooms and showers are spotlessly clean and well maintained, and there is a fully-equipped kitchen. Accommodation is in dorms with basic bunks and single beds made up with duvets. You can go fishing, hiking, or walk down to the beach, and the staff here are extremely friendly and will give you great tips on what to do in the area.
State Highway 6, Kakatopahi River, Ross
☎ *(03) 755 4000*
Dorm bed *$23 ($20 BBH);* ***double/twin room*** *$56 ($50 BBH)*
Reception open *8am-10pm daily*

Maintenance & cleanliness	★★★★½
Facilities	★★½
Atmosphere & character	★★★½
Security	★
Overall rating	★★★½

Pukekura Accommodation

Pukekura is a good place to stop for a night on the way to the glaciers. Attractions here include the Bushman's Centre – a great little museum – and a cheap restaurant with famous possum pies. Across the street is an excellent historic pub full of antiques and old photographs – almost a museum in itself. Accommodation is rustic but well maintained, with good beds made up with nice-looking duvets and ceiling-hung mosquito nets. There is a small kitchen that is old but fairly well equipped and a dining table with a TV. Management are knowledgeable and friendly.
State Highway 6, Pukekura
☎ *(03) 755 4144*
Website *www.pukekura.co.nz*
Dorm bed *$20;* ***double room*** *$45-80*
Credit cards *MC, Visa*
Reception open *9am-10pm daily*

Maintenance & cleanliness	★★★
Facilities	★★
Atmosphere & character	★★★½
Security	★★½
Overall rating	★★½

Okarito

Okarito is a tiny settlement on the edge of the stunning Okarito Lagoon, 28km north of Franz Josef Glacier. The main reasons for a visit to Okarito are the Kiwi tours and water-based activities on the lagoon. Some people use it as an alternative to staying in Franz Josef, but this is only if you are looking for isolation and extreme quiet, as there are no shops or facilities here. Hence, you will need to bring your own supplies.

Accommodation

Okarito YHA

This hostel is a tiny historic building that is run by various people in town, so there is no full time reception on site. There are two rooms: a dormitory with bunk beds and a kitchen/common area that also has three-tier bunks. There are no real facilities besides the kitchen, but it is clean and quiet and the building has a fair amount of character. There is a clean toilet, but showers are across the street at the campground and cost 50c to use.

The Strand, Okarito
☎ *(03) 753 4151*
***Website** www.stayyha.com*
***Dorm bed** $21 ($18 HI/YHA)*

Maintenance & cleanliness	★★★½
Facilities	½
Atmosphere & character	★★½
Security	★
Overall rating	★★

Royal Hostel

This hostel comprises several buildings behind the owners' home. Dorms are clean and nicely furnished. The communal kitchen is well stocked, and the bathrooms are nice and clean. One of the buildings has a very cosy lounge with a log fire. There are not many facilities for backpackers, but they offer laundry facilities and free tea and coffee. There are nice gardens on the grounds with hammocks and a fire pit.

The Strand, Okarito
☎ *(03) 753 4080*
***Dorm bed** $23 ($20 BBH); **double room** $60-80 ($57-77 BBH)*
***Credit cards** MC, Visa*

Maintenance & cleanliness	★★★
Facilities	★
Atmosphere & character	★★½
Security	-
Overall rating	★★

Franz Josef

Franz Josef is a compact tourist town that offers excellent accommodation options for backpackers. Everything here revolves around glacier tours and helicopter flights, but there are heaps of other activities available, including skydiving, quad biking, white water rafting and ice climbing. Kayaking on Lake Mapourika is very popular for the fantastic mountain reflections and sunsets. Franz Josef and Fox Glaciers are similar and offer basically the same thing, but travellers tend to stay in Franz Josef for the facilities. You can visit the Hukawai Glacier Centre to get acquainted with the area and its offerings; there is an indoor ice climbing wall here as well.

Practical Information

Westland Tai Poutini National Park DOC & i-SITE Visitor Centre

Main Road, Franz Josef
☎ *(03) 752 0796*
***Website** www.doc.govt.nz*
***Open** 8am-noon & 1pm-5pm daily*

INTERNET ACCESS

Red Bus Internet

20 Cron Street, Franz Josef
☎ *(03) 752 0230*
***Website** www.glacierkayaks.com/internet_bus_email.html*
***Open** summer 9am-9pm daily; winter 10am-8pm daily*

Coming & Going

Atomic Shuttles *(☎ (03) 349 0697; **website** www.atomictravel.co.nz)*, InterCity Coachlines *(☎ (03) 365 1113; **website** www.intercity.co.nz)* and Naked Bus *(☎ 0900 62533; **website** www.nakedbus.com)* stop in Franz Josef en route between Greymouth and Queenstown. Buses stop at the bus stop on Main Road and some buses also stop outside the YHA hostel.

Accommodation

Chateau Franz

Chateau Franz has quite a bit more character than the others, with just as good facilities. The dorms have comfortable beds with duvets and

clean spacious bathrooms. There are a couple of nice common areas with big televisions and log fires; a small, but adequate, kitchen; internet access, including Wi-Fi ($6 per hour) plus a spa pool and barbecue area. There is a buzzing atmosphere here and staff are gregarious and helpful. They have movie nights with free popcorn, they serve free homemade vegetable soup every evening and also offer two for one drinks at the local pub.
8 Cron Street, Franz Josef
☎ *(03) 752 0738*
Website *www.chateaufranz.co.nz*
Dorm bed *$22-26 ($19-23 BBH);* ***double room*** *$53-55 ($50-52 BBH);* ***twin room*** *$46-48 ($43-45 BBH);* ***camping*** *$10 per person*
Credit cards *MC, Visa*
Reception open *7.30am-9pm daily*

Maintenance & cleanliness	★★★½
Facilities	★★½
Atmosphere & character	★★★★
Security	★
Overall rating	★★★

Franz Josef YHA

Franz Josef's YHA hostel has a warm and cosy atmosphere. Most of the building is very well maintained, although the kitchen is below average for a relatively-new purpose-built YHA. The dorms have thick mattresses and bedside lamps, and the bathrooms are very clean. There is a large sauna that is free to use. The brilliant common room is the perfect place to sit around and socialise. It has a pool table, comfy sofas, a massive stone fireplace and internet access including Wi-Fi ($6 per hour). The hostel has good security, laundry, and helpful staff who can arrange tours for you. The atmosphere is a bit more low-key than the other hostels in Franz Josef.
2-4 Cron Street, Franz Josef
☎ *(03) 752 0754*
Website *www.stayyha.com*
Dorm bed *$24-28 ($21-25 HI/YHA);* ***double/twin room*** *$70-90 ($64-84 HI/YHA)*
Credit cards *MC, Visa*
Reception open *summer 7.30am-9pm daily; winter 7.30am-8pm daily*

Maintenance & cleanliness	★★★★
Facilities	★★★
Atmosphere & character	★★★
Security	★★★½
Overall rating	★★★½

Glow Worm Cottage

This hostel is a motel-style building set around a courtyard with an enclosed spa pool. It is not as nicely maintained as the other places in Franz, but it manages to have a good bit of charm. The accommodation is in dorms with good mattresses and the tiny bathrooms are clean, as is the kitchen. There are also laundry facilities plus a good TV room and internet access ($6 per hour), including Wi-Fi ($4 per hour). Relative to the other hostels, it is a bit more intimate and quiet. It is good value and the friendly reception staff serve free vegetable soup every evening.
27 Cron Street, Franz Josef
☎ *(03) 752 0172*
Website *www.glowwormcottages.co.nz*
Dorm bed *$23-26 ($20-23 BBH);* ***double/twin room*** *$53 ($50 BBH) standard, $105 motel-style*
Credit cards *MC, Visa*
Reception open *summer 7.30am-9pm daily; winter 8am-8pm daily*

Maintenance & cleanliness	★★★
Facilities	★★
Atmosphere & character	★★★
Security	★
Overall rating	★★½

Montrose

Montrose is a nice purpose-built hostel with a good range of facilities. The dorms are tidy and spacious with made-up beds and the brand new bathrooms are squeaky clean. Amenities include two huge lounges with sofas and large screen TVs with plenty of DVDs. They also have a sauna, a barbecue and internet access. There is a young independent traveller vibe here and reception staff are friendly.
9 Cron Street, Franz Josef
☎ *(03) 752 0188*
Dorm bed *$22-24 ($19-21 BBH);* ***double/twin room*** *$60-130 ($54-124 BBH)*

Credit cards *MC, Visa*
Reception open *7.30am-8.30pm daily*

Maintenance & cleanliness	★★★★☆ (4½)
Facilities	★★½
Atmosphere & character	★★★½
Security	★
Overall rating	★★★½

Rainforest Backpackers

Rainforest Backpackers is a purpose-built hostel that also has more upmarket accommodation. They offer an above average range of facilities that includes two spa pools, a sauna ($3 per 30 minutes), a bar and restaurant, a couple of small lounges with big TVs, pool tables, laundry facilities, an undercover barbecue area, internet access (including Wi-Fi) and a kitchen that is pretty good considering there is also a restaurant on site. The dormitory accommodation is fairly standard with thin mattresses, although most rooms have small fridges and en suite bathrooms. The bathrooms are nice and clean, but they have annoying push-button showers. There is a small shop at reception.

46 Cron Street, Franz Josef
☎ *(03) 752 0220 or 0800 873 346*
Website *www.rainforestbackpackers.co.nz*
Dorm bed *$24-27 ($23-26 VIP);* ***double/twin room*** *$50-150 ($48-148 VIP)*
Credit cards *Amex, Diners, MC, Visa*
Reception open *summer 7am-9pm daily; winter 7am-8pm daily*

Maintenance & cleanliness	★★★★½
Facilities	★★★
Atmosphere & character	★★★
Security	★
Overall rating	★★★½

Eating & Drinking

Franz Josef is just a small village but there are several affordable restaurants and pubs, including the **Monsoon Bar** *(46 Cron Street, Franz Josef)* at the Rainforest Retreat Backpackers. There are a couple of cafés in town, the best one being **Full of Beans** *(State Highway 6, Franz Josef)*, next to Franz Josef Glacier Guides. **Guzzi's Pizza** *(Cron Street, Franz Josef)* is a cool little place with cheap pizza, fish and chips, and good espresso. If you are going on a long excursion, stock up on lunch and snacks at the **Four Square** supermarket *(State Highway 6, Franz Josef)* in the centre of town, or grab a cheap sandwich from **Beeches Café** *(State Highway 6, Franz Josef)*.

Sights

Hukawai Glacier Centre

The excellent Hukawai Glacier Centre features the glacier experience; an audio-visual display about New Zealand's glacier region with information on the region's flora, fauna, geology and Māori mythology. A visit to the Hukawai Glacier Experience is a great way to learn more about the region and it will give you a much better appreciation when you visit the glacier. The centre also features an indoor ice climbing wall.

Corner Cowan & Cron Streets, Franz Josef
☎ *(03) 752 0600*

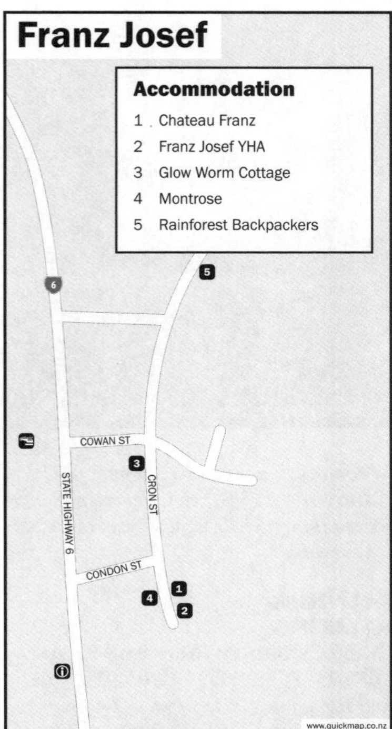

Franz or Fox?

That is the question.

Backpackers are constantly debating over which is better. When you are travelling on a budget, this kind of decision can be hard to make. If you can't see both, which one should you choose?

I am of the opinion that once you have seen one glacier in the Southern Alps, you have seen them all. I mean, essentially, they are the same thing: massive blocks of ice surrounded by pretty mountains. Fox Glacier may be a bit larger than Franz Josef, but you can't really tell since the size of the glacier causes an optical illusion and regardless of square metre-age, you will stand on both of them in awe of their immensity. Fox also claims to have less of an incline to climb up. But let me tell you, after your 800th step in those boots, you might as well take a few more because you will be spending the next few days on your arse.

Both have excellent guides, both have postcard views, and both offer the chance to walk through ice tunnels and peer inside cravasses. The two things you need to decide on are price and location.

Fox Glacier is a bit cheaper. It just is. It doesn't mean it is any less quality. Perhaps Franz Josef just has a more recognizable name. Its like wearing a designer shirt when the cheaper generic brand would be just as comfortable.

Fox is also a quieter town. There is only one backpackers, and it is good, but a bit more laid back than some of the hostels in Franz Josef. There is a bit more nightlife in Franz Josef, and a better supermarket... just more facilities in general. But Fox has the incredibly beautiful and easily accessible Lake Matheson, which is best early in the morning or at sunset. I think it is worth staying in Fox just to see this lake. It takes about an hour to walk around it, but you may want to add a half-hour or so for photo-snapping.

So decide which town suits you, and do it. It is a very rewarding and very good value trip to take while on the South Island. Whichever one you choose, it will be a trip you will always remember.

Tiffany Miller

Lake Matheson near Fox Glacier

Website *www.hukawai.co.nz*
Admission *$15 Glacier Experience, $90 ice climbing, $100 Glacier Experience & ice climbing*

Activities

KAYAKING

Glacier Country Tours and Kayaks
(*☎ (03) 752 0230 or 0800 423 262;* ***website*** *www.glacierkayaks.com)* run kayaking trips on Lake Mapourika, which is part of the Te Waihipaunamu World Heritage area. The three to four hour trip costs $75 and includes a CD-ROM with photos of your trip.

HORSE RIDING

South Westland Horse Treks
(*☎ (03) 752 0223 or 0800 1TREKS;* ***website*** *www.horsetreknz.com)* run one hour to full day horse treks in the surrounding countryside. A one hour

ride costs $50; a two-three hour ride is $90-130 and a five hour ride is $190.

GLACIER HIKES/ICE CLIMBING

Franz Josef Glacier Guides *(☎ (03) 752 0763 or 0800 GUIDES (0800 484 337); **website** www.franzjosefglacier.com)* run guided walks on Franz Josef Glacier, which is by far the most popular activity at Franz Josef. A half-day trip costs $90 and allows 1½-2 hours on the lower reaches of the glacier, a full day trip goes to the glacier's mid-reaches and costs $140 for 6 hours on the ice. The more adventurous can go on a full day ice-climbing excursion for $220.

HELICOPTER FLIGHTS

A helicopter flight offers a birds-eye view of the glacier and several of the helicopter operators are licensed to land on it.

Scenic helicopter flights start from a quick 20-minute buzz over Franz Josef Glacier ($180) to a 30-minute flight over both Franz Josef and Fox Glaciers ($240) or a 40-minute flight that takes in Mount Cook and Fox, Franz Josef and Tasman Glaciers ($340).

Helicopter flights are operated by several companies including **Alpine Adventures** *(☎ (0800 800 793; **website** www.scenic-flights.co.nz)* and the **Helicopter Line** *(☎ (03) 752 0767 or 0800 807 767; **website** www.helicopter.co.nz)*.

HELI-HIKING

Heli-hiking offers the best of both worlds. You get a scenic flight over the glacier and you also get to hike on the ice. Generally walking on the glacier is better on the heli-hikes as you get to the more remote parts of the glacier away from the tour groups.

Franz Josef Glacier Guides *(☎ (03) 752 0763 or 0800 GUIDES (0800 484 337); **website** www.franzjosefglacier.com)* operate heli-hike trips that cost $360.

Fox Glacier

The town of Fox Glacier is even smaller than Franz Josef, although the glacier itself is slightly larger. It offers a similar range of services and activities, but the town has less facilities. Accommodation choices are not as good, and there is only an expensive convenience store rather than a supermarket. But it is a pleasant little Alpine village, and has the added bonus of Lake Matheson, which often has spectacular sunrise and sunset reflections of the Alps.

Coming & Going

Atomic Shuttles *(☎ (03) 349 0697; **website** www.atomictravel.co.nz)*, InterCity Coachlines *(☎ (03) 365 1113; **website** www.intercity.co.nz)* and Naked Bus *(☎ 0900 62533; **website** www.nakedbus.com)* stop in Fox Glacier en route between Greymouth and Queenstown. Buses stop outside Fox Glacier Guiding on Main Road and some buses stop at the Fox General Store.

Accommodation

Ivory Towers

This is now the only backpackers' hostel in Fox; luckily, it is a good one. It would be party central if it weren't for the fact that everyone is either readying for or recovering from a glacier hike. Hence, it has a social but mellow atmosphere. It has a fair amount of character and a colourfully decorated interior, but the doors don't lock so security is an issue. There is a large, well stocked kitchen and some convivial common rooms, as well as a nice veranda that some rooms open on to. Dorms are a bit cramped and cluttered, and they only have one power point, which is inconvenient when everyone wants to charge their camera for the next morning.

Sullivans Road, Fox Glacier
☎ (03) 751 0838
Website *www.ivorytowers.co.nz*
Dorm bed *$26 ($23 BBH);* ***double/twin room*** *$65-80 ($60-75 BBH),* ***family room*** *$90*
Credit card *MC, Visa*
Reception open *summer 8am-8.30pm daily; winter 8am-6pm daily*

Maintenance & cleanliness	★★★½
Facilities	★★★
Atmosphere & character	★★★★
Security	-
Overall rating	★★★

West Coast

Activities

GLACIER HIKES/ICE CLIMBING

Fox Glacier Guiding *(☎ (03) 751 0825; **website** www.foxguides.co.nz)* run guided walks on Fox Glacier. This is a cheaper and less crowded alternative to hiking on nearby Franz Josef. A half-day hike costs $89, a full-day hike costs $135 and ice climbing costs $225.

HELICOPTER FLIGHTS

A helicopter flight offers a birds-eye view of the glacier and several of the helicopter operators are licensed to land on it.

Scenic helicopter flights start from a quick 20-minute buzz over Fox Glacier ($180) to a 30-minute flight over both Franz Josef and Fox Glaciers ($240) or a 40-minute flight that takes in Mount Cook and Fox, Franz Josef and Tasman Glaciers ($340).

Helicopter flights are operated by several companies including **Alpine Adventures** *(☎ (03) 752 0793; **website** www.scenic-flights.co.nz)* and the **Helicopter Line** *(☎ (03) 751 0767 or 0800 807 767; **website** www.helicopter.co.nz)*.

HELI-HIKING & HELI-ICE CLIMBING

Fox Glacier Guiding *(☎ (03) 751 0825; **website** www.foxguides.co.nz)* also operate heli-hiking and heli-ice climbing trips to Fox Glacier. You get a scenic flight over the glacier and you also get to hike or climb on the ice. Generally glacier walks and climbing are better as you get to the more remote parts of the glacier away from the tour groups. Heli-hikes cost $380 or heli-ice climbing is $595.

Haast

This remote area at the southern end of the West Coast has some good hiking trails and offers the chance to see various bird species, including the rare Fiordland crested penguin. It sits beside Mount Aspiring National Park, where the major attractions are outdoors: jetboating, fishing, bushwalks and the popular Haast River Safaris. There is no real centre to Haast; rather, it is split between three areas. Most of the accommodation is located in Haast Township on State Highway 6, while the Tourist Information Centre is in Haast Junction. Haast Beach is at the end of Jackson Bay Road.

Practical Information

Department of Conservation Visitor Centre

Corner State Highway 6 & Jackson Bay Road, Haast Junction
☎ *(03) 750 0809*
Website *www.doc.govt.nz*
Open *Jan-Apr 9am-6.30pm daily; May-Oct 9am-4.30pm daily; Nov-Dec 9am-6.30pm daily*

Coming & Going

Buses running between Wanaka and the West Coast stop in Haast. InterCity Coachlines *(☎ (03) 365 1113; **website** www.intercity.co.nz)* stops opposite Wilderness Backpackers and Naked Bus *(☎ 0900 62533; **website** www.nakedbus.com)* stops outside the Fantail Café on Marks Road.

Accommodation

Haast Lodge

This hostel is well maintained, but doesn't have much atmosphere. There is a spacious common room with TV and internet; a clean, well-maintained kitchen; laundry facilities and a cute garden area with a barbecue. Accommodation is in simple dorms with thick mattresses and nice sheets and the bathrooms are nicely renovated.

Marks Road, Haast
☎ *(03) 750 0703*
Website *www.aspiringcourtmotel.com*
Dorm bed *$24;* ***double room*** *$60*
Credit cards *MC, Visa*
Reception open *8am-8pm daily*

Maintenance & cleanliness	★★★
Facilities	★★
Atmosphere & character	★★½
Security	★★
Overall rating	★★½

Wilderness Backpackers

Wilderness Backpackers is a very well maintained hostel/motel. The clean and brightly coloured dorm rooms have up to five beds each, which are all made up with nice duvets. The bathrooms are brand new and extremely clean. There is a small modern kitchen with lots of appliances, including a pizza oven. All the rooms circle a central atrium with wooden furniture and plants, which acts as the main common area. There are also laundry facilities and internet access. Management are easygoing and friendly, but the atmosphere is very quiet.

Marks Road, Haast
☎ *(03) 750 0029*
***Dorm bed** $22-25; **single room** $50; **double/twin room** $55-65*
***Credit cards** MC, Visa*
***Reception open** 8am-8.30pm daily*

Maintenance & cleanliness	★★★½
Facilities	★½
Atmosphere & character	★★
Security	★★½
Overall rating	★★½

Activities

Jet Boating

Haast River Safari *(☎ (03) 750 0101 or 0800 865 382; **website** www.haastriver.co.nz)* operates jet boat rides on the Haast River. The trip departs from Haast Bridge and takes in the Haast River Valley. The 90-minute trip costs $120.

Canterbury

The Canterbury region covers much of the central east coast of the South Island. The area is home to the sprawling Canterbury Plains, the spectacular Arthur's Pass, Lake Tekapo and the Southern Alps including the majestic Aoraki/Mount Cook – New Zealand's tallest mountain. It is a varied landscape of farms, wineries, ski resorts and coastal towns.

Christchurch is the main city in the region, and the South Island's largest. It attracts crowds of tourists year-round, and has plenty of things to keep you busy. The Banks Peninsula is a huge, rugged landmass left over from a volcano, and is a great place to explore, walk, surf, or chill out in one of its small bay villages. Kaikoura is a cute coastal town with excellent water sports and marine life activities and Hanmer Springs is popular for its thermal pools and alpine setting.

There are heaps of activities to choose from in the Canterbury region. If you are in New Zealand on a working holiday, there are also many places to find fruit picking and vineyard work.

Must do in Canterbury

- Swim with dolphins in Kaikoura or Akaroa
- Watch whales in Kaikoura
- Kayak among the glaciers at Aoraki/Mount Cook National Park

Kaikoura

Kaikoura is an ordinary town in an extraordinary setting. The centre is stretched out along a bay and against a backdrop of majestic snow-capped mountains. Besides a good museum and the opportunity to see remains of ancient Maori settlements, there is not a lot in Kaikoura to keep you on land. Most of its attractions are in the water. The ocean here is famous for its rich marine life, making this a popular place to whale watch or swim with fur seals and dusky dolphins. If you don't have the chance to swim with the seals, you can see them from the Omau Lookout, 20km north of town.

Practical Information

Kaikoura i-SITE Visitor Centre
West End, Kaikoura
☎ *(03) 319 5641*
Website *www.kaikoura.co.nz*
Open *9am-5pm daily*

INTERNET ACCESS

Global Gossip
19 West End, Kaikoura
☎ *(03) 319 7970*
Website *www.globalgossip.com*
Open *8.30am-11.30pm daily*

Coming & Going

BUS

There are regular bus services from Kaikoura to Blenheim, Christchurch, Nelson and Picton.

Northbound InterCity Coachlines *(☎ (03) 365 1113; **website** www.intercity.co.nz)* stop outside Sleepy Whale Backpackers *(86 West End, Kaikoura)* and southbound buses stop opposite the Craypot Café *(77 West End, Kaikoura)*. Atomic Shuttles *(☎ (03) 349 0697; **website** www.atomictravel.co.nz)*, Naked Bus *(☎ 0900 62533; **website** www.nakedbus.com)* and Southern Link K Bus *(☎ (03) 358 8355 or 0508 458 835; **website** www.southernlinkkbus.co.nz)* buses leave from the i-SITE Visitor Centre on West End.

TRAIN

TranzScenic's *TranzCoastal* train stops in Kaikoura en route between Picton and Christchurch. Kaikoura's train station is located behind Beach Road.

Accommodation

Adelphi Lodge

This hostel is right in the centre of town, next to the Adelphi Bar and Restaurant. It is in an old hotel with plenty of character. There is a huge TV lounge with log fire and pool table;

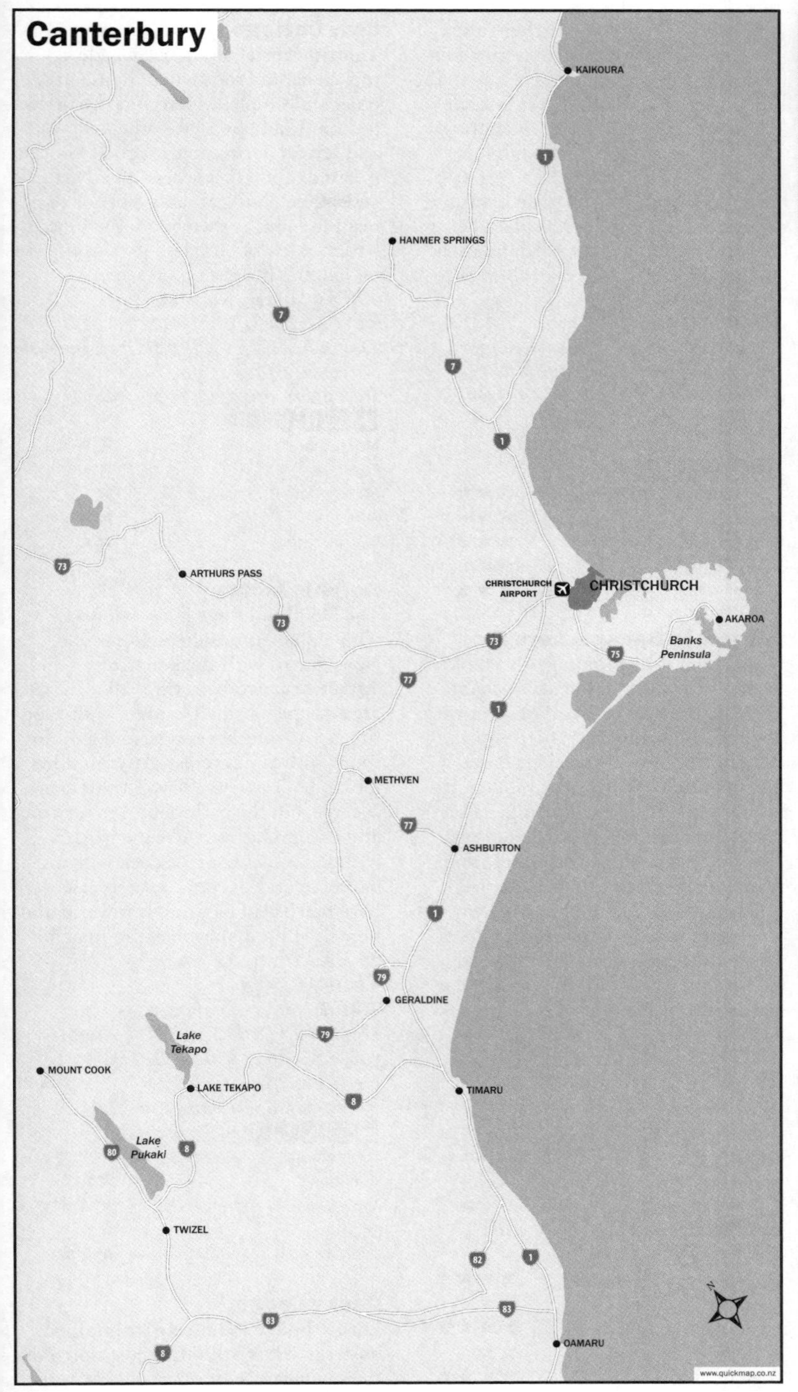
Canterbury
KAIKOURA
HANMER SPRINGS
ARTHURS PASS
CHRISTCHURCH AIRPORT
CHRISTCHURCH
AKAROA
Banks Peninsula
METHVEN
ASHBURTON
GERALDINE
Lake Tekapo
MOUNT COOK
LAKE TEKAPO
TIMARU
Lake Pukaki
TWIZEL
OAMARU
www.quickmap.co.nz

a large fully-equipped kitchen; a spa pool and a rooftop garden with a barbecue, hammocks and great views. The dorms are spacious and comfortable. They have internet access, including Wi-Fi ($6 per hour); although it is slightly cheaper across the street at Global Gossip. It has a great central location and a good atmosphere. Reception staff are friendly and each night, they serve free vegetable soup.

26 West End, Kaikoura
☎ *(03) 319 5141*
Website *www.adelphilodge.co.nz*
Dorm bed *$23-26 ($20-23 BBH);* ***double room*** *$55-65 ($52-60 BBH)*
Credit cards *MC, Visa*
Reception open *8am-9pm daily*

Maintenance & cleanliness	★★★
Facilities	★★★½
Atmosphere & character	★★★★½
Security	★★½
Overall rating	★★★½

Albatross Backpackers Inn

This hostel is in a heritage-listed old post office and it has loads of character. There is a large common area with log fire, TV and sofas where you can usually find lots of travellers hanging out and chatting. The kitchen is nicely kept, although it can get a bit messy and is not very well equipped. The dorms are clean and simple and there are dorm beds in a Turkish-themed room that are less expensive and more fun than the regular dorm beds, although guests then have to go into the other building to use the bathroom. It has a good location and helpful staff.

1 Torquay Street, Kaikoura
☎ *(03) 319 6090 or 0800 222 247*
Website *www.albatross-kaikoura.co.nz*
Dorm bed *$25-28 ($22-25 BBH);* ***double room*** *$65 ($59 BBH);* ***twin room*** *$60 ($54 BBH)*
Credit cards *MC, Visa*
Reception open *8am-9pm daily*

Maintenance & cleanliness	★★★★
Facilities	★★
Atmosphere & character	★★★★½
Security	★★
Overall rating	★★★½

Cray Cottage

This tiny hostel on the Esplanade is tucked behind the owners' house. It is quiet and simple, which could be perfect for some, but boring for others. It has and several dorm rooms, a good kitchen, a laundry, internet access, a barbecue and a quiet lounge that is more of a reading room as there is no TV. Guests have free use of bicycles. Everything is a bit old, but it is kept quite clean.

190 Esplanade, Kaikoura
☎ *(03) 319 5152*
Dorm bed *$23 ($20 BBH);* ***twin room*** *$56 ($50 BBH)*
Reception open *9am-7pm daily*

Maintenance & cleanliness	★★★
Facilities	★½
Atmosphere & character	★½
Security	★★
Overall rating	★★

Dolphin Lodge

The Dolphin Lodge is a small house with a quiet atmosphere. It has spacious dorms with thick mattresses and attractive artwork on the walls. There are a couple of small lounges with a log fire, a TV, internet access, and a dining room with large etched-glass windows looking out over the bay. The kitchen is average, but the bathrooms are very nice and clean. Outside there is a garden with hammocks, a nice deck with a barbecue and spa pool. Guests also have free use of bicycles. It is warm and homely, with management to match.

15 Deal Street, Kaikoura
☎ *(03) 319 5842*
Website *www.dolphinlodge.co.nz*
Dorm bed *$20 ($23 BBH);* ***double room*** *$56-62 ($50-56 BBH)*
Credit cards *MC, Visa*
Reception open *8am-9pm daily*

Maintenance & cleanliness	★★★
Facilities	★★½
Atmosphere & character	★★★½
Security	★½
Overall rating	★★★

Dusky Lodge

Dusky Lodge is a nicely maintained hostel in a large building just north of the town centre. It offers a wide range of facilities including several fully equipped kitchens, comfy lounges with log fires, a TV room that is always full of backpackers, a spa pool and a large heated swimming pool. There is also a good value Thai restaurant on-site. The dorms are nicely appointed, the bathrooms are clean and all the lounges are interestingly decorated with heavy wooden furniture.

67 Beach Road, Kaikoura
(03) 319 5959
Website *www.duskylodge.co.nz*
Dorm bed *$23 ($20 BBH);* ***double room*** *$53-75 ($47-69 BBH)*
Credit cards *MC, Visa*
Reception open *7am-9pm daily*

Maintenance & cleanliness	★★★½
Facilities	★★★★
Atmosphere & character	★★★★
Security	★★★
Overall rating	★★★★

The Lazy Shag

This is a nicely maintained purpose-built hostel on the north side of town. It has a huge, fully-equipped kitchen, two big TV lounges with a log fire and laundry facilities. The dorms are modern with clean en suite bathrooms as well as new mattresses. There is free internet access and guests have free use of kayaks. The only downside is the empty space and slightly institutional atmosphere – it needs some warmth. Bed linen costs $2 extra.

37 Beach Road, Kaikoura
(03) 319 6662
Dorm bed *$22;* ***single room*** *$50;* ***double/twin room*** *$60;* ***triple room*** *$78*
Reception open *8.30am-8pm daily*

Maintenance & cleanliness	★★★★
Facilities	★★★
Atmosphere & character	★★
Security	★½
Overall rating	★★★

Maui YHA

This hostel is in a big white building with a million-dollar view of the bay, town and the mountains. Dorms and

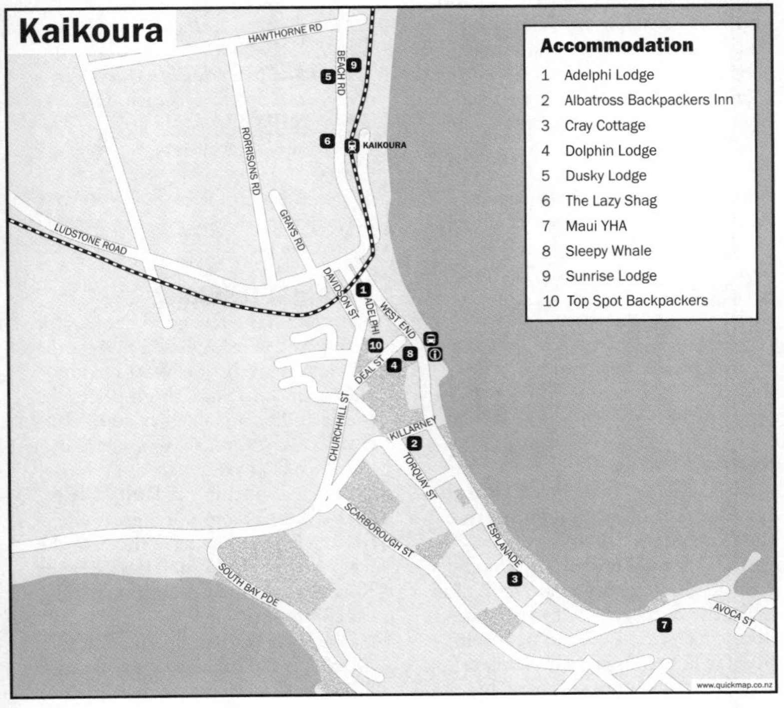

common areas are excellently clean, but the kitchen and bathrooms could use (and will soon get) an update. Amenities include the standard laundry, internet access and a barbecue area. There is a quiet but convivial atmosphere here and the management and staff are very outgoing and friendly.
270 Esplanade, Kaikoura
☎ *(03) 319 5931*
Website *www.stayyha.com*
Dorm bed *$28 ($25 HI/YHA);* ***double/ twin room*** *$57-73 ($54-70 HI/YHA)*
Credit cards *Amex, Diners, JCB, MC, Visa*
Reception open *8.30am-1.30pm & 3.30pm-7.30pm daily*

Maintenance & cleanliness	★★★½
Facilities	★★★
Atmosphere & character	★★★
Security	★★★
Overall rating	★★★½

Sleepy Whale

The Sleepy Whale is a clean and well-maintained hostel in the town centre. It is good value but has basic facilities and lacks the charm of some older hostels. New management had taken over shortly before we visited and assure us that planned renovations will make a big improvement to the hostel.
86 West End, Kaikoura
☎ *(03) 319 7014*
Dorm bed *$18-22;* ***double room*** *$50;* ***twin room*** *$46*
Reception open *summer 7.30am-8pm daily; winter 7.30am-5.30pm daily*

Maintenance & cleanliness	★★★★★
Facilities	★
Atmosphere & character	★★½
Security	★★
Overall rating	★★★

Sunrise Lodge

This is a modest little hostel near the supermarket a few minutes north of the town centre. Facilities include a clean, well maintained kitchen and a cosy TV lounge. There are only nine beds, three in each room and the dorms have good quality beds with bedside lamps. It is a simple place to stay with a quiet atmosphere, but the management make it feel like home. Guests have free use of bicycles, and each night they run a free sunset tour.
74 Beach Road, Kaikoura
☎ *(03) 319 7444*
Dorm bed *$25 ($22 BBH);* ***single room*** *$45;* ***twin room*** *$50*
Credit cards *MC, Visa*
Reception open *8am-9.30pm daily*

Maintenance & cleanliness	★★★½
Facilities	★½
Atmosphere & character	★★½
Security	★½
Overall rating	★★½

Top Spot Backpackers

Top Spot is a homely place just off the main street. It is clean but not very well maintained. Facilities include a nice common room with a log fire, a small TV lounge upstairs with a big TV, a kitchen, laundry and a very nice outdoor deck and barbecue area with hanging grape vines. The dorms have nice innerspring mattresses and made-up beds. There is no internet access and security is a bit weak, but it is in a safe area.
22 Deal Street, Kaikoura
☎ *(03) 319 5540*
Dorm bed *$22;* ***double room*** *$60*
Reception open *8am-8pm daily*

Maintenance & cleanliness	★★½
Facilities	★★
Atmosphere & character	★★½
Security	★★
Overall rating	★★½

Eating & Drinking

Kaikoura has a few good choices for eating and drinking on a budget. Most of the restaurants on West End in the town centre have high prices, but locals and backpackers head to **the Sonic** *(West End, Kaikoura)* for dinner and drinks anyway because it has a great atmosphere. **Pot Belly Café** *(38 West End, Kaikoura)* is a great choice for lunch and they have the best cheap pies in town. Head north on Beach Road for fast food restaurants and cheaper prices.

The **New World** supermarket *(124 Beach Road, Kaikoura)* is a five-minute drive north from the town centre.

Sights

Kaikoura District Museum

This small regional museum has a wide selection of exhibits including dinosaur bones, Māori artefacts and thousands of photos.

14 Ludstone Road, Kaikoura
☎ *(03) 319 7440*
***Admission** $3*
***Open** Mon-Fri 10am-4.30pm, Sat-Sun 2pm-4pm*

Activities

ALBATROSS CRUISES

Albatross Encounter Tours *(☎ (03) 319 6777 or 0800 733 635; **website** www.albatrossencounter.co.nz)* run cruises for bird watchers who want to see ocean-going birds such as mollymawks, petrels and the mighty albatross. You often also see dolphins, seals and whales on these cruises. Albatross cruises cost $80 and you often need to book a few days in advance to ensure space on the boat.

DOLPHINS

One of Kaikoura's big attractions is the opportunity to swim with dolphins. **Dolphin Encounter** *(☎ (03) 319 6777 or 0800 733 365; **website** www.dolphin.co.nz)* run three-hour trips out to swim with the dusky dolphins. You also have the chance to see hectors dolphins, fur seals, orca and pilot whales. It costs $130 to swim with the dolphins or you can come along and watch for $70.

There are restrictions on the number of people allowed to swim with the dolphins and it is often necessary to book well in advance if you are visiting in the peak season (Nov-Apr).

HIKING

The **Kaikoura Coast Track** *(**website** www.kaikouratrack.co.nz)* bills itself as one of New Zealand's finest private walks.

The three-day walk climbs from sea level to 600m, but it is a relatively easy walk. Like the Queen Charlotte Track, hikers have the luxury of having their bags transported between overnight stops so you can walk with just a daypack.

The track is limited to just 10 walkers and eight mountain bikers each day. The track is open Oct-Apr and it costs $185 to walk ($95 for cyclists), which includes accommodation and backpack transport.

HORSE RIDING

Fyffe View Ranch Horse Trekking *(☎ (03) 319 5069; **website** www.kaikourahorsetrekking.co.nz)* offer one-hour horse rides for $45 and more challenging two-hour rides for $70.

SEA KAYAKING

Kaikoura offers excellent sea kayaking that gives you the opportunity to get close to the region's spectacular marine life. **Sea Kayak Kaikoura** *(☎ (03) 319 5641 or 0800 4 KAIKOURA (0800 452 456); **website** www.seakayakkaikoura.co.nz)* offers both guided kayak tours and kayak rental. Half-day guided kayak tours cost $80 and give you the opportunity to see fur seals at close range. You can also rent kayaks for $65 for a half-day or $80 for a full day if you prefer the freedom of exploring at your own pace.

SWIMMING WITH SEALS

In summer (Nov-Apr) **Dive Kaikoura** *(☎ (03) 319 6622; **website** www.divekaikoura.co.nz)* and **Seal Swim Kaikoura** *(☎ (03) 319 6182; **website** www.sealswimkaikoura.co.nz)* run trips that allow you to swim with fur seals. The Seal Swim Kaikoura trip ($70-80) is a shore-based activity where you snorkel out to the seals from Jimmy Armers Beach, while Dive Kaikoura's trip involves taking a boat out to the seals.

WHALE WATCHING

Whale watching is big business in Kaikoura and you have the option of either taking a whale watching cruise or spotting them from a plane or helicopter.

Sperm and humpback whales can be seen Jun-Jul, but orcas are more prevalent during summer.

Whale Watching Cruises

Whale Watch Kaikoura *(☎ (03) 319 6767; **website** www.whalewatch.co.nz)*

has been running whale-watching tours for the past 18 years. The whale watching cruises give you around 2½ hours on the water and you also have the opportunity of seeing dolphins, seals and albatross. Cruises cost $140 and they offer an 80% refund if you don't spot a whale.

Whale Watching Flights

Scenic flights allow you to see whales and other marine life from the air. **Wings over Whales** *(☎ (03) 319 6580 or 0800 2CMOBY (0800 226 629); **website** www.whales.co.nz)* operate flights in fixed-wing aircraft departing from Kaikoura Airport, 8km south of the town centre. Wings over Whales' flights cost $145.

Kaikoura Helicopters *(☎ (03) 319 6609; **website** www.worldofwhales.co.nz)* run helicopter flights from a helipad about a five-minute walk from the town centre. Kaikoura Helicopters' flights cost $195-350 depending on the length of the flight and the number of other passengers.

Hanmer Springs

Hanmer Springs is a small alpine town about 150km northeast of Christchurch. The mineral-rich waters of the Hanmer Springs Thermal Reserve, where you can soak in naturally heated pools and spas, are internationally known and the town has become quite touristy due to the day trippers and pensioners on package tours. The town does not have much else of interest for the backpacker besides some nice walking and cycling tracks, but there are opportunities in the area for jet boating, bungy jumping, heli-skiing, and horse riding. Hanmer Springs is a quiet town and everything closes rather early in the evening.

Practical Information

Hurunui i-SITE Visitor Centre

42 Amuri Avenue, Hanmer Springs
☎ (03) 315 7128 or 0800 442 663
***Website** www.alpinepacifictourism.co.nz*
***Open** 10am-5pm daily*

Coming & Going

Astro Coachlines *(☎ 0800 800 575; **website** www.akaroabus.co.nz)* operate a daily coach service between Christchurch and Hanmer Springs, which costs $25 one-way.

InterCity Coachlines *(☎ (03) 365 1113; **website** www.intercity.co.nz)* and Southern Link K Bus *(☎ (03) 358 8355 or 0508 458 835; **website** www.southernlinkkbus.co.nz)* services between Christchurch and Nelson (via the Lewis Pass) go past Hanmer Springs, although only InterCity stop in town (outside the i-SITE visitor centre on Amuri Avenue). Southern Link K Bus stops at the Hanmer Springs turn-off 9km outside town.

Accommodation

Hanmer Backpackers

This very small hostel is in an alpine-style building just a two-minute walk from the thermal pools. It features a fully-equipped kitchen, a dining area and a cosy upstairs TV lounge. The dorm in the main building has an open beam ceiling and comfortable single beds. The bathrooms are compact but clean. Overall, it has a very warm, quiet atmosphere.

41 Conical Hill Road, Hanmer Springs
☎ (03) 315 7196
***Dorm bed** $22-25*
***Credit cards** MC, Visa*
***Reception open** 8am-9pm daily*

Maintenance & cleanliness	★★★
Facilities	★★½
Atmosphere & character	★★★
Security	★★½
Overall rating	★★★½

Hanmer Springs Forest Camp

This place is a few minutes' drive out of town. It consists of a few long cabins with dorms and double rooms, plus several small huts used as an alternative to camping. These are the cheapest beds in town, and although they are no-frills, they beat sleeping on the ground somewhere else for the same price. There are four large kitchens and common rooms that seem quite dull. The bathrooms are basic but very clean. They have laundry facilities including a free drying room and excellent disabled facilities. Management are extremely nice.

300 Jollies Pass Road, Hanmer Springs
(03) 315 7472
***Dorm bed** $15-20; **double/twin room** $50-75; **camping** $10*
***Credit cards** MC, Visa*
***Reception open** 8.30am-9pm daily*

Maintenance & cleanliness	★★½
Facilities	★½
Atmosphere & character	★★★½
Security	½
Overall rating	★★½

Kakapo Backpackers YHA

This hostel is a section of the Kakapo Lodge. It is very plain, with little in the way of facilities. Amenities include a TV lounge with mismatched sofas and a small TV; a spacious kitchen stocked with lots of cutlery and dishes and an outdoor veranda with a nice view. The dorms have simple wooden bunks with bedside lights. Bathrooms are a bit old, but clean nonetheless. The location is good and reception staff are very friendly.

14 Amuri Avenue, Hanmer Springs
(03) 315 7472
***Website** www.yha.co.nz*
***Dorm bed** $26 ($23 HI/YHA); **double/twin room** $56-76 ($50-70 HI/YHA)*
***Credit cards** MC, Visa*
***Reception open** 8.30am-7.30pm daily*

Maintenance & cleanliness	★★★
Facilities	★★½
Atmosphere & character	★★½
Security	★★
Overall rating	★★½

Le Gite

Le Gite is a lovely little hostel in a cottage two minutes' walk to town. It is warm and cosy, and smartly decorated. Dorms have only three or four single made-up beds, and each is painted in nice colours and has a bedside light. There is a quaint kitchen and TV lounge with sofas, books and a log fire where you can use the internet (including Wi-Fi). There is a nice outdoor veranda with a new barbecue. It is a simple, but clean and comfortable place to stay.

3 Devon Street, Hanmer Springs
(03) 315 5111
***Website** www.legite.co.nz*
***Dorm bed** $25 ($22 BBH); **double/twin room** $54-66 ($50-60 BBH)*
***Credit cards** MC, Visa*
***Reception open** 8.30am-8pm daily*

Maintenance & cleanliness	★★★½
Facilities	★★½
Atmosphere & character	★★★★
Security	★
Overall rating	★★★

Eating & Drinking

There are a few good cafés in town, although most of them cater to an affluent crowd. The Hanmer Springs Bakery has nice fresh bread, pastries and sandwiches. The Pukeko Junction Café also has cheap breakfast and lunch. There are some nice places to hike in the mountains, so many travellers pack a picnic to take on a hike.

Your best bet is to shop in the supermarket in the town centre and cook in the hostel kitchen.

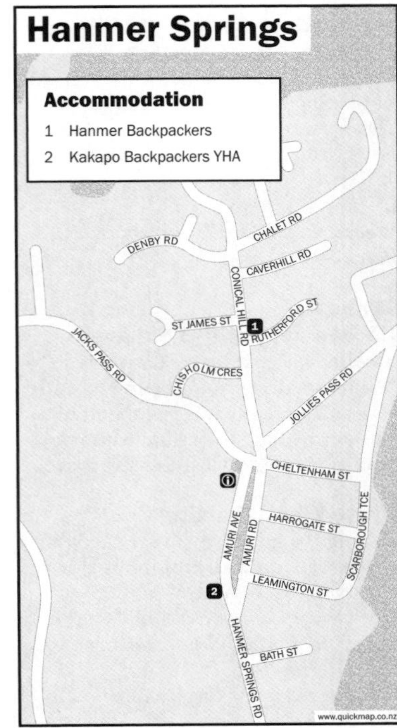

Activities

Bungee Jumping

Thrillseekers have a bungee jumping platform on the historic Waiau Ferry Bridge, 35m above the Waiau River.
Thrillseekers Canyon Adventure Centre, Ferry Bridge, Main Road, Hanmer Springs
☎ *(03) 315 7046*
***Website** www.thrillseeker.co.nz*
***Price** $135*

Hanmer Springs Thermal Reserve

The Thermal Reserve features seven open-air thermal pools, three sulphur pools plus a sauna, steam rooms and a swimming pool with waterslides. The best time to visit the pools is lunchtime or around 7pm-8pm, when there are only a few people around.
Corner Jacks Pass Road & Amuri Avenue, Hanmer Springs
☎ *(03) 315 7511*
***Website** www.hanmersprings.co.nz*
***Admission** $12-15; $22-32 including sauna and steam rooms*
***Open** 10am-9pm daily*

Jet Boating

Thrillseekers run jet boating trips down the Waiau Gorge, which include jet boating down white water rapids.
Thrillseekers Canyon Adventure Centre, Ferry Bridge, Main Road, Hanmer Springs
☎ *(03) 315 7046*
***Website** www.thrillseeker.co.nz*
***Price** $99*

Skiing

The **Hanmer Springs Ski Area** *(**website** www.skihanmer.co.nz)* is a 40-minute drive from the town centre. It's a small area that is geared mostly for intermediate skiers and it's a good value place to ski with $45 lift passes.

White Water Rafting

Rafting is a good way to see the Waiau Gorge Canyon while tumbling down the grade two rapids.
Thrillseekers Canyon Adventure Centre, Ferry Bridge, Main Road, Hanmer Springs
☎ *(03) 315 7046*
***Website** www.thrillseeker.co.nz*
***Price** $135*

Christchurch

The gateway to the South Island sits at the eastern edge of the Canterbury Plains behind the Banks Peninsula.

Known as "The Garden City", Christchurch boasts some beautifully sculpted parks and gardens reminiscent of Victorian England. While much of the city has a decidedly British feel, it also houses the country's largest marae, and you can learn about Māori culture in the museum. The bold new Arts Gallery is a modern architectural masterpiece, and it is juxtaposed with the neo-Gothic colonial remnants of the city centre.

Cathedral Square marks the centre of the city, which is laid out in a grid plan with the Avon River flowing through the middle.

Christchurch has a lively student population as well as some interesting cultural influences which give it a very eclectic and multicultural feel. No place is better to see this melange than Cathedral Square, where you can munch on cheap snack food while watching buskers and walking past colonial-era buildings. It is a very laid-back city, and one which visitors find charming; many have come to stay longer than anticipated.

Practical Information

INFORMATION CENTRES & USEFUL NUMBERS

Christchurch i-SITE Visitor Centre

Old Chief Post Office, Cathedral Square West, Christchurch
☎ *(03) 379 9629*
***Website** www.christchurchinformation.co.nz*
***Open** summer Mon-Fri 8.30am-6pm, Sat-Sun 8.30am-5pm; winter Mon-Fri 8.30am-5pm, Sat-Sun 8.30am-4.30pm*

Department of Conservation Visitor Centre

Level 4, Torrens House, 195 Hereford Street, Christchurch
☎ *(03) 379 9758*
***Website** www.doc.govt.nz*
***Open** Mon-Fri 8.30am-5pm*

INTERNET ACCESS

Most of the hostels in Christchurch offer internet access and many have wireless hotspots. There is also a free Wi-Fi hotspot for customers at **Esquires Coffee** in the PWC Building *(119 Armagh Street, Christchurch)*.

There are a lot of internet cafés around the city, especially in the area around Cathedral Square.

E Blah Blah
77 Cathedral Square, Christchurch
☎ *(03) 377 2381*
***Open** 8.30am-late*

Netopia
751 Colombo Street, Christchurch
☎ *(03) 365 4578*
***Open** 9.30am-11pm daily*

high://NET
230 High Street, Christchurch
☎ *(03) 366 6100*
***Open** 10am-11pm daily*

Cyber Pass Café
27 Chancery Lane (off Cathedral Square), Christchurch
☎ *(03) 365 9000*
***Website** www.cybercafe-chch.co.nz*
***Open** Mon-Fri 9am-10pm, Sat-Sun*

GameZone (convenience store/internet café)
151 Hereford Street, Christchurch
☎ *(03) 379 3185*
***Open** 10am-9pm daily*

Coming & Going
Christchurch is a busy transport hub that is well served by coach, train and air transport.

AIR
Christchurch Airport *(☎ (03) 358 5029; **website** www.christchurch-airport.co.nz)* is 12km west of the city centre. It's the country's second-busiest international airport.

There are several airport shuttle bus services, including Super Shuttle *(☎ 0800 SHUTTLE (0800 748 885); **website** www.supershuttle.co.nz)*, which operate a door-to-door service to hostels. A cheaper option is the airport bus operated by Metro (route 29), which costs $7 and departs from Worcester Street near Cathedral Square.

Another option is the Five Dollar Bus, which runs an express minibus service between the airport and Cathedral Square about once every 20 minutes between 8am and 5pm. This is the best option if you're staying at one of the hostels near the Square (such as Base Backpackers).

BUS
Christchurch is served by many coach and shuttle bus operators. Most buses leave from the streets around Cathedral Square although the stop at 123 Worcester Street is a busy departure point for InterCity coaches. Many smaller shuttle bus operators depart from the information centre or the train station and many will pick you up from your hostel or from any address in the area bounded by Bealey, Fitzgerald, Moorhouse and Deans Avenues.

The following coach and shuttle bus companies operate from Christchurch:

Astro Coachlines *(☎ 0800 800 575; **website** www.akaroabus.co.nz)* and Akaroa Shuttle *(☎ 0800 500 929; **website** www.akaroashuttle.co.nz)* go to Akaroa on the Banks Peninsula. They both depart from the information centre on Cathedral Square. Astro also operate a daily service to Hanmer Springs.

Atomic Shuttles *(☎ (03) 322 8883; **website** www.atomictravel.co.nz)* go to Dunedin, Picton, Queenstown and the West Coast. They will pick up and drop off anywhere within the four avenues and at any backpackers hostel.

InterCity coaches InterCity Coachlines *(☎ (03) 365 1113; **website** www.intercity.co.nz)* depart from the Ritchies Travel *(123 Worcester Street, Christchurch)*. InterCity coaches go up and down the east coast and stop at Picton, Mt Cook, Queenstown and Dunedin.

Naked Bus *(☎ 0900 62533; **website** www.nakedbus.com)* has direct services to Dunedin, Nelson, Picton and Queenstown, which depart from 88 Worcester Street opposite Holy Grail, near Cathedral Square. Southern Link K Bus *(☎ (03) 358 8355 or 0508 458 835; **website** www.southernlinkkbus.co.nz)* also depart from the stop across the road from the Holy Grail. Southern Link K Bus has shuttles to Dunedin, Nelson, Picton and Queenstown.

TRAIN

The *TranzCoastal* train goes north to Picton and the scenic *TranzAlpine* train goes via Arthur's Pass to Greymouth on the West Coast.

The train station is around 3km from Cathedral Square, just west of Hagley Park. It's on a side street between Blenheim Road and Whiteleigh Avenue. The closest local bus route is the Orbiter (route O), which runs along Whiteleigh Avenue, but many hostels will pick you up if you have booked a bed with them.

HITCHHIKING

It is quite easy hitching a ride from Christchurch although you may need to take a bus to get to the good hitching spots.

If you're heading north to Kaikoura and Picton, Main North Road (State Highway 74) before it joins up with State Highway 1 is a good bet. Buses 4, 11, 13, O and R will take you here. You should be able to get to Picton in a day as long as you set out fairly early.

It can take a bit longer to get across to the West Coast, mainly because the traffic is much lighter. Take bus 84 and get off at the corner of Yaldhurst and Russley Roads. Walk west along Yaldhurst Road (State Highway 73) and find a good spot to wait for a lift.

If you're heading south to Dunedin, Invercargill or Queenstown you'll want to get on State Highway 1. Catch bus 5, 82, 83, 84, B to the Hornby Mall and then walk west along the Main South Road (State Highway 1).

Local Transport

Christchurch has one tram route and an extensive bus network, but most people find the city compact enough to walk around.

BUS

Although Christchurch is a pretty easy city to walk around, you may need to take a bus or two if you want to get across town or go to the train station, airport or the good hitchhiking spots. Christchurch's public transport system is surprisingly efficient and most services run every 10 to 15 minutes.

Most buses leave from the City Bus Exchange or from Colombo Street just outside the Bus Exchange. The Bus Exchange is just south of Cathedral Square near the corner of Colombo Street and Litchfield Street. The only major bus routes that don't terminate here are the MetroStar and the Orbiter (route O). The Orbiter is a circular route through the suburbs that connects with most other buses.

Public transport is essential if you're staying at the hostels in New Brighton or Sumner. Buses 5, 40, 51, 60, 83, 84 and M go to New Brighton and bus 3 goes to Sumner.

The Shuttle is a free bus that runs every 10 minutes from the Town Hall, through Cathedral Square and down to the supermarkets on Colombo Street and Moorhouse Avenue.

Most fares in the central area are $2.50 and you can use your ticket to transfer to another service for no extra charge.

The bus information centre in the Bus Exchange gives you timetables and route maps or you can get information online at www.metroinfo.org.nz.

TRAM

Christchurch also has a limited tram service *(☎ (03) 366 6943; **website** www.tram.co.nz)* which runs along a 2.5km loop past the main sights. It's a bit touristy and compared to the bus it is pretty expensive at $14 for a two-day pass.

Accommodation

CITY CENTRE

Akron Lodge

Akron Lodge is part motel, part hostel. The hostel building is very well maintained with warm coloured paint and new carpets throughout. The dorms have nice wooden bunks and good mattresses. The kitchen is small, but it suffices for the size of the place, and the bathrooms are very clean and new. There is a spacious common area/lounge with new plush sofas and Sky TV. The hostel aptly names itself "the Quiet One" and there is a very relaxing feel to it. They offer internet, laundry

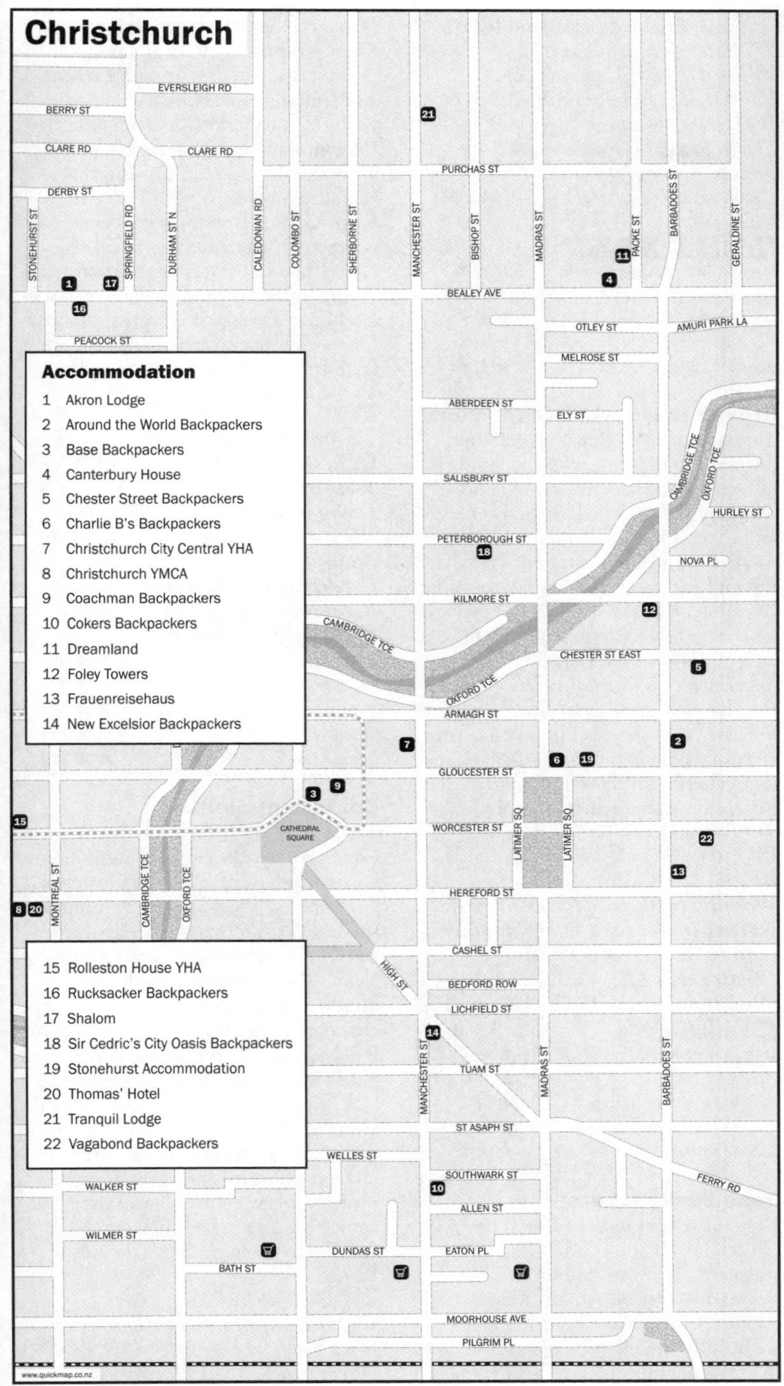

Accommodation

1 Akron Lodge
2 Around the World Backpackers
3 Base Backpackers
4 Canterbury House
5 Chester Street Backpackers
6 Charlie B's Backpackers
7 Christchurch City Central YHA
8 Christchurch YMCA
9 Coachman Backpackers
10 Cokers Backpackers
11 Dreamland
12 Foley Towers
13 Frauenreisehaus
14 New Excelsior Backpackers
15 Rolleston House YHA
16 Rucksacker Backpackers
17 Shalom
18 Sir Cedric's City Oasis Backpackers
19 Stonehurst Accommodation
20 Thomas' Hotel
21 Tranquil Lodge
22 Vagabond Backpackers

facilities, disabled access and lockers.
85 Bealey Avenue, Christchurch
10, 11, 12, 13, 18, 90, 92
(03) 366 1633 or 0800 778787
***Website** www.akronlodge.co.nz*
***Dorm bed** $25; **single room** $40; **double room** $70*
***Credit cards** Amex, Diners, JCB, MC, Visa*

Maintenance & cleanliness	★★★½
Facilities	★★½
Atmosphere & character	★★½
Security	★★½
Overall rating	★★★

Around the World Backpackers

This is a tiny, run down hostel. The dorms are miniscule, cluttered and musty and the showers are old and mouldy. The cramped kitchen is messy, and there is just a TV lounge with a small TV and a few tattered sofas that do not look inviting at all. The outside common area is basically just a picnic table next to a makeshift backyard campground. However, they do offer free internet access, including Wi-Fi, and they have cheap laundry and a locker for each bed. There is not much of an atmosphere here for backpackers, but it is a cheap and central place to crash. Reception staff are helpful and nice.
314 Barbadoes Street, Christchurch
7, 60, 77
(03) 365 4363
***Website** www.aroundtheworld.co.nz*
***Dorm bed** $21 ($18 BBH); **double/twin room** $55 ($50 BBH)*
***Credit cards** MC, Visa*
***Reception open** 8.30am-7.30pm daily*

Maintenance & cleanliness	★★½
Facilities	★★
Atmosphere & character	★★½
Security	★★★
Overall rating	★★½

Base Backpackers

Base is the best located hostel in Christchurch and it offers a good standard of accommodation. The dorms are a bit bland, but they have lockers, comfortable beds made up with fluffy duvets and some have views over Cathedral Square. This means, however, that it can get very noisy at night – especially with the popular bar downstairs. There is also an inexpensive Indian restaurant sharing space with the hostel. Facilities include two kitchens, a laundry, a huge TV lounge with Sky TV and DVDs, internet access including Wi-Fi ($4-5 per hour; Global Gossip), a barbecue area upstairs on a terrace and a full service travel desk. Every night there are events in the bar and they have barbecues once a week. It is a great place to meet other backpackers and reception staff are mostly friendly and upbeat.
56 Cathedral Square, Christchurch
7, 10, 11, 12, 13, 14, 15, 16, 17, 18, 29, 46, 60, 77, 90, 92, Shuttle
(03) 982 2225 or 0800 BASENZ
***Website** www.basebackpackers.com*
***Dorm bed** $27-30 ($26-29 BBH, VIP); **double room** $65-85 ($63-83 BBH, VIP)*
***Credit cards** MC Visa*
***Reception open** 24 hours*

Maintenance & cleanliness	★★★
Facilities	★★★
Atmosphere & character	★★★★
Security	★★★★
Overall rating	★★★½

Canterbury House

This hostel really feels like home – you even have to take off your shoes before going inside. There are cosy lounges with books, TV, a log fire and plush suede sofas. Dorms are cutely decorated and bathrooms are spotlessly clean. The fully-equipped kitchen is quaint and has free tea, coffee and hot chocolate. Outside there is a beautiful flower garden and they have their own pet sheep! The only downside is the lack of internet access, but you could always curl up with a book next to the friendly resident cat. It is a quiet, comfortable place to stay a few minutes' walk from the centre. It's an excellent choice for girls travelling alone.
257 Bealey Avenue, Christchurch
46
(03) 3778 108
***Website** http://canterburyhousebp.kt.fc2.com/*
Dorm bed** $26 ($23 BBH); **single

room *$43 ($40 BBH);* ***double/twin room*** *$62 ($56 BBH)*
Reception open *9am-9pm daily*

Maintenance & cleanliness ★★★★
Facilities ★★
Atmosphere & character ★★★½
Security ★★½
Overall rating ★★★

Celtic Backpackers

Celtic Backpackers is a very run down hostel in an old house in the middle of an upmarket section of Christchurch. It has recently changed owners, and the family who run the place now are very nice. They are planning renovations which are much needed. At the moment, the dorms are cluttered, and the common area is tiny with shabby sofas and chipped paint. The bathrooms are depressingly dated and sterile. But they offer free internet, cheap laundry and they have a very nicely renovated kitchen. We look forward to seeing it when the planned improvements are made.
12 Dublin Street, Christchurch
10, 11, 12, 13, 18, 90, 92
(03) 3661 861
Dorm bed *$22-23 ($19-20 BBH);* ***single/double/twin room*** *$30 ($27 BBH)*
Reception open *9am-9pm daily*

Maintenance & cleanliness ★★
Facilities ★½
Atmosphere & character ★½
Security ★★
Overall rating ★★

Chester Street Backpackers

This is a brilliant little hostel is in a residential area not far from the centre. It is painted in warm colours with quirky decorations and has only 15 beds in nicely decorated rooms. There is a nice fully-equipped kitchen and the bathrooms are small but newly renovated with mosaic accents and nice mirrors. Outside there is an old restored bus, a nice little cottage in the garden, and a "car-becue" – a cool old car boot transformed into a barbecue. It is eccentric but refreshing, peaceful and clean. There are no lockers, but it has a family atmosphere and is in a quiet location. Management and staff are extremely pleasant and welcoming. This place is perfect for backpackers who want to escape the monotony of chain hostels.
148 Chester Street East, Christchurch
7, 60, 70, 77
(03) 3771 897
Website *www.chesterst.co.nz*
Dorm bed *$26 ($22 BBH);* ***double/twin room*** *$56 ($48 BBH)*
Reception open *9am-9.30pm daily*

Maintenance & cleanliness ★★★★
Facilities ★★
Atmosphere & character ★★★★
Security ★★
Overall rating ★★★½

Charlie B's Backpackers

Charlie B's is in a restored old building with nice furnishings and a grand old staircase. There are three floors of huge, clean dorms with brand new carpet. Bathrooms (which are all mixed) are newly renovated and spotless. There are two (large screen) TV lounges with Sky TV and heaps of free DVDs to watch. There is also a games room with a nice piano and pool table. The outside garden is tranquil and has lots of tables and seating. The kitchen is brightly painted, well equipped, and has a café attached with cheap pizza and snacks. This is one of the better places to meet people, and has a good location next to a park. Reception staff are friendly.
268 Madras Street, Christchurch
7, 60, 77
(03) 3798 429 or 0800 224 222
Website *www.charliebs.co.nz*
Dorm bed *$ 20-27;* ***single room*** *$55;* ***double room*** *$65*
Credit cards *MC, Visa*
Reception open *24 hours*

Maintenance & cleanliness ★★★★
Facilities ★★
Atmosphere & character ★★★★½
Security ★★★
Overall rating ★★★½

Christchurch City Central YHA

Christchurch City Central YHA is a great, centrally located hostel. It is

bright, cheerful and spacious. There are two clean fully-equipped kitchens, a games room, TV lounge, and two internet points ($6 per hour including Wi-Fi). The common area has a pool table, table football and a couple of new massage chairs. Dorms are basic, but tiered bunks make them feel spacious. The bathrooms are very clean, although the water pressure in the showers isn't great. The atmosphere is quiet and relaxed, but convivial. They offer free pick up service and a tour desk.
273 Manchester Street, Christchurch
7, 46, 60, 77
(03) 379 9535
***Website** www.yha.co.nz*
***Dorm bed** $27-31 ($24-28 HI/YHA); **single room** $63 ($60 HI/YHA); **double/twin room** $71-73 ($68-70 HI/YHA); **family room** $128-133 ($125-130 HI/YHA)*
***Credit cards** Amex, Diners, JCB, MC, UnionPay, Visa*
***Reception open** 7am-10pm daily*

Maintenance & cleanliness	★★★★
Facilities	★★½
Atmosphere & character	★★★
Security	★★★★
Overall rating	★★★½

Christchurch YMCA
The YMCA is in a large modern building above a great street side café. The dorm rooms are spacious and immaculate. They have lockers, recessed reading lights and thick mattresses. Bathrooms are also well maintained and clean. There is an on-site gym, squash court and climbing wall, as well as a restaurant. It has a slightly institutional feel, though, and the kitchen is far too small for the amount of guests staying here.
12 Hereford Street, Christchurch
29
(03) 3650 502 or 0508 962 224
***Website** www.ymcachch.org.nz*
***Dorm bed** $25; **single room** $40-70; **double room** $60-95*
***Credit cards** Amex, Diners, JCB, MC, Visa*
***Reception open** 24 hours*

Maintenance & cleanliness	★★★½
Facilities	★★
Atmosphere & character	★★
Security	★★★★
Overall rating	★★★

Coachman Backpackers
Coachman Backpackers is a good hostel in a solid old building right behind Cathedral Square. It has an old world feel with dark rich colours when you enter the foyer and ascend the staircase, but the dorm rooms and bathrooms are much brighter and better maintained. The dorms have high ceilings, which make them feel more spacious than they actually are and the metal bunk beds are made up with real inner spring mattresses. The common area is a big dark room with a big TV in one corner and there is also a bar, internet access and a pool table.
144 Gloucester Street, Christchurch
7, 10, 11, 12, 13, 14, 15, 16, 17, 18, 29, 46, 60, 77, 90, 92, Shuttle
(03) 377 0908
***Website** www.coachmanbackpackers.co.nz*
***Dorm bed** $25-28 ($22-25 BBH); **single room** $63-73 ($60-70 BBH); **double room** $66-76 ($60-70 BBH)*
***Credit cards** Amex, Diners, JCB, MC, Visa*
***Reception open** 7am-11pm daily*
ad

Maintenance & cleanliness	★★★½
Facilities	★½
Atmosphere & character	★★★
Security	★★½
Overall rating	★★★

Cokers Backpackers
This hostel is above an old pub, a five-minute walk south of Cathedral Square. The place is pretty run down, with a poorly maintained kitchen that is buzzing with flies; but the dorms are surprisingly pleasant even though you have to go down hallways of peeling paint and old carpet to get to them. The dorms are light and simple yet spacious; they have new good beds with nice blue duvets, and most have en suite bathrooms that are not bad, either. You won't find a great backpacker atmosphere here, except

perhaps some nights in the bar, but it is a cheap and comfortable place to stay for a night or two. Reception staff are very welcoming.
52 Manchester Street, Christchurch
5, 21, 24, 29, 35, 40, 49, 51, 81 84, Shuttle
(03) 379 8580
***Website** www.cokers.co.nz*
***Dorm bed** $24-26; **single room** $60; **double room** $70; **triple room** $90*
***Credit cards** Amex, JCB, MC, Visa*
***Reception open** 24 hours*

Maintenance & cleanliness	★★
Facilities	★★½
Atmosphere & character	★★★½
Security	★★★
Overall rating	★★½

Dorset House
This hostel is in a big old house that dates from 1871 (ancient by New Zealand standards). It features a big common room with tall ceilings, internet access, a TV, pool table and a fireplace. There are three kitchens and several nice outdoor seating areas. The floors are nice polished wood, although most of them are covered in old carpet that needs to be replaced. The dorms are clean and well maintained and they have single beds instead of bunks. The bathrooms have been renovated and are very clean with hairdryers. It has a quiet ambience and offers laundry facilities and disabled access.
1 Dorset Street, Christchurch
10, 11, 12, 13, 18, 90, 92
(03) 366 8268
***Website** www.dorsethouse.co.nz*
***Dorm bed** $28 ($23 BBH); **single room** $51 ($45 BBH); **double/twin room** $69-74 ($58-65 BBH)*
***Credit cards** MC, Visa*
***Reception open** 8am-6pm daily*

Maintenance & cleanliness	★★★
Facilities	★★
Atmosphere & character	★★★
Security	★★
Overall rating	★★½

Dreamland
This hostel consists of two old buildings that are clean and mostly well maintained, but lacking in atmosphere. There are two small kitchens, several lounge areas with internet access and TVs, and a fireplace. The bathrooms are very clean, and most of the dorms are clean and have made-up beds and en suite bathrooms. They also have laundry facilities, free tea and coffee and guests have free use of bicycles. The management are nice, but the place is not very central and has a dull atmosphere.
21 Packe Street, Christchurch
46
(03) 3663 519
***Dorm bed** $24 ($24 BBH); **double room** $58-68 ($52-62 BBH)*
***Credit cards** MC, Visa*
***Reception open** 9am-9pm daily*

Maintenance & cleanliness	★★★
Facilities	★★★
Atmosphere & character	★★
Security	★★★
Overall rating	★★★

Foley Towers
Foley Towers is a small and convivial complex set around a lush garden courtyard. Dorms are large and have good beds and the bathrooms are nice and clean. The well equipped kitchen is painted bright red and there is a cosy lounge with sofas, books and a big bay window. They also have internet access, laundry facilities and a barbecue area. Reception staff are very friendly, and it has a good atmosphere.
208 Kilmore Street, Christchurch
(03) 3669 720
***Dorm bed** $22-24 ($19-21 BBH); **double/twin room** $51-57 ($48-54 BBH)*
***Credit cards** MC, Visa*
***Reception open** 9am-9.30pm daily*

Maintenance & cleanliness	★★★½
Facilities	★★
Atmosphere & character	★★★½
Security	★★★
Overall rating	★★★

Frauenreisehaus
This is a women-only hostel in a lovely old manor house that is maintained with care. There are fireplaces

throughout the common areas and a peaceful garden with hammocks and lounge chairs. There is a cosy TV room with DVDs and plush sofas. The whole place makes you want to curl up with a good book. The fully-equipped kitchen is nice and clean, and dorms have comfortable beds with nice duvets. Bathrooms are clean and come with hairdryers. Since it is women only, the atmosphere here is very quiet and convivial, and it is centrally located and offers internet access ($4 per hour).

272 Barbadoes Street, Christchurch
7, 60, 77
(03) 366 2585
***Dorm bed** $26 ($23 BBH); **single room** $38 ($35 BBH); **twin room** $56 ($50 BBH)*
***Credit cards** MC, Visa*
***Reception open** 8am-9.30pm daily*

Maintenance & cleanliness	★★★½
Facilities	★★
Atmosphere & character	★★★½
Security	★★½
Overall rating	★★★

Kiwi House

Kiwi House is a large newly renovated green building near the centre of town. The bathrooms are especially clean and the kitchen is well equipped. But it is a bit sterile, and has a rather boring atmosphere. The dorms tend to be cramped, but they have new carpet and clean sheets. There is a small TV lounge with plenty of DVDs, and another kitchen in the adjacent building. There are also laundry facilities, internet access ($4 per hour), free pickup from town and secure car parking plus a sauna that is free to use on Tuesdays. It caters mostly to Asian backpackers and long-term workers.

373 Gloucester Street, Christchurch
21, 70, 84
(03) 381 6645
***Website** www.kiwihouse.co.nz*
***Dorm bed** $19-21; **single room** $28-32; **double/twin room** $24-37*
***Credit cards** MC, Visa*
***Reception open** 9am-noon & 4pm-7pm*

Maintenance & cleanliness	★★★½
Facilities	★★
Atmosphere & character	★½
Security	★★
Overall rating	★★½

New Excelsior Backpackers

This hostel is in a beautiful historic building in a very central location. They have a great downstairs bar/café and outside seating on a busy corner at the end of High Street and it is a good place to meet people. The dorm rooms are nothing special – but the double rooms are gorgeous. Facilities include a small fully-equipped kitchen, a homely TV room with big sofas, internet terminals ($6 per hour) and a barbecue. There is a cute centre garden/terrace with flowers and little tables that is refreshingly protected from the noise of the street in front. It has a relatively good backpacker atmosphere, and they have a tour desk at reception.

Corner Manchester & High Streets, Christchurch
7, 10, 11, 12, 13, 14, 15, 16, 17, 18, 29, 46, 60, 77, 90, 92, Shuttle
(03) 366 7570
***Website** www.newexcelsior.co.nz*
***Dorm bed** $22-27; **single room** $45-47; **double room** $58-62*
***Credit cards** Amex, Diners, JCB, MC, UnionPay, Visa*
***Reception open** 7am-8pm daily*

Maintenance & cleanliness	★★★
Facilities	★★½
Atmosphere & character	★★★★½
Security	★
Overall rating	★★★

The Old Country House

This is a lovely hostel in three small, beautifully restored houses. In a quiet residential area, but close to a good cluster of shops and restaurants, it is a cosy place perfect for a getaway. The dorms have nice bunks and large windows and the clean bathrooms are gorgeously maintained. There are two fully-equipped kitchens and several handsomely furnished lounges. There is also a nice yard with fruit trees and an organic herb garden. They have internet access, laundry facilities and a secure car park. Buses 21 and 83 stop right out in front and bus 60 stops around the corner. Management and staff are helpful and friendly.

437 Gloucester Street, Christchurch
21, 60, 83
(03) 3815 504
Website *www.oldcountryhousenz.com*
Dorm bed *$20-23;* ***double/twin room*** *$54-68;* ***triple room*** *$78-90*
Credit cards *MC, Visa*
Reception open *8am-8pm*

Maintenance & cleanliness	★★★★½
Facilities	★★
Atmosphere & character	★★★½
Security	★★★
Overall rating	★★★½

Rolleston House YHA

This hostel has a great location across the street from the Arts Centre. It is in a nicely restored old house, with a huge fully-equipped kitchen. The common area has lots of comfortable sofas, a TV lounge, dining area and internet access ($6 per hour) including wireless. The air-conditioned dorms are simple with good beds and the bathrooms are dated, but are clean nonetheless. They have a laundry, travel desk and snacks are available at reception.

5 Worcester Boulevard, Christchurch
15, 17, 29
(03) 3666 564
Website *www.yha.co.nz*
Dorm bed *$25-29 ($22-26 HI/YHA);* ***double/twin room*** *$68-88 ($65-85 HI/YHA)*
Credit cards *Amex, Diners, JCB, MC, UnionPay, Visa*
Reception open *8am-10pm daily*

Maintenance & cleanliness	★★★
Facilities	★★
Atmosphere & character	★★½
Security	★★★½
Overall rating	★★½

Rucksacker Backpackers

This place has seen a few improvements since its days as Bealey International. The large cosy dorms have good mattresses, and there is new carpet. The TV lounge has a few nice sofas and a new coat of paint. The kitchen is small and bland, though, and the outside common area is just a few picnic tables and a barbecue in a poorly maintained backyard. They have laundry facilities, internet access ($2 per hour) including Wi-Fi. There is a moderately good backpacker atmosphere here, but it is not great because it is on a busy street a few minutes from the centre. Reception staff can be a bit rude.

70 Bealey Avenue, Christchurch
10, 11, 12, 13, 18, 90, 92
(03) 377 7931
Website *www.rucksacker.com*
Dorm bed *$22 ($19 BBH);* ***double/twin room*** *$56 ($50 BBH)*
Credit cards *MC, Visa*
Reception open *9.30am-1.30pm & 3.30pm-9.30pm daily*

Maintenance & cleanliness	★★★
Facilities	★★
Atmosphere & character	★★★½
Security	★★★½
Overall rating	★★★

Shalom

This hostel is under new management and is currently undergoing renovation. It is an old house a few minutes from the city centre. The first thing you notice are the dated and tattered carpets throughout – hopefully they will be replaced. Furnishings are a bit old as well, but the bathrooms are nice and clean, and the dorms are getting there. There is a small kitchen and a new barbecue outside in the courtyard. It also boasts cheap internet access and a great sauna behind the house. The atmosphere is relatively quiet but the new management are friendly and helpful.

69 Bealey Avenue, Christchurch
10, 11, 12, 13, 18, 90, 92
(03) 3666 770
Dorm bed *$20-23 ($18-21 BBH);* ***single room*** *$38 ($35 BBH);* ***double/twin room*** *$56 ($50 BBH)*
Credit cards *MC, Visa*
Reception open *8am-8pm daily*

Maintenance & cleanliness	★★½
Facilities	★★
Atmosphere & character	★★★
Security	★★½
Overall rating	★★½

Sir Cedric's City Oasis Backpackers

Sir Cedric's is a motel in three buildings with surprisingly good facilities. There is a TV lounge with movies, clean bathrooms and a large fully-equipped kitchen. The dorms are spacious and colourful with comfortable bunks. They offer laundry, internet, several lounges, and an outdoor patio with a great spa pool and barbecue area. Security isn't very good, but they are planning to get lockers and video surveillance soon. It is a few minutes from the centre and has a laid-back atmosphere.

180 Peterborough Street, Christchurch
46
(03) 3669 531
***Dorm bed** $22-25 ($20-22 BBH); **double/twin room** $51-53 ($48-50 BBH)*
***Credit cards** MC, Visa*
***Reception open** 7.30am-9pm daily*

Maintenance & cleanliness	★★★
Facilities	★★★½
Atmosphere & character	★★
Security	★½
Overall rating	★★★½

Stonehurst Accommodation

Stonehurst combines several types of accommodation in a nicely maintained old hotel. The dorms are spacious with comfortable beds, but they are a bit dull. The bathrooms and kitchen are clean, although the fridges are only in the dorms; the lounge has internet terminals ($5 per hour) and big red sofas. There are nice outdoor common areas with gardens, a swimming pool and a nice big barbecue area. The only thing that really needs a change is the ugly dated carpet throughout the place. Reception has lockers, a pool table and a tour desk and they sell snacks and drinks. It has a good location, but a mediocre atmosphere.

241 Gloucester Street, Christchurch
7, 60, 77
(03) 379 4620 or 0508 STONED
***Website** www.stonehurst.co.nz*
***Dorm bed** $20-25; **single room** $62; **double room** $70-75; **campervan site** $30-35*
***Credit cards** Amex, Diners, JCB, MC, Visa*
***Reception open** 24 hours*

Maintenance & cleanliness	★★★
Facilities	★★★
Atmosphere & character	★★★
Security	★★★★
Overall rating	★★★

Thomas' Hotel

Thomas's is a tall old building with a nicely maintained interior and a good standard of accommodation. Dorms are a bit small and boring, but they are extremely clean and have a maximum of four beds. The kitchen and bathrooms are also well maintained and tidy and there is a big common room with pool table, books and snack machines plus, a barbecue in the backyard. It is a quiet and comfortable place to stay, right next to the entrance to the Arts Centre weekend market.

36 Hereford Street, Christchurch
29
(03) 379 9536
***Website** www.thomashotel.co.nz*
***Dorm bed** $22-25 ($21-24 VIP); **double room** $65-75 ($63-73 VIP)*
***Credit cards** Amex, Diners, JCB, MC, Visa*
***Reception open** 6.30am-9pm daily*

Maintenance & cleanliness	★★★½
Facilities	★★
Atmosphere & character	★★½
Security	★★★
Overall rating	★★★

Tranquil Lodge

Tranquil Lodge is a quiet and simple hostel. Unfortunately, for some that will surely translate to boring. It has an institutional feel, with long empty halls and a big TV lounge which needs a revamp, although it has a nice pool table. Dorms are also poorly maintained and the kitchen is quite messy. There is not much in the way of facilities except for laundry, a barbecue and a book exchange. Management are nice enough, but there isn't a great backpacker atmosphere.

440 Manchester Street, Christchurch
(03) 366 6500

Website *www.tranquil-lodge.co.nz*
Dorm bed *$23 ($20 BBH);* ***double/ twin room*** *$56 ($50 BBH)*
Credit cards *MC, Visa*
Reception open *24 hours*

Maintenance & cleanliness	★★
Facilities	★★½
Atmosphere & character	★★½
Security	★★
Overall rating	★★

Vagabond Backpackers

This hostel is a nicely maintained house not far from Cathedral Square. The dorms, some of which are in outside cottages, are very clean and breezy. There is a well-equipped kitchen; nice clean bathrooms and a TV lounge with free movies, comfy sofas and loads of books. There isn't much else to it. The atmosphere is convivial and management are warm and friendly.

232 Worcester Street, Christchurch
7, 60, 77
(03) 379 9677
Dorm bed *$23-25 ($20-23 BBH);* ***double room*** *$54-56 ($48-50 BBH);* ***twin room*** *$52-54 ($46-48 BBH)*
Credit cards *MC, Visa*
Reception open *8am-10pm daily*

Maintenance & cleanliness	★★★½
Facilities	★★½
Atmosphere & character	★★★½
Security	★★★½
Overall rating	★★★

SUBURBS

Avon City Backpackers

This is an old, run down hostel with little backpacker atmosphere and a location relatively far from the centre. It consists of two small houses with 18 beds, a small kitchen and ugly furniture. The bathrooms are kept very clean, and guests get towels to use; but some of the dorms smell musty, and there is not much of a common area besides the smoking table outside. The backyard doubles as a campground, and there is no internet access.

563 Worcester Street, Linwood
21, 83
(03) 981 5878
Dorm bed *$20*

Maintenance & cleanliness	★★
Facilities	★★½
Atmosphere & character	★★
Security	★★★½
Overall rating	★★

Drifters

This hostel is set in a big old house with a homely atmosphere. The dorms have thick mattresses and are made up with duvets. There is a TV lounge area with books and maps and most likely a resident dog to hang out with. Bathrooms are squeaky clean. The kitchen could use an update, but it has everything you need to cook, and there is an outside lounge area where guests hang out and have barbecues. They also have a laundry, internet access including Wi-Fi, and free pick up from the city centre. They are close to lots of shops and restaurants. The atmosphere here is not as good as some of the other hostels, but the owners make you feel at home.

408 Gloucester Street, Linwood
21, 83
(03) 9828 228
Website *www.drifters.co.nz*
Dorm bed *$ 22 ($19 BBH);* ***double/ twin room*** *$55 ($49 BBH)*
Credit cards *MC, Visa*
Reception open *7.30am-11pm daily*

Maintenance & cleanliness	★★★
Facilities	★★★½
Atmosphere & character	★★★★½
Security	★★½
Overall rating	★★★

Jailhouse Accommodation

This old prison, which was in use until 1999, has been carefully renovated and turned into an excellent hostel. Dorms are in cells, so most of them are quite small, but they are clean and have good beds. The bathrooms are exceptionally nice and clean, and the kitchen is also small, but fully equipped. There is a movie lounge with bean bags and a huge projection screen; and a café on-site with internet access, including Wi-Fi. Some of the cells, including the solitary confinement, have been kept in their old state, and are an interesting sight to see. Reception staff are outgoing and nice, and as expected, there is excellent security. Location is far from the centre, but near shops and restaurants, and they have free shuttle service.

338 Lincoln Road, Addington
7, 77
(03) 9827 777 or 0800 JAILHOUSE
Website *www.jail.co.nz*
Dorm bed *$25-28 ($22-25 BBH);* ***single room*** *$45 ($40 BBH);* ***double room*** *$69 ($63 BBH);* ***twin room*** *$61-69 ($55-63 BBH)*
Credit cards *MC, Visa*
Reception open *8am-10pm daily*

Maintenance & cleanliness	★★★★
Facilities	★★½
Atmosphere & character	★★★½
Security	★★★★
Overall rating	★★★½

MacKenzie's Backpackers

This hostel adjoins an old pub. The dorms and bathrooms are in need of an update but cleaned regularly. The kitchen is an absolute wreck, with old dirty appliances, cobwebs and a washing machine placed strangely in the middle. It seems not to be used or cleaned, ever. There is also not much common space besides a couple of bench seats with a huge TV plopped down right in front of them. It seems to cater mostly to travellers on working holiday.

51 Pages Road, Wainoni
5, 51
(03) 3899 014
Dorm bed *$20;* ***double room*** *$40*
Credit cards *Amex, Diners, MC, Visa*
Reception open *Mon-Wed 8.30am-11pm, Thu-Sat 8.30am-1am*

Maintenance & cleanliness	★½
Facilities	★
Atmosphere & character	½
Security	★
Overall rating	★

Marine Backpackers

The Marine is a very nicely maintained hostel with a great bar and a bottle shop on-site. It has a beachy feel with modern touches. There are surfboards, maps and colourful tiles in the kitchens and lounges and dorms are a bit plain but spacious. There are two fully-equipped kitchens and a warmly decorated lounge with a log fireplace (but no TV). Bathrooms are clean and modern and hostel also has laundry, internet access and a tour desk. It is just steps from shops and the beach, and 20 minutes from the centre of Christchurch. The family who runs it are warm and friendly. The only problem is security, as there are no lockers and bedroom doors do not lock.

26 Nayland Street, Sumner
3
(03) 3266 609
Website *www.themarine.co.nz*
Dorm bed *$23 ($20 BBH);* ***single room*** *$35 ($30 BBH);* ***double/twin room*** *$50-70 ($45-65 BBH)*
Credit cards *Amex, Diners, MC, Visa*
Reception open *9am-10pm daily*

Maintenance & cleanliness	★★★½
Facilities	★★½
Atmosphere & character	★★★
Security	★½
Overall rating	★★★

Point Break Backpackers

Point Break has been completely renovated and is now a modern, clean and spacious hostel with a good atmosphere. It is located just two blocks from the beach and it's a popular place for surfers. There is a café/restaurant downstairs that gets full at breakfast and lunchtimes. They have almost finished construction on a bar that will host karaoke nights. There is a lounge with a huge TV and a bright, clean fully stocked kitchen. The large dorms have new beds, although they get very cluttered when there are working holiday guests staying there. The hostel has laundry and internet access.

99 Seaview Road, New Brighton
5, 40, 42, 43, M
(03) 3882 050
Website *www.pointbreakbackpackers.co.nz*
Dorm bed *$20-25*
Credit cards *MC, Visa*

Maintenance & cleanliness	★★★½
Facilities	★★
Atmosphere & character	★★★
Security	★★½
Overall rating	★★★

Eating & Drinking

There are heaps of choices when it comes to eating cheap in Christchurch. Fast food places abound in the centre around Cathedral Square, and there are some cheap alfresco cafés around Cathedral Square and along High Street. **Loef's Bakery** *(225 Manchester Street, Christchurch)* is a hole-in-the-wall type of place with excellent coffee and sandwiches at low prices. **The Honey Pot Café** *(112 Lichfield Street, Christchurch)* is a great place for coffee with a groovy ambiance. Locals head to the food hall at **High to Hereford**, off High Street, for a large selection of Asian, Indian and Italian lunch bargains. If you feel like a snack, there are some great food stalls on Cathedral Square – the baked potatoes are a meal in themselves and cost next to nothing and fish and chips are not bad for the price either.

There are a few good value pubs in the city centre as well. **The Bard on Avon** *(corner Gloucester Street & Oxford Terrace, Christchurch)* has a great location and atmosphere, and **Pomeroy's** *(292 Kilmore Street, Christchurch)* is an authentic English-style pub with its own micro brewery. **Dux de Lux** *(41 Hereford Street, Christchurch)* is another brewpub near the Arts Centre that has a great beer garden.

For self-catering, you can save a lot by heading to one of the great value supermarkets. They are all about a 10-minute walk south of Cathedral Square (or a short ride on the free Shuttle bus). Otherwise, there are some smaller convenience stores scattered throughout the centre. The three main supermarkets in town are **New World** *(555 Colombo Street, Christchurch)*, **Pak'n Save** *(297 Moorhouse Avenue, Christchurch)*, and **Woolworths** *(347 Moorhouse Avenue, Christchurch)*.

If you are going to Sumner, the supermarket is just in the centre of town, and there is a groovy little place called the Dot Com Café where you can enjoy delicious food and desserts and use the internet or connect to Wi-Fi. There are also good fish and chips in town near the Esplanade.

Sights

Air Force Museum

Plane spotters will love this aviation museum that features 28 classic aircraft on display plus hands-on exhibits and displays of New Zealand Air Force history.

Wigram Air Base, 45 Harvard Avenue, Sockburn
5, 81
(03) 343 9532
Website *www.airforcemuseum.co.nz*
Admission *$15*
Open *10am-5pm daily*

Antarctic Centre

This tourist attraction near the airport is worth considering if you're interested in Antarctica, but it's no substitute for the real thing. It features a simulated Antarctic environment and you can even ride in a Hägglund Antarctic vehicle.

38 Orchard Road, Christchurch International Airport
29 (airport bus)
(03) 736 4846 or 0508 PENGUIN
Website *www.iceberg.co.nz*
Admission *$30; $48 including Hägglund ride*
Open *Jan-Mar 9am-7pm daily; Apr-Sep 9am-5.30pm daily; Oct-Dec 9am-7pm daily*

Arts Centre & Rutherford's Den

This complex of Gothic Revival buildings was originally the University of Canterbury. The Arts Centre is now a vibrant arts venue with cinemas, theatre and galleries plus shops, bars, cafés and a bustling weekend market.
Ernest Rutherford studied here when it was a university and his den has been made into a multimedia exhibit showcasing the scientist's life and achievements.

Worcester Boulevard, Christchurch
(03) 363 2836
Website *www.artscentre.org.nz & www.rutherfordsden.org.nz*

Admission *free*
Open *9.30am-5pm daily; guided tours 10am-3.30pm daily; Rutherford's Den 10am-5pm daily*

Canterbury Museum

This excellent museum is noted for its exhibitions on Antarctic exploration, Māori culture and natural history.
Rolleston Avenue, Christchurch
15, 17, 29
(03) 366 5000
Website *www.cantmus.govt.nz*
Admission *free; Discovery exhibit $2*
Open *Jan-Mar 9am-5.30pm daily; Apr-Sep 9am-5pm daily; Oct-Dec 9am-5.30pm daily*

Christchurch Art Gallery

The city's impressive new art museum features permanent collections plus a programme of visiting exhibits.
Corner Worcester Boulevard & Montreal Street, Christchurch
15, 17, 29 T
(03) 941 7300
Website *www.christchurchartgallery.org.nz*
Admission *free*
Open *Mon-Tue 10am-5pm, Wed 10am-9pm, Thu-Sun 10am-5pm*

Christ Church Cathedral

Although it is nothing special by European standards, the locals are very proud of their cathedral, which has been around almost as long as Christchurch. Visitors can climb the tower or take a tour of the cathedral.
Cathedral Square, Christchurch
7, 10, 11, 12, 13, 14, 15, 16, 17, 18, 29, 46, 60, 77, 90, 92, Shuttle T
(03) 366 0046
Website *www.christchurchcathedral.co.nz*
Admission *free*
Open *Mon-Sat 9am-5pm, Sun 7.30am-5pm; tours Mon-Fri 11am & 2pm, Sat 11am, Sun 11.30am*

Christchurch Gondola

This gondola ride in Christchurch's southern suburbs offers excellent views of the city centre and surrounding areas including Lyttelton Harbour, the Canterbury Plains, and the Southern Alps.
10 Bridle Path Road, Ferrymead
28
(03) 384 0700
Website *www.gondola.co.nz*
Admission *$22; combined gondola & tram ticket $30*
Open *10am-late daily*

Orana Wildlife Park

This wildlife park is home to a large variety of animals from around the globe with the focus on African animals such as cheetahs, giraffes, lions, monkeys and meerkats. Native animals include birds such as the kaka, kea and kiwi and reptiles like the tuatara.
McLeans Island Road, Papanui
(03) 359 7109
Website *www.oranawildlifepark.co.nz*
Admission *$21*
Open *10am-5pm daily (last entry 4.30pm)*

Southern Encounter Aquarium & Kiwi House

This small aquarium and kiwi house is centrally located right on Cathedral Square. It is home to a variety of local marine life and there is also an enclosure where you can see New Zealand's rare national bird – the kiwi.
Cathedral Square, Christchurch
7, 10, 11, 12, 13, 14, 15, 16, 17, 18, 29, 46, 60, 77, 90, 92, Shuttle T
(03) 359 0581
Website *www.southernencounter.co.nz*
Admission *$15*
Open *9am- 4.30pm daily*

Willowbank Wildlife Reserve

This wildlife park focuses on native bird life and it is best known for its excellent nocturnal kiwi tours. Unlike other kiwi houses that have glassed-in enclosures that recreate an artificial nocturnal environment, only Willowbank is open at night for a more natural look at this unique and rare bird.
Hussey Road, Styx
(03) 359 6226
Website *www.willowbank.co.nz*
Admission *$25 ($20 students)*
Open *10am-10pm daily; guided tours 11.30am, 2.30pm, 7.30pm, 8.30pm, 9.30pm daily*

Activities

Ballooning

Hot air ballooning over the Canterbury Plains is a popular activity that offers spectacular views of the surrounding countryside, although ballooning is said to be better in Methven. **Aoraki Balloon Safaris** (☎ *(03) 302 8172 or 0800 CLOUD 7; **website** www.nzballooning.co.nz)* and **Up Up and Away** (☎ *(03) 381 4600; **website** www.ballooning.co.nz)*. Ballooning trips cost between $285 and $310.

Jet Boating

Jet Thrills (☎ *(03) 385 1478; **website** www.jetthrills.com)* and **Wamak Alpine Jet** (☎ *(03) 318 4881; **website** www.waimakalpinejet.co.nz)* offer jet boat rides on the Waimakariri River. Jet Thrills operates from a site only 15 minutes from the city centre and is the cheaper of the two, costing $70-95. Waimak Alpine Jet cost a little more ($75-105), but they operate in the stunning Waimakariri Canyon.

Punting on the Avon

Christchurch is no substitute for Cambridge, but that doesn't mean that it can't try. Punting on the Avon is one of the more pleasant ways to see the city from the river.

2 Cambridge Terrace, Christchurch
☎ *(03) 366 0337*
***Website** www.punting.co.nz*
***Admission** $20*
***Open** Jan-Apr 9am-6pm daily; May-Sep 10am-4pm daily; Oct-Dec 9am-6pm daily*

Skydiving

The New Zealand Skydiving School offer tandem skydives as well as other skydiving options including a nine-stage accelerated freefall training programme.

Wigram Aerodrome
☎ *(03) 343 5542*
***Website** www.skydiving.co.nz*
***9000ft tandem jump** $265; **12000ft tandem jump** $299*

Wildlife Cruises

You can see Hector's dolphins and a variety of bird life from the wildlife spotting cruises that operate on Lyttelton Harbour.

17 Norwich Quay, Lyttelton
🚌 *28*
☎ *(03) 328 9078 or 0800 436 574*
***Website** www.blackcat.co.nz*
***Price** $52*
***Departs** Jan-Apr 2.30pm daily; May-Aug 1.30pm daily; Sep-Dec 2.30pm daily*

Akaroa & the Banks Peninsula

Formed from the remains of two now extinct volcanoes, the Banks Peninsula today offers the visitor outstanding natural beauty and abundant marine life. It is a great getaway, with scenic bays and harbours, steep green slopes covered in wildflowers and unique wildlife. The Banks Peninsula Track is a great hiking trail that can be completed in several days, staying in mountain huts. There are also opportunities for sailing, kayaking and surfing, and it is a good place to swim with Hector's dolphins, the world's rarest. Okains Bay has a good sandy beach, and is growing in popularity due to its great surf and village atmosphere. Around the peninsula are colonies of seals and nesting penguins.

Akaroa was established by French settlers just after the British colonisation of New Zealand, and the town still has a distinctly French charm. There are great cafés and boutiques along its quaint streets, nice colonial architecture and restaurants serving French cuisine. Even the street names are French. The Akaroa Harbour is spectacular, and is a great place to take a cruise. There are also lavender fields, wineries and specialty cheese shops in and around Akaroa.

Practical Information

Akaroa Visitor Information Centre

80 Rue Lavaud, Akaroa
☎ *(03) 304 8600*
***Website** www.akaroa.com*
***Open** 9am-5pm daily*

INTERNET ACCESS

Le Bon Email
57 Rue Lavaud, Akaroa
☎ *(03) 304 7782*
Website *www.bon-accord.co.nz*

Turenne Dairy, Coffee Shop & Internet
74 Rue Lavaud, Akaroa
☎ *(03) 304 7005*

Coming & Going

Astro Coachlines (☎ *0800 800 575; **website** www.akaroabus.co.nz)* and Akaroa Shuttle (☎ *0800 500 929; **website** www.akaroashuttle.co.nz)* go to Akaroa on the Banks Peninsula. They both depart from the information centre on Cathedral Square.

Accommodation

AKAROA TOWN

Bon Accord Backpackers

This cosy hostel is in the centre of Akaroa. It is a small place comprised of two self-contained cottages that sleep only 14 in several double rooms and a six bed-dorm. The accommodation is quite nice with made-up beds that come with their own hot water bottles and a pair of slippers for you to wear around the house. There is a nice garden area, a couple of kitchens and lounges and wireless internet (Zenbu; 10c per Mb). Guests have free use of bikes.

57 Rue Lavaud, Akaroa
☎ *(03) 304 7782*
Website *www.bon-accord.co.nz*
Dorm bed *$25 ($22 BBH);* ***double/twin room*** *$60 ($54 BBH)*
Reception open *10am-8pm daily*

Maintenance & cleanliness	★★★
Facilities	★★½
Atmosphere & character	★★★
Security	★
Overall rating	★★½

Chez La Mer Backpackers

This hostel is looking a little tired. The bright pink cottage-like exterior is inviting, but inside it is a bit drab. Amenities include two tiny kitchens and a small new outdoor kitchen; clean and well maintained bathrooms; a small common room with a nice sofa and a fireplace plus an outdoor area with a gazebo. Accommodation is in colourful dorms with wooden bunks with thin mattresses.

50 Rue Lavaud, Akaroa
☎ *(03) 304 7024*
Website *www.chezlamer.co.nz*
Dorm bed *$25 ($22 BBH);* ***double/twin room*** *$60-70 ($54-64 BBH)*
Reception open *9am-9pm daily*

Maintenance & cleanliness	★★★½
Facilities	★★½
Atmosphere & character	★★★
Security	★½
Overall rating	★★★

Dolphin Backpackers

This new hostel is a in an old characterless house near the harbour that has mostly double and twin rooms and a few dorm beds. It is comprised of two buildings, one of which doesn't have a kitchen. The dorms are bland but have good beds and are made up with duvets. The common area consists of just a few old sofas plus some books and a TV. Bathrooms are new and clean. It has a mature feel to it and not much of a backpacker atmosphere at all – in fact many young backpackers would find it quite boring. But they do offer discount kayaking tours and the owners are extremely friendly.

108 Rue Jolie, Akaroa
☎ *(03) 304 7136*
Dorm bed *$25;* ***single room*** *$50;* ***double/twin room*** *$60;*
Reception open *9.30am-8pm daily*

Maintenance & cleanliness	★★½
Facilities	★★
Atmosphere & character	★½
Security	★
Overall rating	★★

ELSEWHERE ON THE BANKS PENINSULA

Le Bons Bay Backpackers

This is a wonderful little hostel in a rustic old farmhouse. It is perched on a hillside with stunning views from every angle; even the bathtub has a view. There is a cosy lounge with a piano and fireplace, and nice gardens with hammocks. The dorms are cute and clean, with single beds in A-frame lofts; there are also separate huts with double beds and panoramic views. The kitchen is homely and beautifully maintained. The management and staff are welcoming and pleasant; they make breakfast with homemade breads as well as a famously delicious evening meal which costs $14. It's the perfect alternative to touristy Akaroa town.

Off Summit Road, Le Bons Bay
☎ *(03) 304 8582*
Website *www.lebonsbay.co.nz*
Dorm bed *$25 ($22 BBH);* ***double room*** *$58 ($52 BBH)*
Open *Jan-May & Oct-Dec;* ***reception open*** *7.30am-9.30pm daily*

Maintenance & cleanliness	★★★★
Facilities	★★★½
Atmosphere & character	★★★★★
Security	½
Overall rating	★★★½

Halfmoon Cottage

This hostel is in an old white house with handsome furniture and tasteful décor. The kitchen is light, airy and clean; same with the bathrooms (which have hairdryers). There are only a few dorm beds, but they are clean and spacious. There is a sitting room with log fire, TV, piano and lots of books; a quiet dining area with internet access ($4 per hour) and outside there are flower gardens and a large veranda with chairs and tables. Guests have free use of bicycles and they organise kayaking trips. It has a very quiet atmosphere.

State Highway 75, Barrys Bay
☎ *(03) 304 5050*
Website *www.halfmoon.co.nz*
Dorm bed *$25 ($22 BBH);* ***single room*** *$45 ($40 BBH);* ***double/twin room*** *$68 ($60 BBH)*
Credit cards *MC, Visa*
Reception open *8am-10pm daily*

Maintenance & cleanliness	★★★★
Facilities	★★★½
Atmosphere & character	★★★½
Security	★
Overall rating	★★★

Onuku Farm Hostel

Onuku Farm is a tiny hostel brimming with character. It is located a few kilometres east of Akaroa town on a 1215ha farm and it is a great place to get away. It is also a good place for WWOOFing. The dorms are clean and colourful, there are two cute kitchens (one outside), and there is a nice lounge area with fluffy sofas and a fireplace. There are laundry facilities, a barbecue, and they arrange tours and brew their own beer. They also offer camping, rustic summer huts, and brilliant "stargazers", which are small A-frames with double mattresses, candles and glass ceilings (perfect for couples). It is quiet and reception staff are amiable.

Hamiltons Road, Onuku
☎ *(03) 304 7066*
Website *www.onukufarm.co.nz*
Dorm bed *$26-27 ($22-23 BBH);* ***double/twin room*** *$29 ($26 BBH);* ***camping*** *$12;* ***summer hut*** *(no electric/heat) $14;* ***stargazer*** *$17*
Reception open *9am-1pm & 3pm-9pm*

Canterbury

daily

Maintenance & cleanliness	★★★½
Facilities	★★½
Atmosphere & character	★★★★
Security	★
Overall rating	★★★

Eating & Drinking

Thanks to its French heritage, Akaroa has some wonderful French influenced cuisine, although the more upmarket places may be too hard on the budget. There are quite a few small bakeries that sell freshly baked bread and sandwiches, and many of them are cheap. You will also find a lot of street side cafés with great coffee and pastries. A good, cheap lunch can be found at the **Turenne Café** *(74 Rue Lavaud, Akaroa)* in the centre of town. There is a small supermarket on Rue Lavaud.

The Banks Peninsula's best place to eat isn't in Akaroa, but 14km away at **Le Bons Bay Backpackers** *(off Summit Road, Le Bons Bay)*. If you're staying at Le Bons Bay, you must eat in and enjoy their legendary evening meal, which costs only $14. It's so good that many backpackers stay an extra couple of nights to enjoy more of the scrumptious food.

Sights

Akaroa Museum

This small museum is set in three historic buildings and features exhibits on Akaroa's unique history.

71 Rue Lavaud, Akaroa
☎ *(03) 304 1013*
***Admission** $4*
***Open** summer 10.30am-4.30pm daily; winter 10.30am-4pm daily*

Activities

CRUISES

There are several wildlife spotting cruises operating around the Banks Peninsula.

Black Cat (☎ *0800 436 574; **website** www.blackcat.co.nz)* operates scenic cruises on Akaroa Harbour where you can see the region's marine life. Black Cat cruises cost $55.

Le Bons Bay Nature Tours (☎ *(03) 304 8582; **website** www.lebonsbay.co.nz)* is a great value dolphin-spotting cruise run by Le Bons Bay Backpackers. It's a more personal tour than the cruises that run out of Akaroa as it is just a small boat with a maximum of eight people and it travels to places other boats do not go. This cruise costs only $30.

HIKING

There are several walking tracks on the Banks Peninsula, but the best is the Banks Peninsula Track (2-4 days), which goes from Akaroa to Onuku via several secluded bays.

SWIMMING WITH DOLPHINS

The Hector's dolphin is one of the world's smallest and rarest dolphins. **Black Cat** (☎ *0800 436 574; **website** www.blackcat.co.nz)* run trips on the harbour where you have the opportunity to swim with them. There are only 10 swimmers allowed on each trip, which means that there is a good chance of interacting with the dolphins. This trip gives you two hours on the harbour and costs $110.

Methven & Mount Hutt

Methven is a small town that quietly prepares for the annual onslaught of skiers and snowboarders who come for the snow on Mount Hutt. It has a great range of accommodation, but budget places fill up months in advance for winter. There are not a lot of facilities in town, but there are a couple of good pubs, and during snow season the atmosphere is buzzing day and night. It is surrounded by Canterbury farmland, 92km from Christchurch. In the area there is good salmon fishing, golfing and jet boating in the Rakaia Gorge.

Practical Information

Methven i-SITE Visitor Centre

121 Main Street, Methven
☎ *(03) 302 8955*
***Website** www.methven.net.nz*
***Open** Mon-Fri 9am-5pm, Sat-Sun 11am-4pm*

Coming & Going & Local Transport

Methven Travel (☎ *(03) 302 8106; **website** www.methventravel.co.nz)* run a Christchurch-Methven shuttle service and during the ski season they also operate a bus service linking Methven with the Mount Hutt ski area. Buses depart from their office at 93 Main Street.

Accommodation

Methven gets busy in the ski season so it's a good idea to book your accommodation well in advance if you plan on visiting during winter.

Alpenhorn Chalet

This is a small hostel with great ambience. The dorms are very spacious and have wonderfully comfortable beds made-up with thick duvets. The friendly owner is a chef, so the kitchen is fully equipped, modern and spotless; and there is a small lounge with nice sofas, Sky TV and a fireplace. They also have a great atrium with a glass ceiling and a spa pool, although it only works in winter. There are also laundry facilities and free internet access. It has a very low-key atmosphere and is in a quiet residential area.

44 Allen Street, Methven
☎ *(03) 302 8779*
***Dorm bed** $25*

Maintenance & cleanliness	★★★★
Facilities	★★★
Atmosphere & character	★★★½
Security	★★
Overall rating	★★★½

Big Tree Lodge

This hostel is currently changing management, and will be seeing some changes. For the time being, it is a very well maintained little hostel with single made-up beds and a good amount of charm. There is a big common lounge with a log fire and TV, a small but very well kept kitchen, laundry and internet access. There is also an outdoor herb garden and barbecue plus a ski storage shed. It is next door to Redwood Lodge.

25 South Belt, Methven
☎ *(03) 302 9575*
***Website** www.mt-hutt.com*
***Dorm bed** $28-30 ($25-27 BBH); **double/twin room** $64 ($58 BBH)*
***Credit cards** MC, Visa*

Maintenance & cleanliness	★★★½
Facilities	★★
Atmosphere & character	★★★½
Security	★½
Overall rating	★★★

Kowhai House Lodge & Backpackers

This hostel is a small bright yellow house with good facilities, which include a huge common lounge with TV and big sofas, a massive kitchen, laundry, a ski tuning room, drying room and a spa pool in the back. There are several fireplaces throughout the house and the place is in good condition, although the bathrooms could use some work. Accommodation is in dorms with big comfy beds made up with fluffy duvets. They also have free internet and Wi-Fi access.

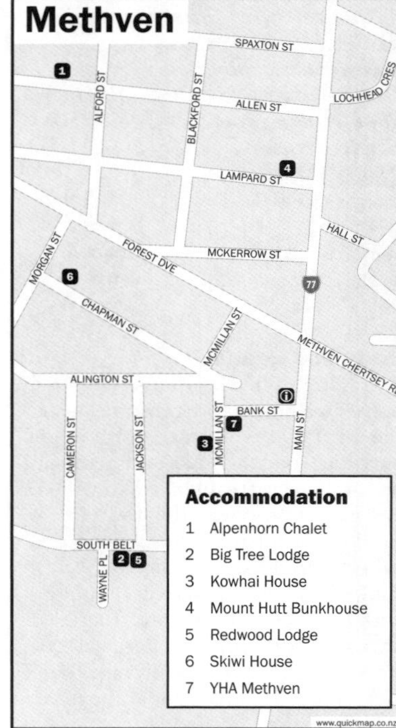

17 McMillan Street, Methven
☎ *(03) 302 8887*
Website *www.kowhaihouse.co.nz*
Dorm bed *$28-30 ($25-27 BBH);* ***double/twin room*** *$33-40 ($29-35 BBH);* ***triple room*** *$36 ($32 BBH); prices include breakfast*
Credit cards *MC, Visa*
Reception open *8am-10pm daily*

Maintenance & cleanliness	★★★
Facilities	★★★
Atmosphere & character	★★★
Security	★
Overall rating	★★★

Mount Hutt Bunkhouse

This hostel has a good location and clean facilities that include a cosy lounge with a log fire and a big screen TV with DVDs, a nice fully equipped kitchen, laundry, a drying room and a ski tuning room. There is also internet access ($6 per hour) including Wi-Fi. It doesn't have as much character as some of the other places, but management are outgoing and friendly, which gives it a good atmosphere.
8 Lampard Street, Methven
☎ *(03) 302 8894*
Website *www.mthuttbunks.co.nz*
Dorm bed *$23-25 ($20-22 BBH);* ***double/twin room*** *$54 ($48 BBH)*
Credit cards *MC, Visa*

Maintenance & cleanliness	★★★½
Facilities	★★★½
Atmosphere & character	★★★½
Security	★½
Overall rating	★★★

Redwood Lodge

This hostel is in a small rose-coloured house in a quiet residential area near the town centre. Themed dorm rooms have big wooden bunks and made-up beds (with electric blankets in winter), and guests are supplied with fresh towels. All the rooms have spotless en suite bathrooms, and there is a well equipped kitchen and a cosy lounge with Sky TV and a log fire. They also have laundry facilities, internet access, a drying room and a ski storage room. Guests receive a discount at the local ski supply shop.
25 South Belt, Methven
☎ *(03) 302 8964*
Website *www.snowboardnz.com*
Dorm bed *$28-30 ($27 BBH);* ***single room*** *$60 ($55 BBH);* ***double room*** *$65-80 ($60-75 BBH);* ***triple room*** *$110 ($105 BBH);* ***family room*** *$110-115 ($105 BBH)*
Credit cards *MC, Visa*

Maintenance & cleanliness	★★★★
Facilities	★★★½
Atmosphere & character	★★★½
Security	★½
Overall rating	★★★

Skiwi House

This is a small hostel with a big personality. It has an excellent lounge/common area, with purple and green walls, funky décor and international feel; guests can chill out here (under a tree) with a book or watch a video. There is also a well equipped kitchen, internet access, laundry, drying room and a barbecue and trampoline in the backyard. The dorms are a bit run-down but clean, although the bathrooms are spotless and nicely renovated.
30 Chapman Street, Methven
☎ *(03) 302 8772*
Website *www.skiwihouse.co.nz*
Dorm bed *$22 ($20 BBH);* ***double/twin room*** *$50 ($46 BBH)*
Credit cards *MC, Visa*

Maintenance & cleanliness	★★★½
Facilities	★★
Atmosphere & character	★★★★
Security	★½
Overall rating	★★★

YHA Methven

Methven's YHA is a brilliant hostel in two almost identical buildings in the town centre. The kitchens are new, clean and fully equipped, the bathrooms and dorms are immaculate, and the dorms have sturdy wooden bunks. There are two common areas with huge windows boasting excellent views of Mount Hutt. The excellent amenities include Sky TV and videos, a ski storage room and a spa pool. There are lots of freebies including free internet (including Wi-Fi), free use of bicycles, golf clubs, fishing gear, tea and coffee, and a great free breakfast. Management are talkative and friendly, and have tons of good advice on activities in the area. This place has the best backpacker atmosphere of the lot.

Corner Bank & McMillan Streets, Methven
☎ *(03) 302 8999*
Website *www.stayyha.com*
Dorm bed *$27-30 ($25-27 HI/YHA);* ***single room*** *$49;* ***double/twin room*** *$76-86; prices include breakfast*
Credit cards *MC, Visa*
Reception open *7am-10pm daily*

Maintenance & cleanliness	★★★★
Facilities	★★★★
Atmosphere & character	★★★½
Security	★
Overall rating	★★★½

Eating & Drinking

Methven is a small town, so there is not much to choose from. There are two supermarkets in the centre of town where you can gather basic cooking supplies. **Charming Thai** *(17 Forest Drive, Methven)* has authentic and relatively cheap food. There are two fish and chip shops in town, the **Blue Pub** *(The Square, Methven)* has the best. Stop in at **Cafe Primo E Secundo** *(38 McMillan Street, Methven)* for a great coffee in an eclectic setting. **Uncle Dominic's Pizza** *(Forest Drive, Methven)* is a local favourite, and they deliver anywhere in town.

Activities

BALLOONING

Methven is said to be the best hot air ballooning destination in New Zealand, boasting spectacular views of the Southern Alps as you gently float over the Canterbury Plains. **Aoraki Balloon Safaris** (☎ *(03) 302 8172 or 0800 CLOUDS;* ***website*** *www.nzballooning.co.nz)* operate balloon rides that cost $295-345.

BUNGEE JUMPING

Mt Hutt Bungy (☎ *(03) 302 9969 or 0800 1 BUNGY;* ***website*** *www.mthuttbungy.com)* claims to be New Zealand's highest, but that's only because it is on top of a mountain. Prices start at $89 for the 43m jump and during winter you can ski or snowboard off a specially designed ramp for a powder touchdown.

JET BOATING

Rakaia Gorge Scenic Jet (☎ *(03) 318 6515)* and **River Tours** (☎ *(03) 318 6574;* ***website*** *www.rivertours.co.nz)* operate jet boat trips in the Rakaia Gorge near Methven. Half-hour rides cost around $70.

SKIING

Mount Hutt *(**website** www.nzski.com/mthutt/)* has a long ski season, which combined with its close proximity to Christchurch ensures that it is a busy resort, both with skiers and snowboarders.

A one-day lift pass costs $87 or $43 for a pass restricted to beginners lifts.

Arthurs Pass

Arthurs Pass is a tiny village seated in a valley surrounded by the high peaks of the Southern Alps. Its main function is as a beginning, end or stopover for hikers traversing the mountains. It is also a stop on the east-west *TranzAlpine* train between Greymouth and Christchurch. The beautiful scenery (especially when snow is covering the peaks) makes for a lovely drive and it's a great place to spend a day or two.

Practical Information

Arthurs Pass National Park Visitor Centre

State Highway 73, Arthurs Pass
☎ *(03) 318 9211*
Website *www.doc.govt.nz*
Open *8am-5pm daily*

Coming & Going

The *TranzAlpine*, New Zealand's most spectacular rail journey passes through Arthurs Pass on the route between Christchurch and Greymouth.

InterCity coaches don't pass through here but Atomic Shuttles (☎ *(03) 322 8883;* ***website*** *www.atomictravel.co.nz)*

do on their Christchurch-Hokitika service.

Accommodation

Mountain House YHA

This hostel consists of a large main building and several smaller ones. The main building has a huge modern fully-equipped kitchen, two lounges with internet access and immaculately clean dorms with wooden bunks and calming colours. The other smaller building has a cosy lounge and a smaller but more colourful kitchen and nice bathrooms. There are log fires and under-floor heating as well as electric blankets throughout. They also offer self-contained cottages, which are adorable and well maintained. This is an excellent hostel with friendly staff.

Main Road, Arthurs Pass
(03) 318 9258
***Website** www.yha.co.nz*
***Dorm bed** $27-29 ($24-26 BBH, HI/YHA); **single room** $67 ($64 BBH, HI/YHA); **double/twin room** $70 ($64 BBH, HI/YHA); **triple room** $93 ($84 BBH, HI/YHA)*
***Credit cards** MC, Visa*
***Reception open** 9am-7pm daily*

Maintenance & cleanliness	★★★★
Facilities	★★½
Atmosphere & character	★★★½
Security	★★
Overall rating	★★★½

Rata Lodge Backpackers

Rata Lodge is really just a house on a hill about ten minutes north of Arthurs Pass. It is secluded and quiet, and consists of a couple of dorm rooms with single beds and some nice double rooms. There is a well equipped kitchen, clean bathrooms and spacious dorms with electric blankets. All rooms have en suite facilities. It is close to the mountains and some glow-worm trails. The atmosphere here is very quiet, and management are friendly.

State Highway 73, Otira, Arthurs Pass
(03) 738 2822
***Dorm bed** $ 28 ($25 BBH); **double room** $70*
***Reception open** 8am-11pm daily*

Maintenance & cleanliness	★★★
Facilities	★★
Atmosphere & character	★★
Security	★
Overall rating	★★½

Hiking

Arthurs Pass National Park has a good selection of hiking trails.

Short walks include the **Devil's Punchbowl Waterfall Walk** *(1 hour return)*, which follows the Bealey River and then climbs to the base of this impressive 131m waterfall. The easy **Bridal Veil Track** *(1½ hours return)* rewards you with nice views of Arthur's Pass village. There is also a good selection of full day walks.

Geraldine

About 40 minutes north of Timaru on the scenic inland route, Geraldine is a pleasant farming town that makes a quiet alternative to Timaru. The area around Geraldine offers white water rafting and great walking trails through lowland podocarp forest. The Rangitata River Valley has spectacular alpine scenery and was the location for some of the *Lord of the Rings* scenes.

The town itself has an evident artistic flair with craft shops lining the main street, and it has nice rose gardens and an historic cinema. It is also home to the Historical Museum and the excellent Vintage Car and Machinery Museum.

Practical Information

Geraldine i-SITE Visitor Centre

Corner Talbot & Cox Streets, Geraldine
(03) 693 1006
***Website** www.southisland.org.nz*

Coming & Going

Buses stop in Geraldine en route between Christchurch and Queenstown.

Atomic Shuttles *((03) 349 0697; **website** www.atomictravel.co.nz)*, InterCity Coachlines *((03) 365 1113; **website** www.intercity.co.nz)* and Naked Bus *(0900 62533; **website** www.nakedbus.com)* stop outside the i-SITE Visitor Centre at the corner of Cox and

Talbot Streets. Southern Link K Bus (☎ *(03) 358 8355 or 0508 458 835;* ***website*** *www.southernlinkkbus.co.nz)* stops outside Oaks Restaurant *(72 Talbot Street, Geraldine).*

Accommodation

Rawhiti Backpackers

This is a nice hostel in an old maternity hospital. It offers clean, spacious dorms with comfortable beds and funky themes. The kitchen is worn but well equipped, and the bathrooms are renovated and spotlessly clean. The huge common room has Sky TV and there is a sunny dining area as well plus the usual laundry and internet facilities, and they offer optional (and good) pizzas in the evening and breakfast in the morning. Management are genial and knowledgeable about the area.

27 Hewlings Street, Geraldine
☎ *(03) 693 8252*
Website *www.rawhitibackpackers.co.nz*
Dorm bed *$24 ($20 BBH);* ***single room*** *$34 ($30);* ***double/twin room*** *$58 ($50 BBH)*
Credit cards *MC, Visa*
Reception open *8am-10am & 3.30pm-8pm daily*

Maintenance & cleanliness	★★★
Facilities	★★
Atmosphere & character	★★★
Security	★★
Overall rating	★★★½

Sights

Geraldine Historical Society Museum

Geraldine's small museum has exhibits of local history including a manual telephone exchange.

5 Cox Street, Geraldine
☎ *(03) 693 7028*
Admission *free*
Open *Mon-Sat 10am-noon & 1.30pm-3.30pm, Sun 1.30pm-3.30pm*

Geraldine Vintage Car & Machinery Museum

This transport museum has 1400 exhibits including a 1929 Spartan biplan and 101 tractors including the oldest working tractor in New Zealand.

178 Talbot Street, Geraldine
☎ *(03) 693 8756*
Admission *$5*
Open *Jan-May & Nov-Dec 10am-4pm daily*

Timaru

Timaru is a port city about 160km south of Christchurch and many travellers stop here on their way along the coast. While not a major tourist destination, Timaru does offer a nice seaside location and a walkable historic centre. The few attractions can be seen in a day or two, but there are several annual festivals including the Festival of Roses and the Caroline Bay Carnival. Worthwhile activities here range from a free brewery tour to New Zealand's third largest public art collection and the sandy beach at Caroline Bay.

Practical Information

Timaru i-SITE Visitor Centre

2 George Street, Timaru
☎ *(03) 688 6163*
Website *www.southisland.org.nz/timaru.asp*
Open *Mon-Fri 8.30am-5pm, Sat-Sun 10am-3pm*

Coming & Going

Atomic Shuttles (☎ *(03) 349 0697;* ***website*** *www.atomictravel.co.nz)*, InterCity Coachlines (☎ *(03) 365 1113;* ***website*** *www.intercity.co.nz)*, Naked Bus (☎ *0900 62533;* ***website*** *www.nakedbus.com)* and Southern Link K Bus (☎ *(03) 358 8355 or 0508 458 835;* ***website*** *www.southernlinkkbus.co.nz)* stop at the old train station on Station Street in Timaru en route between Christchurch and Dunedin.

Local Transport

Timaru has a good local bus service (☎ *(03) 688 5544;* ***website*** *www.metroinfo.org.nz/timIndex.html)* with city bus routes and regional services to Twizel and Lake Tekapo.

A single fare in the city costs $1.15 including free transfers and an all day pass costs $2.30. Buses do not run on Sundays.

Accommodation

1873 Wanderer Backpackers

This large, bright hostel is on the main road into town with easy access to the beach. Dorms have made-up beds and double-paned glass to keep out the noise from the road; bathrooms and common areas are nice and tidy, and the kitchen is a bit worn down but is clean and well equipped. There are laundry facilities, internet access ($6 per hour) including wireless, a TV lounge with DVDs and a back garden with fruit trees. Guests have free use of bicycles.

24 Evans Street, Timaru
Grantlea, Timaru-Temuka
(03) 688 8795
***Dorm bed** $24 ($ 20 BBH); **single room** $27 ($25 BBH); **double room** $54 ($50 BBH)*
***Reception open** 7am-10pm daily*

Maintenance & cleanliness	★★★½
Facilities	★★½
Atmosphere & character	★★★½
Security	★½
Overall rating	★★★

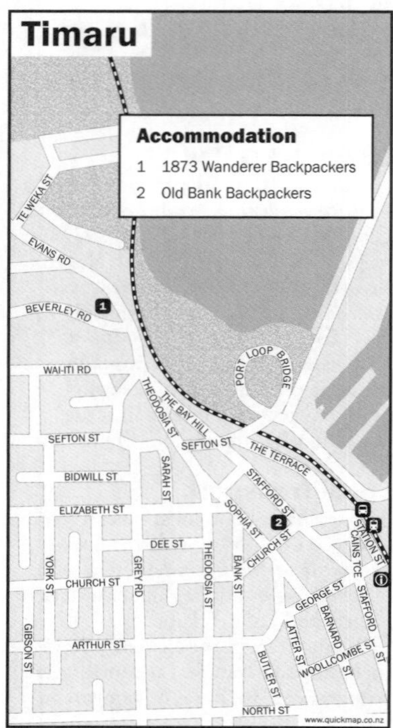

Old Bank Backpackers

This hostel is above a good pub in the town centre. It has recently been renovated and offers a good standard of accommodation. Dorms have new made-up beds in metal bunks (and some single beds), and the bathrooms are clean and bright. The kitchen is small with limited facilities, but it is kept clean by the friendly owners. They offer free breakfast, internet access, and drink vouchers for the bar/café downstairs.

232 Stafford Street, Timaru
(03) 686 9098
***Website** www.oldbankcafe.co.nz*
***Dorm bed** $25-30; **double room** $50*
***Credit cards** MC, Visa*
***Reception open** 8am-11pm daily*

Maintenance & cleanliness	★★★½
Facilities	★★½
Atmosphere & character	★★★
Security	★★
Overall rating	★★★

Eating & Drinking

The city centre has streets lined with cheap cafés and takeaway spots. **Sopheze Coffee Lounge** *(190 Stafford Street, Timaru)* is a great place to chill out with a good espresso. For a good atmosphere, the **Purple Lizard Café** *(332 Stafford Street, Timaru)* is a great spot for lunch. For cheaper fare, head to **May's Bakery** *(292 Stafford Street, Timaru)* for award-winning pies at low prices. There are inexpensive Asian restaurants everywhere, most notably along Evans and Stafford Streets.

Timaru's supermarkets include **Countdown** *(9 Browne Street, Timaru)*, **Pak'n Save** *(Evans Street, Timaru)* and **Woolworths** *(Church Street, Timaru)*.

Sights

DB Mainland Brewery

New Zealand's best value brewery tour lets you take a look at the brewing process at DB's Mainland Brewery on Sheffield Street

Sheffield Street, Washdyke
(03) 688 2059
***Website** www.dbgroup.co.nz*

Admission *free*
Tours *Mon-Fri 10.30am*

South Canterbury Museum
This museum features exhibits relating to the region's nature and history with displays on local Māori history, whaling and European settlement.
Perth Street, Timaru
☎ *(03) 687 7212*
Website *www.timaru.govt.nz/museum/*
Admission *free*
Open *Tue-Fri 10am-4.30pm, Sat-Sun 1.30pm-4.30pm*

Lake Tekapo

This small lakeside village is a hugely popular stopover en route from Christchurch to Queenstown. It boasts incredibly blue water and stunning views of Aoraki/Mount Cook, making it one of the most photographed spots on the island. There are several good accommodation options here, and it is worth staying a night to see the brilliant starry skies from the observatory on Mount John. It is a popular skiing spot in winter and in summer its walking tracks and kayaking are popular.

Coming & Going

Atomic Shuttles *(☎ (03) 349 0697;* ***website*** *www.atomictravel.co.nz)*, InterCity Coachlines *(☎ (03) 365 1113;* ***website*** *www.intercity.co.nz)*, Naked Bus *(☎ 0900 62533;* ***website*** *www.nakedbus.com)* and Southern Link K Bus *(☎ (03) 358 8355 or 0508 458 835;* ***website*** *www.southernlinkkbus.co.nz)* services stop in Tekapo en route between Christchurch and Queenstown. Most buses stop at the Shell Service Station, but InterCity stops outside High Country Crafts.

Timaru's local Metro bus service *(☎ (03) 688 5544;* ***website*** *www.metroinfo.org.nz/timIndex.html)* has a regional route that runs from Timaru to Twizel via Tekapo. The Cook Connection *(☎ 025 583 211;* ***website*** *www.cookconnect.co.nz)* shuttle goes to Twizel and Aoraki/Mount Cook. It departs from the information centre and will also pick up from Tekapo's hostels.

Accommodation

Lakefront Backpackers Lodge
This is a new purpose-built hostel with a pleasant lakeside location. It features a great common room with huge windows, a big log fire and nice TV. Dorm rooms are on the small side, but they have new mattresses and are exceptionally clean; the fully equipped kitchen is modern with lots of stainless steel and brand new appliances and the bathrooms are spotless. There is a nice outdoor barbecue area with a view, and they have internet access, laundry and travel desk. This place has a good backpacker atmosphere.
2 Lake Side Drive, Tekapo
☎ *(03) 680 6227 or 0800 853 853*
Dorm bed *$26*
Credit cards *MC, Visa*

Maintenance & cleanliness	★★★★★
Facilities	★★★
Atmosphere & character	★★★
Security	★½
Overall rating	★★★½

Lake Tekapo Budget Accommodation
This hostel is part of the Lake Tekapo Scenic Resort, but the hostel section isn't as well maintained and is hidden from the lake views enjoyed by the rest of the property. The dorms are huge, with comfortable made-up beds and towels. There is a small lounge with Sky TV, internet access ($9 per hour) including wireless, a ski room and a kitchen that is poorly maintained with the bare minimum of dishes and appliances. It has a very quiet, almost depressing, atmosphere; however you cannot get more central than this.
Lakeside Drive, Tekapo
☎ *(03) 6806 825*
Website *www.laketekapo-accommodation.co.nz*
Dorm bed *$25;* ***double room*** *$80*
Credit cards *Amex, Diners, MC, Visa*
Reception open *7am-9pm daily*

Maintenance & cleanliness	★★★
Facilities	★★
Atmosphere & character	★★
Security	★½
Overall rating	★★½

Lake Tekapo YHA

This is a good YHA hostel in a lakefront location near town. It is bright and colourful, with photos and maps on the walls and stars on the ceiling in the common room. The common room has big cosy sofas, a good log fire, a piano and a million-dollar view. Dorms are on the small side, but they are clean with metal bunks. There is a fully-equipped kitchen, with a rice cooker and chopsticks; clean bathrooms; internet access ($6 per hour); laundry facilities; a travel desk and smiling, helpful staff.

3 Simpson Lane, Tekapo
☎ *(03) 680 6857*
Website *www.yha.co.nz*
Dorm bed *$26-27 ($23-24 HI/YHA);* ***single room*** *$55 ($52 HI/YHA);* ***double/twin room*** *$67 ($64 HI/YHA);* ***camping*** *$12 per person*
Credit cards *MC, Visa*
Reception open *8am-1pm & 3.30pm-7.30pm daily*

Maintenance & cleanliness	★★★★½
Facilities	★★★
Atmosphere & character	★★★½
Security	★★★
Overall rating	★★★★

Tailor-Made Tekapo Backpackers

This is the closest you'll get to feeling like home in Tekapo. The small hostel is comprised of three buildings and offers a warm and cosy lounge and a large, well equipped kitchen. Accommodation is in heated rooms with single comfortable beds. There are nice gardens surrounding the hostel.

9-11 Aorangi Crescent, Tekapo
☎ *(03) 680 6700*
Website *www.tailor-made-backpackers.co.nz*
Dorm bed *$25-27 ($22-24 BBH);* ***single room*** *$48 ($45 BBH);* ***double/twin room*** *$62-74 ($56-68 BBH)*
Credit cards *MC, Visa*
Reception open *8am-8pm daily*

Maintenance & cleanliness	★★★
Facilities	★½
Atmosphere & character	★★★
Security	★
Overall rating	★★½

Eating & Drinking

There are no banks or ATMs in the village and prices are high so you should consider bringing your own groceries. Otherwise, there is a small supermarket in the centre of town. There are some takeaway lunch spots with moderately priced food. Doughboy's Bakery has a line out the door at midday for their cheap meals and delicious pies. Jade Palace Chinese also does a cheap lunch takeaway menu.

Activities

SCENIC FLIGHTS

Air Safaris (☎ *(03) 680 6880;* ***website*** *www.airsafaris.co.nz)* operate 50-minute scenic flights from Lake Tekapo that fly over Lake Tekapo; Franz Josef, Fox, Balfour, La Perouse and Tasman Glaciers and include a loop around Mount Cook. This flight costs $280.

Twizel

Twizel's location in the Mackenzie Basin near the Aoraki/Mount Cook turnoff makes it a cheaper, albeit less scenic, alternative to staying at Mount Cook Village or Lake Tekapo.

It is a dreary planned town that was constructed as a base for the Upper Waitaki Power Development. It has all the charm of an anonymous suburb, but without the infrastructure to make it bearable.

Apart from being a base for visiting Aoraki/Mount Cook National Park, Twizel is also a popular destination for bird watchers as the endangered kaki can be found in the area around Twizel. The Department of Conservation run the Kaki Recovery Programme south of town, maintaining a hide where you can observe these birds.

Practical Information

Twizel Information Centre

Market Place, Twizel
☎ *(03) 435 3124*
Website *www.twizel.com*
Open *Jan-Apr 9am-7pm daily; May-Sep Mon-Sat 9am-5pm; Oct-Dec 9am-7pm daily*

Lake Pukaki Visitor Centre
State Highway 8, Lake Pukaki
☎ *(03) 435 3280*
Website *www.mtcook.org.nz*
Open *summer 9.30am-5.30pm daily; winter 10am-4pm daily*

Coming & Going
Atomic Shuttles (☎ *(03) 349 0697;* ***website*** *www.atomictravel.co.nz)*, InterCity Coachlines (☎ *(03) 365 1113;* ***website*** *www.intercity.co.nz)*, Naked Bus (☎ *0900 62533;* ***website*** *www.nakedbus.com)* and Southern Link K Bus (☎ *(03) 358 8355 or 0508 458 835;* ***website*** *www.southernlinkkbus.co.nz)* services stop in Twizel en route between Christchurch and Queenstown. Buses stop at Market Place near the visitor information centre.

Timaru's local Metro bus service (☎ *(03) 688 5544;* ***website*** *www.metroinfo.org.nz/timIndex.html)* has a regional route that runs from Timaru to Twizel via Tekapo.

The Cook Connection (☎ *025 583 211;* ***website*** *www.cookconnect.co.nz)* shuttle goes to Tekapo and Aoraki/Mount Cook. It departs from the information centre.

Accommodation
Buscot Station Backpackers
The rose bushes leading to the entry of this place give you an idea of what to expect. This lovely house on a huge farm, about 15 minutes south of Twizel, exudes charm. The fully-equipped kitchen is homely and the bathrooms are new and clean. The best part is the common room, with a warm log fire, piano, antiques and photos everywhere; and a nice TV with videos for cold nights. There is a huge dorm in an attached building that has ten or so single made-up beds and a small bathroom. It is a really good place to chill out, with friendly owners and a low-key but convivial atmosphere.
732 Twizel-Omarama Road, Omarama
☎ *(03) 438 9646*
Dorm bed *$20;* ***double room*** *$50;* ***camping*** *$12.50 per person*
Reception open *7.30am-10pm daily*

Maintenance & cleanliness	★★★★
Facilities	★★★½
Atmosphere & character	★★★★
Security	★
Overall rating	★★★½

High Country Lodge
This is a nice holiday park in the centre of town with two backpacker dorm cabins with nice furnishings. The kitchens are clean, if a bit outdated, and the bathrooms are nicely maintained. Rooms have bedside lamps and sinks, and there is a common area with a spacious TV lounge, some books and games, and internet access ($6 per hour) including wireless. There is also a barbecue area outside. It is not the most convivial place, but it is warm and comfortable if you are passing through town.
23 Mackenzie Drive, Twizel
☎ *(03) 435 0671*
Website *www.highcountrylodge.co.nz*
Dorm bed *$25-28 ($22-25 HI/YHA);* ***double room*** *$66-80 ($65-75 HI/YHA);* ***triple room*** *$85-95*
Credit cards *MC, Visa*
Reception open *summer 8am-9pm daily; winter 8am-7.30pm daily*

Maintenance & cleanliness	★★
Facilities	★★
Atmosphere & character	★★★
Security	★★
Overall rating	★★½

Mountain Chalets
This is more of a motel than a hostel, but they offer one "lodge" with backpackers' accommodation. Mountain Chalets has two shared dorm rooms and a few self-contained double rooms in a A-frame cabin. It is not the best maintained cabin of the lot, with a small, messy kitchen and untidy bathrooms. The shared rooms have a set of bunks and just enough room to turn around. There is a common area with a lot of books plus laundry facilities on site and Wi-Fi internet access. It is a good choice if you are travelling with friends and don't mind the very close quarters.
Wairepo Road, Twizel
☎ *(03) 435 0785 or 0800 629 999*

Website *www.mountainchalets.co.nz*
Dorm bed *$20-25;* ***double room*** *$50;* ***twin room*** *$40-50*
Credit cards *MC, Visa*
Reception open *8am-8pm daily*

Maintenance & cleanliness	★★½
Facilities	★½
Atmosphere & character	★★½
Security	★½
Overall rating	★★

Omahau Downs Backpackers

Located about 1km south of town, this modest place offers a range of accommodation including a backpackers' house in the old shearers' quarters. It is quite old, but it tries, although the focus here is more on the bed and breakfast. Amenities include a good kitchen, a cosy living room with log fire and TV, laundry facilities and a barbecue area outside with and views of Aoraki/Mount Cook on clear days. Management are welcoming and helpful, but there is not a very good atmosphere since it is out of town.

State Highway 8, Twizel
☎ *(03) 435 0199*
Website *www.omahau.co.nz*
Dorm bed *$22;* ***double room*** *$55;* ***self-contained cabin*** *$105 for two people*
Credit cards *MC, Visa*
Open *Jan-May & Sep-Dec;* ***reception open*** *7.30am-7.30pm daily*

Maintenance & cleanliness	★★½
Facilities	★★½
Atmosphere & character	★★★
Security	½
Overall rating	★★½

Aoraki/Mount Cook National Park

Aoraki/Mount Cook National Park is home to New Zealand's tallest mountain (Aoraki/Mount Cook) and its largest glacier (Tasman Glacier). Aoraki is a sacred place to Māori, so accessibility and development of the town is limited. This does not mean that it is not crowded with outdoorsy types all year round, though. It is a haven for climbers and hikers; there are excellent walks and scenic flights and guided tours are available. Mount Cook Village is tiny and functional, and offers little to entertain besides a most spectacular view from every window. Walking tracks begin from several points around town.

Practical Information

Aoraki/Mt Cook National Park DOC Visitor Centre

1 Larch Grove, Mount Cook Village
☎ *(03) 435 1186*
Website *www.doc.govt.nz*
Open *Jan-Apr 8.30am-5pm daily; May-Sep 8.30am-4.30pm daily; Oct-Dec 8.30am-4.30pm daily*

Coming & Going

The Cook Connection *(☎ 025 583 211;* ***website*** *www.cookconnect.co.nz)* shuttle goes to Tekapo and Twizel, where you can connect with coaches to Christchurch or Queenstown. It picks up and drops off at the YHA hostel.

Accommodation

Mount Cook YHA

This is a lovely hostel in Mount Cook Village. It features a nice big common area with a big screen TV, a spacious fully-equipped kitchen, a sauna and a barbecue outside. The dorms are well appointed but a bit cramped, and there are sometimes large school groups here. But the location is excellent, and there are stunning views from many of the rooms. It is heated throughout and the staff are very friendly and knowledgeable. You can book all your activities here, and there is a shop at reception for supplies and groceries.

Corner Bowen & Kitchener Drives, Mount Cook Village
☎ *(03) 435 1820*
Website *www.yha.co.nz*
Dorm bed *$29 ($26 HI/YHA);* ***double room*** *$76 ($70 HI/YHA);* ***triple room*** *$99 ($91 HI/YHA)*
Credit cards *MC, Visa*
Reception open *8am-9pm daily*

Maintenance & cleanliness	★★★★★
Facilities	★★
Atmosphere & character	★★★★½
Security	★★
Overall rating	★★★★

Glentanner Park Centre

This purpose-built holiday park is very well maintained and offers a good standard of accommodation. There is a huge 10-bed dormitory, which has sturdy bunks, but is very plain and almost institutional. There is a large fully equipped kitchen, clean bathrooms, laundry facilities, a TV lounge with log fire and internet access. It is about 20km from Mount Cook Village.

State Highway 80, Aoraki/Mount Cook
☎ *(03) 435 1855*
Website *www.glentanner.co.nz*
Dorm bed *$25;* ***double room*** *$70-80;* ***camping*** *$13-15*
Credit cards *Amex, JCB, MC, Visa*
Reception open *8am-9pm daily*

Maintenance & cleanliness	★★★★
Facilities	★★
Atmosphere & character	★★★
Security	½
Overall rating	★★★

Activities

BOAT TOURS & KAYAKING

Glacier Explorers (☎ *(03) 435 1077;* ***website*** *www.glacierexplorers.co.nz)* operate boat tours to Tasman Glacier that cost $120. **Glacier Sea-Kayaking** (☎ *(03) 435 1890;* ***website*** *www.mtcook.com)* run good value sea-kayaking trips to Mueller Glacier that cost $110. Either option allows you to see a glacier from a unique perspective as you glide past icebergs on the lake. These trips operate Oct-May.

SCENIC FLIGHTS

Several companies offer scenic flights over Aoraki/Mount Cook and Tasman Glacier. Flights by both helicopter and fixed wing planes offer glacier landings.

The **Helicopter Line** (☎ *(03) 435 1801;* ***website*** *www.helicopter.co.nz)* has flights departing from Glentanner Park, about a 15-minute drive from Mount Cook Village. These include a 20-minute flight past Mount Brown and Zodiac Glacier ($210), a 30-minute flight over Mount Brown and Richardson Glacier ($295) and a 45-minute flight over Tasman Glacier, Liebig Range and Aoraki/Mount Cook ($415).

Air Safaris (☎ *(03) 680 6880;* ***website*** *www.airsafaris.co.nz)* operate 50-minute scenic flights from Glentanner Park that fly over Lake Tekapo; Franz Josef, Fox, Balfour, La Perouse and Tasman Glaciers and include a loop around Aoraki/Mount Cook. This flight costs $320, but it doesn't include a glacier landing.

Mount Cook Ski Planes (☎ *0800 800 702;* ***website*** *www.mtcookskiplanes.com)* feature snow landings. A 40-minute flight over Tasman Glacier costs $340 and a 55-minute flight over Tasman Glacier with a loop around Aoraki/Mount Cook costs $450. Flights without a glacier landing cost between $230 and $310.

Hiking

There is a good selection of short walking tracks in Aoraki/Mount Cook National Park.

WALKS FROM MT COOK VILLAGE

The most popular hike is the **Hooker Valley Walk** *(4 hours return)*, which passes Mueller Lake and crosses two swing bridges while following the Hooker River to Hooker Lake at the foot of Hooker Glacier.

Other short walks from the village include **Red Tarns Track** *(2 hours return)*, which has a steep climb to a point that affords breathtaking views of Aoraki/Mount Cook and the surrounding alpine country. **Kea Point Walk** *(2 hours return)* leaves from the DOC Visitors' Centre and climbs to a viewpoint looking over Mueller Lake, the Hooker Valley, Mount Sefton and Aoraki/Mount Cook. The more challenging **Sealy Tarns Track** *(3-4 hours return)* branches off from the Kea Point Walk and climbs past abundant wildflowers to offer a stunning view of Aoraki/Mount Cook.

TASMAN VALLEY WALKS

There are also several hikes in the Tasman Valley, about an 8km drive from Mount Cook Village.

These include the short **Blue Lakes and Tasman Glacier View Walk** *(40 minutes)*, which offers views of the Blue Lakes and the lower Tasman Glacier. An alternate route goes to **Tasman Glacier Lake** *(50-60 minutes)*, which freezes over in winter and has icebergs floating in it during summer.

The longer **Ball Shelter Hut Route** *(3-4 hours each way)* follows the old Ball Hut Road alongside the massive Tasman Glacier. People used to stay in the hut overnight and walk back the following day, however this is no longer possible and you now need to complete the return trip on the same day.

Otago

Otago is one of the most popular regions for backpackers in New Zealand – and rightfully so. Early birds can catch the morning surf and watch penguins head to sea on the coast, or watch the sun rise over Mount Aspiring National Park. Night owls will find plenty of places to party in student city Dunedin or backpackers' heaven Queenstown. For the adventurous, Queenstown offers some of the world's best adrenaline-pumping activities. This region has a great tourist infrastructure without (for the most part) feeling too commercial and its residents are fun-loving and welcoming. Getting around is easy, and accommodation options are excellent.

Must do in Otago

- Tour the Speights Brewery in Dunedin
- Bungee jump and canyon swin in Queenstown
- Go white water rafting on the Kawarau and Shotover Rivers

Oamaru

Oamaru is a good place to base yourself while exploring Otago's many coastal attractions. It is most famous for its colony of blue penguins (the smallest in the world) and yellow-eyed penguins (some of the rarest), but it also boasts an impressively restored historic centre. Built of Oamaru stone – also known locally as whitestone – and dating back to gold rush years, this district is charming and full of antique shops and cute cafés, making for a pleasant way to spend a day. It also has the Whitestone Cheese Factory with free viewings in the morning. Otherwise, the town is ordinary, but the nearby town of Moeraki and its famous boulders makes an

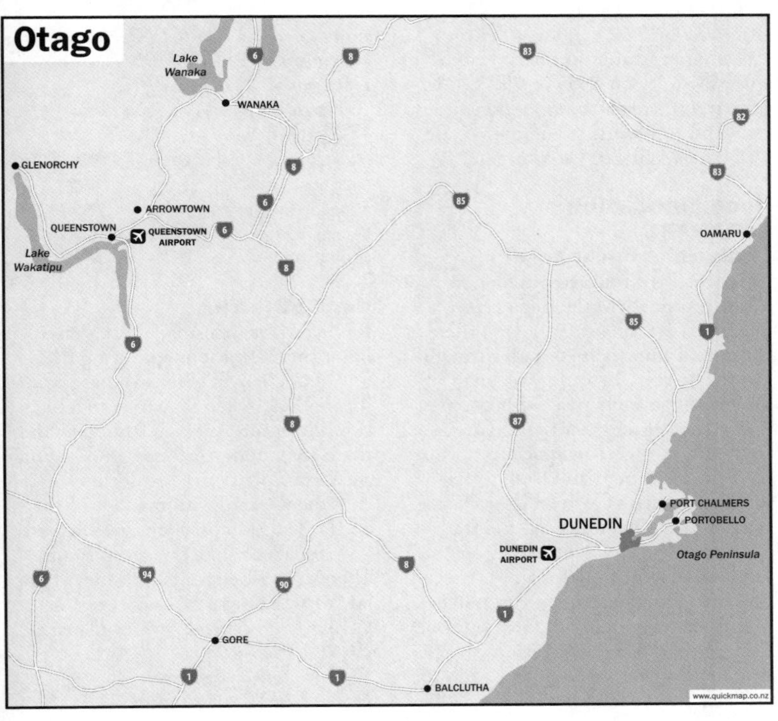

Otago

excellent day trip. It is also a popular stop for backpackers on their way to Aoraki/Mount Cook National Park.

Practical Information

Oamaru i-SITE Visitor Centre

1 Thames Street, Oamaru
☎ *(03) 434 1656*
Website *www.visitoamaru.co.nz*
Open *Mon-Fri 9am-5.30pm, Sat-Sun 10am-4pm*

INTERNET ACCESS

The Empire Cybercafe

15 Thames Street, Oamaru
☎ *(03) 434 3470*

Small Bytes Computing

187 Thames Street, Oamaru
☎ *(03) 434 8490*

Coming & Going

Oamaru lies on State Highway 1 between Christchurch and Dunedin. Atomic Shuttles *(☎ (03) 349 0697; **website** www.atomictravel.co.nz)*, InterCity Coachlines *(☎ (03) 471 7143; **website** www.intercity.co.nz)*, Naked Bus *(☎ 0900 62533; **website** www.nakedbus.com)* and Southern Link K Bus *(☎ (03) 358 8355 or 0508 458 835; **website** www.southernlinkkbus.co.nz)* all stop outside LaGonda Cafe *(191 Thames Street, Oamaru)*.

Accommodation

IN OAMARU

Chillawhile Backpackers

This hostel is a restored old manor house just north of the town centre and it features an art gallery, so there is plenty of interesting art all throughout the hostel. There are two small kitchens; common areas with books, a piano, log fire and comfy sofas and a small TV lounge. The spacious dorms have made-up beds and fresh towels. There are quite a few freebies such as free internet (including Wi-Fi), free breakfast, a free pick up and drop off service and your fourth night is free. The friendly management run movie nights and help out with local information. There is a convivial atmosphere here most of the time.
1 Frome Street, Oamaru
☎ *(03) 437 0168*
Website *www.chillawhile.co.nz*
Dorm bed *$23-25 ($18-20 BBH);* ***single room*** *$50 ($40 BBH);* ***double room*** *$70 ($60 BBH)*

Maintenance & cleanliness	★★★
Facilities	★★★
Atmosphere & character	★★★★½
Security	★½
Overall rating	★★★

Empire Hotel

This hostel is a nice historic building in the town centre that offers free internet, laundry facilities, and a cavernous downstairs billiards room. The kitchen is bare and untidy and dorms are small with old mattresses, but the bathrooms are renovated and clean. There are two big common areas with TVs, but furnishings are rather dated. It has friendly reception, and a great location next to a good café.
13 Thames Street, Oamaru
☎ *(03) 434 3446*
Website *www.empirebackpackersoamaru.co.nz*
Dorm bed *$22-24 ($18-21 BBH);* ***single room*** *$34 ($31 BBH);* ***double/twin room*** *$54 ($48 BBH)*
Reception open *9am-9pm daily*

Maintenance & cleanliness	★★½
Facilities	★★
Atmosphere & character	★★★½
Security	★★
Overall rating	★★½

Red Kettle YHA

Red Kettle is in a small cosy house. It has a common room with a log fire, lots of books and games and big comfy sofas. The kitchen is small and a bit run down, but it is well equipped and there are laundry facilities and internet access ($6 per hour).The dorms are extremely clean, with made-up beds and bedside lamps. Some are themed – we especially like the sheep room. There are gardens outside and it is not far from the town centre.
Corner Cross & Reed Streets, Oamaru
☎ *(03) 434 5008*
Website *www.yha.co.nz*
Dorm bed *$25 ($22 HI/YHA)*

Credit cards *MC, Visa*
Reception open *8am-12pm & 4pm-8pm daily*

Maintenance & cleanliness	★★★½
Facilities	★★
Atmosphere & character	★★★
Security	★★
Overall rating	★★★

Old Bones Backpackers

This is a brand new, purpose-built hostel about five minutes' drive south of town and just a short walk to the beach. It is a lovely place with vaulted ceilings, large windows and high-quality woodwork. The kitchen is spacious and spotless, and the common area has great sofas, books and a warm log fire. There is free internet access and laundry facilities. There are no conventional dorms, just two-bed dorms (shared twin rooms) at backpackers' prices. It doesn't have the usual backpackers' atmosphere, as it caters to a more "mature" crowd most of the time.

Beach Road, Oamaru
☎ *(03) 434 8115*
Website *www.oldbones.co.nz*
Dorm bed *$30;* ***double/twin room*** *$60*

Maintenance & cleanliness	★★★★★
Facilities	★★★
Atmosphere & character	★★★½
Security	★½
Overall rating	★★★½

OUTSIDE OAMARU

There are a couple of nice hostels south of Oamaru that make a nice base for visiting either Oamaru or the Moeraki Boulders.

Coastal Backpackers

This is a small, cosy hostel set on a farm near the beach 20km south of Oamaru, where guests will see lots of sheep and can feed alpacas. It has tidy bathrooms and a small, clean and well maintained kitchen. There is also a cosy TV lounge with a good log fire and a sunny dining room. It has only nine beds, in small shared rooms with

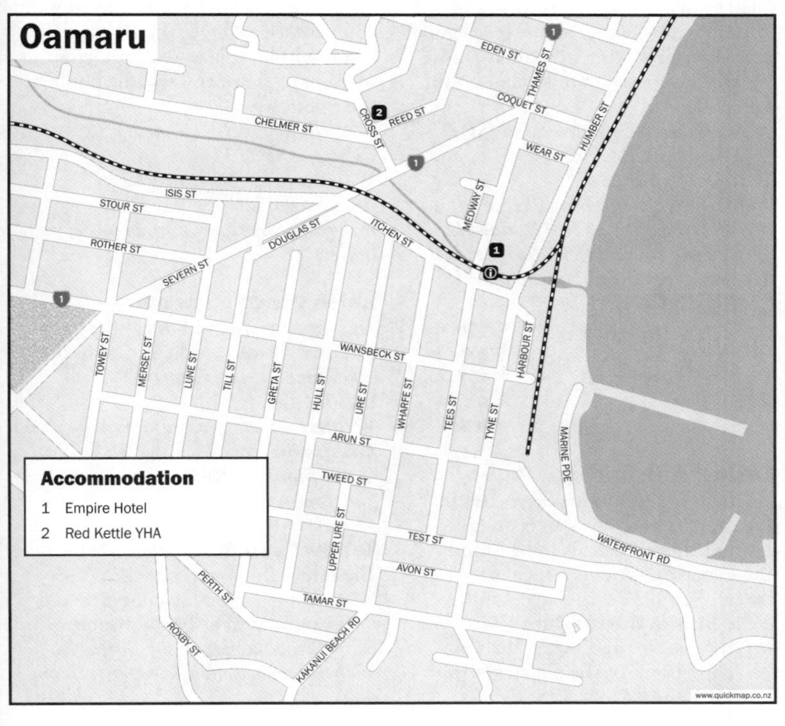

single made-up beds. There is a lovely double room in a separate cabin as well. Management are very friendly and caring.
1050 Waianakarua Road, All Day Bay
☎ *(03) 439 5411*
Website *www.coastalbackpackers.co.nz*
Dorm bed *$24 ($22 BBH);* ***double/ twin room*** *$50 ($46 BBH)*
Reception open *5.30am-10am & noon-7pm*

Maintenance & cleanliness	★★★½
Facilities	★★
Atmosphere & character	★★★
Security	★★
Overall rating	★★★

Olive Grove Lodge

Set on an 11ha organic farm, this hostel has great facilities and an eco-friendly vibe. Dorms are nicely fitted with thick made-up beds. Shared facilities include a large common room with a log fire, comfy sofas, a TV and lots of books; a cutely decorated and well equipped kitchen; laundry; a spa pool and a small sauna. The hostel is surrounded by beautifully kept gardens. It is a good alternative to staying in Oamaru, as it is just 25km south of town, but best if you have a car.
2328 Herbert-Hampden Road (State Highway 1), Waianakarua
☎ *(03) 439 5830*
Website *www.olivebranch.co.nz*
Dorm bed *$25 ($22 BBH);* ***double/ twin room*** *$60-70 ($54-64)*
Reception open *8.30am-8pm daily*

Maintenance & cleanliness	★★★½
Facilities	★★★
Atmosphere & character	★★★½
Security	★½
Overall rating	★★★

Eating & Drinking

Most of the restaurants here cater to day trippers and pensioners on holiday, but there are deals to be found. The historic district is a nice place for a meal, but it is dear – have a coffee at the **Star & Garter Café** *(9 Itchen Street, Oamaru)* and watch the tourists snap photos of the old steam train. **Turrett Takeaways** *(218 Thames Street, Oamaru)* north of town does very cheap quality fish and chips, and **Filadelfio's** *(70 Thames Street, Oamaru)* has great pizza and snacks. **Fat Sally's Pub** *(84 Thames Street, Oamaru)* is a popular place for dinner and drinks.

There are two **New World** supermarkets in town *(Main South Road, Oamaru)* and *(402 Thames Highway Oamaru)* as well as a cheap centrally-located **Countdown** supermarket *(108-116 Thames Street, Oamaru).*

Sights & Activities

Blue Penguin Colony

Blue penguins, also known as fairy penguins or little penguins, can be seen from the viewing platforms at the blue penguin colony at the end of Waterfront Road. This is one of the best spots in New Zealand to see blue penguins, although there are far fewer penguins here than in penguin colonies in Australia. The number of penguins that you can expect to see varies depending on the time of year, for instance between Mar and Aug you may see as few as 15, but in Dec you might be able to see 150 penguins swim in to shore and waddle home to their nests.
Waterfront Road, Oamaru
☎ *(03) 433 1195*
Website *www.penguins.co.nz*
Admission *$20*
Penguins arrive *half an hour before sunset*

North Otago Museum

This small museum has exhibits about the area's history and cultural heritage.
60 Thames Street, Oamaru
☎ *(03) 434 1652*
Website *www.northotagomuseum.co.nz*
Admission *free*
Open *Mon-Fri 10.30am-4.30pm, Sat-Sun 1pm-4pm*

Yellow Eyed Penguin Colony

The rare yellow-eyed penguins are much larger than blue penguins and they can be seen at Bushy Beach.
Bushy Beach Road, Bushy Beach
Website *www.yellow-eyedpenguin.org.nz*

Admission *free*
Penguins leave *just after sunrise;* ***penguins arrive*** *late afternoon before sunset*

Dunedin

Dunedin is a thriving student city with a unique mix of cultural and natural appeal. It is sometimes referred to as the Edinburgh of the South thanks to its rich Scottish heritage and fine Victorian architecture. The 1861 gold rush formed the foundations of the city, but today it is noted mostly for its prominent student population. Despite the steep streets (Baldwin Street is the steepest in the world), it is a largely walkable city with accommodation, sights and restaurants clustered around the central Octagon.

The city has some interesting museums and galleries, as well as some excellent factory tours like the Cadbury Chocolate Factory and Speight's Brewery. These tours are a great alternative to museums and include some tasty samples. The Otago Peninsula, where you can go to the beach or see rare penguins and albatross thriving in their natural habitat, is an easy day trip from the city.

Practical Information

Dunedin i-SITE Visitor Centre

48 The Octagon, Dunedin
☎ *(03) 474 3300*
Website *www.CityofDunedin.com*

INTERNET ACCESS

The Common Room

Corner George & Bath Streets, Dunedin
☎ *(03) 470 1730*
Open *8am-9pm daily*

Netplanet

78 St Andrews Street, Dunedin
☎ *(03) 479 2424*
Open *10am-late daily*

Coming & Going

AIR

Dunedin International Airport *(☎ (03) 486 2879;* ***website*** *www.dnairport.co.nz)* is 30km south of the city centre.

Shuttle buses including Kiwi Shuttle *(☎ (03) 473 7017;* ***website*** *www.kiwishuttles.co.nz)* and Super Shuttle *(☎ (03) 488 1224;* ***website*** *www.supershuttle.co.nz)* charge around $30 to go to the city centre.

BUS

There are direct bus services from Dunedin to Christchurch, Invercargill and Queenstown.

InterCity Coachlines *(☎ (03) 471 7143;* ***website*** *www.intercity.co.nz)* depart from Ritchies/InterCity Travel at 205 St Andrews Street. Atomic Shuttles *(☎ (03) 349 0697;* ***website*** *www.atomictravel.co.nz)*, Naked Bus *(☎ 0900 62533;* ***website*** *www.nakedbus.com)* and Southern Link K Bus *(☎ (03) 358 8355 or 0508 458 835;* ***website*** *www.southernlinkkbus.co.nz)* depart from the train station on Anzac Avenue.

TRAIN

Dunedin is the terminus for the *Taieri Gorge Railway (☎ (03) 477 4449;* ***website*** *www.taieri.co.nz)*, which travels to Middlemarch where there is a connecting coach service to Queenstown. Dunedin's train station is on Anzac Street, about a five-minute walk from the Octagon.

HITCHHIKING

Although Dunedin is a small city, it helps to take a bus to get to the good hitchhiking spots.

Take a bus to Pine Hill and try your luck on State Highway 1 if you're heading north to Christchurch. If you're heading south, take the Mosgiel bus and get off at Kenmont.

Local Transport

Dunedin has a fairly extensive bus network with most bus routes terminating in and around The Octagon. Bus fares start at $1.20 and increase to $4 depending on the distance travelled.

Accommodation

DUNEDIN CITY

Arden Street House

This hostel is in a nice house about a 10-minute walk north of the city

Otago

centre. The main house is quite nice, with a cosy TV room and a modern, well equipped kitchen, but the back house is cramped and stuffy. They also have laundry facilities and internet access. It caters much of the time to long term workers, so it is often quite messy.
36 Arden Street, North East Valley
(03) 473 8860
***Website** www.ardensthouse.co.nz*
***Dorm bed** $20; **single room** $40; **double/twin room** $40*
***Credit cards** MC, Visa*

Maintenance & cleanliness	★★½
Facilities	★★
Atmosphere & character	★★
Security	★
Overall rating	★★

Chalet Backpackers
Set in a converted old hospital, Chalet Backpackers has tons of character and a great international vibe. The dorms have huge windows looking out to the bay and comfortable single beds. There is a big modern kitchen, laundry facilities, a pool room, free tea and coffee, cheerful Swiss management and a cute garden in the back. There is no internet access, but the location is very central.
296 High Street, Dunedin
(03) 479 2075 or 0800 242 538
***Dorm bed** $24 ($21 BBH); **single room** $38 ($35 BBH); **double/twin room** $27 ($24 BBH)*
***Reception open** 9am-9pm daily*

Maintenance & cleanliness	★★★
Facilities	★★½
Atmosphere & character	★★★★★
Security	★★½
Overall rating	★★★½

Downtown Dunedin Backpackers (Leviathan Heritage Hotel)
This hostel is in a huge old hotel in the city centre. It is mainly a hotel, but offers some nice dormitory accommodation as well. Downstairs there is a large restaurant and common area with a piano, log fire and nice old furnishings and there is also internet access (at a hefty $10 per hour), laundry facilities, a nice central courtyard and an old bar that is used only for guests. The dorms have good made-up beds and guests are supplied with fresh towels. The basic kitchen is poorly maintained, and although it is cheap and central, there is not a great backpacker atmosphere here as it often caters to large school groups and sports teams.
27 Queens Gardens, Dunedin
(03) 477 3160
***Website** www.dunedinhotel.co.nz*
***Dorm bed** $25; **single room** $90-105; **double room** $105-130*
***Credit cards** MC, Visa*
***Reception open** 24 hours daily*

Maintenance & cleanliness	★★★½
Facilities	★★
Atmosphere & character	★★
Security	★★★
Overall rating	★★★

Dunedin Central Backpackers
This is a brilliant hostel that has recently been entirely renovated. The kitchen is new and modern, bathrooms are spotless and dorms are tidy with made-up beds and lockers. The small common room has a nice TV, log fire and a guitar. There is warm colour and soft light throughout and security is good. Facilities are minimal, but they have laundry and an internet café next door. It has an excellent location and friendly staff.
243 Moray Street, Dunedin
(03) 477 9985
***Website** www.dunedincentralbackpackers.com*
***Dorm bed** $24-26; **double room** $62; **twin room** $56*
***Credit cards** MC, Visa*
***Reception open** 8am-10pm daily*

Maintenance & cleanliness	★★★★½
Facilities	★★½
Atmosphere & character	★★★★
Security	★★★½
Overall rating	★★★★

Elm Lodge & the Jolly Poacher
This hostel is a bit ramshackle, but it has a homely atmosphere. It also offers good facilities including a spa pool, a sauna, and internet access ($4 per

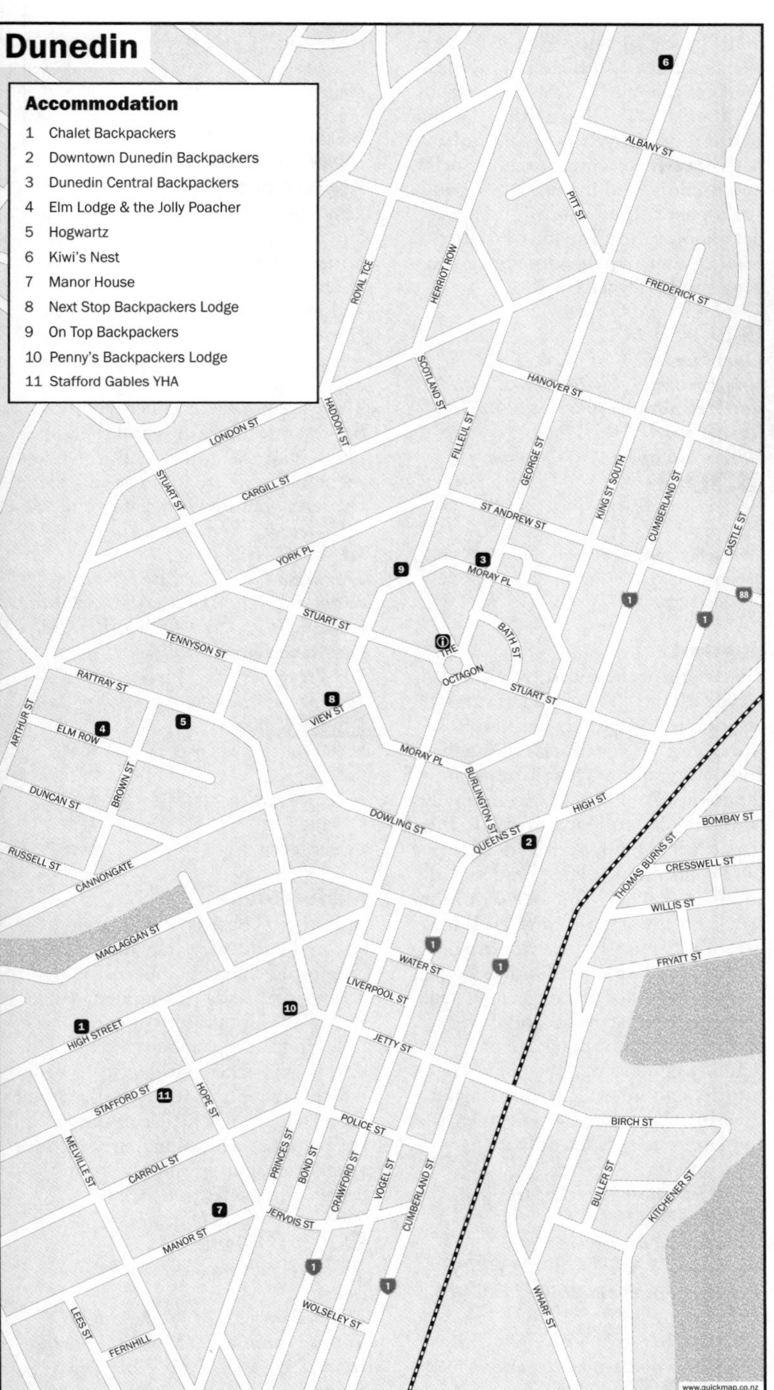
Dunedin
Accommodation
1 Chalet Backpackers
2 Downtown Dunedin Backpackers
3 Dunedin Central Backpackers
4 Elm Lodge & the Jolly Poacher
5 Hogwartz
6 Kiwi's Nest
7 Manor House
8 Next Stop Backpackers Lodge
9 On Top Backpackers
10 Penny's Backpackers Lodge
11 Stafford Gables YHA
ALBANY ST
PITT ST
ROYAL TCE
HERRIOT ROW
FREDERICK ST
SCOTLAND ST
HANOVER ST
HADDON ST
LONDON ST
FILLEUL ST
GEORGE ST
KING ST SOUTH
CUMBERLAND ST
STUART ST
CARGILL ST
ST ANDREW ST
CASTLE ST
YORK PL
MORAY PL
STUART ST
BATH ST
THE OCTAGON
TENNYSON ST
RATTRAY ST
VIEW ST
STUART ST
ARTHUR ST
ELM ROW
BROWN ST
MORAY PL
BURLINGTON ST
DUNCAN ST
DOWLING ST
HIGH ST
QUEENS ST
BOMBAY ST
RUSSELL ST
CANNONGATE
THOMAS BURNS ST
CRESSWELL ST
WILLIS ST
MACLAGGAN ST
WATER ST
FRYATT ST
LIVERPOOL ST
HIGH STREET
JETTY ST
STAFFORD ST
HOPE ST
POLICE ST
BIRCH ST
MELVILLE ST
PRINCES ST
BOND ST
CRAWFORD ST
VOGEL ST
CUMBERLAND ST
BULLER ST
KITCHENER ST
CARROLL ST
JERVOIS ST
MANOR ST
WHARF ST
WOLSELEY ST
LEES ST
FERNHILL
www.quickmap.co.nz

hour) including wireless. The kitchen is well equipped and there is a nice outdoor common area, as well as a small TV lounge with a huge film selection. Dorm rooms have the usual bunks with duvets. Reception staff are helpful and friendly, and the place has a quiet atmosphere. They also run the place next door, called The Jolly Poacher, where guests pay the same price and get a similar level of facilities.
78 Elm Row, Dunedin
(03) 474 1872
***Dorm bed** $23-24 ($19-20 BBH); **single room** $36-46 ($32-42 BBH); **double/twin room** $28 ($24 BBH)*
***Credit cards** MC, Visa*
***Reception open** 9am-7pm daily*

Maintenance & cleanliness	★★★
Facilities	★★★★½
Atmosphere & character	★★★
Security	★★½
Overall rating	★★★

Hogwartz

This is one of the nicest hostels in New Zealand. It is set in a restored bishop's residence that has handsome woodwork, high ceilings, chandeliers and commanding views from many of the rooms. And it is all exceptionally clean and carefully maintained. There is a cosy TV lounge with an extensive DVD collection, a large modern fully-equipped kitchen, and a lovely dining area with a mezzanine and great log fire. While most hostels would cram ten or more bunk beds into its huge rooms, they have just five single beds with quality mattresses and duvets. Double and twin rooms are particularly good value. They have cheap laundry and internet access. It has a cheerful atmosphere, a central location and has extremely friendly management and staff.
277 Rattray Street, Dunedin
(03) 474 1487
***Website** www.hogwartz.co.nz*
***Dorm bed** $26-27 ($22-23 BBH); **double/twin room** $60-72 ($52-64 BBH)*
***Credit cards** MC, Visa*
***Reception open** 8am-8pm daily*

Maintenance & cleanliness	★★★★★
Facilities	★★★
Atmosphere & character	★★★★½
Security	★★
Overall rating	★★★★

Kiwi's Nest

This hostel is an old house near the city centre. It is not the best maintained place, but has a certain amount of charm with bright, airy rooms and made-up beds. There is a large common lounge with a TV and big sofas. The kitchen is quite run down, and the carpets are old and worn. There are not many other facilities besides internet access and the atmosphere is on the dull side. But management and staff are very friendly and the self contained units are good value.
597 George Street, Dunedin
(03) 471 9540
***Dorm bed** $23 ($20 BBH); **single room** $40-55 ($36-45 BBH); **double room** $50-75 ($45-67.50 BBH); **self-contained unit** $90 ($81 BBH)*
***Credit cards** MC, Visa*
***Reception open** 9am-10.30pm daily*

Maintenance & cleanliness	★★½
Facilities	★
Atmosphere & character	★★½
Security	★½
Overall rating	★★

Manor House

This hostel consists of two large restored buildings. They have a fair amount of character, but inside are messy and poorly maintained. There is a cosy TV lounge with pool table, a big telly, and a large modern kitchen. The dorms are packed with up to 10 beds, which have thin mattresses. Bathrooms are also looking a little run-down. Still, the place has a buzzing, party-minded atmosphere and it is not far from the centre. They offer free pick-up.
28 Manor Place, Dunedin
(03) 477 0484
***Website** www.manorhousebackpackers.co.nz*
***Dorm bed** $22-24 ($20-22 BBH); **double room** $60 ($56 BBH); **triple room** $69 ($65 BBH); **camping** $15 per person*

Credit cards *Visa*
Reception open *9am-9pm daily*

Maintenance & cleanliness	★★½
Facilities	★★
Atmosphere & character	★★★½
Security	★
Overall rating	★★½

Next Stop Backpackers Lodge

This hostel is a big old building with a central location. Accommodation is in very spacious dorms with thick mattresses and duvets. There is a library, a pool table and internet access – although the computer they have is quite useless. The kitchen is old and poorly maintained, the bathrooms are dreary and unclean and it has an institutional ambience. It often caters to large school groups, so the backpacker atmosphere here is not very good. You get what you pay for here.

2 View Street, Dunedin
(03) 477 0447 or 0800 463 987
Website *www.nextstop.co.nz*
Dorm bed *$21;* ***single room*** *$38;* ***double/twin room*** *$46-48*
Reception open *9am-9pm daily*

Maintenance & cleanliness	★½
Facilities	★★½
Atmosphere & character	★½
Security	★★½
Overall rating	★★

On Top Backpackers

This hostel has a great atmosphere and an absolute central location. Recently renovated, it has modern, spacious and bright dorms with high quality, made-up beds. The kitchen has huge windows and modern fittings, and there is a lot of common space with an excellent barbecue. Bathrooms are also modern and spotless. There is a pool hall and bar downstairs with a great atmosphere. Guests can use the internet ($4 per hour) and watch Sky TV here as well. Management are good-humoured and cheerful. This place has the best security of Dunedin's hostels.

12 Filleul Street, Dunedin
(03) 477 6121 or 0800 668 672
Website *www.ontopbackpackers.co.nz*
Dorm bed *$25-26 ($23 BBH);* ***double room*** *$60-78 ($54-72 BBH)*
Credit cards *MC, Visa*
Reception open *7.30am-midnight*

Maintenance & cleanliness	★★★★½
Facilities	★★½
Atmosphere & character	★★★★
Security	★★★★
Overall rating	★★★★

Penny's Backpackers Lodge

This hostel is above a cavern bar in the city centre. Behind a run-down façade, Penny's offers surprisingly good accommodation. There is a good common room with free internet, a large screen TV, big sofas and a log fire. The kitchen is small, but modern; the dorm rooms are neat and tidy; the bathrooms are ugly and unclean, though, and security is not good enough for the location and the fact that it is above a bar.

6 Stafford Street, Dunedin
(03) 477 6027 or 0800 PENNYS
Website *www.pennys.co.nz*
Dorm bed *$21-27 ($18-24 BBH);* ***single room*** *$33-38 ($30-35);* ***double/twin room*** *$56-61 ($50-56)*
Credit cards *MC, Visa*
Reception open *8am-10pm daily*

Maintenance & cleanliness	★★★
Facilities	★★
Atmosphere & character	★★★
Security	★
Overall rating	★★½

Stafford Gables YHA

Stafford Gables is a nicely restored heritage building that features a large fully-equipped kitchen; a cool downstairs TV lounge with plenty of DVDs; a laundry; a travel desk; internet facilities ($6 per hour), including Wi-Fi and a rooftop garden with brilliant views. The dorm rooms are spacious with bedside lights and some of them open onto a big balcony. Double and twin rooms are charmingly decorated. Some bathrooms are modern and well maintained, but others look like they are due for a renovation. Cheerful staff and a young crowd give this place a good atmosphere, and it feels more intimate and homely than most other YHA hostels.

71 Stafford Street, Dunedin
☎ *(03) 474 1919*
Website *www.yha.co.nz*
Dorm bed *$26-28 ($23-25 HI/YHA);* ***single room*** *$53 ($50 HI/YHA);* ***double/twin room*** *$71 ($65 HI/YHA);* ***triple room*** *$90 ($81 HI/YHA);* ***family room*** *$94 ($85 HI/YHA)*
Credit cards *Amex, Diners, MC, Visa*
Reception open *summer 7.30am-9.30pm daily; winter 7.30am-8.30pm daily*

Maintenance & cleanliness	★★★★
Facilities	★★½
Atmosphere & character	★★★★
Security	★★★½
Overall rating	★★★½

PORT CHALMERS & SEACLIFF

Port Chalmers and Seacliff are two seaside towns around 20 to 30-minutes drive north of Dunedin. Accommodation here is well suited to travellers with a car who prefer to stay somewhere a little quieter.

Billy Brown's

This hostel requires you to get off the beaten track, but it is well worth the effort. Located up a steep drive on a sheep and deer farm, it is a small and atmospheric place boasting incredible views from all around. There are only nine beds, so it has a quiet ambience, but there is probably no better place for backpackers to get away from the city and relax. It has a warm and cosy lounge with guitars, a log fire, plush couches and an old record player which is a hit with most travellers. The kitchen is perfectly maintained, as are the bathrooms, and everything is super clean. It has friendly management and great atmosphere.
423 Aramoana Road, Hamilton Bay, Port Chalmers
☎ *(03) 472 8323*
Website *www.billybrowns.co.nz*
Dorm bed *$25;* ***double/twin room*** *$30*

Maintenance & cleanliness	★★★★½
Facilities	★★★
Atmosphere & character	★★★½
Security	★½
Overall rating	★★★½

Asylum Lodge

This is a really cool hostel on the grounds of the old Seacliff Lunatic Asylum, which was the largest building in New Zealand when constructed in the late 19th century. Although the original buildings were an impressive castle design, a combination of structural problems, a landslide and fire caused many parts of the structure to fall into disrepair. The hostel is housed in some of the remaining hospital buildings. It features a creatively decorated and well-maintained common room with free internet access. The TV lounge has a collection of 90 DVDs and a pool table; there are interesting photos on the walls, antique furnishings and a fish tank you can see through into the kitchen plus a huge outside deck. Accommodation is in nice dorm rooms with single beds. It is on a farm where you can take horses trekking into the hills for spectacular views. The management also run surfing, spear fishing and kayaking trips. There is a tennis court and guests have free use of mountain bikes. This hostel has a great atmosphere in a relaxing location 32km north of Dunedin's city centre.
36 Russell Street, Seacliff
☎ *(03) 465 8123*
Website *www.seacliffasylum.co.nz*
Dorm bed *$23 ($20 BBH);* ***single room*** *$38 ($35 BBH);* ***double/twin room*** *$54 ($48 BBH)*
Reception open *7.30am-11pm daily*

Maintenance & cleanliness	★★★★
Facilities	★★★½
Atmosphere & character	★★★½
Security	★½
Overall rating	★★★½

Eating & Drinking

Thanks to the substantial student population, Dunedin has great cheap eats. George Street is packed with cheap Thai, Japanese and Chinese places and funky little cafés. Vegetarians are also well catered for; at **Circadian Rhythm Vegan Café** *(72 St Andrew Street, Dunedin)* there is a very good all-you-can-eat buffet. If you are in town on Saturday, be sure to check out the farmers' market at the railway station, where you can find cheap international food and fresh fruit and veggies. There is **New World** supermarket *(Cumberland Street, Dunedin)* in the city centre and a **Pak'n Save** *(86 Hillside Road, Dunedin)* just south of town, but for 24 hours of cheap prices in the centre, the **Countdown** supermarket *(309 Cumberland Street, Dunedin)* is most backpackers' preference.

Sights

Baldwin Street

Baldwin Street in the suburb of North East Valley, 3.5km northeast of the city centre, is recorded as the steepest street in the world with a maximum gradient of 1m in 2.86m, although the steepest gradient applies only to a small portion of the street.
Baldwin Street, North East Valley

Cadbury World

Chocoholics will love the tours of Dunedin's Cadbury chocolate factory where 85% of New Zealand's chocolate is made. The 1¼-hour tour includes a visit to the factory as well as the Cadbury World Visitors' Centre and there are several tasting opportunities. The full factory tour only operates on weekdays, which is why it is cheaper to visit on weekends.
280 Cumberland Street, Dunedin
☎ *(03) 467 7967 or 0800 CADBURY (0800 223 287)*
Website *www.cadburyworld.co.nz*
Admission *Mon-Fri $16, Sat-Sun $10*
Open *9am-3.15pm daily*

Dunedin Public Art Gallery

This large art museum is home to a collection of New Zealand and international art with a notable collection of European art and Japanese prints. An programme of changing exhibits complements the permanent collection.
30 The Octagon, Dunedin
☎ *(03) 474 3240*
Website *http://dunedin.art.museum/*
Admission *free*
Open *10am-5pm daily*

New Zealand Sports Hall of Fame

This sporting museum celebrates the achievements of New Zealand's sporting heroes and features photographs and memorabilia including sporting equipment.
Anzac Avenue, Dunedin
☎ *(03) 477 7775*
Website *www.nzhalloffame.co.nz*
Admission *$5*
Open *10am-4pm daily*

Olveston

This opulent 35-room mansion is home to an astounding array of treasures from around the world that were collected during the extensive travels of its former owners. A visit includes a one-hour guided tour of the property.
42 Royal Terrace, Dunedin
☎ *(03) 477 3320*
Website *www.olveston.co.nz*
Admission *$15 ($14 BBH, HI/YHA)*
Open *9.30am-5pm daily; tours 9.30am, 10.45am, noon, 1.30pm, 2.45pm, 4pm daily*

Otago Museum

The excellent Otago Museum features well presented displays in three major categories: culture, science and natural history. The cultural displays include Maori and Pacific Island artefacts plus a maritime gallery and archaeological treasures from around the world. The natural history section features an animal attic with a huge collection of specimens plus unique displays about extinct birds such as the laughing owl and the massive moa. Discovery World, as the science area is known, has lots of hands-on exhibits such as a water wheel and an indoor waterfall.
419 Great King Street, Dunedin
☎ *(03) 474 7474*
Website *www.otagomuseum.govt.nz*
Admission *free*
Open *10am-5pm daily*

Otago Settlers Museum

This museum focuses on the people of Otago, with an emphasis on its early settlers. There are displays on Māori life, the import and role of Chinese immigrants during the gold rush and more recent European migrants that have made Otago their home. The museum also features a transport gallery with an old Cobb & Co

stagecoach and a collection of old cars, bicycles and steam trains.
31 Queens Gardens, Dunedin
☎ *(03) 477 5052*
Website *www.otago.settlers.museum*
Admission *$4*
Open *10am-5pm daily*

Speight's Brewery
By the time you get to Dunedin you will probably be very familiar with Speight's and the Speight's brewery tour is one of the most popular attractions in the city. The 1½-hour tour takes you through the working brewery and adjoining heritage centre and finishes off with beer tasting.
200 Rattray Street, Dunedin
☎ *(03) 477 7697*
Website *www.speights.co.nz*
Admission *$17*
Tours *Mon-Thu 10am, noon, 2pm, 7pm, Fri-Sun 10am, noon, 2pm, 4pm*

Otago Peninsula
The Otago Peninsula is a popular day trip from Dunedin. It forms Otago Harbour's southern shore and is home to lovely seaside villages and New Zealand's only castle. However its main attraction is the rich variety of wildlife that can be seen here, which includes seals, sea lions and penguins.

Coming & Going
Southeastern Bus Lines run buses to Portobello on the Otago Peninsula. They depart from stand 5 outside the Centre City New World supermarket on Cumberland Street in Dunedin.

Many travellers visit the peninsula by taking one of the many day tours that operate out of Dunedin. These include Back to Nature Tours *(☎ 0800 477 0484; **website** www.backtonaturetours.co.nz)* and Elm Wildlife Tours *(☎ (03) 474 1872; **website** www.elmwildlifetours.co.nz)*. Day tours from Dunedin cost around $80.

Accommodation
Bus-Stop Backpackers
Accommodation at Bus-Stop Backpackers is in the main house with double rooms in a caravan and an old bus. The main house is quite small, with a clean kitchen and a common room with a quiet, homely atmosphere. Shared rooms have made-up single beds and each guest gets a fresh towel. The bathrooms are nice and clean, and there are nice views. Guests can buy fresh vegetables from the organic garden. They also have a small boat that guests can borrow.
252 Harrington Point Road, Portobello
☎ *(03) 478 0330*
Website *www.bus-stop.co.nz*
Dorm bed *$30 ($25 BBH);* ***double/twin room*** *$60 ($50 BBH)*

Maintenance & cleanliness	★★★
Facilities	★½
Atmosphere & character	★★½
Security	★
Overall rating	★★½

Sights & Activities
Fort Taiaroa & Royal Albatross Centre
This military post was developed in 1885 as part of Dunedin's harbour defences. It is now open to the public and features a lighthouse, tunnels and a working Armstrong disappearing gun. The fort is also home to seals, a Stewart Island shag colony and the world's only mainland albatross colony.

The Royal Albatross Centre has displays that provide insight into these enormous sea birds, which have a wingspan of 3m, and it also leads guided tours of the albatross colony between late November and mid-September.
Taiaroa Head, Otago Peninsula
☎ *(03) 478 0499*
Website *www.albatross.org.nz*
Admission *free; albatross tour $30*

Larnarch Castle
New Zealand's only castle is a popular stop on coach tours favoured by the over 60s, but it doesn't really compare to anything in Europe.
Camp Road, Peggys Hill
☎ *(03) 476 1616*
Website *www.larnachcastle.co.nz*
Admission *$25 castle; $10 grounds*
Open *Jan-Easter 9am-7pm daily;*

Easter-Sep 9am-5pm daily; Oct-Dec 9am-7pm daily

New Zealand Marine Studies Centre

Run by Otago University's Department of Marine Science, this aquarium showcases the university's marine research and is home to marine life from southern New Zealand waters including octopus, seahorses and crayfish.

Hatchery Road, Portobello

☎ *(03) 479 5826*

Website *www.otago.ac.nz/marinestudies*

Admission *aquarium $9; guided tour $18*

Open *noon-4.30pm daily; guided tour 10.30am daily*

Yellow Eyed Penguin Conservation Reserve

The world's rarest penguin can be seen at this conservation reserve on the ocean side of the peninsula. The conservation reserve features a system of trenches and observation hides that allow you to see these unique animals at close range.

Harrington Point Road, Otago Peninsula

☎ *(03) 478 0286*

Website *www.penguinplace.co.nz*

90-min tour $35

Open *1 Jan-7 Apr 10.15am-90mins before sunset daily; 8 Apr-30 Sep 3.15pm-4.45pm daily; 1 Oct-31 Dec 10.15am-90mins before sunset daily*

Queenstown

Queenstown lies at the edge of Lake Wakatipu against a backdrop of the beautiful Remarkables mountain range. It is one of the most well-known destinations in New Zealand and a highlight of a visit to the South Island. During summer, this resort town is a well-oiled adventure activity machine, offering bungee jumping, jet boating, paragliding, and white water rafting, among others. It is home to the world's first commercial bungee jump site at Kawarau Bridge, an extremely popular activity with backpackers; as well as the Canyon Swing, the adrenaline junkies' latest craze. In winter the town transforms into a busy ski resort, offering plenty of facilities for skiers and snowboarders.

There is a good range of accommodation, dining and nightlife here as well, although prices are steep. The town centre is an attractive and buzzing cluster of souvenir shops, alfresco cafés, and activity booking agencies. Queenstown can be a lot of fun, but beware of your budget here. If you are after a serious adrenaline rush and have the funds, it is a good idea to take advantage of the combo deals offered on adventure activities.

Practical Information

INFORMATION & BOOKING CENTRES

Queenstown i-SITE Visitor Centre

Corner Camp & Shotover Streets, Queenstown

☎ *(03) 442 4100*

Website *www.queenstown-vacation.com*

Open *7am-6pm daily*

Queenstown Regional DOC Visitor Centre

38 Shotover Street, Queenstown

☎ *(03) 442 7935*

Website *www.doc.govt.nz*

Open *9am-6pm daily*

The Station Information & Booking Centre

Corner Camp & Shotover Streets, Queenstown

☎ *(03) 442 5252*

Website *www.thestation.co.nz*

Open *8am-8pm daily*

INTERNET ACCESS

Budget Communications

Level 2, O'Connells Mall, 309 Camp Street, Queenstown

☎ *(03) 441 1562*

Open *9am-11pm daily*

Ecafe

50 Shotover Street, Queenstown

☎ *(03) 442 9888*

Website *www.ecafe.co.nz*

Open *9am-11pm daily*

Global Gossip Queenstown

27 Shotover Street

☎ *(03) 441 3018*

Website *www.globalgossip.com*

There is free wireless internet access at **Esquires Coffee** at the Sofitel Hotel *(8 Duke Street, Queenstown)* and at **Patagonia Chocolates** on the lakefront *(50 Beach Street, Queenstown)*, which also has New Zealand's best hot chocolate.

Coming & Going

AIR

Queenstown Airport *(☎ (03) 442 3505; **website** www.queenstownairport.co.nz)* is in Frankton about 6km outside the town centre.

Although is close enough to walk into town although most people take a shuttle or the local bus *(☎ (03) 441 4471; **website** www.connectabus.com)*, which costs $5.50 and runs every 30 minutes between the airport and central Queenstown or the Super Shuttle *(☎ (03) 442 3639 or 0800 748 8853; **website** www.supershuttle.co.nz)*, which costs $13-17 and can drop you off at your hostel.

BUS

Several coach and shuttle bus companies connect Queenstown with destinations throughout the South Island.

Atomic Shuttles *(☎ (03) 349 0697; **website** www.atomictravel.co.nz)* go to Christchurch, Greymouth and Wanaka. They depart from the corner of Camp and Shotover Streets.

InterCity Coachlines *(☎ (03) 471 7143; **website** www.intercity.co.nz)* go to Christchurch, Dunedin, Franz Josef, Invercargill, Milford Sound and Wanaka. They depart from the Athol Street car park.

Naked Bus *(☎ 0900 62533; **website** www.nakedbus.com)* go to Christchurch, Dunedin, Greymouth, Invercargill, Milford Sound and Wanaka. They depart from the corner of Camp and Shotover Streets.

Southern Link K Bus *(☎ (03) 358 8355 or 0508 458 835; **website** www.southernlinkkbus.co.nz)* go to Christchurch. They depart from the corner of Camp and Shotover Streets.

Topline Tours *(☎ (03) 442 8178; **website** www.toplinetours.co.nz)* go to Te Anau. They leave from 35 Shotover Street.

Wanaka Connexions *(☎ 0800 244 844; **website** www.time2.co.nz/transport/wanaka_connexions)* have shuttle services to Wanaka plus coaches to Dunedin and Invercargill. They leave from the corner of Camp and Shotover Streets.

If you're going to Arrowtown, the Arrowtown Scenic Bus *(☎ (03) 422 1900; **website** www.arrowtownbus.co.nz)* runs day trips from Queenstown for $25 that return on a different route so you can see more scenery, but a much cheaper option is the local Connectabus *(☎ (03) 441 4471; **website** www.connectabus.com)* which runs every hour and costs $7.50 each way or $13 for a day pass.

HITCHHIKING

Because Queenstown is a small town with a large proportion of backpackers, it can be difficult to hitch a ride out of town. Your best bet is to post notices in the hostels around town advertising that you want a lift and are prepared to pay something toward fuel expenses. Do this a few days in advance and you should have some chance of getting a lift out of town in the company of fellow travellers.

If you're a hard-core hitcher or just someone looking for the cheapest transport option you may end up competing with scores of other backpackers for a lift out of town which could lead to a long wait. Take the Connecta bus or walk out on Frankton Road until you're out of town and find a good spot to wait for a lift. Use a destination sign, since both Christchurch and Dunedin-bound traffic use this road.

Local Transport

The Connecta Bus *(☎ (03) 441 4471; **website** www.connectabus.com)* operates three routes around Queenstown. Services run every 30 minutes to an hour and it is useful for getting to the airport, the supermarket or Remarkables Park Shopping Centre. The one-way fare is $5.50 for travel within Queenstown, although it goes as far afield as Arrowtown ($7.50). A day pass costs $13 and is valid on all services including buses to Arrowtown.

Accommodation

Alpine Lodge

Alpine Lodge is a small hostel with a mellow atmosphere. There is a cosy

lounge with books, guitars and a nice log fire; the small kitchen is well stocked and they offer internet access ($4 per hour), a ski storage room, a laundry and tour bookings. The dorms are a bit dull and some are quite messy. It is just a few minutes' walk from the town centre.
13 Gorge Road, Queenstown
(03) 442 7220
***Website** www.alpinelodgebackpackers.co.nz*
***Dorm bed** $25 ($22 BBH); **double/twin room** $60 ($54 BBH)*
***Credit cards** MC, Visa*
***Reception open** 8am-8pm daily*

Maintenance & cleanliness	★★★½
Facilities	★½
Atmosphere & character	★★★½
Security	★★
Overall rating	★★★

Aspen Lodge

Aspen Lodge is an alpine-style lodge with a good atmosphere and basic amenities. The dorms are well maintained with proper mattresses and most have en suite facilities. There is a well equipped kitchen that could be better maintained; laundry facilities, internet access ($4 per hour) and a barbecue area. The facilities are less than spectacular, but it is popular with backpackers so it has a fun ambience.
11 Gorge Road, Queenstown
(03) 442 9671
***Website** www.aspenlodge.co.nz*
***Dorm bed** $22-27 (18-24 BBH); **double/twin room** $62-78 ($56-72 BBH)*
***Credit cards** MC Visa*
***Reception open** 7.30am-8pm daily*

Maintenance & cleanliness	★★★
Facilities	★★
Atmosphere & character	★★★½
Security	★½
Overall rating	★★½

Base Discovery Lodge

This Base hostel enjoys a central location and has a full-on party atmosphere. It attracts a young backpacker crowd, who attempt each night to cram into the tiny, messy kitchen to cook. The dorms are modern and clean, with good mattresses and beds made-up in Base's trademark black and red. Each dorm has a fridge and telephone and some have a small balcony with mountain views. There are plenty of toilets and showers that are newly renovated, but which quickly get dirty. There is also internet and Wi-Fi access, a laundry and a full service travel agency and tour desk. When we visited we found the reception staff to be abrupt and discourteous.
47-49 Shotover Street, Queenstown
(03) 441 1185
***Website** www.stayatbase.com*
***Dorm bed** $26 ($25 VIP); **single room** $78-98 ($77-97 VIP); **double/twin room** $78-98 ($76-96 VIP); **triple room** $135 ($132 VIP)*
***Credit cards** MC, Visa*
***Reception open** 24 hours*

Maintenance & cleanliness	★★★½
Facilities	★★½
Atmosphere & character	★★★
Security	★★★★
Overall rating	★★★

BJ's Lakeside Backpackers

This hostel shares property with a motel. The dormitory accommodation is set in a run-down building perched on a hill with good views over the lake. Unfortunately, it is terribly maintained, with a kitchen that is barely useful. The bathrooms are filthy and the dorms are plain with old mattresses. They have laundry facilities and internet access, but there is not a very good atmosphere here.
18 Lake Esplanade, Queenstown
(03) 442 8976
***Website** www.queenstownaccommodation.co.nz/lakeside-backpackers.html*
***Dorm bed** $25 ($22 BBH); **single room** $45 ($42 BBH); **double/twin room** $69 ($66 BBH)*
***Credit cards** Amex, Diners, JCB, MC, Visa*
***Reception open** 7.30am-9pm daily*

Maintenance & cleanliness	★★★
Facilities	★½
Atmosphere & character	★★
Security	★½
Overall rating	★★½

Black Sheep Lodge

Black Sheep Lodge is a well maintained hostel with great facilities and a young, energetic vibe. The beds are comfortable and made up with nice blue sheets and duvets. There are tidy bathrooms and a large kitchen with new appliances plus a cosy, spacious common room with Sky TV, a pool table, and a bar and a large outside deck with a spa pool. It is around 500m from the centre of town. They offer free breakfast and a free beer with any activity booking.

13 Frankton Road, Queenstown
☎ *(03) 442 7289*
Website *www.blacksheepbackpackers.co.nz*
Dorm bed *$26 ($23 BBH);* ***double/twin room*** *$62 ($56 BBH)*
Credit cards *MC, Visa*
Reception open *24 hours*

Maintenance & cleanliness	★★★½
Facilities	★★★
Atmosphere & character	★★★★
Security	★★
Overall rating	★★★½

Bumbles Backpackers

Bumbles is a small hostel with a good location by the lake. The building is painted in nice colours, and the common room has a spectacular panoramic lake view. Some rooms also have a balcony. Accommodation is in comfortable wooden bunks and the beds are made up with nice dark blue duvets. Bathrooms are renovated and kept shiny and clean. They have a laundry, internet access and a cheery atmosphere.

2 Brunswick Street, Queenstown
☎ *(03) 442 6298 or 0800 286 2537*
Website *www.bumblesbackpackers.co.nz*
Dorm bed *$27;* ***double/twin room*** *$60*
Credit cards *MC, Visa*
Reception open *7.30am-1pm & 3pm-7.30pm daily*

Maintenance & cleanliness	★★★½
Facilities	★★½
Atmosphere & character	★★★
Security	★½
Overall rating	★★★

Bungi Backpackers

Bungi Backpackers is a funky little hostel with a great atmosphere. The dorm rooms are colourful with comfy beds and central heating. The bathrooms are quite rough, but clean nonetheless, and the kitchen is in the same state. They have cheap laundry facilities, internet access ($6 per hour) including wireless, a common room with a large screen TV and a big video collection plus a large garden area with a barbecue. There is also a great spa pool that is free for guests to use and the friendly staff serve free vegetable soup every night. It is not as central as many of Queenstown's other hostels, although it is only a 10-minute walk to the town centre.

Corner Stanley & Sydney Streets, Queenstown
☎ *(03) 442 8725*
Website *www.kiwi-backpackers.co.nz/bungi_backpackerrs.html*
Dorm bed *$21-24 ($18-21 BBH);* ***double/twin room*** *$51 ($48 BBH)*
Credit cards *MC, Visa*
Reception open *8am-10pm daily*

Maintenance & cleanliness	★★★
Facilities	★★½
Atmosphere & character	★★★★
Security	★½
Overall rating	★★★

Butterfli Lodge

This is a low-key option for Queenstown. It consists of two old houses that are caringly maintained, one with a great common room with log fire and large windows offering stunning views. The kitchen is quite tired and messy, but the spacious dorms are nicer with comfortable single beds made up with duvets. There is a good TV lounge with plenty of DVDs, laundry facilities, cheap internet access and a barbecue area. It is on a quiet residential street close to town.

62 Thompson Street, Queenstown
☎ *(03) 442 6367*
Website *www.butterfli.co.nz*
Dorm bed *$26 ($24 BBH);* ***double/twin room*** *$62 ($58 BBH)*
Reception open *9am-12.30pm & 3pm-7.30pm daily*

Maintenance & cleanliness	★★★
Facilities	★★
Atmosphere & character	★★★
Security	★
Overall rating	★★½

Deco Backpackers

Deco Backpackers is a good hostel with clean and well maintained facilities. The dorms are a bit cramped, but they have wonderfully comfortable beds and fluffy pillows. There is a large fully-equipped kitchen and a dining area that doubles as the common room where backpackers gather to socialise at night and use the free wireless internet. There is also a cosy TV lounge with DVDs and a garden with fruit trees, a barbecue and an awesome view. The hostel is centrally heated and the water throughout is filtered. It has an intimate, convivial atmosphere.

52 Man Street, Queenstown

☎ *(03) 442 7384*

Website *www.decobackpackers.co.nz*

Otago

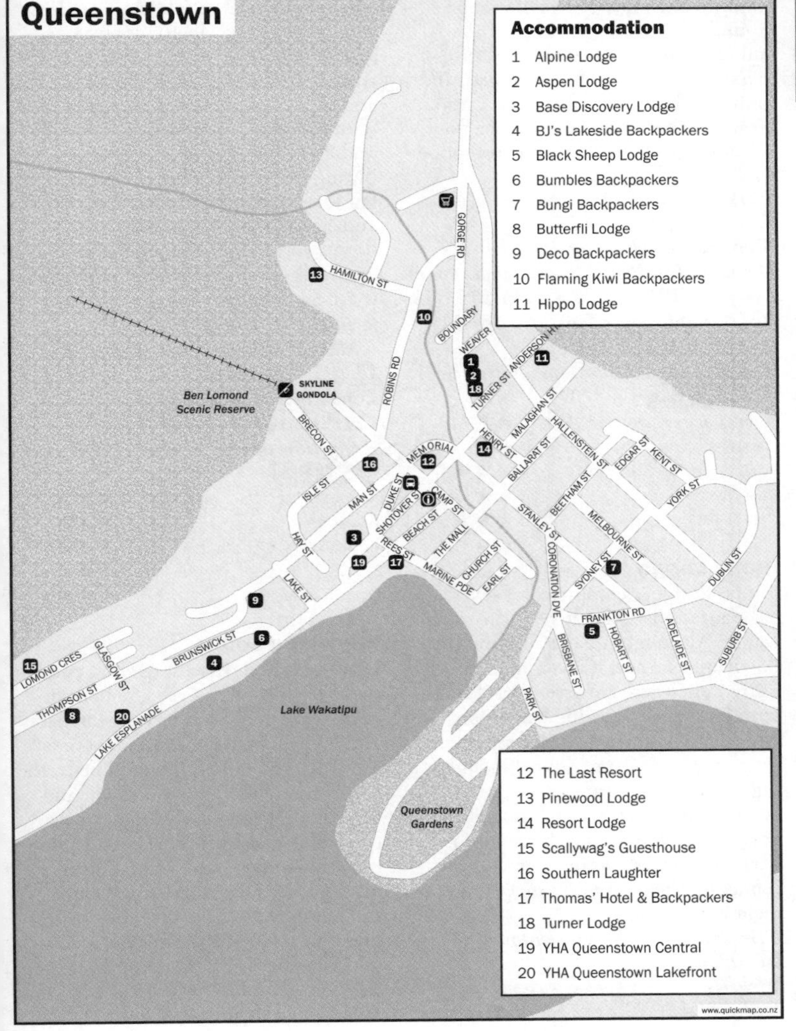

***Dorm bed** $27 ($24 BBH); **double/ twin room** $60-76 ($54-70 BBH); **triple room** $87 ($78 BBH); **camping** $15 per person*
***Credit cards** MC, Visa*
***Reception open** 8am-8pm daily*

Maintenance & cleanliness	★★★½
Facilities	★★½
Atmosphere & character	★★★
Security	★½
Overall rating	★★★

Flaming Kiwi Backpackers

Flaming Kiwi hostel is really rough around the edges. Furnishings are old and tattered, the common areas are messy, the dorm rooms are musty and drab, and bathrooms need renovation. However they do have a free spa pool. It is not very central, but the reception staff are as nice as can be.
39 Robins Road, Queenstown
(03) 442 5494 or 0800 555 775
***Website** www.flamingkiwi.co.nz*
***Dorm bed** $23 ($20 BBH); **single room** $44 ($40 BBH); **double room** $55 ($52 BBH); **triple room** $69 ($60 BBH)*
***Credit cards** MC, Visa*
***Reception open** 8am-8pm daily*

Maintenance & cleanliness	★★½
Facilities	★★
Atmosphere & character	★★★½
Security	★★
Overall rating	★★½

Hippo Lodge

Hippo Lodge is comprised of several old houses on a hillside near the town centre. Although it has a slightly run down appearance, it is maintained fairly well. There are several buildings with kitchens; gleaming bathrooms and cosy TV lounges with log fires and internet access ($6 per hour) including wireless. There are also laundry facilities and a barbecue. Some of the dorms, which have new made-up beds, have stunning views of town and the Remarkables mountain range. It has a mellow atmosphere.
4 Anderson Heights, Queenstown
(03) 442 5785
***Website** www.hippolodge.co.nz*
***Dorm bed** $26-27 ($24-25 BBH); **single room** $40 ($35 BBH); **double room** $65-80 ($60-75 BBH)*
***Credit cards** MC, Visa*
***Reception open** summer 8.30am-8pm daily; winter 8.30am-6.30pm daily*

Maintenance & cleanliness	★★★
Facilities	★★★
Atmosphere & character	★★★
Security	★
Overall rating	★★★

The Last Resort

When all else fails, the Last Resort is a brilliant hostel to fall back on. This small place is excellently maintained with good facilities and a few pleasant surprises. The kitchen is old but clean and well kept; there is a common room with new sofas, a great big-screen TV and 250 films to choose from, a nice dining room with a log fire, cheap laundry, free internet including Wi-Fi and a sundeck with a barbecue. The dorms and bathrooms are immaculate, and beds are made up with high quality sheets. Security is great and management are lovely.
6 Memorial Street, Queenstown
(03) 442 4320
***Dorm bed** $28 ($25 BBH)*
***Credit cards** MC, Visa*
***Reception open** 9.30am-7.30pm daily*

Maintenance & cleanliness	★★★½
Facilities	★★★
Atmosphere & character	★★★★
Security	★★★½
Overall rating	★★★½

Pinewood Lodge

Pinewood Lodge is a sprawling complex of cabins with over 250 beds in total. Each cabin has its own kitchen and bathrooms. The spacious rooms are clean and have with good beds, the Kitchens are modern and clean, and there is a separate TV lounge with a pool table and internet access. There is also a spa pool and a trampoline. It has a good backpacker crowd and a fun atmosphere. It is a few blocks from town, so it is quiet during the day.
48 Hamilton Street, Queenstown
(03) 442 8273
***Website** www.pinewood.co.nz*

***Dorm bed** $25; **double room** $55-100*
***Credit cards** MC, Visa*
***Reception open** 7.30am-9pm daily*

Maintenance & cleanliness	★★★½
Facilities	★★★½
Atmosphere & character	★★★★
Security	★½
Overall rating	★★★½

Resort Lodge

Resort Lodge is a nice building near the town centre. It has brightly coloured rooms and a big balcony with a barbecue and nice views. There is an excellent TV lounge, two good kitchens, laundry facilities, internet access (including Wi-Fi) and a tour and activity booking service. Accommodation is good with made-up beds and phones in each room.

6 Henry Street, Queenstown
☎ *(03) 442 4970 or 0800 082 224*
***Website** www.resortlodge.co.nz*
***Dorm bed** $25 ($22 BBH); **double/twin room** $60 ($55 BBH)*
***Credit cards** MC, Visa*
***Reception open** 8am-8.30pm daily*

Maintenance & cleanliness	★★½
Facilities	★★
Atmosphere & character	★★★
Security	★★
Overall rating	★★½

Scallywag's Guesthouse

Staying at Scallywag's is like staying at an old uncle's house; complete with authentic décor that includes souvenir plates on the walls. It gets mixed reviews from travellers, mainly because it is such as small place where the manager's personality defines the ambience. People who get along with the manager rave about the place, but some travellers find that his presence is a bit too overbearing. It's a quiet place with brilliant views of the lake and the mountains, but it's not the place to stay if you're looking for a party atmosphere. The largest dorm has four beds, each with individual curtains and reading lights.

27 Lomond Street, Queenstown
☎ *(03) 442 4970*
***Dorm bed** $25 ($23 BBH); **double room** $62 ($58 BBH)*

Maintenance & cleanliness	★★★½
Facilities	★★
Atmosphere & character	★★★½
Security	★
Overall rating	★★★

Southern Laughter

Southern Laughter is a great hostel comprised of three timber houses close to the town centre. There are several lounges and kitchens with cool music playing and an antique-style décor. Dorms have TV, kitchenettes, and good beds, although they do get quite cluttered. Bathrooms are new and spotless. They have a pool table, a spa pool, internet access (including Wi-Fi), a barbecue and a sundeck with a great mountain view. It has a funky, laid-back atmosphere.

4 Isle Street, Queenstown
☎ *(03) 441 8828 or 0800 528 4837*
***Website** www.southernlaughter.co.nz*
***Dorm bed** $24-27 ($21-24 BBH); **double/twin room** $56-66 ($50-60 BBH); **triple room** $78 ($69 BBH)*
***Credit cards** MC, Visa*
***Reception open** 7.30am-9pm daily*

Maintenance & cleanliness	★★★½
Facilities	★★★
Atmosphere & character	★★★★
Security	★★½
Overall rating	★★★½

Thomas' Hotel & Backpackers

This hotel-turned-hostel has a great location in the town centre by the lakefront. Facilities include a small TV lounge, a below-average kitchen and a café, but otherwise there is not much in the way of common areas. The spacious dorm rooms have made-up beds and en suite facilities and some even have a stunning view of the lake and mountains.

50 Beach Street, Queenstown
☎ *(03) 442 7180*
***Dorm bed** $30*
***Credit cards** MC, Visa*
***Reception open** 6.30am-9pm daily*

Maintenance & cleanliness	★★★
Facilities	★½
Atmosphere & character	★★★
Security	★★½
Overall rating	★★½

Turner Lodge

This is another property run by the friendly people at Alpine Lodge. It has a quieter atmosphere and more space. It features a huge common room with a retro ski lodge feel, complete with fluffy red carpet and a fully-equipped kitchen. Accommodation is in comfortable rooms with made-up beds, and the bathrooms are very clean. There are spectacular mountain views from the balcony. This property does not have internet access, but guests can also use the internet at Alpine Lodge, which is just around the corner. Guests can also use the ski storage room at Alpine Lodge.

2 Turner Street, Queenstown
☎ *(03) 442 9432*
Website *www.turnerlodge.co.nz*
Dorm bed *$25;* ***single room*** *$75;* ***double/twin room*** *$65-89*
Credit cards *MC, Visa*
Reception open *8am-8pm daily*

Maintenance & cleanliness	★★★½
Facilities	★★
Atmosphere & character	★★★
Security	★★
Overall rating	★★★

YHA Queenstown Central

The Queenstown Central YHA is a nice hostel crammed into a tiny building in the centre of town. The kitchen is open and airy and they have laundry facilities, internet access (including Wi-Fi) and a tour and activity booking service. The dorms are small with big made-up beds and each has an en suite bathroom, although these are outdated and ugly. There is a brilliant view from the upstairs common area. It has a more mature atmosphere than most of Queenstown's other hostels.

48A Shotover Street, Queenstown
☎ *(03) 442 7400*
Website *www.stayyha.com*
Dorm bed *$30 ($27 YHA);* ***double room*** *$82-100*
Credit cards *MC, Visa*
Reception open *7am-9pm daily*

Maintenance & cleanliness	★★★
Facilities	★★½
Atmosphere & character	★★★
Security	★★★½
Overall rating	★★★

YHA Queenstown Lakefront

YHA's original Queenstown hostel is a huge alpine chalet overlooking the lake. Facilities include a large modern fully-equipped kitchen with lots of pots and pans and even rice cookers; there is also a common room with internet terminals, big sofas and tall windows with a spectacular view of the lake and mountains. They also offer laundry facilities, a full tour and activity desk, a small shop at reception and a TV lounge with plenty of DVDs. The dorm rooms are spacious and well-appointed with made-up beds (some are singles) and new carpet and the bathrooms are clean, if a bit tired. For a YHA hostel, it has a good atmosphere.

88-90 Lake Esplanade, Queenstown
☎ *(03) 442 8413*
Website *www.stayyha.com*
Dorm bed *$27-31 ($24-28 HI/YHA);* ***double/twin room*** *$66-76 ($60-70 HI/YHA);* ***triple room*** *$83 ($74 HI/YHA)*
Credit cards *MC, Visa*
Reception open *6.30am-10pm daily*

Maintenance & cleanliness	★★★★
Facilities	★★½
Atmosphere & character	★★★½
Security	★★★
Overall rating	★★★½

Eating & Drinking

Although Queenstown has mostly expensive eateries, there are deals here and there. Of course, the standard fast food can be found everywhere, but there are also some good little cafés, especially outside of the centre.

Most hostels don't offer free breakfast, so you should head to the **FreshChoice** supermarket *(64 Gorge Road, Queenstown)* to stock up on groceries. The **Alpine Supermarket** in the centre *(corner Stanley & Shotover Streets, Queenstown)* has much higher prices.

The **Traffic Café** in Global Gossip *(27 Shotover Street, Queenstown)* does a great breakfast burrito, and for a cheap lunch near the waterfront, head to the green food wagon on the corner of Rees and Beach Streets for good fish & chips. **Fergburger** *(42A Shotover Street, Queenstown)* has a good atmosphere and makes some hearty and delicious burgers for a relatively low price. Another budget option is the food court at the Mall, where you can get great deals on Indian curry and Thai food.

The nightlife in Queenstown is great and many bars offer happy hour drinks. **Pog Mahones Irish Pub** *(14 Rees Street, Queenstown)* is a popular spot with great atmosphere and cheap drink specials and the **Altitude Bar & Café** *(49 Shotover Street,Queenstown)* at Base Backpackers has DJs, karaoke, live music and big screens for watching sport.

Activities

There is no shortage of things to do in and around Queenstown and spending too long here is a sure-fire way to blow through your budget.

ACTIVITY PACKAGE DEALS

If you're planning on doing several activities such as bungee jumping, jet boating and rafting then it may be worth looking at the several combo offers available through booking agents and hostels around town.

Some of the more popular combo offers include Queenstown Rafting's Twin and Triple Challenge packages and the Queenstown Combo packages organised by Totally Tourism.

Queenstown Combos

Totally Tourism *(☎ (03) 442 7318 or 0800 423 836 (0800 4 ADVENTURE); **website** www.combos.co.nz)* have a good choice of activity packages featuring activities on either the Kawarau or Shotover River.

Kawarau River combos include the Queenstown Combo, which combines a helicopter ride, Kawarau Jet and a gondola ride for $210 and the Kawarau Duo, which combines rafting and a ride on the Shotover Jet for $254.

There is an even bigger selection of combo packages on the Shotover River. These combos include bungee jumping, helicopter flights, jet boat rides, skydiving and white water rafting and include:

- Awesome Foursome: Nevis Highwire bungee jump, a helicopter ride, a jet boat ride and rafting on the Shotover River for $509
- Kawarau Bungy Jet: a bungee jump from AJ Hackett's Kawarau Bridge and a Shotover jet boat ride for $254
- Nevis Bungy Jet: the AJ Hackett Nevis Highwire bungee jump and a jet boat ride on the Shotover River for $314
- Nevis Bungy Raft: the AJ Hackett Nevis Highwire bungee jump and white water rafting on the Shotover River for $355
- Shotover Bikeraft: mountain biking and white water rafting on the Shotover River for $295
- Shotover Canyon Combo: the Shotover Canyon Swing, a Shotover jet boat ride, white water rafting on the Shotover River and a helicopter flight into Skippers Canyon for $470
- Shotover Freefall: tandem skydiving from 9000ft, a jet boat ride on the Shotover River, a helicopter flight into Skippers Canyon and white water rafting on the Shotover River for $549
- Shotover Heli Scenic: Shotover jet boat ride and a helicopter flight over Queenstown for $249
- Shotover Heli: a helicopter flight, a ride on the Shotover jet boat and gondola ride for $215
- Shotover Heliraft: a helicopter flight and white water rafting for $239
- Shotover High Five: a helicopter flight, a ride on the Shotover jet boat, a gondola ride, a film and a ride on the Skyline luge for $230
- Shotover High Flyer: a Shotover jet boat ride, a helicopter flight, a bungee jump from AJ Hackett's Ledge and a ride on the gondola for $340
- Shotover Trio: a helicopter ride, a ride on the Shotover jet boat and

white water rafting on the Shotover River for $309
- Skippers Heli Bike: mountain biking and a helicopter flight for $209
- Skydive Raft: a 9000ft tandem skydive and white water rafting on the Shotover River for $395
- Skydive Threesome: a 9000ft tandem skydive, a Shotjet jet boat ride and white water rafting on the Shotover River for $495
- Swing Raft: Shotover Canyon Swing and white water rafting on the Shotover River for $305
- The Shotover Duo combines the Shotover Jet with white water rafting on the Shotover River for $259.
- Whitewater: river surfing on the Kawarau River, a Shotover jet boat ride on the Shotover River and white water rafting on the Shotover River $399

Twin & Triple Challenge

Queenstown Rafting *(☎ (03) 442 9792 or 0800 723 8464 (0800 RAFTING); **website** www.rafting.co.nz)* has combo packages that combine white water rafting with bungee jumping and a jet boat ride.

The Kawarau Twin Challenge ($259) combines white water rafting on the Kawarau River with a jet boat ride on the Shotover Jet. The Kawarau Twin Thriller ($249) is similar, but with a jet boat ride on the Kawarau Jet.

The Nevis Triple Challenge ($509) combines the Nevis Highwire bungee with heli-rafting on the Shotover River and a ride on the Shotover Jet. The Nevis Triple Thriller ($495) is similar, but with a jet boat ride on the Kawarau Jet.

The Shotover Twin Challenge ($259) combines white water rafting on the Shotover River with a Shotover jet boat ride. The Shotover Twin Thriller ($249) is similar, but has a jet boat ride on the Kawarau River instead.

The Shotover Triple Challenge ($309) combines heli-rafting on the Shotover River with a ride on the Shotover Jet. The Shotover Triple Thriller ($299) is similar, but with a ride on the Kawarau Jet instead.

BUNGEE JUMPING

Queenstown is considered the world centre for bungee jumping. Kawarau Bridge (43m) – the world's first commercial bungee site – started operating here in 1988 and this was followed by various attempts at higher jump sites, including the Nevis Highwire (134m), which is the world's third-highest bungee jumping platform.

AJ Hackett, who developed the world's first commercial bungee jump at Kawarau Bridge now operates three bungee sites around Queenstown that range from in height from 43m to 134m.

Transport to all the AJ Hackett bungee sites, except the Ledge, departs from the Station *(corner Camp & Shotover Streets, Queenstown)*.

Kawarau Bridge

This is the world's first commercial bungee site and has been in operation since 1988. This historic bridge offers a 43m jump and is the only Queenstown site that allows a water touch.

☎ (03) 442 4007 or 0800 286 495 (0800 BUNGY JUMP)
***Website** www.bungy.co.nz*
***Price** $160 including t-shirt and transport*

The Ledge

The 47m Ledge is accessible by the Skyline gondola ride and is the closest jump site to the town centre. It offers night jumps during winter.

Bob's Peak via Skyline Gondola
☎ (03) 442 4007 or 0800 286 495 (0800 BUNGY JUMP)
***Website** www.bungy.co.nz*
***Price** $160 including t-shirt and gondola*

Nevis Highwire Bungy

AJ Hackett's highest bungee jump offers a 128km/h freefall from 134m. The purpose-built jump pod is suspended high above the Nevis River and reached by 4WD and cable car. The return trip from Queenstown is four hours making this a good half-day excursion. It's a must if you really want to prove to yourself how hardcore you really are.

☎ (03) 442 4007 or 0800 286 495 (0800 BUNGY JUMP)

Website www.bungy.co.nz
Price $220 including t-shirt and transport

Secrets of Bungy Tour
AJ Hackett runs a behind-the-scenes tour of its bungee jumping operation that is an ideal alternative for those who want a bungee experience but are too chicken to jump. The 45-minute tour takes place at the Kawarau Bridge bungee centre.
☎ *(03) 442 4007 or 0800 286 495 (0800 BUNGY JUMP)*
Website www.bungy.co.nz
Price $45 including transport

3Thrillogy
This combo package is designed for hard-core thrill seeking nutcases. The 3Thrillogy combines the Kawarau, Ledge and Nevis Highwire bungee jumps into one package.
☎ *(03) 442 4007 or 0800 286 495 (0800 BUNGY JUMP)*
Website www.bungy.co.nz
3Thrillogy $425; includes t-shirt and transport

CANYONING

Routeburn Canyoning (☎ *(03) 441 3003; website www.canyoning.co.nz)* run three-hour trips that involve abseiling down waterfalls, swimming slender passages and plunging into pools. Canyoning trips cost $145.

HANG GLIDING

Coronet Tandems (☎ *0800 46 7325 (0800 GO PEAK); website www.tandemparagliding.com)*, **Extreme Air** (☎ *0800 727245 (0800 PARAGLIDE); website www.extremeair.co.nz)*, **Queenstown Hanggliding and Paragliding** (☎ *(03) 442 5747 or 0800 878 4373 (0800 UP THERE); website www.hangglide.co.nz)* and **SkyTrek** (☎ *(03) 409 0625 or 0800 759 873 (0800 SKYTREK); website www.skytrek.co.nz)* run hang gliding trips from Coronet Peak. Flights generally last only 10-15 minutes depending on weather conditions, although the entire trip lasts around 2½ hours including transport to and from Coronet Peak. Most hang gliding companies charge $195 for a tandem flight, although during winter there is a higher launch site that costs a little more. Prices include return transport from Queenstown.

Most of the hang gliding companies also operate tandem paragliding trips.

JET BOATING

While every little town and village in New Zealand seems to have a jet boat operator, it's important to realise that Queenstown played a pioneering role in the jet boating industry and is still regarded by many as the place to go for a spin on a river.

Kawarau Jet
The **Kawarau Jet** (☎ *(03) 442 6142 or 0800 529 272 (0800 KAWARAU); website www.kjet.co.nz)* is the world's first commercial jet boat operation and the 43km ride combines both the Kawarau and Shotover Rivers and features plenty of 360° spins. Kawarau Jet costs $89 and departs from the town pier right in the centre of Queenstown.

Shotover Jet
The **Shotover Jet** (☎ *(03) 442 8570 or 0800 802 804; website www.shotoverjet.co.nz)* operates exclusively on the Shotover River. It is a shorter and more expensive ride than the Kawarau Jet, but it is a more exciting ride taking you deep into the Shotover River Canyon. It costs $109 and includes transport to and from the Station (corner Camp & Shotover Streets, Queenstown).

PARAGLIDING

Coronet Tandems (☎ *0800 46 7325 (0800 GO PEAK); website www.tandemparagliding.com)*, **Extreme Air** (☎ *0800 727245 (0800 PARAGLIDE); website www.extremeair.co.nz)* and **Queenstown Hanggliding and Paragliding** (☎ *(03) 442 5747 or 0800 878 4373 (0800 UP THERE); website www.hangglide.co.nz)* run paragliding flights from Coronet Peak. Flights generally last only 10-15 minutes depending on weather conditions, although the entire trip lasts around 2½ hours including transport to and from Coronet Peak. Most paragliding companies charge $195 for a tandem flight.

Most of the paragliding companies also operate tandem hang gliding trips.

SCENIC FLIGHTS

You have the choice of taking a scenic flight in a helicopter, acrobatic bi-plane or a regular plane. A lot of backpackers take a helicopter flight as part of a combo package or heli-rafting trip.

Actionflite

Actionflite *(☎ 0800 4 788687 (0800 4 STUNTS); **website** www.actionflite.co.nz)* has acrobatic bi-plane rides that are much more than a scenic flight. It's a fast adrenaline-pumping ride of a lifetime that will give you an absolute buzz as your pilot takes the Pitts Special through a series of acrobatic stunts that you would normally only see at an airshow. The flight costs $295.

The Helicopter Line

The Helicopter Line *(☎ (03) 442 3034; **website** www.helicopter.co.nz)* run scenic flights that include a 20-minute flight over the Remarkables ($190), a 50-minute flight over the Southern Alps with a snow landing on Jura Glacier ($420) and a 1½ hour flight to Milford Sound that includes three landings in the mountains ($650).

SKIING & SNOWBOARDING

With all the activities on offer, it's easy to forget that Queenstown started out as a ski resort. The two main ski areas are Coronet Peak and the Remarkables, although Queenstown can also be used as a base for Cardrona and Wanaka's Treble Cone.

Coronet Peak

People have been skiing at Coronet Peak *(**website** www.nzski.com/coronet/)* since 1947, making it New Zealand's oldest ski area. It is the closest resort to Queenstown, has a long season and gets very busy on weekends during the season. A full day lift pass costs $93.

The Remarkables

The Remarkables *(**website** www.nzski.com/remarkables/)* is also a popular ski area but it is less crowded than Coronet Peak. A full day lift pass $87.

Multi-Day Passes

The same company runs both Coronet Peak and the Remarkables and multi-day lift passes work at both resorts. A three-day pass valid at both ski areas costs $263.

SKYDIVING

If a 134m bungee jump isn't high enough you can always jump out of a plane and freefall at 200km/h. Nzone operates tandem skydives where you have the option of jumping at 12000ft (45 seconds freefall) or 15000ft (60 seconds freefall).

35 Shotover Street, Queenstown
☎ *(03) 442 5867*
***Website** www.skydivequeenstown.co.nz*
***Tandem skydive from 12000ft** $299; **tandem skydive from 15000ft** $399*

SKYLINE GONDOLA & LUGE

The Skyline gondola is one of Queenstown's longest established attractions. The gondola ride rises 450m to Bob's Peak where you can find a restaurant, AJ Hackett's Ledge bungee and swing and the Skyline luge track. There are two 800m-long luge tracks, a fast track and a slower, scenic track. The luge is one of Queenstown's best value activities with rides starting at $8.

Brecon Street, Queenstown
☎ *(03) 441 0101*
***Website** www.skyline.co.nz*
***Gondola** $21; **luge ride** $8, **five luge rides** $25, **gondola & five luge rides** $40*

SWINGING

Swings are the adrenaline junkie's latest alternative to bungee jumping. After being strapped into a harness that is attached to twin rope system, you launch yourself off the edge and free fall before the ropes change your direction and swing you in a giant arc.

The Ledge Sky Swing

AJ Hackett's swing operates from the same site as the Ledge bungee. It's only 47m high, but the gondola ride is included in the package.

Bob's Peak via Skyline Gondola
☎ *(03) 442 4007 or 0800 286 495 (0800 BUNGY JUMP)*
***Website** www.bungy.co.nz*
***Swing** $120 including gondola ride*

Shotover Canyon Swing
At 109m, this is the world's highest swing. At the lowest point you are only 7m from the Shotover River.
37 Shotover Street, Queenstown
☎ *(03) 442 9708*
***Website** www.canyonswing.co.nz*
***First swing** $169; **second swing** $49*

WHITE WATER RAFTING

White water rafting on the Kawarau and Shotover Rivers is comparatively good value since a rafting trip takes between a half-day and a full day for not much more than the cost of a 30-minute jet boat ride or three-minute bungee jump.

Both the Kawarau and Shotover Rivers offer grade three to five rapids, but most people find the rafting more exciting on the Shotover, which features the 170m-long Oxenbridge Tunnel. However the 400m-long Chinese Dog Leg rapid on the Kawarau is also one of New Zealand's best white water rides.

During winter (Jun-Sep) rafting companies are only permitted to raft for one hour, which means that they have to begin at Boulder Rapid (only accessible by helicopter), making rafting a more expensive exercise.

Challenge Rafting
☎ *(03) 442 7318 or 0800 4 ADVENTURE (0800 423 836)*
***Website** www.raft.co.nz*
***Kawarau River rafting** $165; **Shotover River rafting** $165; **Shotover River heli-rafting** $239*

Extreme Green Rafting
☎ *(03) 442 8517*
***Website** www.nzraft.com*
***Kawarau River rafting** $165; **Shotover River rafting** $165; **Shotover River heli-rafting** $239*

Queenstown Rafting
35 Shotover Street, Queenstown
☎ *(03) 442 9792 or 0800 RAFTING (0800 723 8464)*
***Website** www.rafting.co.nz*
***Kawarau River rafting** $165; **Shotover River rafting** $165; **Shotover River heli-rafting** $239*

WHITE WATER SLEDGING (HYDROSPEED)

River sledging, or hydrospeed, involves riding a custom-designed river sledge through rapids. Hydrospeed operators point out that you are in control, as opposed to rafting where the guide does the steering. **Frogz** *(☎ (03) 441 2318 or 0800 4 37649 (0800 4 FROGZ); **website** www.frogz.co.nz)* run river sledging trips the Kawarau River (grade 2-4 rapids). A half-day trip costs $135 and a full day trip costs $285.

Arrowtown

This historic gold mining town sprang to life during the 1862 gold rush, and it still retains the Wild West feel of a frontier town, even though it is inundated with day trippers and half the shops in town sell paua and jade souvenirs. It has a quaint main street with lots of little cafés, old wooden buildings and loads of character. Only 20km from Queenstown, it is probably the best preserved gold mining town in Otago and it deserves a visit, even if just for the day.

Practical Information

Arrowtown Visitor Information Centre
49 Buckingham Street, Arrowtown
☎ *(03) 442 1824*
***Website** www.arrowtown.org.nz*
***Open** 8.30am-5pm daily*

Coming & Going

The Arrowtown Scenic Bus *(☎ (03) 422 1900; **website** www.arrowtownbus.co.nz)* runs day trips from Queenstown for $25 that return on a different route so you can see more scenery, but a much cheaper option is the Connectabus *(☎ (03) 441 4471; **website** www.connectabus.com)*, which runs every hour and costs $7.50 each way or $13 for a day pass.

Accommodation

Poplar Lodge

This is a cosy and homely hostel with nicely maintained rooms not far from the town centre. Shared rooms have comfortable beds made up with duvets. There is a small living room with sofas and log fire and there are also tree-filled gardens with pleasant places to chill out

4 Merioneth Street, Arrowtown
☎ *(03) 442 1466*
Website *www.poplarlodge.co.nz*
Dorm bed *$25;* ***single room*** *$60;* ***double/twin room*** *$65-105*
Credit cards *MC, Visa*

Maintenance & cleanliness	★★★½
Facilities	★★
Atmosphere & character	★★★
Security	★½
Overall rating	★★★

Riverdown Guesthouse

This is a nice homely hostel in a very well maintained old cottage. Shared rooms are quaint and cosy, and there is a nice common area/lounge with a log fire. The fully-equipped kitchen is kept clean and includes a dishwasher, and the bathrooms are cute and tidy. There are lovely gardens outside, and overall it has a very quiet, relaxing atmosphere.

7 Bedford Street, Arrowtown
☎ *(03) 409 8499*
Dorm bed *$27;* ***single room*** *$50;* ***double/twin room*** *$60-80*
Open *Jan-Apr & Nov-Dec;* ***reception open*** *8.30am-8pm daily*

Maintenance & cleanliness	★★★
Facilities	★½
Atmosphere & character	★★½
Security	★½
Overall rating	★★½

Sights

Lakes District Museum

The Lakes District Museum is a small museum that features interesting displays on the history of the Southern Lakes district with exhibits about early pioneers and the effect of the gold rush.

49 Buckingham Street, Arrowtown
☎ *(03) 442 1824*
Website *www.museumqueenstown.com*
Admission *$5*
Open *8am-5pm daily*

Glenorchy

Glenorchy is at the northern end of Lake Wakatipu at the mouth of the Dart and Rees River valleys. This rural frontier settlement, a spectacular 45-minute drive from Queenstown, sits below Mount Aspiring National Park. It is most popular with hikers tackling the Caples, Greenstone, Rees, Dart and Routeburn Tracks, and much of the time the village has a good buzz about it with hikers coming off the tracks. There are not many facilities in town and it is advisable that you bring groceries and supplies with you, especially if you are planning a long hike.

Practical Information

Glenorchy Information Centre

Oban Street, Glenorchy
☎ *(03) 441 0303*
Website *www.glenorchyinfocentre.co.nz*

Coming & Going

Backpackers Express *(☎ (03) 441 0303;* ***website*** *www.glenorchyinfocentre.co.nz)* run minibuses between Queenstown and Glenorchy and they also operate a jet boat service to Kinloch Lodge and bus and boat services to the main walking tracks.

Accommodation

Glenorchy Backpackers Retreat

Glenorchy Backpackers Retreat consists of dorm rooms set behind the town's old pub, which has a considerable amount of character. The dorms have bunks and single beds, which are all made-up, in small rooms. The kitchen is tiny, and not very well equipped, but seeing as there are only 14 beds, it suffices. Showers and toilets are nice and clean. They are set in a small garden with a few resident cats. It has a very quiet atmosphere and internet access is available.

Corner Argyll & Mull Streets, Glenorchy
☎ *(03) 442 9902*
Dorm bed *$30;* ***double room*** *$60*

Credit cards *MC, Visa*
Reception open *8am-midnight daily*

Maintenance & cleanliness	★★★½
Facilities	★★
Atmosphere & character	★★★½
Security	★½
Overall rating	★★★½

Glenorchy Holiday Park

Located behind the information centre, this holiday park offers a wide range of accommodation options including one cabin with dorm beds. It is a large timber cabin with sturdy wooden bunks, full of hikers and travellers in town doing adventure activities. A kitchen is available to guests, which is very basic and quite run down. There is a pool table, laundry facilities and a barbecue area. The bathrooms are in a separate block as well, and also could use a bit of maintenance. But for those coming off a long track, it is a good place to clean and rest up before moving on.

Oban Street, Glenorchy
(03) 442 7171
Dorm bed *$25;* ***single room*** *$50;* ***double/twin room*** *$58*
Credit cards *MC, Visa*
Reception open *summer 8am-7.30pm daily; winter 8am-6pm daily*

Maintenance & cleanliness	★★
Facilities	★
Atmosphere & character	★★★½
Security	★
Overall rating	★★

Kinloch Lodge

This place offers hotel and hostel accommodation in a charming old lodge on the edge of the lake, 21km from Glenorchy. There is a good kitchen and dining area with modern fittings, and a nice garden barbecue area. Dorm rooms are well appointed with duvets, freshly painted walls and new carpet. They have internet access, a barbecue and a hillside spa pool with beautiful mountain views. There are also laundry facilities, a cosy TV lounge with DVDs, log fire and tour bookings. It is a great place to chill out and clean up after a long trek.

862 Kinloch Road, Kinloch
(03) 442 4900
Website *www.kinlochlodge.co.nz*
Dorm bed *$27 ($24 BBH);* ***double room*** *$72-110*
Credit cards *MC, Visa*
Reception open *8am-7pm daily*

Maintenance & cleanliness	★★★★
Facilities	★★★
Atmosphere & character	★★★★
Security	★
Overall rating	★★★½

Activities

Canyoning

Routeburn Canyoning *((03) 441 3003;* ***website*** *www.canyoning.co.nz)* run a full-day canyoning trip to Mount Aspiring National Park that involves descending through a semi-granite canyon. This canyoning trip costs $215.

Jet Boating

Dart Wilderness Adventures *((03) 441 0303;* ***website*** *www.glenorchyinfocentre.co.nz)* have a jet boat trip that travels the Dart River between Glenorchy and Sandy Bluff. This 70km adventure is a much longer than most other jet boat trips in New Zealand making it a good value way to see the river.

Dart River Safaris *((03) 442 9992;* ***website*** *www.dartriver.co.nz)* operate a three-hour trip that includes a 90 minute jet boat ride on the Dart River and a guided forest walk for $199. There is also a jet boat trip that gives you a full three hours on the river for $229 and an inflatable kayak trip that costs $279. This is a seven-hour scenic trip that starts with a 75-minute jet boat ride upstream with a two-hour return journey by inflatable kayak, which tackles some grade two rapids.

Mount Aspiring National Park

Mount Aspiring National Park is one of New Zealand's largest national parks. It is at the southern end of the Southern

Alps and offers some of the country's leading hiking tracks including the Routeburn, and Rees-Dart Tracks.

Coming & Going

Backpacker Express *(☎ (03) 441 0303; **website** www.glenorchyinfocentre.co.nz)* runs shuttle buses from Glenorchy to the main hiking tracks.

Activities

Siberia Experience

The **Siberia Experience** *(☎ (03) 443 8666 or 0800 345 666; **website** www.siberiaexperience.co.nz)* trip allows you to get a good feel for the park in just four hours. It starts off with a 25-minute scenic flight that lands in the Siberia Valley and is followed by a three-hour hike to the Wilkin River and ends with a 30-minute jet boat ride to Makaroa. This trip costs $270.

Hiking

REES-DART TRACK

The Rees and Dart Tracks (72km, 4-5 days) combine to form a semi-loop along the Rees and Dart River Valleys. It is a moderately difficult track and most days average six to eight hours of walking.

Backpacker Express *(☎ (03) 441 0303; **website** www.glenorchyinfocentre.co.nz)* runs shuttle buses to the track from Glenorchy and there is also the option of a jet boat transfer as far as Sandy Bluff on the Dart River.

Muddy Creek to Shelter Rock Hut
(16.5km, 6-7 hours)

The first section involves walking along the often muddy Rees River Valley.

Shelter Rock Hut to Dart Hut
(9km, 4-6 hours)

This challenging route connects the Rees and Dart Tracks. It is not very well marked and involves climbing the Rees Saddle. It is possible to make a day trip to Dart Glacier from Dart Hut.

Dart Hut to Daleys Flat
(15.5km, 6-8 hours)

The track goes through beech forest and across the grassy 4km-wide Cattle Flat as it follows the Dart River.

Daleys Flat to Chinamans Bluff Road End
(14.5km, 4-5 hours)

The track follows the Dart River to the road end at Chinamans Bluff. It is possible to save three to four hours walking and be picked up by jet boat at Sandy Bluff.

GREENSTONE & CAPLES TRACKS

Only a tiny part of the Greenstone and Caples Tracks lie within Mount Aspiring National Park, but they are still regarded as some of New Zealand's major walks. The tracks follow the Caples and Greenstone River valleys and there is an option of combining one of the two tracks with the Routeburn Track.

Although the Greenstone and Caples Tracks are two separate walks, they are often combined to make a loop (50km, 4-5 days).

Backpacker Express *(☎ (03) 441 0303; **website** www.glenorchyinfocentre.co.nz)* run shuttle buses to the track from Glenorchy.

Greenstone Road End to Upper Caples Hut
(14km, 4-6 hours)

The track follows the Caples River to Upper Caples Hut, passing Mid Caples Hut after 2½ hours.

Upper Caples Hut to McKellar Hut
(10.5km, 6-8 hours)

The track becomes rougher as it climbs through beech forest and crosses the McKellar Saddle before a steep descent to Lake McKellar and McKellar Hut.

McKellar Hut to Mid Greenstone Hut
(13km, 4-6 hours)

This section is a relatively easy walk along the Greenstone River valley.

Mid Greenstone Hut to Road End
(14.5km, 4-6½ hours)

The final stretch of the Greenstone Track follows the Greenstone River past Sly Burn Hut and through a long narrow gorge. After the junction with the Caples River, it's just a short walk to the road end.

ROUTEBURN TRACK

The Routeburn Track (33km, 3 days) is the shortest of DOC's Great Walks and is among the most popular with around 13,000 people hiking it each year. That makes it almost as popular as the Milford Track. It traverses both the Fiordland and Mount Aspiring National Parks.

You can walk the track in either direction and some people combine this track with the Caples or Greenstone Tracks. The following route describes the track, starting from the eastern trailhead near Glenorchy.

Backpacker Express *(☎ (03) 441 0303; **website** www.glenorchyinfocentre.co.nz)* operates transport from Queenstown and Glenorchy to the eastern trailhead and TrackNet *(☎ (03) 249 7777; **website** www.tracknet.net)* run buses between the Divide and Te Anau and will also take you back to Queenstown. The Routeburn is a one-way track with around 350km of road between the two trailheads and transport can cost around $100 if you want to return to your starting point after hiking the track.

Bookings for hut accommodation on the Routeburn Track are required during peak season (Nov-Apr) when the huts cost $45 per night. Huts cost just $15 per night off-season.

Routeburn Shelter to Routeburn Falls Hut
(8.8km, 3-4 hours)

The first part of the track is mostly easy walking. After two to three hours it passes the Routeburn Flats Hut and starts a steady climb for an hour or so before reaching the Routeburn Falls Hut.

Routeburn Falls Hut to Mackenzie Hut
(11.3km, 5-6 hours)

This exposed alpine section starts off with a climb past Routeburn Falls to Lake Harris and then follows the mountainside to Lake Mackenzie. This is the highest section of the track and during this section it crosses between Mount Aspiring and Fiordland National Parks.

Mackenzie Hut to The Divide
(12km, 4-5½ hours)

The track gradually descends to Howden Hut at the junction where the Routeburn and Greenston/Caples Tracks cross. It then climbs for around 20 minutes before the descent to the end of the track at the Divide.

Wanaka

Wanaka is a pretty alpine resort town on the banks of Lake Wanaka, New Zealand's fourth largest lake and one of its most scenic. Surrounded by high peaks of the Southern Alps, it is a popular destination for skiers and snowboarders, and it offers some great walking and hiking trails for summer months. The town is much quieter than its big sister Queenstown, but offers almost as many adventure activities, the most popular being rafting, skydiving, and canyoning. There are also cruises on the lake and some good museums, including the New Zealand Fighter Pilot Museum, which is great if your trip coincides with the bi-annual air show, Warbirds Over Wanaka. Wanaka is a great alternative to Queenstown if you are looking for a less crowded, more nature-oriented destination.

Practical Information

INFORMATION CENTRES

Wanaka i-SITE Visitor Centre
100 Ardmore Street, Wanaka
☎ *(03) 443 1233*
Website *www.lakewanaka.co.nz*
Open *8.30am-5.30pm daily*

Mount Aspiring National Park Visitor Centre
Ardmore Street, Wanaka
☎ *(03) 443 7660*
Website *www.doc.govt.nz*
Open *Jan-Apr 8am-5pm daily; May-Oct Mon-Fri 8.30am-4.30pm, Sat 9.30am-4pm; Nov-Dec 8am-5pm daily*

INTERNET ACCESS

Bits & Bytes
38 Helwick Street, Wanaka
☎ *(03) 443 7078*

Website *www.comzone.net.nz*
Open *9am-10pm daily*

Dub Dub Dub
48 Helwick Street, Wanaka
☎ *(03) 443 4440*
Website *www.dubdubdubwanaka.co.nz*
Open *8am-10pm daily*

iHub
Pembroke Mall, Wanaka
Website *www.ihub.org.nz*
Open *7am-10pm daily; 24 hour wireless access*

Wanaka Web
3 Helwick Street, Wanaka
☎ *(03) 443 7429*
Website *www.wanakaweb.co.nz*
Open *10am-9pm daily*

Coming & Going

Atomic Shuttles *(☎ (03) 349 0697; **website** www.atomictravel.co.nz)* go to Dunedin and Christchurch. Atomic Shuttles stop outside the i-SITE visitor centre on the lakefront *(100 Ardmore Street, Wanaka).*

InterCity Coachlines *(☎ (03) 471 7143; **website** www.intercity.co.nz)* go to Christchurch and Queenstown. InterCity coaches stop outside the i-SITE visitor centre on the lakefront *(100 Ardmore Street, Wanaka).*

Naked Bus *(☎ 0900 62533; **website** www.nakedbus.com)* go to Christchurch, Greymouth and Queenstown. Naked Bus stop outside the i-SITE visitor centre on the lakefront *(100 Ardmore Street, Wanaka).*

Southern Link K Bus *(☎ (03) 358 8355 or 0508 458 835; **website** www.southernlinkkbus.co.nz)* go to Christchurch and Queenstown. They stop outside Wanaka Travel.

Wanaka Connexions *(☎ 0800 244 844; **website** www.time2.co.nz/transport/wanaka_connexions)* have six daily shuttle services to Queenstown plus coaches to Dunedin and Invercargill. They depart from outside 99 Ardmore Street.

Accommodation

Albert Town Lodge

This is a very nice hostel that also offers motel accommodation. It has a spacious and fully equipped kitchen and a TV lounge with books, TV and new sofas. Dorms are small, but have good beds on wooden bunks. They offer internet access, laundry facilities (including a drying room) and lots of good advice on the area's activities. It has a quiet atmosphere and is about 6km outside of town, so it is best if you have a car.
Corner State Highway 6 & Kingston Street, Albert Town
☎ *(03) 443 9487*
Website *www.alberttownlodge.co.nz*
Dorm bed *$25;* ***double room*** *$65*
Credit cards *MC, Visa*
Reception open *8am-9pm daily*

Maintenance & cleanliness	★★★½
Facilities	★★½
Atmosphere & character	★★★
Security	★★
Overall rating	★★★

Fern Lodge

This hostel is part of a motel. It has dorm rooms (of four beds each) with made-up beds and a common area with a great view of the lake and mountains. Dorms are a bit small, with old furnishings and carpet. The kitchen is also dated and untidy and there are not many facilities besides laundry and TV, although there is an old barbecue in the back. There is no internet access, although there are plenty of internet cafés in town. Fern Lodge has a great location and would be a good option if everything else is full.
122 Brownston Street, Wanaka
☎ *(03) 443 7480 or 0800 555 556*
Website *www.fernlodge.co.nz*
Dorm bed *$22-24;* ***single room*** *$23-25;* ***double room*** *$45-50*
Credit cards *Amex, MC, Visa*
Reception open *8am-8pm daily*

Maintenance & cleanliness	★★★
Facilities	★½
Atmosphere & character	★★
Security	★
Overall rating	★★

Holly's Backpackers

Holly's is a small, homely hostel with fairly basic facilities. The kitchen is a bit rough, but it has a dishwasher. Dorms are tired-looking, but they have thick mattresses and are made-up with duvets. The bathrooms are quite nice and clean, and there is a common room with TV, lots of videos, internet access and a sundeck with an lovely view. The carpets are old and stained throughout, giving the place a dirty and drab appearance. It has a nice, quiet ambience.

71 Upton Street, Wanaka

☎ *(03) 443 8187*

***Dorm bed** $25-27 ($22-24 BBH); **double/twin room** $62 ($56 BBH)*

***Reception open** 8am-6pm daily*

Maintenance & cleanliness	★★½
Facilities	★★½
Atmosphere & character	★★½
Security	★½
Overall rating	★★½

Matterhorn South Backpackers

This hostel is a centrally located motel-style building. Facilities are limited to a kitchen and a small common area with books, a TV, log fire and great views of the lake and mountains. The dorm rooms have en suite bathrooms and some rooms (on the top floor) have a beautiful mountain view; others (on the ground floor) are less impressive.

56 Brownston Street, Wanaka

☎ *(03) 443 1119*

***Dorm bed** $24*

***Credit cards** MC, Visa*

***Reception open** 8am-8pm daily*

Maintenance & cleanliness	★★★½
Facilities	★½
Atmosphere & character	★★★
Security	★
Overall rating	★★½

Mountain View Backpackers

Mountain View Backpackers has spacious dorms with good mattresses with beds made up in lovely shades of blue. There is a small kitchen and a TV lounge with a log fire plus an outside garden with hammocks and a barbecue. The bathrooms are sparkling clean and have great showers. It

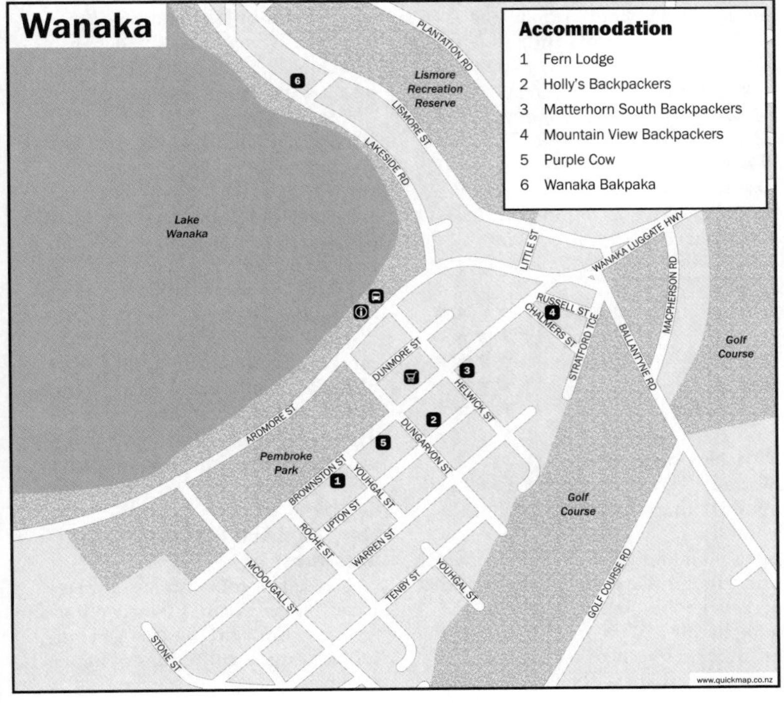

has a very laid-back feel with a central location.
7 Russell Street, Wanaka
☎ *(03) 443 9010 or 0800 112 201*
***Website** www.mtnview.co.nz*
***Dorm bed** $25-27 ($22-24 BBH); **double room** $62 ($56 BBH)*
***Credit cards** MC, Visa*
***Reception open** 8.30am-12.30pm & 3.30pm-8.30pm daily*

Maintenance & cleanliness	★★★★
Facilities	★½
Atmosphere & character	★★★
Security	★
Overall rating	★★★

Purple Cow

The Purple Cow is in a nice timber alpine-style building with stunning views of the lake and mountains. It features a large dining area; a common room with pool table and internet access ($6 per hour), including wireless, and a cinema room where they show free films nightly. Dorms are simple, with en suite bathrooms and plenty of shelving, but the mattresses are thin and uncomfortable. The kitchen is massive and fully stocked, although it is closed for an hour and a half each night for cleaning.
94 Brownston Street, Wanaka
☎ *(03) 443 1800 or 0800 772 277*
***Website** www.purplecow.co.nz*
***Dorm bed** $26-28 ($23-25 BBH); **double room** $72-78 ($68-72 BBH)*
***Credit cards** Amex, MC, Visa*
***Reception open** 8am-8pm daily*

Maintenance & cleanliness	★★★★
Facilities	★★★
Atmosphere & character	★★★½
Security	★★½
Overall rating	★★★½

Wanaka Bakpaka

Wanaka Bakpaka is a great hostel with good facilities. It is set in a hilltop homestead lodge and features a cosy open-plan lounge with funky décor and panoramic views. There is internet access, a book exchange, guitars and a log fire. It is a TV-free hostel, which encourages guests to socialise and organise activities. The large kitchen is newly renovated, modern and fully equipped. Dorms are neat and comfortable with nice new sheets and double rooms are particularly good value. The atmosphere is chilled out.
117 Lakeside Road, Wanaka
☎ *(03) 443 7877*
***Website** www.wanakabakpaka.co.nz*
***Dorm bed** $25-27 ($22-24 BBH); **single room** $45 ($42 BBH); **double/twin room** $62-69 ($56-63 BBH)*
***Credit cards** MC, Visa*
***Reception open** 8am-8pm daily*

Maintenance & cleanliness	★★★★
Facilities	★★★
Atmosphere & character	★★★★
Security	★½
Overall rating	★★★½

Eating & Drinking

Dining options in Wanaka tend to be higher end, so it is best to pick up groceries at the **New World** supermarket *(20 Dunmore Street, Wanaka)* and cook at your hostel.

There are some cheap restaurants, but they can mostly be found out of the centre; **Central Fish** *(54 Reece Crescent, Wanaka)* has excellent fish and chips. Fast food places are found on the outskirts of town as well, but there is a **Subway** *(145 Ardmore Street, Wanaka)* on the lakefront. At most cafés and restaurants along the waterfront, you really pay for the view, but there are a couple of exceptions. The **Snack Shack** *(139 Ardmore Street, Wanaka)* has cheap kebabs and falafel, as well as snacks and good chips. And hidden behind it is **Sagun Café** *(139 Ardmore Street, Wanaka)*, a brilliant little blue café with excellent curry and Indian dishes at great prices. Also in this area, The **Doughbin** *(Lakefront, Wanaka)* has fresh bread, pies and sandwiches at prices that won't kill your budget.

Sights

New Zealand Fighter Pilots Museum

This excellent museum has displays about New Zealand's fighter pilots and features one of the Southern Hemisphere's largest collections of fighter planes.

Wanaka Airport, SH 6, Wanaka
☎ *(03) 443 7010*
Website *www.nzfpm.co.nz*
Admission *$10*
Open *9am-4pm daily*

Wanaka Transport & Toy Museum
This museum features aircraft, cars and motorcycles as well a collection of toys. Exhibits include an Antonov AN-2 (the world's largest bi-plane), a MiG jet fighter and a rare 1924 McLaughlin Buick Limousine.
State Highway 6, near Wanaka Airport
☎ *(03) 443 8765*
Website *www.wanakatransportandtoymuseum.com*
Admission *$8*
Open *8.30am-5pm daily*

Activities

CANYONING

Deep Canyon (☎ *(03) 443 7922;* ***website*** *www.deepcanyon.co.nz)* run exciting canyoning trips in the spectacular canyons of the Matukituki Valley. The trips include abseiling down waterfalls, climbing, swimming and plunging down slippery shutes. The basic trip ($215) is suitable for most people but the "Big Nige" ($280) option is "steeper and deeper" and better suited to fit people with some abseiling experience. A lot of people consider canyoning to be the best activity in Wanaka. Canyoning trips operate Nov-Mar.

JET BOATING

The **Clutha River Jet** (☎ *(03) 443 7495;* ***website*** *www.lakelandadventures.co.nz/jet_boating.htm)* offers one-hour rides on Lake Wanaka and the Clutha River. Jet boat rides depart from the log cabin on the lakefront (100 Ardmore Street, Wanaka) and cost $95.

KAYAKING

Alpine Kayak Guides (☎ *(03) 443 9023;* ***website*** *www.alpinekayaks.co.nz)* run half-day ($135) and full-day ($190) kayaking trips on rivers around Wanaka, including the Clutha River which has mostly grade two rapids. Kayaking trips operate during summer and autumn (Nov-Apr).

ROCK CLIMBING

Wanaka Rock (☎ *(03) 443 6811;* ***website*** *www.wanakarock.co.nz)* has half ($110) and one-day ($190) rock climbing courses as well as more advanced three day courses ($495). A combination of the one-day introductory course ($190) followed by the one-day Explore Wanaka Rock course ($190) will give you a thorough introduction to rock climbing.

SKYDIVING

Doing a tandem skydive over Lake Wanaka allows you to take in the breathtaking views of Aoraki/Mount Cook and Mount Aspiring National Parks as you freefall at 200km/h.
Tandem Skydive Lake Wanaka (☎ *(03) 443 7207 or 0800 786 877;* ***website*** *www.skydivenz.com)* gives you the option of jumping at 12000ft ($279; 45 seconds freefall) or 15000ft ($369; 60 seconds freefall).

WHITE WATER SLEDGING (HYDROSPEED)

River sledging, or hydrospeed, involves riding a custom-designed river sledge through rapids. Hydrospeed operators point out that you are in control, as opposed to rafting where the guide does the steering.
Frogz (☎ *(03) 441 2318 or 0800 4 37649 (0800 4 FROGZ);* ***website*** *www.frogz.co.nz)* run river sledging trips the Kawarau River (grade 2-4 rapids). A half-day trip costs $135 and a full day trip costs $285.

SKIING & SNOWBOARDING

Wanaka is popular with skiers and snowboarders because of its close proximity to Cardrona and Treble Cone ski areas. It can get pretty lively during the ski season.

Cardrona

Located about halfway between Queenstown and Wanaka, Cardrona (☎ *(03) 443 7411;* ***website*** *www.cardrona.com)* is a family-oriented resort with good snowboarding. A full-day lift pass is $81, but a lift, lesson and rental package is better value at $80 for skiers or snowboarders.

Snowpark NZ

Snowpark NZ *(☎ (03) 443 9991; **website** www.snowparknz.com)* claims to be the Southern Hemisphere's top all-mountain terrain park, catering mostly to snowboarders. A day ticket is $65-75.

Treble Cone

With 550ha of terrain, Treble Cone *(☎ (03) 443 7443; **website** www.treblecone.co.nz)* is bigger than most other New Zealand ski areas, and it geared mostly toward advanced skiers who have half the runs while beginners only get 10%. A full-day lift pass costs $89-99. Treble Cone have a first-timers package that gives you ski or snowboard rental, a two-hour group lesson and lift pass for $99 (one-day) or $380 (three-days). Treble Cone is a 35-minute drive from Wanaka.

Waiorau Snow Farm

Waiorau Snow Farm *(☎ (03) 443 7542; **website** www.snowfarmnz.com)* is New Zealand's only dedicated cross-country ski resort. A day pass is $35 and ski rental starts at $25.

Southland

Southland, the South Island's southernmost tip, combines the windswept coastline of the Catlins, the dramatic fiords and pristine wilderness of Fiordland National Park and the rugged beauty of Stewart Island. The area is largely inaccessible national park and offers some of the most fascinating wildlife and ancient landscapes in New Zealand. You will need to put in some extra effort (or cash) to experience all this region has to offer, but in the end, it is one of the more rewarding travel destinations you can find. Milford Sound and the Milford Track are the region's two most famous attractions.

Must do in Southland

- Hike one of the Great Walks in the Fiordland region
- Kayak on Milford Sound

The Catlins

The Catlins are made up of several tiny rural hideaways along the Southern Scenic Route. The area has fantastic scenery and wildlife; it is home to Hector's dolphins and Yellow-eyed penguins – two of the world's rarest species, and there are also many seal and sea lion colonies along the coast. Rolling green hills and windswept trees make for a captivating landscape. Kayaking is great here and it has some of the South Island's best and least crowded surf. You need to have a car (or some luck hitchhiking) to explore the Catlins and most of the roads are unpaved; but the area has some unique natural attractions that reward you for the effort of travelling in this relatively remote area.

Since there are barely any shops, cash machines or facilities in most places, fill your tank and buy groceries in Balclutha

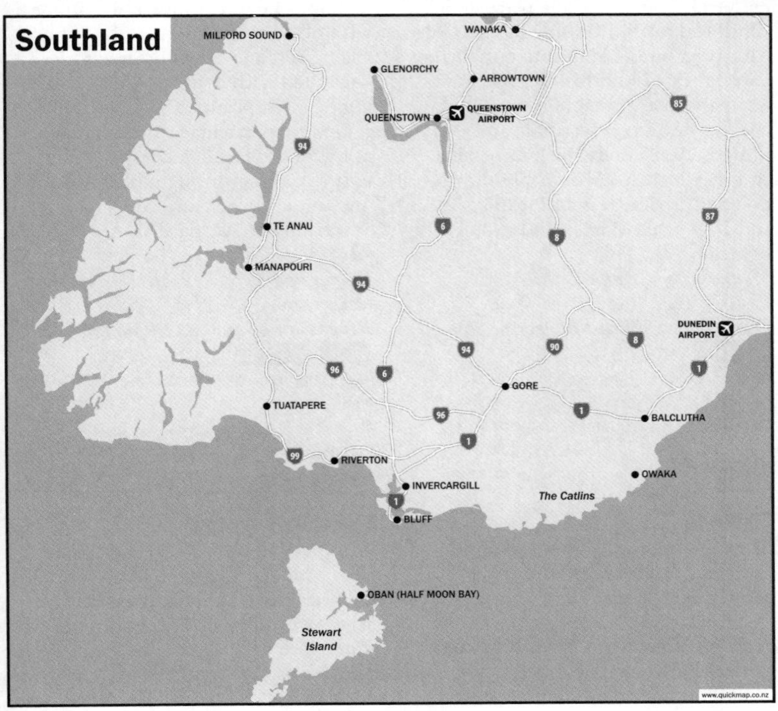

to the north or Invercargill to the south before your journey.

Local Transport

Transport options to, from and through the Catlins are very limited and most visitors to this region drive their own car.

The Catlins Coaster *(☎ (03) 437 0753; **website** www.catlinscoaster.co.nz)* is the main public transport option in the Catlins, and is primarily a backpackers' bus running between Dunedin and Invercargill stopping en route at the small hostels in the Catlins. The Kiwi Experience-affiliated Bottom Bus *(☎ (03) 437 0753; **website** www.bottombus.co.nz)* also includes transport in the Catlins.

Accommodation

KAKA POINT

This small village has a couple of shops and a charming seaside setting. The area around here is home to wildlife including seals and sea lions.

Fernlea Backpackers

Fernlea is a small austere place on a hill above Kaka Point. It only has six beds; with twin bunks built into cosy little nooks they call dorms. The kitchen is worn and the furnishings are dated, but the views are incredible and everything is clean. Beds are comfortable, and they have loads of local information and advice. It is an inexpensive and cosy place to relax and explore the sights of Kaka Point.

Moana Street, Kaka Point

☎ (03) 412 8834

***Dorm bed** $20; **double room** $50*

Maintenance & cleanliness	★★
Facilities	★★
Atmosphere & character	★★★½
Security	★
Overall rating	★★

OWAKA

After driving south from Balclutha, Owaka is the only town of any size before Invercargill.

Catlins Blowhole Backpackers

Catlins Blowhole Backpackers offers an exceptional standard of accommodation in two small red houses on the main road. Each has a kitchen, bathrooms, a lounge, and themed rooms fitted with attractive furnishings, heating and attention to detail. Beds are extra comfortable and made up with thick duvets. Bathrooms are freshly painted and spotlessly clean, and there are cosy lounges with log fires, new sofas and TVs. One of the kitchens is due for renovation, but overall this is an excellent choice. The atmosphere is quaint and quiet.

24 Main Road, Owaka

☎ (03) 412 8111

***Website** www.catlinsbackpackers.co.nz*

***Dorm bed** $27 ($24 BBH); **single room** $60 ($54 BBH); **double/twin room** $62 ($56 BBH)*

Maintenance & cleanliness	★★★★½
Facilities	★★½
Atmosphere & character	★★★½
Security	★½
Overall rating	★★★½

The Split Level

The Split Level features a big lounge with plush sofas, books and TV plus a large veranda. The dorms are nicely decorated with made-up beds, and the kitchen is kept nice and clean. Double rooms are particularly nice. Some parts of the hostel feel dated, especially the ugly carpeting throughout the building; but it is clean and cosy.

9 Waikawa Road, Owaka

☎ (03) 415 8304

***Dorm bed** $25 ($22 BBH); **double/twin room** $55-65 ($52-58 BBH)*

***Reception open** 8am-10pm daily*

Maintenance & cleanliness	★★★
Facilities	★½
Atmosphere & character	★★
Security	★½
Overall rating	★★½

Surat Bay Lodge

This place is more of a beach house than a lodge. It has a kitchen, laundry facilities, central heating, internet access with Skype and a large common room with sofas, a TV and log fire. The dorms are clean and spacious with good bunks. They have kayak hire and an excellent location near the beach where sea lions are almost always seen. Surat Bay Lodge is by the sea, around 5½km from Owaka.

Surat Bay Road, New Haven, Owaka
☎ *(03) 415 8099*
Website *www.suratbay.co.nz*
Dorm bed *$26 ($23 BBH);* ***double/twin room*** *$62 ($56 BBH)*
Credit cards *MC, Visa*

Maintenance & cleanliness	★★★
Facilities	★★★½
Atmosphere & character	★★★½
Security	★½
Overall rating	★★★½

PAPATOWAI & PURAKAUNUI FALLS

This isolated rural locality is a tiny place with just one small shop, but there are a few lovely small hostels nearby.

The cascading Purakaunui Falls are located between Owaka and Papatowai. There is a short 10-minute walk through rainforest to get to the falls from the car park.

Falls Backpackers

This hostel is a small house on a farm overlooking green hills and valleys. With only 10 single beds, which are made-up, it has a warm and cosy ambience. The kitchen and bathrooms are exceptionally clean and well maintained and there is a small common area with log fire and books. The little veranda in front of the house has beautiful views. The rooms are heated and towels are provided for guests. The hostel also occasionally offers animal feeding, and the Purakaunui Falls and glow-worms are just a few minutes away.

Purakaunui Falls Road, Purakaunui
☎ *(03) 415 8724*
Website *www.catlins.co.nz/fallsbprz.html*
Dorm bed *$25 ($22 BBH);* ***double/twin room*** *$62 ($56 BBH)*
Reception open *8am-9pm daily*

Maintenance & cleanliness	★★★★½
Facilities	★★★
Atmosphere & character	★★★
Security	★
Overall rating	★★★½

Hill Top Backpackers

Hill Top is a lovely hostel in a hilltop farmhouse with good quality facilities. The kitchen and common areas are full of character and exquisitely maintained and the dorms have beautiful furnishings and thick mattresses. The lounge has cosy sofas and a warm log fire (no TV), and they have internet access, laundry facilities and a nice sundeck and gardens.

77 Tahakopa Valley Road, Papatowai
☎ *(03) 415 8028*
Website *www.catlins-nz.com*
Dorm bed *$25;* ***double room*** *$65-75*

Maintenance & cleanliness	★★★★
Facilities	★★★½
Atmosphere & character	★★★
Security	★½
Overall rating	★★★

TAHAKOPA

This small settlement is in a valley between the Beresford and MacLennan Ranges. It is not too far from Papatowai.

Wrights Mill Lodge

This hostel is set in a lovely restored villa on a huge tract of farmland. The dorms are cute and clean, with made-up beds and comfortable mattresses. There is a warm lounge with a big TV, a newly renovated kitchen, laundry and nice gardens with a barbecue. Bathrooms are spotless. It has a quiet but very comfortable atmosphere and is the perfect place to get away if you have a car.

865 Tahakopa Valley Road, Tahakopa
☎ *(03) 487 9445*
Website *www.catlinsaccommodation.co.nz*
Dorm bed *$25 ($22 BBH);* ***double room*** *$65-75 ($56-66 BBH)*

Maintenance & cleanliness	★★★★
Facilities	★★★½
Atmosphere & character	★★★
Security	½
Overall rating	★★★

CURIO BAY & SLOPE POINT

The Invercargill end of the Catlins has a couple of nice small hostels with a rural/seaside setting.

Catlins Beach House Accommodation

This tiny hostel is a new house on the beach with new, modern and sparkling clean facilities. There are two well-appointed private double rooms and one dorm room with wooden bunks and thick mattresses made-up with duvets. The kitchen is well equipped and there is a cosy lounge with a log fire, guitar and convivial dining area. There is a lovely view from the veranda and the front lawn.

499 Waikawa-Curio Bay Road, Curio Bay/Tokonui
(03) 246 8340
***Website** www.catlinsbeachhouse.co.nz*
***Dorm bed** $25; **double room** $65-85*
***Credit cards** MC, Visa; $3 credit card surcharge*

Maintenance & cleanliness	★★★★½
Facilities	★★½
Atmosphere & character	★★★
Security	★½
Overall rating	★★★½

Curio Bay Accommodation

This hostel is right next to the Catlins Beach House. The hostel is quaint and intimate inside, with nice furnishings and a well equipped kitchen. The shared rooms are simple and comfortable and there is a good common area with a log fire. It is an older building, but it has character and there is a very quiet and relaxing atmosphere. The beach is steps away.

501 Curio Bay Road, Curio Bay
(03) 246 8797
***Dorm bed** $25 ($22 BBH); **double room** $55-75*

Maintenance & cleanliness	★★★
Facilities	★½
Atmosphere & character	★★★★
Security	★★
Overall rating	★★½

Dolphin Lodge Backpackers

This is a great hostel overlooking the beach at Curio Bay. The two-story house has a large veranda with priceless views along the coast. There is a large common room/kitchen with a log fire and a homely atmosphere plus laundry facilities and an excellent on-site surf school that is run by the knowledgeable and friendly management. The heated dorms have four to six beds.

529 Curio Bay Road, Curio Bay
(03) 2468 577
***Dorm bed** $22; **double room** $55; **twin room** $48*
***Credit cards** MC, Visa*
***Reception open** 8am-10pm daily*

Maintenance & cleanliness	★★★½
Facilities	★★½
Atmosphere & character	★★★
Security	★½
Overall rating	★★★

Penguin Paradise Holiday Lodge

This hostel is in a quiet area of Waikawa, five-minutes from Curio Bay, and has a summer cottage feel to it. It is cosy and quiet, with a small TV lounge with log fire and books and a very clean kitchen. Dorms have thick mattresses and the beds are made-up with duvets. Bathrooms are clean and there is a nice outdoor garden area. It is just across from the beach and next to the museum and the cheapest takeaway food in The Catlins. It is run by the Catlins Surf School instructor, who can give you good advice on things to do in the area.

612 Waikawa-Niagara Road, Waikawa
(03) 246 8552
***Dorm bed** $25 ($22 BBH); **double room** $54 ($48 BBH); **twin room** $50 ($44 BBH)*
***Credit cards** MC, Visa*
***Reception open** 8am-10pm daily*

Maintenance & cleanliness	★★★½
Facilities	★★
Atmosphere & character	★★★
Security	★
Overall rating	★★★

Gore

Gore likes to call itself the "Brown Trout Fishing Capital of the World". It is a small town midway between Queenstown and Invercargill, and is the main commercial centre for the surrounding rural region. Gore is home to the Hokonui Moonshine Museum and is also known for its annual Country Music Festival.

Practical Information

Gore i-SITE Visitors Centre
Gore Arts & Heritage Precinct, 16 Hokonui Drive, Gore
☎ *(03) 203 9288*
Website *www.gorenz.com*
Open *8.30am-5pm daily*

Coming & Going

InterCity Coachlines *(☎ (03) 471 7143; **website** www.intercity.co.nz)* have services to Christchurch, Dunedin, Invercargill and Te Anau. Both Atomic Shuttles *(☎ (03) 349 0697; **website** www.atomictravel.co.nz)* and Naked Bus *(☎ 0900 62533; **website** www.nakedbus.com)* have buses to Dunedin and Invercargill.

Buses stop outside the i-SITE Visitor Information Centre *(16 Hokonui Drive, Gore)*.

Accommodation

The Old Fire Station

This hostel is in, you guessed it, an old fire station. It is a very well maintained place with modern furnishings and good facilities including a small fully-equipped kitchen. The dorms are simple and clean with wooden bunks and the bathrooms are very clean and come with hairdryers. Guests can use the barbecue in the sunny courtyard, and there is plenty of local information available. It has a quiet atmosphere most of the time.
19 Hokonui Drive, Gore
☎ *(03) 208 1925*
Dorm bed *$23-25 ($20-22 BBH);* ***double room*** *$56 ($50 BBH)*
Credit cards *MC, Visa*
Reception open *8am-8pm daily*

Maintenance & cleanliness	★★★½
Facilities	★★
Atmosphere & character	★★★★
Security	★½
Overall rating	★★★

Sights

Gore Historical Museum

This small museum has displays on the region's social history including exhibits on Southland's early settlers and trout fishing.
16 Hokonui Drive, Gore
☎ *(03) 208 7032*
Admission *free*
Open *summer Mon-Fri 8.30am-4.30pm, Sat-Sun 9.30am-3.30pm; winter Mon-Fri 8.30am-4.30pm, Sat-Sun 1pm-3.30pm*

Hokonui Moonshine Museum

This museum has a variety of displays about local history, although the main focus is Hokonui Moonshine – an illicit whiskey that was produced in the surrounding hills during prohibition times.
Corner Hokonui Drive & Norfolk Street, Gore
☎ *(03) 203 9288*
Admission *$5*
Open *summer Mon-Fri 8.30am-4.30pm, Sat-Sun 9.30am-3.30pm; winter Mon-Fri 8.30am-4.30pm, Sat-Sun 1pm-3.30pm*

Invercargill

Invercargill is a large town at the southern end of the South Island. The wide main street is lined with some very nice colonial architecture and Queens Park has beautiful gardens. It has a good museum and is a cheap base for the many travellers who are preparing for a trip to Stewart Island. Unfortunately, it is an otherwise lacklustre town that is mainly a stopover on the way to the natural beauty of the Catlins and the nightlife of Dunedin.

Practical Information

Invercargill i-SITE Visitor Centre
108 Gala Street, Invercargill
☎ *(03) 214 6243*
Website *www.invercargill.org.nz*
Open *summer 8am-7pm daily; winter 8am-5pm daily*

INTERNET ACCESS

Bits & Bytes
55 Dee Street, Invercargill
☎ *(03) 214 0007*
Website *www.comzone.net.nz*
Open *10am-10pm daily*

Global Byte Café
150 Dee Street, Invercargill
☎ *(03) 214 4724*
***Open** 7am-9pm daily*

Tuatara Café & Bar
32 Dee Street, Invercargill
☎ *(03) 214 0954*
***Open** 7am-midnight daily*

Coming & Going
AIR
Invercargill Airport *(☎ (03) 218 6920; **website** www.invercargillairport.co.nz)* has flights to Christchurch, Dunedin and Stewart Island. The airport is only 3km from the city centre.

Stewart Island Flights *(☎ (03) 218 9129; **website** www.stewartislandflights.com)* have good value stand-by flights to Stewart Island, which are an alternative to taking the ferry from Bluff.

BUS
Atomic Shuttles *(☎ (03) 349 0697; **website** www.atomictravel.co.nz)* go to Dunedin; Naked Bus *(☎ 0900 62533; **website** www.nakedbus.com)* go to Dunedin, Milford Sound, Queenstown and Te Anau and InterCity Coachlines *(☎ (03) 474 9600; **website** www.intercitycoach.co.nz)* go to Christchurch, Dunedin, Queenstown and Te Anau.

Stewart Island Experience *(☎ (03) 212 7660 or 0800 000 511; **website** www.stewartislandexperience.co.nz)* run a bus service to Bluff that connects with the Stewart Island Ferry.

Buses stop outside the i-SITE Visitor Centre *(108 Gala Street, Invercargill)*.

Accommodation
Kackling Kea Backpackers
Kackling Kea is a small orange house with a good bit of charm and nicely maintained facilities that include a quiet common room with handsome décor and big plush sofas (but no TV), a nicely renovated kitchen with new appliances, internet access, laundry and a barbecue area. Accommodation is in a few dorms with new carpet and wooden bunks with made-up beds. It has a quiet

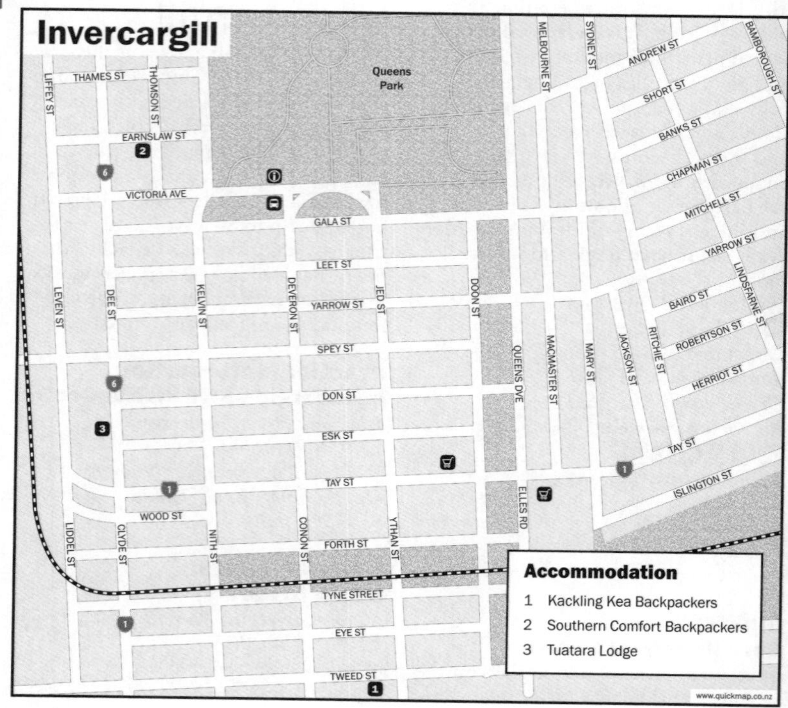

atmosphere and there is freshly baked bread in the morning for breakfast. The location south of the city centre is most convenient if you have a car.
225 Tweed Street, Invercargill
☎ *(03) 214 7950*
Website *www.kacklingkea.com*
Dorm bed *$23-24 ($20-21 BBH);* ***double room*** *$54 ($48 BBH)*
Reception open *8am-1pm & 4pm-9pm daily*

Maintenance & cleanliness	★★★★
Facilities	★½
Atmosphere & character	★★★½
Security	★★★
Overall rating	★★★

Southern Comfort Backpackers

Set in a fine old country house, this hostel has plenty of character. Inside, it is carefully maintained, with a newly renovated kitchen and good showers. There is a quiet common area with log fire, books and internet access as well as a nice outdoor garden with barbecue. The dorms are spacious and clean, some with gorgeous log fireplaces and stained glass bay windows. There are laundry facilities and information about the town and surrounding area. It has a low-key atmosphere and a residential location. It is a good place to relax.
30 Thomson Street, Invercargill
☎ *(03) 218 3838*
Dorm bed *$23 ($20 BBH);* ***double/twin room*** *$52 ($46 BBH)*
Reception open *8.30am-8.30pm daily*

Maintenance & cleanliness	★★★★
Facilities	★★
Atmosphere & character	★★★½
Security	★½
Overall rating	★★★

Tuatara Lodge

This hostel is unexceptional except for the bar and café downstairs. This gives it a good atmosphere, especially when there is live music in the bar. Amenities include a kitchen, laundry, and a tour desk at reception. There is also internet access, including wireless ($5 per hour). The dorms are small, but have wonderfully comfortable beds. However the street side rooms are noisy at night.
32 Dee Street, Invercargill
☎ *(03) 214 0954 or 0800 4 TUATARA*
Website *www.yha.co.nz*
Dorm bed *$25 ($23 HI/YHA, $24 VIP);* ***double/twin room*** *$60-80 ($56-76 HI/YHA, $58-78 VIP)*
Credit cards *MC, Visa*
Reception open *7am-8.30pm daily*

Maintenance & cleanliness	★★★½
Facilities	★★½
Atmosphere & character	★★★★
Security	★★★½
Overall rating	★★★½

Eating & Drinking

Invercargill is not a very expensive town and there are quite a few cheap places to eat in the centre. **Dee Thai** *(9 Dee Street, Invercargill)* has a great lunch special, and the **Fat Indian Curryhouse** *(38 Dee Street, Invercargill)* has super cheap curry deals. There are also fast food places around, like Domino's and KFC.

For the cheapest groceries, go to **Pak'n Save** *(95 Tay Street, Invercargill)*; this is a good place to gather supplies if you are heading to Stewart Island. Other supermarkets include **Countdown** *(172 Tay Street, Invercargill)* and **SuperValue** *(103 Yarrow Street, Invercargill)*.

Sights

Southland Museum & Art Gallery

This excellent musuems has exhibits on New Zealand's remote islands near the Antarctic plus displays on the tuatara-breeding programme.
108 Gala Street, Invercargill
☎ *(03) 218 9753*
Website *www.southlandmuseum.com*
Admission *free*
Open *Mon-Fri 9am-5pm, Sat-Sun 10am-5pm*

Bluff

The New Zealand mainland's southern-most town is renowned for its oysters, but most backpackers come here to take the ferry to Stewart Island/Rakiura.

Coming & Going

BUS

Stewart Island Experience *(☎ (03) 212 7660 or 0800 000 511; **website** www.stewartislandexperience.co.nz)* run a bus service to Bluff that connects with the Stewart Island Ferry. Track-Net *(☎ (03) 249 7777; **website** www.tracknet.net)* run buses from Bluff to Te Anau with connections to Milford Sound and Queenstown.

FERRY

Stewart Island Experience *(☎ (03) 212 7660 or 0800 000 511; **website** www.stewartislandexperience.co.nz)* has regular ferry services linking Bluff with Halfmoon Bay on Stewart Island/ Rakiura.

Sights

Bluff Maritime Museum

This small maritime museum has exhibits on shipwrecks, whaling and the oyster trade, for which Bluff is famous.

227 Foreshore Road, Bluff
☎ (03) 212 7534
***Website** www.bluff.co.nz/museum.html*
***Admission** $2*
***Open** Mon-Fri 10am-4.30pm, Sat-Sun 1pm-5pm*

Stewart Island/ Rakiura

Most of New Zealand's third largest island has now been declared the Rakiura National Park and the majority of the island's tiny population live in the township of Oban (or Halfmoon Bay), which is home to just 400 residents and a cluster of shops and accommodation. The main attractions on the island are the walking tracks, pristine beaches and the bird sanctuary on Ulva Island. Since most of the island is only accessible by foot, there are also tour guides ready to take you on wildlife safaris and overnight wilderness trips. Penguins abound on some of the remote beaches, and this is the only place in New Zealand where kiwis outnumber Kiwis by over 50:1.

Practical Information

INFORMATION CENTRES

Stewart Island i-SITE Visitor Centre
12 Elgin Terrace, Oban
☎ (03) 2191 400
***Website** www.stewartisland.co.nz*

Rakiura National Park Visitor Centre

Main Road, Oban
☎ (03) 219 0009
***Website** www.doc.govt.nz*
***Open** Mon-Fri 8.30am-5pm, Sat-Sun 9am-4pm*

INTERNET ACCESS

Just Café

Main Road, Oban
☎ (03) 219 1422
***Open** Jan-Jun & Oct-Dec 9am-5pm daily*

Coming & Going

AIR

Stewart Island Flights *(☎ (03) 218 9129; **website** www.stewartislandflights.com)* have good value stand-by flights departing from Invercargill. The flight includes transport between Stewart Island's airstrip and the township of Oban on Halfmoon Bay. The airport shuttle departs from the post office on Elgin Terrace.

FERRY

Stewart Island Experience *(☎ (03) 212 7660 or 0800 000 511; **website** www.stewartislandexperience.co.nz)* has regular ferry services linking Bluff with Halfmoon Bay on Stewart Island/ Rakiura.

Local Transport

Despite the unusually large number of cars in Oban, Stewart Island's road network only extends a few kilometres from town and water taxis provide the main transport option on the island. Water taxi companies include Seabuzzz *(☎ (03) 219 1282; **website** www.seabuzz.co.nz)* and Seaview Water Taxi *(☎ (03) 219 1014; **website** www.seaviewwatertaxi.co.nz)*. Most water taxi services depart from the Golden Bay Wharf, about 1km from the centre of Oban.

Accommodation

Michael's House

This place is just a home with a few extra beds thrown into the bedrooms and called a hostel. It is not particularly clean or well maintained, but the beds are made-up and it offers you a chance to chat with the knowledgeable Kiwi host. The kitchen is quite a mess, but there is a small lounge with heaps of books and magazines and a new big screen TV.

1 Golden Bay Road, Oban
(03) 219 1425
***Dorm bed** $25*

Maintenance & cleanliness	★
Facilities	★½
Atmosphere & character	★
Security	½
Overall rating	★

Stewart Island Backpackers

This hostel is in a rundown old school-house. The dorms are small rooms connected by covered boardwalks, and they have old mattresses. There is a huge common area/kitchen with TV, books and sofas. This would be the best place to hang out, but it's not altogether inviting. They have internet access ($2 for 15 minutes), laundry facilities and a barbecue. It has a central location.

18 Ayr Street, Oban
(03) 219 1114
***Dorm bed** $24; **single room** $36; **double/twin room** $55; **camping** $12; **bed sheets** $2*
***Credit cards** MC, Visa*
***Reception open** 7.30am-noon & 1pm-6.30pm daily*

Maintenance & cleanliness	★★½
Facilities	★½
Atmosphere & character	★
Security	★½
Overall rating	★★

The View

This is probably the cleanest and most comfortable place to stay on Stewart Island/Rakiura. The two-storey building has accommodation in clean rooms with comfy made-up beds and individual bedside lights. There is a well equipped kitchen, a spacious lounge with a nice log fire and a garage with a pool table. It definitely lives up to its name with a wonderful view of Half-moon Bay from its hilltop location. It has a tranquil atmosphere and is a place where you will feel at home.

Nichol Road, Oban
(03) 219 1328
***Dorm bed** $30; **double room** $70; **bed sheets** $5*
***Reception open** 9am-9pm daily*

Maintenance & cleanliness	★★★½
Facilities	★★★
Atmosphere & character	★
Security	★
Overall rating	★★½

Eating & Drinking

Bring groceries as food on Stewart Island/Rakiura is expensive, although there is a small **Ship to Shore Four Square** market *(Elgin Terrace, Oban)* for the things you have forgotten.

There are not many options for dining out in town, but the tiny **Just Café** *(Main Road, Oban)* is a popular place

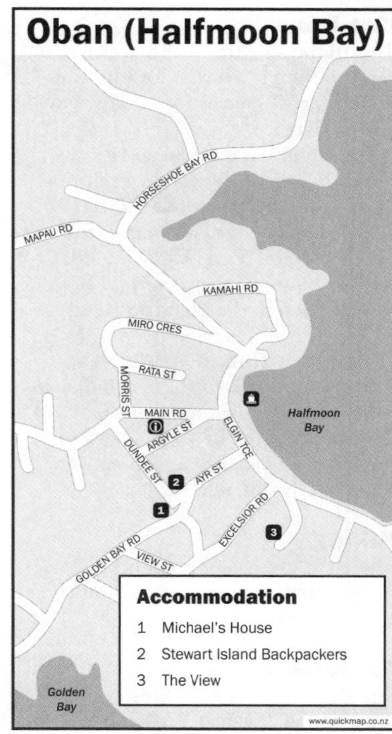

for coffee, sandwiches and baked goods. The seafood here is of course excellent. **Kai Kart** *(Ayr Street, Oban)* has some of the best fish & chips in New Zealand and at takeaway prices it's the perfect spot for lunch or dinner on a budget.

Sights & Activities

Kiwi Spotting

Despite over 20,000 kiwis on the island, it can be very difficult to spot one of them in the wild. **Ruggedy Range Wilderness Experience** *(☎ (03) 219 1066; **website** www.ruggedyrange.com)* run very good, but expensive, kiwi spotting trips that cost $385 for an overnight trip or $785 for a two-night trip.

Sea Kayaking

Stewart Island/Rakiura has lovely sheltered bays, particularly in Paterson Inlet, that are ideal for sea kayaking. **Rakiura Kayaks** *(☎ (03) 219 1160; **website** www.rakiura.co.nz)* run guided kayak trips $50 half day or $75 for a full day. They also rent kayaks for $40 per day.

Ulva Island

This island in Paterson Inlet is free of rats, making it a haven for bird life including 70 species found nowhere else on earth.

It is a popular day trip and it can be reached either by kayak, water taxi or by a tour. Seabuzzz *(☎ (03) 219 1282; **website** www.seabuzz.co.nz)* and Seaview Water Taxi *(☎ (03) 219 1014; **website** www.seaviewwatertaxi.co.nz)* can take you to the island and charge $25 for the return trip.

Ruggedy Range Wilderness Experience *(☎ (03) 219 1066; **website** www.ruggedyrange.com)* and **Ulva's Guided Walks** *(☎ (03) 219 1216; **website** www.ulva.co.nz)* operate day tours to Ulva Island.

Hiking

There are some very good hiking tracks on Stewart Island. The best is of these is the Rakiura Track.

RAKIURA TRACK

The Rakiura Track (36km, 2-3 days) is one of DOC's Great Walks. It is a popular walk with birdwatchers, but lacks the stunning views normally associated with the other Great Walks. Accommodation in DOC huts on the route costs $10 per night.

Halfmoon Bay to Port William Hut
(12km, 4-5 hours)
The track starts at the end of the road north of Oban and follows the coast for most of the first day.

Port William to North Arm Hut
(12km, 6 hours)
This section starts off by backtracking for 45-minutes along the beach and then cuts inland. The track climbs to the summit ridge where there's a lookout tower that offers views to Paterson Inlet. The track climbs for a little longer before descending to North Arm Hut.

North Arm Hut to Halfmoon Bay
(12km, 4-5 hours)
The last section of the track passes Sawdust Bay and Kaipipi Bay, both on the shore of Paterson Inlet. The final stretch from Kapipi Bay to Oban follows the old Kapipi Road, the original access route for the sawmills at Kaipipi Bay that employed over 100 people in the 1860s.

NORTH WEST & SOUTHERN CIRCUITS

If the Rakiura Track is too easy for you, the North West and Southern Circuits (125km, 8-12 days) may be more your style. The complete hike covers most of the northern half of the island, but it can be broken into two segments, both which provide the opportunity to see kiwi in their natural habitat.

This track has huts spaced approximately one day's walk apart.

Riverton

Riverton is a small fishing village, 30km west of Invercargill, with a sheltered harbour and one of the only real safe swimming beaches in Southland. There isn't much to see here, but it has a great hostel and if you're driving it is an alternative to staying in Invercargill.

Accommodation

Globe Backpackers & Bar

This centrally located hostel has a great atmosphere. It has a bar downstairs with Sky TV, a pool table and popular pizzas. Upstairs, the dorms are very well maintained, with shiny bathrooms and sturdy beds with clean new sheets. There is a gorgeous fully-equipped kitchen, laundry and internet access ($4 per hour). Backpackers love this place, no doubt due in part to the gregarious and welcoming hosts.

144 Palmerston Street, Riverton
☎ *(03) 234 8527*
Website *www.theglobe.co.nz*
Dorm bed *$25;* ***double room*** *$60-80*
Credit cards *MC, Visa*
Reception open *9am-10pm daily*

Maintenance & cleanliness	★★★★½
Facilities	★★★
Atmosphere & character	★★★★
Security	★★
Overall rating	★★★★

Tuatapere & the Hump Ridge Track

This small town on State Highway 95 calls itself the "Sausage Capital of New Zealand", however the town's proximity to the spectacular Hump Ridge Track is the main reason most travellers come here. It is a modest and slightly run down old town, with little in the way of attractions other than a few good jet boating excursions. These, coupled with the relatively recent opening of the Hump Ridge Track, have sparked some interest in the area among backpackers.

Practical Information

Hump Ridge Track Visitor Centre

State Highway 95, Tuatapere
☎ *(03) 226 6739 or 0800 486 774*
Website *www.humpridgetrack.co.nz*
Open *8.30am-6pm daily*

Coming & Going

TrackNet *(☎ (03) 249 7777;* ***website*** *www.tracknet.net)* stop in Tuatapere en route between Invercargill and Te Anau.

Accommodation

There are a couple of backpackers' hostels in Tuatapere plus two huts on the Hump Ridge Track.

Five Mountains Holiday Park (Hump Track Backpackers)

This place offers run-down dormitory accommodation behind a café/bar in the centre of town. It doesn't have much of a backpackers' atmosphere and dorm rooms are tattered and worn. The bathrooms are unclean and the kitchen is quite a mess as well. There is a small common lounge, but it is not very inviting. For an up-and-coming tourist destination, this place is more off-putting than inviting.

Corner Halfmile & Clifden Roads, Tuatapere
☎ *(03) 226 6667*
Dorm bed *$22;* ***camping*** *$22-25 per site*
Credit cards *MC, Visa*
Reception open *7am-8pm daily*

Maintenance & cleanliness	★½
Facilities	★
Atmosphere & character	★½
Security	★
Overall rating	★½

Shooters Backpackers

This is a new purpose-built hostel with great facilities. It is in a two-storey wooden building with a large downstairs kitchen and common area with a log fire and sofas. The dorms are clean and have comfy mattresses and made-up beds on wooden bunks. The bathrooms have new fittings and great showers. There are individual security lockers, laundry facilities and internet access. Guests can also use the spa pool and sauna.

73 Main Street, Tuatapere
☎ *(03) 226 6250*
Dorm bed *$25;* ***single room*** *$38;* ***double/twin room*** *$60*
Credit cards *MC, Visa*
Reception open *7am-8.30pm daily*

Maintenance & cleanliness	★★★★½
Facilities	★★★
Atmosphere & character	★★★
Security	★★
Overall rating	★★★½

Activities

Jet Boating

The Hump Ridge Jet *(☎ (03) 225 8174 or 0800 270 556; **website** www.humpridgejet.com)* run jet boating trips on the Wairaurahiri River. This is a lot longer than the average jet boat ride with full-day trips ($180-200) that jet across Lake Hauraoko and then down 27km of grade three rapids on the Wairaurahiri River. The trip includes three to four hours in the jet boat.

Hiking

THE HUMP RIDGE TRACK

The Hump Ridge Track (53km, 3 days) is the country's best privately run hiking track. It starts and finishes at Blue Cliffs Beach, a 20-minute drive from Tuatapere, and follows the Hump Ridge, returning along the coast. It is an excellent walk that features some very impressive bridges including the Percy Burns Viaduct (the world's largest wooden viaduct).

The huts are of a very high standard. In summer it costs $90 for hut accommodation and transfers to and from the trailhead.

It is similar to the Kepler Track and is moderately difficult with some challenging sections and steep climbs on the first day. It involves a lot of walking – around 18km each day.

Refer to the track's website *(www.humpridgetrack.co.nz)* for further information.

Bluecliffs Beach to Okaka Hut *(18km, 7-9 hours)*

The track follows the coast for a few kilometres before cutting inland to Flat Creek. Then it's a steep climb to Okaka Hut on Hump Ridge.

Okaka Hut to Port Craig Village (18km, 7-9 hours)

This section of the track passes several of the towering wooden viaducts, for which the Hump Ridge Track is famous, including the Edwin and Percy Burn Viaducts.

Port Craig Village to Bluecliffs Beach *(17km, 5-7 hours)*

The walk back to Bluecliffs Beach passes through rimu forest, but for the most part is a coastal walk past rock pools and sandy beaches.

Manapouri

Manapouri is a small settlement on the edge of the Lake Manapouri, about 20 minutes from Te Anau. The lake offers some exquisite scenery, with the surrounding Cathedral and Hunter mountain ranges lit up by the sun and giving the area a dramatic ambience. The town itself is barely more than a village and is spread out along the highway with shops and homes sitting humbly beneath the hills. This is mostly a base for travellers going to Doubtful Sound, as well as hikers heading to the Kepler and Dusky Tracks. The lake offers excellent kayaking, and there are horse trekking excursions in the environs.

Coming & Going

Manapouri lies a short distance south of Te Anau on State Highway 95. TrackNet *(☎ (03) 249 7777; **website** www.tracknet.net)* stop here en route between Invercargill and Te Anau.

Accommodation

Freestone Backpackers

Nestled into the hillside about 2km south of Manapouri are five stout cabins and a main house that make up Freestone Backpackers. They were all built by the owner and each has a kitchenette, a pot-belly stove and handsome wooden furnishings. The communal showers and toilets are like-new, and there is a TV lounge in the main building. Views are stunning from everywhere, but are best enjoyed lounging on the small veranda fronting each dorm. There are also laundry facilities and a barbecue area.
Hillside Road, Manapouri

☎ *(03) 249 6893*
***Dorm bed** $25; **triple room** $60; **four-bed private room** $80*
***Reception open** 7am-9pm daily*

Maintenance & cleanliness	★★★½
Facilities	★★
Atmosphere & character	★★★
Security	★
Overall rating	★★★

Possum Lodge

This place is a gathering of self contained cabins and a separate common room. There are also campervan and camping sites on the property. The backpackers' accommodation consists of only 11 dorm beds in two cabins. The common room is a run-down assortment of old furniture and a small TV and there is also a tiny and scant kitchen, laundry facilities, internet access and a barbecue. The atmosphere is low-key (some would say boring) but it has good access to the lake and walking tracks.
13 Murrell Avenue, Manapouri
☎ *(03) 249 6623*
***Dorm bed** $21; **double/twin room** $50-95; **camping** $15 per person*
***Credit cards** MC, Visa*
***Reception open** summer 8.30am-8pm daily; winter 8.30am-1pm & 3pm-8pm daily*

Maintenance & cleanliness	★★½
Facilities	★
Atmosphere & character	★★
Security	★
Overall rating	★★

Te Anau

The small town of Te Anau is the last service centre on the way to Milford Sound and many backpackers stop here for supplies before moving on to the fjords. There are a few good accommodation options in Te Anau and it is a great place for hiking the nearby tracks, so travellers tend to make this their base to explore the Fiordland National Park. Te Anau is known as "the walking capital of the world", and provides easy access to New Zealand's most famous walks – the Routeburn, Milford and Kepler tracks. The town has a lovely lakeside setting and other popular activities here include jet boating, fishing and kayaking. The Te Anau glow-worm caves are another popular night time activity.

Practical Information

Fiordland i-SITE Visitor Centre

Lakefront Drive, Te Anau
☎ *(03) 2498 900*
***Website** www.newzealand.com*
***Open** 8.30am-5pm daily*

Fiordland National Park Visitor Centre

Lakefront Drive, Te Anau
☎ *(03) 249 7924*
***Website** www.doc.govt.nz*
***Open** 1-25 Jan 8.30am-8pm daily; 26 Jan-28 Mar 8.30am-6pm daily; 29 Mar-30 Apr 8.30am-5pm daily; 1 May-27 Oct 8.30am-4.30pm daily; 28 Oct-24 Dec 8.30am-6pm daily; 25 Dec 8.30am-1pm; 26-31 Dec 8.30am-8pm daily*

Coming & Going

Coaches operate from Te Anau to Invercargill, Milford Sound and Queenstown and there are also shuttle bus connections to the hiking tracks.

InterCity Coaches *(☎ (03) 474 9600; **website** www.intercitycoach.co.nz)* go to Invercargill, Milford Sound and Queenstown. They depart from the Real Journey Visitor Centre on Lakefront Drive.

Naked Bus *(☎ 0900 62533; **website** www.nakedbus.com)* and Topline Tours *(☎ (03) 249 7505; **website** www.toplinetours.co.nz)* also have service to Queenstown. Naked Bus departs from Te Anau Lakefront Backpackers *(48 Lakefront Drive, Te Anau)* and Te Anau Lakeview Holiday Park *(77 Manapouri-Te Anau Highway, Te Anau)* and Topline departs from the Miro Street coach stop in the town centre.

TrackNet *(☎ (03) 249 7777; **website** www.tracknet.net)* operate a shuttle service for hikers tackling the Hollyford, Kepler, Milford and Routeburn Tracks. TrackNet also runs buses to Dunedin, Invercargill and Bluff.

Southland

Accommodation

Barnyard Backpackers

This place is full of character. The accommodation is in a row of cute cabins, each with en suite amenities. The main house has a very nice kitchen and a dining area with a huge fireplace in the centre of the room. There is an upstairs common room with a pool table, and the house has open beams and antique décor. It is set on farmland with ponies and other animals and it has a fresh, young buzz and excellent views.

Rainbow Downs, 80 Mount York Road
☎ *(03) 249 8006*
Website *www.barnyardbackpackers.com*

Maintenance & cleanliness	★★★★
Facilities	★★★½
Atmosphere & character	★★★★
Security	★½
Overall rating	★★★½

Fiordland National Park Lodge

This hostel shares space with a luxury lodge on the edge of the lake. Facilities include a good common room with log fire and Sky TV; internet access, including wireless; laundry facilities and there is also a bar and restaurant on site. The facilities, however, are not very well maintained although it still has a pretty good atmosphere. Accommodation is in simple dorm rooms with single, made-up beds. It is a peaceful place 30km north of Te Anau, near the boat departure point for the Milford Track and there are gorgeous views from all over the property.

Te Anau-Milford Sound Highway (State Highway 94), 30km north of Te Anau
☎ *(03) 249 7811 or 0800 500 805*
Website *www.teanau-milfordsound.co.nz*
Dorm bed *$25;* ***double/twin room*** *$70*
Credit cards *Amex, Diners, JCB, MC, Visa*
Reception open *8am-8pm daily*

Maintenance & cleanliness	★★★
Facilities	★★★½
Atmosphere & character	★★★
Security	★½
Overall rating	★★★

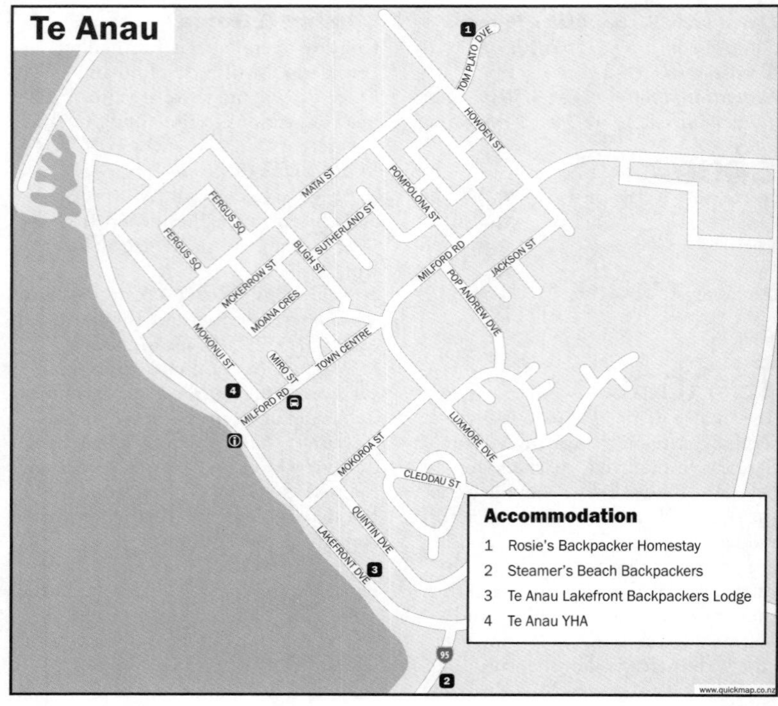

Rosie's Backpacker Homestay

This is a very cosy place in a residential area of Te Anau. It is more of a home stay, as guests share the home with a Kiwi family. There is a lovely lounge with a piano, books and a guitar plus a modern fully-equipped kitchen. There is also a nice outdoor garden area with a barbecue and lovely views. This place is very popular and it is advisable to call ahead.

23 Tom Plato Drive, Te Anau
☎ *(03) 249 8431*
Dorm bed *$30 ($27 BBH);* ***double room*** *$70 ($64 BBH)*
Open *Jan-May & Aug-Dec;* ***reception open*** *8am-10am & 4.30pm-6.30pm daily*

Maintenance & cleanliness	★★★
Facilities	★★½
Atmosphere & character	★★★½
Security	★
Overall rating	★★★

Steamer's Beach Backpackers

This place is in a lodge in a holiday park. It is very well maintained and offers a wide range of facilities, including laundry, spa pool, sauna and a barbecue area. The dorms are neat and spacious with new carpet, and bathrooms are clean. There is also a large well equipped kitchen, laundry facilities, internet access and a good lounge area with Sky TV and a log fire. It is a few minutes outside the town centre.

Corner Lakefront Drive & Te Anau-Manapouri Road, Te Anau
☎ *(03) 249 7737 or 0800 4 TE ANAU*
Website *www.teanau.info*
Dorm bed *$25 ($22 BBH);* ***double room*** *$62 ($56 BBH);* ***twin room*** *$60 ($54 BBH)*
Credit cards *MC, Visa*
Reception open *8am-8pm daily*

Maintenance & cleanliness	★★★½
Facilities	★★★
Atmosphere & character	★★★
Security	★
Overall rating	★★★

Te Anau Lakefront Backpackers

The main building of this hostel has a homey feel to it, but the other two buildings are quite run down motel-style units and some dorm rooms are unclean. If you get lucky, there are two dorms in the main building with a great lake view. They have good facilities in the main building, too, including a huge spa pool, a nice little TV lounge, cheap laundry and internet access as well as a kitchen that could be better maintained. The hostel has a young, buzzing atmosphere and a great location.

48-50 Lakefront Drive, Te Anau
☎ *(03) 249 7713 or 0800 200 074*
Website *www.teanaubackpackers.co.nz*
Dorm bed *$26-28 ($23-25 BBH);* ***double/twin room*** *$70-75 ($65-75 BBH);* ***camping*** *$14 per person*
Credit cards *Amex MC, Visa*
Reception open *summer 7.30am-9pm daily; winter 8am-7.30pm daily*

Maintenance & cleanliness	★★★½
Facilities	★★½
Atmosphere & character	★★★½
Security	★
Overall rating	★★★

Te Anau YHA

This hostel is in a quiet residential area a few minutes' walk from town centre. It offers good amenities, including a cosy TV lounge with lots of DVDs (which you must borrow from reception before 8.30pm), internet access ($6 per hour) including Wi-Fi, a nice garden barbecue area, a volleyball court and a tennis court. Facilities are clean and well-maintained and there is a fully-equipped kitchen. The dorms are spacious and have comfortable beds. The building has a bit more character than most YHAs, but it still has that "school holiday" feel and it caters to a more mature crowd than the average backpackers' hostel. Most people staying here are coming or going from the walking tracks, which gives it a busy atmosphere.

29 Mokonui Street, Te Anau
☎ *(03) 249 7847*
Website *www.yha.co.nz*
Dorm bed *$28-33 ($25-30 HI/YHA);* ***single room*** *$45 ($42 HI/YHA);* ***double room*** *$68-88 ($62-80 HI/YHA);* ***twin room*** *$74-88 ($68-80 HI/YHA)*

Southland

Credit cards *MC, Visa*
Reception open *8.30am-8pm daily*

Maintenance & cleanliness	★★★★★
Facilities	★★★½
Atmosphere & character	★★★
Security	★★
Overall rating	★★★½

Eating & Drinking

Te Anau town centre has a good mix of cafés and bakeries. The **Fiordland Bakery** *(106 Milford Road, Te Anau)* has cheap pies, sandwiches and fresh bread: perfect for a day trip lunch. Restaurants in town are a bit expensive, but there are two supermarkets in town for self-catering. The **SuperValue** supermarket *(1 The Lane, Te Anau)* has lower prices than the **Four Square** supermarket in the town centre.

Fiordland National Park

This spectacular national park at the south western corner of the South Island is largely inaccessible unless you take a scenic flight or hike one of its famous tracks.

Milford Sound is one of the most visited areas within the park and one of the few places with road access. This small village lies under the shadow of the remarkable Mitre Peak and is the launching place for cruises on Milford Sound. There is not much in Milford besides an information point, café and accommodation, so bring food with you if you plan to stay for the night.

This is the finishing point of what many consider to be the greatest walk in the world – the Milford Track. Other excellent walks include the Kepler and Hollyford Tracks, and the demanding Dusky Track. The popularity of the Milford Track means you must book well in advance, and these days many travellers are opting for the lesser known, but equally great alternatives. This is one of the wettest areas in the world, so take good wet-weather gear and plenty of insect repellent for those pesky sand flies.

Coming & Going

Naked Bus *(**website** www.nakedbus.com/milford-sound/)*, InterCity Coaches *(☎ (03) 474 9600; **website** www.intercitycoach.co.nz)* and TrackNet *(☎ (03) 249 7777; **website** www.tracknet.net)* have services linking Milford Sound with Queenstown and Te Anau. Buses stop outside the visitors centre on Milford Wharf.

Naked Bus also have good value day trips from Queenstown to Milford Sound.

Accommodation

In addition to the hostel at Milford Sound, all the main tracks have DOC huts.

Milford Sound Lodge

This is a very well maintained hostel with a good atmosphere. Dorms are spacious with wooden bunks, new clean sheets and central heating, but you have to pay extra for duvets. There is a good kitchen and dining area, and a huge common room with sofas and bean bags. There is a small shop and café at reception, where you can buy expensive groceries and rent movies (but there is no TV). Facilities are all nice and clean and they offer laundry facilities and internet access.

State Highway 94, Milford Sound
☎ (03) 249 8071
Website *www.milfordlodge.com*
Dorm bed *$28 ($25 BBH);* ***double room*** *$70 ($64 BBH)*
Credit cards *MC, Visa*
Reception open *7am-9pm daily*

Maintenance & cleanliness	★★★★
Facilities	★★
Atmosphere & character	★★★½
Security	★½
Overall rating	★★★

Activities

CRUISES ON MILFORD SOUND

Three different companies operate cruises on Milford Sound: **Mitre Peak Cruises** *(☎ (03) 249 8110; **website** www.mitrepeak.com; $60-68)*, **Real Journeys** *(☎ (03) 249 7416 or 0800 656 501; **website** www.realjourneys.co.nz; $65-78)* and **Red Boat**

Cruises (☎ *(03) 441 1137 or 0800 657 444;* ***website*** *www.redboats.co.nz; $65-80).* A lot of the cruises are on big, impersonal boats but Mitre Peak Cruises have the smaller boats and offer a less touristy experience. Real Journeys also have some smaller boats.

The main advantage of these cruises is the view of Mitre Peak, so they are a waste of money when it is covered in low-lying cloud.

SEA KAYAKING

Milford Sound Sea Kayaks (☎ *(03) 249 8500 or 0800 476 726;* ***website*** *www.kayakmilford.co.nz)* run highly recommended sea kayaking trips on Milford Sound including an early morning Sunriser trip. This is the best way to experience Milford Sound in solitude away from the tourist crowds.

SCENIC FLIGHTS

Milford Sound Helicopters (☎ *(03) 249 7845;* ***website*** *www.milfordsound helicopters.com)* and **Real Journeys** (☎ *0800 656 503;* ***website*** *www. realjourneys.co.nz)* offer scenic flights over Milford Sound. Milford Sound Helicopters feature a landing on the Donne Glacier and give you the option of returning to Te Anau.

Hiking

Fiordland National Park has several of New Zealand's Great Walks including the Dusky, Kepler and Milford Tracks. The Routeburn Track lies both in Fiordland National Park and Mount Aspiring National Park; this track is detailed on page 331 in the Otago chapter.

DUSKY TRACK

The Dusky Track (84km, 8-10 days) links Lakes Hauroko and Lake Manapouri. It offers a wide variety of landscapes as it crosses two mountain ranges and three major valleys. It is a very challenging track that is best suited to experienced hikers.

Inclement weather conditions can easily hamper your progress and flooding and avalanches are common. Take extra food in case you are stranded for a day or two.

KEPLER TRACK

The circular Kepler Track (60km, 3-4 days) is the closest major track to Te Anau. It is an increasingly popular track and around 8500 people walk it every year.

The track combines breathtaking views of Lake Manapouri and Lake Te Anau with an exposed alpine crossing.

Control Gates to Luxmore Hut *(13.5km, 6 hours)*

The first 1½-hour is an easy walk to Brod Bay alongside Lake Te Anau. After passing Brod Bay, the track climbs for three hours to reach the tree line and continues up to Luxmore Hut.

Luxmore Hut to Iris Burn Hut *(14.6km, 5-6 hours)*

The most exposed and weather-beaten section of the track crosses mountain ridges before descending back below the tree line to Iris Burn Hut.

Iris Burn Hut to Moturau Hut *(16.2km, 5-6 hours)*

This section of the track passes beech forest as it follows Iris Burn to reach Moturau Hut on the shore of Lake Manapouri.

Moturau Hut to Control Gates *(15.5km, 4-5 hours)*

The last day is an easy flat walk past wetlands to the car park at Rainbow Reach and onwards to the finish point at the Control Gates on Lake Te Anau. During summer you can finish the walk 9.5km early by picking up the shuttle bus to Te Anau at Rainbow Reach.

HOLLYFORD TRACK

The Hollyford Track (56km, 4 days) is the only major low altitude track in Fiordland National Park.

It starts about a two-hour drive north of Te Anau and follows the Hollyford River and Lake McKerrow to Martins Bay.

Road End to Lake Alabaster *(19.5km, 5-7 hours)*

The track starts with a raised boardwalk through flood-prone country and follows the Hollyford River valley to Hidden Falls Hut. It then continues along the valley, climbing Little Homer Saddle, then passes Little Homer Falls and continues on to Alabaster Hut on the southern shore of Lake Alabaster.

Lake Alabaster to Demon Trail Hut *(14.7km, 4-5 hours)*
The track goes through flat forest for a couple of hours before following the eastern shore of Lake McKerrow to Demon Trail Hut. This part of the track is not very well maintained and fallen trees may obscure it.

Demon Trail to Hokuri Hut *(9.6km, 5-6 hours)*
The track continues along the lakeshore to Hokuri Hut. This section is very rocky.

Hokuri to Martins Bay *(13.5km, 4-5 hours)*
After crossing Hokuri Creek, the track follows the shore for a couple of hours and then heads away from the lake and joins the river mouth near Martins Bay Hut.

MILFORD TRACK

The Milford Track (53.5km, 4 days) is New Zealand's most famous walking track and over 13,000 people walk along it every year.

It goes from Lake Te Anau to Milford Sound along the Clinton and Arthur River valleys, passing numerous waterfalls along the way. The Milford Track can only be hiked in one direction.

The number of hikers is restricted to 40 each day and bookings are essential if you're planning on hiking the Milford Track during peak season (Nov-Apr; the Great Walks Season). Booking for each season opens in Jul and the more popular summer months fill up early. You are limited to staying only one night at each hut on the track.

It costs around $300 to hike the Milford Track including $135 for three nights' accommodation in huts on the track, plus another $160 for bus and ferry transfers to and from the track. That's the cheap option! A guided walk can cost over $4000 but your four grand does give you luxury accommodation and gourmet meals.

Glade Wharf to Clinton Hut *(5km, 1-1½ hours)*
You approach the track by ferry from Te Anau Downs. The first day on the track is an easy 5km walk from Glade Wharf on Lake Te Anau to Clinton Hut.

Clinton Hut to Mintaro Hut *(16.5km, 6 hours)*
The second day on the track is a gradual climb to Mintaro Hut.

Mintaro Hut to Dumpling Hut *(14km, 6 hours)*
This section starts with a zigzag climb over Mackinnon Pass followed by a steep rocky descent to Dumpling Hut. Many walkers say that this descent is the most difficult part of the Milford Track.

Dumpling Hut to Sandfly Point *(18km, 5½-6 hours)*
The final leg of the Milford Track follows the Arthur River and the western shore of Lake Ada before reaching the trailhead at Sandfly Point near Milford Sound.

Index

A

Abel Tasman Coastal Track 234–235
Abel Tasman Inland Track 235
Abel Tasman National Park 232–235
Accident Compensation Commission (ACC) 18
Ahipara 95
air travel 27
Akaroa 287–290
albatross 269, 314
Aoraki/Mount Cook National Park 300–302
Arrowtown 327–328
Art Deco 168
Arthurs Pass 293–294
Arthurs Pass National Park 294
ATM cards 20
Atomic Shuttles 29
Auckland 50–68
Auckland Bridge Climb 65–66
Auckland Harbour Bridge 65–66
Auckland Region 50–75

B

backpacker buses 30–44
- Kiwi Experience 31–35
- Magic Travellers Network 35–39
- Stray Bus 39–43

ballooning
- Christchurch 287
- Methven 293

Banks Peninsula 287–290
Barrys Bay 289
Bay of Islands 81–92
Bay of Plenty 136–154
bed bugs 24
bird watching
- Cape Kidnappers 173
- Kaikoura 269
- Stewart Island/Rakiura 346

Blenheim 219–222
Blue Bridge line 49
Bluff 343–344
brewery tours
- DB Mainland Brewery 296
- Lion Brewery 67
- Monteith's Brewery 253
- Speight's Brewery 314

Budget Backpacker.Hostels (BBH) 25
Buller Gorge 242
bungee jumping
- Auckland Harbour Bridge Bungy 65
- Hanmer Springs 272
- Kawarau Bridge 324
- Mokai Gravity Canyon 195
- Mount Hutt 293
- Nevis Highwire Bungy 324
- Queenstown 324–325
- Taihape 195
- Taupo 131
- The Ledge 324

Buried Village of Te Wairoa 152
bus travel 27–44
bushwalking. *see* hiking

C

campervans 46
canoeing
- Whanganui River Journey 190–191

Canterbury 264–302
canyoning
- Matukituki Valley 335
- Mount Aspiring National Park 329
- Queenstown 325

Cape Kidnappers 173
Cape Reinga 94–95, 97
Capital Connection 44
Cardrona 335
car insurance 47
car rental 44–45
car travel 44–47
- buying a car 46–47
- car insurance 47
- car rental 44–45

Cathedral Cove 121
The Catlins 337–340
caves
- Aranui Cave 109
- Metro Cave 248
- Taniwha Caves 253
- Waitomo Glowworm Cave 109

Charleston 247–248
Christchurch 272–287
climbing
- Mount Egmont/Taranaki 177
- Mount Maunganui 141
- Mount Ruapehu Crater Climb 182–183

Clive 172–173
coach travel 27–44
Collingwood 238–239
Coromandel Peninsula 113–125
Coromandel Town 116–118
credit cards 19
Curio Bay 340
customs 16

D

dam dropping 179
Dargaville 100
Department of Conservation 13
discount cards 20–21
diving
  Poor Knights Islands 81
driving 44–47
  buying a car 46–47
  car insurance 47
  car rental 44–45
Dunedin 307–314
Dusky Track 353

E

East Cape 155–161
Egmont National Park 177–178
embassies 15
entry Requirements 13–15

F

ferry travel 49
Fiordland National Park 352–354
Fox Glacier 260, 261–262
Franz Josef 257–261
Franz Josef Glacier 260, 261

G

Geraldine 294–295
Gisborne 155–157
Glenorchy 328–329
Goat Island Marine Reserve 70
Golden Bay 235–239
Gore 340–341
Granity 246
Great Barrier Island 72–75
Great Walks
  Abel Tasman Coastal Track 234–235
  Heaphy Track 239–240
  Lake Waikaremoana Track 161
  Milford Track 354
  Rakiura Track 346
  Routeburn Track 331
  Tongariro Northern Circuit 182
  Whanganui River Journey 190–191
Greenstone and Caples Tracks 330
Greymouth 249–253

H

Haast 262–263
Hahei 121–122
Halfmoon Bay 344–346
Hamilton 102–105
hang gliding
  Coronet Peak 325
Hanmer Springs 270–272
Hastings 169–172
Hatfields Beach 68–69
Hauraki Gulf 71
Hauraki Gulf ferries 49
Havelock 214–215
Havelock North 172
Hawera 179
Hawkes Bay 162–173
health cover 18
Heaphy Track 239–240
Hector 246
Helensville 70–71
Hells Gate 152
Henderson Bay 96–97
Hibiscus Coast 68–69
Hick's Bay 159
high ropes course
  Taupo 131
  Whitianga 121
hiking
  Abel Tasman Coastal Track 234–235
  Abel Tasman Inland Track 235
  Abel Tasman National Park 234–235
  Aoraki/Mount Cook National Park 301–302
  Arthurs Pass National Park 294
  Atene Skyline Track 190
  Ball Shelter Hut Route 302
  Black Valley Walk 241
  Blue Lakes and Tasman Glacier View Walk 302
  Bridal Veil Track 294
  Devil's Punchbowl Waterfall Walk 294
  Dusky Track 353
  Egmont National Park 177–178
  Fiordland National Park 353–354
  Greenstone and Caples Tracks 330
  Heaphy Track 239–240
  Hollyford Track 353–354
  Honeydew Walk 241
  Hooker Valley Walk 301
  Hump Ridge Track 348
  Kahurangi National Park 239–240
  Kaikoura Coast Track 269
  Kea Point Walk 301
  Kepler Track 353
  Lake Rotoiti Circuit 241
  Lake Waikaremoana Track 161
  Loop Track 241
  Mangapurua Track 190
  Matemateonga Track 190
  Milford Track 354
  Mounds Walk 181
  Mount Aspiring National Park 330–331
  Mount Robert 241

Mount Ruapehu Crater Climb 182–183
Nelson Lakes National Park 241
North West and Southern Circuits 346
Nydia Track 218
Queen Charlotte Track 215–219
Rakiura Track 346
Red Tarns Track 301
Rees and Dart Tracks 330
Ridge Track 181
Round the Mountain 183
Routeburn Track 331
Sealy Tarns Track 301
Silica Rapids Walk 181
St Arnaud Range Track 241
Stewart Island/Rakiura 346
Taranaki Falls Walk 181
Tasman Glacier Lake 302
Tongariro Alpine Crossing 181–182
Tongariro National Park 181–182
Tongariro Northern Circuit 182
Travers-Sabine Circuit 241
Whakapapaiti Valley Walk 181
Whakapapa Nature Walk 181
hitchhiking 47–48
Hobbiton 112
Hokianga 98–99
Hokianga Harbour 98–99
Hokitika 253–256
Hollyford Track 353–354
horse riding
Franz Josef 260–261
Kaikoura 269
Hostelling International (HI) 26
hostels 23–26
Hot Water Beach 122
Houhora Heads 96
Houhoura Ha rbour 96
Hump Ridge Track 348
hydrospeed. *see* white water sledging

I

InterCity Coachlines 27–29
Interislander ferry 49
internet cafés 23
Invercargill 341–343
ISE cards 21
ISIC cards 21

J

jet boating
AgroJet 153
Buller Gorge 242
Christchurch 287
Clutha River 335
Dart River 329
Hanmer Springs 272
Huka Jet 131
Kawarau Jet 325
Queenstown 325
Rakaia Gorge 293
Rapids Jet 131–132
Rotorua 153
Shotover Jet 325
Taupo 131
Waiau Gorge 272
Waimakariri River 287
Wairaurahiri River 348

K

Kaeo 92
Kahurangi National Park 239–240
Kaihu 101
Kaikoura 264–270
Kaitaia 93–95
Kaka Point 338
Kapiti Coast 206–207
Karamea 246–247
kayaking. *see also* sea kayaking
Abel Tasman National Park 233–234
Aoraki/Mount Cook National Park 301
Arnold River 253
Clutha River 335
Kaikoura 269
Lake Mapourika 260
Lake Taupo 132
Mueller Glacier 301
Stewart Island/Rakiura 346
Wanaka 335
Whanganui River Journey 190–191
Kepler Track 353
Kerikeri 90–92
Kiwi Experience 31–43
Kowhai Coast 69–70

L

Lake Taupo 125–135
Lake Tekapo 297–298
Le Bons Bay 288–289
Leigh 70

M

Magic Travellers Network 35–43
Manapouri 348–349
Maraehako Bay 160
Marahau 233
Marlborough 210–222
Marlborough Sounds 215–219
Martinborough 208–209
Masterton 207–208
Matamata 111–112
Methven 290–293
Milford Sound 352–353

Milford Track 354
Mitre Peak 352–353
mobile phones 22
Mokai Gravity Canyon 195
money 18–21
Motueka 230–232
Mount Aspiring National Park 329–331
Mount Cook National Park. *see* Aoraki/ Mount Cook National Park
Mount Egmont (Taranaki) 177–178
Mount Hutt 290–293
Mount Maunganui 136–141
Mount Ruapehu Crater Climb 182–183
Mount Ruapehu Ski Area 183
Murchison 241–242

N
Naked Bus 29
Napier 163–169
national parks
  Abel Tasman National Park 232–235
  Aoraki/Mount Cook National Park 300
  Arthurs Pass National Park 294
  Egmont National Park 177–178
  Fiordland National Park 352–354
  Kahurangi National Park 239–240
  Nelson Lakes National Park 240–241
  Paparoa National Park 248–249
  Rakiura National Park 346
  Te Urewera National Park 161
  Whanganui National Park 190–191
National Park Village 183–185
Nelson 223–230
Nelson Lakes National Park 240–241
Nelson-Tasman Region 223–242
New Plymouth 174–177
New Zealand Travelpass 43–44
Ninety Mile Beach 94
Northland 76
Nydia Track 218

O
Oamaru 303–307
Oban 344–346
Ohakune 186–187
Okarito 256–257
Omapere 98–100
Onuku 289
Opononi 98–100
Opotiki 144–145
Opoutere 124
Orakei Korako 125–126
Orewa 68–69
Otago 303–336
Otago Peninsula 314–315
Otorohanga 107
Overlander 44
Owaka 338

P
Paekakariki 206
Paihia 82–88
Palmerston North 191–194
Pancake Rocks 248–249
Paparoa National Park 248–249
Papatowai 339
parachuting. *see* skydiving
paragliding
  Coronet Peak 325
Paraparaumu 207
Parnell 61
passports 13–14
penguins 306, 315
Picton 210–214
Ponsonby 63
Poor Knights Islands 81
Port Chalmers 312
Portobello 314–315
Pukekura 256
Pukenui 96–97
Punakaiki 248–249
Purakaunui Falls 339

Q
quarantine 16
Queen Charlotte Track 215–219
Queenstown 315–327

R
Raglan 105–106
rail travel 44
Rakiura National Park 346
Rakiura Track 346
rambling. *see* hiking
Rangitukia 159
rappelling. *see* abseiling
Rees and Dart Tracks 330
Renwick 222
Riverton 346–347
rock climbing
  Wanaka 335
Ross 256
Rotorua 145–154
Routeburn Track 331
Ruapehu District 180–187
Russell 88–90

S
sailing
  Auckland 66
  Bay of Islands 87–88
scuba diving. *see* diving

Seacliff 312
sea kayaking
  Abel Tasman National Park 233–234
  Bay of Islands 87
  Kaikoura 269
  Stewart Island/Rakiura 346
shweeb 153
skiing
  Cardrona 335
  Coronet Peak 326
  Hanmer Springs 272
  Mount Hutt 293
  Mount Ruapehu 183
  The Remarkables 326
  Treble Cone 336
  Turoa 183
  Waiorau Snow Farm 336
  Whakapapa 183
skydiving
  Christchurch 287
  Mount Maunganui 141
  Queenstown 326
  Taupo 132
  Tauranga 141
  Wanaka 335
SkyJump 66
Skype 23
SkyWalk 66
snowboarding
  Cardrona 335
  Coronet Peak 326
  Mount Ruapehu 183
  Snowpark NZ 336
  The Remarkables 326
  Treble Cone 336
  Turoa 183
  Whakapapa 183
Southland 337–354
St Arnaud 240–241
Stewart Island ferries 49
Stewart Island/Rakiura 344–346
Stratford 178–179
Stray Bus 39–43
surfing
  Mount Maunganui 141
  Raglan 106
swimming with dolphins
  Akaroa 290
  Kaikoura 269
  Mount Maunganui 141
  Whakatane 143
swimming with seals
  Kaikoura 269
swinging
  Mokai Gravity Canyon 195
  Queenstown 326–327
  Shotover Canyon Swing 327
  The Ledge Sky Swing 326–327

T

Tahakopa 339
Taieri Gorge Railway 44
Taihape 194–195
Tairua 123–124
Takaka 235–238
Taranaki 174–179
Taupo 126–132
Tauranga 136–141
tax 17
Te Anau 349–352
Te Araroa 159
Te Aroha 112–113
Te Kaha 160
Te Kuiti 107
Te Urewera National Park 161
Thames 113–116
third-party liability insurance 47
Timaru 295–297
tipping 20
Tokomaru Bay 158
Tolaga Bay 158
Tongariro Alpine Crossing 181–182
Tongariro National Park 180–183
Tongariro Northern Circuit 182
train travel 44
tramping. *see* hiking
TranzAlpine 44
TranzCoastal 44
Tranz Scenic 44
travellers' cheques 19
Treble Cone 336
trekking. *see* hiking
Tuatapere 347–348
Turangi 132–135
Turoa 183
Twizel 298–300

U

ultra light flights
  Auckland 66
Ulva Island 346

V

VIP Backpackers Resorts 25–26

W

Waiheke Island 71–72
Waikato 102–135
Waikawa 340
Waimangu Volcanic Valley 152
Wai-O-Tapu Thermal Wonderland 152
Waipu 76–78

Wairarapa 207–209
Wairoa 162–163
Waitangi 88
Waitangi Treaty Grounds 88
Waitomo Caves 107–111
walking. *see* hiking
Wanaka 331–336
Wanganui 187–190
Warkworth 69–70
Wellington 196–206
Wellington Region 196–209
West Coast 243–263
Westport 243–246
Whakapapa 183
Whakapapa Village 181
Whakarewarewa Thermal Village 153
Whakatane 141–143
whale watching
  Kaikoura 269–270
Whanarua Bay 160
Whangamata 124–125
Whanganui National Park 190–191
Whanganui River Journey 190–191
Whangarei 78–81
Whangaroa Harbour 92
White Island 143–144
white water rafting
  Arnold River 253
  Buller Gorge 242
  Buller River 246
  Kaituna River 154
  Kawarau River 327
  Rangitaiki 154
  Shotover River 327
  Tongariro River 135
  Upper Grey River 253
  Waiau Gorge Canyon 272
  Wairoa River 154
white water sledging
  Kaituna River 154
  Kawarau River 327, 335
  Waingongoro River 179
Whitianga 119–121
Wi-Fi hotspots 23
work 16–18
Working Holiday Scheme 16–17

Y

Youth Hostel Association (YHA) 26

Z

zorbing 154